Issues in
State and Local
Government

Selected Readings

Edited by

RUSSELL W. MADDOX, Jr.

Van Nostrand Political Science Series

Issues in
STATE and LOCAL
GOVERNMENT

Selected Readings

Edited by

RUSSELL W. MADDOX, Jr.

Professor of Political Science
Oregon State University

D. VAN NOSTRAND COMPANY, INC.

Princeton, New Jersey

Toronto   New York   London

D. VAN NOSTRAND COMPANY, INC.
120 Alexander St., Princeton, New Jersey (*Principal office*)
24 West 40 Street, New York 18, New York

D. Van Nostrand Company, Ltd.
358, Kensington High Street, London, W.14, England

D. Van Nostrand Company (Canada), Ltd.
25 Hollinger Road, Toronto 16, Canada

239272
Politics.
C

Preface

This collection of readings has been designed specifically for basic college and university courses in State and Local Government. The selections have been chosen to provide illustrations, strengthen insight, and stimulate thought and discussion. The volume of materials from which to choose is almost limitless, and no claim is made to a representative sample. Furthermore, no effort has been made to undertake the impossible task of presenting "all sides" of important issues. Instead, it is hoped that the presentation of one or two viewpoints will stimulate discussion and elicit contrary ideas. Only use in the classroom can demonstrate whether this hope is justified.

Since a book of readings is generally used as a supplement to a textbook, this collection has been organized so as to parallel standard texts in the field of State and Local Government. An effort has been made to introduce an element of flexibility by dividing the material into ten parts, each concerned with a major aspect of the field. This arrangement is designed to assist the instructor in making specific assignments.

Obviously, a book of readings is the product of the efforts of many persons, both authors and publishers. The editor wishes to express sincere appreciation for the kind permission extended by those whose work contributed to this volume. Acknowledgements accompany individual selections.

A special word of appreciation is due Mrs. Claudia Ballensky for her assistance in typing the manuscript.

R. W. M.

Corvallis, Oregon

VAN NOSTRAND POLITICAL SCIENCE SERIES

Editor

FRANKLIN L. BURDETTE
University of Maryland

HARWOOD L. CHILDS—*Public Opinion*

RUSSELL W. MADDOX, JR.—*Issues in State and Local Government: Selected Readings*

MARTIN C. NEEDLER—*Political Systems of Latin America*

HAROLD AND MARGARET SPROUT—*Foundations of International Politics*

WILLIAM G. ANDREWS—*European Political Institutions*

H. B. SHARABI—*Governments and Politics of the Middle East in the Twentieth Century*

RUSSELL W. MADDOX, JR., and ROBERT F. FUQUAY—*State and Local Government*

GUY B. HATHORN, HOWARD R. PENNIMAN, and HAROLD ZINK—*Government and Politics in the United States*

SAMUEL HENDEL—*The Soviet Crucible: The Soviet System in Theory and Practice,* 2nd Ed.

HAROLD ZINK—*Modern Governments*

HAROLD ZINK, HOWARD R. PENNIMAN, and GUY B. HATHORN—*American Government and Politics: National, State, and Local*

CONLEY H. DILLON, CARL LEIDEN, and PAUL D. STEWART—*Introduction to Political Science*

BENJAMIN BAKER—*Urban Government*

WILLIS G. SWARTZ—*American Governmental Problems,* 2nd Ed.

WILLIAM GOODMAN—*The Two-Party System in the United States,* 3rd Ed.

P. M. A. LINEBARGER, C. DJANG, and A. W. BURKS—*Far Eastern Governments and Politics—China and Japan,* 2nd Ed.

ELMER PLISCHKE—*International Relations: Basic Documents,* 2nd Ed.

M. JORRIN—*Governments of Latin America*

LANE W. LANCASTER—*Government in Rural America,* 2nd Ed.

R. G. DIXON, JR., and ELMER PLISCHKE—*American Government: Basic Documents and Materials*

ELMER PLISCHKE—*Conduct of American Diplomacy,* 2nd Ed.

Contents

Part I

THE STATES IN
THE FEDERAL SYSTEM

THE nature of our federal system is constantly changing. When the national government was formed under the Constitution at the end of the eighteenth century, the people cherished their role as citizens of the separate states—and state citizenship still ranks high in the values of many persons. Yet, as Harvey Mansfield notes in his article on "The States in the Federal System," the passage of years has seen loyalty to the nation assume prime importance. Nevertheless, the states are even more important in the citizens' lives today than at the time of the formation of the Union. The states' continued strength, however, depends in large part on their effectiveness in contributing to the goals that we, as a nation, set for ourselves.

At least until the Civil War was brought to a successful conclusion, a troublesome question plagued our federal union: Was the national government entitled to enforce policies and carry out programs in spite of opposition from the states? In its brief review of the "Evolution of the American Federal System," the Commission on Intergovernmental Relations notes that the first overt challenge to the power of the national government came in 1798 in the form of the Virginia and Kentucky resolutions. These statements clearly implied that the individual states had the right to resist enforcement of federal statutes that they believed to be unconstitutional. (Specifically, the challenge was aimed at the Alien and Sedition laws of 1798 which, among other things, empowered the President to deport aliens considered to be dangerous to the peace of the country and provided punishment for writing or publishing any false, scandalous, or malicious material aimed at the Congress or the President.) The possibility of secession was voiced at the Hartford Convention in 1814, and in 1832 South Carolina threatened nullification of national tariff acts. This threat from South Carolina caused President Andrew Jackson to issue a proclamation to the people of that state stressing the dangers inherent in their position and affirming his unequivocal determination to preserve the Union by force if necessary.

The many threats to national unity culminated in the Civil War, and the question of the ability of states to secede from the Union was answered by force. The United States Supreme Court, in *Texas v. White* (1869), announced that the state of Texas (and by implication, the other states of the Confederacy) was without authority to sever its ties under the Constitution and consequently never, legally speaking, ceased to be a part of the Union.

Among the original purposes of the Constitution was the regulation of relations among the states, and this task has remained a significant function of the national government. An important section of the Constitution relating to this purpose provides that "Full faith and credit shall be given in each State to the public acts, records, and judicial proceedings of every other State." This clause has proved to be especially important with regard to judicial decisions pertaining to a variety of civil matters such as awards for damages, adoption proceedings, and divorce decrees. The last category has been especially troublesome in recent times. It is generally accepted that each state has the legal authority to regulate marriage and divorce among its own residents, and every other state must recognize the validity of such acts. In *Williams v. North Carolina* (1945), however, the U.S. Supreme Court ruled that North Carolina was not required to recognize a divorce granted by a Nevada court to a resident of North Carolina. Instead, it was possible for the Nevada decree to be impeached in the North Carolina courts on the ground that the Nevada courts lacked jurisdiction because the party obtaining the divorce had not acquired bona fide domicile in Nevada.

Although the indivisibility of the Union is well established in the law and political philosophy of the nation, much controversy remains concerning federal-state relations. As the population of the nation grows and becomes increasingly urban, new problems emerge and certain old ones are aggravated. Advocates of federal action to cope with problems relating to such functions as education, welfare, and highway construction urge that only in this way can the resources of the nation be mobilized to meet current social needs. Many persons feel, however, that effective national action is rendered difficult, if not impossible, by the power of special and local interests, including opposition in many instances from state and local governments. Criticism of federal action is often associated with the assertion that state and local governments are "closer" to the people and more responsive to their wishes than the national government and consequently are endowed with some sort of superior quality. Morton Grodzins and Herbert Storing, in their respective articles, question the validity of this idea, and James Jackson Kilpatrick presents "The Case for 'States' Rights.' "

In 1962 the Council of State Governments proposed three amendments to the U.S. Constitution intended to strengthen the position of the states in the federal system. Briefly, these amendments were designed to accomplish three specific purposes:

(1) To enable the states to amend the national Constitution without effective participation by Congress ("Whenever applications from the legislatures of two-thirds of the total number of states of the United States shall contain identical texts of an amendment to be proposed, the President of the Senate and the Speaker of the House of Representatives shall so certify, and the amendment as contained in the application shall be deemed to have been proposed, without further action by Congress.");

(2) To create a Court of the Union, composed of the chief justices of the highest court in each state, with authority to review "any judgment of the [United States] Supreme Court relative to the rights reserved to the states or to the people" by the U.S. Constitution; and

(3) To remove from the U.S. Constitution any restriction with regard to state legislative apportionment and to exclude Congress and the federal courts from this controversial area.

In reference to the proposed change in procedure for amending the Constitution, Professor Charles L. Black, Jr., of the Yale Law School has observed: "It is a proposal for state rule only, on the basis of state-by-state count only, and through state institutions only, with the popular and national principles altogether submerged" ("The Proposed Amendment of Article V: A Threatened Disaster," *Yale Law Journal,* April 1963). Some of the dangers inherent in the proposed Court of the Union are examined by John R. Schmidhauser and Richard L. McAnaw ("Calhoun Revisited"), and the possible consequences of withdrawing federal jurisdiction over apportionment of state legislatures are noted by Jefferson B. Fordham ("To Foster Disunity").

In recent times the interstate compact has attracted increasing attention as a means of fostering cooperation among the states in order to achieve purposes that are of concern to many, and perhaps all, states. Matters handled through interstate agreements include the allocation of river water, conservation of natural resources such as forests and oil, control of stream pollution, public works, civil defense, and education. In "Interstate Agencies and Effective Administration" Richard H. Leach notes certain criticisms commonly leveled against interstate compacts, but concludes that the accomplishments of compact agencies indicate that their performance compares favorably with that of the best federal and state agencies.

1. The States in the American System*

HARVEY C. MANSFIELD

WHEN the Republic was founded the states were going concerns, performing indispensable functions. Their preservation was a prime object of concern, a part of the price of union. A federal system in the beginning was the only feasible means of meeting "the desperate need for a modicum of union where unity is impossible." Over the intervening years the "more perfect union" that the framers of the Constitution sought has largely supplanted the states in the loyalties of the people. The national government has the prestige of victory, accomplishment, and competence, and the advantage of higher visibility. People move about more, they take more interest in national affairs. Moreover, there is little of what the states did in 1787 that the national government could not readily do today. It is perhaps not so evident now that the states are inevitably necessary in the scheme of things. Perhaps they are only more desirable than other conceivable arrangements; or perhaps the grounds of their indispensability have only been altered somewhat.

In any ultimate sense, of course, neither the federal system nor the states

* Reprinted from *The Forty-Eight States: Their Tasks as Policy Makers and Administrators*, The American Assembly, Columbia University, 1955.

are ends in themselves. The final objects of government were never better shortly expressed than in the preamble to the Constitution: to "establish justice, insure domestic tranquillity, provide for the common defense, promote the general welfare, and secure the blessings of liberty. . . ." The serviceability of the states to these goals is the measure of their continuing justification. Nevertheless, in a practical world the successful means of one generation often become the ends of the next. The states have survived the loss of patriotisms they evoked before the Civil War. They do much more today than ever before. They are in no presently realistic danger of atrophy. But their performance also leaves much to be desired, in competence, confidence, and responsiveness. The basic question of public policy they present today, accordingly, is whether, despite their handicaps and shortcomings, they will or should continue to be a primary means of dividing the power and not merely the labor of government in our system. For the main premise of federalism is that such a division is more than inevitable; it is also desirable. That premise falls if the states do not adequately contribute to the final goals of government. The stakes on their realization of their missions are therefore the vitality and viability of the federal system.

What are the missions of the states? No more than a partial answer to this question can come from reading constitutions, for their missions are inherently relative to their situations. Here, along with some common elements, a wide diversity prevails.

THE SITUATIONS OF THE STATES

Every major power except Britain (a compact and relatively homogeneous exception) has a level of governments organized in territorial units between the central authority and the localities. Most of them, as in a unitary system like the French, and even in some nominally federal systems, are subject to a variety of direct and overriding controls from the national government, such as central appointment of their governors or central disallowance of their legislation. Or they may depend on financial support from the center, or, more subtly, be kept in line by the party machinery that sustains a dictatorial regime. Even in comparison with Canada and Australia our states enjoy a high degree of independent political life and autonomous authority.

CONSTITUTIONAL MIDDLEMEN

Some part of the states' independence is traceable to the national Constitution. While the national government must look to that Constitution for its powers, the states look to it only for limitations. So far as the union is concerned they are free to do anything not forbidden. Implicitly they are forbidden to burden interstate commerce unduly, either by taxation or by regulation. Explicitly they are forbidden to make treaties with foreign countries, to coin money, to impair the obligation of contracts, to tax imports or exports, or to deny due process or equal protection in their treatment of individuals. A few other pro-

hibitions, chiefly of historical interest, apply. But these still leave much leeway.

On the positive side, they can make and change their own constitutions, subject to the federal limitations just noted; indeed their own constitutions are the source of most of the legal limits on their powers. They can raise and spend their own funds, though they are no longer self-sufficient financially. They conduct both federal and state elections and are the sources of most of the legal controls over parties and elections. They enact and enforce the main bodies of civil and criminal law; and the state and municipal police, prosecutors, judges, and prisons are their agents. They control the public education systems. They license occupations, charter corporations, and regulate utilities, insurance, and other businesses. They establish and regulate the counties, municipalities, and other political subdivisions.

The practical importance of these powers to the states is reinforced by their constitutional equality of status and their equal representation in the Senate. If a few of the larger or wealthier among them were accorded special prerogatives, such as Prussia enjoyed in imperial Germany, the remainder might become dependent either on these privileged ones or on the national government for protection against them. Either way, the weaker units would lose some freedom of action.

The influence of the states is also greatly enhanced by the ability of state officials and political leaders to infiltrate, sometimes to enfeeble and more often to bend to their interests or inclinations, the powers and agencies of the national government. This shows up in a variety of ways. Very early in our history, senators came to realize the value of collective bargaining with the President over appointments. By the rule of senatorial courtesy many individual senators have taken it as a matter of right that they should name the federal judges, district attorneys and other key national field officials in their states, as well as name a share of the officialdom in Washington. In this way Reed Smoot, Kenneth McKellar, and Pat McCarran with the extra leverage of major committee chairmanships, built up private empires at public expense, responsive to their bidding and the interests of their constituencies. More often, perhaps, senators in suggesting names to the President are only conveyor belts for the wishes of state and county political leaders. These leaders also control the electoral fortunes of a large proportion of the House membership and thereby introduce another decentralizing influence into national councils. The Presidency too, since electoral votes are cast by the unit rule, must ordinarily be sensitive to local political reactions, especially in the larger doubtful states.

Political forces operating through the party system, in sum, commonly keep national actions vis-a-vis the states far inside the boundaries judicially conceded to the national government under the Constitution. The Supreme Court, most insulated from these forces, has been, except on the slavery issue, pretty consistently nationalist in doctrine. But the characteristic deference of Congress to state wishes has shown up again and again: recently, for example, in connection with fair trade laws, the tidelands, the control of insurance, and national school subsidies.

The other face of the states' intermediate position turns downward to the local governments. Here the powers reserved to them under the national Constitution become apparently plenary, save for federal limitations and limitations of the states' own constitutions: in theory, state-local relations are not federal but unitary. Every local unit traces its legal existence and powers to state enactments. State laws and constitutions not only enable local government to exist, but they also place limits, furnish aids, and provide supervision in a great variety of forms. Municipal charters and local taxing and borrowing powers are specialized and limited. Some local administrative actions are subject to state approval or audit. State legislatures intervene in county and municipal affairs with special acts to enable or prohibit. When local officials complain of overcentralization, as they have for the past half century, they have their state capitals in mind.

But just as the influence of the states reaches upward into the national government, so they themselves, and for the same reasons, are infiltrated, sometimes spurred, sometimes paralyzed, by the interests of their organized legal creatures. The multiplicity of elected local officials and their statewide organizations, the county and city political machines, the locally oriented legislators, make state-local relations usually in fact federal, whatever the theoretical plenitude of state powers. Local governments, like the states, want help without controls—all sugar and no medicine.

2. Evolution of the American Federal System*

COMMISSION ON INTERGOVERNMENTAL RELATIONS

THE PROBLEM OF FEDERALISM

THE proper division of labor and authority between the Nation and the States is the key to maintaining the federal nature of our system of government. The lines of division are not static. They have been controversial from the beginning of our life as an independent country. They remain so today. . . .

The federal system devised by the framers of the Constitution was the product of necessity rather than doctrine. There was no dictionary definition of federal government to apply nor any working model to copy. They found the classical examples from Greece and the medieval unions of European cities too remote in time and circumstances to be suitable. Their experience under the Articles of Confederation had taught them what to strive for and what to avoid. They were content to keep the States substantially as they knew them, but they deplored certain economic and fiscal tendencies in some States. Chiefly, they felt a very practical need for a central government of much greater strength and potentialities than the Articles provided.

MIDDLE COURSE CHOSEN

Characteristically, they took a middle course to meet that need—in retrospect probably the only course that was both "adequate to the exigencies of government and the preservation of the union"

* Reprinted from *A Report to the President for Transmittal to the Congress*, The Commission on Intergovernmental Relations, June 1955.

and capable of winning majority support. They rejected summarily the advice of those few, like Hamilton, who sought to build a unitary authority, to abolish the States as autonomous units, and to provide for the appointment of governors from the National Capital. They also overruled decisively the considerably greater number who wanted to keep the union a mere confederation, with a few strengthening amendments to the Articles. . . .

Before the campaign for ratification was well under way, the supporters of the new arrangement were labeled "Federalists," and the fruits of their labors gave a fresh and more precise meaning to the term. The federal system they devised was one of the great innovations in the art of representative government. In building a nation out of diverse elements, the early need in the formative stages is to create a viable measure of union where unity is impossible. The dangers of overcentralization may be foreseen and feared, but they do not materialize until later stages of national development. It was the invaluable merit of the proposed federal system that it promised a means of reconciling the need and the fear.

This system has characteristically been very flexible, leaving a great deal of room for argument and adjustment. The division of powers between the Nation and the States leaves substantial authority with each, but the use and relative importance of powers may shift. The Constitution cannot be formally amended by either level of government without the participation of the other, but interpretation and usage may expand or contract the powers at either level. The National Government deals with the people directly, but it may also utilize the States to reach them indirectly. The States can write and change their own constitutions, but they must meet minimum requirements of the National Constitution. The States are equal in legal status, but not in size, wealth, and influence. In all these essentials the federal relationship is adjustable, within limits. It is affected by controversies over what any government in the system should do, as well as by concepts of what no government should do. Historically, the invocation of States rights has been as much a sign of opposition to a specific National policy as of attachment to local action as such. . . .

THE ISSUE OF NATIONAL SUPREMACY

The basic constitutional question for the federal system from 1789 to 1865 was the issue of National supremacy: whether the National Government was entitled to enforce, over State objections, decisions reached through its own constitutional processes. At bottom this was the same issue posed by the Virginia Plan, and apparently settled by the framers, but it kept reappearing. The first open challenge after 1789 came in 1798 when Jefferson and Madison inspired the Virginia and Kentucky resolutions denouncing the alien and sedition acts. They invited the other State legislatures to instruct their Senators to vote for repeal of the acts and went on to intimate that the States had a right to resist the enforcement of Federal acts they deemed unconstitutional.

In 1814, at the Hartford Convention, New England leaders talked of secession if the Embargo Act were enforced. A few years afterward, Maryland and Ohio took official action to prevent branches of the Nationally-chartered Bank of the United States from operating within their borders; Ohio went so far as to seize the office and the cash on hand. In Jackson's administration, Georgia defied the Supreme Court and

the requirements of a Federal treaty by convicting and hanging a Cherokee Indian under State law. South Carolina threatened nulllification over the tariff issue. Among the efforts of northern States to nullify the Fugitive Slave Act of 1850 was the action of the Wisconsin court in issuing a writ of *habeas corpus* to free a man convicted in a Federal court, after the Supreme Court had specifically denied their authority to do so.

All these challenges from various parts of the country were disposed of peaceably, except for the slavery controversy. Over that issue and secession the North, behind Lincoln's leadership, finally settled by force the ultimate issue of National supremacy. After the war it could no longer be maintained that the Union was only a creature of the States, or a compact among them, liable to be thwarted or dissolved at the will of any of them. From then on, the interpretation of National powers was to be determined, in the main, by some National authority. . . .

RECENT CHANGES

Two related premises regarding the federal system underlay the judicial interpretation of National and State powers for a full half century after 1880. One was that workably clear and distinct boundaries between their respective realms of activity could be drawn in terms of constitutional powers. The other was that the Supreme Court was the final arbiter of the system. Experience showed both assumptions to be illusory. So many judicial precedents of contrary tendency accumulated that the boundary lines became unpredictable and, indeed, a zone of governmental no man's land sometimes appeared to lie between them. . . . The clash culminated in 1937 when the Court began a series of sweeping reversals or modifications of former decisions.

Since 1937, judicial doctrine has recognized the emergence of a new concept of National-State relations, sometimes labelled "cooperative federalism" in contrast with the separatism of the previous era. The concept rests constitutionally on a broad view of National authority, on the abandonment of the due process clause as a source of substantive restraints on State regulation of economic affairs, and on the Court's refusal to entertain taxpayers' suits challenging exercises of the spending power. . . . State and National laws touching economic affairs are no longer held to be deprivations of due process because they conflict with natural rights of property or liberty of contract. The Court has accepted a reading of the general welfare clause that places no discernible judicial limits on the amounts or purposes of Federal spending, although it does not follow that the power to spend carries with it unlimited power to regulate. The potentialities of the spending power were only dimly apprehended before the income tax and Federal Reserve System opened up new reservoirs of Federal revenues and credit. . . .

JUDICIAL REVIEW TODAY

Under judicial doctrine since 1937 the Supreme Court has largely removed itself as a practical factor in determining the economic policies of the States and the Nation. It has not, however, eliminated the historic role of judicial review in our federal system. Two remaining functions are noteworthy here, apart from its task of promoting uniformity of interpretation and filling in the gaps in Federal law. One is the duty of judging when the States have overstepped and encroached on whatever area should be the exclusive domain of Federal regulation, if any, or have actually legislated in conflict with Federal law. The exercise of this function is as old as the Court itself. . . .

The other function is very recent in its present-day significance, dating only from 1925, though its roots go back to the Fourteenth Amendment. This is the guardianship of civil liberties. In the face of its withdrawal from supervision over economic policies, the Court during the past 30 years has become noticeably more stern in construing State responsibilities under the Fourteenth Amendment to protect civil and political rights. . . . In this whole area, in contrast to the field of economic affairs, the Congress has moved slowly, and the Supreme Court has become the principal instrument of Federal surveillance. There is a surface paradox in this extension of National judicial power at the very time the Court is emphasizing its deference to State legislative policy. But the paradox disappears in a view of the purposes of our federal system which puts the strengthening and preservation of basic personal freedoms among the first objects of the Union. . . .

With the passage of the years, the federal division of powers has involved a highly complex distribution of governmental tasks and responsibilities. Because the results are generally approved, the system itself enjoys high prestige. But approval in general should not necessarily imply endorsement of all the details of a going system. Where the problem of our federal system once appeared to be one of creating sufficient strength and authority in the National Government, today contrary concerns have aroused anxiety. The National Government now has within its reach authority well beyond what it requires for ordinary use; forbearance in the exercise of this authority is essential if the federal balance is to be maintained.

Yet prudent limitation of National responsibilities is not likely by itself to prevent overcentralization. A realistic program of decentralization in our contemporary society depends too on the readiness and ability of the States and their subdivisions to assume their full share of the total task of government.

3. Kentucky Resolutions

November 16, 1798

I. *Resolved,* that the several States composing the United States of America, are not united on the principle of unlimited submission to their general government; but that by compact under the style and title of a Constitution for the United States and of amendments thereto, they constituted a general government for special purposes, delegated to that government certain definite powers, reserving each State to itself, the residuary mass of right to their own self-government; and that whensoever the general government assumes undelegated powers, its acts are unauthoritative, void, and of no force: That to this compact each State acceded as a State, and is an integral party, its co-States forming, as to itself, the other party: That the government created by this compact was not made the exclusive or final judge of the extent of the powers delegated to itself; since that would have made its discretion, and not the Constitution, the measure of its powers; but that as in all other cases of compact among parties having no common Judge, *each party has an equal right to judge for itself, as well of infractions as of the mode and measure of redress.*

II. *Resolved,* that the Constitution of the United States having delegated to Congress a power to punish treason, counterfeiting the securities and current coin of the United States, piracies and felonies committed on the high seas, and offenses against the laws of nations, and no other crimes whatever, and it being true as a general principle, and one of the amendments to the Constitution having also declared "that the powers not delegated to the United States by the Constitution, nor prohibited by it to the States, are reserved to

the States respectively, or to the people," therefore . . . the act passed by them on the 27th day of June, 1798, entitled "An act to punish frauds committed on the Bank of the United States" (and all other their acts which assume to create, define, or punish crimes other than those enumerated in the Constitution), are altogether void and of no force, and that the power to create, define, and punish such other crimes is reserved, and of right appertains solely and exclusively to the respective States, each within its own Territory.

III. *Resolved,* that it is true as a general principle, and is also expressly declared by one of the amendments to the Constitution that "the powers not delegated to the United States by the Constitution, nor prohibited by it to the States, are reserved to the States respectively or to the people;" and that no power over the freedom of religion, freedom of speech, or freedom of the press being delegated to the United States by the Constitution, nor prohibited by it to the States, all lawful powers respecting the same did of right remain, and were reserved to the States, or to the people: That thus was manifested their determination to retain to themselves the right of judging how far the licentiousness of speech and of the press may be abridged without lessening their useful freedom, and how far those abuses which cannot be separated from their use should be tolerated rather than the use be destroyed; and thus also they guarded against all abridgment by the United States of the freedom of religious opinions and exercises, and retained to themselves the right of protecting the same, as this State, by a law passed on the general demand of its citizens, had already protected them from all human restraint or interference: And that in addition to this general principle and express declaration, another and more special provision has been made by one of the amendments to the Constitution which expressly declares, that "Congress shall make no law respecting an establishment of religion, or prohibiting the free exercise thereof, or abridging the freedom of speech, or of the press," thereby guarding in the same sentence, and under the same words, the freedom of religion, of speech, and of the press, insomuch, that whatever violates either, throws down the sanctuary which covers the others, and that libels, falsehoods, defamation equally with heresy and false religion, are withheld from the cognizance of Federal tribunals. That therefore . . . [the Sedition Act], which does abridge the freedom of the press, is not law, but is altogether void and of no effect.

IV. *Resolved,* that alien friends are under the jurisdiction and protection of the laws of the State wherein they are; that no power over them has been delegated to the United States, nor prohibited to the individual States distinct from their power over citizens; and it being true as a general principle, and one of the amendments to the Constitution having also declared that "the powers not delegated to the United States by the Constitution, nor prohibited by it to the States, are reserved to the States respectively, or to the people," the . . . [Alien Act of June 22, 1798], which assumes power over alien friends not delegated by the Constitution, is not law, but is altogether void and of no force.

V. *Resolved,* that in addition to the general principle as well as the express declaration, that powers not delegated are reserved, another and more special provision inserted in the Constitution from abundant caution has declared, "that the migration or importation of such persons as any of the States now existing shall think proper to admit,

shall not be prohibited by the Congress prior to the year 1808." That this Commonwealth does admit the migration of alien friends described as the subject of the said act concerning aliens; that a provision against prohibiting their migration is a provision against all acts equivalent thereto, or it would be nugatory; that to remove them when migrated is equivalent to a prohibition of their migration, and is therefore contrary to the said provision of the Constitution, and void.

* * *

VII. *Resolved,* that the construction applied by the general government . . . to those parts of the Constitution of the United States which delegate to Congress a power to lay and collect taxes, duties, imposts, and excises; to pay the debts, and provide for the common defense, and general welfare of the United States, and to make all laws which shall be necessary and proper for carrying into execution the powers vested by the Constitution in the government of the United States, or any department thereof, goes to the destruction of all the limits prescribed to their power by the Constitution: That words meant by that instrument to be subsidiary only to the execution of the limited powers ought not to be so construed as themselves to give unlimited powers, nor a part so to be taken as to destroy the whole residue of the instrument: That the proceedings of the general government under color of these articles will be a fit and necessary subject for revisal and correction at a time of greater tranquillity, while those specified in the preceding resolutions call for immediate redress.

* * *

IX. *Resolved,* lastly, that the Governor of this Commonwealth be, and is hereby authorized and requested to communicate the preceding Resolutions to the Legislatures of the several States, to assure them that this Commonwealth considers Union for specified National purposes, and particularly for those specified in their late Federal Compact, to be friendly to the peace, happiness, and prosperity of all the States: that faithful to that compact according to the plain intent and meaning in which it was understood and acceded to by the several parties, it is sincerely anxious for its preservation: that it does also believe, that to take from the States all the powers of self-government, and transfer them to a general and consolidated government, without regard to the special delegations and reservations solemnly agreed to in that compact, is not for the peace, happiness, or prosperity of these States: And that, therefore, this Commonwealth is determined, as it doubts not its co-States are, tamely to submit to undelegated and consequently unlimited powers in no man or body of men on earth: that if the acts before specified should stand, these conclusions would flow from them; that the general government may place any act they think proper on the list of crimes and punish it themselves, whether enumerated or not enumerated by the Constitution as cognizable by them: that they may transfer its cognizance to the President or any other person, who may himself be the accuser, counsel, judge, and jury, whose suspicions may be the evidence, his order the sentence, his officer the executioner, and his breast the sole record of the transaction: that a very numerous and valuable description of the inhabitants of these States being by this precedent reduced as outlaws to the absolute dominion of one man, and the barrier of the Constitution thus swept away from us all, no rampart now remains against the passions and the powers of a majority of Congress, to protect from a like exportation or other more grievous punishment the minority of the same body, the legislatures, judges, governors, and counselors of the States, nor their other peaceable inhabitants who may venture to reclaim the constitutional rights and liberties of the State and people, or who

for other causes, good or bad, may be obnoxious to the views or marked by the suspicions of the President, or be thought dangerous to his or their elections or other interests, public or personal: . . . that these and successive acts of the same character, unless arrested on the threshold, may tend to drive these States into revolution and blood, and will furnish new calumnies against Republican governments, and new pretexts for those who wish it to be believed, that man cannot be governed but by a rod of iron: that it would be a dangerous delusion were a confidence in the men of our choice to silence our fears for the safety of our rights: that confidence is everywhere the parent of despotism: free government is founded in jealousy and not in confidence; it is jealousy and not confidence which prescribes limited Constitutions to bind down those whom we are obliged to trust with power: that our Constitution has accordingly fixed the limits to which and no further our confidence may go; and let the honest advocate of confidence read the alien and sedition acts, and say if the Constitution has not been wise in fixing limits to the government it created, and whether we should be wise in destroying those limits; let him say what the government is if it be not a tyranny, which the men of our choice have conferred on the President, and the President of our choice has assented to and accepted. . . . In questions of power then let no more be heard of confidence in man, but bind him down from mischief by the claims of the Constitution. That this Commonwealth does therefore call on its co-States for an expression of their sentiments on the acts concerning aliens, and for the punishment of certain crimes herein before specified, plainly declaring whether these acts are or are not authorized by the Federal Compact. And it doubts not that their sense will be so announced as to prove their attachment unaltered to limited government, whether general or particular, and that the rights and liberties of their co-States will be exposed to no dangers by remaining embarked on a common bottom with their own: That they will concur with this Commonwealth in considering the said acts so palpably against the Constitution as to amount to an undisguised declaration, that the compact is not meant to be the measure of the powers of the general government, but that it will proceed in the exercise over these States of all powers whatsoever: That they will view this as seizing the rights of the States and consolidating them in the hands of the general government with a power assumed to bind the States (not merely in cases made Federal) but in all cases whatsoever, by laws made, not with their consent, but by others against their consent: That this would be to surrender the form of government we have chosen, and to live under one deriving its powers from its own will, and not from our authority; and that the co-States, recurring to their natural right in cases not made Federal, will concur in declaring these acts void and of no force, and will each unite with this Commonwealth in requesting their repeal at the next session of Congress.

4. Jackson's Proclamation to the People of South Carolina

December 10, 1832

WHEREAS a convention assembled in the State of South Carolina have passed an ordinance by which they declare "that the several acts and parts of acts of the Congress of the United States purporting to be laws for the imposing of duties and imposts on the importation of foreign commodities, . . . are unauthorized by the Constitution of the United States, and violate the true meaning and intent thereof, and are null and void and no law," nor binding on the citizens of that State or its officers; and by the said ordinance it is further declared to be unlawful for any of the constituted authorities of the State or of the United States to enforce the payment of the duties imposed by the said acts within the same State, and that it is the duty of the legislature to pass such laws as may be necessary to give full effect to the said ordinance; and

Whereas by the said ordinance it is further ordained that in no case of law or equity decided in the courts of said State wherein shall be drawn in question the validity of the said ordinance, or of the acts of the legislature that may be passed to give it effect, or of the said laws of the United States, no appeal shall be allowed to the Supreme Court of the United States, nor shall any copy of the record be permitted or allowed for that purpose, and that any person attempting to take such appeal shall be punished as for contempt of court; and . . .

Whereas the said ordinance prescribes to the people of South Carolina a course of conduct in direct violation of their duty as citizens of the United States, contrary to the laws of their country, subversive of its Constitution, and having for its object the destruction of the Union—

To preserve this bond of our political existence from destruction, to maintain inviolate this state of national honor and prosperity, and to justify the confidence my fellow-citizens have reposed in me, I, Andrew Jackson, President of the United States, have thought proper to issue this my proclamation, stating my views of the Constitution and laws applicable to the measures adopted by the convention of South Carolina and to the reasons they have put forth to sustain them, declaring the course which duty will require me to pursue, and, appealing to the understanding and patriotism of the people, warn them of the consequences that must inevitably result from an observance of the dictates of the convention. . . .

The ordinance is founded . . . on the strange position that any one State may not only declare an act of Congress void, but prohibit its execution; that they may do this consistently with the Constitution; that the true construction of that instrument permits a State to retain its place in the Union and yet be bound by no other of its laws than those it may choose to consider as constitutional. It is true, they add, that to justify this abrogation of a law it must be palpably contrary to the Constitution; but it is evident that to give the right of resisting laws of that description, coupled with the uncontrolled right to decide what laws deserve that character, is to give the power of resisting all laws; for as by the theory there is no appeal, the reasons alleged by the State, good or bad, must prevail. . . . But reasoning on this subject is superfluous when our social compact, in express terms, declares that the laws of the United States, its Constitution, and treaties made under it are the supreme law of the land, and, for greater caution, adds "that the judges in every State shall be bound thereby, anything in the constitution or laws of any State to the contrary notwithstanding." And it may be asserted without fear of refutation that no federative government could exist without a similar provision. Look for a moment to the consequence. If South Carolina considers the revenue laws unconstitutional and has a right to prevent their execution in the port of Charleston, there would be a clear con-

stitutional objection to their collection in every other port; and no revenue could be collected anywhere, for all imposts must be equal. It is no answer to repeat that an unconstitutional law is no law so long as the question of its legality is to be decided by the State itself, for every law operating injuriously upon any local interest will be perhaps thought, and certainly represented, as unconstitutional, and, as has been shown, there is no appeal. . . .

Our present Constitution was formed . . . in vain if this fatal doctrine prevails. It was formed for important objects that are announced in the preamble, made in the name and by the authority of the people of the United States, whose delegates framed and whose conventions approved it. The most important among these objects—that which is placed first in rank, on which all the others rest—is *"to form a more perfect union."* Now, is it possible that even if there were no express provision giving supremacy to the Constitution and laws of the United States over those of the States, can it be conceived that an instrument made for the purpose of *"forming a more perfect union"* than that of the Confederation could be so constructed by the assembled wisdom of our country as to substitute for that Confederation a form of government dependent for its existence on the local interest, the party spirit, of a State, or of a prevailing faction in a State? Every man of plain, unsophisticated understanding who hears the question will give such an answer as will preserve the Union. Metaphysical subtlety, in pursuit of an impracticable theory, could alone have devised one that is calculated to destroy it.

I consider, then, the power to annul a law of the United States, assumed by one State, *incompatible with the existence of the Union, contradicted expressly by the letter of the Constitution, unauthorized by its spirit, inconsistent with every principle on which it was founded, and destructive of the great object for which it was formed. . . .*

The Constitution of the United States, then, forms a *government,* not a league; and whether it be formed by compact between the States or in any other manner, its character is the same. It is a Government in which all the people are represented, which operates directly on the people individually, not upon the States; they retained all the power they did not grant. But each State, having expressly parted with so many powers as to constitute, jointly with the other States, a single nation, can not, from that period, possess any right to secede, because such secession does not break a league, but destroys the unity of a nation; and any injury to that unity is not only a breach which would result from the contravention of a compact, but it is an offense against the whole Union. To say that any State may at pleasure secede from the Union is to say that the United States are not a nation, because it would be a solecism to contend that any part of a nation might dissolve its connection with the other parts, to their injury or ruin, without committing any offense. Secession, like any other revolutionary act, may be morally justified by the extremity of oppression; but to call it a constitutional right is confounding the meaning of terms, and can only be done through gross error or to deceive those who are willing to assert a right, but would pause before they made a revolution or incur the penalties consequent on a failure. . . .

The States severally have not retained their entire sovereignty. It has been shown that in becoming parts of a nation, not members of a league, they surrendered many of their essential parts of sovereignty. The right to make treaties, declare war, levy taxes, exercise exclusive judicial and legislative powers, were all of them functions of sovereign power. The States, then, for all these important purposes were no longer sovereign. . . . How, then, with all these proofs that under all changes of our position we had, for designated purposes and with defined powers, created national governments, how is it that the most perfect of those several modes of union should now be considered as a mere league that may be dissolved at pleasure? It is from an abuse of terms. Compact is used as synonymous with league, although the true term is not employed, because it would at once show the fallacy of the reasoning. It would not do to say that our Constitution was only a league, but it is labored to prove it a compact (which in one sense it is) and then to argue that as a league is a compact every compact between nations must of course be a league, and that from such an engagement every sovereign power has a right to recede. But it has been shown that in this sense the States are not sovereign, and that even if they were, and the national Constitution had been formed by compact, there would be no right in any one State to exonerate itself from its obligations. . . .

If your leaders could succeed in establishing a separation, what would be your situation? Are you united at home? Are you free from the apprehension of civil discord, with all its fearful consequences? Do our neighboring republics, every day suffering some new revolution or contending with some new insurrection, do they excite your envy? But the dictates of a high duty oblige me solemnly to announce that you can not succeed. The laws of the United States must be executed. I have no discretionary power on the subject; my duty is emphatically pronounced in the Constitution. Those who told you that you might peaceably prevent their execution deceived you; they could not have been deceived themselves. They know that a forcible opposition could alone prevent the execution of the laws, and they know that such opposition must be repelled. Their object is disunion. But be not deceived by names. Disunion by armed force is *treason.* Are you really ready to incur its guilt? If you are, on the heads of the instigators of the act be the dreadful consequences; on their heads be the dishonor, but on yours may fall the punishment. On your unhappy State will inevitably fall all the evils of the conflict you force upon the Government of your country. It can not accede to the mad project of disunion, of which you would be the first victims. Its First Magistrate can not, if he would, avoid the performance of his duty. The consequence must be fearful for you, distressing to your fellow-citizens here and to the friends of good government throughout the world. Its enemies have beheld our prosperity with a vexation they could not conceal; it was a standing refutation of their slavish doctrines, and they will point to our discord with the triumph of malignant joy. . . .

Fellow-citizens of the United States, the threat of unhallowed disunion, the names of those once respected by whom it is uttered, the array of military force to support it, denote the approach of a crisis in our affairs on which the continuance of our unexampled prosperity, our political existence, and perhaps that of all free governments may depend.

The conjuncture demanded a free, a full, and explicit enunciation, not only of my intentions, but of my principles of action; and as the claim was asserted of a right by a State to annul the laws of the Union, and even to secede from it at pleasure, a frank exposition of my opinions in relation to the origin and form of our Government and the construction I give to the instrument by which it was created seemed to be proper. Having the fullest confidence in the justness of the legal and constitutional opinion of my duties which has been expressed, I rely with equal confidence on your undivided support in my determination to execute the laws, to preserve the Union by all constitutional means, to arrest, if possible, by moderate and firm measures the necessity of a recourse to force; and if it be the will of Heaven that the recurrence of its primeval curse on man for the shedding of a brother's blood should fall upon our land, that it be not called down by any offensive act on the part of the United States. . . .

ANDREW JACKSON.

5. *Texas v. White*

7 Wall. 700 (1869)

WITH regard to the legal status of Texas during and following the Civil War, Chief Justice Chase, delivering the opinion of the Supreme Court, observed:

. . . It is not to be questioned that this court has original jurisdiction of suits by states against citizens of other States, or that the States entitled to invoke this jurisdiction must be States of the Union. But, it is equally clear that no such jurisdiction has been conferred upon this court of suits by any other political communities than such States.

If, therefore, it is true that the State of Texas was not at the time of filing this bill, or is not now, one of the United States, we have no jurisdiction of this suit, and it is our duty to dismiss it. . . .

In the Constitution the term state most frequently expresses the combined idea . . . of people, territory, and government. A state, in the ordinary sense of the Constitution, is a political community of free citizens, occupying a territory of defined boundaries, and organized under a government sanctioned and limited by a written constitution, and established by the consent of the governed. It is the union of such states, under a common constitution, which forms the distinct and greater political unit, which that Constitution designates as the United States, and makes of the people and states which compose it one people and one country. . . .

The Republic of Texas was admitted into the Union, as a State, on the 27th of December, 1845. By this act the new State, and the People of the new State, were invested with all the rights, and became subject to all the responsibilities and duties of the original States under this Constitution.

From the date of admission, until 1861, the State was represented in the Congress of the United States by her senators and representatives, and her relations as a member of the Union remained unimpaired. In that year, acting upon the theory that the rights of a State under the Constitution might be renounced, and her obligations thrown off at pleasure, Texas undertook to sever the bond thus formed, and to break up her constitutional relations with the United States. . . .

The position thus assumed could only be maintained by arms, and Texas accordingly took part, with the other Confederate States, in the war of the rebellion, which these events made inevitable. During the whole of that war there was no governor, or judge, or any other State officer in Texas, who recognized the National authority. Nor was any officer of the United States permitted to exercise any authority whatever under the National government within the limits of the State except under the immediate protection of the National military forces.

Did Texas, in consequence of these acts, cease to be a State? Or, if not, did the State cease to be a member of the Union? . . .

The Union of the States never was a purely artificial and arbitrary relation. It began among the Colonies, and grew out of common origin, mutual sympathies, kindred principles, similar interests, and geographical relations. It was

confirmed and strengthened by the necessities of war, and received definite form, and character, and sanction from the Articles of Confederation. By these the Union was solemnly declared to "be perpetual." And when these Articles were found to be inadequate to the exigencies of the country, the Constitution was ordained "to form a more perfect Union." It is difficult to convey the idea of indissoluble unity more clearly than by these words. What can be indissoluble if a perpetual Union, made more perfect, is not? . . .

When, therefore, Texas became one of the United States, she entered into an indissoluble relation. All the obligations of perpetual union and all the guarantees of republican government in the Union, attached at once to the State. The act which consummated her admission into the Union was something more than a compact; it was the incorporation of a new member into the political body. And it was final.

The union between Texas and the other States was as complete, as perpetual, and as indissoluble as the union between the original States. There was no place for reconsideration, or revocation, except through revolution, or through consent of the States.

Considered therefore as transactions under the Constitution, the ordinance of secession, adopted by the convention and ratified by a majority of the citizens of Texas, and all the acts of her legislature intended to give effect to that ordinance, were absolutely null. They were utterly without operation in law. The obligations of the State, as a member of the Union, and of every citizen of the State, as a citizen of the United States, remained perfect and unimpaired. It certainly follows that the State did not cease to be a State, nor her citizens to be citizens of the Union. . . .

Our conclusion therefore is, that Texas continued to be a State, and a State of the Union, notwithstanding the transactions to which we have referred. And this conclusion, in our judgment,

is not in conflict with any act or declaration of any department of the National government, but entirely in accordance with the whole series of such
acts and declarations since the first outbreak of the rebellion. . . .

6. *Williams v. North Carolina*

325 U.S. 226 (1945)

MR. JUSTICE FRANKFURTER delivered the
opinion of the Court.

This case is here to review judgments
of the Supreme Court of North Carolina, affirming convictions for bigamous
cohabitation, assailed on the ground
that full faith and credit, as required
by the Constitution of the United
States, was not accorded divorces decreed by one of the courts of Nevada.
Williams v. North Carolina, 317 U.S.
287, 63 S.Ct. 207, 87 L.Ed. 279, 143
A.L.R. 1273, decided an earlier aspect
of the controversy. It was there held
that a divorce granted by Nevada, on
a finding that one spouse was domiciled
in Nevada, must be respected in North
Carolina, where Nevada's finding of
domicil was not questioned though the
other spouse had neither appeared nor
been served with process in Nevada
and though recognition of such a divorce offended the policy of North
Carolina. The record then before us did
not present the question whether North
Carolina had the power "to refuse full
faith and credit to Nevada divorce decrees because, contrary to the findings
of the Nevada court, North Carolina
finds that no bona fide domicil was
acquired in Nevada." . . . This is the
precise issue which has emerged after
retrial of the cause following our reversal. Its obvious importance brought
the case here. . . .

What is immediately before us is
the judgment of the Supreme Court of
North Carolina. . . . We have authority to upset it only if there is want of
foundation for the conclusion that that
Court reached. The conclusion it

reached turns on its finding that the
spouses who obtained the Nevada decrees were not domiciled there. The
fact that the Nevada court found that
they were domiciled there is entitled to
respect, and no more. The burden of
undermining the verity which the Nevada decrees import rests heavily upon
the assailant. But simply because the
Nevada court found that it had power
to award a divorce decree cannot, we
have seen, foreclose reexamination by
another State. Otherwise, as was pointed
out long ago, a court's record would
establish its power and the power
would be proved by the record. . . .
If this Court finds that proper weight
was accorded to the claims of power by
the court of one State in rendering a
judgment the validity of which is
pleaded in defense in another State,
that the burden of overcoming such respect by disproof of the substratum of
fact—here domicil—on which such
power alone can rest was properly
charged against the party challenging
the legitimacy of the judgment, that
such issue of fact was left for fair determination by appropriate procedure, and
that a finding adverse to the necessary
foundation for any valid sister-State
judgment was amply supported in evidence, we can not upset the judgment
before us. . . .

The judgements of conviction now
under review bring before us a record
which may be fairly summarized by
saying that the petitioners left North
Carolina for the purpose of getting
divorces from their respective spouses
in Nevada and as soon as each had

done so and married one another they left Nevada and returned to North Carolina to live there together as man and wife. Against the charge of bigamous cohabitation . . . , petitioners stood on their Nevada divorces and offered exemplified copies of the Nevada proceedings. . . . If the jury found, as they were told, that petitioners had domicils in North Carolina and went to Nevada "simply and solely for the purpose of obtaining" divorces, intending to return to North Carolina on obtaining them, they never lost their North Carolina domicils nor acquired new domicils in Nevada. . . .

The scales of justice must not be unfairly weighted by a State when full faith and credit is claimed for a sister-State judgment. But North Carolina has not so dealt with the Nevada decrees. She has not raised unfair barriers to their recognition. North Carolina did not fail in appreciation or application of federal standards of full faith and credit. Appropriate weight was given to the finding of domicil in the Nevada decrees, and that finding was allowed to be overturned only by relevant standards of proof. There is nothing to suggest that the issue was not fairly submitted to the jury and that it was not fairly assessed on cogent evidence.

*   *   *

In seeking a decree of divorce outside the State in which he has theretofore maintained his marriage, a person is necessarily involved in the legal situation created by our federal system whereby one State can grant a divorce of validity in other States only if the applicant has a bona fide domicil in the State of the court purporting to dissolve a prior legal marriage. The petitioners therefore assumed the risk that this Court would find that North Carolina justifiably concluded that they had not been domiciled in Nevada. Since the divorces which they sought and received in Nevada had no legal validity in North Carolina and their North Carolina spouses were still alive, they subjected themselves to prosecution for bigamous cohabitation under North Carolina law. The legitimate finding of the North Carolina Supreme Court that the petitioners were not in truth domiciled in Nevada was not a contingency against which the petitioners were protected by anything in the Constitution of the United States. . . .

7. Centralization and Decentralization in the American Federal System*

MORTON GRODZINS

FEAR OF THE FEDERAL OCTOPUS: DECENTRALIZATION BY ORDER

THE federal system has been criticized in recent years from two sides. On the one hand, it is said that the strength of special and local interests (including the strength of state and local governments) frustrates national policy. In Congress this critique holds, the power of the peripheries makes consistent national leadership impossible. Members

* Reprinted from *A Nation of States*, ed. Robert A. Goldwin (Chicago: Rand McNally, 1963). Copyright © 1961 by the Public Affairs Conference Center, The University of Chicago. All Rights Reserved.

of Congress, dependent for reelection on local constituencies rather than on national centers of party power, can with impunity sacrifice national goals for special interests. This argument concludes that an expansion of national powers is essential. On the other hand, it is said that the power of the central government is growing to such an extent that it threatens to efface the state and local governments, reducing them to compliant administrative arms of national offices. The "federal octopus" is held to threaten the very existence of the states and to destroy local initiative.

The two critiques are to a large extent contradictory. Yet reforms of the federal system are often proposed as if one or the other of these complaints were the complete truth. Those concerned about the federal system are uniformly found expressing fear of the federal octopus.

Four attempts have been made during the past dozen years to strengthen the states by devolving upon them functions now performed by the federal government. The first and second Hoover Commissions devoted a portion of their energy to this end. The Kestnbaum Commission, although extolling federal-state cooperation in a number of fields, nevertheless operated on the false assumption that "the principal tradition is the tradition of separation." The President's Federal-State Action Committee was established in 1957 at the recommendation of President Eisenhower for the specific purpose of bringing about an orderly devolution of functions from the federal government to the states.

*   *   *

The committee established at Mr. Eisenhower's suggestion was a distinguished one. It had as co-chairmen Robert B. Anderson, Secretary of the Treasury, and Lane Dwinell, Governor of New Hampshire. Two additional cabinet members, as well as the director of the Bureau of the Budget and several members of the President's personal staff, from the federal side, and nine additional governors, from the state side, completed the group. The committee had excellent staff assistance and complete presidential support. There was no disagreement on party or regional lines. The group was determined not to write just another report, but rather it wished to live up to its name and produce "action" toward decentralization via devolution and separation of functions and tax sources. It worked hard for more than two years.

Never did good intent, hopes, and labor produce such negligible results. The committee could agree on only two activities from which the federal government should withdraw in favor of complete state responsibility. One was the federal grant for sewage-treatment plants; the other was federal aid for vocational education (including aid for practical-nurse training and for training in fishery trades and industry). . . . To enable the states to finance these functions, the committee recommended a state offset for a fraction of the federal tax on local telephone calls. It was calculated that the offset tax, plus an equalization grant, would provide each state with at least 40 per cent more money than it would spend on the two functions it would assume. Some states would receive twice as much.

Faithful to his pledge, President Eisenhower recommended all aspects of this program to Congress. Opposition developed from those benefiting from the vocational-education and sewage-plant grants. Many individual mayors, the American Municipal Association, the United States Conference of Mayors, the several professional groups concerned with vocational education, public-health and sportsmen's associations, state departments of education, and even a large number of governors were included in the opposition. As modest as the program was and as generous as the financing provisions seemed to be, no part of the recommendations was made law. The entire program is now dead.

*   *   *

THE DIFFICULTY OF DIVIDING FUNCTIONS: THE ISSUE OF "CLOSENESS"

History and politics are two reasons for the failure of decentralization by order. A third, related reason is the sheer difficulty of dividing functions between central and peripheral units without the division resulting in further centralization.

It is often claimed that local or state governments are "closer" to the people than the federal government, and therefore the preferred instrument for public action. If one carefully examines this statement, it proves to be quite meaningless.

"Closeness" when applied to governments means many things. One meaning is the provision of services directly to the people. Another meaning is participation. A third is control: to say that local governments are closer to the people than the federal government is to say that citizens can control the former more easily and more completely than the latter. A fourth meaning is understanding, a fifth communication, a sixth identification. Thorough analysis of "closeness" would have to compare local, state, and federal governments with respect to all these, as well as other, meanings of the term.

Such an analysis reveals that in few, if any, of these meanings are the state and local units "closer" to the people than the federal government. The big differences are between rural and urban areas: citizens in rural areas are "closer" (in many, but not all, meanings) to both the local and federal governments than are residents of big urban areas.

Consider, for example, "closeness" as the provision of services. All governments in the American system operate in direct contact with people at their places of residence and work, and in important activities the units operate collaboratively. It cannot even be said that the local units provide the most important local services. The important services are those of shared responsibility. Where it is possible to recognize primary responsibilities, the greater importance of local government does not at all emerge.

Where in the American system is the government closest to the people as a provider of services? The answer is clearly neither the local nor federal government in urban areas and not even local government in rural areas. Rather it is the federal government in rural areas that is closest to the people (as provider of services). As a consumer of services the farmer has more governmental wares to choose from than any other citizen. They are largely federal or federally sponsored wares, and they cover virtually all aspects of his personal and economic life.

If he wished to take full advantage of what was offered, an individual farmer could assemble a veritable convention of government helpers in his home and fields. He could have a soil-conservation technician make a survey of his property, prepare plans for conservation practices and watershed protection, and give advice on crops, growing practices, wood-lot planting, and wild-life maintenance. A Forest Service Officer collaboratively with a state forester would provide low-cost tree stock. Extension workers would aid the farmer's wife on all aspects of home management, including gardening, cooking, and sewing; instruct the children with respect to a whole range of health, recreational, and agricultural problems; provide the farmer himself with demonstrations and information aimed at reducing costs, increasing income, and adjusting production to market demands, and give the entire family instruction with respect to "social relations, adjustments and cultural values."

An officer of the Agricultural Conservation Program would arrange federal grants for part of the costs of his soil and conservation practices, including ditching and building ponds. (Another official would provide a supply of fish at little or no cost with which to stock the pond.) A Commodity Stabilization Service worker would arrange for loans on some crops, for government purchase of others, and for special incentive payments on still a third category; he would also pay the farmer for constructing crop-storage facilities. Another officer from the same agency would arrange cash payments to the farmer under the soil-bank program, if he takes out of production acres devoted to designated basic crops (the "acreage reserve") or puts general cropland to conservation use (the "conservation reserve"). An official of the Farmers Home Administration, if credit is not elsewhere available, will make loans to the farmer for the operation, improvement, and enlargement of his property, and (to maximize repayment possibilities) will "service" the farmer-borrower by providing him with comprehensive and continuous technical advice on how to make his operation as profitable as possible. All this just begins the list.

8. The Problem of Big Government*

HERBERT J. STORING

VIEWED from the standpoint of the Founders, American government today seems to have been turned on its head. Generally speaking, and contrary to the Founders' expectations, it is in the state governments that the conservative and propertied interests find their main influence and support. It is the national government that seems most susceptible to pressures from the people at large and least concerned to protect the interests of the few. There lies the irony of the use by the President of the Chamber of Commerce of the Jeffersonian argument that "the government which is best for the people is that which is closest to them." The state governments may be closer to the Chambers of Commerce, but today it is the national government that in all fundamental respects is closer to the people. Indeed the national government, including the Senate and the Supreme Court, seems to have been infused with the popular spirit. And although the President is still obliged to reconcile popular wants and national needs, he has to do so today as a great popular leader rather than as one chosen by a small group of judicious men.

Some argue, therefore, that when conservatives depart from the conception of American government held by their forebears they are only adjusting themselves to new circumstances while remaining true to the traditional end, namely, to support and defend those institutions of government most closely connected with the "temperate and respectable" elements. If the Democracy has occupied the national government and the Presidency, perhaps the party of the Republic must take its stand in the states and, when it can, in Congress.

This argument is untenable for two reasons. First, in seeking to strengthen state governments at the expense of the national, it demands an attitude toward American government that is not only contrary to the best conservative tradition but hopelessly unrealistic. It amounts to a permanent commitment to a series of rear-guard actions in

* Reprinted from *A Nation of States,* ed. Robert A. Goldwin (Chicago: Rand McNally, 1963). Copyright © 1961 by the Public Affairs Conference Center, The University of Chicago. All Rights Reserved.

which there is room only for retreat. Only yesterday many men insisted that social security, agricultural policy, and labor relations were purely local matters, and they sought to enforce this opinion with constitutional shackles on the national government. The effect was only to deprive those men of any influence in deciding how the nation would meet what were manifestly national problems. A rigid insistence today that such matters as unemployment, education, and the condition of our cities are not national problems will have the same kind of consequence. . . .

Second, this argument in favor of weakening the national government fails to recognize that, while a government ought to be ordered so that it will not act badly, it must also and pre-eminently have the capacity to act well. Just as the dangers that the nation may face are illimitable, so are its opportunities. . . . And while the decent operation of government from day to day is served by a plurality of interests,

by divided government, and by checks on ambition, the times of crisis and greatness demand unity and power and leadership. A constitution should so far as possible provide for both. Checks and balances are still important, and let there be no misunderstanding: decentralization of administration, a continued and even increased emphasis on state and local government where that is possible, and internal checks on ill-conceived action are legitimate and necessary. But conservatives defeat their own purposes when they set themselves against an adequate national government and a strong President and administration just because the popular elements are for them. They do no service to themselves or to the Republic when they adopt a policy of strengthening those elements of the American governmental system whose tendency is to emphasize the separateness of the parts at the expense of those in whose hands it lies to maintain the unity of the whole.

9. The Case for "States' Rights"

JAMES JACKSON KILPATRICK

ONE of the reasons for the success of this system is that the States and the localities must always be closer to the people than the central government. In stating this view, I respectfully differ from one of my brother essayists, who paints a pretty picture of the intimacy that exists, especially in the case of the farmer, between the Federal government and the individual citizen. It is a pretty picture, but a false one. On my

* Reprinted from *A Nation of States,* ed. Robert A. Goldwin (Chicago: Rand McNally, 1963). Copyright © 1961 by the Public Affairs Conference Center, The University of Chicago. All Rights Reserved.

own observations (apart from the common observation of mankind), I would find him clearly wrong. Several years ago, in a manifestation of that particular lunacy to which newspapermen historically are prone, I undertook to run a chicken farm. The county agent was indeed a source of comfort, and the home-demonstration worker could be summoned to educate my wife in the mysteries of a churn. But only in a very narrow and technical sense were these neighborly plenipotentiaries ministers of the Federal government. In their appointment and in their daily activities, they were "county people," different in every way from the regional inspectors of the Commodity Credit Corporation sent out to measure one's acres of wheat. Nor were the ministrations of even the county agents and soil conservation committeemen (locally elected) the be-all and end-all of farm life. Of far greater importance were the local schools, and the local tax rate, and the widening of the road that led to the country store. The government that counted most, because we felt the greatest sense of community with it, was the government at the courthouse, and the government at the State Capitol.

A part of this feeling rests in the belief that local government can be controlled in a way that the central government cannot be controlled. Restraints can be applied close at hand, through the devices of referendum and recall, that cannot be applied far away. The county commissioner dwells low on Olympus, and the local alderman is accessible in ways that United States Senators and Cabinet Secretaries are not accessible. When a citizen of Virginia travels to the Capitol at Richmond, he travels with a sure sense of participation and of community; he speaks to the committees of the General Assembly, supporting or opposing particular legislation, as a fellow-citizen in the community of four million that is Virginia. When he travels to the Capitol at Washington, by contrast, he feels insecurity gnawing at his vitals. He finds the palace ringed by the glassy castles of potent baronies—the Machinists, the Mineworkers, the Educationists—and the marbled catacombs of the Senate Office Building are filled with total strangers. In this distant opulence, he stands subdued.

It is out of this sense of helplessness that the citizen draws his prudent fear of "Federal control." He sees Federal control as an inescapable corollary of "Federal aid." He knows that it cannot possibly be otherwise. Nor is he the least impressed by the remonstrances of political doctors who assure him that

the history of numerous grant-in-aid programs fails to support his apprehension.

I am told that Federal controls never have been oppressive, and that Federal outlays almost invariably are administered by State and local functionaries in whom our trust may be freely reposed. I am told that I am conjuring mere spectres and seeing things in the dark. John Marshall long ago (in *McCulloch v. Maryland,* 1819) struck through these specious assurances with a famous line. The tax levied by Maryland upon the Bank of the United States was not large; Mr. McCulloch could have paid it and the Bank would not have gone under. But it was not the particular tax that mattered. It was the power to tax, for "the power to tax involves the power to destroy." . . . If the central government can aid our disabled, and pension our old people, and succour our illegitimate children; if it can fill our fish ponds and level our slums; if it can build our highways and lay our sewers and vaccinate our children and finance our college students, it can dominate our lives in such a way that freedom is lost altogether. It is *the power to control* that is to be feared; and this power to control follows the Federal dollar as surely as that famous lamb accompanied little Mary. And it will follow us to school one day if the principle of general aid to public education, and especially to teacher salaries, ever is approved by the Congress.

Coming events cast long shadows. I see the penumbra approaching and I feel the damp wind cold on my neck. Let the man who imagines there are "no controls" study the disbursement of hospital construction grants under the Hill-Burton Act. Let him gaze upon the thick manual of federally approved regulations by which the interstate highways must be constructed uniformly. Let him ponder the effect of the wage controls decreed under the Davis-Bacon Act—40,000 local determinations a year, and every one of them controlling what shall be paid carpenters, pipefitters, and common laborers. We have lately had the example of what is known euphemistically as the National Defense Education Act, and I find in it incipiently the very philosophy that seems to me so dangerous; for these grants are intended chiefly for students agreeable to studying what the government wants them to study —science, and mathematics, and foreign languages. We have opened our classroom door, like the flap of the nomad's tent, to a very large camel. I see in the history of legislation under the commerce clause what lies ahead in education; for the regulation of commerce that began with the steamboats of Gibbons and Ogden has expanded until even the window washers on a local office building are the objects of Federal control. The scholarship program that begins with a subtle hint of what should be learned will yet end in effective control of what shall be taught, and to whom, and by whom, and in what sort of buildings.

*   *   *

The worst fate that could befall this Republic would be for the centralists to impose upon this broad land a Procrustean uniformity that would impoverish the Hudson Valley to enrich the catfish Yazoo. If our strength be in union, it lies first in apartness. This concept is the spark that kindled the American flame; it is the very soul of our Republic, and we ought never to trade it off to the centralist Mephistopheles who promises a beautiful Utopia but would deliver a dreary Hell.

In thus contending for a tightly limited central government, no thoughtful States' righter would want to be misunderstood. If he urges the importance of the Tenth Amendment, he urges with equal vigor the propriety of Article I, Section 8. In matters of foreign policy, in the waging of war, in the coinage of money, in the full and efficient operation of all those delegated powers that are in fact national in their scope—in all of these, the advocate of strict construction yields to the central authority gladly. He is not asking that Delaware be admitted to NATO, or that a first reliance in some war with Russia be placed on the Georgia militia.

He is urging simply that we cherish a reasoned veneration for established institutions, and that we preserve a decent obedience to the form and spirit and meaning of the Constitution. He knows that fallible man will err, and he conceives it better to risk wrongs imposed upon one State than to hazard misjudgments that fall upon fifty. He is no foe of "national greatness." He is merely convinced that national greatness may best be achieved by building upon the solid foundation of personal liberty, individual attainment, and local responsibility erected by the wisest men the Republic will ever know.

10. Calhoun Revisited*

JOHN R. SCHMIDHAUSER and RICHARD L. McANAW

EVERY few years dissident groups attack our constitutional system under the guise of saving the "sovereign states" from the encroachments of the

* Reprinted with permission from *National Civic Review*, September 1963.

federal government. The current group of "saviors" feel that the U.S. Supreme Court went too far when it acted against racial discrimination and state legislative malapportionment. They seek to curb the power of the Supreme

Court by amending the constitution to provide for a "Court of the Union" composed of the chief justices of the 50 states. This court would meet on the "demand of the legislatures of five states, no two of which shall share any common boundary . . . [to review] any judgment of the Supreme Court relating to the rights reserved to the states." The decisions of this court would be "final" and could not be "overruled by any court."

The catalyst which touched off the current drive for "states' rights" was the decision of the Supreme Court in the recent reapportionment case of *Baker v. Carr*. In September 1962, the National Legislative Conference, composed of state legislative leaders, adopted a resolution deploring the "increasing concentration of power in Washington" and issued a call to "reverse this trend and to strengthen the states." A committee was appointed to "prepare a report exploring a clear-cut approach to the initiation of constitutional amendments through a constitutional convention." Subsequently this committee, called the Federal-State Relations Committee, reported to the Sixteenth General Assembly of the States in December 1962. The committee report called for the proposal of three constitutional amendments. The first provides that the state legislatures may amend the federal constitution without congressional action or the calling of a national convention. The second took state legislative apportionment out of the scope of federal court or federal constitutional authority. The third provided for creation of a Court of the Union to supersede the United States Supreme Court as the highest court of the nation.

The vote of the Assembly of the States tells us something about the backing for the Court of the Union proposal. On this issue, the state delegations at the assembly divided 21 to 20 with five passing. Of the 21 delegations in favor of the resolution, thirteen were either southern or border states

and seven others were controlled by Republican majorities. A northern Republican-southern Democratic coalition similar to the conservative congressional coalition which has successfully blocked civil rights and other legislation of benefit to minority groups and to the urban majority effected passage of this proposed amendment.

Up to now only four states have petitioned Congress with respect to the Court of the Union. Three of these states—Alabama, Arkansas, and Florida—are southern, and the fourth—Wyoming—is among the more conservative of our states. Mississippi rejected all three amendments after apparently seeing some sinister liberal plot to wipe out her "peculiar institution." Although the proponents of the amendments have denied association with "far right" groups such as the White Citizens Council and the John Birch Society, there is a definite parallel in their respective ideologies.

*　　*　　*

Fundamentally, the most serious result of the adoption of the proposed amendment would be the weakening of the nation itself. Professor Charles L. Black, Jr., in a recent *Yale Law Review* article correctly identified the movement for all three amendments as "one more attempt . . . to convert the U.S. into a confederation."

*　　*　　*

Despite the clarity with which the principle of national supremacy was stated in the constitution, strong attacks were launched both upon the principle and upon the Supreme Court's application of it. The early nineteenth century was the great testing period. In *United States v. Judge Peters* the Supreme Court laid down this crucial doctrine:

> If the legislatures of the several states may, at will, annul the judgments of the courts of the United States, and destroy the rights acquired under those judgments, the

constitution itself becomes a solemn mockery; and the nation is deprived of the means of enforcing its laws by the instrumentality of its own tribunals. So fatal a result must be deprecated by all; and the people of Pennsylvania, not less than the citizens of every other state, must feel a deep interest in resisting principles so destructive of the union, and in averting consequences so fatal to themselves.

*   *   *

The contemporary suggestion that the 50 chief justices of the highest appellate courts of the states be made into a judicial institution superseding the venerable Supreme Court is not a conservative suggestion but is radical in the extreme. Such a new institution would completely lack the internal traditions and procedures which have been evolved by the Supreme Court for nearly two centuries. The proposed Court of the Union would be composed of members whose tenure was not stable but frequently dependent upon the vicissitudes of partisan election, some for terms as short as two years.

Of even greater importance is the factor of parochial adherence to regional prejudice which would be built into a court composed of state chief justices. While it is quite true that some of the state appellate courts have produced jurists of high caliber, it is equally true that some of the state appellate courts reflect in the most direct manner the deep regional commitments which inhibit equality of opportunity in law as well as the economic sphere. . . .

In short, the adoption of the Court of the Union to overrule the United States Supreme Court would not only entail the reduction of the nation to a confederacy but would have profound and detrimental effects upon the urgent drive to achieve the American ideal of equality before the law.

11. To Foster Disunity*

JEFFERSON B. FORDHAM

In December 1962 the Council of State Governments put forward three proposed amendments to the United States Constitution. This paper is directly concerned with one of them—that on state legislative apportionment—but in order to identify the package, brief reference will be made to all three. . . . The council seeks action by the legislatures of at least two-thirds of the states memorializing Congress to call a national constitutional convention to propose the desired amendments.

The first amendment would provide a procedure for amending the constitution by state legislative initiation and

* Reprinted with permission from *National Civic Review*, September 1963.

ratification without federal participation as to substance either by congressional action or that of a national convention. The second would place control of state legislative apportionment beyond any federal limitation or control and would exclude completely any congressional or federal court jurisdiction. The third would create a Court of the Union, composed of the chief justices of the highest courts of the states, with jurisdiction to review, on the initiative of five state legislatures . . . "any judgment of the Supreme Court relative to the rights reserved to the states or to the people by this constitution."

The writer's evaluation of the three proposals, as a package, is that they are so bad they defy adequate critical description or characterization. They have a state orientation completely without recognition of the character of the United States as a federal union or the imperative need, in the interest of free men everywhere in this interdependent world, to maintain our strength and effectiveness as a national union. They are, at the same time, insensitive to human rights; as a matter of fact, more than anything else, they are a reaction against decisions of the Supreme Court involving protection of human rights.

The substantive parts of the apportionment proposal read:

> Section 1. No provision of this constitution, or any amendment thereto, shall restrict or limit any state in the apportionment of representation in its legislature.
> Section 2. The judicial power of the United States shall not extend to any suit in law or equity, or to any controversy relating to apportionment of representation in a state legislature.

The recommendation of the initiating committee of the General Assembly of the States (an arm of the Council of State Governments) identified the proposal as "an amendment to eliminate federal judicial authority over the apportionment of state legislatures." This is patently inaccurate; the first paragraph expressly removes such apportionment from the restrictive application of any provision of the federal constitution as amended and thus goes far beyond the asserted purpose of eliminating federal court jurisdiction.

The proposal is, of course, a reaction to the Tennessee reapportionment case, *Baker v. Carr* (369 U.S. 186, 1962). . . .

*   *   *

It must be apparent that, as a practical matter, the apportionment amendment is the key proposal in the "disunion" package even though the other two are the ones which broadly attack the union. Apportionment is of direct concern to state legislators the country over. Thus, it is a rallying focus for counteraction by legislators in all regions. State's rights proponents in the South need help from other quarters to muster the legislative support necessary to initiate the call of a constitutional convention.

While one is mindful that in some states constitutional provisions on legislative representation may be vulnerable because they work invidious discrimination, it is clear enough that the fault lies with the legislatures in many states. It is common knowledge that legislatures have been flagrantly in default with respect to redistricting and reapportionment. This being the case, the moral position of state legislative proponents of the present proposed amendment is weak. What they seek is to assure their freedom and impunity to continue to deal callously with the political interests of citizens.

*   *   *

All this is not to assert that to supplant malapportionment with fair representation in relation to population would of itself convert the legislatures into strong and effective organs. Other changes . . . are needed. It is proper to suggest, however, that fair representation is likely to bring about greater state legislative sensitivity in two of the greatest problem areas of our time —the areas of human rights and of urban affairs in an increasingly urbanized society.

*   *   *

The proposed amendment is a blunderbuss attack on *Baker v. Carr*. It does not stop with denying federal court jurisdiction in cases involving state legislative apportionment. It provides that nothing in the constitution shall restrict or limit any state as to legislative apportionment. This covers the whole ground. The equal protection clause would not apply. The Fifteenth Amendment guaranty of the franchise without regard to race or color would not apply to the election of state representatives and racial discrimination could be practiced in any state with no recourse open to the victims. It is significant that there could be no redress on federal grounds even in state courts since the amendment would have removed them.

. . . The amendment would enjoy the odious distinction of being the first change in the constitution to reduce the protection of individual rights and, with supreme irony, would do this at a time when we are at a critical point in the struggle for equality of opportunity.

*   *   *

12. Interstate Agencies and Effective Administration*

RICHARD H. LEACH

DESPITE the recent trend toward broader use of interstate compact agencies, there persists a fairly widespread feeling that they entail a great many "pitfalls" and thus that they should be used only *in extremis*. It is true that compact agencies, like any other governmental device, cannot be guaranteed to operate perfectly, but it does not follow that they should therefore be avoided.

Unfortunately, the literature on interstate compacts, while rich in historical and legal studies, is poor in operational studies. As Emil Sady pointed out in 1957, the administration of interstate agencies is one of the areas most requiring study in the whole field of federal-state relations. Case studies, Sady noted, need to be made of "the special problems involved in the creation, organization, financing, public control and use of interstate bodies. . . ." Until a number of such analyses are made, precise data on the operational capacities of compact agencies will be lacking.

* Reprinted with permission from *State Government,* Summer 1961. Footnotes omitted.

RECORDS MATCHING THE BEST

I have followed the careers of all the major compact agencies now operating in the United States rather closely over the past five years, however, and I have become convinced that the common arguments advanced against compact agencies . . . do not amount to much. The record shows that their performance records can match the best of those of state and federal agencies. As consideration is given to their use in attacking the problems of the 1960's, these arguments ought to be reexamined, and any concern which may have been felt about the use of a compact agency on administrative grounds should be abandoned. There is no evidence to indicate that compact agencies warrant special concern on operational grounds.

FOUR MAIN CRITICISMS

*   *   *

Perhaps the most common charge against interstate agencies is that they are irresponsible, beyond reach of the people's control once they are set up. Since nowhere are compact commissions elected by the people of the party states, and thus cannot be made responsible to them in the ordinary way, they are *ipso facto* irresponsible. Nor, runs the argument, is their responsibility either to the state legislatures which establish them, or to the Governors who in most cases appoint their members, any more clearly defined. In almost no case have legislatures or Governors developed an effective procedure to make compact commissions responsible to them. And, continues the charge, compact agencies are not responsible to Congress, either. Although for the most part they cannot come into existence without Congressional consent, Congress has not developed any more satisfactory procedure than have the states to enforce responsibility. Indeed, the argument concludes, compact agencies, once launched, are relegated to a limbo of neglect, and from then on they operate as essentially irresponsible bodies. "The special authority," warns William Zeckendorf, "can be an efficient governmental entity; it can also be an autocratic and unresponsive agency."

The charge also is often made that compact commissions are staff dominated. With one outstanding exception (the Waterfront Commission of New York Harbor), commissioners give only part of their time and attention to compact agency affairs. They are state and federal officials, educators, industrialists, farmers, and legislators first, and compact commissioners second. Their first loyalty must necessarily be to their first interest. Compact operation and staff direction, it is said, can at best be but a secondary concern to them. Morever, compact commissioners generally serve with no compensation, or with only token compensation, and thus, it is advanced, they tend to feel less personal responsibility for agency operation than they would if they were salaried.

In fact, few compact commissions meet more often than twice or three times a year. When they do come together, they are forced by the circumstances of the case to receive staff recommendations and approve staff action rather than to make recommendations to the staff and suggest staff action. These factors, opponents of compacts point out, combined with the freedom which commissions have from civil service requirements in hiring staff, lead to staff domination and control of compact agency operation. In many cases, it is charged, the staff of a compact agency, to all intents and purposes, *is* the agency. Acting virtually independently of the commission, the staff initiates and executes policy. If the commissions themselves are irresponsible, the argument assumes, the staff must be even more so, removed as it is still a step further from popular control.

The third criticism levelled against compact agencies is that—as islands offshore from the *terra firma* of responsible democratic government—they fail to coordinate their operations with those of other governmental units. Thus, it is pointed out, the Port of New York Authority frequently acts without prior consultation with officials of the City of New York. Faced with the pronouncement of a new Authority program as a *fait accompli,* city officials have no recourse but to work out the best accommodation they can to it. Nor is the Port Authority alone in this respect. Virtually every compact agency works in a field where municipal, state or federal agencies also are at work, and, the charge is made, because coordination is lacking, duplication and overlapping on the one hand and conflict and ill will on the other often result.

The other complaint most commonly made about compact agencies is that there is no adequate way to judge their effectiveness. This is called a most grievous fault because the people cannot bring the same sanctions to bear on compact officials that they can on state and federal officers. Existing as they do in a sort of twilight zone of the public consciousness, compact agencies may not make the contributions they might or should. Indeed, they may not even justify their continued existence. Other governmental units, it is said, are at least subject to the scrutiny of legislatures every year or two at appropriations time, and they are subject to the possibility of special legislative investigation. Compact agencies, however, while not exempt from either possibility, have not in practice been subjected at all frequently to such review. And because compact agencies are not in the regular administrative family of either the states or the federal government, the parental control exercised by Governors and the President is likewise light. Nor do many compact agencies have easily identifiable publics which they must please. In short, it is maintained, they operate without benefit of systematic or even casual review of their operations and of their effectiveness, and as a consequence are often less concerned with their performance than with being successful in their public relations.

THE PROBLEMS AREN'T PECULIAR

It is not my contention that the case against compact agencies is altogether overstated. When once set up they do operate beyond the reach of the people; their operations are largely staff directed; they do sometimes fail to coordinate their activities with those of other governmental agencies; and it is hard to tell when they are doing a good job. It is my contention, however, that these are not the peculiarities of compact agencies alone. The same strictures may be made of any governmental unit. It is not fair to try to single out compact agencies and indict them with faults which are common to the whole species.

The kinds of problems compact agencies create in their operation run across the board in public administration and offer perhaps the greatest challenge to students of American government. The rebuttal of the case against them thus cannot be made on the grounds that it is false, but on the grounds that compact agencies, perhaps more than any other governmental agency, have developed operating procedures which minimize these dangers. If anything, their record suggests that they offer a model which might be followed by other units of government.

THE QUESTION OF RESPONSIBILITY

It is true, of course, that compact agencies are not directly responsible to the people of the states in the same way that elected officials are. But in the complex world of modern American government, how close are the people to any governmental agency? In every state and in the federal government as well, the trend has been increasingly toward placing important aspects of government in the hands of appointed boards and commissions, the members of which are beyond the immediate reach of public opinion. If the charge of irresponsibility be raised against compact agencies on this ground, it must be raised likewise against a great many other governmental agencies as well. To what extent, for example, is the Federal Trade Commission or the Interstate Commerce Commission responsible to the people? Or a state department of motor vehicles or parole board to the people of its state? Or, for that matter, the city planning commission of many a city to its citizens? The argument that the essence of responsibility lies in external, popular checks on governmental bodies simply cannot be used effectively today, with regard to compact agencies or any other similarly constituted governmental agency.

Nor does it follow that the lack of a direct relationship to the people automatically results in the abuse of power, in irresponsible action. A governmental agency does not need to be directly responsible to the people to be responsive to the public interest. The latter is accomplished in the case of compact agencies in a number of ways. Formally, it is accomplished in the compact itself, which in virtually every case more or less severely limits the power of the commission it creates, by imposing strict financial and budgetary controls on it, or by endowing the Governors with a form of veto power over its actions, or, most frequently, simply by denying it the power of enforcement altogether.

In addition, reports to popularly elected officials or bodies are required of all compact agencies at regular intervals, on the basis of which they can be taken to task, if need be, in the same way their sister agencies in the individual states can be. Very few agencies, moreover, are free from the necessity of securing appropriations for continued operation from the legislatures of the party states. It is not logical to assume that the states will long continue to support an "autocratic and unresponsive" agency. Nor is there anything to prevent the party states from requiring whatever additional guarantees they think necessary to secure responsiveness. Still further, the actions of compact agencies are subject to review by the courts.

Important as all these formal devices are for assuring compact agency responsibility, they are not nearly as important in the last analysis as the internal, subjective sense of responsibility—of dedication to the public welfare—which has developed in most of the compact agencies now in operation. Lacking, in almost every case, effective *governmental* power, they are forced to fall back on consent and persuasion to accomplish their ends. And it does not take much to demonstrate that consent and persuasion are the handmaidens of responsible, responsive, not arbitrary action.

This internal sense of responsibility is adequate almost by itself to make external checks unnecessary. In addition, the habit has been developed of appointing members of compact commissions on an essentially nonpolitical basis. Many compacts specify the persons who shall serve as commissioners; others leave selection to the discretion of the Governor. Either way, the selection is made on the basis of professional qualifications or office held, and not on the basis of political alignment. Commissioners are thus inclined to consider the problems before them in a clinical rather than a political way. They are not concerned about political rewards and relationships. This, too, serves to orient them in the direction of the public interest: of the interest of the whole public and not of themselves or a narrow part of the public.

Indeed, my acquaintance with compact agencies leads me to believe that there are few better administered—i.e., administered from the point of view of the public interest—governmental agencies than compact agencies. The proof of the pudding is in the eating, and the record of compact agencies in operation firmly refutes the charge of irresponsibility.

'STAFF DOMINATION'

As for staff domination, what governmental agency does not have its activities largely in the hands of its staff? The Interstate Commerce Commission, for example, consists of eleven commissioners; its staff totals about 2,360. Is it not true that the commission is more the 2,360 than the eleven? How would the eleven function at all without the 2,360? The Federal Trade Commission has five members and a staff of more than 800. Is the conclusion any more valid here that the commissioners can do the job alone? Certainly anyone who has studied the Presidency knows the need for presidential staff assistance, and it is often difficult to distinguish staff action from that of the President himself. The same situation applies throughout the federal government, in state and local agencies, in private industry and in universities. What faculty would not complain if the university were actually run by its trustees? Indeed, so important is staff to the operation of any enterprise that the personnel problem is today generally recognized as of prime importance in both government and industry.

What really counts, therefore, is not the surface indications that compact agencies are staff run, but what kind of staffs the compact agencies employ. Here the evidence is clear. Freed from civil service regulations and salary limitations which often make it more difficult for the states to get good people for various posts, compact agencies on the whole have employed top-flight staffs, and having hired them are able to keep them. . . .

Certainly the compact agency staff picture is devoid of any indication of empire-building. Compare, for example, the total number of staff employed by all the compact agencies now operating in the United States with the number of employees of one state department. There are less than 500 of the former; the Highway Department of virtually every state is larger. Nor are bad results evident. Compact staffs have performed their work well. Streams are being cleaned up, crime is being reduced, education is being furthered, transportation is being facilitated, wherever you look on the compact front.

*   *   *

CONCERNING COORDINATION

Nor is the failure to coordinate their activities with those of other governmental bodies peculiar to compact agencies alone. Lack of coordination is common on all levels of government, perhaps more on the federal level than anywhere else. The failure of the Bureau of Reclamation and the Corps of Engineers to coordinate their programs over the years is one outstanding example. The findings of the various "Little Hoover Commissions" in the states are replete with evidence of poor or nonexistent coordination among state agencies.

Coordination is chiefly a matter of leadership, in a compact agency or any other unit, and because the executive directors of most compact agencies realize the necessity of cooperation for the success of their activities, they push in that direction all the time. Indeed, the failure to coordinate results more often from the intransigence of the older and better established state and local agencies than from the failure of the compact agency to extend an invitation to cooperate. The record of cooperation achieved between compact agencies and the federal government by itself belies the assertion that they automatically result in poor coordination.

MEASURING EFFECTIVENESS

Finally, the charge that it is hard to tell when they are doing a good job applies to a great many more institutions than compact agencies. It is hardly a ground for avoiding that particular form of organization. Moreover, many compact agencies are treading new ground, working in areas where no precedents exist. Thus it is hard to develop adequate standards to judge effectiveness, much less to apply them. As for compact agencies playing the public relations theme for all it is worth, this does not seem to be motivated, as compact critics think, by a desire to gloss over poor performance, but instead by a real need to introduce compact agency work to the public— to make the people aware of the role it is playing in meeting the governmental needs of the community.

THEY HAVE PROVED THEMSELVES

Every time a compact agency is proposed as a solution to a problem, one or more of the arguments noted above against its creation is usually raised. Precisely because there is so little in the way of definitive studies of compact operation, it is hard to counter the arguments with statistical evidence. Yet they should be countered. For well over thirty compact agencies are now in operation, the oldest dating back forty years, and acquaintance with them makes it clear that they perform as well as, and often better than, older and more familiar governmental agencies.

Compact agencies have proved themselves, and they may safely be relied upon to help solve a great many of the difficult problems of the next several decades. At least, when proposals for their use are made, as they increasingly will be, there will be no need to abandon the idea on operational grounds. Compact agencies have won a place in the American governmental composite. They can be used without fear that they will be crippled by "administrative pitfalls." Indeed, in the years ahead they may well be recognized as models for other agencies to follow in the administration of their programs.

Part II

STATE CONSTITUTIONS

As Robert B. Dishman has so ably noted, constitutions need to evidence certain requirements in order to perform effectively their role as basic law. They should be confined to fundamentals, kept up to date, consistent in their provisions, simply written, and logically arranged (*State Constitutions: The Shape of the Document,* National Municipal League, 1960). If such considerations are to have effect on our state constitutions, a first step is to study the existing documents in order to obtain appreciation of their nature and knowledge of their provisions. Although each state constitution is unique, understanding can be facilitated by use of a frame of reference for study. Charlotte Irvine and Edward M. Kresky give assistance to the student in *How to Study a State Constitution.* Especially helpful is their list of questions to be kept in mind while examining the content of a state constitution.

Additional insight into the nature of state constitutions as they exist today is provided by David Fellman in "What Should a State Constitution Contain?" His specific examples, illustrating the problem of detail, are especially helpful. Also, Professor Fellman examines factors that have contributed to the wordiness of the states' basic laws as well as reasons why excessive detail is undesirable. A careful reading of this article assists in an appreciation of the politics of state constitutions as well as their formal structural nature. After all, many provisions find their way into state constitutions because some group has successfully urged their inclusion.

A chief purpose of every constitution in the American system of government is to protect the people in the enjoyment of civil liberties, as the prominent place occupied by a bill of rights in each state constitution attests. Although judicial extension of certain guarantees found in the national Constitution as limitations upon state action has reduced the significance of some provisions in state bills of rights, not all the rights belonging to citizens of the various states are protected under federal law. Consequently, many guarantees found in state bills of rights continue to have real significance. The purposes served by a state bill of rights are examined in relation to the drafting of the Alaskan constitution.

In 1921 the Committee on State Government of the National Municipal League prepared the first edition of the Model State Constitution. Since that time six versions, or editions, of the Model have appeared, the most recent in 1963. Although no one seriously claims that this document is perfect or that it should be adopted *in toto* in any state, it deserves the careful attention of all students and practitioners in the field of state and local government. Unquestionably, the influence of the Model is apparent in recent state constitutions, especially those of New Jersey, Alaska, Hawaii, and Michigan. Mr. John Bebout describes briefly the role of the Model in his "Introduction" to the sixth edition of that important document.

13. How to Study a State Constitution*

CHARLOTTE IRVINE and EDWARD M. KRESKY

A PLAN FOR STUDY

Studying a constitution has two aspects, analyzing the form and content of the constitution and gathering the information needed to evaluate the content.

A preliminary look is sometimes the quickest way to become familiar with patent difficulties. In our more colorful constitutions may be found a provision against duelling, a page on the world's fair, or an exhortation on the importance of selected virtues. There may be pinpointed detail regulating matters that have long since ceased to merit special protection or to tempt special pressures. A contradiction may be obvious. Passages that defy comprehen-

* Reprinted with permission from *How To Study a State Constitution*, National Municipal League, 1962. Footnotes omitted.

sion may encourage or discourage further reading.

But there will be a fair bulk of material embodying policies from which no one would wish the state to depart. Do these belong in the constitution? What would happen if they were withdrawn? What harm does it do to give good laws constitutional protection?

BACKGROUND READING

In looking for answers to these questions, some background reading before proceeding further with the constitution itself would be profitable. The chapters on constitutions and constitutional history in any college level text on state government are helpful. Other reading might include *Major Problems in State Constitutional Revision,* edited by W. Brooke Graves, the National Municipal League's Constitutional Studies Project volumes, especially *State Constitutions: The Shape of the Document, Salient Issues of Constitutional Revision* and *The Future Role of the States.* These publications not only can help the reader understand more clearly the difference between statutory and fundamental matters but also will indicate generally the role state constitutions should play in the operation of our system of government.

MODELS AND COMPARISONS

After completing some background reading, examination of certain "model constitutions" would be helpful. The classic model is the United States Constitution. Another is the *Model State Constitution* of the National Municipal League, studied especially in the light of the brief explanations of each article.

The constitutions of the states of New Jersey, Hawaii and Alaska and also that of the commonwealth of Puerto Rico are examples of modern basic charters. While none is free of reference to passing issues, all are confined on the whole to establishing uncomplicated frameworks, and any one of them demonstrates how much can be omitted from a constitution without plunging a state into chaos.

The following words of caution concerning comparative study of state constitutions are worthy of note:

> In every age, some things are too unsettled, too vulnerable, or too momentous to the people, to entrust to the legislative process, which by its very nature is subject to constant pressure. What these things are varies from state to state, and a chart comparing state constitutions sharpens the sense of separate histories more than it yields advice on California's needs.

Looking at other constitutions, however, at least shows that comparable states have managed without constitutional protection in this or that special province.

Subjects covered in the constitution under study but not commonly mentioned in other constitutions at least raise questions. Does this provision embody important public policy? Might it profitably be modified or eliminated? Would omitting it, along with a number of other such provisions, give the state assets in flexibility?

STUDYING THE FORM

DEADWOOD

"When, on occasion, a state makes a serious effort to prune away its constitutional deadwood, it is likely to be surprised at the amount of debris that results." Identifying the deadwood is especially useful in diagnosing general faults. Obvious repetitions, sections that have been superseded but never eliminated, references to extinct programs and institutions, resounding but inoperative admonitions are not hard to find. Professor Dishman's discussion in *The Shape of the Document* of provisions that are inconsistent either with federal law or with other sections of the constitution can help identify nominations to a list of expendables.

POOR ORGANIZATION

The index, if there is one, helps to locate examples of unhappy form such as treatment of the same matter scattered through the document or amendments tacked on at the end. One section may appear to be the final law, yet the genuine last word may be embedded in an entirely different article or articles.

INSCRUTABLE LANGUAGE

If there are passages that on careful reading fail to yield any firm sense of meaning, it is fair to conclude that the document is deficient in this important particular. The constitution is a compact between the citizen and his government; it is essential that he be able to understand the terms of that compact.

If the constitution can be criticized on matters of form, editorial improvement would seem a simple solution. The remedy is not, in fact, always so simple. Frequently what looks like a matter of language develops on closer examination to be a larger problem involving other sections and raising fundamental questions.

Unnecessary clutter, confused form, and obscure language are rarely the ailments in themselves but rather are complications. Relatively harmless, they add to the not-so-harmless length and obscurity. Critical standards tend to diminish. Haphazard and obscure content breeds haphazard and even unnecessary addition. In a sense, no one is in charge. Legislators grow less careful in submitting amendments, since final decision rests with the voters. Voters make their decision in terms of the intent of the amendment, assuming the form has satisfied legislative scrutiny and ignoring entirely the question whether the particular law even belongs in the constitution. This lack of responsibility regarding both form and content exists in spite of the fact that "almost every word of the constitution, though it purports to be enabling, is apt to operate in some way as a limitation upon legislative action."

Thus a general judgment on the form of the document, even without precise knowledge of the effect and meaning of all provisions, is an important and valid yardstick in citizen study.

STUDYING THE CONTENT

A study of the content of a state constitution may be aided by the asking of certain questions. For the document in general the following questions can be raised regarding the various provisions:

1. Is the provision needed?
2. Does the provision protect the people in their rights and treat them equally and impartially?
3. Do the provisions hamper the agencies of government in their attempts to discharge their responsibilities?
4. Are the provisions flexible enough to permit orderly change? Have they made change so difficult that badly needed improvements are long overdue?
5. Are the provisions so narrowly drawn or so statutory in character that they have become "amendment breeders"?
6. Are the provisions logically organized and free of deadwood?
7. Do the provisions make sense to the informed lay reader?
8. Are the provisions rendered inoperative because they conflict with, or have been superseded by, other sections of the constitutions or by federal law?

On matters of taxation and finance the reader can consider such questions as the following:

1. Are the tax and finance provisions drawn broadly enough to permit the executive and legislative branches to make meaningful fiscal policy?
2. Do the provisions permit development of an equitable tax structure flexible enough to meet changing needs?
3. Do the provisions allow the governor to apply sound principles of fiscal management?
4. Do the provisions insure legislative oversight of financial affairs while protecting gubernatorial prerogatives?

On provisions concerning local government these questions are pertinent:

1. Do the provisions encourage and insure responsible home rule?
2. Do the provisions also protect genuine state concerns in the grant of home rule power to local governments?
3. Are the provisions flexible enough to permit the state and local govern-

ments to act jointly and cooperatively in solving urban problems that cut across established political boundaries?

On matters pertaining to the executive these questions might be raised:

1. Does the article facilitate executive leadership in regard to the governor's responsibilities toward state government and the people?
2. Does the constitution permit the governor to exercise the requisite authority for modern government? Is his term of office adequate? Can he succeed himself? What of salary and perquisites? Veto powers?
3. Do the provisions relating to the organization of state administration serve to integrate and unify the executive branch under the governor?

Regarding the judiciary these are some basic points to look for:

1. Does the article provide for a simple system of courts with clearly defined jurisdictions?
2. Is the process for the selection and tenure of judges conducive to competent judicial work?
3. Does the article permit—or stimulate—modern administrative machinery for the carrying out of the day-to-day functions of the court system?

* * *

14. What Should a State Constitution Contain?*

DAVID FELLMAN

FOR a variety of historical reasons, and not because of abstract cogitation, the American people have always regarded the written constitution as the essential basis of legitimate government. The colonial experience with the common law and written charters, to which appeal was constantly made in recurring disputes with the home government; the concept that the state rested on contract, which dominated political thinking in the eighteenth century; and the appeal to a higher law as justification for revolution established for us the proposition that government is not the state, but only its agent, deriving its just powers from the consent of the governed as set forth in a written constitution emanating from the people. Thus, Chief Justice John Marshall

* Reprinted with permission from W. Brooke Graves (ed.), State Constitutional Revision, Public Administration Service, 1960. Footnotes omitted.

spoke in an authentic American genre when he wrote in one of his most celebrated opinions:

That the people have an original right to establish, for their future government, such principles as, in their opinion, shall most conduce to their own happiness, is the basis on which the whole American fabric has been erected.

THE AMERICAN IDEA OF A CONSTITUTION

Pursuant to a resolution adopted by the Continental Congress on May 15, 1776, the people of the various states began to write constitutions, and they have been at it ever since. The original state constitutions summarized the political ideas which then prevailed. It is an interesting paradox that these documents of the Revolution were essentially conservative in tone; they did not break much new ground, but sought largely to conserve the prevailing values of their age. They were very brief documents, running from about 6 to 16 pages of ordinary print, and they stated very concisely certain basic principles regarding popular sovereignty, the separation of powers and checks and balances, individual liberty and the supremacy of law, and the superiority among governmental institutions of the legislative body as the authentic voice of the people.

In the ensuing years, however, as new states entered the Union and old constitutions were occasionally revised, these documents necessarily changed in response to the evolving patterns of American life. It has well been remarked that a study of our state constitutions "affords a perfect mirror of American democracy," since they have always articulated the varied and changing interests and conditions of the American people. They reflect the steady growth of executive power, the erosion of popular confidence in the legislature through the multiplication of constitutional limitations, the extension of popular participation in government as a consequence of the flowering of a democratic spirit, the rise of corporations to a dominant position in the economy, the Civil War and Reconstruction, the steady growth of commerce and industry, and the development of vast new urban communities.

*　　*　　*

Though no two state constitutions are alike in all details, all of them conform roughly to a common pattern. First there is a preamble, repeating in rather stock phrases certain first principles regarding the nature and purposes of government. Then there is a bill of rights, spelling out in familiar language the basic rights of conscience and of property and the rights of persons accused of crime. The next three articles usually deal with the legisla-

tive, executive, and judicial branches of the state government, in that order, describing their structure, powers, and limitations. At the end is an article dealing with the methods of constitutional amendment or revision and a schedule for the transition to the new dispensation. In addition, most state constitutions have articles of varying length and detail on a wide variety of additional subjects, notably education, local government, the suffrage, public finance, corporations, and other business organizations. While the state constitution generally is not regarded as a grant of powers to the legislature, since the legislature has all powers not denied to it by either the federal or its state constitution, the contemporary documents reflect the modern interest in new social services by authorizing or even directing legislative activity in regard to welfare and health activities, care of the aged, social security, unemployment, workmen's compensation, and the like.

However detailed state constitutions may be, as in the case of the federal Constitution, custom plays a large role in the actual functioning of state government. No document can say everything, though some states have overloaded their constitutions with details. Some of the most significant aspects of state government are not provided for in constitutional language. Many of the most important activities of the political parties fall within the scope of custom. The party caucus in the legislature, which may very well dominate the formal proceedings, is a product of custom, as is the representation of minority parties on legislative committees. The elaborate body of practices that defines the relationships between the governor and the legislature is largely unwritten.

CONTEMPORARY CRITICISMS OF STATE CONSTITUTIONS

If students of contemporary state government agree upon anything, it is that modern state constitutions are seriously defective and need considerable revision. While very little has been written in a systematic way about the proper contents of a state constitution, the consensus of informed opinion holds that most state constitutions need a great deal of attention both to style and content. . . .

THE PROBLEM OF DETAIL

The most obvious, and in many ways the crucial, fault of state constitutions is that they are too detailed. They simply attempt to say far too much on too many subjects. This was not always so. The Virginia Constitution of 1776 had about 1,500 words; the New Jersey Constitution of 1776 about 2,500 words; the New York Constitution of 1777 some 3,000 words; and the longest of them, that of Massachusetts (1780), had about 12,000 words, which, incidentally, is the size of the Model State Constitution. Today, 37 state constitutions are longer than the original Massachusetts document. Of the 8 state constitutions which have under 10,000 words each, 7 were drafted before the Civil War. . . .

Almost any constitution will supply examples of details that hardly rise to the dignity of a place in such a document. The Oklahoma Constitution devotes 20 pages to the division of the state into counties and the definition of their boundaries (Art. XVII), has over 300 words on the piddling subject of free transportation by railroads (Art. IX, sec. 13), and even stipulates that home economics must be taught in all public schools (Art. XIII, sec. 7). At the same level of importance is a provision in the South Dakota Constitution which authorizes a twine and cordage plant at the state penitentiary (Art. XI, sec. 1) and a clause in the Constitution of South Carolina which defines what shall constitute a "durable hard surface" street in the city of Greenville (Art. X, sec. 14). Many state constitutions spell out in precise sums the salaries of public officers and prescribe the election of a large variety of public officers (e.g., the Constitution of Texas provides for the popular election of the inspector of hides and animals and the public weighers, Art. XVI, secs. 64, 65). Small wonder that someone recently suggested to the Kentucky Constitution Review Commission that a clause be added stipulating that "no whiskey be sold in the State under four years old and made from 100 percent corn or Rye, No neutral spirits added." Why not?

Local government is one of many subjects which state constitutions are apt to treat with excessive detail. For example, about one-sixth of the long California Constitution is concerned with details of city and county government (Art. XI), and the Louisiana Constitution devotes 28 pages to the government of New Orleans (Art. XIV, secs. 20-31.1).

Another subject upon which state constitutions lavish words is public finance. The South Carolina Constitution sets up local debt limitations and then devotes almost 14 pages to spelling out exceptions (Art. VIII, sec. 7); it also has 12 pages of exceptions to the revenue provisions (Art. X, sec. 5). The Louisiana Constitution has several thousand words on the one-cent-per-gallon tax on nonmotor fuels, even going so far as to define the term as meaning "all volatile gas-generating liquids having a flash point below 110 degrees F. . . ." (Art. VI-A). Ten per cent of the California Constitution deals with revenue and taxation (Arts. XIII, XVI). The Texas Constitution spells out the upper limit of taxation by rural fire-prevention districts (Art. III, sec. 48-d).

*　　*　　*

Why have the state constitutions become such wordy documents? All observers agree that the principal reason has been the growth of popular distrust of the legislature; and some provisions are really commands to the legislature to make sure that it does certain things. For example, the Oklahoma Constitution directs the Legislature to revise the statutes periodically (Art. V, sec. 43) and legislate against monopolies (Art. V, sec. 44), and the Illinois Constitution directs the General Assembly to enact safety laws for miners (Art. IV, sec. 29). Many state constitutional provisions reflect the growing complexity of the social and economic order in regard to such matters as corporations, public utilities, and social legislation. Some constitutional provisions, such as those dealing with social security and labor, were designed to overcome the anticipated opposition of conservative courts. Court decisions have often been overruled by constitutional amendments. The triumph of Jacksonian democracy explains the elaboration of provisions dealing with the suffrage and the election of more and more public officers. The need for new governmental machinery to handle emerging problems has led to the expansion of constitutions to create new administrative agencies. The rapid growth of government business in recent decades has resulted in new constitutional sections dealing with such topics as the civil service, public works, and the letting of contracts.

Very often an item is inserted into a state constitution because, as in the case of homestead exemptions, the makers of the document feel that it is particularly important and should be put beyond the possibility of legislative tinkering. Furthermore, members of constitutional conventions often get into the odd habit of assuming that in some special way they are endowed with more wisdom and righteousness than members of future legislatures are likely to have. . . . In addition, many constitutional provisions represent either the hopes or fears of special interest groups who want their particular views nailed down.

Finally, it remains to be noted that a democratic people will necessarily find the quickest and surest means of having their way. In some states it is as easy to amend the constitution as it is to adopt a statute by the initiative and referendum. Writing a new constitution, or amending it, has often been found to be a quicker and simpler method of securing reforms than legislative action. The American people, Lord Bryce observed in his celebrated book on our governmental system, have "a conscious relish for power," and "there is an unmistakable wish in the minds of the people to act directly rather than through their representatives in legislation."

Of course, the more detailed a constitution is, the more often it has to be amended. Thus, it is the fate of a long constitution that in the very nature of things it has to grow longer. There is simply more to amend. It follows that wordy constitutions must be changed frequently, so that they get wordier still. It is an inexorable vicious circle.

*   *   *

Excessive constitutional detail is bad for many reasons. It solidifies the entrenchment of vested interests. It makes temporary matters permanent. It deprives state legislatures and local governments of desirable flexibility and diminishes their sense of responsibility. It encourages the search for methods of evading constitutional provisions and thus tends to debase our sense of constitutional morality. It makes frequent recourse to the amending processes inevitable. It hinders action in time of special stress or emergency. It stands in the way of healthy progress. It blurs the distinction between constitutional and statute law, to the detriment of both. It creates badly written instruments full of obsolete, repetitious, misleading provisions. Above all, it confuses the public, and in fact makes certain that few will ever bother to read the state constitution. This is extremely unfortunate, since one of the main purposes of a constitution is to educate the public in first principles. How can the people be expected to respect a constitution they never read, and which may in fact be altogether unreadable? Long ago Chief Justice John Marshall made this crystal clear:

> A constitution, to contain an accurate detail of all the subdivisions of which its great powers will admit, and of all the means by which they may be carried into execution, would partake of the prolixity of a legal code, and could scarcely be embraced by the human mind. It would probably never be understood by the public. Its nature, therefore, requires, that only its great outlines should be marked, its important objects designated, and the minor ingredients which compose those objects be deduced from the nature of the objects themselves.

*   *   *

THE UPDATING OF STATE CONSTITUTIONS

State constitutions need frequent attention to make sure they are in tune with the times. Many traditional clauses in bills of rights are ripe for reexamination, and some deadwood, such as clauses dealing with the right to bear arms, the quartering of troops, and the granting of titles of nobility, can be pruned away. While most of the traditional guaranties are still acceptable, recently-revised documents spell out such rights as the right of labor to organize and bargain collectively, the right of the worker to just compensation and to a reasonable working day, the right to social security, and the right of employed minors and women to special protection. While provisions against discrimination are by no means novel, the newer constitutions are especially meticulous and, indeed, often quite eloquent on the subject. There are new clauses dealing with such current problems as wiretapping and fairness in legislative investigations. The Model State Constitution includes a clause which is designed to strengthen the whole conception of a bill of rights by specifying that any citizen may go to court to restrain the violation of any constitutional provision. . . .

A great many clauses dealing with the legislature need rethinking, as the interesting suggestions of the Model State Constitution on this subject would indicate. . . .

Constitutional articles relating to the state executives are also subject to widespread debate. . . . What is required for the state executive branch is concentration of authority and responsibility, functional integration, the removal of boards and commissions from purely administrative work, the coordination of staff services, and provision for an independent audit. While the office of governor has become much more powerful than it was in the early days of the Republic, its power still is kept dispersed and disintegrated and does not measure up to the requirements of modern administration. . . .

It is equally necessary to create a judicial department, since all that most states have today is a congeries of various types of courts having various sorts of jurisdictions. Roscoe Pound has made it abundantly clear that in each state the whole judicial power should be vested in one single great court, divided into departments or divisions and containing a great deal of internal flexibility. Such is the central point of the article of the Model State Constitution on the judiciary, for it would make all courts of the state parts of a unified "general court of justice," . . . Both the Missouri and New Jersey constitutions have taken important strides in this direction, as have the new constitutions of Alaska, Hawaii, and Puerto Rico. Most state constitutions, however, still have a long road to travel before they begin to approximate the desired goal of judicial integration.

Most other major sections of state constitutions need rethinking. Certainly this is true for provisions that deal with local government. It is time to reconsider all the restrictions imposed upon the legislature in connection with local government that often make desirable flexibility impossible. The emphasis in the newer state constitutions is upon local home rule. It is also imperative that adequate provision be made for urgent problems growing out of urban growth, such as annexation and consolidation of local units, intergovernmental cooperation, city-county consolidation, debt limitations, local budgeting, slum clearance, and urban renewal. Equally pressing in a great many states is the question of reviewing the sections dealing with state finance. Here, too, the current tendency is to reduce restrictions upon the legislative power and to simplify and liberalize provisions on this subject.

Finally, attention should be directed toward the amending procedures set forth in state constitutions. If a state constitution is to serve its proper purposes, the door must be open to change by reasonable procedures. Where the amending process is too difficult, such as the requirement of an extraordinary popular vote, the document tends to get out of date; on the other hand, if the amending process is too easy, then the constitution tends to get out of hand. Ideally, the amending process should be more difficult than the ordinary legislative process, but not impossibly difficult. Furthermore, every generation has a right, and indeed an obligation, to review its constitution, and a few documents make periodic review, or at least its possibility, automatic. Such provisions are altogether consistent with sound democratic theory, for in the last analysis the constitution belongs to the people and should express their will. Finally, there has been a highly desirable tendency in recent years to provide for adequate preliminary spadework through the use of commissions or other special bodies charged with the function of doing research and writing informed reports on the problems that are likely to arise. . . .

THE QUALITIES OF A GOOD CONSTITUTION

What, then, are the proper attributes of a good constitution? It is difficult to generalize, since a constitution must be both stable and flexible. Serving as the legal underpinning for the commonwealth, it must supply the stability which orderly government requires; yet it will fail of its purposes if the door is closed too tightly against change and adaptation. Indeed, in many ways the central problem is to find a proper balance between stability and change. . . . Furthermore, there has never been an ideal state constitution, and no constitution could possibly be ideal for all states. A document which is suitable for the needs of a maritime state might not do very well for an arid, inland state. Also, every viable constitution must necessarily reflect the power structure of the particular society it is designed to serve; it cannot and will not function in a vacuum. Nor will a good constitution retain its quality for very long, in our sort of dynamic society, unless it can be changed to keep with the times. . . .

Certainly, the first requisite of a good constitution is brevity. It is a very great mistake for the authors of a constitution to attempt to say too much. A constitution is no place for legal codes or the appeasement of temporary interests. It should do no more than set down fundamental and enduring first principles. It must describe the basic framework of government, assign the institutions their powers, spell out the fundamental rights of man, and make provision for peaceful change. But it should do all of these things in general rather than in overly detailed language, and should attempt no more. And there is reason to believe that prevailing conditions are such that the goal of a concise constitution is now feasible, since courts today rarely stand in the way of social legislation, there has been an observable decline in the legislative appetite for special legislation, the Fourteenth Amendment of the federal Constitution sets limits to many types of state misbehavior, and modern means of mass communication are tremendously important checks upon improper legislation. An effective free press is probably a more efficacious check than formal constitutional limitations. Furthermore, there is a growing public awareness that holding legislators politically accountable for what they do protects the public interest more surely than constitutional caveats which hamstring any sort of action.

A second quality of a good constitution is readability, for one of its central purposes is to educate the public in first principles. If it is to fulfill this objective it must be something the average citizen will undertake to read. It should therefore be written in good, modern English; obsolete terminology should be avoided; ambiguous phraseology should be clarified; and repetitious or contradictory language should be corrected. The articles, sections, and clauses should be arranged in a logical and orderly way. In short, the constitution should be intelligible to ordinary people, if it is to command confidence and, indeed, general reverence. It is not merely or primarily a lawyer's document to be manipulated in litigation. It is above everything else a people's charter, a statement of their essential conceptions about government.

*　　*　　*

A sound constitutional revision, even if undertaken on a comprehensive scale, will never change the basic pattern to which the American people are thoroughly habituated and which they obviously want to preserve. The Missouri Constitution of 1945 illustrates this point, since it is by no means a new document, many sections dating from the original Constitution of 1820. Though the new Constitution is shorter than its predecessor, that of 1875, by some 11,000 words, all of the traditional provisions were included. But some antiquated sections were eliminated, a great deal of detail was dropped, language was clarified and simplified, and many provisions were rearranged. New provisions were added to deal with modern problems relating to agriculture, education, forestry, health, hospitals, libraries, museums, parks, recreation, and welfare.

This, then is another aspect of a good constitution, that it makes provision for emerging problems and reflects the best in current thinking. A constitutional convention today will have to concern itself with problems of urban growth and metropolitan government, reapportionment, aids to legislation, the short ballot, court reorganization, the extension of the merit system, revenue sources, debt limitations, the organization of local government, terms of office, highways, and the expansion of welfare services, including housing, reclamation of blighted areas, mental care, conservation, and the like. Changes in all these areas are now in the air.

Above all, as the Model State Constitution emphasizes, reality must be given to the concept of the "department." Every state constitution goes through the motions of asserting that power is divided among three departments, but in most states executive and judicial departments are largely fictions. Where the governor shares power and influence with 10 other popularly-elected officials and a large number of quasi-independent boards and commissions, one can hardly talk about an executive department as a reality. Nor is a mere congeries of courts a department in any realistic sense.

And wholly apart from the new problems, there are plenty of old problems that need rethinking. Bills of rights should be clarified and modernized. Legislatures shoud be made smaller and more representative, and given more effective organization. Relations between the governor and the legislature can certainly be improved through institutional changes. The last word has not yet been said on the subject of the executive budget. The governor's term of office is still a lively issue in many states. The best method of selecting judges is another. Existing initiative and referendum procedures and amending provisions are ripe for reevaluation. Intergovernmental cooperation can and should be encouraged. Even the minimum age for voting is now being discussed; after all, the age limit of 21 years was not decreed in heaven.

Finally, it is desirable that the writers of constitutions should stick as close as possible to reality and avoid making claims or staking out generalizations which, though theoretically desirable, are impossible of fulfillment. Otherwise, people are likely to find a constitution something of a snare and a delusion. . . . As far as possible, a state constitution should be a reasonable document.

15. Civil Rights and Liberties*

THE PURPOSE OF A BILL OF RIGHTS

TODAY, on the demand of the people expressed through their duly elected representatives, government on all levels has assumed a greater and greater variety of service functions and activities. Hence, bills of rights have assumed ever greater importance. At the same time, a number of the traditional rights protected under the original federal and state bills of rights have become so deeply ingrained in the American governmental system and in American tradition that few citizens are conscious of the initial grievances that called them into being.

A bill of rights is, in a very real sense, an expression of political faith and ideals—it sets the bounds of political authority and reserves to the individual certain freedoms believed essential to human happiness. It guarantees protection for those areas of individual difference necessary for the operation of popular government and political democracy.

Few areas of public law form the basis for as many legal actions as do federal and state bills of rights. The very growth of governmental authority and activity has involved over the years an ever greater encroachment on the privileges and liberties enjoyed by individuals and their privately organized enterprises and institutions. Liberty is relative in that it cannot be so utilized that its exercise by one individual deprives another of his just freedoms. The courts of our land are ever called upon to delimit the boundaries of individual freedom as individual well-being comes into conflict with the well-being of society. Likewise they must decide in case after case at what point the long-run cause of free institutions assumes greater significance than an immediate and apparent social advantage or benefit. To a degree greater than in any other country, judges in the United States have the duty of assuring that statutes and administrative action accord with the principles expressed in state and federal bills of rights.

There can be little question that the Alaskan Constitution must have a bill of rights. Protection of individual freedoms, tradition, and the expressed policies of the United States Congress in proposed enabling legislation all demand its inclusion. The basic question, therefore, is what should and should not be included in a bill of rights for the Alaskan Constitution.

* Reprinted from *Constitutional Studies: Prepared on Behalf of the Alaska Statehood Committee for the Alaska Constitutional Convention,* Public Administration Service, 1955. Footnotes omitted.

RELATIONSHIP BETWEEN THE FEDERAL BILL OF RIGHTS AND STATE BILLS OF RIGHTS

It is to be noted that from a legal standpoint the existence of the federal Bill of Rights has obviated to some extent the need to include certain specific provisions in state bills of rights. The federal Bill of Rights was for many years a limitation on the action of the federal government and was held to impose no limitations on the scope of state action. However, after adoption of the Fourteenth Amendment to the federal constitution, a new relationship gradually emerged whereby a number of the prohibitions of the federal Bill of Rights were held to limit state authority as well as that of the national government. The major change in judicial interpretation came in 1925 when the United States Supreme Court was considering the legality of a New York law designed to suppress seditious utterances. . . . The dual character of the civil rights structure in the United States has now been partially bridged by judicial interpretation.

What rights and "liberties" of the first ten amendments to the federal constitution are included in the Fourteenth Amendment and therefore protected by the national constitution against state action? The fact of the matter is that the Supreme Court has *not* blanketed in *all* of the first ten amendments but only those that it has deemed "basic and fundamental" to a "scheme of ordered liberty." Consequently, even though a state Bill of Rights may contain many expressions of principle which, because of the bridging action of the Fourteenth Amendment, duplicate statements in the federal Bill of Rights, both literally and in legal force, a state cannot assume that all rights of its citizens are adequately and fully protected by the federal document. A state Bill of Rights covering the fundamental features of the federal Bill is generally regarded as desirable and necessary.

Many states have gone far beyond the fundamental freedoms protected in the federal Bill of Rights and have added others reflecting particular attitudes and problems of the citizens of the state community. Viewed in retrospect, however, many of the "rights" included in some of the state Bills of Rights seem neither fundamental nor proper in a constitutional document. For instance, the agricultural state of Minnesota declared constitutionally that "any person may sell or peddle the products of the farm or garden occupied or cultivated by him without obtaining a license." California and Rhode Island, where fishing is important, have guaranteed in their Bills of Rights that their citizens shall "enjoy and freely exercise all the rights of fishing." Many other examples of a similar nature might be cited. Over the years it has become increasingly clear as our society has become more complex and the area of government action has been extended so that limitations on government authority related to particular local circumstances and times eventually become handicaps rather than benefits. If a so-called "right" is not so fundamental as to have almost universal applicability in times of normal political life, its inclusion in a Bill of Rights is of dubious merit.

* * *

The great majority of rights which appear in various state Bills of Rights and in the federal Bill of Rights are primarily against the arbitrary actions of government and government officials. They are tangible and justiciable. When violated, action may be taken in a court of law. The extension of governmental activity has narrowed the meaning of some of these rights and guarantees, but they still stand as the bulwark protecting the freedom of the American people.

As government has assumed an ever greater role in the social and economic order, many people have favored the recognition of a new category of "rights." This category would not prohibit or restrict government action.

Rather, it would guarantee active government protection or intervention on behalf of particular interests or individuals. In other cases it would guarantee to every individual certain material or social benefits.

Many states have launched forth into this new area of positive "rights." Where one group, such as organized labor, is favored by a so-called right, opposing groups seek embodiment in the constitution of a counter right. Thus guarantees of collective bargaining are answered in other states by guarantees of a right to work irrespective of membership in a labor organization. . . .

* * *

It is to be noted that declarations of this sort involve highly controversial matters. It cannot be said that they reflect a basic consensus about which there is general and universal agreement. Traditionally, Bills of Rights have protected individuals in their person and in their property. Newer provisions on industrial relations mark an effort to establish the preferred positions of one or another economic or social group in a constitutional document.

* * *

It is perhaps pertinent to note that the federal Constitution and the consti-

tutions of most states have been effective and vigorous charters because they have been realistic documents consolidating fundamental ideas and principles concerning which there was general agreement and on the basis of which people could act and depend upon the courts to uphold them in their rights. Constitutions which outreach the fundamental freedoms and rights of the people framing them become objects of little effect and frequently of ridicule. The Constitutions of France, Italy, and many of the Latin American republics suffer from such defects.

A bill of rights section of a constitution should be restricted to a statement of the inalienable and unassailable rights and freedoms which characterize democratic people. These rights and freedoms should be those symbolic truths which are not only universally accepted by school children as well as adults and by all social and economic groups, but which they are willing to defend at all costs.

To venture beyond the fundamental and universal rights in a bill of rights section of a constitution by including controversial assertions of economic privilege accomplishes little more than a derogation of democracy's self-evident truths.

16. Introduction to *Model State Constitution**

JOHN E. BEBOUT

STRICTLY speaking there can be no such thing as a "Model State Constitution" because there is no model state. Consequently, when one essays the role of model builder in this field, he is immediately beset by a host of conflicting urges. At one end of the scale he is

* Reprinted with permission from *Model State Constitution*, Sixth Edition, National Municipal League, 1963.

tempted to imagine the ideal state that never existed and never will and write a constitution for it. One trouble with this is that the ideal state would probably need no constitution or, rather, no written constitution.

Only a little short of this ideal state one is tempted to imagine a state in which all citizens are active and responsible and in which the only need would be for an extremely short document expressing the basic principles of republican government and delineating the essential features of the legislative, executive and judicial departments. The very mention of these three departments, however, calls to mind that all that is really necessary to inaugurate republican government is to establish a representative legislature which may then exercise the constituent function with respect to the other agencies needed to carry out public policy and to administer justice and law.

The new *Model State Constitution* is, like its predecessors, designed to be a practical help to persons interested in improving the constitutions of actual states in the union. Admitting the nonexistence of a "model" or even a "typical" state, the architects of the sixth edition are not interested in a blueprint for Utopia. The *Model* is, therefore, quite traditional; indeed, more traditional in its conformity to basic American political ideas than either its predecessor *Models* or most existing state constitutions.

In going back to earlier American constitutional traditions, this *Model* looks more like the newest state constitutions—those of Alaska, Hawaii and New Jersey—than the middle-aged, heavily inflated documents of most of the states. The reason for this may be expressed in the words of *A Report to the People of Alaska from the Alaska Constitutional Convention,* which explained in the following paragraph why it adopted "a simple plan of state government that is characteristically American":

This system in its essential features is very similar to that of the national government in Washington. This is because the convention found that the state governments that worked best were those that conformed most closely to the simple design given to the government of the United States by the convention that met in Philadelphia in 1787.

The departure of many state constitutions from the simplicity and clarity of the national prototype prepared by the convention of 1787 has been due, of course, to a number of causes, perhaps the least of which have been unclear thinking and bungling workmanship. For the most part, the overelaboration of checks and balances, the built-in weaknesses in all branches of government, and the proliferation of "thou shalt nots" on the one hand and of essentially statutory declarations of public policy in the guise of constitutional provisions on the other stem from disillusionment with representative institutions and the desire either to prevent sin or to enforce the good (as seen by those making the constitutions).

All previous *Model State Constitutions* have deplored the tendency of these hedges against human weakness to enfeeble state and local institutions and to undermine civic responsibility. It seems, however, to those who have prepared the present *Model* that earlier *Models* have reflected too much of the same tendency. Consequently, while providing for a presumably representative one-house legislature, earlier *Models* included numerous compensatory devices such as the initiative and referendum, self-executing home rule, prescriptions for a legislative council and the like which are necessary only if the legislature is not in fact representative and responsive. Those *Models* have been curious combinations of the ideal (not meaning Utopian) and provisions which clearly indicate lack of confidence in the efficacy of the basic arrangements for responsible government. Yet a review of the existing highly imperfect constitutions for our imperfect states indicates that many states do very well without some of the hedges against sin or the admonitions for virtue contained in past *Models*.

Moreover, times, customs and public morals do change and so should constitutions, even model constitutions. Many of the prolix provisions designed to confine or narrowly direct the exercise of public authority—what Henry Jones Ford once called "a strait-jacket and handcuffs on government"—were designed after the event to prevent evils far more characteristic of an earlier day than of this generation. Yet provisions of a limiting nature, whether cast in the negative terms of prohibitions or in the positive terms of statutory prescriptions, are hard to change or eliminate no matter how altered the circumstances. There is always someone who feels advantaged by them, or at least someone who says, "It did happen once, how do we know it won't happen again?" For this reason it seems clear that a model state constitution should push as strongly as possible for a hard-headed review of all except the clearly basic provisions to determine whether or not they meet present and future needs. If a model state constitution does not help those who consult it to distinguish the ephemeral and transitory provisions inherited from a far different past from those of enduring value, it is not performing its function.

It is not suggested that our states have begun to approach the millennium with respect to their readiness for responsible government; but they certainly have outgrown the need for many of the strictures that they imposed upon themselves in a less sophisticated era of political development.

Speaking of the need for occasional constitutional revision, Jefferson once observed that he knew "that laws and institutions must go hand in hand with the progress of the human mind. As that becomes more developed, more enlightened . . . institutions must advance also and keep pace with the times."

The limitations on state and local government action were devised for the most part during an age when less was demanded of government than is the case today. In a period of expanding governmental activity, special limitations on state and local government may have a very different effect on the balance of power in the federal system than they had when they were originally adopted. Even near the beginning of the century Professor Ford saw in these limitations one of the reasons for expanding federal power. Retention of these limitations in the latter half of the century is even more clearly conducive to this end, a fact which is entitled to serious consideration by revisers of state constitutions.

In order to be of practical help to constitutional revisers who feel the need for additional protections against unsatisfactory performance, supplemental or alternative provisions are suggested at various points. For example, a self-executing provision for the making of home rule charters is included as an alternative for the benefit of states whose experience makes it seem unsafe to count on the legislature to make adequate provision for home rule charters.

This *Model,* the work of many informed minds, presents a plan of government that would be workable on the basis of a modicum of political maturity and civic responsibility and is therefore unencumbered by any limitations, checks or "compensatory devices" not likely to be needed.

Part III

STATE EXECUTIVES

THROUGHOUT the nineteenth century and even into the twentieth, state executives occupied a position of secondary importance among the branches of government. The fear and distrust directed toward the colonial governors appointed by the Crown or the Proprietor were reflected in the early state constitutions, which established legislatures as the dominant branch of government. Disenchantment with the results of legislative dominance accompanied by increasing demands for governmental activity and leadership have contributed to an enlargement of the role of the states' chief executives.

Coleman B. Ransone, Jr., describes the role of the governor in terms of three broad areas of operations: policy formation, public relations, and management. He then stresses the importance of the governor's role in the area of policy formation, particularly in relation to legislation. He notes, however, that the degree to which a governor assumes such a role depends upon a combination of factors in his state, including his role as party leader, customs and traditions, and his own concept of his proper function. The combination of roles that a governor is usually expected to assume, concludes Professor Ransone, "places on any but the most exceptional individual an almost impossible burden." The many facets of gubernatorial responsibility are further explored by Professor Bennett Rich, who also provides insight into the evolution of the office of governor.

In an effort to determine the career patterns of state governors, Joseph A. Schlesinger examines data on all the governors elected between 1870 and 1950. His study is designed "to reveal both the historical developments in the office careers of the American governors and the differences among the states in the way they select this particular group of leaders." It appears that membership in the state legislature has been the most important office experience for governors; more than half of those studied had served in this capacity. At the other extreme, very few persons have been elected governor without prior service in some public office. Schlesinger concludes that although there is no rigid promotional ladder followed by governors in any state, there is a typical office career followed by a third or more governors in over half of the states.

A major contribution to the strengthened position of the governor, especially in the field of management, has been made by various state departments of administration. Joe Nusbaum examines the chief purposes behind the development of centralized staff agencies, with special emphasis on improved practices in accounting, purchasing, paperwork systems, records management, and budgeting. He also assesses the future of state departments of administration and concludes that their role "will be one that promotes management adaptability to keep pace with social and technological change."

17. The Office of Governor Today*

COLEMAN B. RANSONE, Jr.

THE governor of the modern American state is concerned primarily with three broad areas of operations: policy formation, public relations, and management. Of these three, the governor's principal role seems to be that of policy formation, since the compelling force of policy considerations runs like a thread through all the governor's other functions. Most governors, sooner or later, find themselves enmeshed in the problem of formulating a legislative program and securing the acceptance of that program by the legislature. They also discover that they must be concerned with establishing the administrative policies which will govern the execution of this program and other programs which have been established on a continuing basis. Intertwined with both of these attempts are the gover-

* Reprinted with permission from *Office of Governor in the United States*, by Coleman B. Ransone, Jr., University of Alabama Press, 1956. Footnotes omitted.

nors' endeavors to exercise policy control over their party or over the faction of the party with which they are associated. This control may be either a direct control, as an adjunct to an attempt to establish legislative or administrative policy, or it may be more indirect in that the governors' concern with the control of the party organization may be based on a desire to influence the nominating process in connection with their renomination as governor or their nomination for some other office. Policy considerations also are an important force in the governors' role in public relations, since much of that effort is directed toward explaining or justifying their programs, either actual or proposed, to the people of the state. The American governor is deeply concerned with policy—legislative, administrative, and political—and while he is seldom conscious of the particular area in which he is operating and may be operating in all three areas simultaneously on a given problem, he is certainly active in the field of policy-making and decision-making.

Perhaps his most easily identified activity as a policy-maker takes place in the legislative policy field. The governor of the modern American state does not wait for policy to be handed to him by the legislature in the form of a legislative statute and then set about to carry out this policy. As numerous studies of the legislative process in the states have revealed, . . . the majority of important legislative policies embodied in the major pieces of legislation passed by the average state legislature emanate from the governor's office or from the offices of his department heads. The separation of powers theory, which still enjoys lip service among state legislators and constitution makers, is no great impediment to the governor in his role in the legislative process. In all states the governor is recognized by the constitution as having some part in the formation of legislative policy, and the development of the office has been such in most states that the governor has emerged as a powerful force in legislative affairs. The entering wedge in the governor's development as a leader in legislative policy is his power to report to the legislature on the condition of the state and to make such recommendations for legislation as he deems appropriate. Gradually over a period of time this power to recommend has been implemented by such powers as the veto, the executive amendment, and the power to call special sessions of the legislature. These formal powers have become more meaningful because the governor's popular election has greatly increased the prestige of the office. This prestige also has been increased through the example of forceful leadership presented by recent occupants of the office. The effectiveness of the governor's leadership in legislative matters also has increased with the development of informal arrangements to secure the passage of legislation. These arrangements seem to form an "influence cycle" which begins with the organization of the legislature, continues through such persuasive techniques as personal conferences with individual legislators and the judicious use of patronage, and finally ends with the veto, which generally is used as a last resort if other methods fail. All of these powers and techniques place the governor in a position to wield considerable influence in the legislative process. Whether he in fact assumes the role of legislative leader is another matter and depends on such factors as his party leadership, the customs and traditions of the state, and the governor's own view of his proper function.

The southern governors tend to place more emphasis on this aspect of policy formation than do those from other sections of the country. In the South, legislative leadership probably would be ranked first in a listing of the governor's functions. In the rest of the nation, the governor's role in administrative policy formation probably would receive equal emphasis. However, the problem of legislative policy formation and the corollary problem of securing the enactment of a legislative program is one with which all governors are concerned. . . .

The governor's role in forming party policy or acting as party leader generally is not considered by the governors to be separate or distinct from their roles in legislative or administrative policy formation. In practice, the governor seldom acts as a party leader except with some specific objective in mind, such as using this power to insure the passage of a particular piece of legislation. Demands on the governor when acting in this role also generally take specific form, such as pressure by party leaders for recognition in the determination of the governor's appointments. Furthermore, party leadership in most states is apt to be split between the governor and some other leading political figure. This rival is likely to be the senior United States Senator of the state but may be another elected officer of the state or even a political boss who holds no elective office. The use of the term "party leader" is, therefore, somewhat restricted in a consideration of the governor's functions.

*   *   *

The fact that the governor in the South and in the normally Democratic and Republican states is primarily a factional leader, coupled with the fact that many of the so-called two-party states fail to follow the prescribed pattern, leads to the conclusion that if the governor is a party leader, he acts in a fashion which does not follow the prescribed pattern. In practice, it seems to the writer that the governor must build a block of votes from whatever source he can and that in only a few states are the members of his party alone a sufficient basis for such a bloc. Consequently, while the governor's effectiveness as a party leader should not be judged entirely in legislative terms, it seems clear that the term cannot be used in its generally accepted sense in referring to the governor of most states. While the governor may be a party leader in terms of the state party's relations to the national party, he is a factional leader in terms of the organization of the party within the state. The term "party leader" as used in this book in connection with the governor's role in policy formation should be understood to mean the governor's leadership of a faction of his party in most states and of the majority of his party in those states where a true two-party situation prevails. This function is so closely connected with the governor's functions in legislative and administrative policy formation that we will not attempt to consider it in a separate chapter. . . .

The governor's role in management is also a policy role to a considerable extent, since the governor is concerned primarily with the establishment of the policies which will govern the operation of the executive branch during his administration. This aspect of policy formation has been distinguished from the governor's role in legislative and party policy formation primarily for the sake of emphasis, but it does have a different character because of the nature of the individuals with whom the governor deals. In attempting to establish administrative policy, the governor must deal with the heads of the agencies which make up the executive branch. In many ways the governor is in a weaker position *vis-à-vis* some of these agency heads than he is with the legislature. While the governor is supposed to be the state's chief executive, he is actually the chief executive only in the sense that he is the first among several executives. Because many of the other executive offices [*sic*] also are popularly elected, they are on the same level with the governor and draw their authority from the same source. Consequently, the governor is not in an ideal position to establish administrative policy because he does not control the department heads who will theoretically be bound by that policy and who will carry out the governor's programs. The postion of the governor is further weakened by the fact that in many states he has only a two-year term and some of his department heads may have terms longer than that of the governor. This means that in addition to being confronted with other elected officers who share his executive power he also is faced with one or more department heads who have been appointed in previous administrations and who are probably of the opposite political party. These are only a few of the complicating factors which make the governor's role in management a very difficult one. . . . In attempting to achieve his goals, the governor is forced to depend primarily on such persuasive devices as cabinet meetings and personal conferences and on the executive budget and financial controls in those states where he is given these powers. . . . Under such conditions it is small wonder that his primary concern is with legislation rather than administration.

The governor's role in public relations also is closely related to his roles in policy formation and management. The preceding analyses of the governor's daily routine and the governor's own views on the gubernatorial function have covered this aspect in some detail. . . .

The governor's function in the field of public relations is considered as separate in this formulation of his duties because so much of his time is devoted to public appearances, press conferences, correspondence, and interviews with the state's citizens on matters which have importance primarily in terms of the governor's relation to the public. It is perfectly true that in his major speeches he may be dealing with questions of policy or may be attempting to build up public support for his legislative program. It is true that his press conferences may be devoted to the announcement of appointments or to answering questions on some phase of administrative affairs. It is true also that the citizens of the state come to see him with personal problems in relation to state employment, old age assistance payments, highways, and a multitude of other matters which are directly related to administration. However, when the governor makes a public address explaining policy, or answers the questions of the press on a prison riot, or talks to a citizen about a job for a son-in-law, he is primarily engaged in explaining his program or the workings of one of the programs of the state government to the public, the press, or the individual citizen. . . . The governor's position is such that he must be constantly engaged in exposition. He must not only prepare a legislative program and see that it is enacted and establish administrative policies and see that they are adhered to, but he must also constantly assure the citizens that these functions are being well done and that he is carrying out the promises which he made in the election. It is, indeed, extremely difficult to combine the talents for policy formation, management, and exposition in one person, but any governor must constantly attempt to perform this difficult feat.

Perhaps this need for constant exposition is the feature which most clearly distinguishes the occupant of a key government post whether it be legislator, cabinet member, or governor, from important positions in business. While public relations is now recognized in both fields, it reaches much further into the inner workings of the government than it does in business. The government's whole scheme of fiscal operations is an open public record. Every policy which is considered by the legislature, not just those which are successful, is put before the public for scrutiny. While the press occasionally complains of closed hearings of certain boards and commissions, the general tendency at the state level is for the operations of the executive as well as the legislative branch to be open to the press and the public. Pitiless publicity can be focused at any moment on any part of the whole governmental process and the office of governor is a favorite target of the spotlight.

The governor's every move is worthy of front page reporting. He has no private life and his day's work is not finished when he goes home from the office. One governor, who also had served several terms in Congress, said that he would rate the difficulties of the duties of the two offices about even but that the governorship was a much more strenuous position than that of Congressman because the governor had no private life at all. . . .

All of this emphasis on exposition means that the governor spends a tremendous amount of time on what has been called here the public relations aspects of his functions. It seems fair to say that the governor spends at least half of his time on such activities. This means that public relations is so time consuming that it limits the governor's other functions. The governor has only 24 hours in the day, and while it is not uncommon for him to devote twelve to fifteen of these to public business, there is a limit to what one man can accomplish.

The concept which we have developed in this country of a chief executive, whether he be President or governor, is that of a man who is expected to be simultaneously a legislative leader, a political chief, a general manager, and the ceremonial and public representative of the state. This concept places on any but the most exceptional individual an almost impossible burden. It seems abundantly clear that the average governor does not have the time to perform all of the functions which he is now called upon to carry out. The only way to give him sufficient time is to reduce the number of functions, reduce the time spent on certain of his functions, or to give him sufficient institutional aid to assist him in coping with these many responsibilities.

*   *   *

It does not appear that the governor can abandon his major functions as policy maker, public relations man, and general manager, nor is it desirable that he give up any of these roles entirely. However, it is possible, as the experience of several states has shown, to reduce materially the minor duties of the governor, most of which have been saddled on him by legislative enactment, as for example, the commissioning of notaries public, appointment of justices of the peace, the approval in writing of all state contracts, and the like. This reduction in minor duties will save some time which can then be used for more important functions. In addition, better office management in the handling of correspondence and interviews should result in a reduction of the amount of time spent on these functions. This reduction in minor functions

and the reduction of time spent on those functions remaining is not a real frontal attack on the problem. What most governors need is some high-level assistance in performing their major functions, most of which cannot be completely delegated because of their very nature.

In the policy field, for example, the governor himself in the last analysis must make the policy decisions. Even in this role, however, he can be given some help. If the burden of decision-making cannot be transferred from his shoulders, much of the spade work preliminary to those decisions can be done by an able staff. Our experience with the Presidency and with developments in some of our states shows the desirability of what might be called a policy staff. . . .

Some progress can also be made through proper organization, scheduling, and staffing in reducing the governor's work load in the field of public relations. . . . The primary complicating factor is that the governor's public-relations role is so closely affiliated with his role in partisan politics and with his future political aspirations that it will be exceedingly difficult as a practical matter to curtail.

The field in which the greatest progress has been made in delegation and staff assistance is in management. Here, we already have an example of what can be done in the Executive Office of the President, in the well-developed executive offices of several of our larger states, and in the recent development of the concept of a department of administration in some states. While none of these solutions has a complete transfer value, the experience at the federal level and in those states which have tried these devices should prove valuable to those states which have not yet explored such an approach. . . .

18. The Governor as Policy Leader*

BENNETT M. RICH

THE 50 governors occupy the top legal and political positions in the states. As demanding as these positions are they do not mark the limits of the governors' responsibilities and opportunities, for in the increasingly important web of intergovernmental relations the governors occupy 50 strategic positions in the federal-state complex. A strong and effective state government which can serve as an equal partner in the federal system requires a strong and effective chief executive. Obviously, there are many other requirements, but the position of the governor has been transformed in this century and has increased in importance more rapidly than any other facet of state government. Policy leadership throughout our governmental framework has come to mean executive leadership. The American public accepts this enhanced role as a necessary and, indeed, desirable development.

Few governmental issues outweigh in importance those of providing a climate for the governorship which will attract the ablest persons to the office and of providing powers adequate to their task. Much, of course, depends upon personality, individual qualifications and political support, but much also depends upon the constitutional framework within which the governor must work. State constitutions play a significant role in determining the kind of leadership the chief executive can provide. This is the focus of the present chapter; the next treats the governor as administrator. Admittedly the separation is artificial and only a matter of convenience for the roles are interwoven and reciprocal.

* Reprinted with permission from *Salient Issues of Constitutional Revision*, National Municipal League, 1961. Footnotes omitted.

THE GOVERNORSHIP IN HISTORY

The earliest governors were objects of suspicion. They represented English power, either directly from the king or through a proprietor who had been authorized to establish a colony. For the most part neither the king nor the proprietors were interested in elaborate forms of government but were content with the minimum governmental machinery necessary to accomplish their primary objectives, chiefly economic and commercial. For example, in 1610 the instructions to the governor of Virginia gave him complete authority to "rule, punish, pardon, govern."

Not all the pre-revolutionary governors exercised unlimited power. Indeed, in Virginia, only a few years later, the chief executive was required to share his authority with a Council of State and Assembly of Burgesses. In most colonies the settlers were quick to seek ways in which to reduce the authority of the governor, such as limitations on his power to raise revenues and to initiate legislation. Fighting for advantage between the assemblies and the governors became standard practice and from bitter experience the colonists learned to distrust the executive.

EARLY STATE CONSTITUTIONS

One observer, commenting on the distrust of the executive evident in the Maryland constitution of 1777, declared, "The constitutionalists forgot that the governor was from 1777 just as much a representative of the people as the members of the legislative body." No longer was the chief executive the representative of a foreign power but neither was he yet to be classified as the representative of all the people. In only four states was the governor elected by the voters and in two of these, Connecticut and Rhode Island, this had been the practice in colonial times. Massachusetts and New York adopted a similar practice but in almost all the other states the new constitutions provided for the annual election of the governor, or president as he was sometimes called, by joint ballot of both houses.

The legal powers of the first state chief executives were in sharp contrast with those exercised by colonial governors. Now there were legislative checks at every turn. In New Jersey, for example, the governor presided over the upper house and voted in case of a tie but he had no separate power of veto. All appointments, whether to administrative or judicial positions, or to the militia, were in the hands of the legislature. The constitution declared that he was to exercise "supreme executive power," but nowhere was there an indication of the nature of this grant.

*   *   *

CHANGING PERSPECTIVES

A principal factor in the changing position of the office of governor may be traced to the failure of the early state legislatures. They proved unable to view either national or state problems in national or state terms. Instead, local or private interests were dominant. Public confidence in the theory of legislative supremacy slowly waned; reaction came in the form of constitutional amendments designed to place limitations on special privilege. The governorship was the beneficiary of this development. Not only were special devices such as the veto adopted to curb legislative excesses; of equal, if not greater, importance was the change in public attitude. As the legislature lost public favor, the governor gained.

Another factor responsible for the development of the gubernatorial office was the early nineteenth century em-

phasis upon greater popular participation in the governmental process. A majority of the first constitutions provided for the election of the governor by the legislators, not by the people. Constitutional changes were soon adopted, however, which resulted in the use by a majority of the states of a system of direct election. Coupled with the system of direct election there developed the movement for an enlarged electorate. For example, property qualifications for voting and for holding office were eliminated.

The adoption of a system of direct election, the enlargement of the suffrage, the introduction of the veto— these changes were of paramount importance. The governor now had a degree of independence, he had the interest of a greater segment of the population and, through the veto, he had a voice, albeit a negative one, in the formulation of state policy.

The office of governor has advanced toward a position of relative equality with the legislature by slow and halting steps. An evidence of the complete superiority of the legislature during the nineteenth century may be obtained from the comments of two eminent foreign observers. De Tocqueville declared in 1831 that "In America the legislature of each state is supreme; nothing can impede its authority." In 1889 Lord Bryce confirmed this observation: "Everything in the nature of state policy belongs to the legislature and to the legislature alone."

THE MODERN GOVERNORSHIP

The early twentieth century witnessed the governor assume a much more active leadership role. No longer did he fit the description of the New York governor of the 1820's, "a sort of nominal governor, standing disconnected with the business and interests of the state, with his arms folded, looking on like a sentinel." Instead he was to use not only the powers given him by the state constitution but other so called extra-legal powers which accrued to him as the principal elected representative of all the people.

The constitutional right to recommend measures to the legislature was interpreted to include also the right to recommend to the people. Woodrow Wilson declared that the people were "impatient of a governor who will not exercise energetic leadership, who will not make his appeals directly to public opinion and insist that the dictates of public opinion be carried out in definite legal reforms of his own suggestion." The possibilities of the office were demonstrated in the early 1900's by several strong governors, including Wilson of New Jersey, Hughes of New York, La-Follette of Wisconsin and Johnson of California, demonstrating that even in a period of political bossism the chief executive could through personal influence exercise a commanding voice in party and thus governmental decisions.

For several decades the principal emphasis in state government reform has been upon problems incident to the administrative organization of the governor's office. The urge to create separate elective offices in the early 1800's was matched by a later zeal for the creation of separate administrative agencies having no responsibility to the governor. As a consequence, the chief executive had little control over the executive branch. Professor George W. Spicer observed that "The developments of a century and a half in the office of the governor of Virginia carried him to a position of legislative leadership and administrative impotence."

More recently, as a part of the general movement to unify the executive office, attention has been centered upon a variety of controls relating to matters such as budgeting, accounting, purchasing, personnel, records management and other service activities. In many states the office of governor has become an enormously complex institution. Unhappily, as a consequence of the lag in constitutional revision, the philosophies of an earlier day are still dominant.

THE CONSTITUTIONAL OFFICE TODAY

The state constitution should be an instrument which enables the chief executive to supply the maximum leadership of which he is capable. But too often constitutional language and institutional arrangements designed in past decades to obtain improved government now serve to impede the attainment of that objective. Not only must obsolete constitutional provisions, ambiguous wording and requirements generally recognized as outmoded be removed from state constitutions but also reconsideration—in the light of contemporary needs and expectations—should be given to many institutional factors that impinge upon the office of governor. Some factors are obvious in their impact, others less so. Many have substantial bodies of theory to support them, most have political support of some kind. All should be judged by modern standards. The following discussion concerns some aspects of the tenure of governors and the impact of these upon gubernatorial power.

TERM OF OFFICE

The length of a term of office may seem of little constitutional importance but it is, in fact, a stumbling block of considerable magnitude. True, early restrictive provisions have been eliminated, a clear demonstration of the increased public confidence in the chief executive. The one-year term common in the post-revolutionary period has given way to two-, three- and four-year terms. . . . The pressures of reform are now pitted against the two-year term, which is generally considered too short a period for a governor to develop and implement his program. Even where he may succeed himself he seems continually caught up in the throes of electoral politics. While several states have recently abandoned the two-year term . . . fifteen states still retain it.

A correlative question involves the

number of terms a person may serve. In fifteen states a governor may not succeed himself; in seven he may not serve a third consecutive term. Curiously, only two states with two-year terms place any restriction upon succession; New Mexico and South Dakota (the latter by state legislation) have maximums of two consecutive terms. The main argument favoring restriction is based upon fear of "bossism" or perpetuation in office by unscrupulous means. While this always is a remote possibility, the critics of restriction have the better case. A. Harry Moore, former governor of New Jersey, argued unsuccessfully for unlimited succession with the members of that state's 1947 constitutional convention, but the question he posed still defies answer by the advocates of restriction. "Why," asked Governor Moore, "should we eliminate from the prospective field of candidates from whom the people can make a choice, the one individual whose qualifications they are best able to judge—the then current governor?"

The present trend is toward freeing constitutions of term limitations. Colorado, Connecticut, Maine, Minnesota and Ohio have in recent years eliminated restrictions. Tennessee, on the other hand, while extending the term to four years prohibited succession.

*   *   *

GOVERNOR'S ROLE AS REPRESENTATIVE OF ALL THE PEOPLE

The governor's greatest challenge lies in his role as the representative of all the people of his state. Legislators can speak for their own districts although some, through long and active service, may attract a statewide following. Separately elected heads of major departments may have special clienteles. But normally neither legislator nor department head can compete with the chief executive. He is the official voice—and in some states the only voice—of all the people.

*   *   *

Certain kinds of issues seem to gravitate upward awaiting a gubernatorial pronouncement. Fos example, a strike on the Long Island Raiload in the summer of 1960 was settled only after Governor Nelson Rockefeller met with the warring groups. Efforts on the part of employee representatives and management to reach a settlement had proved of no avail. Governmental mediation machinery, similarly, had not succeeded. . . .

In considering the role of the governor as chief representative, one may properly ask whether the constitution impedes full and free exercise of the chief executive's leadership potential. We are concerned here not with checks against abuse of power; the legislature of every state has ample authority for this purpose. Rather, the problem is one of providing constitutional language which facilitates, rather than restricts, the governor's efforts to safeguard and to promote the public interest.

Some governors attempt little, others much. The constitution should not hinder those in the latter group. Many constitutions, however, hinder those in both groups. Constitutional language which goes beyond the minimums essential to provide the desired governmental structure and to guarantee basic individual rights may introduce rigidities which hamper the chief executive in the greatest of all his roles.

CHIEF LEGISLATOR

The governor's is the most important single voice in lawmaking. Perhaps a more accurate statement is that his voice may be the strongest provided he wishes to use the formal and informal powers at his command. Obviously much depends upon the personality of the chief executive.

The governor today occupies a position in marked contrast to that of his predecessors. Some of the early constitutions did not recognize the governor's role in introducing legislation through reports and messages. When Lord Bryce described the governorship in the late 1880's he reported that the chief executive may "recommend measures" to the legislature but that he "does not frame and present bills." A quarter-century later Woodrow Wilson took an entirely different view:

It seems perfectly clear that it is the explicit prerogative of practically every American executive to recommend measures if he pleases in the form of bills. It is no presumption on his part, therefore, and no invasion of the rights of any other branch of government, if he presses his views in any form that he pleases, upon the lawmaking body.

But the message power was only one means by which forceful governors in the early 1900's responded to public demands for greater gubernatorial activity with respect to legislation. Over the years the veto power was increased but it was a negative instrument. More positive measures were required. In 1912 Professor John M. Mathews reported that "whether rightfully or not" the people are holding the governor responsible for legislation "because he alone stands out conspicuously among state officers."

The governor's influence stemmed in part from his pre-eminent position as the chief representative of the whole people, in part from his position as top administrator and in part from his position as leader of his party. Governors began to introduce "administration bills," to meet with legislative leaders of one or both parties, to exercise control of the legislative program through constitutional budgetary powers and often to appeal publicly for support. Patronage also was a factor. In 1945 Governor Walter Evans Edge of New Jersey made perfectly clear to the legislature that there would be no appointments until his legislative program had

been adopted. Some years later he wrote:

I do not wish to seem cynical but it is difficult for a modern governor to be a great administrator and a great legislator at the same time. The appointing power, for better or for worse, is an important factor in his legislative program.

* * *

THE VETO

The legislative accomplishments of a governor constitute one of the principal measures of his success as chief executive. The other side of the coin relates to what he is able to prevent the legislature from doing through his constitutional power of veto. The veto remains a potent weapon. From the point of view of constitutional language, the governor's veto powers today are stronger than at any time in history. Viewed in terms of his total position as chief legislator, however, recent emphasis has been upon positive legislative achievements. Thus today the veto plays a less vital role than it did in the late nineteenth century when Lord Bryce observed that "the use of the veto is, in ordinary times, a governor's most serious duty and chiefly by his discharge of it is he judged."

The device was not included in most of the early state constitutions. Indeed the first grievance listed in the Declaration of Independence related to the king's refusal to "assent to laws, the most wholesome and necessary for the public good." South Carolina, Massachusetts and New York alone among the original states allowed the veto and South Carolina later dropped it in a revised constitution. The adoption of the veto in the constitution of the United States may have stimulated some action but in general the states were slow to add the device, Ohio and Rhode Island waiting until 1902 and 1909 respectively. Now all the states except North Carolina provide for it.

Constitutional language concerning the veto varies from state to state. There is wide variation, for example, in the amount of time at the discretion of the governor following passage of a bill; from three days in nine states to 30 days in Georgia. In some states, by inaction at the end of the session—that is, the pocket veto—a bill may be killed. In others, unless rejection is filed, a bill becomes law. There is variation also in the number required to overrule the veto. Six states require a majority of those elected in each house; in Connecticut the requirement is a majority of those present. This pattern is repeated with three-fifths of those elected and three-fifths of those present; and two-thirds of those elected and two-thirds of those present. In Virginia the two-thirds of those present must include a majority of those elected.

Forty-one states provide the item veto on appropriation bills, a device that, if used, can considerably strengthen the governor in legislative matters. It has had extensive use in some states such as California and Pennsylvania but it has been almost completely ignored in others. Frank W. Prescott concludes that the device "remains a useful albeit somewhat rusty 'gun behind the door,' to be aimed at an occasional predatory prowler."

Although the hand of the governor has been strengthened, there has been a tendency to hold him more closely accountable. The pocket veto has been almost completely eliminated in New Jersey. While New York's constitution permits the pocket veto, recent governors have in practice modified its effect by issuing short memoranda on the more important measures vetoed after adjournment of the legislatiure. Governor Lehman "felt a 'personal responsibility' to affix his signature, in approval or disapproval, to every bill submitted to him by the legislature." In 1959 Governor Nelson Rockefeller issued memoranda on each of the 322 bills which he vetoed.

In some states the veto is an extraordinarily powerful weapon. From 1872 to 1951 the legislature of New York never overrode a full veto and only a few times turned back item vetoes. M. Nelson McGeary reported in 1947 that "only once in the present century has the legislature of Pennsylvania overridden a veto." "Realization of the potential power of the governor's veto weapon," he observed, "appears unduly to have tamed the legislators." In both New York and Pennsylvania the legislative bodies pass most of the bills in the closing days of a session. Legislators of these states accept, and perhaps often welcome, the fact that during the 30 days following adjournment, as provided by the constitution, vetoes will be forthcoming.

The virtually absolute nature of the veto is demonstrated in a study by Frank W. Prescott covering all the states for the year 1947:

Bills introduced	62,304
Bills passed in both houses	24,928
Bills vetoed and pocket vetoes	1,253
Vetoes overridden	22

Of 1,253 vetoes only 22, or 1.7 per cent, were overridden. While these figures do not reveal the importance of the issues overridden, the extremely small number is significant. In 23 states two-thirds of the entire membership of each house is necessary to override the governor. Thus the chief executive in these states is in a much stronger position than the president whose veto may be overridden by two-thirds of a quorum in each house of Congress.

The greatest restriction on legislative action with respect to the veto is contained in the Alaska constitution. Three-fourths of the membership is required to override the veto of revenue and appropriation bills or items. Repassage of other bills requires two-thirds of the membership.

The trend toward a strong veto may now be overreaching the bounds of reasonableness. The veto provision is one which merits careful examination in each state to determine whether the constitutional language and the interpretations of the language as evidenced by current practice fall within reasonable limits. Improvement of the end product—the law—may be effected through features such as the executive amendment, or conditional veto as it is called in New Jersey, by which the executive may return a bill with suggestions for change. If the legislature accepts, the bill is sent again to the chief executive. This procedure is written into the constitutions of Alabama, Virginia, Massachusetts and New Jersey. It is used in some states on an informal basis. The extension of procedures such as this, requiring a closer working relationship between the governor and the legislature, would seem to be more productive potentially than would a further increase in the fraction of the legislative membership necessary to override the chief executive. The veto is now uncomfortably close to being absolute in some states, hardly a democratic development.

CONCLUSION

The office of governor has been characterized by William H. Young as proceeding "from detested minion of royal power, to stepson of legislative domination, to popular figurehead, to effective executive." The transition from figurehead to effective executive is a difficult one to achieve.

The constitutional climate in many states does not encourage the development of gubernatorial leadership. Indeed, as one observer has noted, "State constitutions almost uniformly are more restrictive than facilitative." Thus the constitution may act as a negative influence, making the position of governor less desirable and preventing the achievement of programs desired by the people.

Revision could free constitutions of "restrictive" language. A "facilitative" approach is essential in order to enhance the attractiveness of the chief executive's position and to challenge an able governor to extend himself in supplying the high quality leadership which every state so desperately needs.

19. The Office Careers of Governors in the United States*

JOSEPH A. SCHLESINGER

THE means of advancement from office to office is an important characteristic of any political system. In American politics the empirical study of movement between office is of special importance, because there is little, if any, prescribed relation between offices, either in law or in conscious custom. Given

* Reprinted with permission from *How They Became Governor,* Governmental Research Bureau, Michigan State University, 1957. Footnotes omitted.

an abundance of elective offices in a constitutional framework of federalism and the separation of powers, many paths are open to the politically ambitious. However, as is readily evident, all paths do not lead equally to higher office. No legal prescription keeps the county clerk from the presidency. Nevertheless, the major national conventions have yet to nominate a county clerk for the highest national office. Despite a multiplicity of possible career lines in local, state, and national politics, it is certain that the paths actually followed by successful politicians have not been completely haphazard.

The object of this study is to determine the offices which have led to a pivotal position in American politics, the governorship of the states. In attempting to describe the governors' office careers, both historical and comparative methods have been used. From career data on all of the governors elected in the 48 states from 1870 to 1950, patterns of regularity in the office backgrounds of the governors have been drawn, with particular reference to their variation from state to state. At the same time, the eighty-year time span has made possible the observation of changes in particular career patterns. Thus the study attempts to reveal both the historical developments in the office careers of the American governors and the differences among the states in the way they select this particular group of leaders.

There is probably no public office, with the exception of the presidency, which has not at some time been held by a future state governor. However, only a few of these offices have been important numerically as stepping-stones to the governorship. Therefore, in order to gain a faithful picture of gubernatorial career patterns, it is necessary first to reduce the thousands of possible offices to a set of categories which is, at the same time, meaningful and descriptive of the major office career lines. The following, then, are the categories of offices careers used in the study.

1. *State legislative office* is isolated as a typical position which has been of exceptional importance in the careers of governors.

2. *Statewide elective offices* include such positions as lieutenant-governor, secretary of state, superintendent of public instruction, and the like, wherever they are elective. Excluded from this category are all judicial or legal offices such as attorney general or su-

preme court justice, despite the fact that in many instances they are elected at large by the state. The latter have been included in the next category.

3. *Law enforcement offices* cover such positions as attorney and judge at all levels of government. Law enforcement positions such as police commissioner and sheriff have also been included. No distinction is made here between elective and appointive positions. These positions have been singled out and grouped together because they are generally related in the political process, and it was felt therefore, that they should be given a separate category in the promotional scheme.

4. *Federal elective offices* include all United States representatives, senators, vice presidents, and presidents.

5. *Administrative offices* are defined here as all appointive positions at all levels of government, with the exception of those appointed in the law enforcement category. However, at the local level of government many positions have been included in the administrative category which may in some instances actually be elected positions. The only local offices classed as local elective for this study are those described below in category six. Such positions as superintendent of schools, county assessor, city clerk, fence viewer, etc., are frequently elective and frequently appointive. The task of dividing them according to mode of selection would be impossible because of the range of varying procedures in an eighty-year period. Furthermore, such executive positions are easily distinguishable from the major local elective, policy directive posts.

6. *Local elective offices* include the office of mayor, councilman, or alderman, school committeeman, and county commissioner. Again, elective law enforcement positions are not included in this category.

7. *No office* means no public office experience at all prior to the governorship.

In analyzing office patterns on the

basis of the above categories we are concerned with (a) the frequency with which an office category appears in the *experience* of governors, and (b) the *position* which the office category holds in a career leading to the governorship. The number of governors who have held a particular office indicates the general significance which the office has had in state politics. Of equal importance is the time placement of the office in the governors' careers. Many governors may have held a particular office at some point in their careers, but few may have gone directly to the governorship from it. This office becomes significant then primarily as a form of *experience*. On the other hand, those offices which are immediate stepping stones to the highest office in the state are specially designated. These we have called *end offices*. In describing the patterns of promotion in the states, the major emphasis has been upon these two measures—experience and end office.

If we assume a national pattern of office recruitment for governorship, we see (Table I, Column A) that from the point of view of experience the state legislature has been the most important office. More than half the governors had been in a state legislature at some time. The next most important group of offices is the law enforcement category; 32 per cent of the governors from 1870 to 1950 at some point held such an office. Administrative, local elective, state-wide elective, and federal elective offices were important in the experience of governors in that order. Only 9 per cent of the governors fell into the no office category. Roughly the same ordering of offices is found if they are ranked in terms of the office which came first in the governor's career (Table I, Column C). Most governors began their careers in the state legislature, whereas very few began in either a state-wide or federal elective position.

Although the order of the office categories according to experience and first office is approximately the same, their ranking according to end office differs (Table I, Column B). It is true that legislative and law enforcement positions still rank first and second as end offices in governors' careers. But their position of importance has been considerably reduced in comparison with the state-wide and federal elective offices.

TABLE I   *Pattern of Office Experience of All Elected Governors in the United States, 1870-1950*

Office Types	A No. with This as Experience	B No. with This as End Office	C No. with This as First Office	D No. with This as Only Office	Index of Finality (B/A)	Index of Sequence (D/B)
State Legislature	521	200	312	130	38	65
Law Enforcement	319	162	200	85	51	52
Administrative	292	136	167	58	47	43
Local Elective	197	74	118	35	38	47
Statewide Elective	188	157	21	21	84	13
Federal Elective	138	112	26	25	81	22
No Office	88	88	88	88		
Other		66	63			
Total		995	995			

Footnotes omitted.

Local elective office, which had ranked fourth according to experience and first office held, drops to last position as an end office. Obviously some offices are more characteristically end offices and others transitional.

Two numerical indices provide a refined measure of the relative positions of the offices in the careers of the governors. The first index is that of *finality*. The index of finality is the percentage of those holding a particular office who held it as an end office (Table I). It tells, therefore, the place which an office has had in the governors' careers, whether it has been transitional or an immediate stepping-stone to the governorship. In this respect, the lowest ranking office is the state legislative, because only 38 per cent of the governors with legislative experience held the position as an end office. Local elective follows closely with an index of 39. On the other hand, state-wide and federal elective offices are strong end offices with indices of 84 and 81. They are at the top of the career line, second only to the governorship itself.

The second measure of position indicates which offices leading to the governorship also required prior office experience. This particular measure is called the index of *sequence*. It is the percentage of governors holding a particular office type who held only that office type in their careers prior to governorship (Table I, last column). The larger the numerical index for an office, the less the office required some form of prior experience. This index results in a ranking opposed to that found by the index of finality. At the bottom, numerically, as those which required the most previous office experience, are the state-wide and federal elective offices. Of the governors who came directly from state-wide elective office only 13 per cent had no previous office experience. That is, governors who had been lieutenant governors or state treasurers and the like were men who had held other offices as well. On the other hand, 65 per cent of the governors coming directly from the leg-

islature had no other office experience. They started in the legislature and went to the governorship directly from that office. Thus promotion from the legislature is a mode of advancement composed of fewer offices than promotion from state-wide elective positions. Law enforcement, administrative, and local elective offices ranked intermediately according to the index of sequence, with about half of their holders having no previous experience.

The analysis of a national pattern of promotion reveals, then, that almost all American governors have had some previous office experience. The most predominant types of experience have been state legislative and law enforcement. These offices, however, tend to be transitional. The offices at the top of the hierarchy, just below the governorship, are the state-wide or federal elective. This ordering of positions gives a general impression of the relative importance of these offices in the politics of the states.

The national pattern, however, does not focus upon any particular office career, despite differences in positional importance. If we use the end office to designate the pattern, we find that nationally only 20 per cent of the governors held the same end office, the state legislative position. In fact, the distribution of office categories is such that it is impossible to assert that governors' careers are structured nationally, or that one type of career is dominant in the United States. The office of governor, however, is not a national office. When we examine it within the context of the state, we find that for many of the states the governors' careers do tend to follow similar patterns.

The relative importance of the office types in the governors' careers as they differ by states may be derived from Tables II and III. In Table II the states are grouped according to the proportion of their governors who held a particular type of office at any time in their career. The states are thus classified according to the major transitional offices, the state legislative, law enforcement, administrative, and local elective. As is readily apparent, the national figures hide a wealth of variation among the states. In Table III are found those states whose governors derive consistently enough from the same type of office to warrant describing their careers as patterned. There are twenty-five states in which 30 per cent or more of the governors came directly from the same office type. These states, therefore, have well-defined paths of recruitment. No state, by this standard, falls into more than one pattern of office recruitment. In Table III the states with a tendency (20-29 per cent) to fall into one or another category are also indicated, although none has a sufficient concentration to warrant describing it as patterned.

THE USE OF OFFICE CAREERS BY STATES

STATE-WIDE ELECTIVE OFFICE

The most clearly defined path to the governorship is through state-wide elective office. As we have seen, state-wide elective offices are predominantly end offices. Men usually come to these positions with previous experience and hold them just prior to the governorship. The pattern consists of a minimum of two offices before the governorship: (1) legislative office, and (2) state office (usually the lieutenant governorship). As we shall see later, legislative leadership, i.e., speaker of the house or senate president, is frequently a third stage in the process of advancement. Thus we have here a highly ordered pattern, which enables one to project the future governors of a state over a period of from four to six years and possibly more. Promotion directly from state-wide elective office has occurred often in only a few states. In only four was this the case for more than 30 per cent of the governors; but of these, Massachusetts, Vermont, and Iowa had

over 40 per cent of their governors coming from state-wide elective office, evidence of a very strong pattern.

STATE LEGISLATIVE OFFICE

To ten states can be ascribed the legislative pattern of promotion. These states satisfy our requirement that at least 30 per cent of all their governors have come directly from the state legislature. In most instances legislative office was the only one held prior to the governorship. In some states, however, the legislative method of advancement consists of at least two stages, membership in the legislature per se and legislative leadership.

Legislative experience in the careers of governors is distinctly a regional phenomenon. The highest concentration of such experience is found along the eastern seaboard, ranging from New England through the South to Mississippi. A second belt of concentration is found in the midwestern states from Iowa through Nebraska. The concentration is greatest in New England, where 70 per cent of the governors of each state had legislative experience, with the exception of Connecticut (68 per cent). Ohio and Pennsylvania form an area whose governors had little legislative experience (under 15 per cent each). The career of the governor which includes a stay in the state legislature is thus typical of only some states.

The positional importance of the legislature varies likewise. (Compare Tables II and III.) The legislature tends to be important as an end office in those states where it is also important as a form of experience. Yet the relationship between experience and end office is not unitary. The proportion of those with legislative experience who go directly to the governorship differs from state to state. If we look at New England, which had the highest concentration of legislative experience, we find that 72 per cent of Massachusetts' governors had legislative experience, whereas only 3 per cent of the total

TABLE II *The Major Forms of Political Office Experience—Distribution by States*

Per cent of Governors with Office Experience	State Legislative	Law Enforcement	Administrative	Local Elective
80-89	Vt.	Mont.		
70-79	Me., Mass., Miss., N.H., R.I.			N. Mex.
60-69	Ala., Conn., Fla., Ga., Ia., Neb., N.J., N.C., S.C.	Ill.		
50-59	Ark., Del., Ida., Kans., Md., Ore., S.D., Tenn., Utah, Va., Wyo.	Ark., Ky., N.C., Tenn., Tex., W. Va.	N.H.	S.D., Wyo.
40-49	Ariz., Calif., Ill., Ind., Mich., Minn., Mont., N.M., N.Y., W.Va.	Ala., Fla., Ga., Mo., N.Y., Ohio, Pa., S.C.	La., Mich., N.J., N.M., Utah, Vt., Wis., W. Va.	Mass., Wash., N.Y., Utah
30-39	Colo., Ky., La., N.D., Tex., Wis.	Colo., Md., Mich., N.J., Okla., S.D., Vt., Wid.	Cal., Ill., Kans., Me., Md., Wyo., Minn., Neb., Nev., N.Y., S.C.	Idaho, Me., Mich., Neb., N.C., W.Va., Wis.
20-29	Mo., Nev., Wash.	Ariz., Calif., Ind., Ia., Kans., La., Me., Mass., Minn., Miss., N.M, N.D., Va.	Ariz., Ark., Del., Ida., N.C., Ore., R.I., Ind., Miss., Mo., Mont., Okla., Pa., Va.	Cal., Colo., Conn., Fla., Minn., N.H., Ore.
10-19	Ohio, Okla.	Conn., Neb., Nev., N.H., Ore., R.I., Wash., Wyo.	Ala., Colo., Conn., N.D., S.D., Tex., Ga., Ia., Ky., Ohio, Tenn., Wash., Mass.	Ala., Del., Ill., Ind., Kans., Md., Miss., Mo., Mont., N.D., S.C., Tenn., Vt.
0-9	Pa.	Del., Ida., Utah	Fla.	Ariz., Ark., Ga., Ia., Ky., La., Nev., N.J., Ohio, Okla., Pa., R.I., Tex., Va.

68

TABLE III *The Major Office Promotion Patterns in the States*

Per cent of Governors	No Office	State Legislature	Law Enforcement	Statewide Elective	Federal Elective	Administrative	Local Elective
50-53			Montana	Mass.			
40-49	Utah		Ark.	Vt., Iowa	Ohio	N. Mex.	
30-39		Ala., Me., Ariz., Miss., Del., Neb., Ga., N.H., Kans.	Mo., Tenn. Tex., W. Va.	La.		Wyo., Utah	Idaho
States with a tendency toward one or another pattern							
20-29	Colo., Del., Fla., Ind., Ore.	Cal., Conn., Fla., Ida., Ill., Ia., Minn., N.J., N.D., Ore., R.I., Vt., W. Va.	Colo., Fla., Ga., Ill., Ky., La., Md., Minn., N.J., N.C., N.D., Ohio, Pa., S.C., S.D.	Ark., Conn., Ind., Mich., Minn., Mont., N.C., R.I., S.C., S.D.	Ind., Ky., Ind., Mass., Minn., Mont., N.Y., Tenn.	Ariz., Del., Ill., Kans., Mich., Neb., Nev., N.J., Okla., Pa., S.D., W. Va.	

went straight to the governorship from that office. Thus legislative office appears to be an essential prerequisite for the governorship of Massachusetts, but only as preparation for some other office which is closer to the governorship. On the other hand, Maine drew 37 per cent and New Hampshire 30 per cent of all of their governors directly from the legislature. What in Massachusetts has been an office of transition is an end office in Maine. Legislative office has been even more of an end office in Kansas, where, although only 59 per cent of the governors had legislative experience, 37 per cent of all the governors came directly from the legislature. In the South the legislature is typically an office of transition. Although many southern governors have had legislative experience, only in Mississippi and Georgia has it been significant as an end office. Frequency and position thus vary by state and region.

LAW ENFORCEMENT OFFICE

The law enforcement category is composed of a number of offices which are related internally to each other in a hierarchy of promotion. At the top of the hierarchy are state judges and attorney generals; at the bottom are state and local attorneys. Typically, then, the pattern consists of at least two law enforcement offices. Other experience, particularly legislative, is frequently a part of the law enforcement career.

The regional character of the third major office pattern is as distinctive as that of the legislative. The two states where this pattern has been most concentrated are Montana and Illinois. Regionally, however, the states bordering the Deep South, Texas, Arkansas, Tennessee, Kentucky, West Virginia, and North Carolina are those with the highest concentrations. Areas where law enforcement offices have been of least importance, on the other hand, are New England (except Vermont) and most of the far western states.

Here again the positional importance of the offices varies. States where law enforcement offices have been clearly transitional are Vermont, New York, Illinois, and Michigan. The number of their governors to come directly from law enforcement office was low in comparison to the number who had had such office experience. On the other hand, law enforcement offices were distinctly end offices in Arkansas, Missouri, Texas, Tennessee, and Montana.

If we compare the geographic incidence of the law enforcement and legislative patterns, we find that the two types of careers are often opposed. In New England this is most clearly seen, since law enforcement offices have been unimportant, even as types of experience, whereas the legislature has been very important. In the South and Border States both types have been important as office experience, but only in West Virginia, Florida, and Alabama did *both* legislative and law enforcement offices account for as much as 20 per cent each of the end offices of their governors.

ADMINISTRATIVE OFFICE

Non-elective public administrative offices have played an important part in governor's careers, primarily as office experience. About 30 per cent of all governors have held such positions, but less than half of these became governor directly from them. The offices within the category, of course, vary widely in type and importance.

Regionally, administrative positions have been most important in the West. The three Mountains States, Wyoming, Utah, and New Mexico had over 30 per cent of their governors coming directly from these offices. Adjoining states, Nevada and Arizona, and the tier of states from South Dakota to Oklahoma exhibited tendencies in this direction. Illinois, Michigan, West Virginia, Pennsylvania, New Jersey, and Delaware also had more than 20 per cent of their governors come from administrative office. The South, the Border States, and New

England are conspicuously areas in which administrative offices did not lead directly to the governorship. Since these areas exhibited the strongest patterns for the other offices it would be impossible for them to make much direct use of administrative offices in their promotional systems.

As a type of office experience, administrative posts were important (over 30 per cent) in less than half the states. The areas of concentration are much the same for administrative positions as for end offices. In northern New England, in Maine, Vermont, and New Hampshire, however, administrative offices were important as experience, but played no part at all as end offices.

FEDERAL ELECTIVE OFFICE

The distinctive character of the federal elective career in state politics is evident in its lack of concentration. Only one state can be said to have a federal pattern, Ohio, which has had 42 per cent of its governors come directly from Congress. States which have used federal offices to some extent as an end office are Maryland (28 per cent of its governors), Kentucky, Minnesota, Tennessee (24 per cent), New York (23 per cent), Massachusetts (22 per cent), and Indiana (21 per cent). Three of these are northern, highly populated states. The geographic distribution, however, does not indicate that the more congressmen a state has, the more likely one is to become governor.

LOCAL ELECTIVE OFFICE

Quantitatively at least, local elective office is one of the least significant paths to the governorship, there being even more governors with no office experience at all than those coming directly from a local elective post. The distribution of local elective experience among the states shows that in only half did as many as 20 per cent of the governors have this type of experience. In New Mexico, South Dakota, and Wyoming, however, over half of the governors had such experience. In Washington and Utah in the West, and in New York and Massachusetts in the East, over 40 per cent of the governors in each state had local experience. In all of these states, however, local office was purely transitional; in none of them did even 20 per cent of the governors come directly from such a position. Only in Idaho were there enough governors who came from local office to warrant describing a pattern of local elective office.

NO OFFICE

The "no office" category resembles most closely the local elective office in the infrequency of its occurrence as lack of any real concentration in any of the states. The largest single concentration of governors with no previous experience was in Oregon (29 per cent). Other states with over 20 per cent were Colorado, Delaware, Florida, Indiana, and Texas. There is no regional concentration here, and the percentages do not warrant describing any state as having a pattern of no office experience for its governors.

From this overview of governors' careers we can draw the following conclusions: (1) In no state is there a rigid ladder of promotion followed by all governors; (2) however, in more than one half of the states there is a typical office career followed by about a third or more of the governors; and (3) the typical careers are not distributed among the states haphazardly, but tend to cluster regionally. The latter point gives support to our original assumption that career lines of political leaders are an "expression" or facet of the states' political systems. For the similarity of career lines of governors of states within a region is, in all likelihood, the product of a broader regional similarity in history and political structure. . . .

20. State Departments of Administration: Their Role and Trends of Development*

JOE E. NUSBAUM

A "BOLD NEW CONCEPT" to improve management direction of business firms —the integration of staff services under a vice-president of administration—was discussed at an American Management Association seminar in the fall of 1960. This new concept in business is a well-established organizational pattern in state government. The single thread of similarity in the states' sporadic attempts to make some sense of the maze of agencies, boards, departments and commissions has been the consolidation of staff services into a central administrative agency.

While state governments as a group have made wide use of the integrated organizational structure for staff services, large business firms appear to be more advanced in the development of the individual services and in relating them to top management. An analysis of a department of administration by businessmen in one state indicated that large businesses are more willing to make expenditures for technical and professional help.

Competition forces businesses to give constant attention to administrative policies and procedures and to maintain a high quality of staff services. Perhaps more importantly, business firms make more use of these services as effective management tools as contrasted with the provision of routine housekeeping services. However, large organizations in both public and private spheres are recognizing the need for organizing and using these tools of management to work more effectively on behalf of the entire organization.

*Reprinted with permission from *State Government*, Spring 1962. Footnotes omitted.

Due to mounting pressures on state programs, resulting in ever greater complexity in governmental operations, there is almost universal concern among Governors for better ways of giving administrative direction to state services. In tracing the development of state administrative structures over the recent past, the one common effort toward coordination has been the consolidation of staff services into a department of administration or finance.

DEVELOPMENT OF CENTRALIZED STAFF AGENCIES

Consolidated agencies for central administrative operations have been in existence for almost forty years. Departments of finance were first established in Illinois in 1917 and in California in 1921. The first formally designated Department of Administration was set up in Minnesota in 1939. About two-thirds of the states have now integrated previously separate aspects of financial and administrative operations into single staff agencies. The functions most commonly included in the earlier departments were budgeting, accounting, purchasing and routine housekeeping duties; but recent developments have seen the addition of personnel administration, records management, data processing and long-range planning.

Of thirty-four states with departments of administration (not necessarily so named) thirty-three include budgeting, and thirty purchasing, and twenty-three are responsible for central accounting. States whose departments of administration include the broadest range of functions include Indiana, Kansas, Maryland, Pennsylvania, Rhode Island, Vermont and Wisconsin.

Typical central staff agencies, which will be referred to hereafter as departments of administration, are headed by a director or a commissioner appointed by and serving at the pleasure of the Governor. In some states the department head serves for a specified term, usually coincident with that of the Governor. In a few states, notably in Maine and in New Hampshire, he serves for a term longer than that of the Governor. The heads of bureaus and divisions within departments of administration are usually career administrators employed under a merit system, but in some cases they serve at the pleasure of the department head.

PRIMARY PURPOSES

The creation of departments of administration has meant greater central control of those administrative functions which are common to all agencies. Outmoded practices often have existed in the fields of accounting, purchasing, paperwork systems, records management and budgetary planning. More central direction and control over these functions was necessary. Also, conflicts in policies between staff functions could be eliminated by placing them in one department.

Those who have expected a substantial direct savings simply by consolidating a number of units into a department of administration have been disappointed. Even the modest economies made possible by consolidation have not been realized if the divisions of the department continued, in fact, to operate independently of each other.

Moreover, the potentially greater economies that could be produced in the major state spending programs did not materialize automatically, but had to be developed by aggressive pursuit of objectives, use of competent staff and strong support of Governors and legislatures.

Departments of administration have been established, in part, to assist the Governor in his constitutional responsibility for the faithful execution of state programs. Because the Governor is the chief political and ceremonial head of the state, and is much occupied with legislative programs, he has had relatively little time to devote to purely administrative functions. Thus, it has often fallen to the director of the department of administration to be the Governor's alter ego in the area of state administrative operations (at least in those states where the head of this department serves at the pleasure of the Governor). In many respects the head of the department of administration has become the Governor's chief administrative officer, responsible for keeping the machinery of government running smoothly. For example, in recognition of this role, the Commissioner of Administration in Minnesota has often been referred to as the state's "business manager."

In order to assure himself of an independent source of information, the chief executive has leaned heavily on the department of administration for collecting facts, sifting statistics and making objective analyses of data supplied by various state agencies. In most states the Governor is conspicuously isolated from the operations of state programs by a sprawling multiplicity of agencies, departments, boards and commissions over which he has little direct control.

Yet, the Governor is expected to carry out his constitutional responsibility as chief executive of the state. This has pointed to the obvious necessity for his chief administrative officer, the head of the department of administration, to be directly responsible to him.

RECENT DEVELOPMENTS

Many changes have taken place in the activities carried on by departments of administration in the last ten years, both in terms of added new functions and in changes in existing functions. Whole new functions are being added to existing departments or included in newly organized departments.

Personnel administration is a prime example. There is a growing awareness among public administrators of the relationship between effective personnel administration and the other staff functions. In states with a merit system, fears of political interference are slowly disappearing, and personnel administration is beginning to assume its rightful place among the tools available for strengthening administrative operations. Fifteen of thirty-four departments of administration are now responsible, in varying degrees, for personnel management, including, in some states, the maintenance of a statewide merit system.

State governments are following on the heels of private business in making use of modern electronic data processing equipment in paperwork processing. Only in the past few years have states begun to provide this service on a centralized basis. To gain the benefits of electronic data processing for many operations which could not justify a complete range of equipment of their own, a central service had to be provided, and the logical heir to this function has been the department of administration. It is certain that many more states will be moving in this direction and add to the nineteen departments of administration already providing a central data processing service.

Management analysis is increasingly becoming an effective tool of departments of administration for improvement of state programs. One unique approach to systematic management improvement has been undertaken in Wisconsin. In 1960 the first management audit, a comprehensive review of the state's investment functions, was conducted by a team of specialists from the Department of Administration and staff members of the State Investment Board. . . .

This management audit uncovered one simple practice which was costing the state $50,000 annually in lost investment income. Twenty-one recommendations resulting from the management audit dealt with statewide investment policy, cash flow management and interdepartmental responsibilities. Adoption of these recommendations and the rebidding of the state's banking business will earn additional investment income far in excess of the immediate savings of $50,000.

The management audit technique illustrates graphically the advantages of an integrated department of administration. All of the staff specialties can be brought to bear at once in analyzing the various facets of an administrative operation.

In the field of purchasing, major advances are also being made by departments of administration. Central warehousing in some states has increased volume purchasing and has reduced the cost of supplies and equipment. Another recent development is the consolidation of state purchasing requirements with those of local governments. . . .

The desirability of an integrated approach to central staff planning can also be illustrated in the area of space analysis and assignment. A chronic handicap in the operations of state government is the lack of sufficient, usable office space. Serious overcrowding exists in most state offices. State agencies have spilled over into nearby private office buildings, vacated stores and, in some cases, empty homes. This fragmentation in the geographical location of departmental functions has seriously curtailed the ability of state agencies to carry on efficient operations. Departments of administration have usually been given the task of analyzing agency space requirements and maintaining some balance between the competing needs of a multiplicity of state departments. Also, new buildings must be designed with enough flexibility to meet the immediate and future needs of state departments. To perform the space analysis and assignment task effectively, a department of administration must make use of specialists in records management, systems analysis, organization analysis and architectural design in arriving at an independent judgment.

THE FUTURE ROLE

Will departments of administration continue in substantially the same role they have played in the past? A change in emphasis can be detected now and will likely produce the following changes:

—Many service operations will be delegated to the state agencies under standards developed centrally;

—departments of administration will become more involved in management processes as technological developments and integration of programs require more detailed coordination in the management of state programs; and

—coordination and supervision of program planning will become an increasingly important function.

The department of administration as a provider of direct services to other agencies will become less significant. There is growing awareness that once the necessary administrative guidelines and standards have been established and accepted by line departments, many service functions should be decentralized. This is especially true in relation to departments responsible for the major state programs, such as welfare, highways and higher education.

In this connection, some departments of administration are presently giving direction and training to agency staffs in records management, systems analysis and other management improvement activities. Some departments have begun to delegate such activities as position classification, routine purchasing and large volume data processing, subject to central policies and audit.

Departments of administration will inevitably become more involved, as the vehicle for executive coordination and direction, in the curernt management of programs. As the social problems at the state government level—in urban growth, economic development, education beyond the high school and health and welfare—become more complex, broad, interdepartmental efforts to tackle the problems will challenge the formal organizational arrangements between departments. New federal programs, such as the program for area redevelopment, will require participation by a number of state agencies. Technological changes which permit rapid and large volume processing and communication of information have no respect for formal organizational lines.

The role of the departments of administration will be one that promotes management adaptability to keep pace with social and technological change. The best current example of the effect of technological change on state government management is the development and use of high-speed computers, which offer a tremendous opportunity to increase productivity in paperwork operations. To achieve the objectives of a data processing program inevitably requires substantial changes in state policies and practices. For example, new policies have to be established for agencies to share the use of equipment; central processing of payrolls may require a change in pay dates and elimination of some decentralized payroll units; integration of processing functions may completely eliminate work units; and work flow relationships may have to be altered considerably.

In promoting the revision of present systems, departments of administration will clash head-on with some time honored concepts of organization. The principles of line and staff, for example, may not be a useful guide in these new management situations. States may have to impose fundamental changes in cumbersome processing systems—changes which will mean some loss of control over routine processing operations by the separate agencies—if the states are to absorb the change in the nature and volume of work.

Departments of administration will

not only be involved in the coordination and review of current management of programs but will be increasingly used by Governors in longer range planning and development of programs and in recommending organizational arrangements to implement the changing program emphases.

Over a long period of time, there has been a reluctant but inevitable awareness of the chief executive's responsibility for keeping the organizational structure of the state attuned to changing programs. While alterations in state organization have normally resulted from special legislative studies, recent developments indicate a recognition that proposals for revamping the administrative structure can be, and often should be, initiated in the executive branch. Again, the department of administration, with its knowledge of state operations and its capacity for independent review of organizational problems, can provide assistance in carrying out this responsibility.

The head of the department of administration will continue to play a major role on behalf of the Governor as liaison with the state's agencies in financial and administrative matters. Also, as the chief buffer between political leadership and professional bureaucracy, it appears that he and his department will become more involved in program development.

An example of how this is likely to occur was the development of the student loan program in Wisconsin. Governor Nelson advocated a much greater state effort in providing financial assistance to students seeking a higher education. After this executive policy was determined, the financial and administrative problems of implementing it were turned over to the Department of Administration. A student loan proposal was developed and enacted into law which makes up to $5 million available in loans to needy Wisconsin students, without the necessity for appropriations from state funds except for an appropriation to cover any losses of principal and interest. This unique solution to the problem of assistance for students in higher education was made possible by authorizing the State Investment Board to purchase student loans from the agency that administers the loan program. Thus, cash balances were put to use for a state program with no loss of investment earnings.

ALTERNATIVE DIRECTIONS

The above projections of the future role of a department of administration could be altered considerably by what happens to the organizational pattern of the rest of state government. If, as seems likely in the short run, the traditional pattern of state organization is maintained, with the chief executive isolated to a large extent from the departmental operations by the existence of many boards, commissions and departments, headed by persons with long and overlapping terms of office, the department of administration will be a primary tool of the Governor in program planning and management coordination.

On the other hand, in those states where the structure is moving in the direction of a cabinet type of organization, with larger agencies headed by a single individual appointed by and serving at the pleasure of the Governor, the department of administration is likely to diminish in importance as a tool in bringing overall direction of state programs.

The latter approach, however, is just now beginning to appear. The constitutions of the new states of Hawaii and Alaska both place limitations on the number of principal agencies which may be created in state government. In these cases, the Governor is able to deal effectively with his department heads in much the same manner as the President with his cabinet.

A similar approach has been taken in California with its new "agency" plan. Under this system, existing departments are to be grouped together under a cabinet type of officer, called the agency administrator, who serves as the Governor's chief advisor in a broad functional area.

SOME BASIC ASPECTS

Major emphasis has been placed here on the extent to which a department of administration can be of assistance to the Governor in carrying out his executive responsibilities. Some would argue that this increases the Governor's power unduly, and infringes on the legislature's ability to serve as a check on the power of the executive branch. However, an imbalance will occur only if legislators fail to equip themselves with the necessary tools to establish broad policy and to review the effectiveness of administrative programs. Legislatures, too, must be provided with sufficient staff, an adequately organized staff, to carry out these responsibilities. Steps already have been taken in this direction in many states, where permanent researchers are assigned to interim legislative bodies, legislative fiscal analysts have been attached to appropriation committees, and trained staff have been assigned to other standing committees and to legislative leaders.

In addition, legislatures must review their procedures and policies to determine if they are organized to meet the demands of the future.

Finally, whatever the future role of departments of administration, the importance of staff cannot be overemphasized. Departments must, if they are to serve effectively, attract and hold competent professional staffs to deal with the new complexities of state government. More specialized talents are needed, such as in the fields of data processing and systems analysis. But there is also a need to have adequate staffs of trained "generalists," with the imagination and perspective to handle broad administrative problems. Professional staffs must also provide management continuity when political leadership changes.

A KEY TO RESPONSIVE GOVERNMENT

It is a political truism that the average voter holds the Governor responsible for the effective and efficient conduct of state administration. But, to carry out this responsibility, he must have an administrative arm able to deal with increasingly complex management problems in state administration. The role of a department of administration should be to assist the Governor to more effectively fulfill his responsibility as chief executive officer.

Part IV

STATE LEGISLATURES

THE U. S. Constitution stipulates that each state shall be guaranteed a republican form of government. In essence, republican government is representative government. In each of the fifty states the voters choose members of the state legislature to represent them in the important task of determining the significant (and sometimes not so significant) issues of public policy. Then, in many ways, the people evidence distrust of their representatives and adopt attitudes and follow courses of action that make it difficult if not impossible for legislators to perform their appointed task in an effective manner. In her article, "The Legislature," Patricia Wirt proposes certain standards by which legislative bodies may be judged and then delineates factors that explain at least partially why state legislatures do not and cannot meet these requirements.

In 1962 the U. S. Supreme Court decided *Baker v. Carr,* holding that federal courts may take jurisdiction over cases involving alleged denial of rights under the federal Constitution stemming from the manner in which representation is apportioned in state legislatures. In their dissent, Justices Frankfurter and Harlan strongly criticized what they termed "a massive repudiation of the experience of our whole past" and expressed the fear that the majority decision might well lead to an impairment of the Court's position as the final arbiter of legal issues that are "often strongly entangled in popular feelings." They were concerned that the consequences of the decision might be worse than the evil it was designed to remedy.

Specifically, *Baker v. Carr* resulted from the failure of the Tennessee General Assembly to reapportion its membership since 1901. The background facts that resulted in the issue being brought to the courts are cogently detailed by Wilder Crane in "Tennessee: Inertia and the Courts," accompanied by brief comments on the reaction in Tennessee to the Supreme Court's decision. Developments in other states where judicial action has been invoked to correct inequities in legislative apportionment are examined in Will Maslow's "Reapportionment: Breaking the Rural Strangle Hold."

When the Supreme Court remanded the case of *Baker v. Carr* to the federal district court for further action, it provided no criteria to guide the lower court in its deliberations. As might be expected, decisions that have been rendered by the courts in subsequent years have produced no uniformity of standards. Consequently, it is pertinent to inquire as to what type of legislative apportionment the courts will accept. James E. Larson, "Awaiting the Other Shoe," classifies apportionment decisions of recent years and attempts to summarize the positions taken by the courts in an effort to provide some insight into the kinds of apportionment schemes acceptable to the courts.

A "solution" to the apportionment problem popular in some quarters is adoption of the "federal plan" whereby representation in one house is based on population while representation in the second house is based on area. The proponents of this scheme, which already exists in some states, argue that the success of this arrangement at the national level augurs well for its application to state legislatures. In his *Reapportionment and the Federal Analogy,* Robert McKay observes that this proposal "has a surface appeal that has led to uncritical acceptance of the analogy without noting the reasons for which application of that scheme might be inappropriate in the state legislative forum." He then analyzes briefly some difficulties associated with any attempt to apply the federal analogy to state legislatures.[1]

[1] In six cases decided on June 15, 1964, the U.S. Supreme Court ruled that the selection of members to both houses of state legislatures must be based on population. The leading case is *Reynolds v. Sims.* (See p. 108.)

21. The Legislature*

PATRICIA SHUMATE WIRT

FEW American political institutions today enjoy as little prestige as state legislatures. Many are excessively large, most are malapportioned; they are also restricted constitutionally in their powers to legislate, are poorly organized

* Reprinted with permission from *Salient Issues of Constitutional Revision,* National Municipal League, 1961.

and often hampered by archaic rules and procedures. Theoretically the states' chief policy-making institutions, they have lost much of the respect and support which the people gave in the early days of the republic. Serious efforts to reform state institutions have gone on for over half a century but those directed at legislatures have generally met with the least success. Yet many other problems of state government and of the federal system can be solved only by state legislative action—and this in turn depends on something being done about state legislative powers, organization and representation. Major surgery is called for if these organs of the body politic are to make their essential contribution to contemporary government.

The ideal democratic legislature meets several tests: (1) It is responsive to the needs of the state and endowed with sufficient power to formulate necessary policy; (2) its seats are distributed according to the principle of "one man, one vote"; (3) it has high "visibility," performing its duties responsibly and in such a fashion that the public can oversee and judge its actions; (4) its rules permit majority rule while protecting against arbitrary action; (5) it has sufficient time and resources for informed deliberations; (6) competent citizens are attracted to and honored by legislative service. These are the standards by which the legislature should be judged.

* * *

THE "MANACLED STATE"

"Much of the work of constitutional revision so far as the legislature is concerned is . . . a matter of determining not what should be added to the constitution but what might properly be taken out of it." Provisions which prohibit the assembly from legislating on certain subjects and those which in themselves legislate hinder the legislators in their overall function of "policy making and articulation." . . . Constitutional restrictions bear most heavily upon the fiscal powers of legislatures—to tax, to appropriate, to incur and finance debt and to establish the administrative structure necessary to implement these powers. But the general legislative power is similarly restricted. Individual fetters not only affect specific efforts by legislatures but seem to have

a cumulative effect in discouraging legislative imagination and creativity.

Of equal importance in hampering legislative action are the many essentially statutory provisions which have been given constitutional status. The constitution of Louisiana has long been the textbook example of the worst on this score and is replete with provisions noway fundamental:

> In a single 40-page section the constitution sets up a general highway fund and specifies minutely the license fee private automobiles are to pay each year, the tax to be imposed on gasoline and other motor fuels, the amount of bonds that may be issued and the rate of interest they may bear, the proportion of the fund to be used for improving gravel roads and, finally, the places at which bridges and paved highways were to be built. Lest there be misunderstanding on the last point, a map showing the highway routes to be paved was attached and made an official part of the section.

This is typical of literally hundreds of items in that constitution. Similar specimens may be drawn from many others. Florida's, for example, "contains the complete method for administering the distribution and use of motor vehicle licensing funds dedicated to the County Capital Outlay and Debt Service School Fund" (Art. XII, sec. 18). The constitution of Pennsylvania directly regulates general corporate powers, corporate elections, qualifications of foreign corporations to operate within the state, and specifically corporate fiscal powers. It is "fundamental law" in Oklahoma that public schools teach the "elements of agriculture, horticulture, stock feeding and domestic science" (Art. XIII, sec. 7). Local government particularly is subject to detailed treatment in state constitutions, necessitating much legislative action as well as constitutional amendment and generally negating the principle of home rule.

Obstructions to the exercise of legislative power become increasingly more troublesome. While it is still a pastime of many people to berate government and public officials and to honor laissez-faire concepts, Americans are turning more and more to government for assistance in the satisfaction of their needs and in the solution of their problems.

Also at issue here is our belief in representative government. The specific constitutional problem is implementation of the statement found in the constitution of Hawaii: "The legislative power of the state shall be vested in a legislature. . . . Such power shall extend to all rightful subjects of legislation not inconsistent with this constitution or the constitution of the United States" (Art. III, sec. 1).

STRUCTURE, ORGANIZATION, PROCEDURE

If a legislature is representative and has sufficient power to meet its responsibilities, its actions can still be hampered and its goals jeopardized by problems of structure, organization and procedure. As we shall see below some provisions on these matters which present the greatest difficulties are traditional ones which have become dated. Others were cemented into state constitutions during the period of distrust of legislatures. All should be re-examined, most modified, some erased. The fundamental law should certainly provide for the number of houses, the basis of apportionment and terms and qualifications of legislators. But such timely matters as frequency and duration of sessions, legislative salaries, staff requirements and rules of procedure should be left to periodic legislative review and change.

ONE HOUSE OR TWO?

In 1959 two members of Pennsylvania's Commission on Constitutional Revision appended a minority statement to the commission's report which among several things said:

In undertaking to vitalize the legislature and to render it equal to the responsibilities of its key policy-making and power distribution role, we need to make a fresh start. The unicameral or single-chamber form would be structurally a fresh start of a dramatic character calculated to fix political and institutional responsibility and to make legislative processes more understandable to the people. The unicameral plan could be expected to add stature to membership. The operation of a bicameral legislature is diffuse and dilatory—something we should find quite insupportable in local government and in business organization.

*   *   *

Yet America has had considerable experience with the one-house legislature, most of it highly successful. Although by 1790 both had added a second house, Pennsylvania and Georgia entered the union with a unicameral legislature. Vermont—copying almost verbatim the Pennsylvania constitution—maintained the one-house legislature until 1836; it was then abandoned by a narrow vote in a constitutional convention largely for extraneous reasons. Bicameralism has practically disappeared at the municipal level. Why does bicameralism maintain such a strong hold over state government? Historical precedent, inertia and vested interests seem to be among the reasons.

Bicameralism was originally adopted at the national level not for its intrinsic qualities but largely because of political necessity. It was one of the historic compromises that brought large and small states together under the new constitution and it was a device by which the system of federalism was supported—equal representation of all states in the Senate. Yet this action—necessary though it was—set a bad example for the states, for proponents of bicameralism, ignoring the practical basis for the national system, argued in effect that what's necessary for the country is good for the state. Proponents have gone so far as to support the federal analogy for the states, ignoring the quite different constitutional relationship between state and local units of government.

But there are more substantial arguments for bicameralism which experience has not fulfilled. It is claimed that consideration of bills by two houses leads naturally to better policies and more carefully written laws. Yet legislative houses are notorious for "buck-passing," for hastily passing legislation on the expectation that the other house will give careful consideration or will assume the political responsibility for action. It is claimed that the second house is a check against "popular passions." This grew out of an early American fear of democracy and hardly seems a respectable argument for democrats to use. Ours is a system of limited government but sufficient checks seem present in the executive veto, judicial review and public opinion.

It has been claimed that two houses provide protection against corruption and undue influence by lobbies. Logic and the Nebraska experience, however, support unicameralism on this count. Where the organization is simple and membership is small "visibility" is higher. There are fewer havens for the unscrupulous and legislative activity is made clearer and more understandable to the public. "Certainly in eliminating the need for conference committees the unicameral legislature has removed one focal point of undue influence or corruption."

Finally, it is argued that bicameralism permits the use of different bases of representation—population in one house and local units of government in the other. In practice in most states both houses have roughly the same representative base. In theory the proposition is unacceptable for it calls for malapportionment in one house, a violation of the principle of "one man, one vote." It is possible, however, to provide in a unicameral legislature for different bases of representation which do not violate the principle; some members can be chosen from single-member districts, others at large.

Most of the claimed virtues of unicameralism have been realized in the Nebraska experience. In the single house of 43 members (called senators) responsibility can be more easily pinpointed than in the previous two-house legislature. The legislative process has been facilitated with fewer bills introduced and a higher percentage of them passed. With a smaller number of legislators the prestige of membership has risen and with it the quality of candidates for legislative office. Significantly, costs have been lowered.

But in reality many of these same improvements can be made within a bicameral system. States having and retaining two houses—and this includes all but Nebraska—should carefully review the structure and procedures followed and the quality of members elected. Perhaps this will remain the chief means of improving legislative institutions for the road to unicameralism seems a rough one indeed. The Kansas Commission on Constitutional Revision, recognizing "the hold of tradition and the widely varying views that exist" on this issue, "decided that an effort to achieve the practicable, less-than-perfect, is to be preferred to a vain attempt for the ideal."

HOW MANY LEGISLATORS?

* * *

No ready principle or rule of thumb has been devised to determine the proper size for any given state legislature. Population and area are factors but can hardly be regarded as determinants since there is obviously no relationship between the size of the state and the size of the legislature. The main argument for large bodies is that they are necessary to secure adequate representation for the different elements of public opinion. Those favoring smaller legislatures think that every member should have the chance to participate in debate and to shape policy.

In 1954 the American Political Science Association recommended that state legislatures be small enough to permit deliberation but large enough to provide adequate personnel for committee work. The lower house or a unicameral legislature should not have less than 40 members. In bicameral bodies, the association added, "a ratio of one senator to three representatives is desirable." The Committee on State Government of the National Municipal League believed that small houses would tend to make membership in the legislature seem more important, increase each member's responsibility, facilitate increasing legislative salaries, reduce the tendency to leave important decisions to irresponsible committees and enable the legislature to act more as a deliberate assembly. There is little room for doubt that reducing the size of some American legislatures would enable them to function more effectively.

LEGISLATIVE SESSIONS

*   *   *

In recent years strong opinion has developed in favor of more frequent sessions of legislatures in the majority of the states. The Committee on State Government of the National Municipal League advocated continuous legislative sessions, explaining in part that "the need for legislation does not arise once in two years, or from January to March of each year. Normal legislative problems should be faced when the need arises as a regular process, not in period spasms nor as emergencies for special sessions."

One compromise made by some states is the holding of special budgetary sessions during alternate years. The overwhelming uncertainties of trying to prophesy revenues and expenditures from two to three years in advance has caused this development. Yet this compromise has created its own problems and seems no long-term answer to the difficulty. The line between fiscal and non-fiscal matters is difficult to draw and provides another feature of the legislative process which can be exploited for purposes of delay. One legislator from a state with budget sessions comments, "Much of our time at the fiscal session is wasted arguing and debating over what is fiscal and what is non-fiscal. . . . I have serious doubt that one of the annual sessions should be restricted to fiscal matters."

Another relic from the days of distrust of legislatures is the time limit for sessions. About one-third of the states have direct constitutional time limits, usually of 60, 90 or 120 days. A half dozen more have provisions which stop the pay of legislators after a specified number of days, usually 60 or 90. Nearly 40 years ago a distinguished legislator attacked with vigor such restrictions:

> Putting on a time limit is perhaps the most preposterous device men ever conceived for the remedy of political ills. No railroad, banking or manufacturing corporation would be so silly as to try to improve an inefficient directorate by a vote compelling directors' meetings to adjourn after two hours or restricting such meetings to two months in the year. If the administration of justice became conspicuously defective, nobody would risk his reputation for sanity by advising that the courts should sit only from New Year's Day to Easter.

In states without time limits the legislature is meeting longer and longer in each session and this, surprisingly enough, is leading to some advocacy of placing restrictions. In those states with time limits conflicting views are revealed. Many people—legislators and the public alike—are embarrassed and seriously concerned by the frequent scenes of chaos at the end of sessions when legislators are forced to such demeaning tactics as stopping the clock. As problems of modern government multiply, the futility of trying to cope with them in short, limited biennial sessions is obvious. Less obvious perhaps are the ways in which limited sessions accent other deficiencies of state legislatures. They encourage militant minorities to resort to delaying tactics to thwart the will of majorities. They encourage the hasty and inadequate consideration of "must" bills that pile up at the end of the session. They place a premium on a legislator's knowledge of parliamentary strategy and not on the substance of his arguments.

*   *   *

THE PROCESS OF LEGISLATION

Legislative procedure should be left for legislative determination. There seems to be obvious inconsistency in vesting the legislative power of the state in a body but denying that body the right to prescribe its daily work. State constitutions are replete with procedural requirements which legislatures must meet. Some are substantively sound but could better be left to legislative action while others are archaic and some unnecessarily provide the basis for later litigation. Here the U.S. Constitution did not provide the example, for that document is almost clear of such provisions, leaving it to Congress to run itself and to the voters to pass judgment upon the quality of congressional actions. The U.S. Constitution designates the presiding officers of each house—the speaker and the vice president, defines a quorum as a majority of the house, requires that a journal be kept and specifically requires a yea-nay vote in the reconsideration of vetoes (Art. I, secs, 2,3,5,7). With these exceptions "each house may determine the rules of its proceedings" (Art. I, sec. 5). The question is not whether state legislatures should have rules of procedure; they should, quite definitely, and these should be realistic and binding. The question is whether these should be placed in the state constitution.

Probably the most archaic and most widely condemned procedure is that requiring that a bill be read in full on three separate days. This requirement antedates the development of rapid printing devices and has been slavishly copied as something fundamental ever since. It is almost universally circumvented, however, except when used as a dilatory device. There is certainly no assurance that all legislators read carefully all bills printed and placed upon their desks, but it is obvious that the perfunctory and usually "droneful" reading of bills or their titles adds little to the understanding a legislator has of the issue before him.

That bills should be referred to committee for consideration, that they should be printed and in the hands of legislators a minimum period before final action, that legislatures should be able to resolve themselves into a committee of the whole—all these may be desirable but it should be possible to leave them for legislative determination. If for some reason a statement to these effects is necessary it should be kept simple for over-elaboration can in practice lead to excessive restriction.

Most state constitutions contain provisions relating to titles and contents of bills, designed to prevent abuses such as logrolling and trick legislation. The most common of these provisions specifies that each bill shall relate to a single subject and that the subject be expressed in the title. These provisions are sound in purpose but in some states they have led to troublesome and unnecessary litigation without achieving uniform enforcement. If such provisions are included, consideration should be given to exempting legislation from judicial review on their account.

Of doubtful value also are detailed provisions relating to the establishment of legislative councils and the facilitation of executive-legislative cooperation. If such provisions are included they should be permissive and questions of form, organization and procedure left for legislative and executive action.

PAYING THE LEGISLATORS

The constitutional specification of legislative (and other) salaries has been thoroughly discredited by experience. There is no respectable body of opinion that today advocates a continuation of this practice. If the states are to raise the quality of their legislative action, they must first raise the quality of their legislative personnel. The latter requires facing up to the inadequacies of legislative salaries in the majority of states. The abandonment of constitutional prescription will not, of course, guarantee the forthcoming of adequate compensation. It seems the first formal step to be taken, however. Actually some of the specified salaries approach respectability but specification promises difficulty at some time.

*   *   *

Low pay—whether constitutionally or otherwise prescribed—has forced legislators at times into questionable practices. For example, they vote themselves additional living or travel allowances. In one state legislators practiced the subterfuge of appropriating for "postage" which gave them about $300 more for the session; subsequently they were given a salary increase via an amendment and such practices ceased. Such practices, however, drive from office public-spirited citizens who view them as unethical, thus confounding the situation by putting in office those persons more inclined to practice subterfuge.

*   *   *

CONCLUSION

Any genuine improvement in legislative organization and performance will certainly not come by putting legislators in constitutional strait jackets or by merely tinkering with the legislative article. Legislatures which are restricted can and often do find ways to avoid constitutional restraints but this encourages subterfuge and adds unnecessarily to expense in time and money. Furthermore, hindering provisions impede those legislatures which are trying to do their work effectively and responsibly, and they diminish the stature of the legislature in the eyes of the public.

Reforms must be directed toward making the legislature a decision-making body with power commensurate with responsibility. They should contribute toward making legislative service attractive to men of ability. As one authority has outlined the path of reform:

If we will but free our legislatures from their constitutional hobbles, pay them decently, organize them so that they can serve adequately, and create a vigilant public opinion which insists upon responsible service of a high caliber (these are not simple reforms, to be sure), there is no inherent reason why they cannot assume the rightful place of representative assemblies in a representative government.

22. Baker v. Carr

369 U.S. 186 (1962)

ACTION under the civil rights statute, by qualified voters of certain counties of Tennessee for a declaration that a state apportionment statute was an unconstitutional deprivation of equal protection of the laws, for an injunction, and other relief. A three-judge District Court, for the Middle District of Tennessee, 179 F. Supp. 824, entered an order dismissing the complaint, and plaintiffs appealed. The Supreme Court, Mr. Justice Brennan, held that complaint containing allegations that a state statute effected an apportionment that deprived plaintiffs of equal protection of the laws in violation of the Fourteenth Amendment presented a justiciable constitutional cause of action, and the right asserted was within reach of judicial protection under the Fourteenth Amendment, and did not present a nonjusticiable political question.

Reversed and remanded.

MR. JUSTICE BRENNAN delivered the opinion of the Court.

. . . The complaint, alleging that by means of a 1901 statute of Tennessee apportioning the members of the General Assembly among the state's 95 counties, "these plaintiffs and others similarly situated, are denied the equal protection of the laws accorded them by the Fourteenth Amendment to the Constitution of the United States by virtue of the debasement of their votes was dismissed by a three-judge court. . . . The court held that it lacked jurisdiction of the subject matter and also that no claim was stated upon which relief could be granted. . . . We hold that the dismissal was error, and remand the cause to the District Court for trial and further proceedings consistent with this opinion.

*   *   *

[*Prior to 1901 apportionment of members to the General Assembly was based on an enumeration of qualified voters in each county conducted by state authority.*] In 1901 the General Assembly abandoned separate enumeration in favor of reliance upon the Federal Census and passed the Apportionment Act here in controversy. In the more than 60 years since that action, all proposals in both Houses of the General Assembly for reapportionment have failed to pass.

Between 1901 and 1961, Tennessee has experienced substantial growth and redistribution of her population. . . . The relative standings of the counties in terms of qualified voters have changed significantly. It is primarily the continued application of the 1901 Apportionment Act to this shifted and enlarged voting population which gives rise to the present controversy.

. . . Appellants also argue that, because of the composition of the legislature effected by the 1901 Apportionment Act, redress in the form of a state constitutional amendment to change the entire mechanism for reapportioning, or any other change short of that, is difficult or impossible. . . .

*   *   *

In light of the District Court's treatment of the case, we hold today only (a) that the court possessed jurisdiction of the subject matter; (b) that a justiciable cause of action is stated upon which appellants would be entitled to appropriate relief; and (c) because appellees raise the issue before this Court, that the appellants have standing to challenge the Tennessee apportionment statutes. Beyond noting that we have no cause at this stage to doubt the District Court will be able to fashion relief if violations of constitutional rights are found, it is improper now to consider what remedy would be most appropriate if appellants prevail at the trial.

*   *   *

We come, finally, to the ultimate inquiry whether our precedents as to what constitutes a nonjusticiable "political question" bring the case before us under the umbrella of that doctrine. . . . We find none: The question here is the consistency of state action with the Federal Constitution. We have no question decided, or to be decided, by a political branch of government coequal with this Court. Nor do we risk embarrassment of our government abroad, or grave disturbance at home if we take issue with Tennessee as to the constitutionality of her action here challenged. . . .

*   *   *

We conclude that the complaint's allegations of a denial of equal protection present a justiciable constitutional cause of action upon which appellants are entitled to a trial and a decision. The right asserted is within the reach of judicial protection under the Fourteenth Amendment.

*   *   *

MR. JUSTICE FRANKFURTER, whom MR. JUSTICE HARLAN joins, dissenting.

The Court today reverses a uniform course of decision established by a dozen cases, including one by which the very claim now sustained was unanimously rejected only five years ago. The impressive body of rulings thus cast aside reflected the equally uniform course of our political history regarding the relationship between population and legislative representation—a wholly different matter from denial of the franchise to individuals because of race, color, religion or sex. Such a massive repudiation of the experience of our whole past in asserting destructively novel judicial power demands a detailed analysis of the role of this Court in our constitutional scheme. Disregard of inherent limits in the effective exercise of the Court's "judicial Power" not only presages the futility of judicial intervention in the essentially political conflict of forces by which the relation between population and representation has time out of mind been and now is determined. It may well impair the Court's position as the ultimate organ of "the supreme Law of the Land" in that vast range of legal problems, often strongly entangled in popular feelings, on which this Court must pronounce. The Court's authority—possessed of neither the purse nor the sword—ultimately rests on sustained public confidence in its moral sanction. Such feeling must be nourished by the Court's complete detachment, in fact and in ap-

pearance, from political entanglements and by abstention from injecting itself into the clash of political forces in political settlements.

A hypothetical claim resting on abstract assumptions is now for the first time made the basis for affording illusory relief for a particular evil even though it foreshadows deeper and more pervasive difficulties in consequence. The claim is hypothetical and the assumptions are abstract because the Court does not vouchsafe the lower courts—state and federal—guidelines for formulating specific, definite, wholly unprecedented remedies for the inevitable litigations that today's umbrageous disposition is bound to stimulate in connection with politically motivated reapportionments in so many States. In such a setting, to promulgate jurisdiction in the abstract is meaningless. . . . For this Court to direct the District Court to enforce a claim to which the Court has over the years consistently found itself required to deny legal enforcement and at the same time to find it necessary to withhold any guidance to the lower court how to enforce this turnabout, new legal claim, manifests an odd—indeed an esoteric—conception of judicial propriety. . . .

*   *   *

We were soothingly told at the bar of this Court that we need not worry about the kind of remedy a court could effectively fashion once the abstract, constitutional right to have courts pass on a state-wide system of electoral districts is recognized as a matter of judicial rhetoric, because legislatures would heed the Court's admonition. This is not only a euphoric hope. It implies a sorry confession of judicial impotence in place of a frank acknowledgment that there is not under our Constitution a judicial remedy for every political mischief, for every undesirable exercise of legislative power. The Framers carefully and with deliberate forethought refused so to enthrone the judiciary. In this situation, as in others of like nature, appeal for relief does not belong here. Appeal must be to an informed, civically militant electorate. In a democratic society like ours, relief must come through an aroused popular conscience that sears the conscience of the people's representatives. . . .

*   *   *

MR. JUSTICE HARLAN, whom MR. JUSTICE FRANKFURTER joins, dissenting.

I can find nothing in the Equal Protection Clause or elsewhere in the Federal Constitution which expressly or impliedly supports the view that state legislatures must be so structured as to reflect with approximate equality the voice of every voter. Not only is that proposition refuted by history, as shown by my Brother FRANKFURTER, but it strikes deep into the heart of our federal system. Its acceptance would require us to turn our backs on the regard this Court has always shown for the judgment of state legislatures and courts on matters of basically local concern.

In the last analysis, what lies at the core of this controversy is a difference of opinion as to the function of representative government. It is surely beyond argument that those who have the responsibility for devising a system of representation may permissibly consider that factors other than bare numbers should be taken into account. . . . To consider that we may ignore the Tennessee Legislature's judgment in this instance because that body was the product of an asymmetrical electoral apportionment would in effect be to assume the very conclusion here disputed. Hence we must accept the present form of the Tennessee Legislature as the embodiment of the State's choice, or, more realistically, its compromise, between competing political philosophies. The federal courts have not been empowered by the Equal Protection Clause to judge whether this resolution of the State's internal political conflict is desirable or undesirable, wise or unwise.

*   *   *

MR. JUSTICE CLARK, concurring with the majority, notes the importance of certain political considerations:

The controlling facts cannot be disputed. It appears from the record that 37% of the voters of Tennessee elect 20 of the 33 Senators while 40% of the voters elect 63 of the 99 members of the House. . . . However, the root of the trouble is not in Tennessee's Constitution, for admittedly its policy has not been followed. The discrimination lies in the action of Tennessee's Assembly in allocating legislative seats to counties or districts created by it. Try as one may, Tennessee's apportionment just cannot be made to fit the pattern cut by its Constitution. This was the finding of the District Court. . . . The frequency and magnitude of the inequalities in the present districting admit of no policy whatever.

*   *   *

The truth is that—although this case has been here for two years and has had over six hours' argument (three times the ordinary case) and has been most carefully considered over and over again by us in Conference and individually—no one, not even the State nor the dissenters, has come up with any rational basis for Tennessee's apportionment statute.

*   *   *

Although I find the Tennessee aportionment statute offends the Equal Protection Clause, I would not consider intervention by this Court into so delicate a field if there were any other relief available to the people of Tennessee. But the majority of the people of Tennessee have no "practical opportunities for exerting their political weight at the polls" to correct the existing "invidious discrimination." Tennessee has no initiative and referendum. I have searched diligently for other "practical opportunities" present under the law. I find none other than through the federal courts. The majority of the voters have been caught up in a legislative strait jacket. Tennessee has an "informed, civically minded electorate" and "an aroused popular conscience," but it does not sear "the conscience of the people's representatives." This is because the legislative policy has riveted the present seats in the Assembly to their respective constituencies, and by the votes of their incumbents a reapportionment of any kind is prevented. The people have been rebuffed at the hands of the Assembly; they have tried the constitutional convention route, but since the call must originate in the Assembly it, too, has been fruitless. They have tried Tennessee courts with the same result, and the Governors have fought the tide only to flounder. It is said that there is recourse in Congress and perhaps that may be, but from a practical standpoint this is without substance. To date Congress has never undertaken such a task in any State. We therefore must conclude that the people of Tennessee are stymied and without judicial intervention will be saddled with the present discrimination in the affairs of their state government.

23. Tennessee: Inertia and the Courts*

WILDER CRANE

IN March 1962, the United States Supreme Court made the unprecedented decision that a U.S. District Court had jurisdiction in a suit brought by urban taxpayers to challenge the apportionment of a state legislature. This paper is an account of the developments in Tennessee that led to a decision which is expected to have nation-wide consequences.

THE PROBLEM

The Tennessee General Assembly, a Senate of thirty-three members and a House of Representatives of ninety-nine members, was not reapportioned between 1901 and 1962. The state constitution adopted in 1870 requires that the General Assembly reapportion its two houses the year following each national census, but the requirement was ignored by the legislators for sixty years.

*Reprinted from *The Politics of Reapportionment, edited* by Malcolm Jewell, with permission of the author, Wilder Crane, and the publisher, Atherton Press, A Division of Prentice-Hall, Inc., 70 Fifth Avenue, New York.

The constitution does not, moreover, contain the common provisions guaranteeing small counties a minimum representation or restricting populous counties to a maximum. It restricts the House of Representatives to ninety-nine members and the Senate to one-third that number. Though it provides that counties having only two-thirds of the ratio shall be entitled to one member in the House of Representatives, it contains other provisions which allow compensation for fractional inequities in apportioning the Senate. Thus, the constitution's only provision which might complicate reapportionment is its use of the terms "qualified voters" and "qualified electors" rather than population as the basis for apportionment. All parties to the court hearing in June 1962 used the adult population statistics.

The other distinctive institutional facts about the Tennessee legislature concern the basis of apportionment. Tennessee does not have a uniform system of single-member districts. All of the four metropolitan counties which have several representatives elect them all on a county-at-large basis; these metropolitan counties are Shelby (Memphis), Davidson (Nashville), Hamilton (Chattanooga), and Knox (Knoxville). A more distinctive Tennessee institution is the "floterial" district. In addition to their respective representatives, some counties share an extra representative with adjacent counties; some counties have no direct representative. Twenty-two of the ninety-nine districts in the House of Representatives under the 1901 apportionment were floterial. The seats are rotated among the counties in accordance with party agreements which are made with little regard to their respective populations, and sometimes with votes cast only in the candidate's county. This arrangement has required Davidson County (population 399,000) to allow neighboring Wilson County (population 27,000) to nominate this representative periodically and similarly requires Knox County (population 250,000) to defer to Loudon County (population 24,000). Similar rotation agreements apply to some senatorial districts.

The failure of the legislature to reapportion from 1901 to 1962 resulted in the obvious underrepresentation of urban areas and overrepresentation of rural areas. In broadest terms, one-third of Tennessee's voters elected two-thirds of the legislators. The four metropolitan counties were most seriously underrepresented; . . . these counties had over 40 per cent of the population but less than 20 per cent of the representatives.

* * *

However, the malapportionment was not as simple as mere discrimination against the four metropolitan counties. Tennessee, like Gaul, is divided into three parts, known as "grand divisions": mountainous east Tennessee, centering on Knoxville; bluegrass middle Tennessee, centering on Nashville; and what is virtually a northern extension of Mississippi, centering on Memphis. The geographic, economic, and cultural differences among these divisions are probably greater than such

differences among neighboring states in the North. For example, all the Midwestern states would have much more in common with one another than the three grand divisions of Tennessee have. The greatest contrasts exist between east and west Tennessee. East Tennessee was loyal to the Union during the Civil War, remains overwhelmingly Republican, is developing its industries at a rapid rate, and is growing in population. West Tennessee (with the single exception of Memphis) is a declining Southern rural area which is losing population at a rapid rate and whose segregationist policies (especially in Haywood and Fayette counties) have recently attracted nation-wide concern.

Malapportionment in Tennessee was most striking when one compared west and east Tennessee. Every county in west Tennessee except Shelby (Memphis) was overrepresented. Here one found counties such as Chester and Lake, which have less than 10,000 population but had a direct representative. In contrast, in east Tennessee one found non-metropolitan counties such as Sullivan (population 114,000) and Washington (population 64,000), which had only one representative.

THE INTERESTS

This overrepresentation of the stagnant and declining sections of the state has some cultural effects which may be as serious as the more obvious discrimination against metropolitan centers in the distribution of state aid. Overrepresentation of west Tennessee may be one of the explanations why the Tennessee legislature adopted resolutions condemning the Supreme Court decision on school segregation, whereas such Tennessee cities as Nashville have been cited as models for their effective and constructive steps toward school integration. Similar examples are the refusal of the 1961 legislature to repeal the prohibition of the teaching of evolution, for which Scopes was tried, and

its refusal to allow bars and only grudg-
ing legalization of package liquor stores
(with restrictive price controls) in five
counties.

The consequences of malapportionment are more obvious in the distribution of state aid. The brief filed by the
appellants in the Tennessee apportionment case before the Supreme Court
summarizes the problem as follows:

In the 1957-58 apportionment of
the county aid funds, the General
Assembly permitted 23 counties to
receive 57.9% more state aid than
would be the case on a basis of state
aid per capita, and it turns out that
these counties had 23 more direct
representatives than permitted under
the state constitution. Ten counties,
having 25 less direct representatives
than permitted under the Tennessee
Constitution, among them Shelby,
Knox, Hamilton, and Davidson, received 136.9% less state aid than on
a per capita basis. Expressed another
way, a voter in Moore County (with
a voting population in 1950 of 2,340)
has 17 times as much representation
in the Lower House as does a voter
in Davidson County (1950 voting
population 211,930), and Moore
County receives 17 times the apportionment per vehicle of state gasoline
taxes as does Davidson county.

Accordingly, officials of the four metropolitan centers have taken the initiative in attempts to achieve reapportionment. Mayor Ben West of Nashville
has been particularly active in this effort, but the other three metropolitan
cities have also provided funds and legal
assistance in efforts to achieve apportionment.

Nonetheless, it is not possible to assert that the reapportionment controversy is a simple rural-versus-urban conflict, because metropolitan area government officials have not been successful
in mustering support from those other
urban interests which might have been
expected to support reapportionment.
With the exception of the League of

Women Voters, which has campaigned
for reapportionment and cooperated in
the attempts to achieve it by court action, other urban interests have given
metropolitan city officials little assistance. Representatives of such clearly
urban interests as labor, liquor, and the
Tennessee Municipal League have on
occasion stated that they did not favor
reapportionment because it would
merely increase the number of poor-
quality metropolitan legislators. Even a
state official of so clearly an urban interest as the AFL-CIO maintained that
he found more sympathetic cooperation
with the problems of labor from intelligent rural legislators than from the
"bums" who reach the legislature from
the county-at-large electoral lotteries in
the metropolitan centers.

Partisan interests are probably as important in Tennessee as rural-versus-urban interests in the apportionment controversy. In contrast with most of the
Northern states, however, the Republicans have most to gain from a reapportionment more accurately reflecting
population. Thus, the few Republican
legislators (partly because they are more
competent than the Democratic metropolitan legislators) have taken the lead
in fighting for reapportionment.

On a partisan basis, the apportionment of 1901 was not proportional, and
recent trends have accelerated this discrepancy. In 1901, ten Republican counties with the requisite population were
denied a representative, whereas thirteen Democratic counties without the
requisite population were awarded a
full representative. Though there have
been some partisan changes among the
counties subsequently, east Tennessee
remains solidly Republican, and its two
Congressional districts are among the
most safely Republican in the nation.
The Republicans have carried Tennessee in the last three presidential elections, with Nixon carrying the state by
a 75,000-vote margin. In state-wide elections, the Republicans can be certain of
a minimum of 40 per cent of the votes.
Nonetheless, in the 1961 General As-

sembly, the Republicans had merely 19 per cent of the total: six of the thirty-three senators and nineteen of the ninety-nine representatives. Although their leader, Sen. Robert Peters (Kingsport), was the only member to enliven a legislature completely dominated by the governor, the Republicans cannot really compete under the present apportionment.

Senator Peters has regularly introduced reapportionment bills and resolutions. Republicans and metropolitan Democrats have supported him unanimously, but this combination can at best result in fourteen of the thirty-three votes in the Senate and thirty-six of the ninety-nine votes in the House of Representatives. East Tennessee Republicans also took the initiative in court actions and subsequently enlisted the aid of city officials and the League of Women Voters in the metropolitan counties.

In 1961, after the U.S. Supreme Court had agreed to hear the Tennessee case, some observers had hoped that the Minnesota precedent would be followed, and that the Tennessee General Assembly would act on its own initiative with some minimal reapportionment. However, Senator Peters, although waging a series of verbal battles on the floor, failed in his efforts to have his reapportionment bill taken from committee. The most Peters could achieve was to join the Senate speaker in co-sponsoring measures to have the qualified voters enumerated and the problem studied. The Legislative Council began another study after the General Assembly adjourned in 1961 but announced it had nothing to report even after the Supreme Court decision in 1962.

It has been customary for Tennessee governors to include a few remarks in their messages to the General Assembly about the constitutional requirement of reapportionment. There is no indication that any of the recent governors has done anything more. The incumbent governor, Buford Ellington, a farm boy from Mississippi, squeezed through to victory in an eight-way race in which he failed to win a plurality in any metropolitan county. The *Nashville Tennessean* suggested that it was not simply lack of intelligence which led him to state, when questioned on the issue, that he was "not smart enough" to know how to achieve reapportionment.

Tennessee governors are so powerful —with their four-year terms, complete control over their administrations, and vast patronage—that they have little trouble dominating their amateurish seventy-five-day-maximum biennial legislatures, the majority of whose members are first-termers. Thus, Governor Ellington pushed through his budget and complete administrative program this year in the first two weeks of the session.

Several techniques for reapportionment available in other states are not available in Tennessee. There are no constitutional provisions for initiative or referendum. The governor has no authority to call a constitutional convention. The General Assembly, which can call a convention by majority vote in two successive sessions, has consistently refused to do so. Even if a convention were called, it would be chosen according to the present legislative apportionment.

The General Assembly itself may initiate amendments to the constitution by action in two successive sessions, but this device would hardly be a means of reapportioning. As a matter of fact, during the reapportionment controversies the only proposals for constitutional amendments came from the rural legislators, who proposed amending the constitution to give every county one representative in the event that the federal courts found that the violation of the Tennessee constitution also violated federal law.

THE COURTS AND REAPPORTIONMENT

With all other routes barred, proponents of reapportionment began court action in 1955. The initiative was taken by persons in east Tennessee, primarily a group of Knoxville attorneys. Subsequently, city officials and members of the League of Women Voters contributed their support to these efforts.

In 1955, proponents of reapportionment brought an action in Chancery Court in Davidson County. As taxpayers, they alleged that the General Assembly was violating the state constitution. The Chancery Court accepted this allegation, but the Tennessee Supreme Court overruled; it held that to declare the 1901 act unconstitutional would deprive the state of a legislature.

This decision closed the last door to state relief and thus led proponents of reapportionment to the federal courts. Money was obtained from city governments, more parties were enlisted, and a suit was brought in the U.S. District Court for the Middle District of Tennessee. The suit sought a declaratory judgment as well as an interlocutory and permanent injunction restraining state election officials from the execution of the apportionment act of 1901. Without taking testimony, a three-judge district court in 1959 granted a motion of attorneys from the Tennessee attorney general's office to dismiss on the ground that the court lacked jurisdiction. Notice of appeal was filed with the U.S. Supreme Court in March 1960, and the Court noted probable jurisdiction in November 1960. Thus, the 1961 Tennessee legislature met with the threat of U.S. Supreme Court action hanging over it, but nonetheless did not act.

The Supreme Court heard arguments in April 1961 and heard further arguments at the beginning of the fall term in October. The appellants, as taxpayers and voters, brought their action under the U.S. Civil Rights acts, as amended in 1957 and 1960, to invalidate the 1901 Tennessee statute, which, they alleged, denied them equality of voting rights guaranteed by the constitution of Tennessee and by the equal-protection clause of the Fourteenth Amendment to the U.S. Constitution. They argued that the Tennessee case was distinguished from *Colgrove v. Green* in that, unlike *Colgrove,* there was no alternative to judicial assistance if relief were to be obtained; they also pointed out that in *Colegrove* there was no constitutional requirement for apportionment. Instead, they relied on *Gomillion v. Lightfoot,* in which state legislative action in setting local boundaries was found to be a deprivation of constitutional rights.

The U.S. solicitor general entered the case in an *amicus* capacity to argue that U.S. courts should assume jurisdiction. Remedies suggested by the appellants included remanding the case to the district court to allow state officials to present an acceptable apportionment plan, an injunction against further elections under the 1901 apportionment, an order to conduct state legislative elections at-large, or the direct application by the Court of the mathematical formula of the state constitution for reapportionment. Appellants stressed that the district court should be asked to attempt the first or least drastic of these remedies and move to the other remedies only in the event that the state legislature failed to act.

Attorneys for Tennessee argued merely that apportionment was an exclusively state matter, and that the federal courts had no jurisdiction. They did not attempt to defnd the apportionment as equitable or constitutional and thus found themselves defending a violation of the state constitution.

On March 26, 1962, the Supreme Court announced its decision. Although the justices disagreed on the implications of their six-to-two holding, the majority agreed as a minimum that U.S. courts had jurisdiction, that the case was justiciable, and that the plaintiffs had standing to bring the action. The two dissents and the three separate concurring opinons created some ambiguity. More important, however, was the failure of the Supreme Court to provide any guidance to the district court to which the case was remanded.

The immediate reaction of Tennessee officials to the Supreme Court decision gave little promise that they would assume the initiative for reapportionment. Governor Ellington was hesitant to call a special session of the legislature in the last months of his term. On reading the decision, the Governor declared that he was "more confused than ever," but he did apparently understand the implications of having received five hundred letters and calls urging him to defend the present apportionment, as contrasted with only three requests to call a special session of the legislature. Instead of immediately taking the initiative, the Governor blithely suggested that the state remain neutral to allow the urban and rural groups to fight the issue out in court. His attorney general immediately declared that this course of action was impossible, since his office had an obligation to defend the state against the plaintiffs' challenge.

The announced candidates for governor publicly expressed relief that the reapportionment question was in the courts and thus removed from campaign controversy. Similarly, legislative leaders adopted a wait-and-see attitude. The administration leader in the House of Representatives, long a leader of the rural faction, announced that the court would have to order a specific plan of reapportionment, because the legislature was unable to do so. The Legislative Council, to which the problem had been assigned in the 1961 session, met a few days after the Supreme Court decision and announced that it had nothing to report and would have nothing to report until after the fall elections of 1962.

Following the Supreme Court decision, the only concrete proposal by rural legislative leaders was one to amend the constitution to give legal validity to rural overrepresentation in at least one house of the legislature. This proposal, which has been held in reserve for many years as a counterthreat to other reapportionment proposals, would give each of ninety-five counties one representative and each of the four metropolitan counties two representative in the lower house. Paradoxically, therefore, the only rural legislators proposing to act before the district court made a decision suggested a reduction in urban representation.

A month after the Supreme Court announced its decision, Governor Ellington, observing the swift and decisive action by courts in Alabama, Georgia, and Maryland, changed his mind and began attempts at compromise. On May 2, the Governor announced that, though he had been unable to get advance legislative agreement on a reapportionment plan, he was calling a special session of the legislature. He warned that the federal courts might reapportion the state if the legislature failed to do so. In the meantime, the attorney general asked the court to delay hearing the case until the legislature had had an opportunity to act.

The Tennessee legislature met in special session on May 29, 1962. On June 7, Governor Ellington signed Tennessee's first reapportionment measure in sixty-one years. The new apportionment was the work of the Governor's legislative leaders, particularly House Speaker James Bomar and Senate Speaker William D. Baird, who skillfully steered the bills through both houses. The Governor stayed in the background, though he made some efforts to get a compromise acceptable to urban interests. He described the final bills as "good bills" that "went farther than I had expected." Reapportionment was accomplished through separate bills for each house, each of which increased representation for metropolitan and eastern Tennessee counties but neither of which conformed fully to population requirements in the state constitution. The four metropolitan counties, which have 43 per cent of the adult population, increased their Senate seats from six to ten out of thirty-three and lost one of the two Senate floterial seats. They increased their House seats from twenty to thirty-two out of ninety-nine and lost both floterial seats there. The eastern Tennessee counties, with 27 per cent of the adult population, continued to receive seven Senate seats but increased their number in the House from twenty to twenty-six. The Baird measure allotted the Senate seats somewhat equally among the nine Congressional districts with little regard for population equities. The Bomar measure for the House was based more closely on the state constitution, except that the principle of allotting a reprsentative to counties with only two-thirds of a ratio was extended to the floterial districts.

Almost all metropolitan legislators opposed both bills in the roll calls. Two-thirds of the Republicans opposed the Senate bill, but a large majority of them (outside Knoxville) voted for the House measure, which had been amended by the leadership to grant concessions to Republican eastern Tennessee. Thus, the unusual coalition of metropolitan and eastern Tennessee legislators, formed with some difficulty at the start of the special session, failed to hold together. The coalition did propose a measure which was based completely on the voting-population standards in the state constitution, but it won only fifteen votes in the Senate and twenty-nine in the House.

The special session also voted to propose to the voters a limited constitutional convention pertaining to certain legislative articles, including apportionment. Metropolitan and Republican legislators generally voted against the proposed convention, not only because it might open the way to diluting the population principle set forth in the constitution, but also because the bill prescribed that representation at the convention would be the same as that prevailing for the lower house *before* reapportionment. Sponsors of the proposal for a convention, which could not meet until 1965, obviously hoped that judicial decisions before that time would clearly permit a modification of the population principle for one house.

After passage of the reapportionment legislation, the three-judge federal court held a hearing, on June 11, to consider whether the new law met constitutional standards. The plaintiffs argued that the new apportionment set no rational standards and made arbitrary distinctions even among urban counties and among rural counties. They argued that the court could and should draw up its own apportionment plan, and they offered several plans described as adhering to the state constitution. The court did not appear to welcome the invitation to accept one of these or devise its own. The defense position, argued most effectively by an attorney for the Farm Bureau, was that the House apportionment adhered quite closely to the state constitution, with most of the population inequalities resulting from the provision of a seat to counties with two-thirds of a ratio, as required by the constitution. There was a less vigorous defense of the Senate plan, which admittedly was based in part on the political necessity of winning votes in the legislature. The defense argued that, if there were inequities in either plan, the legislature should be given an opportunity to correct them in 1963.

On June 22 the three-judge court held that "at least one house should be based fully on population," and it said that neither house met that standard under the new apportionment. The reapportionment was judged to have removed glaring inequities in the House but to have retained enough inequality to cause serious doubts about its constitutionality, while the Senate reapportionment was said to be "devoid of any standard or rational plan or classification." Though accepting most of the plaintiff's arguments, the court accepted the remedy suggested by the defense. It said that the legislature could be elected in 1962 on the basis of the new apportionment and that the 1963 legislature should have an opportunity to make revisions in the apportionment. . . .

24. Reapportionment:
Breaking the Rural Strangle Hold *

WILL MASLOW

THE momentous decision of the U.S. Supreme Court in *Baker v. Carr,* the Tennessee reapportionment case, and the thirty-odd state and federal decisions which it evoked, indicate that we are on the threshold of a development that may vastly improve our legislative bodies. More than fifty suits have been started in thirty-eight different states in the twelve months that have elapsed since the Supreme Court ruled that "invidious discrimination" in the apportionment or districting of a state legislature violated the Fourteenth Amendment. Although none of these suits has yet resulted in the permanent and equitable "remap" of a state legislature, enough has already been accomplished to quicken hope that the rural strangle hold of our state legislatures may soon be broken. There has been more action on reapportionment in this last year than in the prior twenty-five years. However, no equivalent attack has yet been mounted on the gerrymandering of Congressional seats.

The decision in *Baker v. Carr* was handed down on March 26, 1962. Heroic efforts were at once made to disfranchised voters to enjoin the 1962 primaries to compel reapportionment of the state legislatures to be chosen in the general elections. But while fifteen state and federal district courts moved with unprecedented speed to find that existing legislative apportionments denied certain voters equal protection of the laws, they were not prepared, in the summer of 1962, to fashion judicial remedies until this year's state legislatures had an opportunity to correct glaring discrepancies in voting power. However, federal courts in Alabama, Florida, Georgia and Tennessee, and the state courts in Maryland, prodded state legislatures into special session, and temporary arrangements were hurriedly devised which increased urban representation in one or both chambers.

Forty-seven of the state legislatures will be in session this year. Even those that have not been warned by the courts are on notice that failure to reapportion equitably may result in judicial remedies for malapportionment.

Perhaps the greatest gains from last year's litigation were achieved in Georgia. The infamous "county unit" plan—whereby candidates for state offices and Congressional districts were required to obtain not a popular majority, but only a majority of the units assigned to counties and districts—was invalidated. On March 18, the Supreme Court not only sustained this decision, but went further: by a vote of 8 to 1, it outlawed any voting system in which votes were weighted. The Court stated that our "conception of equality . . . can mean only one thing—one person, one vote." The opinion, of course, does not affect apportionment of state legislators, but the overtones are unmistakable.

Another law suit in Georgia led to a reapportionment of the state senate hastily enacted by a special legislative session. Metropolitan Atlanta and other urban areas were assigned twenty-three of the fifty-four senate seats. In one senatorial district in Atlanta, two Negroes ran against each other in the general elections and Leroy Johnson, the Democratic candidate, was elected—the

* Reprinted with permission from *The Nation*, April 6, 1963.

first Negro to serve in the Georgia legislature since Reconstruction.

In Tennessee, the legislature was called into special session even before the Supreme Court had remanded *Baker v. Carr* to the Federal District Court. The legislature enacted measures increasing the representation of the state's four metropolitan counties from about one-half to three-quarters of the number to which they would have been entitled on population standards. The federal court held, however, that the remap was still inadequate, and decided that the legislature to be elected in 1962 on the basis of the improved apportionment should have until June, this year, to revise the apportionment. The Court stated that "at least one house [*of the legislature*] should be based fully on population."

There have been surprisingly few setbacks in the coast-to-coast effort to overcome districting frozen for a generation. (Twenty-seven states have not reapportioned their state legislatures in twenty-five years; in eight states in more than fifty years.) A three-man federal district court upheld the reapportionment in New York State fixed by its 1894 constitution; an appeal to the Supreme Court is now pending. New Hampshire's singular arrangement, whereby senate seats are divided according to direct taxes paid, was ruled constitutional. (The plan, though odd, is probably equivalent to representation based on population.) Suits in South Dakota and Wyoming were dismissed on technical grounds and efforts to challenge the reapportionment of Congressional seats in Florida, Georgia and Texas failed.

The federal and state courts that were suddenly confronted with reapportionment issues had little guidance from the Supreme Court. *Baker v. Carr* laid down no guide lines, substantive or procedural, and deliberately refused to indicate the extent of discrimination that would render an apportionment plan unconstitutional. After its decision in the Tennessee case, the Supreme Court reversed the decision of the Michigan Supreme Court and of a district court in New York, remanding both cases for further consideration in the light of *Baker v. Carr,* but giving no further clarification. Whether the Court can continue to avoid coming to grips with the thorny problems involved remains to be seen. On its fall docket are no less than ten reapportionment cases from Alabama, Georgia, Maryland, Michigan, New York, Oklahoma and Virginia.

Many questions must be decided. Must a state apportion both houses of its legislature on a population basis, or is a "federal plan" (with representation in one house based on geography or political subdivisions) sufficient? May a federal court set aside an inequitable distribution that was approved originally by popular vote? Must a federal court refrain from judicial intervention if a state allows its voters by initiative and referendum to by-pass the state legislature and place an apportionment plan on the ballot? Are federal courts limited to situations, like Tennessee, where apportionment plans violate state constitutions, or may they strike down discriminatory plans required by such constitutions? May an apportionment originally valid become unconstitutional by reason of the passage of time or changed circumstances? Is an apportionment constitutional because it is rational, i.e., based on some plan or principle, such as geography, even though it is obviously inequitable and discriminatory? And, finally, and perhaps most difficult: How discriminatory must a system be to violate the Fourteenth Amendment?

Some courts have been beguiled into sanctioning the so-called federal plan under which one house of a state legislature is apportioned on the basis of geography, not population. Others have explicitly rejected the federal analogy. . . . After all, small states gained equality in the original Constitution because, without such representation, there would have been no union. . . .

Apart from the sixteen states which sanction the federal plan, there are twenty-five others in which the population basis of apportionment is qualified, usually by the requirement that each county, no matter how small, is entitled to at least one representative in one or both houses. The inevitable result of such qualifications is rural over-representation.

*   *   *

Perhaps the best way of appreciating the speed and forthrightness of the courts in coping with these unprecedented problems is to describe some of the most striking cases. On April 14, 1962, a three-judge federal district court, having before it an application for a temporary injunction to prevent the holding in Alabama of the state primary elections of May, 1962, and the general elections of November, 1962, did not wait for the introduction of evidence. It quoted the Alabama constitution requiring that "representation in the legislature shall be based upon population" and revised decennially, and took judicial notice of an Alabama state court decision that there had been no reapportionment based on population changes since 1901. It then postponed the suit until July 16, 1962, to give the Alabama legislature opportunity to comply with the state constitutional mandate.

The Alabama legislature was called into special session on June 5 and on July 12, four days before the judicial deadline, approved a proposed constitutional amendment (subject to popular ratification) reapportioning the state senate and lower chamber. It also adopted a stand-by statute, apportioning each chamber on a different basis to become effective if the constitutional amendment were rejected by the federal court or the people.

On July 21, the federal district court found that both the constitutional amendment and the stand-by measure were inacceptable and voided both. It then promulgated a temporary reapportionment plan solely to elect the 1963 legislature, incorporating the house apportionment of the constitutional amendment and the senate apportionment of the stand-by measure, choosing for each house the plan closest to true equality of representation. The court specifically rejected a "federal plan" which, indeed, would have been worse than the existing malapportionment. This was the first time a federal court had ever actually reapportioned a state legislature and was the first reapportionment in Alabama since 1901. Two days later, Gov. John Patterson . . . accepted the order of the federal court. An effort to obtain a stay of the order from Supreme Court Justice Hugo Black proved unsuccessful and a second primary election was held in August, 1962.

The representation of urban areas has been increased in the new legislature, the Birmingham delegation enlarged from seven to seventeen and that from Mobile County from three to eighteen. Nevertheless, 27.6 per cent of the people of Alabama still elect a majority of the Alabama senate.

The district court has meanwhile retained jurisdiction of the case (*Sims v. Frink*) in order to give this year's Alabama legislature an opportunity to provide for a true reapportionment of both houses and to break what the court called "the strangle hold." But the court warned that if the 1963 legislature failed to act, it would exercise its "solemn duty" to prevent a denial of the equal protection of the law.

Not all courts have been as forceful in seeking to achieve equality of representation. On July 23, 1962, a federal district court invalidated Florida's 1961 reapportionment and ordered a new plan to be promulgated for the 1962 elections, warning that if it were not done, the court would itself "fashion a remedy of judicial apportionment by judicial decree." The legislature met in special session in August, 1962, and drew up a new plan, which the court approved on September 6.

The apportionment plan was, however, rejected by the voters, the opposition being greatest in the more populous counties and cities. The Florida legislature was again called into special session to draft a new apportionment, but after twenty days of deadlock it adjourned without any action, leaving the matter once more in the hands of the federal court.

State courts were no less forceful than federal courts. On April 23, 1962, the U.S. Supreme Court, in a one-sentence opinion, reinstated a complaint in an apportionment suit brought by August Scholle, head of the Michigan State Federation of Labor, which the Michigan supreme court had dismissed (by a 5-to-3 vote) in 1960. On July 18, 1962, Michigan's highest court invalidated (by a 4-to-3 vote) the apportionment for the state senate which had been frozen into the constitution and approved by the voters in 1952. It also enjoined the primary election only three weeks off. The court "respectfully advised" that a new apportionment was urgently required, but warned that if it were not forthcoming, state senators would be chosen at large in a state-wide primary to be held on September 11.

The majority of the court found the largest senate district contained twelve times as many people as the smallest, and that 53 per cent of the state's population chose only 29 per cent of the senate. It ruled that such a discrepancy violated the Fourteenth Amendment.

At this junction, Supreme Court Justice Potter Stewart stayed the Michigan court's ruling pending an appeal to the U.S. Supreme Court, thus reinstating the August primaries and making impossible any revision of Michigan apportionment until 1963. If the Supreme Court now agrees to hear *Scholle v. Hare,* it will have to decide whether one house of a state legislature may be chosen on the basis of geography, not population.

The litigation in Maryland demonstrates that rural domination of a state's legislature can only be broken by a court or the threat of court action. The Maryland constitution allots one senator to each county and six to Baltimore City, and also apportions the 123 members of the House of Delegates. The state legislature is given no express power to apportion. As a result, Baltimore and its four suburban counties, which contain 76 per cent of the state's population, elected only 34 per cent of the senate and 49 per cent of the house. Bills to call a constitutional convention have repeatedly failed because of rural opposition, even after proposals for such a convention had been approved by the voters.

On April 25, 1962, after reciting the above facts, the Maryland supreme court directed a lower court to receive evidence whether unconstitutional discrimination existed in the apportionment of either Maryland house. On May 24, 1962, Chancellor Duckett ruled that the Maryland senate might properly be chosen on the basis of geographical areas, but that the house apportionment was illegal. On May 24, the Maryland General Assembly met and reapportioned the Maryland house by creating nineteen new seats, which for the first time gave Baltimore and its four suburban counties control of that chamber. On July 23, the Maryland supreme court approved the house reapportionment, but ruled that the senate did not have to be chosen on a population basis. An Appeal has been taken to the U.S. Supreme Court.

*   *   *

Legislative redistricting referenda were on the ballot in twelve states in the last elections. In seven states, the voters approved easier procedures for future apportionments or defeated plans unfair to urban voters. In five others, however, including California, voters either rejected plans to give urban areas more representation or else approved plans unfair by population standards.

A great debate is now developing and political scientists and good-government groups can testify that more hard thinking is being done about legislative apportionment than the country has witnessed in decades. "One man, one vote" is becoming a rallying cry. Voter apathy is being replaced by voter determination and the courts are playing a catalytic role in stimulating legislation, shaping popular attitudes and preserving the fundamental principle of our democracy: the equality of man under the rule of law.

Much remains to be done. A recent study by the National Municipal League shows that less than 30 per cent of the population is able to elect a majority of the lower house in thirteen state legislatures and a majority of the upper houses in twenty states.

* * *

25. Awaiting the Other Shoe*

JAMES E. LARSON

WHAT type of legislative apportionment will the courts accept? To answer this question is not without its difficulties. It is of little or no help to turn to the reapportionment decisions of the past few months. To follow this course is but to seek confusion, for the courts speak with many voices. They speak most firmly and in close unison where legislative inaction over a long period has abrogated state constitutional provisions and created sizable inequities in representation. They speak less firmly when inequities of voting strength can be traced to the state constitution themselves.

Indeed, if we ask "What have the courts accepted?," it is possible to set up at least seven broad classes into which the reapportionment decisions of the last several years may be divided:

1. Those in which the court merely asserted jurisdiction (Hawaii, Minnesota, New Jersey);

2. Those in which apportionment statutes, valid when enacted, were found to be invalid because of the passage of time and legislative inaction (Indiana, Tennessee, Kansas, Alabama, Oklahoma, Vermont);

3. Those in which existing acts of apportionment were upheld (Idaho and Wisconsin);

4. Those in which constitutional provisions were held invalid (Georgia, Michigan, Florida, Maryland, Oklahoma);

5. Those in which state constitutional provisions creating inequities were upheld (New York, Michigan, New Hampshire, Maryland);

6. Those which only implied that state constitutional provisions were invalid (Rhode Island);

7. Those in which the court made its own reapportionment (Alabama).

From a review of these cases, it seems that the position of the courts can be summed up about as follows:

(1) The courts will accept a pattern of apportionment which bases representation in both houses of a bicameral legislature upon population, provided the apportionment is reasonably up to date.

(2) The courts will accept an apportionment of either house on a population basis.

(3) The courts, with one notable exception, have accepted patterns of apportionment permitting some deviation from the population standard in one house, provided there are historical, geographical, political or other so-called

* Reprinted with permission from *National Civic Review*, April 1963. Footnotes omitted.

rational reasons for the departure and the other house is population based.

(4) The courts are not innovators. They have insisted that wherever possible, the legislature do its own reapportioning. They have avoided novel solutions in the form of elections at large and weighted voting. They have taken minimum rather than maximum steps.

As every person is aware, a great constitutional question is involved under the third category, namely, whether the Fourteenth Amendment permits the states to adopt patterns of representation which in one house give weight to factors other than population and, if so, to what factors and to what extent? In recent cases the learned counsels and judges have marshaled impressive evidence in support of both sides. The conflict of views have found in cases relevant to the problem is remarkable, from:

> In a democratic country nothing is worse than disfranchisement. And there is no such thing as being just a little bit disfranchised. A free man's right to vote is a full right to vote or it is no right to vote. (*Gomillion* v. *Lightfoot,* 270 F. 2d 594,612, Wisdom J. concurring.)

To:

> Universal equality is not the test; there is room for weighing. (*Baker* v. *Carr,* 369 U.S. at 226, Douglas J. concurring.)

And to Justice Harlan's dissent in *Baker:*

> It is surely beyond argument that those who have the responsibility for devising a system of representation may permissibly consider that factors other than bare numbers should be taken into account. (369 U.S. at 333.)

*   *   *

But what will the courts accept? On the record thus far the courts (state and federal) have been unwilling to upset state patterns of representation except to require that at least one house be based upon population. The exception is the Michigan reapportionment case, *Scholle* v. *Hare.* In Oklahoma, a federal three-judge court ruled that both houses of the Oklahoma legislature must be reapportioned on the general principle of substantial numerical equality, holding, however, that such an apportionment was consonant with the intent and spirit of the Oklahoma constitution as well as the equal protection clause of the Fourteenth Amendment. No federal court has yet fully held that the principle of numerical equality shall apply to both houses of a state legislature unless that intent can be drawn from the state's constitution. At present, then, this is the answer to our question.

Unfortunately, the answer does not clear the air or stifle the controversy implicit in the original question. Recognition of the fact that cases from Alabama, Maryland, Michigan and New York are now before the United States Supreme Court forces us to rephrase our question to read "Does the Fourteenth Amendment permit state legislative apportionment on a nonpopulation basis?"

In this connection it may be appropriate to suggest several approaches to the question which may throw some illumination on the problem. In large part, the judgment of the court will hinge on its conceptions of (1) the nature of representation in a democracy and (2) the role of a second house in a bicameral legislature. These two matters are, of course, closely related. It is not possible to discuss either of these subjects in any full sense, but several aspects of each may be noted.

THE NATURE OF REPRESENTATION

No good political scientist will attempt an exposition of representation without a formal salutation to the Declaration of Independence, to Thomas

Jefferson and perhaps to John Stuart Mill. We know, in fact, too little about representation. Politically it is something of a Johnny-come-lately. Of itself, representation is an illusive concept, mysterious in its operations. In simple terms representation involves making present something or somebody that is not present. Hence, representation involves ideas, "for only through an idea can the making present of one thing or person be conceived." This is helpful but we are less than clear on what we are looking for, or expect, with regard to representation. Our uncertainty is the cause of our difficulties. As Joseph Tussman notes:

"To represent" has several different senses. In one sense it means "to stand for" or to symbolize, as a flag represents or a figurehead or a monarch who reigns but does not rule represents; it is a ceremonial representation. But in another sense "to represent" is not "to stand for" but "to act for." . . . Does "acting for" mean simply carrying out orders or does it mean acting in the interests of the represented? There is quite a difference, and there are different conceptions of representative government stemming from this difference. Sometimes we expect the representative to act as our instructed delegate. But sometimes we expect him to do his Burkean best, in spite of our harrassment. We are not too clear, unanimous or consistent at this point.

Ambiguity appears also when we think of the representative body, a parliament or a legislature. On the one hand its representativeness is thought to be that of a "sample"; a legislature is representative when it contains within itself the same elements, in the same proportion, as are found in the body politic at large. It is typical of us: we are all in it in microcosm. As such it mirrors or reflects; what we think, it thinks; what it does, we do; it is simply the body politic writ small. Behind this conception are marshaled the attempts to make our representative institutions more representative. They should be like us so they will act like us—no worse, no better.

On the other hand there still lingers the conception of representative government as a form of elective aristocracy. And on this view we want to be represented by our best, our wisest and our fairest. The representative body should be the cream, not a homogenized sample. It should not mirror, but focus; its sense should be uncommon; its vision clearer.

Restlessly, we move between these two concepts, rejecting, according to Tussman, the politician for not being a statesman and scorning the statesman for the politician. It is unlikely then that the problem of *equality* of representation can be divorced from the problem of *quality* of representation. Plato advised on the necessity of securing "competent judgment" in those who must hold political power. Hence, "What kind of legislators do we want?" is as important a question as "Shall legislators be apportioned equally?" What is the relevance of the question "What kind of legislators?" to the problem of equality of representation? From the political scientist's point of view, much more research is needed to determine the extent to which different apportionment patterns reflect the popular attitudes on the nature of representation and to what degree these attitudes have a rational basis.

If we rely upon history for an interpretation of the role of the second house in a bicameral legislature, we are forced to recognize that republican government was established in the United States with the clear intent of preventing popular control of government. The Founding Fathers were fearful of the unbridled excesses of democracy; they sought stability. The bicameral legislature was to act as a brake on government. The Senate was specifically designed to be small and stable of membership in order to restrain the "propensity of . . . single and numerous assemblies to yield to the impulse of sudden and violent passions and to be seduced by factious leaders into intemperate and pernicious resolutions." The Senate, then, was the focal point of the anti-democratic attitudes of such illustrious Americans as Hamilton, Randolph and Madison. Indeed, as the majority opinion of the Maryland Court Appeals noted in the Maryland reapportionment case, the federal constitution-framers did look to Maryland in their search for a desirable model. Randolph of Virginia, in the opening speech of the convention, took note that "Maryland has a more powerful senate, but . . . that it is not powerful enough" against the dangers arising from the democratic parts of its constitution. Is there reason to believe that the fear of political turbulence associated with mass rule which weighed so heavily with the constitution-makers of 1787 is a factor of no significance today?

RATIONALITY AND REPRESENTATION

In much of the legal discussion of apportionment plans, the word "rational" is prominent. A plan will stand or fall in terms of its rationality. Most of the searching for a rational plan of representation has been down the corridors of mathematical equality. Rationality in a scheme of representation requires that representation relates to people in an acceptable numerical fashion—exact equality is not required, but reference to historical, geographical or political considerations must prove rationality. Yet the basic problem may be viewed in another light, or be brought into different focus, by asking whether it is irrational for a majority of the people to accept the idea that the masses are prone to make overrapid political judgments and to provide protection for itself in terms of an upper house in the legislature that shall function as a bal-

ance wheel, stabilizing the government against undue strains.

The problem, dual in nature, is one of fundamental importance. Realistically, for a number of states, rural domination of the legislature will not be broken if one house continues as a stronghold for minority interests. In other states the problem takes another form. Stated over-simply it is whether a population majority has the freedom to divest itself of the power to rule. In the former case it is a matter of the will of the majority being thwarted by a minority, while in the latter it is a question of a majority preference. How shall the Fourteenth Amendment affect the two cases? One solution perhaps is to turn to the concept of the will of the people, however ambiguous that term may be. The courts might do well to accept Edmund Burke's principle that in all governments the people are the true legislature. Examples are readily at hand. In Florida, Mississippi and Oregon, referenda on constitutional amendments for the purpose of adopting new apportionment formulae were defeated in November 1962—largely, it may be supposed, because the formulae were not sufficiently rational, i.e., departed too far from the population standard. It is unlikely that a majority in many states will adopt a pattern of representation that departs in any unreasonable or irrational way from the concept of equal voting rights. Where, as notably in California, Michigan and Washington, there has been a popular rejection of a strict population basis for representation, special factors can be considered as making such a choice rational or reasonable in the eyes of the majority—among them, rapid population influx and concentration and big unionism.

Wherever possible, not in all cases, the courts might adopt this solution to the representation dilemma. Ultimately the courts might assume a view roughly analogous to the "preferred position" doctrine of the First Amendment liberties: that there be a presumption of constitutionality of apportionment provisions which reflect the free exercise of the will of the majority. The test should be whether the people of the state are possessed of the means to formulate freely a system of representation or whether they are captives of a recalcitrant legislature or of inflexible constitutional provisions. Here the people must rely on the courts. The courts in turn must judge "invidiousness" derived from these sources and where found set it aside.

26. Reapportionment and the Federal Analogy*

ROBERT B. McKAY

. . . It is clear that a state apportionment scheme, to be "rational," must demonstrate some relationship to population. The complainants in *Baker* did not challenge the provision in the Tennesee Constitution, in which the standard for allocating legislative representation was closely geared to population. The complaint rather was based on legislative violation of this standard, particularly in the failure to reapportion every ten years since 1901, sometimes described as "silent gerrymandering." . . .

Equally obvious is the corollary proposition that the members of at least one house in a bicameral legislature must be chosen on a population basis. The remaining question, whether both houses must reflect population in their manner of selection, is not answered in *Baker v. Carr;* and there have been conflicting views on this matter in other courts that have since passed on the question. The Michigan Supreme Court, in *Scholle v. Hare,* ruled on July 18, 1962, that Michigan senatorial districts, as well as those of the house, must satisfy standards of reasonable equality in terms of population. To the same effect, a three-judge federal district court held just three days later, in *Sims v. Frink,* that population must be used to some extent as a guide for re-

apportioning both houses in the Alabama legislature.

On the other hand, the Maryland Court of Appeals, in *Maryland Committee for Fair Representation v. Tawes,* held on July 23, 1962, that constitutional requirements are satisfied when one house has a population-related base. Similarly, a three-judge federal district court sitting in Georgia has held that at least one house must be elected by the people apportioned to population but declined to decide whether the other house must take population into account. *Toombs v. Fortson. . . .*

The issue, now sharply drawn, may be stated as follows: Since the United States Senate provides equal representation for all states regardless of population, while the House of Representatives provides representation according to population, is not a similar arrangement permissible by analogy in state legislatures? The contention is that, since the national governmental structure has proved reasonably satisfactory, and since the system was approved by the framers of the Constitution, a similar formula should be acceptable in state legislatures.

The argument has a surface appeal that has led to uncritical acceptance of the analogy without noting the reasons for which application of that scheme might be inappropriate in the state legislative forum. Typical of the unrea-

* Reprinted with permission from *Reapportionment and the Federal Analogy*, National Municipal League, 1962.

soned acceptance of this too-easy argument is the statement of Mr. Justice Harlan in his dissent in *Baker:*

> It is surely beyond argument that those who have the responsibility for devising a system of representation may permissibly consider that factors other than bare numbers should be taken into account. The existence of the United States Senate is proof enough of that. 369 U.S. at 333.

But the answer is not as delusively simple as Mr. Justice Harlan suggests. Indeed, careful analysis of the issue suggests an exactly opposite conclusion, namely, that the federal analogy is not relevant in determining whether a state apportionment plan is or is not consistent with the equal protection clause of the Fourteenth Amendment. Uncritical application of that standard may well lead into constitutional error.

*   *   *

FEDERALISM IN STATE LEGISLATURES

In devising plans for legislative representation, states have frequently taken into account factors other than population, including geography, political subdivisions, urban-rural conflicts, other economic interests, the extent of political participation, and even (in New Hampshire) the amount of direct taxes. . . . The concern here, then is . . . to examine the justifications advanced, based on the federal analogy, for abandoning altogether reliance on population in fixing election districts in one house of a state legislature.

The issue is important in view of the substantial number of states in which the congressional scheme has apparently served as a model for state legislatures. In eight of the fifty states the members of one house represent political subdivisions regardless of population; *i.e.,* in Arizona, Idaho, Montana, Nevada, New Jersey, New Mexico and South Carolina the Senate is composed of an equal number of senators (usually one) from each county, while in Vermont the House of Representatives is made up of one member from each town. In a few states, such as Delaware and Mississippi, by constitution or statute the districts from which both senators and representatives are chosen are fixed without regard to subsequent changes in population. In a number of other states one house (or sometimes both houses) must include at least one member from each county, after which some adjustment is made to accommodate the more populous counties.

The arguments favoring the application of the federal system to the states were summarized by Judge O. Bowie Duckett of the Circuit Court for Anne Arundel County, Maryland, in his opinion in *Maryland Committee for Fair Representation v. Tawes* (May 24, 1962):

> Such an arrangement protects the minorities. It prevents hasty, although popular, legislation at the time. It is based upon history and reason and helps to protect the republican form of government guaranteed by Article IV, sec. 4, of the United States Constitution. It preserves the checks and balances of the state government which has worked so well under the federal. Moreover, there would be little advantage in having a bicameral legislature if the composition and qualifications of the members were similar.

*   *   *

FEDERAL ANALOGY AND MAJORITY RULE

Proponents of the federal analogy claim as an advantage of two houses, one of which is less responsive to popular will, a healthy restraint upon excessive majoritarianism. This formulation of the argument leaves unstated two underlying premises, neither of which can withstand analysis.

First there is a suggestion that majority rule is not altogether desirable, or at least that minority groups are likely to be unreasonably disadvantaged if the majority has its way. But is this true? Minorities are accorded constitutional protection in bills of rights and elsewhere to assure adequate hearing for their views and to protect against oppression by the majority. Once minority rights have been assured in these important respects, no sound reason appears for denying the majority its will in ordinary legislation. Indeed, if the two houses of a legislature are chosen in ways that will ensure representation of radically different interests, an opposite and perhaps greater danger is threatened, the legislative stalemate. Even in Congress this has sometimes occurred, but the risk there is minimized by the greater physical expanse and cultural diversity represented in Congress as compared with the more parochial interests within any single state. The interest groups that operate in the United States Senate and House of Representatives are so numerous and diverse that ordinarily there is little risk that the two houses can be separately controlled by opposing interest groups. In short, there are few issues that would pit the area-based Senate against the population-based House.

In the states the problem is very different, as illustrated most dramatically in the urban-rural conflict that is the pattern today in nearly all the states that have departed significantly from the principle of equal population in one or both houses. Sufficient evidence of this legislative impasse on urban-rural issues is found in the repeated refusal of many state legislatures to follow their own constitutional mandate of periodic reapportionment. It becomes almost axiomatic that the more severe the malapportionment the less is the opportunity for legislative correction. All too often the "federal" system in state legislatures has worked not to protect the minorities but to frustrate all sense of legislative responsibility. When legislatures become incapable of any action on important matters and when they flout

the constitutional imperative of periodic reapportionment, state government falls into disrepute. Only through reassertion of state legislative responsibility can the decline of respect for the state governmental process be reversed.

A second major postulate underlying the check-and-balance arguments advanced in support of the federal analogy is the common belief that the organization of state governments is not essentially different from that of the national government. The assumption could scarcely be more false. The short answer is that the United States, as the very name implies, is a union composed of the sovereign states, consenting to centralized responsibility as to certain enumerated powers but reserving to themselves the balance. The constituent states, on the other hand, have uniformly adopted a unitary structure of government in which no subordinate political subdivision retains any sovereignty but exercises only such functions as are conferred upon it for the convenience of, and at the pleasure of, the state government.

* * *

FEDERAL ANALOGY AND BICAMERAL LEGISLATURE

A final argument advanced by advocates of the federal analogy is that there must be differentiation of representation between the two houses not only to serve the check-and-balance function already discussed but as well to justify the existence of a bicameral legislature. As with many plausible-sounding arguments, the difficulty is that the logic has been pressed beyond defensible limits. The proponents of this argument must necessarily defend *completely* different representation formulas in the two houses, that is, one house related to population and the other totally unrelated.

In fact, however, there are a number of less drastic ways in which the two houses may be made to represent quite different interests. Most important is the fact that under any system no member of one house has the same constituency as any member of the other house. When the lower house is several times larger than the upper, as is ordinarily the case, the members of the more numerous house typically represent persons whose interests are often closely identified with each other in terms of geography, economics and ethnic grouping. Members of the less numerous house, on the other hand, represent larger, more diverse segments of the state, whose problems and interests may be quite different in total impact from those of the smaller group represented by their opposite numbers.

26A. *Reynolds v. Sims*

84 S.Ct. 1362 (1964)

While this book was in production, the U. S. Supreme Court ruled in six cases that districts for election of members to both houses of bicameral state legislatures must be based on population. The leading case was *Reynolds v. Sims,* where the Court provided some insight into the rationale of its position with these observations for the majority by Mr. Chief Justice WARREN:

Legislators represent people, not trees or acres. Legislators are elected by voters, not farms or cities or economic interests. As long as ours is a representative form of government, and our legislatures are those instruments of government elected directly by and directly representative of the people, the right to elect legislators in a free and unimpaired fashion is a bedrock of our political system. . . . If a state should provide that the votes of citizens in one part of the State should be given two times, or five times, or 10 times the weight of votes of citizens in another part of the State, it could hardly be contended that the right to vote of those residing in the disfavored areas had not been effectively diluted. It would appear extraordinary to suggest that a state could be constitutionally permitted to enact a law providing that certain of the state's voters could vote two, five, or 10 times for their legislative representatives, while voters living elsewhere could vote only once. And it is inconceivable that a state law to the effect that, in counting votes for legislators, the votes of citizens in one part of the State would be multiplied by two, five, or 10, while the votes of persons in another area would be counted only at face value, could be constitutionally sustainable. Of course, the effect of state legislative districting schemes which give the same number of representatives to unequal numbers of constituents is identical. Overweighting and overvaluation of the votes of those living here has the certain effect of dilution and undervaluation of the votes of those living there. The resulting discrimination against those individual voters living in disfavored areas is easily demonstrable mathematically. Their right to vote is simply not the same right to vote as that of those living in a favored part of the state. . . . Weighting the votes of citizens differently, by any method or means, merely because of where they happen to reside, hardly seems justifiable. . . .

We hold that, as a basic constitutional standard, the Equal Protection Clause requires that the seats in both houses of a bicameral state legislature must be apportioned on a population basis. . . .

Part V

LAW AND THE COURTS

WHEN a layman becomes directly involved with the law as, for example, a party to a suit for damages or as a defendant in a criminal case, he is usually impressed and perhaps perturbed by the obscure expressions, the "gobbledygook," employed by the members of the legal profession. Even more disturbing, however, is the lack of precision with regard to the meaning of ordinary words such as fence, house, game, daylight, accident, and collision. The confusion surrounding the use of these and similar words in court decisions is delightfully detailed by Harry Hibschman in "Humpty Dumpty's Rule in Law."

Although Americans characteristically stress the importance of "fair play" in judicial proceedings, the fact is that the most elementary requirements of justice are often disregarded in state courts. An example of flagrant denial of defendants' rights because of community prejudice toward a minority, inflamed to the point of threatening violence, is found in *Moore v. Dempsey*. More common causes of injustice are illustrated by *Gideon v. Wainwright* and *Townsend v. Sain*. In the *Gideon* case a Florida court refused to appoint counsel for an indigent defendant accused of breaking and entering. The U. S. Supreme Court, overturning its twenty-year-old precedent of *Betts v. Brady*, held the guarantee of counsel found in the Sixth Amendment to the U. S. Constitution to be a fundamental right that must be observed in state courts because of inclusion in the concept of due process imposed upon the states by the Fourteenth Amendment. The second case involved an appeal by one Charles Townsend from a conviction of murder in an Illinois court. Over the objection of his attorney, Townsend's confession was introduced as evidence in his trial. The facts indicated that the confession was obtained while Townsend was under the influence of drugs. The U. S. Supreme Court ruled that use of a confession obtained under such circumstances constituted a deprivation of the defendant's constitutional rights.

"Justice delayed is justice denied." In spite of general acceptance of this old saw, the disposition of cases in our courts is often a slow and tedious process. Months and even years may elapse between the initiation and conclusion of litigation. In their study of the Supreme Court of New York County (Manhattan), Zeisel, Kalvern, and Buchholz shed some light on the nature and causes of the delay often experienced in the courts of the states.

No element in the administration of the law is more important than the qualifications of judges. Arthur T. Vanderbilt discusses the essential characteristics of a "true judge": impartiality, independence, and immunity. He maintains that popular election is not the best way to select judges who possess these requirements, especially when they are elected on a partisan basis along with other national, state, and local candidates. Regardless of the method of selection used, some judges will prove unsuited for their office. Murray Teigh Bloom considers the problem of "Unseating Unfit Judges." Mr. Bloom illustrates the desirability of having adequate machinery available to remove judges who have demonstrated that they do not adequately meet the demands imposed upon them by their office. Brief attention is directed to the California Commission on Judicial Qualifications as illustrative of effective arrangements for handling this problem.

The practices observed in each of the fifty states to select judges are summarized in the table on the "Final Selection of Judges of All State Courts," followed by the provisions of the California Constitution governing the selection of judges in that state. The "California Plan" is often cited as an exemplary system for the choice of state judges.

27. Humpty Dumpty's Rule in Law*

HARRY HIBSCHMAN

"WHEN I use a word," said Humpty Dumpty, "it means just what I choose it to mean—neither more nor less."

But Alice objected, "The question is

* Reprinted with permission from *The Atlantic Monthly*, April 1932.

whether you can make words mean so many different things."

And Humpty Dumpty airily replied, "The question is which is to be master, that's all."

We are not living in Wonderland, as

we have reason to know every time we come to grips with actualities; and yet in this very real world what Humpty Dumpty said is true—words mean what their masters say they mean. And the masters are the courts of last resort, the Supreme Court of the United States and the appellate courts of the various states. This statement a study of their decisions will speedily confirm; and it will at the same time show what a myth is that certainty of the law which laymen are assured exists.

To begin with the highest court in the land, it held many years ago that the expression "high seas" includes the Great Lakes, though the question arose in connection with the interpretation of a statute written originally by a Congressman who later became a judge, and who as a judge declared that the Great Lakes were not included. A dictionary in common use even now, in defining the words "high seas," uses the Great Lakes as an example of what the words do not cover; and to ordinary folks the dictionary definition for "high seas" as the open ocean seems still to be good.

But would it occur to you that a fence is a building? A New York Court said it was. And the highest court of Massachusetts has held a tent to be a building. A railroad car is a building in Nebraska, but not in Arkansas. A corncrib is also a building in Iowa, but not in Florida—perhaps because they raise corn in the former state and not in the latter. At any rate the Florida Supreme Court argued, "We have been unable to find this word 'corncrib' in Worcester's Dictionary; and it is not necessarily a building, a ship or a vessel. . . . 'Crib' has various meanings, as the manger of a stable, a bin, a frame for a child's bed, a small habitation, and it is used in the latter sense by Shakespeare. Nowhere else do we find it used in the sense of a building." That was in the year of the Lord 1882, and as a consequence of the court's conclusions a defendant who had been convicted of burglary went free.

On the other hand, a Texas court, in order to sustain a conviction of burglary, held that an office in one corner of a hardware store, made of pickets about four feet high, three inches apart, with a plank on top used as a shelf, was a building, though it is clear that it was nothing more or less than a corner fenced off within a building. By the same reasoning the part of a court-room railed off from the public is a building.

A jackass is a horse. The Tennessee Supreme Court settled that many years ago. And, according to the Illinois Supreme Court, asses are cattle. So are goats under a ruling of the North Carolina Supreme Court. The latter court cited in support of its conclusions the well-known case of Laban and Jacob.

Snakes are "implements, instruments, and tools of trade," at least when Uncle Sam is collecting his revenues. For the same purpose a new metal called "bouchan," used in watches, is a jewel. In Georgia a minor who has a separate estate is an orphan. In Pennsylvania a bicycle is an animal, and in the Federal courts it is also a business vehicle.

Chinamen in California were formerly held to be Indians, which disqualified them as witnesses against white folks and made it possible for good white men to rob and assault them with impunity. A Chinese merchant sent to the penitentiary is no longer a merchant, but a laborer, so that the exclusion acts may be applied to him. For the same purpose a gambler is a laborer. According to a very recent decision, however, an air pilot is not a laborer.

In New York, under the sanitary code, candies are vegetables; and in Georgia a watermelon is both a fruit and a vegetable. Pipes, tobacco, cigars, and newspapers are not "articles of comfort" for a poor husband, but mere luxuries. So says the Alabama Supreme Court, which might be expected to have a deeper sympathy for the downtrodden male. In Massachusetts a college education is not a necessary under present-day conditions, according to a decision rendered last year.

In Michigan a dentist is a mechanic. In Mississippi he is not a mechanic. And in North Carolina he is not a physician, within a statute allowing the sale of liquor on the certificate of a physician. Otherwise, says the court, "toothache would be more welcome and more prevalent than snake bite."

A gelding is not a horse. At least both the Montana and the Kansas Supreme Courts have held that, where an indictment charges a defendant with having stolen a gelding, his conviction cannot be sustained if the evidence merely shows that he stole a horse. And a charge of stealing a hog cannot be supported by testimony of the stealing of a dead hog. In other words, a dead hog is not a hog. We have the word of the Supreme Court of Virginia for that.

A question that often arises in connection with certain crimes is the meaning of the term "daylight," or "daytime." This is also an important matter in connection with the service of search warrants. In such a case decided in 1923, it was held by a Federal court that a search warrant providing for a search in daytime only was no justification for a search made at 5:15 P.M. on December 22. In another case decided in 1927, however, it was decided that thirty-eight minutes after sunset was "daytime" in Georgia. The test applied was the so-called burglary test, which is whether there is sufficient light from the sun to recognize a man's features. Judge Sibley said in that case: "Daytime does not in law or by common understanding begin at sunrise, and end at sunset, but includes dawn at one end and twilight at the other."

But in 1929, in a case involving a search under a daytime warrant, Judge Norton, another Federal district judge, reached a conclusion directly contrary to that of Judge Sibley. Judge Norton said:

"Daytime" in this statute is used in its ordinary meaning at the present time. . . . What seems to me to be the correct rule is stated in Murray's Dictionary, where "day" is defined as "in ordinary usage including the lighter part of morning and evening twilight, but, when strictly used, limited to the time when the sun is above the horizon." This rule has great practical advantages. . . . Sunrise and sunset will make a much better working rule than the vague and shadowy boundaries adopted for humanitarian reasons for defining burglary.

So there you are. Which is right? I confess I do not know.

Is an airplane a "self-propelled vehicle"? A Federal district court held it was and convicted a defendant of crime of having transported a "self-propelled vehicle," which had been stolen, from one state to another, where the facts showed that he had flown a stolen plane across the state line. But the United States Supreme Court held only a few months ago that the district judge was mistaken—that an airplane is not "a self-propelled vehicle."

In Missouri a pistol so defective that it could not be discharged even if it were loaded is a firearm. In New York it is not.

Nowhere is it more evident that the prejudices and predilections of the courts determine the meaning of words than in the decisions interpreting Sunday laws, particularly with reference to baseball. Thus, the Supreme Court of Kansas has held that baseball is not a game under a statute forbidding "games of any kind." The Missouri Supreme Court has laid down a similar rule, saying that baseball is a sport. But the Nebraska Supreme Court has held baseball to be a game within a statute forbidding "sporting" on Sunday. The New Mexico Supreme Court, on the contrary, has held that baseball is neither a sport nor labor. But it is labor in Virginia, at least when played by professional players, though no admission is charged. In Tennessee it is not the exercise of any "common avocation of life"; and in Oklahoma it is a public sport and banned if played by professionals, but a private sport and not within the statute when played by amateurs.

Turning away from the criminal law for a moment, let us take a look at the exemption laws and the laws of estates. How would you define the words "household effects"? In Vermont it was held some years ago that they did not include a piano. In Michigan there has been a similar holding; but in Missouri, Oklahoma, and Texas the term "household effects" has been held to include a piano. In New York it has recently been held that "household effects" included two automobiles, a riding horse, and a speedboat; and an earlier New York decision was to the effect that wines in a well-stocked cellar were "household goods." It may be interesting in this connection to note that the Iowa Supreme Court held in 1929 that a radio had "no likeness or kindred relationship with a musical instrument."

Another word that has puzzled the courts from time to time and led to conflicting rulings is the word "accident." According to a Pennsylvania court, the bite of a dog is an accident. So is being shot by an assailant or robber; and so was the shooting of a husband by his wife, when, following a quarrel, the husband approached the house, swearing and carrying an axe, and the wife took a pistol and killed him. The latter holding was made to enable the wife to recover on an insurance policy containing a provision that there could be no recovery by the beneficiary if the insured met his death at her hands other than by accident. Suicide in a fit of delirium or insanity is an accident; but electrocution following a conviction of murder is not an accident according to a decision of the United States Circuit Court of Appeals handed down last June. However, death by lynching is an accident in the opinion of the Kentucky Supreme Court, whatever it may appear to the victim.

"Colored person" in Virginia means one having one-fourth or more of Negro blood. In North Carolina, on the other hand, it means a person having Negro blood of any degree. In Oklahoma it is held to mean Negro so clearly that a white person charged with being colored can maintain an action for libel. But in Mississippi it has been held that the term "colored races" includes all races except white. The Court of Appeals of the District of Columbia, on the other hand, held in 1910 that "colored" referred only to persons of the Negro race, and that, regardless of the slight amount of Negro blood that might be in their veins, —the determining factors being "physical touches, whether of shade, hair, or physiognomy,"—they were "colored" if there was the least admixture of Negro blood.

The word "collision" is another that has demanded a great deal of attention on the part of the courts, and their conclusions as to its application have been varied and conflicting as usual. The Michigan Supreme Court, for instance, held in 1920 that "an object coming from above" might be considered as constituting a collision, the object in that case being the shovel of a steam shovel that fell upon a loading motor truck. The Texas Court of Civil Appeals, on the contrary, decided in a somewhat similar case that an object falling from above could not be considered as constituting a collision, the object being the upper floor of a garage that gave way and crushed a car on the floor below.

In New Jersey a recovery on an insurance policy on the ground of a collision was allowed where the car went through the guard rail of a bridge and was damaged by falling to the ground below. Where a car was backed into an open elevator shaft and fell to the floor below it was held to be a collision by the Pennsylvania Superior Court. But in Wisconsin it has been held that where a car ran off the road, and down an embankment into a river, the facts did not justify recovery as for a collision. In Missouri, on the other hand, recovery as for a collision was allowed under almost identical circumstances. Where, in order to avoid striking an approaching car, a driver turned out and his car left the road, fell down an embankment, struck a rock, and turned over, it was held in New York that the injury to his car was due to a "collision," the court saying, "In simple words, it is a striking together of two objects. The road is an object, likewise the earth. Whether vertical or horizontal makes no difference." But the Washington Supreme Court held in 1924 that it was not a collision where a car skidded off the road and rolled and bounded down a mountain side, striking stumps and trees as it went. Again, on the contrary, the Alabama Supreme Court held that same year that where a car was left standing on a hill and started by the force of gravity, going over a cliff and hitting the ground a number of feet below, damages were recoverable as for a collision.

There is one other troublesome word that needs to be noted—namely the word "drunkenness." The Nebraska Supreme Court held that a man might be under the influence of liquor without being drunk, and gave as the test the one of whether or not he had lost control of his bodily and mental faculties. But the Iowa Supreme Court in a case involving the removal of a mayor on the ground of intoxication, after saying that intoxication and drunkenness meant the same, held, "It means not necessarily that he is so drunk as to be unable to walk straight or show outward signs to a casual observer, but is satisfied if he is sufficiently under the influence of liquor so that he is not entirely himself."

A Texas court more wisely said, "A person may be intoxicated and not drunk. One drink will not ordinarily make a man drunk. Defendant had the appearance of a man who was drinking some but was able to attend to his business." But the same court had said previously with even a greater exhibition of wisdom, "It is extremely difficult to draw the line on a 'drunk.' There are various stages, such as quarter drunk, half drunk and dead drunk. There are the stages of being vivacious, foxy, tipsy, and on a 'high lonesome,' and it is as difficult to determine when a young lady gets to be an old maid as it is to tell when a man has taken enough alcoholic stimulant to pass the line between 'jolly sober' and 'gentlemanly drunk.'"

And now, approaching the end, let us see what "end" means according to an august appellate tribunal. Said the Virginia Supreme Court: "It imports what will be when the Apocalyptic Angel, with one foot on the sea and other upon the Earth, shall lift his hand to Heaven and swear, by Him that liveth forever and ever, that there shall be 'Time no longer.'"

It is well, however, to note that at least in one instance a high court was stumped by a problem of definition. It was the Supreme Court of Georgia, which in 1925 admitted and explained:

From the days of Socrates and Xantippe, men and women have known what is meant by nagging, although philology cannot define or legal chemistry resolve it into its elements. Humor and threats are idle. Soft words but increase its velocity and harsh ones its violence. Darkness has for it no terrors, and the long hours of the night draw no drapery of the couch around it. It takes the sparkle out of the wine of life and turns at night into ashes the fruits of the labor of the day. In the words of Solomon, "it is better to dwell in the corner of the housetop than with a brawling woman in the wide house."

And further deponent sayeth not.

28. *Moore v. Dempsey*

281 U.S. 86 (1923)

. . . THE appellants are five negroes who were convicted of murder in the first degree and sentenced to death by the Court of the State of Arkansas. The ground of the petition for the writ [*of habeas corpus*] is that the proceedings in the State Court, although a trial in form, were only a form, and that the appellants were hurried to conviction under the pressure of a mob without any regard for their rights and without according to them due process of law.

The case stated by the petition is as follows, and it will be understood that while we put it in narrative form, we are not affirming the facts to be as stated but only what we must take them to be, as they are admitted by the demurrer: On the night of September 30, 1919, a number of colored people assembled in their church were attacked and fired upon by a body of white men, and in the disturbance that followed a white man was killed. The report of the killing caused great excitement and was followed by the hunting down and shooting of many negroes and also by the killing on October 1 of one Clinton Lee, a white man, for whose murder the petitioners were indicted. . . .

A Committee of Seven was appointed by the Governor in regard to what the committee called the "insurrection" in the county. The newspapers daily published inflammatory articles. On the 7th a statement by one of the committee was made public to the effect that the present trouble was "a deliberately planned insurrection of the negroes against the whites, directed by an organization known as the 'Progressive Farmers' and 'Household Union of America' established for the purpose of banding negroes together for the killing of white people." According to

the statement the organization was started by a swindler to get money from the blacks.

Shortly after the arrest of the petitioners a mob marched to the jail for the purpose of lynching them but were prevented by the presence of United States troops and the promise of some of the Committee of Seven and other leading officials that if the mob would refrain, as the petition puts it, they would execute those found guilty in the form of law. The Committee's own statement was that the reason that the people refrained from mob violence was "that this Committee gave our citizens their solemn promise that the law would be carried out." According to affidavits of two white men and the colored witnesses on whose testimony the petitioners were convicted, . . . the Committee made good their promise by calling colored witnesses and having them whipped and tortured until they would say what was wanted, among them being the two relied on to prove the petitioners' guilt. However this may be, a grand jury of white men was organized on October 27 with one of the Committee of Seven and, it is alleged, with many of a posse organized to fight the blacks, upon it, and on the morning of the 29th the indictment was returned. On November 3 the petitioners were brought into Court, informed that a certain lawyer was appointed their counsel and were placed on trial before a white jury—blacks being systematically excluded from both grand and petit juries. The Court and neighborhood were thronged with an adverse crowd that threatened the most dangerous consequences to anyone interfering with the desired result. The counsel did not venture to demand delay or a change of venue, to challenge a jury-man or to ask for separate trials. He had no preliminary consultation with the accused, called no witnesses for the defense although they could have been produced, and did not put the defend-ants on the stand. The trial lasted about three-quarters of an hour and in less than five minutes the jury brought in a verdict of guilty of murder in the first degree. According to the allegations and affidavits there never was a chance for the petitioners to be acquitted; no jury-man could have voted for an acquittal and continued to live in Phillips County and if any prisoner by any chance had been acquitted by a jury he could not have escaped the mob.

The averments as to the prejudice by which the trial was environed have some corroboration in appeals to the Governor, about a year later, earnestly urging him not to interfere with the execution of the petitioners. One came from five members of the Committee of Seven, and stated in addition to what has been quoted heretofore that "all our citizens are of the opinion that the law should take its course." Another from a part of the American Legion protests against a contemplated commutation of the sentence of four of the petitioners and repeats that a "solemn promise was given by the leading citizens of the community that if the guilty parties were not lynched, and let the law take its course, that justice would be done

and the majesty of the law upheld." A meeting of the Helena Rotary Club at-tended by members representing, as it said, seventy-five of the leading indus-trial and commercial enterprises of Helena, passed a resolution approving and supporting the action of the Amer-ican Legion post. The Lions Club of Helena at a meeting attended by mem-bers said to represent sixty of the lead-ing industrial and commercial enter-prises of the city passed a resolution to the same effect. In May of the same year, a trial of six other negroes was coming on and it was represented to the Governor by the white citizens and officials of Phillips County that in all probability those negroes would be lynched. It is alleged that in order to appease the mob spirit and in a measure secure the safety of the six the Governor fixed the date for the execution of the petitioners at June 10, 1921, but that the execution was stayed by proceedings in Court. . . .

*   *   *

. . . We have confined the statement to facts admitted by the demurrer. We will not say that they cannot be met, but it appears to us unavoidable that the District Judge should find whether the facts alleged are true and whether they can be explained so far as to leave the state proceedings undisturbed.

Order reversed. The case to stand for hearing before the District Court.

29. *Gideon v. Wainwright*

372 U.S. 335 (1963)

PETITIONER was charged in a Florida state court with having broken and en-tered a poolroom. . . . This offense is a felony under Florida law. Appearing in court without funds and without a lawyer, petitioner asked the court to

appoint counsel for him, whereupon the following colloquy took place:

"The Court: Mr. Gideon, I am sorry, but I cannot appoint Counsel to represent you in this case. Under the laws of the State of Florida, the only time the Court can appoint Counsel to represent a Defendant is when that person is charged with a capital offense. I am sorry, but I will have to deny your request to appoint Counsel to defend you in this case.

"The Defendant: The United States Supreme Court says I am entitled to be represented by Counsel."

Put to trial before a jury, Gideon conducted his defense about as well as could be expected from a layman. He made an opening statement to the jury, cross-examined the state's witnesses, presented witnesses in his own defense, declined to testify himself, and made a short argument "emphasizing his innocence to the charge contained in the Information filed in this case." The jury returned a verdict of guilty, and petitioner was sentenced to serve five years in the state prison. Later, petitioner filed in the Florida Supreme Court this habeas corpus petition attacking his conviction and sentence on the ground that the trial court's refusal to appoint counsel for him denied him rights "guaranteed by the Constitution and the Bill of Rights by the United States Government." Treating the petition for habeas corpus as properly before it, the State Supreme Court, "upon consideration thereof" but without an opinion, denied all relief. Since 1942, when Betts v. Brady, 316 U.S. 455, 62 S.Ct. 1252, 86 L.Ed. 1595, was decided by a divided Court, the problem of a defendant's federal constitutional right to counsel in a state court has been a continuing source of controversy and litigation in both state and federal courts. To give this problem review here, we granted certiorari. . . .

The facts upon which Betts claimed that he had been unconstitutionally denied the right to have counsel appointed to assist him are strikingly like the facts upon which Gideon here bases his federal constitutional claim. Betts was indicted for robbery in a Maryland state court. On arraignment, he told the trial

judge of his lack of funds to hire a lawyer and asked the court to appoint one for him. Betts was advised that it was not the practice in that county to appoint counsel for indigent defendants except in murder and rape cases. He then pleaded not guilty, had witnesses summoned, cross-examined the State's witnesses, examined his own, and chose not to testify himself. He was found guilty by the judge, sitting without a jury, and sentenced to eight years in prison. Like Gideon, Betts sought release by habeas corpus, alleging that he had been denied the right to assistance of counsel in violation of the Fourteenth Amendment. Betts was denied any relief, and on review this Court affirmed. It was held that a refusal to appoint counsel for an indigent defendant charged with a felony did not necessarily violate the Due Process Clause of the Fourteenth Amendment, which for reasons given the Court deemed to be the only applicable federal constitutional provision. . . . Treating due process as "a concept less rigid and more fluid than those envisaged in other specific and particular provisions of the Bill of Rights," the Court held that refusal to appoint counsel under the particular facts and circumstances in the Betts case was not so "offensive to the common and fundamental ideas of fairness" as to amount to a denial of due process. Since the facts and circumstances of the two cases are so nearly indistinguishable, we think the Betts v. Brady holding if left standing would require us to reject Gideon's claim that the Constitution guarantees him the assistance of counsel. Upon full reconsideration we conclude that Betts v. Brady should be overruled.

* * *

We think the Court in Betts had ample precedent for acknowledging that those guarantees of the Bill of Rights which are fundamental safeguards of liberty immune from federal abridgment are equally protected against state invasion by the Due Process Clause of the Fourteenth Amendment. This same principle was recognized, explained, and applied in Powell v. Alabama, 287 U.S. 45, 53 S.Ct. 55, 77 L.Ed. 158 (1932), a case upholding the right of counsel. . . . In many cases other than Powell and Betts, this Court has looked to the fundamental nature of original Bill of Rights guarantees to decide whether the Fourteenth Amendment makes them obligatory on the States. Explicitly recognized to be of this "fundamental nature" and therefore made immune from state invasion by the Fourteenth, or some part of it, are the First Amendment's freedoms of speech, press, religion, assembly, association, and petition for redress of grievances. For the same reason, though not always in precisely the same terminology, the Court has made obligatory on the States the Fifth Amendment's command that private property shall not be taken for public use without just compensation, the Fourth Amendment's prohibition of unreasonable searches and seizures, and the Eighth's ban on cruel and unusual punishment. On the other hand, this Court in Palko v. Connecticut, 302 U.S. 319, 58 S.Ct. 149, 82 L.Ed. 288 (1937), refused to hold that the Fourteenth Amendment made the double jeopardy provision of the Fifth Amendment obligatory on the States. . . .

We accept Betts v. Brady's assumption, based as it was on our prior cases, that a provision of the Bill of Rights which is "fundamental and essential to a fair trial" is made obligatory upon the States by the Fourteenth Amendment. We think the Court in Betts was wrong, however, in concluding that the Sixth Amendment's guarantee of counsel is not one of these fundamental rights. Ten years before Betts v. Brady, this Court, after full consideration of all the historical data examined in Betts, had unequivocally declared that "the right to the aid of counsel is of this fundamental character." Powell v. Alabama, 287 U.S. 45, 68, 53 S.Ct. 55, 63, 77 L.Ed. 158 (1932). While the Court

at the close of its Powell opinion did by its language, as this Court frequently does, limit its holding to the particular facts and circumstances of that case, its conclusions about the fundamental nature of right to counsel are unmistakable. . . .

. . . The fact is that in deciding as it did—that "appointment of counsel is not a fundamental right, essential to a fair trial"—the Court in Betts v. Brady made an abrupt break with its own well-considered precedents. In returning to these old precedents, sounder we believe than the new, we but restore constitutional principles established to achieve a fair system of justice. Not only these precedents but also reason and reflection require us to recognize that in our adversary system of criminal justice, any person haled into court, who is too poor to hire a lawyer, cannot be assured a fair trial unless counsel is provided for him. This seems to us to be an obvious truth. Governments, both state and federal, quite properly spend vast sums of money to establish machinery to try defendants accused of crime. Lawyers to prosecute are everywhere deemed essential to protect the public's interest in an orderly society. Similarly, there are few defendants charged with crime, few indeed, who fail to hire the best lawyers they can get to prepare and present their defenses. That government hires lawyers to prosecute and defendants who have the money hire lawyers to defend are the strongest indications of the widespread belief that lawyers in criminal courts are necessities, not luxuries. The right of one charged with crime to counsel may not be deemed fundamental and essential to fair trials in some countries, but it is in ours. From the very beginning, our state and national constitutions and laws have laid great emphasis on procedural and substantive safeguards designed to assure fair trials before impartial tribunals in which every defendant stands equal before the law. This noble ideal cannot be realized if the poor man charged with crime has to face his accusers without a lawyer to assist him. . . .

The judgment is reversed and the cause is remanded to the Supreme Court of Florida for further action not inconsistent with this opinion.

30. *Townsend v.. Sain*

372 U.S. 293 (1963)

. . . In 1955 the petitioner, Charles Townsend, was tried before a jury for murder in the Criminal Court of Cook County, Illinois. At his trial petitioner, through his court-appointed counsel, the public defender, objected to the introduction of his confession on the ground that it was the product of coercion. A hearing was held outside the presence of the jury, and the trial judge denied the motion to suppress. He later admitted the confession into evidence. Further evidence relating to the issue of voluntariness was introduced before the jury. The charge permitted them to disregard the confession if they found that it was involuntary. Under Illinois law the admissibility of the confession is determined solely by the trial judge, but the question of voluntariness, because it bears on the issue of credibility, may also be presented to the jury. . . . The jury found petitioner guilty and affixed the death penalty to its verdict. The Supreme Court of Illinois affirmed the conviction, two justices dissenting. . . .

*   *   *

Having thoroughly exhausted his state remedies, Townsend petitioned for habeas corpus in the United States District Court for the Northern District of Illinois. That court, considering only the pleadings filed in the course of that proceeding and the opinion of the Illinois Supreme Court rendered on direct appeal, denied the writ. The Court of Appeals for the Seventh Circuit dismissed an appeal. 265 F.2d 660. How-

ever, this Court granted a petition for certiorari. . . .

*   *   *

The undisputed evidence adduced at the trial-court hearing on the motion to suppress showed the following. Petitioner was arrested by Chicago police shortly before or after 2 a.m. on New Year's Day 1954. They had received information from one Campbell, then in their custody for robbery, that petitioner was connected with the robbery and murder of Jack Boone, a Chicago steelworker and the victim in this case. Townsend was 19 years old at the time, a confirmed heroin addict and user of narcotics since age 15. He was under the influence of a dose of heroin administered approximately one and one-half hours before his arrest. It was his practice to take injections three to five hours apart. At about 2:30 a.m. petitioner was taken to the second district police station and, shortly after his arrival, was questioned for a period variously fixed from one-half to two hours. During this period, he denied committing any crimes. Thereafter at about 5 a.m. he was taken to the 19th district station where he remained, without being questioned, until about 8:15 p.m. that evening. At that time he was returned to the second district station and placed in a line-up with several other men so that he could be viewed by one Anagnost, the victim of another robbery. When Anagnost identified another man, rather than petitioner, as his assailant, a scuffle ensued, the details of which were disputed by petitioner and the police. Following this incident petitioner was again subjected to questioning. He was interrogated more or less regularly from about 8:45 until 9:30 by police officers. At that time an Assistant State's Attorney arrived. Some time shortly before or after nine o'clock, but before the arrival of the State's Attorney, petitioner complained to officer Cagney that he had pain in his stomach, that he was suffering from other withdrawal symptoms, that he wanted a doctor, and that he was in need of a dose of narcotics. Petitioner clutched convulsively at his stomach a number of times. Cagney, aware that petitioner was a narcotic addict, telephoned for a police physician. There was some dispute between him and the State's attorney, both prosecution witnesses, as to whether the questioning continued until the doctor arrived. Cagney testified that it did and the State's attorney to the contrary. In any event after the withdrawal symptoms commenced it appears that petitioner was unresponsive to questioning. The doctor appeared at 9:45. In the presence of officer Cagney he gave Townsend a combined dosage by injection of 1/8-grain of phenobarbital and 1/230-grain of hyoscine. Hyoscine is the same as scopolamine and is claimed by petitioner in this proceeding to have the properties of a "truth serum." The doctor also left petitioner four or five 1/4-grain tablets of phenobarbital. Townsend was told to take two of these that evening and the remainder the following day. The doctor testified that these medications were given to petitioner for the purpose of alleviating the withdrawal symptoms; and the police officers and the State's attorney testified that they did not know what the doctor had given petitioner. The doctor departed between 10 and 10:30. The medication alleviated the discomfort of the withdrawal symptoms, and petitioner promptly responded to questioning.

As to events succeeding this point in time on January 1, the testimony of the prosecution witnesses and of the petitioner irreconcilably conflicts. However, for the purposes of this proceeding both sides agree that the following occurred. After the doctor left, officer Fitzgerald and the Assistant State's Attorney joined officer Cagney in the room with the petitioner, where he was questioned for about 25 minutes. They all went to another room; a court reporter there took down petitioner's statements. The State's attorney turned the questioning to the Boone case about 11:15. In less than nine minutes a full confession was transcribed. At about 11:45 the questioning was terminated, and petitioner was returned to his cell.

The following day, Saturday, January 2, at about 1 p.m. petitioner was taken to the office of the prosecutor where the Assistant State's Attorney read, and petitioner signed, transcriptions of the statements which he had made the night before. When Townsend again experienced discomfort on Sunday evening, the doctor was summoned. He gave petitioner more 1/4-grain tablets of phenobarbital. On Monday, January 4, Townsend was taken to a coroner's inquest hearing where he was called to the witness stand by the State and, after being advised of his right not to testify, again confessed. At the time of the inquest petitioner was without counsel. The public defender was not appointed to represent him until his arraignment on January 12.

Petitioner testified at the motion to suppress to the following version of his detention. He was initially questioned at the second district police station for a period in excess of two hours. Upon his return from the 19th district and after Anagnost, the robbery victim who had viewed the line-up, had identified another person as the assailant, officer Cagney accompanied Anagnost into the hall and told him that he had identified the wrong person. Another officer then entered the room, hit the petitioner in the stomach and stated that petitioner knew that he had robbed Anagnost. Petitioner fell to the floor and vomited water and a little blood. Officer Cagney spoke to Townsend five or 10 minutes later. Townsend told him that he was sick from the use of drugs, and Cagney offered to call a doctor if petitioner would "cooperate" and tell the truth about the Boone murder. Five minutes later the officer had changed his tack; he told petitioner that he thought him innocent and that he would call the doctor, implying that the doctor would give him a narcotic. The doctor gave petitioner an injection in the arm and five pills. Townsend took three of these immediately. Although he felt better, he felt dizzy and sleepy and his distance vision was impaired. Anagnost was then brought into the room, and petitioner was asked by someone to tell Anagnost that he had robbed him. Petitioner then admitted the robbery, and the next thing he knew was that he was sitting at a desk. He fell asleep but was awakened and handed a pen; he signed his name believing that he was going to be released on bond. Townsend was taken to his cell but was later taken back to the room in which he had been before. He could see "a lot of lights flickering," and someone told him to hold his head up. This went on for a minute or so, and petitioner was then again taken back to his cell. The next morning petitioner's head was much clearer. Although he could not really remember what had occurred following the injection on the previous evening, an officer then told petitioner that he had confessed. Townsend was taken into a room and asked about a number of robberies and murders. "I believe I said yes to all of them." He could not hear very well and felt sleepy. That afternoon, after he had taken the remainder of the phenobarbital pills, he was taken to the office of the State's attorney. Half asleep he signed another paper although not aware of its contents. The doctor gave him six or seven pills of a different color on Sunday evening. He took some of these immediately. They kept him awake all night. The following Monday morning he took more of these pills.

Later that day he was taken to a coroner's inquest. He testified at the inquest because the officers had told him to do so.

Essentially the prosecution witnesses contradicted all of the above. They testified that petitioner had been questioned initially for only one-half hour, that he had scuffled with the man identified by Anagnost, and not an officer, and that he had not vomited. The officers and the Assistant State's Attorney also testified that petitioner had appeared to be awake and coherent throughout the evening of the 1st of January and at all relevant times thereafter, and that he had not taken the pills given to him by the doctor on the evening of the 1st. They stated that the petitioner had appeared to follow the statement which he signed and which was read to him at the State's attorney's office. Finally they denied that any threats or promises of any sort had been made or that Townsend had been told to testify at the coroner's hearing. As stated above counsel was not provided for him at this inquest.

There was considerable testimony at the motion to suppress concerning the probable effects of hyoscine and phenobarbital. Dr. Mansfield, who had prescribed for petitioner on the evening when he had first confessed, testified for the prosecution. He stated that . . . the dosage administered would not put a person to sleep and would not cause amnesia or impairment of eyesight or of mental condition. The doctor denied that he had administered any "truth serum." However, he did not disclose that hyoscine is the same as scopolamine or that the latter is familiarly known as "truth serum." Petitioner's expert was a doctor of physiology, pharmacology and toxicology. He was formerly the senior toxicological chemist of Cook County and at the time of trial was a professor of pharmacology, chemotherapy and toxicology at the Loyola University School of Medicine. He testified to the effect of the injection upon a hypothetical subject, obviously the petitioner. The expert stated that the effect of the prescribed dosage of hyoscine upon the subject, assumed to be a narcotic addict, "would be of such a nature that it could range between absolute sleep * * * and drowsiness, as one extreme, and the other extreme * * * would incorporate complete disorientation and excitation * * *." And, assuming that the subject took 1/8-grain phenobarbital by injection and 1/2-grain orally at the same time, the expert stated that the depressive effect would be accentuated. The expert testified that the subject would suffer partial or total amnesia for five to eight hours and loss of near vision for four to six hours.

The trial judge summarily denied the motion to suppress and later admitted the court reporter's transcription of the confession into evidence. He made no findings of fact and wrote no opinion stating the grounds of his decision. Thereafter, for the purpose of testing the credibility of the confession, the evidence relating to coercion was placed before the jury. At that time additional noteworthy testimony was elicited. The identity of hyoscine and scopolamine was established (but no mention of its properties as a "truth serum" was made). An expert witness called by the prosecution testified that Townsend had such a low intelligence that he was a near mental defective and "just a little above moron." Townsend testified that the officers had slapped him on several occasions and had threatened to shoot him. Finally, officer Corcoran testified that about 9 p.m., Friday evening, before the doctor's arrival, Townsend had confessed to the Boone assault and robbery in response to a question propounded by officer Cagney in the presence of officers Fitzgerald, Martin and himself. But although Corcoran, Cagney and Martin had testified extensively at the motion to suppress, none had mentioned any such confession. Furthermore, both Townsend and officer Fitzgerald at the motion to suppress had flatly said that no statement had been made before the doctor arrived. Although the other three officers testified at the trial, not one of them was asked to corroborate this phase of Corcoran's testimony.

It was established that the homicide occurred at about 6 p.m. on December 18, 1953. Essentially the only evidence which connected petitioner with the crime, other than his confession, was the testimony of Campbell, then on probation for robbery, and of the pathologist who performed the autopsy on Boone. Campbell testified that about the "middle" of December at about 8:30 p.m. he had seen Townsend walking down a street in the vicinity of the murder with a brick in his hand. He was unable to fix the exact date, did not know of the Boone murder at the time and, so far as his testimony revealed, had no reason to suspect Townsend had done anything unlawful previous to their meeting.

The pathologist testified that death was caused by a "severe blow to the top of his [Boone's] head * * *." Contrary to the statement in the opinion of the Illinois Supreme Court on direct appeal there was no testimony that the wounds were "located in such a manner as to have been inflicted by a blow with a house brick * * *."

*   *   *

Numerous decisions of this Court have established the standards governing the admissibility of confessions into evidence. If an individual's "will was overborne" or if his confession was not "the product of a rational intellect and a free will," his confession is inadmissible because coerced. These standards are applicable whether a confession is the product of physical intimidation or psychological pressure and, of course, are equally applicable to a drug-induced statement. It is difficult to imagine a situation in which a confession would be less the product of a free intellect, less voluntary, than when brought about by a drug having the effect of a "truth serum." It is not significant that the drug may have been administered and the questions asked by persons unfamiliar with hyoscine's properties as a "truth serum," if these properties exist. Any questioning by police officers which *in fact* produces a confession which is not the product of a free intellect is inadmissible. The Court has usually so stated the test.

* * *

Thus we conclude that the petition for habeas corpus alleged a deprivation of constitutional rights.

* * *

Reversed and remanded.

31. Delay in the Court*

HANS ZEISEL, HARRY KALVERN, Jr., and BERNARD BUCHHOLZ

DELAY in the courts is unqualifiedly bad. It is bad because it deprives citizens of a basic public service; it is bad because the lapse of time frequently causes deterioration of evidence and makes it less likely that justice be done when the case is finally tried; it is bad because delay may cause severe hardship to some parties and may in general affect litigants differentially; and it is bad because it brings to the entire court system a loss of public confidence, respect, and pride. . . .

THE MEASUREMENT OF DELAY

Everyone has a rough common sense notion of what court delay means and everyone realizes that delay results from a backlog of pending suits which forces the litigants to stand in line and wait their turn. Yet the accurate measurement of delay turns out to be a complex and interesting matter. In popular discussions, the two most frequently used measures of delay have been the size of the backlog, and the age of the last case tried in regular order. On closer analysis, neither of these emerges as an altogether satisfactory measure.

Because delay does result from the existence of a backlog, and because the large numbers associated with the backlog tend to have a dramatic impact, talk of delay in terms of the size of the backlog has become quite customary. But, preoccupation with backlog figures is, in fact, misleading and may have the effect of making the removal of delay seem an impossible task. Since the backlog may run into ten thousand cases, and the court can only try a few hundred of them each year, the popular impression has been created that it would take decades to dispose of such a backlog.

But . . . the cardinal fact about the disposition of cases in our courts is that only a fraction of the suits reach the trial stage, and it is only at this stage that they become a serious burden to the court. This is why the size of the backlog is so frequently a paper figure of limited significance. The numerical size of the backlog tells us little unless we also know the size of the court, the proportion of cases settled before assignment, and the time it takes to dispose of assigned cases. A large backlog of pending suits may be disposed of quite speedily if the court is large, or if the average time required for disposition is small, or if a large proportion of cases is disposed of voluntarily without court

* Reprinted with permission from Hans Zeisel, Harry Kalvern, Jr., and Bernard Buchholz, *Delay in the Court*, Little, Brown and Co., 1959. Footnotes omitted.

action. And since any or all of these
factors may change over time, the nominal backlog is a poor measure of delay
even within the same court system.

* * *

It is true, of course, that if we look at
delay only from the viewpoint of the
litigant who knows that he has no
chance of preferment, the delay in regular order is what he would like to
know. Similarly, if a litigant is reasonably certain of preferment, the average
delay of preferred cases is the measure
appropriate for his case. But when delay is viewed from the perspective of
the court system as whole, in an attempt to assess its overall efficiency, the
proper measure of delay is the average
of the preferred *and* regular order
cases. And this, incidentally, is the delay that interests a litigant who really
does not know whether he will get any
preference or not.

* * *

. . . Is the total interval between the
moment the case becomes official and
the date of its trial really delay? In a
real sense the parties are not delayed
until they are ready to try and are prevented from doing so solely by the un-
availability of the court. This means
that the question as to the correct starting point of delay can be determined
only by taking the subjective expectations of the parties into account. It is
widely recognized that trial immediately after the cause of action arises
would be highly undesirable, if not impossible, in most cases, especially in
those involving serious personal inju-
ries. Some time is required for the
preparation of the case and for the
clarification of damages both from the
point of view of the litigants and of
the court. But where the calendar is
substantially delayed litigants may be
tempted to file suit prematurely, not
because they are ready for trial but in
order to cut down their total waiting
time. . . .

The companion problem to when to
begin counting delay is at what point
the count ought to end. Almost every
court system will have among its pending cases some which, because of con-
tinuances and voluntary adjournments,
are far older than cases being tried in
regular order. Certainly the court
should not be charged with this total
waiting time. It would seem that such
cases should be counted as delayed only
up to the point at which the court offered trial. For measurement purposes,
the interval of voluntary delay ought
to be subtracted from the total age of
the case when it reaches trial. . . .

32. The Essential Characteristics of Judicial Office*

ARTHUR T. VANDERBILT

In the eight centuries or more in which
the judicial office has evolved in the
Anglo-American system of law, three

* Reprinted with permission of the publisher from *Judges and Jurors: Their Functions, Qualifications and Selection*, by Arthur
T. Vanderbilt, Boston University Press, 1958.
Footnotes omitted.

essentials stand out in any definition of
a true judge. These are impartiality,
independence and immunity. Of these
impartiality is the most important;
independence and immunity are the
means of achieving impartiality. Judges
should be free from every tie which
may sway their judgment. They should

be answerable to no one and immune from liability for judicial acts, to the end that justice may be administered without favor. The independence that judges must have to administer the law impartially was achieved only after the courts became separated from other governmental organs and only . . . when it was recognized that justice was a mockery and a farce if the judges were dependent on other departments of government for their income or for the retention of their office. Without these all the personal qualifications of the judge—his character, courage, honesty, wisdom and learning—are of little import or value save in unusual crises, where the judge is called to stand up to a test that it is not fair or wise to impose on any man.

*   *   *

Impartiality is part of the definition of a good judge. . . . As long as a judge is subject to removal or the threat thereof, or to pressure, or influence, his judicial decisions obviously cannot be expected to be impartial. And so not until judges of the English courts were commissioned to hold office during good behavior, with certain compensation, may they be said to have achieved those measures necessary to the independence that make for impartiality. Quite as important as the effect of these statutes on the judiciary was their effect on litigants and the public. With their passage any doubt that they might have entertained as to the independence in fact of judges from governmental pressure was entirely dissipated. . . .

We have been discussing the independence necessary to the judicial office without which the independent individual cannot function freely and impartially, but there is another kind of independence and impartiality that is equally important—that relates to the character of the judge himself. He must be able to think things through for himself and not be so easily swayed by arguments on one side as to cause him to close his mind to the other side of the case. He must be independent in mind so as to evaluate both precedents and contemporary needs, to balance them and, fearless of public opinion, to render impartial judgment. He must be independent in the sense that he is self-reliant and not submissive, able to make decisions freely without being subject to bias and influence. This is a matter of individual personality; it is independence in the sense of the courageous character of a particular person. It is quite as important as the independence that is accorded any constitution or statute. But it can only be obtained through the proper selection of judges.

Judicial independence has been enhanced by the development of the common-law doctrine of judicial immunity that has enabled judges to be free from fear of recrimination for the consequences of their judicial decisions. Gradually it became a principle of English law that judges were not liable civilly for judicial acts within their jurisdiction. . . .

*   *   *

The problem of the tenure to be given judges is inextricably interrelated with the question of the degree of independence necessary for the fulfillment of judicial functions. To a public for whom equality is a by-word lengthy terms of office or tenure during good behavior may seem aristocratic. The popular feeling that all can equally administer justice and that experience in these tasks is of little importance makes it difficult for the public to realize the value of continuity in judicial office. It is too often forgotten that the judicial task is a specialized one. Historically short terms of office have gone hand in hand with the selection of judges by the electorate. This may be explained as the result of the democratic fervor which swept the country a century or more ago. Limitations on judicial tenure and popular election of judges were the first expedients of a people critical of their courts and desirous of influencing and controlling judicial decisions. Because of the manifold difficulties in selecting those fit for such specialized tasks short terms may be used as a device to check the abuse of the office by those temporarily placed there and as a means of removal of those unfit for office, but without any assurance that the replacement will be any better than those whom they replace. Unless tenure is secure it is difficult to attract the ablest men to the bench or for them to develop their abilities to administer justice impartially. . . . Moreover, under a system of short terms of office, tenure may not depend on the judge's performance, but on the turn of the wheel of fortune at the polls, something quite beyond his individual control when one party sweeps into office by such an overwhelming vote that all other officeholders of the other party, no matter how valuable their work may have been, are turned out of office by an electorate voting a straight ticket. . . .

*   *   *

At present in the federal courts, and in Delaware, Maine, Massachusetts, New Hampshire and New Jersey, the majority of all judges are appointed by the executive subject to confirmation by some body such as the senate or governor's council, while in Rhode Island trial court judges are so appointed. In several other states various classes of judges are appointed. All judges with some minor exceptions are selected by popular vote in thirty-six states, in twenty of which they are elected under party labels.

In many of the states where judicial offices are nominally filled by the legislature or by popular election many judges originally receive their commissions to office by virtue of *ad interim* appointments by the governor. These *ad interim* appointees as a class are better than the judges nominated in partisan contests. When they run for election at the end of their appointments, the prestige of their position frequently insures their election. In this manner the caliber of the elected judiciary is vastly improved. It is rather generally conceded that the elective system would long since have proved unworkable in practice had it not been that in state after state a majority of judges owe their original selection to such *ad interim* appointments.

*   *   *

The difficulty of the public as a whole in getting to know and judge the qualifications of many practitioners of law in the rush of life in today's predominantly urban society presents a major obstacle to the effective use of the elective process. Moreover, judges are not essentially representatives of the people as are legislators and the executive. The experience of the past years and the many abuses of the elective process which have developed indicates that the nomination of judges thereunder will be the work of a few irresponsible party leaders. How is the judicial candidate to campaign effectively for office? What is the platform on which he may stand? What may he validly promise? Political campaigns are costly and if a judge must participate in such a campaign, how is he to escape sharing the costs, directly or indirectly?

The basic criticism directed at the elective system is that, linked as it is with tenure for a term of years necessitating repeated stands before the electorate, it lessens the independence of the judiciary by making politics a primary element in their selection and continuance in office. Unqualified and inferior men are often elected judges in a system which is permeated by politics especially in cosmopolitan communities. Where political connections are necessary to become a judge, many lawyers do not wish to become candidates because they do not wish to be involved in what is so often, in this respect, a very "dirty game." Where the populace cannot in most cases make a valid judgment on the merits of the many judicial nominees on the ballot, the judges are not really elected but are appointed by political leaders whom the public does not know and over whom it has no real control. . . . The major defect of the elective system is that it renders judges subservient . . . since in a sense they hold office only during pleasure, for a term, and are subject to dismissal for political or other invalid reasons. . . .

* * *

No method of selection is foolproof. No system could be worse, however, than popular election on the party ticket along with a host of other national, state and local party candidates running for a variety of offices especially in cosmopolitan areas. In such circumstances there is not the slightest chance of a judge being thus selected on the basis of his qualifications for the office. . . . But good judges are not to be expected under any system in this country without the cooperation of the bar and the public.

33. Unseating Unfit Judges*

MURRAY TEIGH BLOOM

IT is rare that a judge goes wrong. But, with 6,700 judges in the country, inevitably a few turn out incompetent or incapable of administering justice. And when it happens it is, in most states, a near impossibility to get them off the bench.

For example, in March 1961, the complaint of Mrs. Sylvia Goszkowski of Detroit came before the Michigan attorney general. Henderson Graham, the 43-year old probate judge of Tuscola County who had handled the settlement of her parents' will, was pressuring her to give him an unsecured loan of $20,000. If she didn't give it to him, he threatened, he would increase her bond as guardian of her younger sister's estate.

The Michigan attorney general's office started an investigation. Twice more Judge Graham visited the two sisters, who told him their answer was "No." He then warned them that the guardianship bond of $3,000 would have to be increased.

The attorney general's office presented evidence to the State Supreme Court, which held hearings and heard Judge Graham's explanations of his

* Reprinted with permission from *National Civic Review*, February 1963.

conduct: a nonlawyer, he said he was not familiar with judicial ethics. (Michigan is one of many states which do not require probate judges to be lawyers.) The court then unanimously recommended that the state legislature remove him from office. "Such conduct on the part of a judge is both intolerable and unpardonable," the court found.

In Michigan, as in most other states, the only effective way of removing a judge from office is through legislative removal proceedings. Two-thirds of the House and Senate must approve the resolution ordering a judge's removal before the governor can take action. In April 1962 the Michigan House of Representatives met to consider the Judge Graham case and voted 100-3 to *turn down* the Supreme Court's recommendation to remove the judge.

The State Supreme Court promptly stripped Judge Graham of the power to act in any probate cases, but it was not able to stop his salary of $9,500 a year which he will draw until the end of his term in 1964.

Contrast this with what happened in April 1961 when a California woman wrote to her state's newly established and unique Commission on Judicial

Qualifications about a local judge. He was often drunk on the bench and had recently been arrested in another county for drunken driving. "Please check on this situation so that we may have decent justice in here," she pleaded.

Within a week a state investigator was assigned to look into the accusation. Ten days later the investigator's carefully detailed report was studied by the full commission meeting in its permanent offices in San Francisco. The nine members agreed the judge was guilty of "habitual intemperance" and wrote him they would recommend his removal by the Supreme Court. Late in May 1961 the judge resigned rather than face public charges.

The Graham case is typical of the great difficulty most other states encounter. In 1960 George E. Brand, former president of the Michigan Bar Association, checked court records as far back as possible and found that, out of 40 states, legislative attempts to invoke impeachment proceedings against judges had been made in only seventeen states. As a result nineteen judges were removed and three resigned—out of 52 impeachments.

The judicial salary Henderson Graham will continue to draw will be only a tiny part of the billion dollars we spend every year to pay our 6,700 judges and run the courts in which they sit. In most states once a judge assumes the bench his reelection as an incumbent is little more than a formality, and he can serve indefinitely with almost no danger of being unseated.

This almost certain job security plus the traditional deference for a judge is too heady a mixture for some. In a detailed analysis of the Los Angeles trial courts made for the American Bar Association in 1956, James G. Holbrook, professor of law at the University of Southern California, described what happens to a lawyer who is suddenly elevated to a judgeship:

"He finds himself surrounded by an almost fawning group. It is 'Yes, your honor, this' and 'Yes, your honor, that' from morning until night. Court attachés are dependent upon him for what at his whim can be a pleasant or unpleasant task. Lawyers are dependent upon his pleasure as to the time of trial, conduct of trial and result of trial. Citizens have their property, their independence and even their lives dependent upon his judgment. There is no real control over his hours, his industriousness or his thoroughness. It must be a breath-taking sensation when all this finally dawns upon a judge. It takes both humility and untold strength of character to emerge unscathed."

Clearly, not all judges have the requisite qualities to emerge unscathed. During the American Bar Association convention last August an informal poll of ten trial judges and court administrative officers from different states revealed that each knew of at least one judge in his state who was unfit because of unjudicial conduct, senility or downright incompetence.

The problem also exists in federal courts where judges are appointed for life. It has happened even on the U.S. Supreme Court, as was disclosed only recently by Walter F. Murphy, associate professor of politics at Princeton University, after he was given access to the private papers of former Chief Justice William Howard Taft. In 1924 Taft was in poor health but was afraid to take any time away from court work because the senior associate justice, Joseph McKenna, 81, was no longer capable of sustained mental effort and had shown gross signs of senility for several years. In desperation the other justices agreed not to hand down decisions in cases where McKenna's vote was the deciding one. Finally after a reluctant showdown meeting in 1925 McKenna was persuaded to resign.

The court administrative officer of an eastern state told me of a judge, apparently mentally disturbed, now sitting on the bench of his state. "Sooner or later his antics are going to make headlines," the official said. "But under our state constitution only the legislature can remove a judge and so far they never have."

Sometimes, in desperation, harassed lawyers will try to unseat an unfit judge by political methods. The county bar association president in one western state told me how he and several other lawyers bucked a senile but politically powerful judge: "We got a good lawyer to run for the nomination and we had to raise a war chest to finance his campaign. Well, our man squeaked through —but if the old man had won, a lot of us could just as well have started building a law practice elsewhere."

In 1959 the American Bar Association, the American Judicature Society and the Institute of Judicial Administration, meeting in Chicago, unanimously concluded that we needed "a less cumbersome method to bring about the discipline or removal of a judge whose conduct has subjected or is likely to subject the court to public censure or reproach, or is prejudicial to the administration of justice."

That same year a California state legislative committee on the administration of justice found that certain judges "delayed decisions for months or even years." Some of the state's 898 judges took long vacations and worked short hours despite backlogs of cases awaiting trial. Some refused to accept assignment to cases they found unpleasant or dull. Some tolerated petty rackets involving "kickbacks" to court attachés. Some failed to appear for scheduled trials or took the bench while obviously under the influence of liquor. Some clung doggedly to their positions and salaries for years after they had been disabled by sickness or age. In one case a 68-year-old judge who continually pleaded ill-health was found to have received more than $33,000 in salary for nine mornings of work in two years. Yet in nearly a century California had had only two impeachment trials, one at the time of the Civil War when a conviction was changed by a later legislature. The second resulted in acquittal.

In November 1960 California voters overwhelmingly approved a constitutional amendment creating a state Commission on Judicial Qualifications empowered to recommend to the State Supreme Court the removal of a judge for cause, and granting the State Supreme Court power to act on the recommendation. The commission has nine members: five judges appointed by the Supreme Court, two experienced attorneys selected by the State Bar, two citizens named by the governor.

In its first two years the commission received 163 complaints, all carefully looked into even though many obviously came from disgruntled litigants who were simply bad losers. Of the 163 complaints, 46 merited further investigation. In ten cases the judges involved resigned or retired because of the commission's inquiry In three of these cases, drinking was the problem. In three it was absenteeism. In three other cases it was emotional disturbance: one judge made improper comments to jurors, went out of his way to embarrass witnesses, had fits of rage at counsel; another was admitted by his psychiatrist to be "very disturbed" and emotionally unsuited to making judicial decisions. In only one instance was there intentional mishandling of court proceedings.

"Just the fact the commission is around has made many of our shortday judges sit much longer," says Justice A. Frank Bray, chairman of the commission. Also, there has been an improvement in the conduct of some judges. One complaint was about a judge who wouldn't permit the plaintiff to speak and told her if she didn't get out of the courtroom she would be arrested. Another was about a judge whose only reply to an attorney's lengthy, earnest argument was, "Horse feathers." These judges have been warned that no judge has a right to be crusty, arbitrary or short-tempered in his dealings with lawyers, litigants or witnesses.

Jack E. Frankel, executive secretary for the commission, is an attorney who for five years handled major disciplinary matters for the State Bar. One of the commission's most useful accomplishments, he says, is that at last it gives people an effective place to lodge complaints against judges. "Right now there are, I'm certain, hundreds of such complaints floating around in the other 49 states. The great majority of these are unmerited. But as long as a state doesn't have an agency to run down the grievances against judges and take action, these criticisms remain unchecked and dangerous rumors. In this way the few misfits on the bench can help accumulate a reservoir of distrust that tends in time to discredit the entire judiciary in the eyes of the public."

34. Final Selection of Judges of All State Courts*

Alabama .... All elected on partisan ballot except that some juvenile court judges are appointed either by the governor, by the legislature, or by county commissions.

Alaska .... Supreme Court Justices and superior court judges appointed by governor from nominations by Judicial Council. Approved or rejected at first general election held more than three years after appointment. Non-partisan ballot. Re-elected by popular vote—Supreme Court Justices every 10 years, Superior Court Judges every 6 years. Magistrate judges appointed by and serve at pleasure of Presiding Judge of Superior Court.

Arizona .... Supreme and superior court judges elected on non-partisan ballot; justices of the peace elected on partisan ballot; police magistrates appointed by city councils.

Arkansas .... All elected on partisan ballot.

California .... Supreme Court and district courts of appeals judges appointed initially by governor with approval of Commission on Judicial Appointments. Run for re-election on record. All judges elected on non-partisan ballot.

Colorado .... All elected on partisan ballot except that municipal judges and police magistrates are appointed by the local governing body unless home rule charter provides otherwise.

Connecticut ...... All selected by legislature from nominations submitted by governor except that probate judges are elected on partisan ballot.

Delaware .... All appointed by governor with consent of the senate.

Florida .... All elected on partisan ballot.

* Adapted from The Book of the States 1964-65, Council of State Governments, p. 126.

Georgia	All elected on partisan ballot except that county and some city court judges are appointed by the governor with the consent of the senate.
Hawaii	Supreme Court Justices and circuit court judges appointed by the governor with consent of the senate. District magistrates appointed by Chief Justice of the state.
Idaho	Supreme Court and district court judges elected on non-partisan ballot; probate judges elected on partisan ballot; justices of the peace appointed by board of county commissioners and probate judge with approval of senior district judge.
Illinois	All elected on partisan ballot; run on record for re-election. Magistrates, appointed by circuit judges, serve at pleasure of judges.
Indiana	All elected on partisan ballot except that judge of Municipal Court is appointed by governor.
Iowa	Judges of Supreme and district courts appointed by governor from lists submitted by nominating commission. Run on record.
Kansas	Supreme Court Judges appointed by governor from list submitted by nominating commission. Run on record for re-election. All other judges elected on partisan ballot.
Kentucky	All elected on partisan ballot.
Louisiana	All elected on partisan ballot.
Maine	All appointed by governor with consent of Executive Council except that probate judges are elected on partisan ballot.
Maryland	Judges of Court of Appeals, Circuit Courts and Supreme Bench of Baltimore appointed by governor; elected on non-partisan ballot after at least one year's service. Trial magistrates appointed by governor. People's Court judges in Baltimore City appointed initially; incumbents run on record for re-election. People's Court judges in Baltimore County appointed initially by governor with consent of senate, thereafter appointed by governor. People's Court judges of Montgomery County appointed by County Council. Judges of Municipal Court of Baltimore City elected on non-partisan ballot.
Massachusetts	All appointed by governor with consent of the Council.
Michigan	All elected on non-partisan ballot.
Minnesota	All elected on non-partisan ballot.
Mississippi	All elected on partisan ballot.
Missouri	Judges of Supreme Court, appellate courts, circuit and probate courts in St. Louis and Jackson County and St. Louis Court of Criminal Corrections appointed initially by governor from nominations submitted by special commissions. Run on record for re-election. All other judges elected on partisan ballot.
Montana	All elected on non-partisan ballot except that some police court judges are appointed by local governing bodies.

Nebraska	Judges of Supreme and district courts and some juvenile and municipal judges appointed by governor from lists submitted by nominating commissions. Run on record. Most other judges elected.
Nevada	All elected on non-partisan ballot.
New Hampshire ..	All appointed by governor with confirmation of the Council.
New Jersey	All appointed by governor with consent of senate except that surrogates are elected; magistrates of municipal courts serving one municipality only are appointed by governing bodies.
New Mexico	All elected on partisan ballot.
New York	All elected on partisan ballot except that governor appoints judges of Court of Claims and designates members of appellate division of Supreme Court; mayor of New York City appoints judges of some local courts.
North Carolina ...	All elected on partisan ballot except that a few county court judges are appointed by governor or county commissioners; some magistrates are appointed by governor or General Assembly; juvenile court judges are appointed by county commissioners or city boards.
North Dakota	All elected on non-partisan ballot.
Ohio	All elected on non-partisan ballot.
Oklahoma	All elected on partisan ballot except judge of Tulsa County Juvenile Court, who is appointed from a list submitted by a committee of lawyers and laymen.
Oregon	All elected on non-partisan ballot.
Pennsylvania	All elected on partisan ballot.
Rhode Island	Supreme Court justices elected by legislature. Superior and family court judges appointed by governor with consent of senate; probate judges appointed by city or town councils.
South Carolina ...	Supreme Court and circuit court judges chosen by legislature. City judges, magistrates, and some county judges appointed by governor. Probate judges and some county judges elected on partisan ballot.
South Dakota	All elected on non-partisan ballot, except county justices of the peace, who are appointed by the senior circuit judge of the judicial circuit in which the county is located.
Tennessee	All elected on non-partisan ballot.
Texas	All elected on partisan ballot.
Utah	All elected on non-partisan ballot except that juvenile court judges are appointed by governor with consent of Department of Welfare and town justices are appointed by town trustees.
Vermont	Supreme court and county court presiding judges elected by legislature. Municipal judges appointed by governor. Assistant judges of county courts and probate judges elected on partisan ballot.

Virginia .... Supreme Court of Appeals and all major trial court judges elected by legislature. Most judges of courts of limited jurisdiction appointed by judges of major trial courts. A few are elected by popular vote, some by the legislature, and some by city councils.

Washington ...... All elected on non-partisan ballot.

West Virginia .... All elected on partisan ballot.

Wisconsin .... All elected on non-partisan ballot.

Wyoming .... Supreme Court justices and district court judges elected on a non-partisan basis and other judges on a partisan basis.

35. Selection of Judges in California

CONSTITUTION of California, Article VI, Section 26:

Within 30 days before the sixteenth day of August next preceding the expiration of his term, any justice of the Supreme Court, justice of a District Court of Appeal, or judge of a superior court in any county the electors of which have adopted provisions of this section as applicable to the judge or judges of the superior court of such county in the manner hereinafter provided, may file with the officer charged with the duty of certifying nominations for publication in the official ballot a declaration of candidacy for election to succeed himself. If he does not file such declaration the Governor must nominate a suitable person for the office before the sixteenth day of September, by filing such nomination with the officer charged with said duty of certifying nominations.

In either event, the name of such candidate shall be placed upon the ballot for the ensuing general election in November in substantially the following form:

For ....
    (title of office)

Shall ....
       (name)

be elected to the office for the term expiring January

.....................?
       (year)

	Yes
	No

No name shall be placed upon the ballot as a candidate for any of said judicial offices except that of a person so declaring or so nominated. If a majority of the electors voting upon such candidacy vote "yes," such person shall be elected to said office. If a majority of those voting thereon vote "no," he shall not be elected, and may not thereafter be appointed to fill any vacancy in that court, but may be nominated and elected thereto as hereinabove provided.

Whenever a vacancy shall occur in any judicial office above named, by reason of the failure of a candidate to be elected or otherwise, the Governor shall appoint a suitable person to fill the vacancy. An incumbent of any such judicial office serving a term by appointment of the Governor shall hold office until the first Monday after the first day of January following the general election next after his appointment, or until the qualification of any nominee who may have been elected to said office prior to that time.

No such nomination or appointment by the Governor shall be effective unless there be filed with the Secretary of State a written confirmation of such nomination or appointment signed by a majority of the three officials herein designed as the Commission on Qualifications. The Commission on Qualifications shall consist of (1) the Chief Justice of the Supreme Court, or, if such office be vacant, the acting Chief Justice; (2) the presiding justice of the District Court of Appeal of the district in which a justice of a District Court of Appeal or a judge of a superior court is to serve, or, if there be two such presiding justices, the one who has served the longer as such; or, in the case of the nomination or appointment of a justice of the Supreme Court, the presiding justice who has served longest as such upon any of the District Courts of Appeal; and (3) the Attorney General.

If two or more presiding justices above designated shall have served terms of equal length, they shall choose the one who is to be a member of the Commission on Qualifications by lot, whenever occasion for action arises. The Legislature shall provide by general law for the retirement, with reasonable retirement allowance, of such justices and judges for age or disability.

In addition to the methods of removal by the Legislature provided by Sections 17 and 18 of Article IV and by Section 10 of this article, the provisions of Article XXIII relative to the recall of elective public officers shall be applicable to justices and judges elected and appointed pursuant to the provisions of this section so far as the same relate to removal from office.

The provisions of this section shall not apply to the judge or judges of the superior court of any county until a majority of the electors of such county voting on the question of adoption of such provisions, in a manner to be provided for by the Legislature, shall vote in favor thereof.

If the Legislature diminishes the number of judges of the superior court in any county or city and county, the offices which first become vacant, to the number of judges diminished, shall be deemed to be abolished.

Part VI

POLITICAL PROCESSES

Athough generalizations about the nature of politics in the states are not lacking, significant insights into the manner in which the political process functions in the individual states are uncommon. Dayton D. McKean advances several explanations for the lack of information on state politics, including their complex nature, the lack of funds for research, and the low esteem in which political affairs are commonly held. Mr. McKean calls attention to important considerations that must be weighed in any effort to understand the politics of a state, such as one-party and two-party arrangements, tight and loose party organizations, the existence or absence of bosses and machines, and the nature and role of interest groups.

Some insight into the way a political machine may work is provided by Warren Moscow's description of the theft of an election by Tammany Hall in New York City some thirty years ago. Mr. Moscow also provides a partial explanation for the decline of such machines. One of the most successful political bosses of all time was Huey Long of Louisiana. Much of Long's success may be attributed to his personal temperament and tactics, which are briefly described by Allan Sindler in his examination of the kind of politics that appealed to the people of Louisiana. Sindler calls attention to the demoralizing effects of "Long's version of absolute power, which was lawlessness, not merely legally entrenched but highly visible and candid in its operation and enjoying continued popular endorsement."

That the image of the political boss, although somewhat paled, has not disappeared from state politics is demonstrated by Ed Cray in his description of the career of Jesse Unruh of California. The political opportunities available to those who are interested in working shrewdly and untiringly have been demonstrated by Mr. Unruh's career. His meteoric rise from obscurity to dominant position in California politics within fifteen years is a modern Horatio Alger story in the political vein.

Among the most significant recent developments pertaining to the nature of local political processes has been the nonpartisan election. Among cities with a population over 5,000, slightly over two-thirds now use the nonpartisan ballot. Charles Adrian examines certain characteristics that seem to reappear wherever nonpartisan elections are used.

36. The Politics of the States*

DAYTON D. McKEAN

IT is much more difficult to understand politics than atomic physics, Albert Einstein once said, because politics is much more complicated than physics. Politics is, indeed, infinitely complex; two atoms of hydrogen will, under given conditions, behave in identical and predictable ways, but no two voters have the same personalities or life experiences, and consequently their political attitudes and behavior are likely not to be the same. Virtually nothing of importance, therefore, can be said of American politics without adding important qualifications and exceptions unless, perhaps, that the Democratic party is organized in every state. Writers who blandly assert that all farmers, or all union members, or all politicians behave, believe, or vote some way or other are usually making only unsupported assertions.

Such writers, unfortunately, get away with their sweeping generalizations because this democracy, which has put billions into the study of the atom, has put only thousands into the study of the voter. We do not know, therefore, such elementary facts as how many persons in the United States are legally eligible

to vote. All we have are census estimates of the number of people—not even citizens—over 21 years of age. On such flimsy bases, however, American voters are castigated for their alleged apathy, when actually they may be as politically active as the voters in any other country. We do not know. We particularly need more studies of state politics.

THE LOW VISIBILITY AND ESTEEM OF STATE POLITICS

When American society was simple and largely rural it may have been a fair assumption that the citizen could, in his spare time, keep himself informed about the personnel and policies of his governments, so that he could make intelligent decisions at town meetings or in elections. Today, however, not even a person who gives his whole time to following the government and politics of one state, such as New Jersey or California, can keep up with more than what seem to be the most important problems and trends. When not even a governor can do it, the citizen can do it even less, for the citizen has other matters on his mind besides governing—such pressing items, for example, as making a living.

National and world events, more-

* Reprinted from *The Forty-Eight States: Their Tasks as Policy Makers and Administrators,* The American Assembly, Columbia University, 1955.

over, call for their share of what time the citizen can devote to public affairs; and his county, town, and school district call for another share. In this blooming, buzzing confusion of issues and personalities the voter is likely to give some attention to those matters that the communications industries put before him and to ignore the rest. We do not have one public opinion study of the information on and the attitudes toward the politics of a state, but in the absence of such a survey it is probably safe to assume that the level of information is very low. Probably not one percent of the voters have read their state constitutions or know the name of any state official except the governor. It is also probably safe to assume that, since most newspapers find the greatest news value in the scandals, crimes, and other misdeeds in state politics, they omit or give little space to what is well and honestly accomplished. Accordingly the pictures of state affairs the voters have in their heads are mostly of strife and struggle among a lot of fools and crooks. Most daily papers present one or more columnists on national and international politics, but few carry a column on state politics, and those that do usually have a cynical commentator who emphasizes the sensational, the illegal, or the trivial.

We cannot hope to reverse the major trends of American society to make life once again simple, so that the citizen might follow politics easily. We cannot expect that he will abandon his job to get behind what the papers and the radio present to him. But we may wish that the politics of the states could be presented to the busy voter as a series of broad and meaningful choices between parties, so that, without having to know the names and records of thousands of officials, he could make an intelligent choice between parties and then hold answerable the party that did or did not do what he wanted. It is impossible for a voter to hold responsible an appointed official, or one elected from another county or district, though it may

be possbile to hold their parties responsible for their behavior. One of the sentiments most dangerous to democracy may, therefore, be the attitude commonly expressed in such words as "I never vote for the party; I vote for the man."

SOME TRENDS IN STATE POLITICS

American politics, like American life, is in process of constant change. A generalization that was valid in 1900 may not be true today, and vice versa. Some of the changes that occur are so great as to represent a complete reversal of party position. The states' rights issues, for example, had seemed for more than a century to be under a sort of copyright held by the Democratic party, but on March 4, 1933, this copyright passed into the public domain, and the Republican party, long the advocate of national supremacy, took up the issue.

Some channels of party policy, like the Constitution, remain from generation to generation little changed, but among the important observable developments discussed in this and other papers are the increasing urbanization of the states; the continued growth of metropolitan areas, some of which pay no attention to state lines; the rise of militant new interests, such as racial minorities; the decline of all minor parties and the disappearance of some; the absence of any important third-party movement; the rise of new means of political communication, such as radio and television; and the development of a system of interest groups so potent as to challenge the parties as the originators and advocates of public policies.

Most serious students of American politics would probably be in substantial agreement upon the trends just mentioned. Others, but not all, assert that we are also in the midst of more developments, such as the nationalization of political issues (the acceptance of positions by national party organizations, which positions the state and local parties must then accept); the rise of class politics; the development of a new sectionalism; the passing of the boss system; and a new nonpartisan, intergovernmental politics such as that alleged to be growing up as a result of interstate compacts. Before much of anything can be said with certainty about these developments we need more research in them than we have had.

THE MAJOR IMPORTANCE OF STATE POLITICS

American major parties are commonly described as loose confederations of state parties. The absence from this definition of any references to issues has confused some foreign observers and appalled others. Lord Bryce, for example, quoted with approval an unnamed newspaper reporter of his day who said that the two parties were like bottles bearing different labels, but both were empty. They were not quite empty in 1888 when Bryce wrote, and they are not today. Yet not principle but the hope of office has usually been the chief binding force of our major party organizations; issues come and go, while the parties continue from one century to another. In most states even the candidates wear their party labels, if at all, lightly, and they pick up and put down issues largely as they please. A British voter may not be aware of a particular candidate's set of attitudes, but he knows how a Laborite or a Conservative will, if elected, generally vote in Parliament. The American voter, on the contrary, may cast a Republican ballot and get an Ives, a Langer, a McCarthy, a Millikin, or some one in between; and his Democratic friend across the state line may elect a Humphrey, a Lehman, a Byrd, or a person of some other type. Those names are chosen from the national scene because they are well known; similar comparisons could as readily be made among recent state governors: Harriman, Lausche, and Talmadge all call themselves Democrats; Dewey, Stratton of Illinois, and Bracken Lee of Utah, are Republicans. The American voter, when he selects one bottle or the other, takes a gamble that his British contemporary does not; perhaps his often blind choice adds a sporting element to the great game of politics—at any rate, it adds to the confusion.

The uncertainty of our politics is such that Woodrow Wilson once said that no man of middle age should despair of becoming President. While there is no single clear avenue to preferment for the would-be statesman as there is, for instance, in England, still service in state politics is perhaps the commonest avenue to national office. A term or two in the legislature, election as district attorney, then governor, then congressman or senator is, with variations, a path frequently followed. Many of our national officials, therefore, come to their new responsibilities, not from such an apprenticeship in dealing with national issues as might be gained by service in the diplomatic corps or in the federal bureaucracy, but rather with experience in state politics only. This use of the states as training grounds for national politicians has, no doubt, its desirable features, for most men so trained never forget the importance of the attitudes held by the folks back home; but it also fixes upon Congress a parochialism that not all national legislatures seem to display. A partial explanation for the kind of stuff that fills the pages of the *Congressional Record* is that some of the speakers learned to talk that way when, years before, while running for the legislature, they harangued the people at the forks of the creek.

THE AUTONOMOUS CHARACTER OF STATE PARTIES

When the leaders of a state party draft the party platform—which in some states attracts so little public interest that it is never printed—they are not bound by any national platform. The state platform, in fact, may be adopted weeks before the national one, and in any event it may take positions on such issues as fair employment exactly the opposite of that taken by the same party in its national platform. These heresies do not and cannot lead to excommunication by the national committee, for each party is as independent of Washington as it is of every other state party.

Probably each state has certain issues that are peculiar to itself, such as the dispute over water for Denver between the eastern and western slopes of Colorado; but the existence of such strictly state issues does not guarantee a party division along lines of the principal alternatives so that the voter may make a clear choice. On the contrary, in a two-party situation both parties may straddle or avoid such issues.

Few issues of importance are, moreover, without their national aspects. Problems of financing highways, schools, or unemployment relief are necessarily related to what the national government does. Some state issues—for example, the current drive to prohibit the closed shop—grow out of federal statutes or activities. The great majority of the issues in American politics do not stop at state lines, and for a single state to attempt a solution of a broad problem, such as farm price supports, might throw upon its economy an intolerable burden or produce an impossible competitive situation for its industries. In such circumstances state parties and candidates cannot be blamed if they treat issues with certain cautious vagueness.

The independent character of state parties is further encouraged by the differences in their sources of financial support. Probably no state party obtains from national headquarters funds to assist in the election of candidates for state offices; instead, it has to collect its money wherever it can, and it may accept help from sources which are hostile to the policies of its national organization. Each national organization obtains some funds from state parties in the wealthy states, and each national committee sends some of these funds into close or doubtful states to help candidates for Congress. In general, however, the financing of parties is done at each level, and so money cannot be used as a means of discipline.

* * *

THE VARYING PATTERNS OF STATE POLITICS

SECTIONALISM

People tend to think and act politically the way their families, their friends, and their neighbors think and act. Notable similarities of behavior described in terms of geographical area are called sectionalism or regionalism. Sometimes an identity of interest among the people in an area may be observed which presumably explains why they mostly vote the same way— dairy farming or silver mining, for example. Again, they may tend to vote alike because of social pressure—it is not good form to be a Democrat in Vermont or a Republican in Georgia. Sometimes attachment to one party or the other goes back to some ancient party battle, some struggle long ago, such as those in the aftermath of the Civil War. But probably the strongest influence is family. Various students of the matter have estimated that somewhere between 65 and 85 percent of the voters get their politics in the same place they get their religion—at home. To the extent that this generalization can be demonstrated from election statistics and survey materials it forms the strongest rebuttal to the Marxian hypothesis that economic interest is determining to behavior.

In American life the existence of sections is so well known that the common names for the sections have passed into our ordinary speech: New England, the South, the West, and so on. Sectional consciousness is somewhat intensified by differences of dialect or accent, by certain problems of long standing such as race relations, and by variations in religion and country of origin. Although we know what we mean by the New England states, the description of no other section is exact, not even of the South, for some writers will include Oklahoma and the so-called border states, others will not. Out where the West begins is a poetic and not a political place.

THE ONE-PARTY STATES

The states that formed the Confederacy were, from the end of Reconstruction to 1928, a section commonly called the Solid South. Al Smith's religion cracked it then, and it broke again in 1948 and 1952 primarily over civil rights for Negroes. But only in presidential elections. In the choice of governors and legislatures the South is about as Democratic as it ever was. . . . The much discussed development of a two-party system in the South has still to appear in state politics, even though some southern states now occasionally go Republican in presidential elections.

There is no solid North. Only Vermont can be said to be uniformly and dependably Republican in both state and national elections, but Democrats in appreciable numbers get elected to the Vermont legislature. In Kansas, Maine, and the Dakotas the legislature is almost always Republican by an overwhelming majority. Possibly Nebraska would belong in this list except that its legislature is elected on a nonpartisan ballot. . . .

It would be a common-sense expectation that in the one-party states a pattern of factionalism would develop within the dominant party which would be something of a counterpart to the two-party system elsewhere. There are, indeed, some examples, such as the Byrd and anti-Byrd, Long and anti-Long factions in Virginia and Louisiana; and sometimes a sort of subsectionalism—piedmont versus tidewater in the Carolinas, east versus west in Kansas, north versus south in Vermont—may be rather dimly seen. For most of the one-party states, however, common sense lets us down, and the typical pattern of politics seems to be temporary, shifting factions of the followers of different leaders. The foremost student of the subject, V. O. Key, Jr., whose *Southern Politics* is the standard book, says that this personal factionalism might best be described as a no-party politics. In this welter of factions there is not the slightest approach to a system of party responsibility where a party stands answerable for the behavior of its nominees if they win; instead, the voter must choose in a single party primary among the conflicting claims and extravagant promises of many candidates for office, all running on their own. The complexity of this factional politics is so great that for the South it cannot be described except in a long book, and no book-length attempt has been made for the northern one-party states.

THE TWO-PARTY STATES

The positions of the major parties in the remaining states vary from those where either party may win any state-wide office, as in Connecticut and Massachusetts, to those where one party or the other usually wins—the Democrats in West Virginia, for instance, the Republicans in Iowa. In all of the two-party states each of the parties has a going organization and offers candidates for all or almost all of the state-wide offices, whereas in some states in the deep South the Republican party does not regularly even go through the motions of nominating candidates for governor.

In the two-party states, however, there are one-party islands, cities or counties that always or almost always go Democratic or Republican as the case may be. The general tendency is for the cities to be Democratic, the rural counties and suburbs Republican. It has been estimated, in fact, that about half of the electoral areas in the United States are one-party. In them, whether they appear in two-party states or not, the voter has no real choice for the legislature unless he can exercise it in a majority party primary.

* * *

Some people who are familiar with a tight precinct-by-precinct, ward-by-ward organization such as Tammany had in its most successful periods leap to the conclusion that all parties in all states are so constructed. Actually, the farther West one looks the looser the organizations appear. . . .

In attitudes of conservatism-liberalism a certain sectional difference may be detected between the major parties, but no political terms are more slippery than these two. The Republican party tends everywhere to be conservative, although the Republican party in Delaware and Pennsylvania is more conservative than in North Dakota or California. In the North the Democratic party tends to be the liberal party, but in the South, especially on matters of race relations, it is conservative. On certain issues, however, such as public power, the southern Democratic party is more liberal than much of its northern wing. In the two states that elect their legislatures on nonpartisan ballots, Nebraska and Minnesota, it is said that the voting in the houses tends to divide along conservative versus liberal lines, and that the conservatives are mostly Republicans, the liberals, Democrats. Any of the generalizations on this legislative behavior, however, are bound to be based upon personal judgments, particularly upon what constitutes conservatism or liberalism.

The conservative attitudes of many southern Democrats in Congress, which since around 1938 have led them to vote on many issues with northern Republicans rather than with northern Democrats, have made some people hopeful that a new sectional realignment of the parties could be brought about. Senator Karl Mundt and others set up a formal organization that tried between the elections of 1948 and 1952 to produce a new arrangement. Nothing came of it. Other people, devoted to democracy, have long urged in print and speech that our party system should be in fact more nearly a system, one that the voters could understand and in which they could record their choices.

* * *

BOSSES AND MACHINES IN STATE POLITICS

The term *boss* is one that Americans added to the English language, but in spite of the fact that we have had scores of state bosses we are at the moment short of conspicuous examples. The best known of the contemporary machines is the Byrd machine in Virginia, which the *New York Times* once called "the most urbane and genteel dictatorship in America." No doubt bosses take on the coloration of the age in which they live, and perhaps the successful ones are not anxious for publicity these days. Newspaper reports, however, turn them up now and then. . . .

Although the word *boss* is sometimes used as an epithet for any political leader the speaker dislikes, its difference from *leader* lies in the fact that a real boss governs through his control of the machinery of his party, and that he governs beyond the office, if any, that he holds. It was this irresponsibility of ruler to ruled that Elihu Root denounced as the "invisible government" of New York:

Then Mr. Platt ruled the state; for nigh upon twenty years he ruled it. It was not the governor; it was not the legislature; it was not any elected officers; it was Mr. Platt. And the capitol was not here; it was at 49 Broadway with Mr. Platt and his lieutenants.

Among the state bosses of recent years, other than those already mentioned, have been Edward H. Crump of Tennessee, Huey Long of Louisiana, David C. Stephenson of Indiana, Boies

Penrose of Pennsylvania, and J. H. Roraback of Connecticut. Others whose power over their states was never fully consolidated were Frank Hague of New Jersey, Edward J. Flynn of New York, Eugene Talmadge of Georgia, "Alfalfa Bill" Murray of Oklahoma, Tom Pendergast of Missouri, and Theodore Bilbo of Mississippi.

These were men well known to the public. But there have been and remain others who rule quietly. Lew Smith of the New Hampshire Jockey Club is recognized by the politicians of that state as the boss, but he is scarcely known outside. Sometimes the boss is the head of a business, like William F. Wyman, or of a newspaper, like Roy Roberts of the *Kansas City Star,* and his other interests make him want to keep his control inconspicuous.

Every time some big boss dies, retires, or goes to jail the newspaper headlines refer to him as "the last of the bosses," "the last of the great bosses," or "the last of the old-fashioned bosses." We may, of course, hope that the statements are right, for the existence of these domestic dictators contradicts everything that American democracy stands for. But in view of the long history of bossism and in view of the fact that the causes of the system are still with us, we might better hesitate before joining in obsequies that may prove to be premature.

Observers differ on the causes of bossism, and some ascribe more weight than do others to different causes, but there is a rough measure of agreement. First, there is an observable tendency in all human associations for one or a few ambitious individuals to rise to the top, the "iron law of oligarchy" as Robert Michels called it. This centralizing tendency is particularly notable when a group like a political machine must make binding but secret decisions, or when it engages in some illegal or extra-legal undertakings. Second, all the constitutional and legal forms that make real party responsibility difficult or impossible make boss government easier. If real leadership cannot be exercised by and within the legal government, an extra-legal government may grow up outside. A boss may rise who can bring the separated powers together—who can within limits control governor, legislature, and courts. So Jim Curley was not disliked by all the well-to-do in Massachusetts; he was expensive, but "He gets things done." Third, the vast multiplication of the units of local government—there are some 117,000 in the United States with the resulting conflict and overlapping of authority—is so bewildering to the half-interested citizen that he makes no attempt to understand the labyrinth. The boss, however, needs to understand it, because he must utilize its possibilities for patronage; for a high brokerage fee he may produce a kind of administrative unity in what would otherwise be an administrative wilderness. Other reasons are long ballots; short terms of office; the ineligibility of officials, no matter how successful, to succeed themselves; frequent elections; the complexities of the primary system; and the large amounts of money available to any machine that can offer protection compared with the inadequate amounts available to anti-organization or reform groups or candidates. Probably no single cause produces the boss and the machine. Rather, the natural tendency of some persons to rise to the top of any association may produce a boss in the right set of political and social circumstances.

Assuming that the majority of Americans want to get rid of the boss system—not an entirely safe assumption—the most promising cure . . . is the simplification of governments and the development of a strong and responsible party system.

INTEREST GROUPS AND STATE POLITICS

The most complete knowledge about the operations of the parties and factions of a state is only half, and perhaps the smaller half, of understanding its politics. Limited as they are by constitutional and statutory requirements, our parties mainly pursue a politics of place and position and leave the politics of public policy to organized interest groups. It is policy rather than place, however, that touches the voter: it will not much matter to him who is auditor, secretary of state, or warden of the prison; but when the American Legion gets through a bonus that he has to pay for, or when the Dairymen's League gets through a law that increases his milk bill by 30 percent, it matters. The weakeness of party has been the strength of organized groups. William Allen White, one of the most astute of American political observers, saw this clearly and expressed his view of it vividly:

> The fiction of one vote for one person is still maintained politely in high-school classes in civil government; but men and women who touch practical politics, if only obliquely, know that they now may have as many votes in government as they have interests. . . . The ruling classes are those who use their craft societies, medical associations, farm bureaus, labor unions, bankers' associations, women's leagues, and the like to influence government. Of course, it takes time and intelligence, and a little money, but not much. For fifty dollars a year [in membership dues] the average family ought to be able to buy half a dozen powerful votes in government, each vote ten times as powerful as the vote guaranteed by the Constitution.

THE NUMBER AND VARIETY OF GROUPS

In the capital city of most states 200 or more organizations with some interest or an exclusive interest in what the state government does will have their headquarters. Scores, even hundreds of other organizations, will send an officer or a delegation to town when something comes up that affects them. Alphabetically, the associations may run from the American Automobile Association to the YWCA, and the policies in which they are interested will run from alcohol to zoning. Studies in northern cities indicate that there is approximately one formal organized group for each seven persons. . . .

THE LOBBY

The terms *lobbyist* and *lobby* carry no odor of sanctity, but actually a lobby is good or bad, or neither good nor bad, depending upon one's interests and attitudes toward the group and its methods. Thus, the Women's Christian Temperance Union and all the other organizations that go to make up what is often called the dry lobby regard the Distilled Spirits Institute, the liquor dealers' association, and the rest of the wet lobby as being engaged largely in the work of the devil. The wets, for their part, believe that the drys are aiming to bring back Prohibition with all the evils of the speakeasy and the gangster. Whether an organization is good or bad depends upon the point from which one looks at it. Whether its methods are reprehensible depends upon one's standards, which among individuals will vary from "any port in a storm" to "no good end can be reached in a bad way." And because certain lobbyists will never knowingly let any legislator hunger or thirst we must not conclude that all lobbyists are ready to trample each other to pick up the check.

A more fundamental difficulty with the term *lobbyist* is that it ignores what is an increasingly important part of the work of the representatives of the groups: following the administration and the courts. The Legion, say, obtains a statute to give veterans various preferences in civil service examinations, appointments, and tenure in jobs. But the law is far from being self-executing; in fact, civil service commissions will tend to make rulings inconsistent with it, and appointing officers will avoid it by a seemingly endless variety of devices. Instead of spending his days in the lobby of the legislature, therefore, the statehouse man for the Legion must spend his days arguing with the civil service commission, appealing for and staging hearings, registering complaints with personnel officers, and if these fail, fighting their rulings or decisions in the courts. Much the same sort of life is led by the representatives of the state Chamber of Commerce, the state teachers' association, and many others. While the word *lobbyist* does not cover these important activities, we lack one that does.

* * *

THE PRINCIPAL PATTERNS OF INTEREST-GROUP POLITICS

No two states have identical sets of groups or identical group politics; some, in fact, are unique. The Mormon Church, for example, holds a position in Utah politics that no religious organization holds in that of any other state. Colorado alone has an old-age pension group called the National Annuity League that appears to be on pension matters stronger than either or both political parties. But in spite of differences a few clusters of interests may be identified that are influential in most state politics. Books have been written about these interests. All that can be attempted here is to point them out.

Farmers and farm organizations have been active in politics since colonial times. The Proclamation of 1763, which shut off westward expansion, attracted farmers to the Revolution. From that date to this, farm groups have sought cheap land, low taxes on land, easy laws for debtors, good rural roads, and regulations of elevators, stockyards, and freight rates. There are about 30,000 farm organizations, some confined to a single state or to a specialized kind of agriculture, but the Big Four are the Grange, the Farmers' Union, the Farm Bureau, and the National Council of Farmer Co-operatives.

Labor too has been a force in politics since the organization of the first union in 1790. Although there are hundreds of unions, the great bulk of the 15,000,-000 members belong either to the CIO or to the A.F.L., now in process of merger. Union labor is reputed to be strongest in the politics of Michigan and strong elsewhere in the North, but weak in the South and West. Its concentration in the underrepresented cities weakens its influence in the legislatures, even though it can tip the balance to elect governors in many industrial states.

Business and industry are everywhere active in interest group politics, although obviously the kind of business that is influential varies widely: insurance in Connecticut, finance in New York, oil and gas in Texas, and so on. No one organization in any state speaks with authority for all its businesses, although the broadest associations are the state chambers of commerce. Every state has some trade associations, such as the retail merchants' associations, that are necessarily active at the capitol, and every state also has businesses whose very existence depends upon licenses or franchises—utilities, liquor, horseracing, for example—enterprises which are commonly supposed to be immersed in politics of every kind, at every level.

There are a dozen or more veterans' organizations, but the American Legion with its 3,000,000 members overshadows them all. It is the only one that is influential in the politics of every state. Its list of legislative and administrative victories—state bonuses, teachers' oath laws, veterans' tax preferences and exemptions, and many others—is more impressive than the list any other group can show.

Scores, perhaps hundreds, of the actions of state governments affect religious bodies, from health regulations (such as vaccination) to the food served on certain days of the week to the inmates of institutions. Broad questions of public policy such as education stir the sects deeply. The principal religious groups have, therefore, representatives —sometimes a whole staff of them—in capital cities to make their wishes known to state officials.

Some 200 professions, from architects to undertakers, are licensed in some or all states, commonly by separate licensing boards for each profession, and more professions seek licensing laws every year. The politics involved in getting the bills passed, obtaining satisfactory appointees on the boards, issuing rules, policing the professions, opposing other professions (lawyers versus realtors, M.D.'s versus osteopaths and chiropractors) is infinitely complex and never ending.

The public employees of any state, whether or not they are politically appointed, are an important interest in state politics. They commonly have a large number of associations that work together, with the possible exception of the teachers' groups, which usually go their own way. . . . As the shortage of teachers becomes more acute the influence of their associations may be expected to increase.

The formal governments in the states have their associations, such as the leagues of municipalities, to present their views to appropriate agencies of the state. It seems odd that the constitutional representative system appears to the local governments so inadequate that they must hire their own staffs and have an office near the statehouse. But the states have their own organizations like the Council of State Governments, and some cities and states have full time paid lobbyists in Washington. The process operates in all directions.

In the politics of certain states various racial or nationality groups are important, such as Negroes, French-Canadians, Spanish-Americans. In still other states some other interests, such as the League of Women Voters or a taxpayers' association, will be influential. Only the most intimate acquaintance with the politics of a particular state will enable any one to describe with confidence its interest groups and their objectives.

*   *   *

BENEFITS OF GROUP POLITICS

Group politics have come to be as much a part of the political scene as party politics, and the groups do many good things that the parties cannot. They superimpose upon geographical representation a rough kind of functional representation; the parties, resting upon areas, are insufficiently refined instruments to represent the multitude of interests in society. Second, some of the groups initiate public policies, pointing out the need for legislation or administrative or judicial action. Third, they perform a critical function in examining bills, rules, judicial decisions, and administrative actions. Fourth, they seek to get candidates for office to express themselves on the issues in which the groups are interested, when often the candidates would much prefer to say nothing as eloquently as possible. If a candidate wins, some groups will try to hold him to his promises. Fifth, they may have an educational function, bringing both to the public and to their own members materials on issues. Finally, they help to overcome to some extent the difficulties inherent in the system of separated powers. Essentially nonpartisan and working on all branches, they may get a government to move that is constitutionally inclined to deadlock and stalemate. All of these services, some people would say, are only part of the good that bad men do. But they are done, nevertheless.

37. The Machines*

WARREN MOSCOW

THE last time an election was stolen in New York City was in 1933, when Tammany, fighting a losing battle to save its power and prestige, elected a Borough President and a District Attorney by a margin of about 12,000 votes, all fraudulent. Those were the only offices it managed to salvage that year out of the anti-machine landslide that elected Fiorello La Guardia as Mayor for the first time. In the long run Tammany, known nation-wide as the prototype of machine politics, would have been better off if it had not stolen the prosecutor's office. Its District Attorney was picked by men interested in protecting rather than prosecuting the underworld, and the state-sponsored Dewey investigation two years later was the inevitable result.

The theft of an election, like that of 1933, probably won't happen again, or not for a long time. Tammany was desperate, but still strong, because it had the racket mobs and the police department was under its control. Squads of mobster "storm troopers," trade-marked for their own purposes by identical pearl-gray fedoras, marched in on polling place after polling place south of Fourteenth Street in Manhattan and took over the voting machinery.

They told the policeman assigned to the place to "beat it," and he, knowing where the interest of his superiors lay, took a walk around the block instead of sounding a riot call. The citizenry, waiting in line to vote, was shoved out of the way. One gorilla—one who was able to write—would take over the

registry book and sign for those who had not yet voted, while another rang up the votes on the voting machine, as if it were a cash register. From start to finish it was just a show of force and, because of that, was limited in its application to the sections of the county where lived the poorer and less educated voters—where such tactics had the most chance of success without interference.

Interference was tried. Fiorello La Guardia's campaign manager, William M. Chadbourne, raised his bull-like voice in protest, but was arrested for disorderly conduct and marched off to the hoosegow. Things really were rough that day.

But all this was the adrenalin-inspired struggle of a dying political machine, the Tammany Hall whose name had been synonymous with power and corruption in municipal politics. And even for the limited success it achieved, it needed the connivance of a police department whose members had grown used to the system, the theory of political action that permitted the underworld to get away with murder.

* * *

Immigration built the political machines in New York City, starting 'way back with the flood of the Irish, and the machines were struck a death blow when the nation embarked, after World War I, on a policy of restricted immigration through the quota system. The machines did not show the effects until much later, but the cutting-off of large-scale immigration deprived them of most of their annual crop of prospective voters, people whom they could help become citizens, people in a strange country, having to learn a new language. These people needed the helping hand extended by Tammany and its allies and were in return willing, even eager, to hand over their family bloc of votes. The second generation in these families, born here, better educated, better off financially, usually grew away from the dependence their parents had had on the district leader and his leg-man, the election district or precinct captain. But up to the cutting off of immigration, there was always a new group of arrivals to be taken into the fold.

The second most important factor in the decline of the machines was the social-welfare program put into effect under the New Deal. It is a political paradox that the machines all over the country turned in their greatest majorities for and under Franklin D. Roosevelt, implementing the social program that was cutting their own throats.

In the old days—in fact, up to 1931 —it was against the law in New York State for public funds to be used for the support of anyone outside a public institution. To be fed or housed, you had to go to the poorhouse as far as any agency of government was concerned. This meant that the man who was temporarily down and out got his aid from his local political machine. The leader had a ready two bucks in his pocket—in days when two bucks meant something—and his card, with a scribbled notation, was always good for a job shovelling snow for the city or digging a ditch for the gas company. The Christmas and Thanksgiving baskets meant holiday cheer for those who otherwise would not have had the means to celebrate; the annual outing of the Umteenth Ward Democratic Club meant a neighborhood picnic for those in whose lives picnics were rare.

The Roosevelt program produced home relief and unemployment relief, which kept families together; it brought aid to widows and dependent children—aid they got as a matter of right from government and not as a favor from a political machine. It is true that the people on WPA and home relief voted for Roosevelt en masse in the 1936 election, but in New York at least, they did it as a matter of economics, or in gratitude, not as the result of compulsion.

Which leads to the basic and fundamental fact about the political machines of today. It is that even when a machine wins and wins overwhelmingly, it does so without actually controlling the vote cast.

The people vote for machine candidates when they want to, not because they have to. There is no personal obligation to the machine for money, food, or jobs. The old intimate contact between ward captain and voter does not exist. It was a long time before political observers noted this trend. It was well hidden because during the period when the decay was eating at the vitals of the machines, they happened to have, in New York City and state, a remarkable series of vote-getting candidates at the top of their tickets who attracted the electorate.

*   *   *

The basic trouble with Tammany is that the present members still look back to the days when it was the dominant organization in the city. They have tried to keep their machine geared to the old ratio of power and patronage, to maintain that higher standard of political living which was theirs when they ran the city, and no longer can be kept up on the purse of a single county organization.

Tammany had so much, in the old days, that it suffered far more than any of the other county organizations when it lost control of City Hall in 1933, with the election of La Guardia. The others had lived off their county patronage, plus the bits Tammany let them have from the city trough. It is probable that Tammany could have survived one or two terms of La Guardia as Mayor, still possessing, as it did for a while, control of the magistrates' courts and the county offices. But before La Guardia was through, county offices and county government had been wiped out, or placed on a civil-service merit basis. And magistrates serve only ten-year terms.

By the time the Little Flower left City Hall, at the end of twelve years of independent, anti-machine rule, there was not—there could not be—a single person outside of the state and county courts who owed his job and therefore his primary allegiance to Tammany rather than to La Guardia.

* * *

In weighing Tammany's position, one must remember that the votes it once controlled are no longer there, even if Tammany could control them. Manhattan, for twenty years, has been in the process of being transformed into a business and management terminal, with no room for low-rent slums. A single improvement like the Holland Tunnel wiped out six blocks of tenements for its plaza, and the voters never came back. Once the largest of the five boroughs . . . , it probably will slip into fourth place in the next decade, below the Bronx and Queens. With the loss of people, it has also lost congressional and legislative representation and the prestige that goes with large blocks of votes. . . .

38. One Man Wore the Crown*

ALLAN P. SINDLER

To great numbers of Louisianians, Huey Long was either the salvation or the ruination of Louisiana. It is not surprising, therefore, that most judgments of the Kingfish, whether derived from adulation or detestation, are essentially one-dimensional. A more accurate view of Huey must stress the mixture of types he actually was and the many-sided impact of his reign on succeeding state politics. The importance of a full understanding of Long scarcely can be exaggerated, for to him must be attributed much of the form and content of recent Louisiana politics through 1952. [Editor's note: Long was assassinated in Baton Rouge in September, 1935.]

TEMPERAMENT AND TACTICS

* * *

Too much of the daringness and imaginativeness which Huey brought to his career was devoted to devising ways to punish his political foes. Long understated the streak of vengefulness in his nature when he observed in his autobiography, "Once disappointed over a political undertaking, I could never cast it from my mind." His rudeness and his predilection for engaging in personal abuse, both stemming from his egocentricity merited the observation that ". . . Huey P. Long . . . would not have been allowed to live a week if the code duello had still been in force."

Yet the vilification and occasional crucifixion of his political adversaries were part of that intense personalization of politics by which Huey was able to erect and maintain a highly personal dictatorship. Many Louisianians idolized Long: some of the Kingfish's devoted Catholic followers, for example, unofficially canonized him. The state presented a statue of Huey

* Reprinted with permission from *Huey Long's Louisiana*, by Allan P. Sindler, Johns Hopkins Press, 1956. Footnotes omitted.

as one of its two great sons entitled to recognition in Statuary Hall in Washington, purchased Long's New Orleans home for a museum, and made his birthday a legal holiday. By capitalizing on the political potency of Long's name, his successors in 1936 were able to retain the loyalty of his following while at the same time to mock his memory by enacting a state sales tax and by burying Share-Our-Wealth. . . .

The emotional loyalties which Huey Long aroused, in Louisiana and in the nation, reflected the fact that, at his oratorical best, Huey expressed the yearnings of the "have-nots" for a material level of living consonant with the equality of citizens proclaimed in the Constitution. In the midst of the depression, here was a homely philosopher who applied, in the vernacular of the uneducated man, the verities of the Bible and the American Constitution to the terrifying and bewildering economic problems of the day. Here was a dedicated leader for the "forgotten men." . . .

That Huey could alternate between vindictiveness and disarming rusticity testified to his capacity to adapt skillfully his tactics to his objective and his audience. Particularly noteworthy was his deliberate exploitation of a comic role through which he sought favorable press attention to enhance his class leadership and to obscure the uglier aspects of his regime. Huey observed of his sobriquet, "Kingfish," derived from "Kingfish of the Mystic Knights of the Sea" from the "Amos and Andy" radio show, that "it has served to substitute gaiety for some of the tragedy of politics." Outrageous burlesque, however, also was a most useful disguise for grim purpose. . . .

Back home in Louisiana . . . in view of the events of state politics, Long's pose of comic relief was a bit difficult to sustain. The press in Louisiana, therefore, was raped rather than seduced. By ridiculing the urban press as biased spokesmen for "the interests," Long not only minimized the impact of their anti-Longism but also made them suspect as prejudiced reporters of the political news of the day. The country parish weekly press supported the Long faction, either willingly or because they were in too precarious a financial position to withstand intimidation by the state administration. Not content with undermining the influence of the daily newspapers and with controlling the weekly press, Long spread the gospel through his own organ, the *Progress,* "the most cheerfully venomous regular publication in the nation." For those special occasions when Long's viewpoint had to be communicated swiftly to all parts of the state, Huey perfected an efficient system of direct distribution of circulars which involved the use of state printing equipment, the state highway police, and factional leaders in the parishes. Long's treatment of the Louisiana press helped explain his creation of a dictatorship based upon mass loyalty to his person. As Huey liked to boast, "When I lie from the stump, I lie big, because no matter what the newspapers say, 90 per cent of the people will believe me."

Long applied a similar heavy hand, for the most part, in solving the troublesome problems of political finances. Huey's power and magnetism attracted the backing of some wealthy adventurers and businessmen, most prominent of whom was Robert S. Maestri, appointed by Huey as Commissioner of Conservation and by Huey's heirs as Mayor of New Orleans. Financial contributions also were forthcoming from the usual groups anxious to do business with the state, particularly since Huey's bent for power assured the partisan administration of many functions of government. Another important source of funds was suggested by the admission of Seymour Weiss that commissions from Louisiana highway surety bonds were held for the benefit of the Long political machine. The public boast of the Long forces that theirs was a people's movement applied quite clearly to the raising of campaign funds. Salary deductions and forced subscriptions to the *Progress* were imposed upon public employees and justified as "a legitimate and honorable way of raising funds from people who owe their jobs to the administration and who would have nothing otherwise. . . ." Besides, averred the Longites, was it preferable to rely upon big business for the money necessary to win elections?

On balance, it was the brazenness of Long's tactics more than any other feature of his dictatorship which distinguished his rule from the practices of other American political bosses. . . . It would have been better for Louisiana if Long had been either the old-fashioned despot who dispensed with the Legislature, the courts, and the ballot box or the hidden boss who pulled the strings via his office telephone. Either way would have been less demoralizing to Louisianians than Long's version of absolute power, which was lawlessness, not merely legally entrenched but highly visible and candid in its operation and enjoying continued popular endorsement. These circumstances suggest the pertinence of the story of Huey P. Long to those who are concerned about the capacity of constitutional democracy to endure.

* * *

A THREE-DIMENSIONAL JUDGMENT OF HUEY LONG

What may be termed the classic defense of the Kingfish was rendered by Senator Overton in his Memorial Address for Huey Long delivered on the floor of the United States Senate on January 22, 1936. In that speech, Overton candidly recognized that "it has been repeatedly contended by many of his critics that Senator Long rose to political power by ruthless and unscrupulous methods." Overton chose not to attempt denial of the truth of the charge but to blunt its force by asserting that Long's methods had to be understood in the context of "both the

modern political history of Louisiana and the political career of the man. . . ." The crux of the ensuing argument was that "ruthless warfare against Governor Long" conducted by the discredited "political aristocracy" he had displaced, culminating in the 1929 impeachment effort, compelled Long, "in order to save himself [*and*] his friends and associates from political annihilation . . . to build and maintain an organization as ruthless perhaps, as was the opposition." In short, Overton's defense was made largely on relative grounds, with the "better elements" and the Choctaws used as constant foils.

There was much of persuasive substance in Overton's hymn to the memory of Huey. If, as has been argued here, the class reforms of Long were limited both in scope and content, then the popular inflation of his reputation for liberalism commented strikingly on the inadequacies of prior state administrations. That a majority of the citizenry acquiesced in tyranny because of the benefits it yielded them condemned the conservative predecessors of Huey far more than it did the Kingfish. As Long liked to say, Louisiana had been suffering from a Tweedledum-Tweedledee administration: "one of 'em skinned you from the ankles up, the other from the neck down." Compared with past governors, Huey gave more to the people, and few of his followers looked, or apparently even cared, to see if he also took more for himself.

* * *

The fact of Huey's ruthless bossdom, admitted even by Overton, became virtually the single datum in the confirmed anti-Long's judgment of the Kingfish. Long, according to this view, was nothing but a neurotic seeker of power, a political racketeer who would have slashed his way to autocracy in any state. The inferences followed that the substance of Huey's policies did not necessarily reveal anything about the true nature of his class sympathies and that a meaningful analysis of Long should confine itself to the dissection of the techniques by which he achieved and wielded power.

To date there is not available, and perhaps there never will be available, the kinds of materials and data which would permit an assessment of the validity of the foregoing anti-Long judgment. In the opinion of this writer—and it remains only an opinion—it is highly likely that Long was possessed

of deep proletarian sympathies. Those sympathies, however, became so enmeshed with a lust for power and with a determination to avenge every real or fancied personal grievance as to make futile any attempt to gauge the sincerity of his policies. It seems likely also that, far from being born with a scepter on his mind, Long did not plan much in advance, if at all, either the fact or the details of his dictatorship. . . .

39. Jesse Unruh: "Big Daddy" of California*

ED CRAY

* * *

[*Jesse*] Unruh's Roman-candle political career could only have happened in the fireworks factory of California politics, where skyrockets and meteoric rises are commonplace. Discharged from the Navy at the end of World War II, he enrolled at the University of Southern California, soon became a prime mover in the campus veterans' organization, Trovets, and flirted with the political Left. His greatest success was to force the administration of the Methodist-founded school to remove the usual question about religion from the university's admission application. He gathered around him a group of friends, many of whom have since climbed in political status with him—and largely because of him. In 1948, he split off from the "extreme" Left when, as he put it, he objected to the Communist-run campaign of the Independent Progressive Party and Henry Wallace. Unruh preferred to stay within the Democratic Party—his boyhood in Texas taught him that politics meant "Democrat." Moreover, he was busy running for state office, entering the Democratic primary. Poorly financed,

he lost to a man generally considered to be more conservative.

In 1949, he was one of the founding members of the Democratic Guild, a local political club in southwest Los Angeles. Active in Helen Gahagan Douglas' campaign for the Senate, he was rewarded with a patronage appointment in the 1950 census count. (He suspects that he was far down on the list, but was the only candidate the Census Bureau would accept.) His stint as director of the census in southwest Los Angeles taught the journalism graduate the sociological minutiae which make for winning political campaigns.

Elected to the Los Angeles Democratic County Committee in 1950, Unruh was one of a group of reformers who attempted to breathe life into that stagnant body and to do battle as a "good government" group against "bossism." The reformers included a number of men who have since become opponents of Unruh, including Lt. Gov. Glenn Anderson, former State Senator Richard Richards and former chairman of the Los Angeles County Committee, Don Rose.

Part of the reform was to include the organization of volunteer clubs whose preprimary endorsements could bring

* Reprinted with permission from *The Nation*, March 9, 1963. Footnotes omitted.

some order to the chaos of the cross-filed primary, which permitted a candidate, without party label, to enter both party primaries. . . . In 1948, there were approximately twenty-five clubs in Los Angeles County; four years later, there were a hundred clubs, but the vast volunteer enthusiasm ignited by Adlai Stevenson's campaign in 1952 had yet to be effectively organized.

Eisenhower took California in spite of volunteer enthusiasm and Unruh was beaten in his attempt to unseat a veteran Assemblyman who had the backing of Los Angeles' conservative labor unions. Two years later, Unruh had digested an important political lesson: volunteer efforts without labor's backing and, even worse, without money, weren't enough. With a war chest of $2,800 and the party label attached to his name due to a change in the state law, Unruh ran again. His opponent, who had beaten him two years before, chose to switch his registration from Democrat to Republican and then lost the labor support he had earlier enjoyed. Heavy contributions from lobbyists were not enough to beat Unruh's volunteers who, by then, had become an effective Assembly District organization.

Jess Unruh went off to Sacramento in 1954 as a member of a liberal caucus within the Democratic minority in the State Assembly. Artie Samish, long the dominant force in state politics, had been convicted of income-tax evasion and sent off to a federal prison, leaving behind a power vacuum. Goodwin Knight was Governor now, replacing Warren who had moved up to the Supreme Court.

*   *   *

The 1957 legislature was leaderless. The affable Goodie Knight's program was designed to alienate no one, since his political strength lay in the middle-of-the-road posture which Warren had studiously maintained and passed on. The lobbyists were still seeking a replacement for Samish, fighting among themselves for the first time in their unrecorded history.

Bill Munnell, today a Superior Court judge in Los Angeles, was elected minority leader, and two more members, Gordon Winton and Robert Crown, had joined the liberal caucus, which took over the balance of power in the legislature. Munnell's leadership came by virtue of his seniority and the chairmanship of the Finance and Taxation Committee; Unruh's came by virtue of his membership on that committee and his friendship with the chairman. The lobbyists sought out Unruh as a man close to the minority leader and one who might ease their bills through. In return, they offered campaign contributions. Unruh, however, had little need of a lavish war chest; he was in a safe Democratic district. But he knew of deserving Democrats who did need funds and he was glad to steer lobbyists accordingly. He handled no money himself, acting only as an adviser. (Unruh has never had direct personal control over campaign contributions or party funds. The CDC [California Democratic Council] has sought in vain for proof of charges of "corrupt machine politics" which they would like to lay at Unruh's doorstep.)

Politically astute, a parliamentarian with a growing reputation as the fastest gavel in the West, a man to whom legislators owed a favor, Unruh was picked in October, 1957, by Fred Dutton to manage the Southern California gubernatorial campaign for the then Attorney-General Edmund G. "Pat" Brown. He went on the Brown payroll at $10,000 per year while continuing to serve in the legislature. First he had to overcome the objections of the party's big financial contributors, who felt he was too close to the maverick CDC; then he had to make his peace with the conservative unions that have long dominated the Los Angeles County Labor Council.

The gubernatorial campaign of 1958 was the best organized, and offered the Democrats' first united front, in the history of the state. "Pat" Brown was running against William F. Knowland, Oakland newspaper publisher, conservative Republican and a Chiang Kai-shek supporter in the U.S. Senate. The ideological lines were clearly drawn: Knowland supported a right-to-work measure on the ballot; Brown was advocating a liberal program of legislation which the state had long needed and never received. Labor, for the only time in the state's history, backed its claims of delivering the vote. The CDC, now grown to 100,000 members, had become a political veteran. Two unsuccessful Stevenson campaigns and a losing Senatorial race in 1956 (when Senator Kuchel defeated Richard Richards) had added professional skills to amateur enthusiasm.

In the maelstrom of precinct operations in California, there are no ward heelers, no patronage appointments, no jobs on the city rolls, no welfare handouts. In short, there is nothing to compel the voters' loyalty to the machine. Without party loyalty (and Democratic switching once ran as high as 30 per cent), the only solution is voter education. This the CDC handled with great skill. By 1958, many club members were walking precincts for the third time and had come to know the residents on a first-name basis. Months prior to the election, key precincts were combed, then worked again and again. Some precincts had workers make as many as three door-to-door sweeps, talking issues, explaining the Democratic platform, extolling the merits of the *entire* ticket.

Brown's campaign manager, Fred Dutton (now an Assistant Secretary of State for Congressional Affairs) and Don Bradley, campaign manager for Senatorial candidate Clair Engle, built a state-wide operation unprecedented in thoroughness and efficiency. Jess Unruh learned a great deal about politics from these two while serving as Brown's Southern California chairman.

Brown beat Knowland by more than a million votes. Democrats elected six of seven state-wide candidates, reversed the Republican edge in the House delegation from 17-13 to 16-14, and gave Brown sizable majorities in both houses of the state legislature.

The legislature which convened in Sacramento in 1959 offered Brown's program little opposition, primarily because Jess Unruh had political muscle and a willingness to use it. Unruh had some claim to high office in the Assembly as a reward for the Southern California campaign. The speakership—probably the second most important office in Sacramento—was open. Assemblyman Gus Hawkins, a twenty-four-year veteran who, for the first time in his career, was a member of the majority, was a front-runner for the office. Munnell was heir apparent to the majority leader's post. In one of the most politically important of his many moves, Unruh backed Assemblyman Ralph Brown for the Speaker's chair. To this end, he rounded up the support of Richfield Oil, pointing out to its lobbyists that Hawkins was heavily backed by Superior Oil Co.

The battle of the oil companies is another of California's unique and ubiquitous political problems. The oil industry here is divided into two large groups—"Big Oil" and "Little Oil." Aside from a common endorsement of the 27.5 per cent depletion allowance and an aversion to state gasoline taxes, the two have little in common. "Big Oil"—Standard, Shell, Signal, Tidewater, Union and Texaco—are huge companies which not only drill and refine oil, but maintain their own retail outlets. "Little Oil" constitutes such companies as Superior, Wilshire, Pauley and some others little known outside the state. Richfield shifts between the two groups, a maverick with a large retail operation but a dependence upon the major producers for a large share of its crude. With one person of every five in the state employed directly or indirectly in the service of the internal combustion engine, and with gasoline tax revenues of $357.6 million second only to the retail sales tax in state income, the state legislature figures heavily in the considerations of the various oil companies.

At work even before the legislature opened, Unruh lined up support for Ralph Brown. Many Assemblymen owed Unruh a favor for having steered campaign contributions their way. Brown was elected Speaker and Unruh's reward was chairmanship of the powerful Ways and Means Committee. For the first time he had an official position which made him the equal in prestige of his tutor, William Munnell. Additionally, Unruh was the funnel through which campaign contributions now poured. Assemblymen who had received assistance now paid their debts; Assemblymen who might need assistance—in both parties—listened to the powerful Unruh.

Around Unruh gathered a group of legislators who had once been the core of the liberal minority. On the Assembly floor, the group was dubbed the Praetorian Guard, the phalanx of the advocates for the Governor's program. Off the Assembly floor, a handful of convivial, though not necessarily well-heeled, lobbyists were added. The "Cub Scout Den," as it came to be called— Unruh was known familiarly as "the Den Mother"—became the source of Unruh's political strength.

"Pat" Brown's legislative program was long overdue. His principal spokesman, especially on matters of taxation, was Jesse Unruh. Cross-filing was repealed, a Fair Employment Practices Act was passed, state aid to education and unemployment compensation were increased, $75 million in workers' benefits were approved. The Governor was later to say that Unruh made his reputation on his, Brown's, program and that Brown made his on the strength of Unruh's ability to push it through.

There was one major failure. As part of an eight-point program to raise $245 million in taxes, Brown asked for an oil-severance tax which would have raised $23 million a year. Brown fought hard, but Unruh was not enthusiastic for the measure; neither were the various Assemblymen who had come to appreciate the value of Unruh-apportioned oil contributions. The proposal was defeated.

Unruh had waited through two fruitless sessions for the heavy Democratic majorities needed to pass the two bills of which he is the most proud. His Civil Rights Act flatly prohibits racial or religious discrimination in all business transactions in the state and has come to be the one item that confounds those who view the man as a conservative. (Naturally, the measure did nothing to hurt its author in the Negro precincts of his own district, while the lobbies it antagonized—real estate, for example—were already opposed to him.) The second act to which he put his name was brilliant in its Machiavellian design. The Retail Credit Act established interest rates and effectively stifled the loan sharks who had pillaged lower-class neighborhoods for years. In halting the politically powerless loan sharks and appearing as the friend of the little man, Unruh also set a 1.5 per cent per month (18 per cent per year) interest rate on revolving credit funds favored by the metropolitan department stores. The 18 per cent per year rate— which he tacitly concedes may be high, "but we had no previous experience anywhere to draw on"—obtained for him the backing of James S. Sheppard, former president of the state bar, a conservative Democrat and counsel for most of Los Angeles' largest department stores. A member of Democratic Associates, the party's largest fundraising source, Sheppard was also influential with the multi-million-dollar, Republican-owned firms he represented, and was thus able to tap conservatives of both parties. And Unruh had a claim upon him.

Unruh was planning ahead, knowing full well that John F. Kennedy did not like California's political climate, despite the considerable support from the California delegation he had received in his abortive bid for the Vice-Presidential nomination in 1956. In California, there was no machine to deal with, no party discipline, the Congressional delegation was a collection of "me-firsts" with local machines and little party loyalty. Worst of all, there was the CDC, that collection of wild-eyed liberals who took part in political campaigns for the fun of it or out of democratic (small "d") idealism without thought of political preference or monetary reward for themselves. . . .

Late in 1959, Unruh met with Kennedy's two political tacticians, Lawrence O'Brien and Kenneth O'Donnell. The three saw eye-to-eye, pocketbook-to pocketbook. Unruh had a growing appreciation of image-politics, thanks to his apprenticeship in California's cross-filing campaigns. At that meeting, Unruh acquired the inside track to the White House because "Pat" Brown was simultaneously making a serious political mistake: he was picking the state's delegation to the Democratic convention in a democratic (small "d" again) fashion.

In 1950, as an early step to broaden the base of the Democratic Party, Glenn Anderson, then Los Angeles County Committeeman, worked out a scheme whereby the delegation to the Democratic National Convention would be picked literally from the grass roots. In addition to office-holders and their petty-patronage appointees, one or two people were to be selected from each Congressional district after the district had caucused and presented a list of six or eight to the head of the delegation.

Ten years later, Brown followed this formula to the letter. He had problems which the Kennedys, in their machine-politics wisdom, could not and would not appreciate. If Brown was for Kennedy as he had said, then, dammit, he should appoint a delegation which, like those of the Eastern states, would stay in line. There was steady pressure on Brown from Unruh and others to do just that. But Brown had to run for re-election whether Kennedy won or

not, and he needed the support of all elements in the party. (California's gubernatorial election does not fall in the same year as the Presidential; with no top-down support, the candidate in California must do it from the bottom up.)

* * *

Unruh, who had filled a vacuum in Sacramento left when Samish was involuntarily retired, was there to fill another one. Brown now projected the image of a man of hair-trigger indecision and, in national party terms, was therefore unfit for the mantle of leadership. The National Committeeman was Attorney General Stanley Mosk. Mosk had been elected just prior to the Democratic National Convention to replace Paul Ziffren, an eight-year veteran who had made no bones of his dislike for Lyndon Johnson. The order to dump the liberal Ziffren came not from Kennedy, as has been whispered, but from Speaker of the House Sam Rayburn, who was promoting Lyndon Johnson's candidacy. Rayburn passed the word to the House delegation that Ziffren had to go or they might have trouble getting bills through.

The Kennedy campaign in California was hardly an unqualified success. Dutton had overall charge; Bradley was to handle the northern half of the state. Unruh, who again was the paid campaign manager in Southern California, ignored the CDC, partly out of a growing suspicion of volunteer politics and partly because the Kennedy men were running a different sort of campaign, one with a heavy reliance on television. The CDC, in turn, volunteered little; for many, the joy was gone from politics. . . .

Late in the campaign, with the Kennedy drive hardly a model of efficiency, Representative James Roosevelt and Manny Rohatiner, a field secretary for Los Angeles County Supervisor Ernest Debs, went to Unruh, suggesting that he install a get-out-the-vote drive

on Election Day in addition to everything else that was planned. The result
was a last-minute operation. The effort
was focused in those lower-class, traditionally Democratic districts where the
vote turnout is also traditionally poor-
est; its intent was to produce an extra
10 per cent of the registered Democrats
who normally wouldn't come out to
vote. According to Rohatiner, the effort
turned a loss of 75,000 in Los Angeles
County into a narrow 25,000 Kennedy
victory. Nixon, however, won the state
by 35,000 votes (of six million cast).
Neither Dutton nor Unruh was charged
by the White House with the loss;
after all, Unruh had delivered Los
Angeles County and its 40 per cent of
the state-wide vote—at a cost of $313,-
000.

Kennedy safely in the White House,
Unruh was involved in the apportionment of political favors. To provide
regional balance in the Cabinet, the
Postmaster General was to come from
California. Governor Brown reportedly
favored Hugo Fisher, the liberal State
Senator from Republican-voting San
Diego who had carried much of the
Governor's program in the upper house.
Unruh wanted someone less closely
aligned with the party's "liberal" wing
and the CDC. The new President
named J. Edward Day, then chairman
of Democratic Associates, former legal
and legislative assistant to Adlai Stevenson in Illinois, and vice president of
Prudential Insurance Co. CDC leaders
grumbled privately.

Similarly, Unruh's suggestion that
George E. O'Brien, head of the elec-
tricians' union and the dominant force
in the Los Angeles Labor Council,
would make an excellent U.S. Marshal
was acted upon. O'Brien had provided
many of the people for the get-out-the-
vote drive, paying some of the unem-
ployed union people from COPE funds.
In Sacramento, Unruh's power had
grown substantially. His assistance to
selected candidates to whom he also
channeled money from the ever-eager
lobbyists now was to be repaid. Mean-

while, the CDC was struggling with a
host of problems.

In many areas, the volunteers had
worked for local Assembly and Congressional candidates, but had ignored
the top of the ticket. . . . The volunteers reserved the right to refuse service
to anyone. Although individual clubs
were strong, weaknesses in the organization as whole were painfully obvious.
The CDC was a grass-roots organization, but it is some of the highest-price
grass around. There are few clubs in
the areas of high minority-group registration. Labor, that huge bloc of lower-
middle-class voters, is virtually un-
represented in it. Individually, and collectively as COPE, the unions have dis-
dained the CDC as an organization unresponsive to labor's demands and far
too cerebral. The CDC's greatest
strength lies largely in those upper-
middle and upper-class areas where
Democrats have the slimmest chances
of election. Individual clubs promote
discussion of issues—some more than
others—and these discussions cruise
along at a university-seminar level, far
above the rank and file's collective
head. Formed to educate the voter, the
CDC has served to educate precisely
those people least in need of help.

The organization's leadership is well
aware of these weaknesses and has
taken steps to correct them. But a basic
conflict remains.

Once elected, politicians become extremely cagey about taking public
stands. Even more, they want to avoid
having positions thrust upon them.
Those in office before the CDC became
a force in California politics have carefully avoided the organization. Representative James Roosevelt, liberal
enough for the CDC, represents a district which is a hotbed of volunteer
activity, but has never been a CDC
supporter.

At its height during Brown's campaign in 1958, the volunteer movement
numbered 100,000; just two years later,
it had fallen to half that. Those remaining were the most dedicated; but,

to the anger of the politicians, the dedication was not to the party, but to the issues which had led the volunteers to the party in the first place.

* * *

By the opening of the 1961 session of the state legislature, Jesse Marvin Unruh was running the Assembly. Presiding as chairman of Ways and Means (which, like its Washington namesake, is a kingpin committee), he helped the Speaker appoint committees, fought a running feud with the upper house, and perfected his ability to appraise each bill for its inherent worth, financial or otherwise, for the party. Three terms in the Assembly had given him the background he needed, and the keys to enough skeleton closets, to suggest in strong terms to lobbyists that this or that bill was worth this or that sum of money.

According to one lobbyist, Unruh views all bills as being one of three types: it will help only the lobby at the expense of the taxpayer; it will help the taxpayer at the expense of the lobby; or it will help one without harming the other. The first type does not move; Unruh's stock response is, "I don't think this is the year for your bill." Bills favoring the taxpayer at the expense of the lobbyist will pass the Assembly if the lobby is not particularly strong. The bills which hurt no one (although they usually mean that the lobbyist will benefit financially) acquire unspoken values—sometimes blocks of $25-a-plate dinner tickets, sometimes outright contributions to one campaign or another, sometimes the promise not to oppose a bill in which another group is interested. There are many rumors and few facts about this general weighing of legislation. One thing is clear: Unruh has become a past master at it.

* * *

Ralph Brown was still the Speaker, and though an important figure in getting the Governor's program through the legislature, he was more and more overshadowed by Unruh. Brown let it be known that he was interested in retiring from Sacramento—a District Court of Appeals judgeship would be adequate, he thought. Unruh was the heir apparent, although Speaker pro tem Carlos Bee would automatically move up if Brown were to resign after the legislature ended its session in June. Late in April, Unruh announced that he had the necessary votes to be elected —seven weeks before the legislature was to adjourn and four months before Ralph Brown's judgeship would be available. Brown chose not to view this as an affront; he only wanted out. Unruh maneuvered to have an urgency clause written into the judgeship bill, but was thwarted by state law. (The urgency clause would have set the court up before September, permitted Brown to resign as soon as the post was available and set the stage for Unruh's immediate election before the session ended.)

Lower house members offered no opposition to the judgeship bill, fearing what Unruh might do in the upcoming reapportionment were they to vote against the bill. Moreover, Unruh suggested to those who might oppose him that pet legislation might not find its way out of his committee. The judgeship for Brown went through; Brown resigned from the legislature at the end of the session and Bee moved up temporarily. Flexing his political muscle, Unruh managed an unprecedented, between-sessions call of the Assembly at which he was elected Speaker.

He was now officially the second most powerful man in Sacramento, a role he had filled unofficially for almost three years.

* * *

Invested now with both the power and the glory of the Speakership, Unruh began planning for "Pat" Brown's re-election campaign. As he had in 1958 and 1960, he would handle the south. Don Bradley, Brown's political pro, would be in charge of the state-wide organization. In addition, Unruh was to handle the coordination of both Assembly and Congressional races in Southern California. On Jan. 12, 1962, 1,200 people, one-third of them Republicans, paid $50 to attend a testimonial dinner for the new Speaker. He frankly admitted that the money from the dinner would be spent on deserving Assembly candidates. Lobbyists were conspicuous by their presence.

* * *

The smoldering fight between the CDC and Unruh erupted with the June primary. In Los Angeles' 31st Congressional District (Unruh's own), Assemblyman Charles Wilson was facing the CDC-oriented liberal, Jerry Pacht. Unruh had promised Wilson a Congressional district to his liking; Unruh wanted to add much of the high Democratic registration in Wilson's Assembly district to his own, but to do so would leave Wilson out on a limb. So Wilson was to run for Congress.

Pacht's long identification with the CDC, his forthright liberalism and his backing by Californians for Liberal Representation, a peace-oriented, civil-liberties-advocating group, all combined to make the fight a "natural." It is doubtful if Unruh thought that Wilson was the most brilliant legislator the party had sent to Sacramento, or even if he was the best man for Congress. But if Unruh demanded party loyalty in the legislature, he returned it in the campaigns. Into the district poured troops and money.

Unruh told Pacht that he would do "everything possible" to beat him. "Everything possible" included Red-baiting (which Unruh may not have been responsible for, but made no effort to stop) and sending out a mailing to every Democrat in the district. The mailing, appearing as a telegram, bore the legend: "Kennedy Repudiates Pacht." The text was taken from a telegram sent at Unruh's request to Wilson by Larry O'Brien in the White House. Circled in red ink was the statement, "The President has neither by letter nor in any other way endorsed the candidacy of Mr. Pacht or. . . ." The heavy red circle blotted out the rest of the sentence: ". . . or any other candidates for the nomination." It was a professional job of misrepresentation only slightly mitigated by the fact that it had been promoted by the circulation of a letter sent to Pacht in 1960 by then-candidate Kennedy when the President-to-be endorsed Pacht's bid for Congress in another district. Although Pacht had reproduced the entire Kennedy letter, the date could easily be overlooked or discounted; the effect of the letter was to make it appear that Pacht had the President's support in the primary.

Wilson won by 5,000 votes of 57,000 cast, and Unruh had beaten the CDC in their first open battle.

* * *

Brown's re-election win over Nixon by 297,000 votes has been credited to everyone but Brown. Those who worked on the get-out-the-vote drive immediately issued victory statements; Unruh was characteristically more modest. He estimated that the get-out-the-vote drive garnered 100,000 votes for the top of the ticket. Even without these votes, Brown would have won. The CDC people, fearing that their efforts would be ignored, countered with claims of their own. Some 3,000 of the get-out-the-vote workers, paid or not, were CDC members. And in the precincts which Unruh had left untouched, even those with high Republican registrations, the Democratic turnout had been gratifying.

The CDC did contribute to the Brown victory, but the figures offered to support their claims to laurel wreaths are explained by something other than shoe-leather and persuasion. The highest voter turnouts were in districts worked by the CDC, but these districts are, by and large, the highest in income and socio-economic status. Democrats there would have turned out anyway.

The Unruh people claim a vote haul of 100,000—a figure which campaign strategists close to the Governor suspect might be more realistically pegged at 75,000. But the percentage of Democratic registration voting for Brown was lower in Los Angeles County (69.85 per cent) than in the two comparable counties in the San Francisco Bay Area (San Francisco, 74.69 per cent; Alameda, 73.5 per cent) and neither county had a paid operation going. In the only other county in the state with a registration over 250,000, Republican San Diego, the loyalty figure was 63.4 per cent, in spite of the fact that 200 of its 1,991 precincts were covered by the Unruh drive.

The man who, in successive elections, had beaten the two biggest Republicans in California, William Knowland and Richard Nixon, was given no credit for his victory. The image of the indecisive, good-natured, but bumbling "Pat"

Brown, lingered longer in the minds of the party functionaries than it did in the minds of the voters.

* * *

Unruh's political future is a matter of some speculation. It is widely believed that he wants to succeed Brown as Governor; his denials are discounted as the politician's usual remarks in such a situation. If the Governor's Victorian mansion is Unruh's goal, the "bossism" image would prove to be the largest roadblock, a fact of which Unruh is well aware. There are other problems too. Unruh has one base of strength: the support, if not the undying devotion, of elected legislators. In Los Angeles, he also controls the county committee. But he has no popularity with the voters outside of his Assembly district and little contact with local politicians outside of Los Angeles County.

40. Some General Characteristics of Nonpartisan Elections*

CHARLES R. ADRIAN

Out of the middle-class businessman's "Efficiency and Economy Movement" that reached full strength in the second decade of the twentieth century came a series of innovations designed to place government "on a business basis" and to weaken the power of the political parties. The movement was inspired both by the example of the success of the corporate structure in trade and industry and by revulsion against the low standards of morality to be found in many sectors of political party activity around the turn of the century. The contemporary brand of politician had

* Reprinted with permission from *The American Political Science Review*, September 1952. Footnotes omitted.

recently been exposed by the "muckrakers" and the prestige of the parties had reached a very low level.

Of the numerous ideas and mechanisms adopted as a result of the reform movement, one of the most unusual was that of election without party designation. Early in the twentieth century, under the theory that judges are neutral referees, not political officers, and that political activities should therefore be discouraged in the choosing of them, many communities initiated "nonpartisan" elections (the term that is usually applied) in the balloting for judicial posts. Next, using the argument that local officials should be businesslike administrators—there being no Republi-

can way to pave a street and no Democratic way to lay a sewer—and that
politics on the national scene have
nothing in common with local problems, the movement spread to other
offices. In a number of states various
district, county, township, judicial,
school, and city offices were made nonpartisan. And in 1913 largely as the
result of a strange political accident,
Minnesota not only made its county
and municipal offices nonpartisan, but
extended the principle to the election
of the state legislature.

The principle lost much of its fasci-
nation for the public after the early
years of the 'twenties, although it enjoyed some revival after Nebraska applied the method to the choice of its
widely discussed unicameral legislature
authorized in November, 1934. . . .

As a term, "nonpartisanship" is at
best somewhat ambiguous, and to the
poorly informed voter it may often be
misleading. The expression cannot be
said to denote the absence of adherence
to factional groups or political interests.
No matter how ephemeral the organizational structure, wherever men are
elected to offices that require the making of *public policy* decisions, there are
always persons and groups interested in
getting certain candidates elected and
in defeating others. All elections are
partisan in the sense that people and
groups take sides and struggle against
one another for victory; and offices
filled "without party designation" are
partisan enough according to this
meaning. As it is used in the United
States, "nonpartisanship" actually describes a situation in which (1) public
offices are filled without party designations being placed on the ballot and
(2) the long ballot is used. . . .

While nonpartisan elections have not
been given close study by many scholars, the materials available indicate that
the system has certain characteristics
which reappear wherever the plan is
used. The purpose of this study is to
submit some tentative propositions

which seem to be characteristic of nonpartisanship. These propositions are
based upon available empirical evidence, and all require verification
through additional research. Owing to
space limitations little evidence is actually presented here; personal observations and studies of the state legislatures of Minnesota and Nebraska and
of the city councils of Minneapolis and
Detroit have furnished most of the data
suggesting the hypotheses.

Certain qualifications must be made
in establishing a frame of reference.
First, where comparisons with partisan
situations are made, a general two-party
system is presumed—not necessarily an
"ideal" two-party system, but one in
which members of one party may conceivably replace members of another
party in office. In one-party situations,
a quasi-nonpartisanship obtains that
makes comparisons with nonpartisanship meaningless. In addition, where
local, rather than general, parties are
found, it is probable that some of the
characteristics postulated for nonpartisanship would be valid while others
would not. Second, what might be
called an impersonal type of politics is
presumed. Where elections are held in
constituencies small enough to have
government by personality, it would be
unsafe to say that the material below is
applicable.

The following are offered as propositions:

1. *Nonpartisanship serves to weaken
the political parties in those areas where
it is in effect.* This is what its creators
intended that it should do. They felt
that the established political parties,
closely tied up with the system of spoils
and other Jacksonian precepts, were not
to be trusted. Ideally, they wanted to
see the principles of "sound business
management" applied to government,
not by professional politicians, but by
established and successful business men
of the community.

The removal of the party label from
certain parts of the ballot has resulted

in the weakening of political party organizations for several reasons. The reduction in the number of offices to be filled by the parties has weakened them by making active participation in their activities less attractive to the citizen: with fewer elective or appointive jobs available as rewards, there is less incentive for the individual to give his energies. There is not even the incentive of seeking to influence party members in the many areas where the parties are no longer effective in the determination of policy. Furthermore, the removal of some or all of the state and local offices from the party ballot has served to cut away the local roots of the party; weak local organizations in turn have made effective campaigning difficult by removing the ordinary citizen from regular and frequent contact with the parties.

Altogether, in states where nonpartisanship applies to an important sector of the ballot, the party organizations have been weak. This remains true, for example, in California, Michigan, Minnesota, Nebraska, and North Dakota; and further evidence of the debilitating effect of nonpartisanship upon the established parties is to be found in the attitudes of professional politicians. When the system was first proposed in Minnesota, Republican leaders in large measure stood in opposition to the elimination of the party label. While some Democrats at first believed that the party had nothing to lose in a situation in which it was already extremely weak, they later changed their mind, and leaders of all three of the state's major parties eventually took strong stands against the plan. In Michigan, Democrats at first supported the nonpartisanship movement, but subsequently regretted their action. Party leaders viewed nonpartisanship in the Nebraska legislature with apprehension.

2. Segregation of political leaders strictly to either partisan or nonpartisan areas is the general rule. The effect of

this tendency upon Minnesota politics when the legislature of that state was removed from the party ballot is clearly described in the following quotation:

> The new law which requires county officers and members of the legislature to be elected as nonpartisans takes all of the vitality out of a party campaign. Heretofore it has been the county officers and legislative candidates who have paid most of the expenses and harrowed up the country for the benefit of state candidates. This year it is all different. Only two of the county offices have contests and as they are nonpartisan they are taking no part in the state campaign nor are they paving the way for the state contestants.

Here was a basic alteration in traditional campaign techniques. The local organizations had been the very heart of the political parties in Minnesota, but it now became necessary for the parties to establish regional campaign personnel separate from politicians on the local scene. (The obverse situation obtained as well: party state central committees immediately chose virtually to ignore legislative and county contests.) With some exceptions, as indicated below, parallel sets of office-seekers, aides, and organizations had to be created, with very little intercourse between them. This was the case in all four of the areas observed for this article; an individual who wished to become active in politics had to choose one road or the other.

3. Channels for recruitment of candidates for partisan offices are restricted by nonpartisanship. It is unusual for a successful nonpartisan politician to move up into higher partisan ranks. Thus the fact that personnel for the two ballots are kept largely separate creates a problem for the parties, which ordinarily use local and legislative positions as the training ground for higher offices.

The problem has not been acute in

Minnesota (though certainly it is present), because a workable, particularly competitive two-party system has in recent years provided impetus for recruitment of able personnel. But in Michigan where Detroit, most of its suburbs, and other cities have nonpartisan elections, the system appears to have had a definitely adverse effect upon the quality of party personnel. This is particularly true of the Democratic party, which draws most of its strength in the state from the city of Detroit, and the results are especially apparent in the consistently low overall quality of the Wayne county legislative delegation.

In exceptional circumstances an outstanding campaigner from nonpartisan ranks will receive overtures from one or both political parties, but even in these rare cases there are many obstacles to success. For example, Edward J. Jeffries, Jr., the greatest vote-getter ever to serve as mayor of Detroit, was wooed by both major parties as a gubernatorial candidate and after having served four terms as mayor (the longest tenure in city's history), he filed for the Republican nomination for governor in 1946. He ran a poor fourth in a field of four. Some members of the Minnesota legislature have looked fondly toward the governor's chair; but party regulars understandably take a dim view of bringing in candidates "from outside the party," and success is rare. Since the overwhelming majority of the members of the Nebraska and Minnesota legislatures are inactive in the regular parties and so without chance for further advancement there, their services are not available for positions of higher party leadership. Similarly, almost no members of the Minneapolis or Detroit city councils have been active in party affairs, and the same, with only a few exceptions, may be said of the mayors of the two cities. These officeholders are not available to the political parties, or, at the very least, the parties do not wish to avail themselves of their services.

4. Channels for recruitment of candidates for nonpartisan offices are restricted by nonpartisanship. The securing of active political party members to fill nonpartisan positions is difficult. In Minneapolis, a party regular seeking a nonpartisan council or mayoralty seat is at a disadvantage and seldom makes good, especially in the case of the former. In Detroit, where nonpartisanship has become a refuge of conservatism, any attempt by an active party member to penetrate into the city's nonpartisan elections, and especially an effort to carry along "partisan politics," is greeted by powerful and effective blasts from the newspapers and from the Detroit Citizens' League. And status as active party members almost invariably places legislative candidates at a disadvantage in Minnesota and Nebraska.

Occasionally it is possible for an active party member to enter the nonpartisan lists and sometimes even to go on from there to higher positions within the party. Frank Murphy, the only mayor of Detroit to achieve national fame in the more than three decades since the city's present charter was adopted, was an active Democrat both before and after his tenure in the city hall. Murphy's election, however, was the result of a combination of unusual circumstances—including the recall in 1930 of the incumbent mayor, whose unethical behavior in office had temporarily weakened public confidence in some of the groups ordinarily most influential in choosing the chief executive, the extreme economic depression that affected Detroit even more than the rest of the nation and the very strong support given him by the *Detroit Times*; and Murphy made a strenuous effort to keep his partisan and nonpartisan political activities separate from one another. A few other Detroit mayors have had loose party connections and one had served in Congress before becoming mayor, but that was in the earliest days of nonpartisanship in the city government.

Hubert H. Humphrey, an active

Democrat, became mayor of Minneapolis in 1945, but on a largely nonparty campaign to "clean up" the city and with support from the Republican Cowles newspapers. Very active in partisan affairs while mayor, he moved on from that position to the United States Senate, while his successor, who had never been active in partisan activities, returned to the customary nonpartisan pattern. It is also to be remembered that James Michael Curley was for a time head of both the nonpartisan city government and the Democratic party in Boston, although his once vast support was always more of a personal than a party matter.

Certainly cases of party actives successful in obtaining nonpartisan offices are always exceptional. The usual picture find nonpartisan mayors rising from nonpartisan councils and nonpartisan councilmen coming from political obscurity—successfully reaching the council usually only after several tries have afforded the chance for the public to become familiar with their names.

5. *Limited new channels for recruitment of candidates for nonpartisan offices are opened by nonpartisanship.* Proponents of nonpartisanship have always argued that the system encourages many able, successful, well-known citizens of the community to run for office who would never become candidates under the traditional method since they would be unwilling to become entangled in the ordinary processes of party politics. There is evidence in all nonpartisan jurisdictions to support this contention. To be sure, the candidate under any elective system (except, perhaps, in very small communities with a purely personal type of government) must have a yen, or at least a tolerance, for electioneering; but many persons who have established reputations as business or professional men would fear the condescending attitudes often taken by Americans toward candidates who engage in party activities. These individuals sometimes can be persuaded to hold a nonpartisan office

in the council or legislature as a civic duty. Such persuasion appears to be effective from time to time and probably helps bring many capable persons into law-making bodies or mayoralty offices.

Nonpartisanship does not, however, *insure* the filling of available seats from among the community's successful. The individual who has never "made good" at anything else, who is a perennial office-seeker, and who depends for a livelihood upon scraps from the political table—the "political hack" of the vernacular—is a familiar figure around the Minneapolis council table and certainly is not unknown in the Detroit council or the Minnesota and Nebraska legislatures.

6. *Segregation of funds for financing nonpartisan and partisan election campaigns is nearly complete.* Nonpartisanship has produced parallel financing systems. In Michigan this separation of funds is required by law, but even in Minnesota, where rapport with the regular parties is close to being established, most individual candidates must shift for themselves. In that state, the Republicans, indirectly and *sub rosa,* give aid to certain needy candidates who agree to join the Conservative caucus in the legislature; but the Democratic Party has given no similar assistance, and the general practice in nonpartisan jurisdictions is for the individual candidate to seek out his own support. This is hardly surprising in light of the fact that political parties are almost never really rich and, needing money to support their own candidates, can scarcely be expected to give assistance to persons over whom they probably would exercise little or no control, granted election.

Individual financing has a tendency to confuse the voting public, leading many persons into believing that, while the political parties are beholden to those who pay their bills, nonpartisans are "independent." This naive belief is often encouraged in nonpartisan jurisdictions and results in a definitely undesirable development, for it means that the public is quite unaware of the nature of the commitments made by, or the type of support being given, a candidate. (The fact that state law may require the filing of a statement of campaign contributions does not fundamentally alter this situation.)

7. *Facilities for fund-raising by candidates for nonpartisan offices are restricted by nonpartisanship.* Under the traditional political system, the party carries on much of the financing burden as a staff function. If a candidate can secure organizational backing, he is free to carry on his campaign with little or no worry about the requisite funds: the party has machinery to care for this problem. On the other hand, the nonpartisan candidate is an individual who, when he first enters politics, has no organized support or money-raising mechanism. When he knows that he must spend his own money, or that of friends, or persuade an important interest group to give him aid, the burden of campaigning is made so heavy that the likelihood of an individual's trying to gain a seat is decreased. When this situation is combined with the discouraging advantage held by the incumbent (discussed below), it is not surprising that relatively few persons run for nonpartisan offices and that those who do become candidates do not, and cannot campaign extensively.

8. *Nonpartisanship encourages the avoidance of issues of policy in campaigns.* Since voting "for the man" and other frontier concepts have kept American political parties from exercising responsibility, the lack of definite platforms and the failure to carry out concrete campaign promises under nonpartisanship have not been as apparent as would otherwise be the case. The system does not make campaigning upon issues profitable, but discourages it even more than does the present party system. Seldom does a nonpartisan candidate take a firm, widely-publicized stand upon the important issues

of the day, and this is especially true if he is running for a seat in a collegial body. He prefers to take no stand at all, or an ambiguous one, or to discuss irrelevancies. He would rather try to be all things to all people, depending upon a well-known political name, or upon religious, ethnic, or other extraneous associations. In fact, fence-straddling is much more tempting than under the conventional election system, since in the latter the presence of a party label suggests some sort of "position" to the electorate. And since under nonpartisanship the voter seldom can associate a candidate with a position, he comes, as a last resort in his confusion, to choose "name" candidates. This means that there is a premium upon personal publicity; that the individual with newspaper backing often has an inordinate advantage; and that the *incumbent* nearly always (unless he has somehow managed to develop notoriety) is in a very strong position simply because his name has appeared more or less regularly before the public during his years in office.

9. *Nonpartisanship tends to frustrate protest voting.* This is so because the electorate, when disgruntled, tends to vote on a party basis and, of course, cannot do so without party labels. American politics is characterized by an "in" party versus an "out" party. Even if there is little philosophical cohesion within each, there is at least the label to serve as a guide for the voter. Under ordinary circumstances, the voter will accept the "in" group; but in times of grave dissatisfaction he can turn to the "out" party for the hope of relief. In nonpartisan jurisdictions, this is impossible. In the first place, there is no collectively identifiable "in" or "out" group. Whether or not there is within a legislative body a majority clique, caucus, or set indebted to the same interest groups, its members are to the voter, who seeks to hold them accountable, merely a collection of individual names. In the second place, if the voter seeks to "turn the rascals out," he has

no guide for doing so. He may, if interested enough, determine the incumbents 'names, but he usually has no way of knowing whether the opposing candidates will follow a policy of reform, or whatever it is that the voter desires. In partisan politics, the "out" party under such circumstances would promise changes akin to what the voter wanted and could be held accountable for producing them after the election. But the non-incumbent nonpartisan candidate usually prefers the middle-of-the-road; even if he makes definite commitments, his eventual voting behavior can be known to the individual voter only with the greatest difficulty; and under no circumstances need he bear responsibility for the acts of the body to which he belongs.

Although violent changes have taken place in partisan legislative bodies, as in the early days of the great depression, no similar drastic changes can be found in nonpartisan bodies. In 1931 the Michigan House of Representatives was under Republican control by a majority of ninety-eight to two; in 1933 the Democrats organized the House with a fifty-five to forty-five majority. A similar result took place in the Senate, where in 1931 the Republicans held a majority of thirty-one to one; two years later the Democrats were in control with an advantage of seventeen to fifteen. Evidence of the effectiveness of protest voting was even more spectacular in the state of Washington. There, the Republicans held a majority in the 1931 House of Representatives of ninety to eight. In 1935 the relative positions had been completely reversed and the Democrats were in control, ninety-one to eight. Similarly, in the 1931 Washington Senate the Republicans were in charge, forty-one to one; four years later the Democrats held a majority of thirty-seven to nine. No such changes took place in the nonpartisan Minnesota legislature during the same period, despite drastic changes in the partisan state offices. In 1931 when the Farmer-Labor radical Floyd B.

Olson was swept into the governorship, the House Liberals were too weak even to have a candidate for the speakership. In 1933, fifty-eight per cent of the House and fifty-five per cent of the Senate were made up of incumbent holdovers from the previous conservative era. Olson never held a working majority in either house, although he won three consecutive decisive victories for himself. The voters apparently did not know how to give him a legislative majority.

10. Nonpartisanship produces a legislative body with a relatively high percentage of experienced members, making for conservatism. This follows from the lack of provision for protest voting, the scarcity of campaigns based upon issues, and the resultant advantage given the incumbent as the voter casts about for a familiar name.

In Minnesota, nonpartisanship has produced a continuing trend toward a large number of holdovers from one legislature to the next. In Nebraska, the trend has been striking and uninterrupted since the adoption of nonpartisanship and in Detroit the incumbent's advantage has been one of the most definite characteristics of elections to the council. In the 1951 Detroit election, in fact, all nine incumbents were returned to office. An incumbent in that city is rarely defeated so long as he contests for a seat.

A study of ten non-southern states made a number of years ago indicated that Minnesota had a more experienced legislature than any except the most populous states, where the salary is outstanding (among state legislatures) and a high degree of political organization aids stability. Unlike the situation in many state legislatures (as in the Michigan and Washington cases cited above), where first and second-term members must be called upon to shoulder committee chairmanships and other important positions, the Minnesota legislature has almost never had to place inexperienced persons in key positions. This is also true in the Nebraska legislature and in nonpartisan city councils.

The tendency to reëlect members of the policy-making body has helped to make nonpartisan organizations lean toward conservatism. As indicated above, traditional legislative bodies are often called upon to sacrifice experience for flexibility in the face of demands of the public. Sessions that result are often chaotic, but they are ordinarily productive and responsive. Under nonpartisanship, a much more conservative approach may be expected, and as a result there is a tendency for legislators to diverge from contemporary public thinking on issues.

In Detroit, and to a lesser extent in Minneapolis, the vacuum caused by the absence of party labels as a guide for the voter has been partly filled by newspaper activity. Since daily newspapers are for the most part conservative, especially on local affairs, and since they have a disproportionate advantage in nonpartisan elections by the dissemination of all-important publicity, the conservative tendency of nonpartisan bodies is enhanced. (In legislative constituencies of rural Nebraska and Minnesota, newspapers are of less influence than they are in metropolitan areas, probably because of the more personal nature of a rural campaign.)

11. There is no collective responsibility in a nonpartisan body. This follows from the fact that there is no unifying organization or symbol. Each individual stands alone, responsible to his constituents for his own acts only, and for them but vaguely, since nonpartisan campaigns do not ordinarily center upon definite issues. Individual political behavior is not tempered by the fact that a political party has "a past to honor and a future to protect," in the words of a former Minnesota governor.

Without collective responsibility and a well-knit internal organization, a legislative body is likely to be lacking in a collective, comprehensive program. This often results either in a great deal of wasted motion and ineffective floundering or in the leadership's passing to an individual outside the legislative body who is in the public eye—the governor or mayor. In Nebraska, the former appears to have resulted, while in Minnesota the governor has become the dominant policy-maker, taking away much of the potential legislative leadership. In Detroit, the mayor has completely overshadowed the council in policy leadership—aided, to be sure, by the fact that the city has a strong-mayor form of organization.

Without collective responsibility, no one, except possibly the governor, is answerable for the budget in Nebraska or Minnesota. The individual legislator can always, and frequently does, assert that he voted for those items of interest to his district, while disclaiming responsibility for the budget as a whole, or for the legislative pork barrel. From the beginning of legislative nonpartisanship in Minnesota, claims have been made that the system encourages excessive legislative expenditures and logrolling for this reason. The writer has heard similar charges voiced against the Minneapolis and even the Detroit councils, although the fact that the latter is elected at large probably mitigates the tendency there. The Nebraska legislature has been charged with being a "fraternity of tolerance" because of vote trading and pork barreling. Nonpartisan legislatures could hardly be called unique in this respect, but the lack of a party answerable for padding of the budget surely places legislators in sore temptation.

It should be noted that although the Minnesota legislature is organized into two caucuses, "Liberal" and "Conservative" to which nearly all members nominally belong, these two groups do not bear collective responsibility for legislative actions. Caucus labels do not appear on the ballot, and the voter often finds it very difficult to discover the allegiance of a non-incumbent candidate, especially since membership is largely optional and often is not announced publicly until after election.

Furthermore, caucuses do not directly parallel the two major parties and are not party adjuncts; caucus membership may be very nominal; and both caucuses are without effective methods of disciplining "members."

The twenty-six member Minneapolis city council is likewise divided into two caucuses, "Liberal" and "Progressive," but the same statements may be made about this structural arrangement as have been made concerning the Minnesota legislative caucuses. The Nebraska legislature, in a proper respecting of the spirit of nonpartisanship, does not have caucus organizations, while the Detroit and many other nonpartisan city councils are too small to have even a nominal bifurcation.

Part VII

FINANCE AND PERSONNEL

SOME of the most vexatious problems in American government today relate to finances and personnel, and they are especially troublesome at the state and local levels. Although the situation of each
state is unique, certain difficulties are shared by most, if not all, states
and local governments. In his article, "Some Tax and Revenue Problems of the States," Charles Conlon briefly examines a few common
problems, stressing that future growth and change in the composition
of the country's population will inevitably impose greater demands
upon government. He notes briefly two chief sources of state and local
revenue, namely sales and property taxes, and emphasizes the importance of effective administration to the realization of income adequate
to finance governmental services. John F. Due examines sales taxes intensively, with special emphasis on arguments pro and con. Mr. Due
concludes that "the sales tax must be regarded as a second-best tax—
one to be employed only if various circumstances make complete reliance on income and other more suitable taxes undesirable."

In spite of the fact that the property tax is widely condemned on
theoretical grounds and censured for the inept manner in which it is
commonly administered, it continues to be the most important tax for
local governments. The role of the property tax is dispassionately examined by the Advisory Commission on Intergovernmental Relations
in its review of "The Place of the Property Tax in the State-Local
Revenue System." Roger Freeman provides further insight into the
nature of this tax in his look at "What Ails Property Tax?" He notes
that although the property tax is the chief tax for local purposes, it is
really "a minor item in our tax bill," accounting for about 11 per cent
of taxes. Mr. Freeman describes some of the pitfalls associated with
the administration of the property tax, including exemptions, rate
limitations, and fractional assessments. He also calls attention to the
problems sometimes posed by judicial decisions. The underassessment

of property and the role of the states in combatting this practice are explained by the Advisory Commission on Intergovernmental Relations, which stresses the importance of state action to eliminate some of the worst inequities associated with the property tax.

Local governments, especially the larger cities, are constantly in search of additional sources of income. One new source that has proved to be especially lucrative for cities in a few states is the sales tax. The growth of the municipal sales tax and the administrative problems accompanying its use are detailed by John F. Due. A second recent addition to the sources of municipal revenue is the income tax. Robert A. Sigafoos examines the history and problems of the municipal income tax and concludes that it can contribute appreciably to meeting the fiscal problems of cities and, if imposed on all salaries and wages earned in a city, is particularly well suited to requiring commuters to share significantly in the costs of city government.

Among the less well known but increasingly important sources of local revenue is the special assessment. Although practices differ from community to community, the manner in which Ann Arbor, Michigan, handles its program, described by Guy C. Larcom, Jr., illustrates the chief administrative concerns associated with the use of this "bane of the property owner."

Ever since the first Hoover Commission published its reports, one of the "bright, white hopes" of fiscal management has been the performance budget. In varying degrees, this fiscal tool has been adopted by many units of government across the nation. One of the early converts was the city of Los Angeles, which adopted performance budgeting in 1952. In the light of eight years' experience, Ali Eghtedari and Frank Sherwood examine the manner in which this fiscal device has functioned in that major city. They conclude that the performance approach *can* result in strengthening the executive budget, but it *may* at the same time inhibit legislative participation in the budget process. The authors also note some questions relating to the use of the performance budget that remain unanswered. Often the terms "performance budget" and "program budget" are used interchangeably. In his article on "Reappraising Program Budgeting," Ralph W. Snyder calls attention to the confusion of terms and distinguishes between the two budgeting procedures.

Among the more controversial techniques of fiscal management is central purchasing. William E. Stevenson notes briefly some considerations that have contributed to the widespread adoption of this practice and enumerates certain "cornerstones" on which a successful program of central purchasing must be founded. He also stresses the viewpoint that "Purchasing is not an end in itself but a vital service to an end."

During the last thirty years or so, great strides forward have been made in both the philosophy and techniques of personnel management. Felix Nigro, in his "Agenda for the Sixties," calls attention to the "mountain of work" that still lies ahead, but some comfort may be obtained from the realization that the mountain "is not as big as it used to be." Mr. Nigro's contrasting of conditions in the Thirties and those today is very heartening to all persons concerned with personnel management in the public service. At the same time he notes areas in which room for great improvement still exists and wisely observes that "The key to further progress in public personnel administration, as in many other things, is the willingness of the public to invest more money in it." Efforts must be directed, according to Nigro, toward more effective handling of such vexing operating problems as the strengthening of career services, balancing considerations of merit and seniority, improving compensation plans, discovering more effective schemes for performance evaluation, making better use of probationary periods, devising more satisfactory removal procedures, and coming to grips with the manifold problems associated with employee-management relations.

In the United States most people, including many in government service, have been hesitant to accept collective bargaining as a legitimate means of determining working conditions in public employment. Sterling Spero observes that traditionally such matters have been settled "by legislation or unilateral decision by the employing authority." The traditional viewpoint is allied with the concept of government as "the custodian of ultimate authority" with which none of its employees may bargain. This idea has sometimes enabled public administrators to justify their unwillingness to bargain by claiming that such a course of action was impossible. The fact is that collective bargaining has been used in areas of the public service for many years and is being employed with increasing frequency. Mr. Spero examines the nature of collective bargaining in the public service and considers its relation to the anti-strike policy characteristic of public jurisdictions in the United States.

41. Some Tax and Revenue Problems of the States*

CHARLES F. CONLON

EACH state has its own tax and revenue problems, but there are various aspects of these in which many states have a common interest. I will touch on a few of these, emphasizing those points which appear to be of special significance from the legislative standpoint. As a preliminary step, it would be well to indicate the extent of the expected growth in the operations of state and local government, because this is the factor which more than any other will determine revenue requirements and fiscal policies.

POPULATION THE MEASURE

The projected growth and change in the composition of the population, taken together, constitute the simplest and perhaps the most practical measure of the increase in the governmental workload. During the decade of the 50's the 5-19 year age group increased 42 per cent. In the decade 1960-1970, it will increase another 31 per cent. In short, from 1950 to 1970, the population in the 5-19 age group is expected to jump from 35.1 million to 65.3 million. This is the measure of the school problem. Since 1950, the 65 and over age group has increased 28 per cent. In the decade 1960-1970 it is expected to increase another 23 per cent. In contrast, the 25-34 year age group, an important one from the standpoint of productivity, will decline to about 22.5 million in 1965. Thus, in the middle of the next decade we will have about 2.25 million fewer people in the 25-34

* Reprinted with permission from *State Government*, Spring 1960.

year age group than we had four years ago, while the population in the school age groups and in the 65 year and over group will continue to increase substantially.

This projected workload may be related to expenditure and revenue requirements in dollars by comparison with the governmental costs involved during the present period of growth. Specifically, on a combined state and local basis, direct general expenditures, as reported by the Census Bureau, rose from $150 per capita in 1950 to $237 in 1957. About 65 per cent of this increase is accounted for by expenditures for education and highways. With the school age group and the total population both growing substantially, it may be assumed that the factors which have necessitated higher expenditures in recent years will continue to be operative in the next decade; and the likelihood is that the order of growth in expenditures and supporting revenues will not be greatly different from that observed since the beginning of the present decade—if we have reasonably stable prices.

CONTINUED PRESSURE ON TAX SYSTEM

What does this mean in terms of taxes? On an over-all basis, it indicates there will be continued pressure on the state-local tax system, and particularly on state systems. While the latter have been responsive to the rise in business activities, prices and income payments, taxes have had to be increased from time to time during the present decade, and it is fairly certain that additional revenue will be required in the next few years if expenditure programs are carried forward at the levels now assumed. . . .

STATE TAX SOURCES AND TRENDS

Major sources of general tax revenue, excluding property taxes, are now in use in the several states as follows: Of the fifty states, thirty-seven tax corporation net income; thirty-one tax personal income (excluding New Hampshire and Tennessee); thirty-three impose general sales taxes . . . ; forty-six tax cigarettes or tobacco products; and all tax alcoholic beverages. [*Editor's note: As of 1963, 35 states taxed personal income; 36 used the general sales tax; and 48 imposed a special tax on cigarettes.*] A combination of general sales and personal and corporate income taxes is found in twenty states, and a combination of sales and corporation income taxes in four states. Ten states have sales taxes but no kind of income tax. A combination of personal and corporation income taxes is found in eleven states. . . .

. . . There have been no adoptions of personal income taxes since the 30's. It is apparent that there is a trend toward increased reliance on taxes on consumption. The frequency with which general sales taxes have been enacted since World War II, the number of increases in sales tax rates, and the movement toward broadening the sales tax base to include some types of service, all point in this direction. Indeed, much of the revision in personal income tax laws has had somewhat the same effect, insofar as the coverage of the tax has been broadened and its impact increased through reductions in exemptions and increases in initial bracket tax rates.

This recital indicates that in some states there are substantial revenue sources which may be tapped. The difficulty is that the existence of untapped tax sources may not always be in the states where the requirements for higher expenditures are most pressing. The impact of population changes varies considerably with respect to schools, highways, and particularly urban access highways and streets, water and sanitation facilities and transportation; and the impact of these changes may be most severe in some jurisdictions where all the major revenue sources have already been tapped. On a state-by-state basis, therefore, we may run into situations where the tax problem will be acute in the next four or five years, even though for the states as a whole there appear to be sufficient tax sources to meet foreseen requirements.

SALES TAXES

Assuming that we will continue to increase our reliance on general sales taxes, there are several points concerning which legislative scrutiny will become increasingly important. Among these are the use of sales taxes by local governments, the inclusion of a broad range of services within the base of the tax, and the application of the tax to purchases by businesses.

Local governments are exerting pressure for access to non-property tax revenue sources, and particularly the sales tax. Where this is the case, the state-administered state and local sales tax—on the pattern developed in California, Illinois and Mississippi—merits careful study. Under this approach the tax base is uniform, and the taxpayer's compliance problems are simplified. For the local government the plan is advantageous because administrative burdens and costs are marginal; no separate local administrative staff is required. Moreover, the local government unit retains the power to decide whether the tax shall be imposed, which is not the case when a mandatory addition to the state rate is enacted, with subsequent distribution of the yield of this additional tax among all local governments.

Legislators in many states have expressed an interest in broadening the tax base. In the sales tax field this is evidenced by proposals to include recepits from specific services, or even to include all services within the tax base. However, the inclusion of services generally would add a large number of taxpayers to the rolls; it would possibly entail further dilution of field audit forces, which in many states are even now too small to provide adequate coverage of retailers selling tangible personal property. For this reason, in a state where a substantial portion of business purchases (materials consumed in industrial production, etc.) are not taxed, it might be the more practical policy to obtain the equivalent amount of new revenue simply by raising the existing sales tax rate, rather than by amending the sales tax law to include all services. This action would involve the assumption that non-business consumers of personal services are, by and large, the same people who are non-business consumers of tangible personal property. Whether these two categories of consumers are for all practical purposes the same remains to be determined, but in the absence of any evidence to the contrary the doubt might well be resolved in favor of holding down the number of reporting taxpayers.

Another point of concern to legislators is the matter of taxes which enter into production costs, and consequently affect the state's ability to maintain or expand its industrial status by attracting new industries. General sales taxes are within this category when they apply to materials consumed in manufacturing and processing, to machinery and equipment, and to electricity, fuels, etc. If we think the states will rely to an increasing extent on sales taxes, some consideration might be given to measures designed to minimize the impact of this policy on both local consumers and local producers. Sales tax costs are no different from other business costs, and by and large they show up with overhead markups in the retail prices of the goods produced. Thus, the consumer pays more sales tax in the long run, while the manufacturer who competes in regional or national markets may be less favorably situated than his competitors who are located in states where either there is no sales tax or, if there is one, sales of producers' goods and materials consumed directly in manufacturing or processing are excluded from the base of the tax.

This is a particularly important question for legislators in any state where the adoption of a retail sales tax is under consideration, or in a state where the sales tax has not been in effect so long that its main provisions have assumed the status of permanency. Once the taxation of producers' goods and materials consumed in production becomes fixed as a matter of practice, any proposal to change the law runs into the roadblock of replacement revenue, with the result that it is likely to fail. The situation is analogous to that commonly found in the property tax field, whereby work in progress, inventories and stock in trade continue to be taxed in spite of a host of official tax study committee recommendations that those types of property be exempted or be given preferential treatment.

PROPERTY TAXES

One tax which, more than any other, deserves the attention and careful study of legislators is the property tax. There is some tendency to dismiss the property tax with the once-over-lightly treatment, on the ground that it is becoming less and less important. But this is far from the truth. The property tax is now and will continue to be the base on which the state-local tax structure is built. Excluding highway-user revenues, which are largely dedicated to road purposes, property taxes now account for more than half of all state-local tax revenues, and while their relative importance may decline somewhat, they may still be expected to produce about half of all state-local revenues in the next ten to fifteen years.

The main difficulty about the property tax is the lack of uniformity in assessments, a factor which affects the distribution of the tax burden both directly and indirectly—indirectly because property tax assessments often constitute an important element in formulas for the distribution of state aid funds. Constitutional and statutory prescriptions of uniformity have been all too frequently overlooked; meantime, the wide differences which exist between statutory standards and actual levies of assessment have been demonstrated by assessment ratio studies in many states, and nationally by the study conducted as a part of the 1957 Census of Governments.

The legislatures in many states have been alert to the need for improvement in property tax administration. They have enacted laws designed to improve assessment organization and administration—by providing for districts of adequate size, by prescribing minimum qualifications for assessment personnel, by strengthening the supervisory powers of state agencies in the assessment field, by providing funds for training, technical assistance and reappraisal projects, etc. These programs are now showing their value in actual operations.

The outlook for continued improvement in the quality of assessments is at least fair, subject to one condition. The condition is that state legislators be willing and able to maintain the pressure for improvement in the assessment field, even though such action may affect the existing distribution of state grants, or may result in the shift of some part of the tax burden from one type of property tax to others, or from state-assesssed property to locally assessed property. These possibilities have to be faced in any jurisdiction where a long-continued but illegal practice of using different assessment ratios for various classes of property has in effect been frozen into the system.

Whether this situation is resolved rests with the legislatures, perhaps more than with any other branch of government, but, as of this time, the outlook is at best uncertain. At any rate, proposed corrective action involving shifts in the property tax burden has thus far had a lukewarm reception, even in legislatures which have been among the most forward in enacting legislation and providing facilities to improve the administration of the property tax.

TAX ADMINISTRATION

The quality of tax administration is another area which merits the attention of state legislative leaders. It is important under any circumstances to provide the funds and facilities for adequate and effective tax administration, and it is all the more so if, as seems to be the case, we are moving toward a broader use of taxes measured by business receipts, and particularly by receipts of businesses where the ratio of net profit to gross receipts is small.

The quality of state tax administration has improved considerably since World War II, although the degree of improvement varies within a fairly wide range among the states. There has been much progress in developing enforcement techniques and practices; in establishing criteria for the selection of audit cases; in determining the scope and number of audit cases necessary to ensure effective tax enforcement; in training personnel and in adapting the newest types of electronic computing, accounting and record keeping systems to use in tax administration. Nevertheless, there is still considerable room for improvement in this area.

The operation which could be strengthened in many states is the field audit of taxpayers' accounts. The field audit organization is the key to effective tax administration, and this is particularly true in respect to excises measured by business receipts, because here the states do not have the umbrella of the federal audit force as is the case in the income tax field.

There are indications that legislatures are loath to recommend appropriations for additional auditors unless each additional dollar spent will bring in $8 to $10 new revenue. Actually, if there is a prospect of returns of that magnitude, expansion of the audit force is imperative—not merely desirable. Yields of $3 to $4 for each additional dollar spent in field audit operations would reflect a less serious situation, but they would clearly indicate that tax enforcement activities are inadequate.

The range in field audit coverage in the sales tax field varies greatly among the states. Here are a few examples derived from data compiled within the past two years. The ratio of field auditors to registered taxpayers (sales tax accounts) among the several states varies from 1/468 to 1/3800. Several states report ratios of one auditor to 2,500 or more accounts, and there are many states where the ratio is in excess of one to 3,000. Field audit costs as a percentage of the total tax changes made by auditors range from 8.8 per cent to 48 per cent. These range points are roughly equivalent to field audit yields of $11 and $2 respectively for each field audit dollar spent. Most of the states surveyed fall in the group which reports a recovery of $4 to $6 for each field audit dollar spent.

Are these differences reflected in actual tax collection experience? The answer is an emphatic yes. For example, the per capita yield for each 1 per cent of sales tax levied was $14.02 in the 1/468 ratio state mentioned above, while the comparable figure in the 1/3800 ratio state was $10.76, even though food was exempt from tax in the first state and taxed in the second. Economic differences, of course, account for much of the difference in yields in these two states, but there are states with fairly similar economic characteristics where there is a difference of $1.00 in per capita yields of sales taxes on a 1 per cent rate basis. This may not appear to be a great difference, but in a state with a population, say, of 3 million, and a 3 per cent sales tax rate, it amounts to $9 million annually.

The revenue derived immediately as the result of field audit activities is by no means the most important thing about them. Legislators should remember that one of the real benefits of a field audit program, conducted over a period of years, is the improvement in the quality of the original returns filed by taxpayers; thus the important revenue effects of the program will show up more and more in the form of current payments and less in the form of deficiency assessments made after audit.

Even where there is a strong desire to improve the effectiveness of tax administration, the states run into another real problem, that of the retention of trained personnel. Too often state tax departments, and other departments, function as training grounds for industry and private professions, which hire away the good prospects. Generally speaking, the difficulty is inadequate salary scales for professional personnel —accountants, auditors, lawyers, valuation engineers, etc. There is a considerable variation in the salaries paid in these posts among the states, and even the highest may be less than the going rate for equal competence in private industry or private practice. Needless to say, there is also a great variation among the states in the quality and competence of professional personnel.

Although this situation is often attributed to a shortage of funds, it is difficult to accept that explanation. First, the strengthening of staff would surely increase revenues in most states. Second, and of greater importance, is the fact that in many states more than a sufficient amount of public funds are already allocated to the support of tax administration, in the broadest sense of the term; the difficulty is that a considerable proportion of these funds are returned directly to taxpayers and are not spent for enforcement purposes in the strict sense of the term. This is the case in those states where the taxpayer is permitted to retain a percentage of his tax as a compensation for his time and trouble in filling out the return and remitting the tax. There was approximately $37 million collected from the public in state sales taxes in 1959 which never found its way into state treasuries. Instead this amount was withheld and retained by reporting retailers as provided by law.

These retained taxes are substantial, relative to the amounts actually spent by the state for sales tax enforcement. For example, in state A the amount thus retained by retailers was $2.2 million; total expenditures by the tax department for sales and use tax administration were about $750,000. In another state retained collections were $1.68 million, and the costs of operating the sales tax division about $100,000.

In the long run it would be sound policy to discontinue these allowances and to make an equivalent sum, or as much of this sum as is necessary, available to improve the effectiveness of tax administration. The fact is that a good deal of this money is divided in small amounts among a very large number of small retailers; the bigger stores realize substantial amounts, but the payment only goes to increase net income and the United States Treasury takes half of it anyway. If these funds were available for tax enforcement, they could be spent under unified direction and control in a manner that would produce optimum results. It would very definitely be to the advantage of businessmen generally to have the assurance that the tax laws, and particularly sales, gross receipts and excise tax laws, were being enforced fairly and effectively. There is no better way of obtaining this assurance than to see to it that tax departments are properly staffed.

TAX RESEARCH

In the biennial session of 1957, about 3,000 tax laws were enacted in the states. It was estimated that the 1959 output was similar. Assuming that one bill of three introduced becomes law, this means that 9,000 to 10,000 tax bills go into the hopper. Some of these may be dismissed out of hand, but many require careful study. Since most bills proposed amendments to existing tax laws, it is logical that they be referred to the tax department for a report on their probable effects on one class or another of taxpayers, on the revenue, and on administration. This is precisely the procedure followed in many states, and while the legislature ultimately decides the policy involved, it does so with a full understanding of the probable consequences of passage or rejection.

In some states, however, this procedure cannot be followed because there are no organized research facilities in the tax department. In such cases a hastily drafted report, perhaps more intuitive than factual, is about all that may be expected. The committee chairman or a few of its hard working members may be, for all practical purposes, left on their own to develop, as best they can, with the very limited time and resources available, an understanding of what is involved in a bill.

Here is an area to which legislative attention—not in all states, but in some—might be directed with profit. Organized tax research isn't expensive; it is a facility which every state should have but which not all do, and it seems to me that it would be worth while to see that it is provided. This kind of facility will help the legislature to obtain a better understanding of the meaning and probable effect of proposed tax legislation. In the long run it should help to produce better tax legislation.

*   *   *

42. Justification for the Use of Sales Taxation*

JOHN F. DUE

THE basic arguments for the use of a sales tax center around three primary points: (1) the superiority of the expenditure basis of taxation to the income basis, from the standpoint of incentive effects, economic growth, and inflation-control, (2) the superiority of the sales tax from an administrative standpoint, compared to both the income tax and the spendings tax, the alternative form of expenditure-based taxation, and (3) the need for autonomous revenue sources on the part of the states in a Federal system. Each aspect will be discussed.

Incentive Effects and the Expenditure Basis of Taxation—A primary argument for the use of the consumption-expenditure basis of taxation, that is, the establishment of a tax structure in which tax liability depends upon consumption rather than income, is the claim that the expenditure basis avoids the adverse effects on economic incentives which an income tax, particularly a highly progressive one, creates. The complaints against the income tax on the basis of incentive effects are well known, and need not be repeated in detail. The income tax, by taking a portion of all earnings from investment, may restrict the development of new businesses and the expansion of old, in part by lessening the supply of money capital available for expansion, in part by lessening the incentives to expand. Incentive to avoid risky investment is particularly strong if capital gains are taxable as income. On the other hand, the sales tax does not affect the earn-

ings from new capital equipment directly (assuming that the total demand for goods produced with the equipment is unaffected by the tax) and does not even do so indirectly so long as the earnings are not used for the purchase of taxable goods.

Furthermore, the income tax, by taking a portion of all earnings from work, may alter the incentives to undertake work, particularly marginal activity, such as overtime work or that of additional members of the family. The effect may be in the direction of increasing the amount of work, if the family strives to maintain its old level of living despite the tax; it may reduce it if the elasticity of demand for income in terms of work is high. In cither case the tax can be charged with distorting work-leisure patterns. On the other hand, the sales tax will have no such effect, so long as additional income is desired for purposes free of sales tax, particularly saving. However, to the extent that additional income is sought for the purpose of acquiring additional goods subject to tax, the effects of the two taxes will be more nearly the same. Even in this case, however, there is apparently a tendency for workers to react more strongly to reductions in take-home monetary incomes than to reductions in the real values of their incomes through price increases. This phenomenon is illustrated by the much greater tendency of unions to strike against a reduction in real income arising out of a cut in money income than they are to strike against an equal reduction arising out of a rise in the price level.

Some advantages could be claimed

---

* Reprinted with permission from *Sales Taxation*, by John F. Due, Routledge & Kegan Paul, Ltd., 1957. Footnotes omitted.

for the sales tax with respect to incentive effects even if the income tax regarded as the alternative had proportional rates. But in practice most income taxes are progressive, and the sales tax may be regarded as a substitute for higher marginal rates of the tax. If the problem is posed in this form the relative advantages of the sales tax in avoiding adverse incentive effects are greater; high marginal rates of the income tax are particularly likely to restrict both investment and marginal labor activity of various forms. But this additional superiority of the sales tax can scarcely be attributed to the expenditure basis of the tax, but to the lack of progression; the extreme incentive effects of the income tax could be eliminated in such a case by alterations in the income tax, as well as by shift to the expenditure form. But in practice such a revision of the income tax might prove to be politically unpalatable, and thus establishment of a sales tax might be the only way to avoid the adverse effects of the high progression. Once a certain degree of progression is established, it is commonly regarded as political suicide to espouse the cause of lower progression, even though the existing degree may have been established with little rhyme or reason.

Long Range Capital Formation and Economic Development—A closely related advantage claimed for the sales tax because of its expenditure basis is the argument that such a tax restricts the long-range rate of capital formation and economic development less than income taxes. The sales tax does not lessen the *incentive* to save as does the income tax, and its burden is concentrated more heavily upon those persons who will be compelled to reduce consumption rather than savings. Thus, for a given sum of tax revenue, a greater portion of the sales tax will be absorbed from sums which would otherwise be spent on consumption than in the case of the income tax; thus the overall ratio of savings to national income will remain higher,

and the rate of capital formation which is possible without inflation will be greater. This effect is distinct from any effect which the income tax may have upon the incentives to undertake business expansion.

This argument, of course, is valid only if the total level of consumption, after taxes, is high enough to insure that investment does not lag behind savings at full employment levels. If investment is inadequate, all potential savings will not be utilized, and the actual rate of capital formation will lag behind the potential rate. The significance of the argument, even if investment is adequate, depends, of course, upon the actual extent to which the income tax reduces the overall ratio of savings to national income, and this cannot be determined at all precisely.

The argument, to the extent to which it is valid, has greatest significance in undeveloped countries, ones having obviously inadequate capital equipment relative to manpower. In such cases an increase in the rate of capital formation may allow a very sharp rise in the overall standard of living. In more highly developed countries, an increased rate of capital formation is not necessarily advantageous; the optimum rate of capital formation in such circumstances is difficult to define.

Equity Considerations—Despite the widespread acceptance of the principle that the income basis of taxation conforms most closely with accepted standards of equity, arguments are advanced that at least supplementary use of the sales tax can increase the overall equity of the tax structure. In most extreme form, this argument maintains that expenditures, not income, appropriately measure economic well-being and thus taxpaying ability, and that inclusion of the portion of income saved within the measure of the tax is basically inequitable. Closely related is the argument that inclusion results in discriminatory double taxation, since both the original income and the earnings on it are taxed. The taxation of the original income reduces the amount which can be saved and thus the amount of return on the savings, while the return itself is again subject to tax. This argument is open to serious question; the opposite point of view, that additions to savings constitute, in themselves, elements in the measure of economic well being, and that taxation of both saved income and the earnings from them does not constitute discriminatory double taxation in any meaningful sense are much more widely accepted.

In more moderate form the sales tax is defended on an equity basis on the grounds that the income basis tends to discriminate against persons who have not yet accumulated wealth compared to those who have, and places an inadequate burden on persons making large current consumption purchases out of previously accumulated wealth. The sales tax permits those persons who have not yet accumulated to do so without suffering tax burden on the portion of income used for this purpose, and it reaches effectively those persons spending from accumulated wealth. Also, the sales tax insures some payment from persons who, legally, or illegally, are able to escape adequate payment under the income tax.

Furthermore, the income tax does not differentiate between various forms of income on the basis of differences in spending power, in any satisfactory way. The greater the accumulated wealth which a person already has, the greater is the spending power of additional income, since he is under no compulsion to save for purposes of emergency. Furthermore, the greater the assurance of continuation of the income, the greater is the spending power involved. The sales tax provides the differentiation because it applies only to the actual amounts spent.

Ease of Administration—One of the primary arguments for the use of the sales tax in preference to both income taxes and spending taxes is the greater ease of administration. In the first place, the sales tax is collected from a relatively small number of business firms, instead of from a large number of individuals, and thus control is easier and less expensive. Secondly, the tax is collected on the basis of figures of total sales, which are much easier to ascertain and subject to less interpretative questions than net earnings, which must be calculated for the portion of the income tax applying to any type of business activity. Thirdly, it avoids the fundamental problems of delimiting income in the case of capital gains in a period of changing prices.

This argument is of particular significance with respect to the lower income groups, for which income tax administration may become expensive, relative to revenue. In a country with large numbers of persons in the lower income groups, an income tax with reasonable exemptions is likely to reach only a small proportion of the population; if the remainder are to make some contribution to tax revenue, the sales tax may be the only feasible basis.

Administrative considerations also serve as an argument in favor of the sales-tax type of expenditures tax relative to the spendings tax, which would be based upon consumer expenditures, but would be collected directly from individuals by means of returns.

The argument of administrative effectiveness has played a particularly important role in the development of sales taxation in countries in which standards of tax administration, tax compliance, and literacy are relatively low. In such countries effective collection of income taxes is almost impossible, and reliance upon sales taxation becomes imperative. This is a partial explanation of the dominance of commodity taxation in many countries two and three centuries ago, and of its continued importance in some countries down to the present time.

The Sales Tax in Federal Government Structures—A further argument has relevance only to countries with Federal or semi-Federal governmental structures.

In such countries, there is a tendency for the Federal governments to dominate the income tax field; with high Federal rates it becomes difficult, as a practical, political matter, for the states to rely heavily upon this source of revenue. As a consequence, particularly if they receive only limited financial support from the Federal government, there is a tendency for them to turn to sales taxes in order to obtain a significant autonomous source of tax revenue. The importance of state sales taxation in the United States can be attributed in part to this situation.

The Merits of Sales Taxes Compared to Excise Taxes—The preceding discussion has centered around the relative merits of the sales tax relative to income taxes. But the tax may also be compared with its cousin, a system of excise or special sales taxes. As compared to this type of tax, the sales tax has three major advantages. In the first place, because of its greater coverage, a lower rate is possible for the raising of a given sum. The lower the rate, the less is the incentive given to evasion and the less serious are the objectionable results of the tax, other features being the same. But more significantly, the sales tax avoids the inevitable discrimination created by the excise taxes against those persons who have relatively high preferences for the taxed articles. This discrimination may in some instances be justified on the basis of deliberate social policy, as in the case of the tax on liquor. Or it may be regarded as justifiable because of special benefits received by the persons paying the tax, as in the case of the gasoline tax. But with most commodities, the consequent discrimination is contrary to usually accepted standards of equity. A sales tax, if properly designed, is uniform on all consumption expenditures.

Finally, the excise taxes will lead to reallocation of consumer demand and thus a reallocation of resources. If it is assumed that the allocation of resources is at the optimum, in terms of consumer demand, before the tax is introduced, the reallocation may reduce economic welfare. If a tax on theatre tickets causes persons to take walks for amusement when they would prefer to go to the theatre, the persons lose satisfaction (find themselves on lower indifference curves), yet the government gets no revenue. If, of course, the optimum was not previously attained, the tax could conceivably result in a more optimum resource allocation. But it is almost inconceivable that a widespread excise tax system could do this by accident on any scale, and review of excise tax systems, such as that of the United States, suggests on the basis of common-sense observations that the opposite is much more likely to be true. . . .

THE OBJECTIONS TO SALES TAXATION

The primary objections to the use of sales taxation are likewise so well known that detailed analysis is unnecessary, but a review of them is desirable.

Equity Arguments—The basic and most widely accepted objection centers around the distribution of the burden of the tax by income group, under the assumption that the tax is shifted forward to the final consumers of the products. The tax tends to place a relatively heavy burden on all persons whose expenditures on taxable goods constitute relatively high percentages of their incomes. Such a distribution pattern is not necessarily inherently objectionable. A defense could be made for placing a heavier tax on a person who spends substantial amounts in excess of his income for consumption purchases than that on a person with the same income who spends less on consumption and uses the balance for business expansion. But it is argued that the relatively heavier burden is in many cases inflicted on persons ill able to pay it, with consequent inequity. In the first place, persons in the lower income groups tend to spend higher percentages of their incomes and save lower percentages than those in the higher income groups; as a consequence, if the sales tax applies to all consumption expenditures, the tax will tend to be regressive relative to income. In Chapter II, the results of several studies of the actual pattern of distribution of burden were summarized; in general, with food taxable, the burden is highly regressive. These results must be interpreted with some care; in any particular period, the lower income groups will include some persons who are in these income levels only temporarily, and whose consumption patterns are largely conditioned by past and expected future income. But nevertheless, the results have some significance.

In many cases, governments have sought to reduce the degree of regressiveness by the exemption of food. As shown in Chapter II, food exemption materially reduces not only the relative regressiveness of the tax, but also the absolute burden on the lowest income groups. In other cases, governments have sought to introduce some degree of progression by applying higher rates to a number of commodities regarded as "luxuries". . . . But this policy results in some discrimination among consumers on the basis of taste, as does food exemption to a somewhat lesser extent.

The general regressiveness of the tax is not so much an argument against use of the sales tax, but against excessive reliance upon it as an element in the overall tax structure. So long as the sales tax remains a minor segment of the total, any regressiveness which it may have is more than offset by the progressiveness of the income tax, at least for those income groups affected by the income tax. Unfortunately the income taxes of some countries, of which the United States is an outstanding example, are not significantly progressive for the great majority of taxpayers which fall into the first income

tax bracket and are all taxed at the same rate.

Apart from the overall tendency to place a relatively heavy burden on persons in the lower income groups, the tax tends to penalize any groups whose circumstances compel them to spend higher percentages of their incomes to attain a given standard of living. Thus the tax tends to burden large families more heavily than smaller families with the same income, since the former must spend a higher percentage of income to attain a given living standard. Essentially the large family has less taxpaying ability than the smaller, yet the sales tax burden upon it will be greater. Newly married couples spending high percentages of income for consumer durables, persons losing property by casualty and forced to replace it, persons who are ill and required to buy expensive medicines are all subjected to relatively heavy burden, compared to that on others with comparable incomes. At the very best, the sales tax is a relatively crude method of distributing burden among various people— although admittedly it does place a more satisfactory burden than the income tax on persons spending large amounts from accumulated wealth and on those able to escape the income tax.

*　　*　　*

Deflationary Effects—The argument that a sales tax is superior to an income tax as an instrument of inflation control . . . suggests a relative disadvantage of the sales tax, compared to the usual type of income tax, in any period in which there is a tendency toward unemployment. The sales tax not only impinges more heavily on the lower income groups, which spend, on the average, higher percentages of their incomes, but likewise gives at least a limited incentive to spend less and save more. Not only is the direct restrictive effect upon consumption greater, per dollar of tax revenue, than that of the income tax, but as a consequence of the decline in consumption, the restrictive effect upon investment may also be greater. The direct and immediate restrictive effect of an income tax upon the incentive to undertake investment may be greater than that of a sales tax, as outlined above, but investment depends in large measure upon the volume of consumption sales. Thus to the extent to which the sales tax curtails the latter to a greater extent than an income tax, the net final deflationary effect may be greater.

Effects upon Allocation of Resources and Methods of Production—A universal sales tax, completely shifted to the final consumer, and applying only to final consumption goods, should be completely neutral with respect to allocation of consumer income among commodities—and thus resource allocation—and with respect to choice of methods of production. But . . . sales taxes are typically not of this character. Any exemption from the tax will tend to increase relative consumption of the commodities affected; if this cannot be defended on the basis of general economic or social policy, it must be regarded as contrary to optimum economic welfare. . . .

*   *   *

GENERAL EVALUATION

In terms of usual standards of equity, a sales tax, no matter how carefully established, is inferior to the income tax. It tends to penalize persons whose circumstances compel them to spend relatively high percentages of their incomes to attain given standards of living, and it cannot be adjusted satisfactorily in terms of various considerations which effect taxpaying ability at given income levels, such as numbers of dependents and medical expenses. It frequently operates in perverse fashion, striking more heavily the persons least able to pay. Certain modifications, such as the exemption of food, may alleviate the basic objection of the heavy burden

placed on the poor, but cannot solve all inequities and often create new ones. The basic case for permanent use of a sales tax must rest upon three primary arguments:

1. The danger that the raising of income taxes beyond certain levels will seriously impair economic incentives, and thus reduce the level of national income and the rate of economic growth.

2. The need for autonomous revenue sources for states and Federal governments in a Federal system.

3. The difficulties of administering a broad-coverage income tax in countries with relatively low standards of tax administration and compliance, and the difficulties of administering a spendings tax. . . .

Thus the case for use of sales taxation is strongest under the following circumstances:

1. When the overall level of governmental expenditures is so high that the income tax, together with other suitable taxes, cannot yield adequate revenues without serious incentive effects. The case for the sales tax, of course, increases as these incentive effects become more clearly demonstrated; in many countries, such as the United States, there is actually little evidence of them at the present time.

2. When a rapid rate of economic growth is imperative if standards of living are to be improved, and it is obvious that high income taxes will lessen the potential rate of capital formation by reducing significantly the overall propensity to save. A sales tax compels a temporary reduction in consumption and insures that the savings of the higher income groups will be available for capital formation. This argument is, of course, of primary importance in undeveloped countries.

3. In countries in which administrative standards and taxpayer attitudes do not permit effective enforcement of income taxes applying to a high percentage of the population. If income levels are such that very large numbers of per-

sons would be paying only small amounts of income tax, the problems with income tax enforcement are multiplied.

4. In countries with Federal governmental structures, to insure autonomous revenue for one of the levels of government, particularly the state level. Unfortunately in some Federal countries the Federal governments have preempted both the income and sales tax fields.

In countries in which there is relatively little inequality in income distribution, and thus the significance of the regressiveness of the pattern of burden distribution is minimized.

On the whole, the sales tax must be regarded as a second-best tax—one to be employed only if various circumstances make complete reliance on income and other more suitable taxes undesirable. A carefully designed sales tax is not perhaps as objectionable as it was once regarded; it offers definite advantages over widespread excise tax systems, with their inevitable discrimination among various consumers and business firms and their tendency to distort consumption patterns; and it is definitely superior to high rate "business" taxes with uncertain incidence and possible serious economic effects. But it must be regarded as secondary to income taxation, in terms of usually accepted standards of taxation.

43. The Place of the Property Tax in the State-Local Revenue System*

ADVISORY COMMISSION ON INTERGOVERNMENTAL RELATIONS

OF the $18.0 billion of property tax revenues in 1961 nearly $17.4 billion went to the local governments and only $0.6 billion or 3.5 percent to the State governments; but this huge revenue item was of as much concern to State governments as if all of it were their own money. Each State and its localities share in one governing job and must draw from the same aggregate of resources to pay the costs. Since the State creates the local governments and determines their share of the governing role, it must see to it that their financial resources match their responsibilities. To the extent that sufficient revenue is not raised locally the State must provide it—or rely on the Federal Government to provide it.

* Reprinted from *The Role of the States in Strengthening the Property Tax*, Advisory Commission on Intergovernmental Relations, 1963. Footnotes and table omitted.

The property taxes of local governments in 1961 represented 87.7 percent of local tax revenue, virtually the same proportion that prevailed through the 1950's. The bulk of the remainder was accounted for by the sales, gross receipts, and income taxes that some of the larger municipalities are using successfully as partial replacements for the property tax. These replacement sources, however, are identical with the major sources on which the States rely actually or potentially for the bulk of their tax revenue. To the extent that they are used locally they are not available to the State governments. While the local governments are using most of the property taxes, dipping into the major nonproperty tax sources that form the base of the State level tax structures, and drawing on various kinds of minor local tax and nontax revenue, they are depending on the upper levels of government for a substantial portion of their general revenue needs—about 30 percent in 1961.

No lessening of the pressure for more State-local revenue is in prospect. State and local government responsibilities are bound to continue their growth as a rising and increasingly urban population requires more and higher-type services. The State governments face a dual demand that points to higher rates for their sales, gross receipts, and income taxes, or the need for adopting such taxes if they do not already have them—a demand for more State purpose revenue and a demand for more fiscal aid to local governments. Inevitably the property tax, a broadly productive tax that is exclusively in the realm of State-local government, will have to carry its share of the load.

INTERSTATE VARIATIONS IN USE OF THE PROPERTY TAX

On a nationwide basis the property tax, although it has declined in relative importance over the years, continues to be the largest single source in the State-local tax system. It accounted for 46.3 percent of all State-local tax revenue in 1961 and had not deviated much from this relationship for several years. This national figure, however, conceals vast differences among the States in property tax policy. In the individual States property tax revenues in 1961 ranged from 13 to 70 percent of total tax revenues, with the percentages for only 14 of the States concentrated in the 40-50 percent range. The distribution was as [shown in the accompanying table].

The States have impelling reasons, as can be seen, for a new look at the property tax. Their views as to its proper role in their overall tax systems are sure to vary, but none of them can afford to disregard its potential value for the demanding years ahead. Those States that place substantial dependence on the property tax can increase its reliability by raising the quality of its administration. The few States that have not found it necessary to put much dependence on this tax can turn to it for a better-balanced revenue system. Those States that have permitted it to decline to a minor position through pressure or neglect, or have reduced its productivity through maladministration, or fear to put more reliance on it because its management is defective, have weakened their financial outlook. The States now undertaking remedial action are showing foresight, because constructive changes in the management and use of the tax are not effected overnight and smooth adjustment can avoid harsh emergency measures at some later date.

THE PROPERTY TAX AND LOCAL SELF-GOVERNMENT

One factor that should be kept in view in determining the future position of the property tax is its close alignment with the outlook for local self-government. It is the only major tax adaptable to local use generally, regardless of the size and nature of the local jurisdiction. Aside from being a good revenue producer it has the dependability and adjustability that local governments need. The required revenue yield can be obtained from year to year with a convenient range of flexibility and a satisfactory degree of precision, and the collectability of most classes of property taxes is assured by an enforceable lien on the property. These virtues are vitiated in practice, however, if highly restrictive tax rate limits combine with deep underassessment to relegate the property tax to an inflexibly minor role in local government finance and inferior assessment administration stultifies the tax's reputation.

In at least a few States the spleen against the property tax has been so intense as to generate constantly increasing fiscal aid to local governments regardless of whether the local fiscal

Under 20 percent	20 to 29.9 percent	30 to 39.9 percent	40 to 49.9 percent	50 to 59.9 percent	60 and over
Hawaii.... 12.7	Alabama... 20.8	Georgia.... 30.4	Florida.... 40.6	North Dakota... 50.8	Kansas ... 60.4
	Delaware.. 22.7	Kentucky.. 31.1	Maryland.. 42.2	Maine...... 51.1	New Hampshire.... 62.8
	South Carolina.. 23.0	Washington. 31.5	Vermont... 44.6	Ohio...... 51.9	New Jersey...... 67.2
	Louisiana.. 23.0	Oklahoma... 32.2	New York.. 44.7	Wyoming... 52.6	Nebraska.. 70.5
	Alaska...... 24.4	Tennessee.. 32.7	Arizona... 45.4	Illinois..... 54.2	
	New Mexico .. 26.4	Pennsylvania... 34.0	Missouri.... 46.1	Wisconsin... 55.0	
	North Carolina . 28.3	Nevada..... 35.7	Utah....... 46.8	Minnesota... 55.1	
	Mississippi . 28.4	Virginia..... 36.7	Rhode Island.... 47.5	Indiana..... 55.3	
	Arkansas... 28.7		Idaho..... 47.7	Connecticut. 56.4	
	West Virginia.. 29.0		Oregon...... 48.2	Montana..... 57.0	
			Texas...... 48.7	Iowa....... 57.4	
			Colorado... 48.9	South Dakota.. 57.7	
			California... 49.7	Massachusetts...... 59.1	
			Michigan... 49.7		
Number of States... 1	10	8	14	13	4

effort is adequate, or to deprive them of the opportunity to develop sound budgeting and capital financing policies. That inept and inequitable property assessment should be a barrier to reasonable dependence on the property tax, as it is in numerous communities, is a reflection on the State governments that have permitted such a condition to continue. Determination of the property tax base is strictly an administrative function demanding technical competence. The State itself could provide this service uniformly and efficiently on a statewide basis without encroaching on local prerogatives to determine fiscal policy and make financial plans.

An increasing recognition by tax study commissions and State legislatures that neglect and underuse of the property tax have been detrimental to both local and State governments is an encouraging development. The following are representative conclusions:

In Alabama, which has been depending on the property tax for only one-fifth of its State-local tax revenues, a tax study commission reported in 1957:

> In summary, many of the considerable pressures on the legislature to increase State appropriations are a direct result of the comparable low tax effort made by the local governments of Alabama. Conversely, the preemption of the most productive sources of revenue by the State, together with virtual neglect of the property tax, has left localities, particularly cities, with limited revenue resources. The trend has clearly been toward a highly centralized revenue system; the results, in part, have been low levels of services at the municipal level, and a heavy reliance on the several taxes administered at the State level . . . The comparative decline of the tax in Alabama may be attributed to constitutional rate limitations, numerous exemptions, and faulty assessment administration.

In South Carolina, where the property tax also is a relatively minor revenue factor, Prof. G. H. Aull, a tax economist who has made a number of notable studies of the property tax in the State, has characterized the State's property tax system as being "in a state of utter disgrace" and has declared:

> Because of the breakdown in this important source of local revenue the State has poured a substantial amount of other tax revenue into an attempt to shore up the structure of local government. In choosing this course (rather than forcing a modernizing of property tax laws), the State has neglected other important functions and weakened its own financial position without at the same time making any permanent contribution to the cause of local self government.

A tax study commission in Washington, reporting in 1958 on how to close the impending gap between expenditure needs and the yield of the existing revenue system, said, among other things:

> Fundamental to the concept of strong, effective local government is the proposition that the service responsibilities of local government should be balanced by fiscal capacity to maintain them at the level desired by the local taxpayers. This is of the essence of local self-government. Failure to insure this principle in Washington by a history of assessments below the level required by the State constitution and statutes has resulted in the need for increased State grants and shared revenues, and has contributed heavily to the shift of responsibilities from local government to the State . . . *A vigorous effort must be made to rehabilitate the property tax, to make it more equitable among property owners, and at the same time make it more responsive to the revenue needs of the various units of local government . . .*

In West Virginia, where the State

government is supervising a statewide revaluation of taxable property, a tax study commission concluded in 1960 "that the property tax should be called upon to bear more of the increasing costs of local government and the public schools," and recommended "the furtherance of the statewide property revaluation program as rapidly as possible as a means of eliminating or reducing the inequities of property assessment and making more money available on the local level for public schools, county and municipal governments."

MORE REVENUE THROUGH BETTER ASSESSMENT ADMINISTRATION

More dependence can be placed on the property tax when assessment administration meets high standards, i.e., when all taxable property is on the tax roll, all property is assessed uniformly in relation to market value, and the assessment level has not been allowed to deteriorate. In fact, the establishment of these conditions where they have not prevailed in the past may increase the productivity of the tax without increasing the burden of the taxpayers who have been paying their fair share of the total.

In the great majority of States there probably is little taxable real property that is escaping assessment. Even in recent years, however, searching reappraisals in some States have discovered considerable areas of land and numerous improvements that were not on the assessment rolls, and have found many assessing offices that were not equipped with adequate maps and other guides that would prevent such omissions.

In many of the 46 States that tax some or all kinds of personal property there would appear to be large amounts of such property that have been eluding the assessor entirely or have been assessed very nominally. Personal property has been losing ground relatively

as a tax base; it represented only 15.9 percent of all locally assessed property in the United States in 1961, compared with 17.4 percent in 1956. Undoubtedly there is a sizeable revenue potential in personal property taxes that is awaiting development; but . . . the tax must be worthy of enforcement, the tax law must be made administrable, and the administrative provisions must be adequate.

The derogatory mythology that has been built around the property tax in many parts of the country is partly a product of maladministration. Raising the quality of administration of the tax to that of other major taxes may not make the taxpayer enjoy paying the tax, but he is much more likely to pay it without resentment if he has assurance that assessments are reasonably uniform, that all taxable property is sharing proportionately in the burden, and that the tax holds a carefully considered position in a well-balanced State-local revenue system. Establishment of competent professional tax administration, regular publicizing of reliable data on the level and quality of assessment, and facilitation of appeal of assessments by the taxpayer are the important keys to maintaining the productivity of the property tax in areas where it is in substantial use and to increased dependence on it in areas of subnormal use.

STATE USE OF THE PROPERTY TAX

Thirty-seven States, according to the Census Bureau, still levy some kind of State property tax that produces at least $1 million annually. The aggregate of such taxes in 1962, however, was only $640 million or 3.1 percent of total State tax revenue; in many of the States the amount levied is relatively negligible; and over one-half of the total amount comprises special property taxes rather than general property taxes.

The general property tax, which supplied about half of all State tax revenue in 1902, has been abandoned largely or entirely for State use by State after State. In 1932 it still accounted for 22 percent of all State tax revenue, but by 1942 the proportion had dropped to 3.5 percent and in 1962 it was only 1.3 percent. Of the 27 States that still levy a State general property tax, only a few place much dependence on it. In 1962 it accounted for 28.6 percent of State tax revenue in Nebraska, 18.0 percent in Wyoming and 13.3 percent in Arizona. In five States it provided between 5 and 10 percent and in seven other States between 3 and 5 percent. . . .

Prior to 1930 six States had given up the general property tax for State purposes, influenced largely by the theory that it was desirable to separate State and local revenue sources and the belief that this policy would discourage competitive underassessment. The 1930's brought sweeping replacement of State general property taxes by new sources of State revenue and a dozen States withdrew entirely or almost entirely from the tax. In some instances this policy was directed primarily to helping hard-pressed local governments; but depression conditions gave property tax relief great popular appeal and some States combined abandonment of the tax for State purposes with increased restrictions on its local use. In the late 1940's, when the States were still enjoying their war-generated affluence, five more States—Arkansas, Connecticut, Massachusetts, New Jersey, and Tennessee—withdrew from the tax. Texas adopted a constitutional amendment in 1948 (effective in 1951) prohibiting State use of the tax for general purposes, though continuing its use for confederate pensions and part of the State aid for schools. Maine withdrew from the tax (except in unorganized areas) in 1951, but authorized local governments to continue levying the State rate for local purposes. Neither of the two newest States levies a general property tax, Alaska having discontinued its use for territorial purposes in 1953 and Hawaii having dedicated it to local use in 1911.

State general property taxes are used mainly for the financing of State government but some of the proceeds are directed to local purposes, mostly public schools. An analysis by McGehee H. Spears of the U.S. Department of Agriculture indicated that the total of such taxes in 1957 was distributed 31 percent for the State general funds, 24 percent for public schools, 18 percent for other education, 15 percent for debt service, and 12 percent for various earmarked purposes. An indeterminate portion of the tax going to the general funds is directed to local aid; Missouri, for example, has been allocating one-third to counties for the support of schools. Public schools have been receiving all of the State tax in Utah, around four-fifth of it in Texas and Wyoming, and smaller portions in several other States. A dozen States use the State tax to pay principal and interest on some or most of their general purpose debt. Maryland uses its tax entirely for this purpose, and Iowa and Ohio, which previously had abandoned the tax, readopted it to service veterans' bonus bonds. Some States, among them Illinois, New Jersey, and Oregon, while they do not levy general property taxes for debt, specifically provide for standby support from such taxes for this purpose.

THE CASE FOR A STATE GENERAL PROPERTY TAX

The abandonment of the State general property tax by nearly one-half of the States and the contraction of its use for State purposes to a minimal level by most of the others have relinquished to local governments a major tax that all of them can use; but the results have disclosed fallacies in the theory of separation of State and local sources of revenue.

Administratively, the withdrawal of the States from the general property tax has had some detrimental effects. It removed the most obvious need for statewide equalization of assessments, tended to make State supervision of local assessing even more perfunctory than it had been, and obscured the need for joint State-local responsibility for conducting, coordinating, and standardizing assessment administration. Some legislatures have been reluctant to appropriate money for the State's share of administering a tax that produced little or no State revenue. It must be said, however, that in a number of cases State responsibilities had been so badly met that there was little room for deterioration, and in some States such detrimental effects as did develop are being overcome by constructive State action. The necessity for statewide equalization of assessments for collateral purposes has been emphasized by the widespread development of equalizing school aid programs, and the more alert legislatures are realizing that skilled State participation in local property tax administration can strengthen the tax and lessen the need for State aid from other revenue sources.

A main defect of the separation of sources policy that assigns the general property tax to be levied by local governments for their basic support is the failure of the distribution of taxable property in a State to coordinate with the distribution of population and the cost of local government. The inequity is intensified in many States by the highly subdivided local government structure. Two residential suburbs, for example, may have equal governmental needs, but the taxable property per capita in one may be vastly higher than in the other. A huge industry may enrich the taxing power of the taxing district which it dominates while its employees inhabit an adjoining district whose taxable property comprises mainly their modest dwellings. Among rural areas there is a similar lack of such coordination. Some well-to-do communities have been able, by incorporating as local governments, to insulate themselves from payment of a proportionate share of the property taxes levied in the State.

An increasing local awareness of this uncoordinated situation, particularly among small suburban communities, has induced local protectionist planning and zoning policies that are a hindrance to sound metropolitan area planning. The fractionalized character of the local government structure in metropolitan areas is in itself a deterrent to land use planning for the well-balanced economic development of such areas; but when the planning and zoning in each small community seek to produce a local economic balance that will hold down tax rates, i.e., are more or less dominated by local fiscal considerations, the important area wide objectives are additionally thwarted. In proposing a partial solution for this problem through the levy of a State property tax for local apportionment, Lynn A. Stiles has observed that "The whole idea of 'economic balance' in so narrow a context is absurd. And if the tax structure is a force animating the drive for balance of this sort, then clearly something needs to be done about the tax system."

How to moderate the inequalities in local property tax burdens that arise because of the varying local relationships between fiscal ability and public service needs is one of the really perplexing problems in State-local fiscal relations. By eliminating abnormally high tax rate areas at one extreme and opportunities for tax shelter in low tax rate areas at the other extreme, there would be fewer local communities facing the alternatives of deficient public services or excessive tax burdens, more flexibility for well-planned metropolitan area development, and the potential for a larger overall contribution from the general property tax to State-local revenues without injustice to any locality.

Expanding the jurisdiction of taxing districts has an equalizing effect. Some equalization is accomplished by the consolidation of school districts, and a few States provide for an equalizing county school tax to help support local school districts. Some consideration has been given to the creation of metropolitan area taxing districts for equalizing as well as revenue producing purposes, and there are a few large multi-county metropolitan districts with property taxing powers that illustrate this effect. The ultimate in this equalizing development would be a statewide taxing district; i.e., a state property tax could be levied at a uniform rate for local use, to be distributed in such manner as to help equalize the cost of providing locally administered public services that should meet minimum standards on a statewide basis.

Various means of using this device are worth consideration. State assessed public utility property might be taxed by the State at the statewide average rate in lieu of locally imposed taxes, as is done in Michigan and Wisconsin, with the proceeds distributed locally on some equitable formula. The States might take over the assessment of all industrial property, which has a notably uneven local distribution, and follow the tax procedure suggested for utility property. A great majority of the States purport to follow the equivalent of this device for public schools, but by means that are less satisfactory than the actual levy of a State property tax.

The need for equalization of the local property tax effort has been recognized increasingly by the States in the area of public school financing by their adoption of school foundation programs. The theoretical intent of such programs is to set a minimum standard for local school expenditure per pupil, require a uniform tax effort in all districts by the application of a specified tax rate to the equalized valuation, provide for State aid, usually from some nonproperty tax source, to supply the difference between the local tax yield and the standard requirement, and leave it to each district to raise additional revenue if it wishes to conduct a more costly program.

What seems in theory to be a workable device for statewide equalization of a major portion of local property taxes turns out in practice to be defective in its operation in some States and usually is not only distorted from its equalizing purpose but is submerged in a cumbersome hocus pocus of school aid formulas that are completely unintelligible to the general public. In a number of States the mandated local tax rates are still based on unequalized or defectively equalized local assessed valuations, thus encouraging competitive underassessment. Where there is State equalization of assessments the basis in most instances is a fraction of full value which understates fiscal ability, and the laborious and costly task of equalization is directed primarily to interarea equalization, including equalization of assessing mistakes, rather than to improving the quality of local assessment.

* * *

44. What Ails Property Tax?*

ROGER A. FREEMAN

It has been said that the property tax is like a mule: no pride in ancestry, no chance of progeny. History records innumerable attempts to make the property tax fair and equitable; few of them succeeded for any length of time. Evasion and inequity have characterized property taxation through the ages.

*Reprinted with permission from *National Municipal Review*, November 1955.

The principle of ad valorem taxation is ancient. The settlers of the Massachusetts Bay Colony, 300 years ago, "levied every man according to his estate." They took this concept from Elizabethan forms of taxation which can be traced back as far as William the Conqueror's Domesday Book. The earliest mention seems to be a real estate tax which the legendary Roman King Servius Tullius slapped on his unsuspecting subjects in the sixth century before Christ. The Romans soon after abolished the kings but they were never able to abolish the tax.

In the United States property was undoubtedly burdened with too great a share of the cost of government until about twenty years ago, when property tax collections totalled more than all other taxes—federal, state and local—together.

The picture changed drastically in the past quarter century: the property tax turned from a major into a minor item on our tax bill. For some years now it has accounted for only 11 per cent of all taxes. To be sure, property tax collections have not declined. . . . But other taxes outpaced them. Governments in the United States now derive 63 per cent of their tax revenues from income taxes and 26 per cent from excise taxes.

Property taxes claimed about 5 per cent of our national income in the early part of the twentieth century, took 6 per cent in 1929, jumped to 12 per cent during the depression years and fell back to 6 per cent by 1939. Since then our income has climbed faster than property taxes. In recent years property taxes have equalled about 3 per cent of the national income.

*   *   *

But the property tax still is an essential part of our tax structure. As long as the over-all burden is as heavy as it is, we must of necessity diversify the forms of taxation by which we measure each man's contribution. Ad valorem taxes which are gauged by the owner-ship of property as a major economic resource serve to provide a better balance of the burden of government. No other tax is equally well suited for imposition by local jurisdictions. Land and houses stay put. The continued existence of local government is inextricably tied to the property tax base.

PROPERTY TAX DECLINE

In the past two decades other sources of municipal income have sprung up —sales, business and income or payroll taxes. . . . Municipal non-property taxes will keep growing at a moderate pace. But the property tax will continue to be called upon to supply the bulk of local government revenues.

The relative decline of the property tax was caused by several developments:

1. State government, which used to receive a substantial part of its income from property taxes, virtually withdrew from the field.

2. Several major functions which had been responsibilities of local government were partially or completely shifted to state or federal governments. This is particularly true of public welfare, roads and schools.

3. The pasture of state and federal aid looked greener. . . .

Looking toward the future we seem to face a choice between two alternatives:

1. We can continue the trend of transferring activities and responsibilities to higher levels of government. We can easily foresee that such a policy will slowly but surely turn local governments—and eventually state governments—into mere field offices of the federal government.

2. We can strengthen the fiscal powers of local government so that it can cope with its residual responsibilities. This process will inevitably include a program of vitalizing the property tax.

3. If we are to follow the second alternative we shall need to correct the

major shortcomings of the present property tax administration. They are:

1. *Exemptions.* The number of tax exemptions has been increasing to a point where we are dealing less and less with a "general" property tax. Thirteen states grant homestead exemptions, sixteen states veteran exemptions from $500 up to $5,000 assessed value. Because assessed values are only a fraction of current values, far more residential property escapes taxation than was intended. About a dozen states permit the exemption of new industrial property. Eight states do not tax personalty and a number of states make other concessions. Various studies have shown that exemptions are an ineffective and costly method of attracting industrial location. Exemptions are of course popular with the groups for whose benefit they were enacted but it is not sufficiently realized how much of an additional burden they place on non-favored classes of property owners.

IN LIEU PAYMENTS

The federal government enjoys immunity from local taxation. A few agencies make payments in lieu of taxes; e.g., Tennessee Valley Authority, Atomic Energy Commission, Housing and Home Finance Agency. Other departments share revenues with state and local governments (forests, grazing, minerals). Some assistance is given to schools in federally affected areas. But many of these payments fall short of a fair contribution to local government. What is needed—and was recommended by the Commision on Intergovernmental Relations—is a comprehensive system of payments in lieu of taxes in those cases where the federal government has acquired land or buildings in recent years and operates facilities which serve essentially national purposes or commercial operations.

Much state and local government property which is used for proprietary operations, particularly in the utilities

field, escapes taxation. Its share is shifted to the general taxpayer.

2. *Rate Limitations.* Limitations on property tax rates have been used for almost a century but became more widespread in the early 1930s. Nine states now have over-all rate limitations. Almost all states limit the property taxing powers of their political subdivisions and municipal corporations to a maximum millage. Some states permit these rates to be exceeded by popular vote; others do not.

These millage limitations were established at a time when the scope and standards of public services were much lower than they are today. Debt limits which in almost all states are based on assessed valuations frequently prevent local governments from financing school buildings and other badly needed improvements.

These taxing and bonding limits are often cut to a half, a third or less of their statutory level by the practice of assessing property at a fraction of its full value.

3. *Fractional Assessment.* Constitutional and statutory provisions notwithstanding, property has, with rare exceptions, probably never been assessed at full value. In 1929 real estate assessments in the U.S. totalled $135 billion. It was estimated at the time that the true value was about as twice as high. The value of real estate may now be estimated at between $600 and $700 billion. Real estate assessments in the United States total only $200 billion. In other words, real estate is on the average assessed at less than one third of its current value. . . .

Sometimes fractional assessments are rationalized by claiming that current prices are inflated. That is a confusion of terms. What is inflated is not the prices but our currency: we are dealing in 50-cent dollars. The price of real estate is expressed in the same dollars with which we pay taxes and with which cities and schools must pay their salaries and other costs. The statement that assessments are set at "normal" values is an attempt to evade by dialectic means the clear mandate of the law. Appraisals of real estate for other than tax purposes—for banks, insurance, loan companies, prospective buyers—do not seem to be plagued with a concept of "normal" value.

In the 25 states where the state government still receives some share of property tax collections, there is positive encouragement to competitive under-assessment as means of minimizing local contributions. Half the states distribute grants-in-aid on formulas based on local wealth as evidenced by assessed values. This system penalizes correct assessment and rewards under-assessment. The so-called equalization ratios used in some states are with few exceptions fictitious. . . .

4. *Uniformity of Assessments.* The laws of most states prescribe that property be assessed uniformly (if sometimes by classes). No law is more flagrantly broken. Governor Langlie said in his message to the 1953 and 1955 sessions of the Washington legislature: "Valuations are now a mockery of the uniformity provisions of our state constitution."

RATIO VARIES

John Sly said in his New Jersey property tax study, which he significantly captioned *A Century of Inequities:* "Never has so much money been raised from so many people so inequitably as in the current administration of the local tax on real estate." Uniform treatment, he said, was undiscoverable except in isolated instances. The ratio of assessed to full value varied among the 21 New Jersey counties from 16 per cent to 56 per cent. A Pennsylvania study showed variations from 20 per cent to 78 per cent, a Washington study from 13 per cent to 38 per cent. Variations within counties are even greater than among counties.

Variations among individual pieces of property and omissions are due to incompetence of assessments, to insufficient staffing and to failure to use up-to-date technical aids. Assessors' offices are frequently given inadequate budgets.

Variations among classes are due to a deliberate if illegal policy. The New Jersey study found that commercial property was assessed at an average of 49 per cent, residential property at 29 per cent. In Washington residential property is assessed at an average of 19 per cent, commercial property at 27 per cent to 38 per cent. The reasons for these discrepancies are patent: there are more votes among owners of residential property than of commercial property.

What all this adds up to is a breakdown of local property tax administration. In no other tax could such conditions exist. They can exist in the property tax field only because taxpayers do not know how bad the situation is. Many governors have bitterly criticized the sorry condition of property tax assessments. With rare exceptions, legislatures have closed their eyes to the disgraceful situation or at best have taken half-hearted action.

COURTS HAMPER ACTION

Courts have a record of more often hampering rather than helping attempts to correct these injustices. They seem to have difficulty distinguishing between the appraisal of property, which is a technical process, and the power of taxation, which is a political process. There has been a reluctance to interfere because of a mistaken concept of "home rule." We may wonder whether there is an inherent right of local officials to break the constitution and laws of the state and inflict flagrant injustice under the cloak of home rule. State government has a duty to act if law enforcement breaks down within its borders, if some local units of government are prevented from exercising their legitimate duties by the failure of some officials to uphold the law.

The maladministration of the property tax has probably done more to weaken home rule than anything else. This condition if continued much longer will destroy home rule by ruining the financial integrity of local government. There is in the long run no political independence without fiscal independence.

I have mentioned that there have been many attempts to improve property tax administration. All but 8 states have taken some action since the end of World War II to equalize property tax assessments. Ten states have enacted measures toward this end in the past year. In a majority of the states, the results have been modest or disappointing.

Why is it that the property tax is in such bad shape while other taxes seem to be fairly well administered? What distinguishes the property tax from all others?

The property tax in the United States originated long before the others; its organization and methods are hopelessly outdated. In no other tax field do we elect administrative officials. But the great majority of property tax assessors are elective. It is quite likely that our income tax administration would be in no better shape if the employees of the Internal Revenue Service were locally elected without regard to technical qualifications.

The appraisal of property—just as the verification of income tax or sales tax returns—is a technical job which requires professional skill and knowledge. It is not supposed to be a policy-making job. The employees of the Internal Revenue Service or of the state tax department do not claim the discretion to apply the tax rates to 30 per cent or 50 per cent of a taxpayer's income or sales volume. But property tax assessors exercise such an authority.

The question is sometimes asked what difference it makes whether the size of the tax levy is raised or lowered by manipulating assessments or by adjusting the rates. The difference is that in the former case under legal millage limitations the policy decision is shifted from the legislative body—the city council, board of county commissioners, school board—which under the law has the power, to a single official who usurped it. Instead of the representative bodies which are responsible for the operation of their governmental units, it often is the tax assessor who decides how much they can spend.

ASSESSOR SETS RATES

It has been said that the tax assessor has made himself the budget officer for all local governments. That is not quite correct. A budget officer administers a budget but does not set its size or the amount of the tax bill. That power belongs to legislative bodies. The property tax assessor is the only single public official in the United States who can in effect determine tax rates and set the amount of taxes which the residents of a jurisdiction must pay. He exercises that authority not by law but arrogation. He has made himself in effect a one-man legislature. Often he makes vital decisions about the operations of cities, counties or school districts although he has no responsibility for their activities.

A long and disgraceful record has proven that local property tax administration except in rare circumstances will fail. Sporadic attempts at improvement by local initiative or under state stimulation have at best been temporarily successful. If we want property tax assessments to cease to be a political football then we must put them on a scientific and objective basis. An increasing number of people are coming reluctantly to the conclusion that this will not be accomplished until the appraisal of property is divorced from local administration and made uniform by the same method by which inter-county utility property is appraised in most states: under uniform standards on a statewide basis. Home rule will be more effectively guaranteed by leaving the decision on tax rates in fact as well as in name to locally elected responsible bodies.

It is unlikely that local governments will be able to cope with the task that lies before them in the next decade without a restoration of the property tax. The need for added services and facilities is vast and urgent, present inequities are drastic and widespread. Minor corrections or palliative measures will not do the job.

* * *

45. Eliminating Underassessment*

ADVISORY COMMISSION ON INTERGOVERNMENTAL RELATIONS

FULL value assessment versus fractional assessment is not the issue under consideration here. About one-third of the States, as shown in chapter 4, legally authorize fractional assessment for all or part of their taxable property. Underassessment means assessment at a level clearly below that required by law.

Policymaking is a legislative function. When assessors change the laws in their conduct of the assessment process or State regulatory agencies "equalize" assessments at a level which is remote from the constitutional or statutory requirement, there is administrative usurpation of legislative power. This administrative recasting of legislative policy, as has been shown, can and often does have widely detrimental effects. Some of it has been forced by the legislature's abdication of its responsibilities, but to give permanence to such conditions would do violence to constitutional principles.

FEASIBILITY OF FIXED-LEVEL ASSESSMENT

Technically, if the assessors are competent and adequately equipped and are allowed a reasonable range of tol-

* Reprinted from The Role of the States in Strengthening the Property Tax, Advisory Commission on Intergovernmental Relations, 1963. Footnotes omitted.

erance, the maintenance of a specified level of assessment is feasible. Regardless of whether property is assessed for taxation at full value, at some uniform fraction of full value set by statute, or at some unauthorized fraction set by the assessor, the process must start with an appraisal of the full value of the property, which is its market value. In all instances the task of the assessor, unless he is just guessing or copying the preceding roll year after year, is the same. He must find the market value of the property. It then can be assessed for taxation at that value or any fraction thereof.

The technical feasibility of this objective must be qualified, as noted, by allowance for a reasonable range of tolerance. Precision as to the level of assessment is no more attainable than precise uniformity of assessment. Market values must be approximated in many instances and, additionally, they undergo constant change of cyclical as well as secular character. Not all these changes, moreover, are uniform within a community; some occur variously in different sections as these sections improve or deteriorate. A complete reassessment each year may not be feasible or desirable; but if the checking of significant changes is a continuous process and adjustment for secular trend is made every few years, assessing can achieve what Tax Commissioner Thomas A. Byrne calls "a conservative full value rather than a precise reflection of the market level in any year."

The assessor must have the guidance, in working for a reasonable approximation of the legal basis of assessment, of a clear, usable legal definition of full value—one that avoids forcing him to become an economic forecaster and restrains his "precautionary regard for inflation tendencies." The assessor should not have to contend with such equivocal statutory instructions as: (relating to real property) "The term full cash value . . . shall mean current value less an allowance for inflation, if in fact inflation exists," and (relating to certain personal property) "The term full cash value as used in this subsection shall mean current value without any allowance for inflation."

Troubles caused by fuzzy definitions of value may be illustrated by what happened in Oregon. After launching its comprehensive reappraisal program in 1951, the State Tax Commission soon found that the statutory definition of true value, as construed by the courts, was a serious impediment to doing a sound job. According to statute, "True cash value of all property, real and personal, means the amount the property would sell for in the ordinary course of business, under normal conditions in accordance with rules and regulations promulgated by the State tax commission." The State Supreme Court ruled that under the "normal conditions" provision, determination of the true cash value of real property required adjustment of market value to a "constant value which levels the effects of depressions and booms." (Appeal of Kliks, 153 Or. 669.) This put the Tax Commission into the forecasting business, precluded a firm standard of assessment for real property and, because the ruling had been extended only to some classes of personalty, prevented complete equalization between realty and personalty.

In 1955 the legislature changed the definition to provide that true cash value shall be "market value as of the assessment date."

FEASIBILITY VERSUS PRACTICABILITY

Notwithstanding the technical feasibility of reasonable conformity with the law, nowhere on a statewide basis, so far as can be ascertained, does the level of assessed valuation approach a legal basis that has been long established. For this discrepancy both the assessors and the State governments are responsible. Professionally well-qualified assessors have tended to concentrate their efforts on meeting the legal requirement of uniformity and to give much less attention to the level of assessment at which they achieve uniformity. Many assessors, however, have ignored the law for less professional reasons. Underassessment was less controversial, more pleasing to the taxpayers; or it enabled the assessor to serve as a self-constituted budget officer in lowering a community's taxing and borrowing power; or it had interarea competitive advantages; or it was a convenient way of obscuring mistakes. In postwar years the gap between law and practice has widened as in Byrne's words, "the market has literally run away from assessors" while they kept their eyes glued too long to 1940 values.

A large share of the responsibility for this conspicuous breakdown in law enforcement belongs to the State governments. Quite obviously they have failed to enforce the law, but their culpability goes deeper than this because of their adoption of policies that have made the law virtually unenforceable. By their use of assessed valuation as a base for various regulatory purposes, they have placed a premium on underassessment.

Property owners are convinced that an increase in their assessed valuations means an increase in their tax burdens, and beneficiaries of partial tax exemption know that such an increase means lower benefits. Thus public resistance to increases in assessment levels intimidates assessors and ties the hands of even the most scrupulous State tax administrators. Such increases stir popular resentment much more readily than inequities in local assessment rolls. According to a well-documented statement of an authority who has studied this issue intensively:

> Undoubtedly the most impressive factor blocking compliance with the constitutional full value mandate is the paralyzing fear that any decision to raise depressed local assessment levels to full value would meet with overwhelming public opposition.

In a number of States the State agency responsible for property tax regulation has the legal power to order local property tax administrators to raise assessments to the legal level, and in recent years some States have strengthened these agencies; but even the most competent have been baffled by the wide gap between the assessment level and the legal base, the derangements that would be caused by disturbing the status quo, and the political unfeasibility of closing the gap and have resorted to compromise equalization policies that mitigate some of the ills of, but do not eliminate, underassessment.

ALTERNATIVES FOR REMEDIAL ACTION

The States have a choice among three possible courses of action to eliminate underassessment. (1) They can provide for effective enforcement of existing law. (2) They can change the law to conform more nearly to prevailing practice and then concentrate on effective enforcement. (3) They can abolish fixed assessment levels and abandon the use of assessed valuation for ancillary purposes.

Least likely to succeed is the first of the three alternatives when the legal and actual levels are far apart. Theoretically, it might be initiated in a very simple manner by the State tax commission's exercise of its authority to compel the adjustment of all assessments to the legal basis. Actually, this would be a good way to start a political revolution. Leadership that could induce the legislature to make all of the essential supporting legal adjustments and convince a rebellious public that the policy was desirable would be almost a miracle.

The second alternative has a better chance of acceptance. It requires less basic adjustments and is easier to sell to the taxpayers since the changed legal assessment level bears a closer resemblance to existing local levels. If the groundwork for this adjustment has been laid by State supervised reappraisals in all assessment areas where they were needed and by the development of competent and adequate State supervision of local assessing, the actual adoption of the plan is facilitated and simplified. In any event, adoption of such a program, unless it is virtually forced by court action, will depend on strong administrative leadership, cooperation by the legislature, active support by civic groups and local governments, and an effective program of education for the public. The effort is not worth undertaking, moreover, unless it includes adoption of satisfactory means to enforce the new law.

Varying versions of this plan have been adopted recently by a few States. Oregon, Arkansas, and New Jersey provide good examples. In Oregon, the way had been smoothed by a statewide reappraisal program in progress since 1951. Prior to 1953 all taxable property was required to be assessed at true cash value; then, because of general disregard of this standard, the legislature changed the law to permit each assessor, with the concurrence of the county board of equalization, to determine the ratio to be used. The requirements, noted in the preceding chapter, for verifying and publicizing the ratios seem to have worked fairly well; but in 1959 the legislature set a statutory level of 25 percent of true cash value to become effective in 1961 except for a few counties still undergoing reappraisal and for counties assessing at higher levels which they did not want to reduce. In 1957 the county ratios had ranged from 48 to 22 with a median of 30, but for the 1962 tax year the State verified ratios were at 25 percent for all but three counties—one electing to maintain its higher ratio and two still under reappraisal.

The broad program to rehabilitate property tax administration initiated by the legislature of the State of Arkansas in 1955 included the requirement that all property should be assessed at 20 percent of actual value, creation of an assessment coordination division, provision for regular ratio studies to check performance, and stimulation of local compliance by provision that if, by 1957, any county's assessed valuation level was below 90 percent of the established standard (i.e., below 18 percent) the county would lose a proportionate share of its State aid. While there was temporary postponement of sanctions, one county was penalized in 1960 and there was rapid improvement in the uniformity of assessment levels as disclosed by the ratio studies. Prior to initiation of the program the inter-area range in the level of assessment was from under 10 percent to over 20 percent. In 1961 the range was from 16 to 22 percent, with only four counties below 18 percent. Three of these were raised to the required level within the short period allowed for adjustment.

In New Jersey the courts forced abolition of underassessment, thereby aiding the long efforts of the proponents of property tax reform. In 1957 the Supreme Sourt of New Jersey declared that the legal standard of assessment would be enforced by the courts at the suit of any taxpayer, and so long as the standard set by statute is 100 percent of real value the courts would mandate that standard; but the court permitted postponement of compliance to give the legislature time to change the basis of assessment if it wished to do so. In 1960 the State legislature provided, for taxes due in 1962 (later postponed to 1965), that each county board of taxation could set the level, in multiples of 10 but not less than 20 percent, at which all real property is to be assessed, with 50 percent to be the level if a county fails to set the ratio.

THE PREFERRED ALTERNATIVE

A third and, all things considered, the most satisfactory means of abolishing underassessment is (1) to purge assessed valuations of all uses except that of serving as a tax base, and (2) to eliminate all constitutional and statutory requirements for fixed levels of assessment; but only in conjunction with the requirement that a well qualified and equipped State administrative agency make a reliable determination annually of the average level of assessment and the market value of taxable property in each of the State's assessment districts. The market value, thus determined, would be used as a measurement base, doing away with the vagaries of fractional assessment for this purpose; the State determined average level of assessment for each district would show the taxpayer what the level of assessment for his property should be and give him a firm basis for appealing from an inequitable assessment; and data also would be available to control the distribution of equalizing State grants and to equalize tax rates of taxing districts served by more than one assessment district.

ADMINISTRATIVE ADVANTAGES

Under this arrangement, just one basic legal requirement is imposed on the assessor—he must obtain reasonable intra-area uniformity in his assessing.

He is freed from the legal responsibility of achieving uniformity at some fixed level specified by constitution or statute, and, because taxing and borrowing power are no longer controlled by assessed valuations, he is freed from pressure to hold down the assessment level. This plan, however, needs one qualification. Because assessing has a tendency to become progressively less uniform at low fractions of full value, it would be wise to set a minimum level. State enforcement of this minimum poses no difficult problems.

Broadening the reliance on the statistical measurement studies produced by State supervisory agencies would put pressure on these agencies to produce more reliable studies, which, in turn, should contribute to more scientific property tax administration. Also, State supervision of local assessment, freed largely from concern as to assessment levels, would be able to concentrate more on producing greater interclass and intraclass assessment uniformity.

AID FOR THE TAXPAYER

Fractional assessment, legal or illegal, is confusing to the taxpayer. He compares tax rates that lack comparability, and quite commonly has little readily available means of knowing, to say nothing of proving, whether his assessment is reasonably equitable. Full-value assessment would remove some of this confusion, but since it does not appear to be practicable, the State has a responsibility for removing as much mystery as possible from fractional assessment.

The means here advocated for eliminating underassessment would be unsatisfactory without full, clear disclosure for the taxpayer. The State's statistical determinations as they affect each taxing district should have prompt and wide publicity, in readily understandable form and with clarifying explanation. Among the more obviously required data would be comparisons of market values and assessed values, not only for taxable property as a whole but by major classes of property. Removing the mystery from such factors would be painful in some jurisdictions, but in the long run it could remove a considerable amount of taxpayer injustice.

For the protection of the taxpayer, the State determined or verified ratio of assessed to market value should be made legally available to him as a basis for protesting and contesting an assessment which he believes to be inequitable. Oregon not only has made such statutory provision, as noted earlier, but has set up a small claims division of a new tax court to aid the small property taxpayer. In New York, a statutory amendment of 1961 permits the State determined "equalization rate" (which is on a full-value basis) to be introduced as evidence in judicial proceedings to review an assessment.

FULL VALUE AS A MEASUREMENT BASE

The irrationality of using assessed valuation as a measurement base has been emphasized in chapter 4. If a State government believes that local governments should be limited in the amount of their taxing and borrowing, its limiting action should be based on careful consideration of their fiscal capacities and the extent to which they may draw safely on these capacities. If taxable property values are to be used in evaluating fiscal ability, then full value, rather than a tricky and elastic assessed-valuation yardstick or an equalized value that does not represent full value is the true index of such ability. It measures the entirety of this entity, not just a variable fraction of it, and provides a clear concept of fiscal ability as the basis for studying and imposing rational limitations. Likewise, if partial tax exemptions to homeowners, veterans or other beneficiaries of this type of legislative largess are to be based on dollar amounts of property value, they should be in dollars of full value, rather than of assessed value, so that the legislature can make a clear determination of the size of its munificence.

All such regulation and dispensation should be placed on a full-value basis, regardless of whether, or how, underassessment is abolished. This change, when it can be effected by statutory means, would require the State legislatures to review all existing formulas involving assessed valuation and to recast them so that they have a rational relation to full value. One of the immediate advantages of the change, in fact, would be the pressure placed on legislatures to study and regenerate tax limit and debt limit formulas that no longer reflect legislative intent and do a disservice to local government. When constitutional provisions are involved the obstacles to change are more formidable but still worth overcoming— including, if possible, the removal of such details from the constitution.

The use of full value as a measurement base is being demonstrated effectively in New York and Wisconsin, where local assessing continues at varying fractions of full value. Its use as a base for debt limitation was authorized by statute in 1961 in Pennsylvania, which provides extensive local option as to the level of assessment, but was declared unconstitutional. A plan in Illinois to use full value as a base for tax and debt limitation, however, has fallen short of its purpose.

Local assessment levels in New York, legally required to be at full value, still range from under 30 to over 60 percent of full value; but these variations have no effect on the legal taxing and borrowing powers of local governments. In early postwar years, when the State constitution still restricted borrowing and taxing by local governments to specified percentages of their assessed valuations, the effect of underassessment was an erratic and planless determination of such powers that threatened the ability of some local governments to function and brought outcries for more State aid. In 1949 and 1951 the constitution was amended to base the limitations of taxing and borrowing power on the full value of taxable property. (A 5-year moving average of full values, rather than that for a single year, is used as the base.) In the debt limit amendment small reductions were made in the controlling percentages to bring them into what was deemed good conformity with the full-value base. A special State agency was established to provide reliable full-value data by means of regular assessment ratio studies.

One of the established functions of the property tax division of the Wisconsin Department of Taxation is the annual determination of the full value of taxable property in all taxing districts of the State. Operating through six district offices and with a trained field staff, the division is able to do an efficient job by supplementing its assessment ratio studies with continuous field appraisal work. These State full-value figures have increasingly numerous statutory uses—more than 80 according to a tabulation through 1961 by the department. In addition to exceptionally varied applications for which State equalized assessments are invaluable, they serve as the bases for most statutory tax limitation and constitutional and statutory debt limitation.

To recapitulate, one of the truly important prerequisites for strengthening the property tax is to disassociate assessed valuation from all functions except service as a tax base. It is essential, for one thing, to get rid of primitive concepts of budget control that conjure with assessed valuations and tax rates, and place emphasis on budgeting and financial planning that make judicious use and apportionment of a community's basic fiscal ability, one good measure of which is the full value of taxable property. It is essential, for another thing, to divest property tax administrators of their illegal power to dictate local ceilings for taxing and borrowing and confine them to their proper function of doing a competent job of tax administration.

46. Municipal Sales Taxation*

JOHN F. DUE

SALES taxation at the municipal level in the United States is in general a product of financial problems created by the depression of the 'thirties and the inflationary pressure of the postwar period. But its development in various areas has been so diverse that an understanding of it and of the problems which it creates, and a general evaluation is possible only if the actual experience in various areas is reviewed.

NEW YORK CITY

The first municipal sales tax in North America was enacted in December of 1934 by the City of New York as a part of a program of financing unemployment relief. New York State had enacted a 1 per cent tax in 1933 but allowed it to expire permanently in 1934, thus paving the way for the city levy. The initial 2 per cent city rate was lowered to 1 per cent in 1941, raised back to 2 per cent in 1946 and increased to 3 per cent in 1951. The tax yielded $312 million in 1955, or more than any state sales taxes except those of California and Michigan. The sum constituted about 27 per cent of total municipal tax revenue and about 18 per cent of total municipal general revenue.

The tax resembles the state sales taxes very closely, applying to all retail sales except those of food and medicine. The only services taxed are public utilities and certain ones performed on tangible property, such as printing. Purchases of producers' goods other than materials are taxable. A bracket

* Reprinted with permission from *Sales Taxation,* by John F. Due, Routledge & Kegan Paul, Ltd., 1957. Footnotes omitted.

system is prescribed, and retailers are required to pay to the city any amounts collected in excess of the sum calculated by applying the tax rate to total sales.

A compensating use tax is imposed upon purchases made outside the city and brought in for use within the city. The city is able to enforce the use tax to roughly the same extent that the states are able to enforce their taxes of this type.

*   *   *

On the whole, the New York tax has proven to be highly productive of revenue, despite an inadequate audit program, and is firmly established in the city's revenue system. Because of the size and population of New York City, its importance as a shopping center, and its location relative to the rest of the state, the New York City tax has not created the types of problems, particularly with respect to loss of business to out-of-city retailers, which have arisen with other city sales taxes. In general it is no more difficult for the city of New York to operate a sales tax than it is for a state to do so.

In the postwar years, the use of the sales tax in New York state has spread to additional cities and counties, including Auburn and Erie county (Buffalo) with 1 per cent rates; Monroe county (Rochester), with a 3 per cent rate, and Niagara Falls, Poughkeepsie, and Syracuse, with 2 per cent rates. These taxes are locally administered, and are similar in scope to the New York City tax.

CALIFORNIA'S EXPERIENCE

The experience with municipal sales taxes in California, the first state in which these taxes came into general usage, is particularly interesting, because it illustrates so clearly the evils which arise when local governments are free to impose and administer their own sales taxes without restriction.

Development—In 1943, the California state legislature reduced the state sales tax from 3 per cent to 2½ per cent because of current budget surpluses. Municipalities, hard pressed to meet growing demand for services from a rapidly rising population and higher costs in the face of strong opposition to property tax increases, soon saw that the use of a 2½ per cent sales tax rate by the state paved the way for a relatively painless source of revenue. They could impose a ½ per cent rate, and not raise the burden over that prevailing prior to the reduction in the state figure, and, on smaller sales, without producing any higher price to the consumer than that with the 2½ per cent state tax, since the same brackets could be retained without undue burden on the retailers. The first city tax (in San Bernadino) became effective in January, 1945; by the end of 1947 the number of the taxes was almost 100, and by 1953 162, despite the restoration of the state rate to 3 per cent in 1949. The initial ½ per cent city rates soon gave way to 1 per cent rates in many areas to bring the combined state and local rate in most of the urban centers of the state to 4 per cent. . . . The taxes were employed by the four largest cities in the state, and 28 out of the 35 cities having population in excess of 25,000. . . .

There was no coordination in administration with the state sales tax, the cities administering their own taxes, and requiring separate tax returns from the retailers. Only 7 cities had any audit programs at all, and these were very limited; the others relied on the honesty of the taxpayer and the effectiveness of state audit. While in a general way the local taxes followed the pattern of the state tax with respect to coverage (food being exempt, for example), they were not identical with the state tax nor uniform in various cities. Greatest divergence arose with respect to intercity transactions; in general a sale for delivery outside of the city was not taxable, while compensating use taxes were imposed by most cities (but not effectively enforced) against purchases made outside of the city and brought in.

It was estimated that on the average the city collections constituted only about 70 per cent of the amount which would have been yielded by a state tax of comparable magnitude collected in the cities using the tax.

Difficulties—As these city taxes spread and the rates increased, several types of problems grew in intensity:

1. Retailers found it necessary to file separate state and local returns, and multiple-unit stores were required to file a separate return to each sales-tax-using city in which they operated. The tasks of the retailers were greatly complicated by the non-uniformity in the various taxes; the figure of taxable sales for city tax would virtually never be the same as that of taxable sales for state tax on sales made in the city.

2. The exemption of sales for delivery outside of the city created problems for store clerks to determine tax status of a certain sale, especially in metropolitan areas in which cities are contiguous, and seriously complicated record keeping. In addition, retailers experienced increased demand for delivery to persons living outside of the city.

3. The use tax provisions could not be enforced effectively except on a few types of transactions, and thus discriminated against the particular consumers and retailers who were subjected to tax. If a customer made a purchase from an out-of-town store of a firm also operating a store in the city, payment of the tax by the store could be enforced, whereas if purchases were made from other out-of-town stores, there was no possibility of enforcement.

4. The possibility of escape from sales tax by making purchases, especially

expensive ones, outside of the city provided an artificial factor affecting location of retail stores and discrimination
against retailers already established
within the city. Particularly, the tax
encouraged the location of new suburban shopping centers outside of the
city limits, and provided an additional
argument against the incorporation of
suburban areas into the city. The extent of these effects is difficult to assess,
but there was inevitably some influence. . . .

5. Enforcement standards varied
widely among different cities, and costs
of collection were often substantial.
One study of municipal collection costs
showed a range from .4 per cent of
yield to 8.5 per cent, with substantial
concentration between 2 and 4 per cent,
despite the fact that the cities did not
maintain any significant audit program.

These problems led to increasing demands for reform, the most strenuous
ones coming from the retailers' organizations. Consideration was given to a
plan for an increase in the state tax rate
to 4 per cent, with the additional 1 per
cent being shared with the cities (and
perhaps the counties, which were also
seeking sales tax revenue). This plan
would have eliminated virtually all of
the evils of the existing structure, insuring uniformity of tax rate throughout
the state and eliminating duplication. . . . But some question arose with
respect to the constitutionality of this
technique because of prohibitions on
the expenditure by the state of funds
for local functions, and the plan was
opposed by the League of Municipalities and various city governments on
the basis of interference with local autonomy. Questions arose with respect to
the position of those few municipalities
which were not interested in sales tax
revenue, and over allocation of revenue
between cities and counties.

The New System—As a consequence
of these objections, a compromise proposal was developed and enacted by the
legislature, becoming effective April 1,
1956. Under this new plan, the counties
are authorized to enact 1 per cent sales
taxes, provided that they are identical
(apart from certain minor features)
with the state sales tax, and provided
that the counties contract with the
State Board of Equalization (which administers the state tax) for collection.
In turn, retailers are allowed credit
against the county tax for amounts due
under a city sales tax, provided that
this city sales tax conforms with the
same requirements established for the
county taxes; that is, that the structure
of the city tax is identical with the state
levy (with minor modifications) and
contract is made by the city for collection by the State Board. The city taxes
may be 1 per cent or less. Thus, in conforming counties, that is, those conforming with the plan:

1. Sales in cities which impose the
tax are subject to both county and
city tax, but the latter constitutes a
credit against the former; thus if the
city tax is 1 per cent, all of the revenue accrues to the city.

2. Sales in incorporated areas and
in cities not imposing the tax are subject only to the county tax, all revenue accruing to the county.

In non-conforming counties, cities can
continue to impose their own locally
administered taxes. Such counties cannot impose a sales tax.

In all cases, the tax is collected from
the consumer on the basis of a combined state and local tax schedule.

*   *   *

Counties are not compelled, of
course, to enact a sales tax; if they do
not, cities in the county are free to continue their own sales taxes, but cannot
contract for state collection. Actually
the counties have considerable incentive to enact the tax as a source of revenue for themselves, from sales in
unincorporated areas, and in areas in
which the city tax is less than 1 per
cent. Once a county tax is enacted, the
cities are virtually compelled to make
their taxes conform with the system, or

retailers will be subject to both city and county tax without credit for the former against the latter. If a city in a conforming county fails to enact a tax, the county receives the entire tax revenue from sales in the city.

*   *   *

ILLINOIS

The state of Illinois has followed a third path with respect to local sales taxation. In 1947 the legislature gave all municipalities the power to impose a sales tax, but attached the requirement that the proposed tax be submitted to popular vote before becoming effective. About 12 cities attempted to get such approval, but in all cases the plan was turned down by the voters, often because of organized opposition of retailers. But the financial position of many municipalities grew steadily worse, and some action became essential. In 1955, following an agreement between the Governor and the Mayor of Chicago, the legislature approved a measure removing the referendum requirement. At the same time the state sales tax rate was increased from 2 to 2½ per cent. An alternative proposal of a 3 per cent state rate with distribution of ½ per cent to the localities was rejected, partly on the grounds of preservation of local financial autonomy, partly because of the dislike by the state administration of further increases in state tax rates and state expenditure figures.

The municipalities were given discretion only over the rate, being authorized to impose a rate up to ½ per cent, a figure which in practice all have used. The base of the local taxes is identical with the base for the state tax, all sales being taxed upon the basis of the location of the retail store, regardless of place to which delivery is made. No local use taxes are permitted. State administration is mandatory. The retailer indicates the amount of local tax in a separate space on the form and remits the amount to the state; this sum is returned to the cities imposing the taxes on the basis of place of collection, less a 6 per cent charge for collection.

Upon the removal of the referendum requirement, the cities acted rapidly. By January of 1956, six months after the legislation became effective, 617 cities had imposed the tax. . . . The sales tax cities include Chicago, all other cities above 25,000 population, and all except four with population over 10,000, plus numerous small towns and villages. The total yield attained an annual rate of about $50,000,000 by the summer of 1956. About half—$24 million per year—constitutes Chicago's share; this is roughly 15 per cent of the city's total tax revenue. The local tax has gone into effect with relatively little complaint or difficulty, although some cities claimed initially that multiple unit stores were not reporting receipts accurately by municipality. The tax has avoided most of the difficulties of the old California system, but is inferior to the new California system—to the extent to which the latter comes into general use—in one respect: incentive to shop outside the city limits is provided by the tax. . . .

Illinois experience suggests that the local autonomy argument against sharing of the state tax is not too significant. The local taxes spread like wildfire, despite the obvious fact that some localities were in much less need of additional revenues than others. In some towns the tax was enacted first, and attention was then given to ways to spend the money. [*Editor's note: According to the Advisory Commission on Intergovernmental Relations, some 1120 municipalities and 56 counties in Illinois levied general sales taxes as of January 1, 1961. Local Nonproperty Taxes and the Coordinating Role of the State, p. 34.*]

OTHER STATES WITH STATE COLLECTION

Mississippi—The pattern in Mississippi is much the same as that in Illinois, except that the city taxes came much more slowly. Demand for the tax arose out of the inadequacy of property tax revenues in the face of rising costs, and the eventual exhaustion of war-accumulated state surpluses, which had been used to help the cities in the immediate postwar period. Power was first granted to cities to levy sales taxes by legislation of 1950, but a 3/5 referendum requirement and other restrictions limited the use to a few cities. The restrictions were gradually relaxed, and by 1953 10 cities were imposing the tax. In 1954 the size-of-city requirement was eliminated and in 1955 the compulsory referendum rule was removed (a petition of 20 per cent of the voters can still force a referendum, but only a majority vote is required for approval of the tax). . . .

The local tax rate is now set by law at ½ per cent, with a ¼ per cent rate on gas and electricity. Only retail sales are taxable, although the state tax is broader in coverage. The base of the tax is the same as the retail portion of the state tax, and state collection is mandatory. A 5 per cent collection charge is now made, although the cities are seeking a reduction in this figure. Taxpayers merely report local tax in a separate space on the tax form. Multiple unit stores must localize collections by city. The state reports few problems for itself in the collection of the local taxes.

New Mexico—The only other instance of state collection is in New Mexico, in which the city of Albuquerque imposes a 1 per cent tax collected by the state as a supplement to the state tax.

OTHER LOCALLY COLLECTED TAXES

New Orleans—The second-oldest municipal sales tax in the United States is that of New Orleans, first imposed in 1936 in the form of a luxury tax of limited scope, to meet depression-in-

duced deficits. In 1938 the scope of the tax was broadened to include most commodities. In 1940, both the city and state sales taxes were repealed, but the city reinstated the tax in 1941. Since the state tax was not in operation, the city was forced to develop its own sales tax administration, which it retained after the state tax was reintroduced in 1942. Separate returns are required of retailers for state and local levies. The coverage, however, is similar to that of the state tax, including not only sales of tangible personal property, but also transient rentals, laundry, cold storage, repairs, and printing. . . .

*   *   *

Alabama—A third state of the deep south, Alabama, also permits local sales taxes. These are now imposed by 8 cities and 5 counties, most of the rates being 1 per cent, with a ½ per cent figure in 2 cases. Like the Louisiana taxes, they are locally administered. [*Editor's note: According to the Advisory Commission on Intergovernmental Relations, at least 63 municipalities and 13 counties in Alabama levied general sales taxes as of January 1, 1961. Local Nonproperty Taxes and the Coordinating Role of the State, p. 34.*]

Virginia—In the state of Virginia (which does not use a sales tax) one city, Bristol, imposes a sales tax. This levy is an outgrowth of a peculiar geographical situation; half of the city area is in the state of Tennessee. When Tennessee levied a tax in 1947, the Virginia city saw the possibility of a similar tax levy as a solution to its financial problems, and in 1950 enacted a local tax virtually identical to the Tennessee law—a move which no doubt found great favor on the part of merchants in the Tennessee portion of the city. The tax is imposed at the same 2 per cent rate as the Tennessee tax, with a compensating use tax, which is remitted largely by Tennessee dealers making deliveries in the city. Seventeen per cent of the sales use tax revenue comes from the use tax—a very high figure.

Since Virginia has no state sales tax, the city maintains its own collection and audit staff. Stress has been placed in audit on taxable items bought outside the state and brought in. Costs of collection are reported to be less than 2 per cent of revenue. . . . No serious loss of business to other non-tax Virginia communities has been experienced by the merchants. The Bristol tax is an interesting experiment in cooperation on the part of two segments of a border city community to avoid the worst evils arising from imposition of a sales tax in one.

Colorado—Another pioneer city sales tax is that of Denver, which was imposed in 1948 to meet a growing crisis in city finance. The tax is operated independently of the state sales tax, and the base is substantially different. Unlike the Colorado tax, the city exempts food and prescription drugs. In addition, sales to manufacturing and other firms for use outside the city are tax free, as well as articles sold for delivery outside the city. No use tax is employed, largely because an original proposal for such a tax met with strong

public opposition. A 1 per cent rate is imposed, with a bracket system for collection; retailers are liable for payment of 1 per cent of their total sales. . . .

* * *

Arizona—The final locally-collected sales tax is that of Phoenix, Arizona, imposed at a ½ per cent rate on retail transactions, and a lower rate (usually ¼ per cent) on certain other activities. The State of Arizona imposes a sales tax, but there is no coordination of collection of the two taxes.

Abandoned Local Sales Taxes—Apart from the taxes now in effect, several others have been used and abandoned. The best known was that of Philadelphia, a 2 per cent retail sales tax which was collected for 11 months in 1938. The tax was highly unpopular, with organized opposition by labor unions and retailers, and was allowed to expire. It was ultimately replaced by a municipal earnings tax. The city of Atlantic City imposed a 3 per cent retail sales tax for a short period until the New Jersey Supreme Court ruled it to be invalid. Several West Virginia cities imposed fractional rate sales taxes for a time during the 'thirties.

47. The Municipal Income Tax*

ROBERT A. SIGAFOOS

THE GROWTH OF MUNICIPAL INCOME TAXATION

The development of the municipal income tax in the United States is largely a post World War II phenomenon. Since the 1930's, municipalities have been faced with the problem of ever-increasing revenue deficiencies.

* Reprinted with permission from *Municipal Income Tax: Its History and Problems* Public Administration Service, 1955. Footnotes omitted.

The public demand for new and improved municipal services, constitutional and statutory limitations on property tax rates, debt limitations, the increasing pre-emption by the state and federal governments of tax sources, and the effects of post-war inflation on the cost of municipal services have all caused local government officials to look for new and more productive sources of funds.

The municipal income tax appears to offer a possible solution to many such municipal financial difficulties. In 1954, Cincinnati and Pittsburgh each needed over six million dollars to balance its operating budget; St. Louis required eight million dollars. To raise the necessary new revenues these three municipalities chose the municipal income tax over other possible alternatives. Cincinnati rejected by popular vote a property tax rate increase, and the city administration responded with an income tax to yield the required operating revenue. St. Louis feared that higher property tax rates might encourage further migration of population and industry to the suburbs. Pittsburgh was concerned with a similar problem, aggravated by the failure of certain city-county financial arrangements to materialize.

Textbooks on public finance have given only superficial treatment to the municipal income tax as a source of local revenue. Their authors continue to regard the traditional property tax as the only tax of major significance for local governments. Even the development of 434 [*as of 1963, some 1200 —Editor*] relatively simple but highly productive income tax systems in municipalities and school districts has not resulted in more than passing mention of this form of taxation in public finance courses in most of our universities. Nevertheless, the recent enactment of these broad-based, low rate income taxes and the pressures that have brought them into existence give every indication of the discovery of an important tax potentiality. This fact cannot fail to strongly influence an increasing number of local jurisdictions faced with a compelling need for additional revenue.

The first appearance of a form of municipal income tax in the United States occurred in the early nineteenth century in Charleston, South Carolina. For many years in Charleston, personal income of all types was assessed and taxed in much the same manner as property. After a prolonged period of increasingly ineffective administration, the tax was eventually abandoned.

In more recent times, particularly during the first thirty years of this century, the local income tax came into extensive use in Canada. However, as a consequence of Dominion-provincial wartime readjustments in taxing authority in 1942, local governments were forced to relinquish their income taxing powers. While the Canadian taxes were still in use, the idea of local governments taxing incomes was reintroduced in the United States in the State of Pennsylvania. In 1932, that state granted permission to Philadelphia to levy taxes on nonproperty sources not already being used as a tax base by the state itself. Under this act Philadelphia created a city sales tax and municipal income tax in 1938. Shortly, however, this income tax was declared unconstitutional because of its exemption provisions. This difficulty was subsequently overcome, and in 1940 Philadelphia was able to re-establish a successful wage and income tax. The revised levy has been used as a pattern by many other jurisdictions desirous of establishing a comparable tax. General permission to tax income was granted to almost 3,600 municipalities and school districts by the Pennsylvania state legislature in 1947 through passage of the widely known Act 481. This so-called "tax anything" law was patterned after the measure granting broad taxing power to Philadelphia fifteen years earlier. . . .

New York City enacted a municipal income tax in 1934, the ordinance providing for a tax rate equivalent to 15 per cent of the federal income tax paid by the residents of that city. No collections were ever made under the law, however, owing first to an initial postponement of the effective date of the tax and then to outright repeal of the ordinance in 1935. The municipal income tax was again considered in New York City in 1952 by the special Mayor's Committee on Management Survey, and findings were presented in what has been publicly called the Haig-Shoup report. The committee reported on the potentialities of various types of taxes but took rather a dim view of the income tax. It reasoned, however, that if additional tax measures were found to be absolutely necessary a municipal income tax should be enacted. . . . The city has never acted on this proposal believing it to be politically hazardous. However, the state legislature of New York in 1953, without petition from the city, authorized New York City to levy a special payroll tax. The tax would be levied at a rate of one-half of 1 per cent on all wages and salaries, one-fourth of 1 per cent to be paid by employees and the other one-fourth of 1 per cent by the employers. The tax would apply only to wages and salaries in excess of $30 per week on $1,200 per year. Other types of earned income, all types of property income, and net profits would apparently be excluded. The New York City administration has emphatically called this tax possibility "a last resort."

The first city in Ohio to tax incomes was Toledo, which imposed the levy in 1946. Toledo was followed in 1948 by Columbus, Springfield, and Youngstown. Dayton and Warren enacted the tax in 1949, and recently Canton and several smaller Ohio cities have likewise imposed the levy. Cincinnati imposed the tax for a seven-month period in 1954, and again for a nine-month period in 1955. In November, 1954, the electorate of that city approved a property tax rate increase which would have done away with the further need of the income tax, but the city reimposed the latter tax when the Ohio Supreme Court invalidated the property rate increase. The Court held that the City had exceeded its authority, and misled the voters with the statement on the ballot that if the property levy were approved, there would be no income tax in 1955 or 1956. While the income tax has gradually spread among Ohio cities, moves to introduce the levy have not always been successful. . . .

St. Louis is the only city in Missouri that has taxed incomes. The first levy was imposed in 1946 but was invalidated by the Missouri Supreme Court for lack of state authorization. The Missouri legislature then granted St. Louis authority to tax incomes for a two-year period from 1948 to 1950. Authorization was allowed to lapse until 1952 when the legislature again extended the necessary taxing power for two years. Authority was renewed in 1954 for a three-year period.

In Kentucky, the income tax is in use under the guise of an occupational license tax. Such a tax was first enacted by Louisville in 1948. Paducah followed with a similar levy in 1951, and more recently Lexington and Newport have adopted comparable measures.

Various proposals for the adoption of municipal income taxes have been considered in recent years in other parts of the United States, but for one reason or another they have failed to receive final acceptance. Minnesota affords an example. The legislature in 1947 authorized Minneapolis to submit to the electorate an income tax proposal and the measure was defeated. The following year a proposed amendment to the home-rule charter of Minneapolis would have authorized a graduated income tax, but the amendment was never submitted to a vote. In Duluth, voters twice overwhelmingly rejected income tax proposals.

There can be little doubt that interest in the municipal income tax is growing. Even where no concrete proposal has emerged, it has been the subject of much discussion. The Los Angeles City Council studied municipal income tax possibilities early in 1954, but dropped the matter after encountering widespread public protest. Similar reaction developed in Chicago when the city was preparing to petition the Illinois legislature for new nonproperty tax sources. Other communities where the possibility of the tax has been considered or mentioned include Cleveland; Denver; San Francisco; certain smaller Ohio, Kentucky, and Tennessee cities;

Dallas and Ft. Worth in Texas; and Boston, Massachusetts.

*   *   *

In the great majority of states, no specific statutory authorization has been enacted by the legislatures permitting municipalities to tax incomes. In a few states there are constitutional prohibitions against municipal income taxation. On the other hand, six states have by law authorized one or more local governmental units to levy such taxes. . . .

*   *   *

GENERAL TAX PRINCIPLES AND THEORY APPLIED TO THE MUNICIPAL INCOME TAX

ABILITY TO PAY

Under the present municipal income tax pattern the well-accepted modern principle, that of taxing according to a person's ability to pay, has been ignored. Exemptions and progression features are almost entirely absent. Because the tax is based on gross earnings of individuals, except in one or two Ohio cities where some very limited exemptions are given each taxpayer, no distinction is made between differing income levels and family responsibilities. One taxpayer, regardless of the size of his family, pays as much tax as another taxpayer with the same gross income but without dependents; while use of a common flat rate applicable to all earned income ignores the individual taxpayer's ability to pay. This concept, briefly stated, is a general, overall rule that loss of economic goods through taxation becomes less important as a person acquires more of such goods. Implicit here is the idea, at least as far as basic exemptions are concerned, that taxpayers should be assured a minimum protection against tax encroachment on income needed for basic living expenses. Even with exemptions, however, a flat rate on the remaining tax base still does not compensate for the different abilities to pay of taxpayers at varying income levels above an exemption line.

Failure to include unearned income in the income tax base extends still further the inequality of treatment among taxpayers. This type of income generally accrues to persons in higher income brackets. These persons are assumed to have greater capacity to pay than low and moderate wage earning classes.

One defense of the present pattern, however, is that distribution of the over-all tax burden on all taxpayers through federal, state, and local taxes puts an individual's annual tax payment on a progressive basis, and in line with his separate ability-to-pay. . . .

*   *   *

TAXING NONRESIDENTS

More than half of all cities with populations above 10,000 draw a fairly large part of the daily labor force from surrounding fringe areas. The employment centers are still predominantly in central cities despite a postwar trend of some new industry to begin operations in suburban areas, and a lesser tendency of existing firms to migrate to suburban or semi-rural areas. Cities, however, still largely retain their advantageous industrial location features, such as presence of skilled labor pool, transportation outlets, complementary industries, market distribution centers, and many similar features holding industry to its traditional locations. Mass migration seldom occurs except in the case of declining industries moving in an attempt to lower production costs as, for example, the textile industry in its movement out of many Northeastern cities in recent years.

Unquestionably, this attraction of nonresidents to city job opportunities has considerable bearing on municipal finance. These persons, who number in the several millions throughout the United States, receive free many municipal services or facilities which are now being paid for out of existing property tax receipts and lesser municipal revenues. These direct and indirect services of protection, subsidized transportation in many cities, streets, and other benefits must be borne principally by residents because most central cities find themselves with political boundaries that do not coincide with their economic areas. Often in large cities such as New York, Chicago, and Los Angeles the city's area of employment influence may extend as far as 50 to 75 miles. The bulk of the commuting nonresident employees, however, live reasonably close to the city limits. The very challenging problem for the core cities is to construct an adequate revenue system to overcome some of the resulting pressure on municipal costs.

*   *   *

In the immediate future, the income tax, despite obvious shortcomings in its present form, would seem to offer one fairly easy way to assess both residents and nonresidents at least to the extent of their earnings allocable to the central city. This may be the only direct opportunity, since a municipal sales tax offers an alternative to residents and nonresidents alike to make their purchases beyond city boundaries.

Philadelphia and St. Louis, and most of the other large income taxing cities, collect somewhere between 15 and 25 per cent of their income tax revenues from nonresidents. Cities elsewhere with heavy movement of employees into their boundaries daily might well consider this potential opportunity to spread the financial support for municipal services. . . .

At the present very low rates the tax burden is not exorbitant for nonresidents. . . . Such a tax contribution gives little cause for complaint that central cities are attempting to shift the burden of their revenue program on the shoulders of outsiders. Philadelphia's nonresidents, for example, contribute only 5 per cent of the city's total receipts from all sources. There is a growing interest among municipal finance officials in making greater use of service charges to consumers of measurable services. This concept could conceivably be altered and expanded to cover in a more general way the costs of city facilities used daily by nonresident employees.

*   *   *

TAX STABILITY

As just noted, personal income and its principal component, wages and salaries, have moved consistently upward over recent years on a national scale; but for any one of several reasons, local economies have sometimes experienced contrary trends. Local governments in specific areas encounter possible dangers of relying too heavily on income tax revenues. When wages are not paid, taxes are not paid. There can be no back taxes to collect on income which has never been earned. Many jurisdictions cannot easily make up a large revenue loss caused by local economic difficulties. This often means that certain municipal services have to be dropped or seriously curtailed because of the general lack of reserve funds to draw on.

A feature lacking with the present municipal income tax is stability of yield fairly closely aligned with annual municipal expenditure programs, which customarily do not vary substantially from year to year. As payrolls and business profits rise, yield of the flat rate taxes climbs in the same proportion; and when the reverse is true, the fall is also in the same proportion. With local income taxes applicable primarily to payrolls and overwhelmingly so in Pennsylvania where corporate profits are excluded, the brief income tax history proves how sensitive this form of tax is to prolonged or even temporary payroll shrinkages.

Many of the recent proposals which suggest putting municipal finance policy in line with national countercyclical fiscal policies stress tax programs whose yields rise proportionally with upward income movements and hold off on individuals or businesses when the economy falters. Most of such suggestions overlook the status of fixed community services. Usually these services are planned annually on a direct needs basis within the limits of expected revenues from principal sources, whether the sources be property taxes, the income tax, receipts from municipally-owned utilities, state grants-in-aid, or any other income source. Many of the suggestions relate to powers available to the federal government rather than to those of municipal governments. They overlook the limited fiscal means available to these latter units when asking for the establishment of counter-cyclical financial programs to coincide with anti-recession or anti-inflation policies of the federal government. One of the theoretical proposals most often heard is for the accumulation of tax reserve funds. These funds would be derived from excess revenues gathered during inflationary years and set aside for release during periods of business decline. Borrowing for public works during recessions to help sustain employment is another suggestion; and there are several other ideas that would be helpful if it were possible to overcome the very close allegiance of state legislatures and local councils to traditional policies in municipal finance. There is no indication that any substantial movement toward modernizing municipal fiscal policies is near at hand in any state.

48. Special Assessment Policies for a Growing City*

GUY C. LARCOM, Jr.

ANN ARBOR, Michigan (67,340), like many other rapidly growing cities, has found it necessary to change its policy regarding special assessment of utilities and improvements. In 1956 the city began assessing 100 per cent of the cost of improvements against benefited land. This decision was made because the city literally was "running out of money" due to the demands for sewers, water lines, road improvements, and other services to new subdivisions and newly annexed and developing areas. Within the limitations of city general revenues, there was not enough money to finance these costs without infringing on other city services or without exceeding established tax limits.

Prior to 1956, city policy varied with each type of improvement. For example, the city absorbed 50 per cent of the cost of storm sewers. Water lines were installed and assessed on a front-foot basis, sometimes less than the actual cost of the installation. Other utilities and improvements were installed under a proration of about 80 per cent of the actual cost.

The new policy was put into effect by the adoption of an ordinance on "Financing Local Public Improvements," providing that: "It shall be the general policy of the City to finance construction by the City of local public improvements by special assessment," including sidewalks, water mains and connections, storm and sanitary sewers, street grading and graveling, street pav-

* Reprinted with permission from *Public Management*, September 1961.

ing, and curb and gutter. For water mains and storm and sanitary sewers, the ordinance provides not only for the assessment of cost within an assessment district but also for the assessment of a portion of the cost of water transmission mains and storm and sanitary trunk sewers to connect a new area to the existing city systems.

ASSESSMENT METHODS

For each project to be assessed, the city council first adopts a resolution of necessity which authorizes the city administrator to bring in plans, specifications, and cost estimates. These are prepared by the city engineer and show the size and cost of the utility or improvement, the district that will benefit, and the cost distribution: city share, private property share, and other public agencies. If council approves the report, an assessment roll is prepared. If the project is at all controversial, the city administrator will hold an informal administrative hearing, and a formal public hearing always is held. When the project is completed and final costs are in, the assessment roll is revised uniformly upward or downward.

The method of assessment is left to the city administrative departments and is determined by the city assessor and the city engineer, with the approval of the city administrator. Every effort is made to adhere to uniform policies.

Streets. Sidewalks, street grading, graveling and paving, and curb and gutter are all, when installed new, assessed 100 per cent against abutting properties on a front-foot basis. The total cost generally is distributed among the various benefiting properties on the basis that the frontage of each property bears to the total length of the improvement.

Street paving and curb and gutter assessments are set up each year on a city-wide basis—i.e., all streets to be paved are included in the assessment district and the lineal foot costs are broken down on the basis of the width of the various streets in the district. Thus all 28-foot streets have one unit cost, all 30-foot streets another, and so on. In the case of paving, curb and gutter, and sidewalks, no formula for reducing the cost is made for irregular or corner properties.

Water. A water system may be divided into water distribution mains directly serving properties and water transmission mains bringing water from the existing city system to the new area. Benefiting properties usually are charged for the entire cost of the distribution system and a portion of the cost of the transmission main—that portion needed to serve the distribution area. Water assessment may be on a front foot basis, on a unit basis when most of the properties are of the same size and type, with each property representing one unit, or on an area basis when the land parcels vary greatly in size.

Sanitary Sewers. A sanitary sewer system includes lateral sewers serving individual properties and the trunk sewers necessary to connect the lateral system in an area to the existing city system. Assessments usually include all of the cost of the lateral system and a portion of the cost of the trunk sewer—that portion of the trunk sewer that can be attributed to serving the new area. Sanitary sewers in developed or platted areas are assessed on a unit basis, with each parcel of land of the same size representing one unit. In unplatted areas, sanitary sewers are assessed on an acreage or area basis.

Storm Sewers. A storm sewer system involves lateral and trunk sewers. Again, the assessment is 100 per cent of the cost of the lateral sewers in the street and a portion of the cost of the trunk sewer—that portion of the trunk sewer that can be attributed to the flow or runoff of water from the area served. Storm sewers are assessed on a drainage area basis, depending on the size of each property and its relationship to the total area served.

BENEFIT

The question of "benefit" from any individual improvement is one that is frequently debated. The fact is, however, that over a period of years, by practice and through court action, bases for special assessment have been established. Ann Arbor's practices probably do not differ greatly from those of many other cities.

For example, the practice of charging off the cost of a storm sewer on a drainage area basis, regardless of whether or not the properties front on the storm sewer, is standard. It is frequently misunderstood because upland areas contributing to water runoff during rainfall do not feel any benefit from a sewer constructed at a lower level to protect areas from flooding. On the other hand, it is unfair for the properties at the lower level to pay all the costs of removing storm water accumulated by drainage from their upland neighbors.

SPECIAL ASSESSMENT DISTRICT

The special assessment is, in effect, a levy or special charge for the improvements that distinctly benefit an area. It is assumed that the benefit does not extend beyond the area and that any area outside of the district cannot be so assessed. In the case of storm and sanitary sewers, the assessment district is usually a drainage district, determined by the city engineer. Once the size and shape of the district and the type of improvement is established, it becomes the assessor's duty to spread the cost throughout the area. Each assessment district is a matter of official and public record, with engineering and assessment details available, and an analysis of cost distribution.

ASSESSING SUBDIVISIONS

Ann Arbor's policy requires subdividers to put in the necessary utilities and improvements serving their respective subdivisions. The subdivider, in effect, accepts the obligation for the utilities and improvements, installs them, and charges them off against properties as they are sold. This has the advantage of enabling the eventual home owner to meet the cost of improvements over a longer period as part of his mortgage.

The city has a standard subdivision agreement which covers not only all arrangements for the utilities and improvements but also shade tree planting on lawn extensions, street name signs, conformance to city engineering standards, and contribution of land for park facilities. With each plat of any sizable subdivision, an effort is made to obtain some park or recreational land area, either as a free contribution to the city or on the basis of raw land costs.

For properties not subject to the plat law, such as shopping centers and large apartment houses, the city requires a site plan to be approved by the planning commission and the city administrator. In conjunction with this site plan, an agreement may be drawn up providing that the developer will install necessary utilities and improvements.

This procedure for subdivisions has greatly reduced the amount of public friction involved in special assessments. It should be stressed, however, that subdivision and site plan agreements cannot require installations at the expense of the developer that would exceed what could normally and legally be assessed. The agreements do provide an opportunity for bargaining between the subdivider and the city for certain improvements which are not clearly assessable but which contribute to the worth of the development. In the cast of major improvements of benefit to special types of developments, such as an industrial research park or a new university center, which require a heavy public investment in transmission mains and trunk sewers, the city will negotiate a contract rather than establishing an assessment district, and the charges will be paid under the contractual arrangement.

As can be seen, the city imposes its charges either in advance of or at the time of the installation of assessable utilities and improvements. However, the city has made one exception to this policy. In the case of a new research park, established by a nonprofit corporation to attract research industry to Ann Arbor, the city has agreed to install the utilities and improvements serving the research park without the assessment procedure and to accept payment on a per-acre basis as the land in the research park is sold.

TAX-FREE PROPERTY

Ann Arbor, a city with an unusually high percentage of tax-free property, has had to find a way for tax-free agencies to participate in the capital costs of city expansion. The University of Michigan has evolved a joint policy with the city under which the University pays its share of the cost of improvements on the same basis as a private land owner. The University does not admit to public assessment; it does, however, admit to benefit and is willing to pay its fair share of the cost of utilities and improvements once benefit is shown.

The University also has adhered to a policy of growth within the city limits by bringing new land needed for University development within the city boundaries by annexation. The University's very fair approach to the cost problem of serving the new areas has enabled city utilities to keep pace with University growth.

The city has attempted to achieve a similar policy with other public agencies. The school board and the county participate in most of the cost of assessable city services just as the University does. The city has run into difficulty, however, with the federal government and the state highway department.

Public agencies should recognize that utilities and improvements serving a land area are a necessary part of the development cost and should be budgeted as part of the project cost along with land, site preparation, and structures. In the case of city-owned property served by assessable improvements, the city absorbs its share of the cost out of the general fund on the same basis as private property.

LAND OUTSIDE THE CITY

The city cannot, of course, assess properties outside the city limits, despite the fact that the property may benefit from the improvements. A trunk sewer, for example, may serve a drainage district outside the city as well as within the city limits. In these cases, Ann Arbor participates extensively in the cost of assessable improvements because it must pick up as a "city share" that portion of the cost that is chargeable against properties outside the city. The city assessor and engineer make a memorandum record of these charges. Then if the property is annexed to the city, the cost of the improvement is collected through an "improvement charge" against each property. The improvement charge is no more nor less than a means of collecting from property newly annexed to the city the special assessment that would have been paid if the property had been in the city when the improvements were installed.

EXCEPTIONS

The city attempts to assess or to collect the cost of all new improvements, but there are some exceptions. The cost of paving major roads and of widening and improving already paved streets is not assessed. Rebuilding curb and gutter is not assessed nor are relief sewers and water mains. Major water transmission mains and trunk and interceptor sewers, the benefit of which cannot be allocated to a geographical area of the city, are financed as part of the general capital costs of these utilities and are not assessed. The determination of whether a trunk sewer or water transmission main is or is not assessable against a definite district is sometimes difficult to make.

CONCLUSIONS

Should the city assess to the extent it does the cost of improvements and utilities, or should these be financed in some other way?

The alternative method would be to charge off the cost of such improvements against city operating funds. There are several arguments against this. The city changed to the current policy in 1956 because it found it could not continue to pay for these projects in a rapidly growing community. These are *capital improvements* and should be financed separately from operating services. If they were financed as operating services, the city charter limit on tax millage would have to be raised excessively. More important would be the inequity of the city as a whole paying, as part of the normal tax burden, the cost of utilities and improvements that help to develop raw land.

The crux of this problem is that utilities and improvements benefit the land, and the land is made usable by these utilities and improvements. The value

of land can be expressed in raw land cost plus the cost of improvements. If the owner of the land, the developer, and the ultimate user are spared the cost of improvements, then the land is, in effect, subsidized by the city taxpayer. Developers and other public agencies should acquire land at a price that allows for the payment of the additional cost of the benefiting utilities and improvements.

Special assessments are the bane of the property owner. They are costly and frequently run several times the amount of what would be the normal property tax. The taxpayer often figures that the services that are charged by special assessment should be included in his general property tax. Usually at public hearings there are the "poor widows" who own property but, having no income, cannot bear their share of a special assessment improvement.

Cities that are expanding less rapidly or with a highly productive tax base and low tax rate may prefer to finance all or a portion of their improvements from general revenues. This is a matter of legislative choice.

For a growing city, the policy of making all new properties pay their fair share of the cost of the improvements that make the property usable can enable the city to expand in size without an increase in the general tax levy or in the city debt.

49. Performance Budgeting in Los Angeles*

ALI EGHTEDARI and FRANK SHERWOOD

It was about a decade ago that the first Hoover Commission coined a term which has found a secure niche in the literature of public administration: *the performance budget.*

* Reprinted with permission from *Public Administration Review,* Spring 1960, by permission of the American Society for Public Administration. Footnotes omitted.

Since that time, many publications have filled untold pages with expositions on the subject. Most of the early writing was bright and hopeful; much of it explained early installations and attested to successful experience. Indeed probably no major management study of the '50's omitted a section urging some variation on the performance budget theme. Now, however, we are beginning to build some long-term experience with our new device, and we can begin serious evaluation. One such evaluation—of the experience of the City of Los Angeles from 1952 to 1958, particularly the Building and Safety and Library Departments—is condensed here along with additional observations.

Los Angeles was a pioneer of performance budgeting. Its able and aggressive staff, under the leadership of City Administrative Officer Samuel Leask, Jr., in 1952 succeeded in a really herculean effort to transform municipal budget practice. Nearly all departments of the city participated. It is perhaps fair to say that no governmental jurisdiction (excluding such proprietary agencies as the Port of New York Authority) has committed itself so fully and so effectively over so long a period to the proposal of the first Hoover Commission.

There has been much written about what the performance or program budget can do, largely directed toward improving decision-making both by legislators and executives. To a marked extent this new emphasis is the consequence of greater awareness of the budget as (1) a power and control instrument and (2) a policy statement. If there is anything of a formal nature which is now regarded as the bonding agent in the coordination of a complex program, it would certainly seem to be the budget. Thus the old style line-item budget has fallen into disrepute, as every management survey attests. . . .

There has been a rather strong conviction that the performance budget can do much to rectify the failures which have characterized detailed line-item budgeting. Some of the favorite hypotheses are that the performance budget: (1) helps to improve planning, (2) provides more effective control, (3) sharpens decision-making at all executive levels and particularly by the legislature, (4) helps to decentralize decision-making and thus encourages

placing authority at the level of real responsibility, and (5) helps to improve public relations by providing clearer information on each program. Thus the aspirations for the performance budget have been very high.

PLANNING AND CONTROL

What kind of a planning instrument has performance budgeting turned out to be? Has it really improved decision-making?

Los Angeles is a weak mayor city. A group of citizen commissions with administrative powers are layered between the mayor and his department managers. Reporting to *both* the mayor and the city council is a city administrative officer, who possesses essentially no line authority. He is appointed and dismissed by the mayor with council approval. He may also be dismissed by a two-thirds vote of the council alone. Thus weak in the structural trappings of power, the CAO has had one major channel through which to make his influence felt, the exercise of his responsibility under the mayor for budget preparation and administration. In addition, he is empowered by the charter to investigate the administration of the various departments for the purpose of recommending to the mayor and council such reforms as will promote greater effectiveness.

Since 1951, when the office of city administrative officer was created and Leask was appointed to it in [*June*], there can be little doubt that Los Angeles, though weighted down with an unusually cumbersome structure of government, has moved very substantially in the direction of centralized management. The CAO's office without question has improved the quality of program planning, has brought about a higher degree of coordination among the essentially independent departments than ever existed before, and has made some contribution to the over-all efficiency of municipal operations.

Certainly the greatest credit for these achievements must go to the eminently capable Mr. Leask, who over nearly a decade has worked very effectively with two mayors, numerous councilmen, and scores of commissioners and bureaucrats in what is obviously an ambiguous and tenuous relationship. He has been supported in this effort by a very able and dedicated career staff.

Personalities aside, however, the performance budget seems to have played a very important role in the growth of the CAO's influence. Leask and his staff have relied heavily on it, at any rate. Only six months after his appointment, Leask proposed and the mayor announced (in January, 1952) that *all* city departments would prepare their 1952-53 budgets on a performance basis. Thus the city was operating with a performance budget just one year after the CAO plan in Los Angeles began.

Underlying all other aspects of the performance budgeting program has been the insistence that the budget be regarded as a *contract* between the mayor and the council on the one hand and the departments on the other. This is certainly not a new idea in budgetary theory. What is unique is that it is more than an ambiguous homily in Los Angeles. The CAO sees that the contract *is* observed.

The CAO is effective in the discharge of this responsibility partly because he has a large staff of high calibre. But it is more than a matter of staff. The new contract control depends heavily on the idea of work programs. These are called the "foundation of the budget" and they constitute reference points out of which flow questions with regard to the timing, size, and nature of expenditures. As a consequence we find a close tie-in between budget preparation and execution. The work programs form the bases for the original appropriations; then a government-wide reporting system which relates units of work performed to man-hours expended provides a check of actual versus proposed performance.

Such a system has enabled the CAO to keep at least a finger on a multitude of diverse operations without plowing through a labyrinth of often misleading verbiage. Furthermore the information collected has also found its way into the many other recommendations and reports of the CAO to the council and mayor. Thus the reporting and programing set in motion by the performance budget in 1952 have operated in a thousand subtle ways, as information can, to make the CAO a real power figure in the government and thereby to promote centralized management.

BUDGET DECISION-MAKING

In its report, the first Hoover Commission laid great stress on the performance budget's potential to improve legislative decision-making; in most of the other writing, a similar point has been made. It has been argued that emphasis on objects of expenditures in the budget leads to arbitrariness and irrationality. Since there is no way to tell how much program is being purchased under the object of expenditure approach, the legislator, and indeed the administrator, are ill-equipped to understand the effect of a budget slash. The argument runs that legislators particularly should concentrate on the size of program required, relative importance of programs, and priorities among programs, relating these questions to the amounts of money to be made available for government operations. By the same token, there should be less concern with numbers of personnel required, amount of postage stamps to be used, and so forth.

Though it may seem superfluous, it is important to recognize that in performance budget theory the desirability of legislative review and adoption of the budget package has always been assumed. Indeed it was hoped that more emphasis on program and less on fiscal detail would excite greater interest in the adoption phase. The Los Angeles experience, however, raises the question of whether formal legislative debate and decision on the total budget "package" is as vital as tradition suggests.

There are two facts which seem particularly significant:

1. In the five year period, 1954-55 to 1958-59, a comparison of the mayor's proposed budgets with the council's total appropriations reveals substantially no difference. In short, the proposed budget emanating from the mayor's office became the appropriation law. In general, council hearings on the budget have developed little participation and little debate.

2. Interviews of the 15 councilmen revealed almost no understanding of the performance budget rationale. Indeed those who had served prior to 1952 generally were not aware that any change in budget procedure had taken place. In most of the interviews, the councilmen seemed to agree that they had *abandoned* the formal budget review phase as an occasion for policy decisions.

Thus one conclusion seems inescapable. For better or for worse, the legislative adoption phase of the traditional budget cycle has been fairly well obliterated in Los Angeles. How significant is this development? For those who see legislative control of the purse as essential to democratic government, it may be highly worrisome. But administrative officials in Los Angeles feel the problem is more apparent than real. They emphasize the environment in which the Los Angeles city government operates. They point out that councilmen are full-time officials, meeting daily in regular and committee sessions. Thus the council, the CAO, the press, and the various interest groups have plenty of opportunity throughout the year to get together on matters of policy. . . .

The case of police appropriations provides a concrete illustration. The police chief has announced to the public for

the last several years that he needs to approximately double the size of the force, from 5,000 to 10,000 men. As budget preparation was getting under way in 1957, he made this statement again.

A special committee of the council reviewed this request and also heard the CAO report that 5,000 additional policemen would require $30,000,000 more in the budget. It decided the money could not be raised, and the chief himself submitted a departmental budget which called for only 1,078 new positions. When the mayor's budget was finally sent to the council, the number had been whittled to 320, and this was routinely approved by the council. There was no policy debate at the time of formal budget review.

The police experience suggests that the budget is a policy statement which already has been approved in various informal ways by the time it reaches the council formally. Here it is important to remember that the city administrative officer works for *both* the council and the mayor. Unlike the U.S. government where the Bureau of the Budget is regarded as purely the President's agency, Los Angeles legislators feel that the budget has been prepared by their man. Because of their contacts with him throughout the year and because they feel assured of his loyalty to their policy view, the legislators seem little inclined to do any second guessing.

Has performance budgeting been a significant factor in these developments? Obviously there are some peculiar factors in the Los Angeles environment which have nothing to do with the type of budget. Nevertheless the interviews did reveal that the performance budget may have fostered these developments. The budget is a well-researched document. It cannot be attacked in its details; and, if anything, the councilman is glutted with information supporting all proposals. Thus the old lines of inquiry are pretty well closed to the legislator. If he starts worrying about the cost of a waste-basket, he may soon find himself wondering why he started the whole business.

As a consequence, the only avenue of debate left is broad policy, just as performance budgeting theorists intended. But the unanticipated consequence is that legislators seem to have found an alternative: *not* to participate in the debate at all. Politically, it must be realized, the decision not to participate is very sensible. As the police case suggests, budget policy lines in Los Angeles carry a high degree of consensus, representing a series of painstaking and painful accommodations among the interests of a large and complex organization. Anyone who ventures onto this treacherous ground does so at considerable risk. The effect, then, of the performance budget has been to kill off some of the old legislative irrationalities and most particularly "across-the-board" economy slashes. It has not, however, forced the legislator to pick up a new mantle as budget policy statesman.

DECENTRALIZATION

It has long been a favorite theme that the performance budget should promote delegation of authority and thus secure a higher degree of participation and motivation at the line supervisory level. Some studies do show that delegation of budget responsibility is one of the most effective means of securing "cost consciousness" among supervisors. Since the performance budget relies heavily on factual data from all levels, it has seemed logical to argue the desirability of building the budget from the bottom.

The design and installation of a performance budgeting program on a scale required for Los Angeles has undoubtedly required much leadership and control from the top. The interesting point is that performance budgeting *itself* has not set into motion any clear pressures for devolution of authority.

In cooperation with the CAO and his staff, the general managers of the larger city departments have developed departmental budget preparation manuals which require the various line supervisors to initiate the budget requests for their respective units. After review at the successive levels of authority, the complete departmental budget request emerges and is submitted to the mayor and the CAO for consideration.

While a definite effort is being made by top management to secure the involvement of lower echelon management in performance budgeting, this has turned out to be a rather difficult task. In some respects it raises questions along the lines suggested by March and Simon in their use of the term *uncertainty absorption,* which takes place ". . . when inferences are drawn from a body of evidence and the inferences, instead of the evidence itself, are then communicated." March and Simon point out that both the *amount* and the *locus* of uncertainty absorption affect the power structure in an organization. In short, there are good reasons to assume that lower levels do *not* want information communicated upward, because it affects their power interests adversely. In a lower echelon of one of the departments studied, it was found that work programs were being developed *after* expenditure proposals had been roughly arrived at on an object basis. This would seem to support March and Simon's contention that what a lower manager may be interested in communicating upward is his judgment, not the facts.

On the whole, the Los Angeles experience suggests that decentralization is not the ready hand-maiden of performance budgeting some of us thought. In Los Angeles the performance budget has worked wonderfully to centralize management. It has brought all the disparate units of the city under the contract-oriented eye of the CAO. Within this context, is real decentralization also possible? There is at least a shred of evidence to suggest that this may be another basic problem area in the practice which was not anticipated in the theory.

ANALYZING PERFORMANCE

The performance budgeting idea seeks to promote rational decision-making through the presentation of objective program data, in which costs and size of program are related. This means ideally the quantification of information: *x* number of units of work to be performed at *x* dollars per unit. In such a system there are two problems: developing numerical units which give an accurate picture of the cost per unit of work and relating qualitative to quantitative data.

SETTING WORK UNITS

Performance budgeting in Los Angeles has laid great stress on the measurability of work. As a consequence, a rather phenomenally high percentage of all the tasks in the city have been subjected to such quantification. In both the Department of Library and of Building and Safety, for example, about 85 per cent of all personnel are engaged in work which is being measured. Given such an all-encompassing effort to quantify work, it might be expected that many of the work units would prove, in practice, to be quite inappropriate. This does not appear to have been the case.

A detailed analysis of the behavior of the various work units used in the Departments of Building and Safety and the Library over a three-year period show only a modest fluctuation. One exception was in the measurement of reference work performed in certain subject departments in the Central Library where a unit of "100 Questions Asked" exhibited a variation up to 100 per cent over a three-year period.

Perhaps the most serious reservation that may be noted with regard to the use of such data is its relevance only to *quantity* of work performed. Such production units obviously do not tell anything about *quality*. For example, television has apparently caused a rather substantial shift away from cheap fiction, leaving the library's main task the more time-consuming selection and distribution of better books. More time is thus required to process fewer books, with no decline in efficiency of operations. Productivity—output per unit of manpower applied—requires one method of measurement whereas quality control utilizes an entirely different method. Administrative officials report they assume that the same quality of service is being supplied for each unit of work performed. . . . Line supervisors are relied upon to make periodic observations and checks of service quality. Top management appraises quality to some extent by the number of service complaints received.

THE REPORTING SYSTEM

It is of great significance that Los Angeles has made such major performance budgeting strides without a close tie-in to the accounting system. The city administrative officer does not have responsibility for accounting and was not able to get from the city's accounting program the kind of information he felt necessary for effective performance of his mission. As a matter of fact, the need for management data was undoubtedly a strong motivating force in the development of performance budgeting.

Yet the CAO could not establish a duplicating set of books. As a consequence, his reporting system is built on the most important single item of resource expenditure, personal services. Sometimes known as the "manhour approach" to budgeting, this reporting system seeks to gather data on two critical items: (a) the number of units of work performed; (b) the number of manhours required to perform those units. In all cases, particularly those where personal services have not been the most significant expenditures, this substitute for a more effective accounting program may not be ideal. But the fact is that Los Angeles *did* install performance reporting; and, as we indicated earlier, it has aided the city administrative officer greatly in the performance of his tasks. All in all, this must be judged one of the most effective aspects of Los Angeles' performance budgeting venture. It is interesting that an approach which has seemingly yielded so much in Los Angeles and is so well packaged in the U.S. Bureau of the Budget publication, *A Work Measurement System: A Case Study* (U.S. Government Printing Office, 1950), has caught on so little elsewhere.

STANDARDS

Even though performance budgeting may be well established as a system, the Los Angeles experience suggests that evaluation and management use of the data may remain difficult. Essentially, quantitative standards of performance must be set which can serve as budget guides and also as targets for administrative improvement.

The evaluation of performance still occurs on a largely subjective basis in Los Angeles. Some attempts have been made to develop standards; but the job is such a major one, requiring a wealth of operational experience, that administrative officials are not yet ready to claim anything for publication. The data do supply leads to improvement possibilities, of course. For example, the manhours per work unit in the Department of Building and Safety have been slowly rising; in the Department of the Library they have been slightly declining. While such information is important in itself, there is a need for a device which suggests the significance of these shifts and the point at which they should come to the attention of top management.

SOME CONCLUSIONS

The purpose of this article has been to compare certain elements of performance budgeting theory with the practice in Los Angeles, which has given the concept perhaps as thorough and intensive a trial as any governmental jurisdiction in the United States.

Some of the answers which the Los Angeles experience suggests are:

1. The performance approach *can* result in a strengthening of the executive budget and in this sense can have an effect on program planning and the central control of decisions going into the executive budget.

2. The measurement of work in a governmental jurisdiction is practical and feasible, and there are positive benefits to be gained from such measurement.

3. The performance budget need not be based on the accounting system.

On the other hand, certain questions are raised:

1. Does the performance budget tend to inhibit legislative participation in the budget process? Or does formal legislative participation in the budget process become less important (and perhaps unnecessary) when the legislative body is kept continuously aware of the financial condition and needs of the jurisdiction throughout the year?

2. If we assume that such an abdication of legislative involvement *does* take place, are we prepared to pay such a price for an increased grasp of budget decisions by the chief executive, plus the managerial benefits?

3. How should performance information be used in managerial appraisal? Will we be able to develop an appraisal system (i.e., standards) sufficiently rational to make the accumulation of such hordes of data a useful expenditure of time?

4. In strengthening the executive, does the performance budget also set into motion forces incompatible with organizational decentralization?

50. Reappraising Program Budgeting*

RALPH W. SNYDER

FEDERAL, state, and local government administrators, challenged by the 1949 "Hoover Commission" proposal on program or performance budgeting, broke new trails in the decade of the 50's toward the discovery of the budget as a major policy-making device and all-important tool of administrative control. While new techniques and concepts are emerging to strengthen the role of the budget in decision-making and management, real budgetary reform lags, and program or performance budgeting yet remains something of a curiosity.

The budgeting and accounting report of the Commission on Organization of the Executive Branch of the Government, commonly known as the Hoover Commission report, recommended that the federal budget be formulated in terms of governmental activities, functions, and programs rather than in terms of things bought. The major objectives of the proposal were to (1) reduce the federal budget to a more understandable and meaningful form, and (2) facilitate legislative and administrative review and control by relating the units of work involved in any specific program with their appropriate costs.

Some municipal governments have been quick to recognize the potentialities of program or performance budgeting. Currently 60 cities are reported to be using some form of program or performance budget. Most municipalities, however, still cling to the line-item budget, apprehensive of the problems and pitfalls brought to light by some of the literature in this area and unwilling to assume the responsibilities of change. Those that have broken with tradition, however, have discovered a powerful tool of effective administration.

* Reprinted with permission from *Public Management,* Spring 1960. Footnotes omitted.

BUDGETS AND COMMUNITY GOALS

Significantly the proponents of program or performance budgeting are usually members of the policy-making body, top-level administrators, and laymen engaged in the intricate and baffling job of making sense out of the annual budget. These adherents find the program or performance budget an indispensable aid to making value judgments of specific programs, supported by the budget, in relation to institutional goals. At least one American city (Evanston, Illinois) has cast the entire budget in these terms, relating each major budget item to the achievement of specific community objectives.

The various publics no longer need to conduct a grand-scale survey for fiscal information. Here, for their surveillance, are the streets to be paved or resurfaced, the health services offered, the level and scope of library and other cultural opportunities, the urban redevelopment areas, the hopes, schemes, and plans of the municipal government —and, *at what costs.* Subjective analysis of the governmental program can be adequately detailed and explained through the instrument of program or performance budgeting. The reaching of the understanding of the public is the first step in achieving its support of worthy governmental activities and programs.

PROGRAM OR PERFORMANCE?

Throughout this discussion the terms "program" and "performance" budget have been used conjunctively. This interchangeability of terms is reflected in much of the literature dealing with the subject and has resulted in considerable confusion. In reality the concept involves two related although not totally synonymous applications of a type of budgeting. A *program budget* is inherently a policy-making tool, subject to review and decision by the legislative body. It deals primarily with things *to be done*. A *performance budget* is a valuable instrument of management through which the administrator guides the *execution* of policy and controls costs.

Program budgets deal principally with broad planning and total program costs. A performance budget is based upon work load and cost information and the content matter of programs, abstracted from the past and projected into the future. Each has its own separate and distinct function, although the one is built upon the other. Limitations of language seem to doom us to this confusion of terms. Because, however, the realization of the policy-making implications of budgeting are transcendent in importance, the term "program budgeting" will be used henceforth in this article.

In preparing a program budget several general considerations should be recognized. Basic is the identification of program objectives. This is the joint responsibility of the city council and the city manager. It is necessary to determine the direction in which the city government's energies and resources will be expended. Here, prior programs will be reviewed, reduced, increased in scope, or even eliminated. New programs will be considered for their contribution to community objectives.

Second, specific activities need to be selected which fulfill program objectives. For example, if a determination is made that the control or elimination of Dutch Elm disease is a desirable program objective, are tree spraying, tree trimming, and tree sanitation activities which will accomplish this end? Would spraying alone achieve the desired results? Should inventory and inspection be continuing parts of the program?

Third, the relative value of the results of such a program must be weighed and evaluated. Is it possible that ultimate dollar savings could be achieved through this program by the reduction of tree removal costs? Or could there be more value in removing all American Elms subject to the disease and replacing them with some disease-resistant species? These factors require both qualitative and quantitative analysis with the administrator furnishing sufficient data for an intelligent and informed decision to be made.

Finally, contingent risks need to be examined. What other programs may have to suffer, and to what extent, as a consequence of an all-out attack upon D.E.D.? If the tree-spraying and trimming activities were abandoned or reduced in scope, what results could be anticipated? These judgments involve financial, legal, aesthetic, and even political factors.

It is the policy-making implications of the program budget which represent its greatest asset. Properly presented, the city council has the opportunity to make decisions on policies and programs, not on the minutiae of data. The city council is better able to fulfill its public responsibility without the need to solve the riddle of how paper clips, asphalt, and kilowatt hours of electricity to be purchased contribute to the carrying out of their grand plans for the community. These commodities, as commonly presented in the line-item budget, give no clue as to what is to be accomplished thereby.

CHALLENGES OF PROGRAM BUDGETING

While the city council can content itself with these broad strokes on a large canvas, the chief administrator requires more detail for effective execution and control of the program. It is the kind of required detail that has provoked a long-standing controversy among adherents of the program budget and is a factor frequently cited as an impediment to its development. There is a feeling among many public administrators that program budgets are necessarily dependent upon cost accounting and, since adequate cost accounting involves additional expenditures for personnel and equipment for fact-gathering, work-load analysis, and so on, program budgeting is not worth the cost or trouble. Furthermore, they maintain some activities do not lend themselves to precise measurement, counting, or weighing—for example, the ministerial activities of the city manager.

This, as one writer described it, "slavish linkage to cost accounting" has handicapped the growth of program budgeting. Significant departures from the cost accounting concept have been made and there is no valid reason why other equally productive standards of measurement cannot be used such as the man-hour or man-year relationship to the volume of output. These non-cost accounting approaches to program budgeting deserve further exploration and development.

Whatever the standard of measurement for work output, it is important that the level of work accomplishment be consistently compared with the budgeted work program. Development of a program budget and the use of such an instrument are sometimes two different matters. Understanding and knowledge by department heads and subordinates are essential to the full realization of the advantages of the program budget as a managerial tool.

Too frequently the program budget is developed by staff technicians without line participation and, if such is the case, the value of program budgeting as a control and reporting device is lost. Indeed the city manager may find that desirable programs and objectives are only partially realized or completely fail of accomplishment. In this area new methods of budget reporting, in terms of program achievement as well as in dollars expended, are in need of development.

A concern expressed by many public administrators is the selection of meaningful standards of work production and their allied costs. How can the city manager be certain that the price tag affixed to a unit of work is correct and valid? One interesting approach has been the seeking of intercity cost comparisons for equivalent work units. For example, what does it cost to collect a ton of garbage in New York, in Fort Worth, in Council Bluffs, and in Tacoma? Can the variables in cost, such as prevailing wage scales, weather and topographic factors, equipment utilization, and so on, be isolated and identified so that an index might be developed for comparing other unit costs?

Investigations to date seem to indicate not only a lack of common terminology but also such great variations in conditions of service as to make comparisons virtually impossible. The study does, however, demonstrate the desirability of cost comparison between governmental units within smaller territorial limits, such as metropolitan areas, or between communities with identical or near identical social, ethnic, economic, and environmental characteristics. If the variables can be identified, it is conceivable that a wide range of cost information could be exchanged between communities as easily as exchanging information about the weather.

PROGRAM BUDGET BARRIERS

Qualitative as well as quantitative performance standards also require further refinement and the qualitative relationship to costs established. The fact of measurement of the number of curb miles swept by a patrol street sweeper at so many dollars and cents per mile loses meaning if the streets are not swept clean and in a manner acceptable to the community. It follows that norms of quality of performance need to be set in addition to the level of units produced and realistic cost relationships developed.

Still another area for refinement is the budget relationship of recurring and non-recurring costs. The identification of items of purely custodial or continuing expense and those representative of service or program advancement and capital improvement can be a key feature of the budget as a policy-making instrument. The city of Cincinnati has been a forerunner in this facet of budget-making which will be further amplified in the next article in this series. It is sufficient here to point out that the separation of the items composing the basic or standby budget from the items representative of program and service advancement is a further aid to the legislative body and the public in reaching decisions for new policies and programs.

In most cities the most serious barrier to program budgeting is antiquated legislation which mandates the line-item appropriation budget. Although there are encouraging signs of budgetary reform in the air, many municipal administrators to circumvent such requirements budget by activity and program and appropriate by line item. The program budget then becomes the blueprint of public policy and program activity and the line-item appropriation ordinance merely the fulfillment of the legal authorization to expend public funds. Although troublesome and time-consuming, this procedure is better than attempting to administer far-reaching and important public programs without a program budget at all.

Change is also desirable in the traditional organization of budgets by funds and departments. Programs of governmental services and activities frequently cut across fund and departmental lines.

The program budget, for its ultimate value, will be organized in terms of activities and functions. This will require a reduction in the number of separate funds and the grouping of departments into a structure of functional similarity. Reexamination of the organization pattern in these terms may reveal less need to maintain separate engineering and public works departments or indicate the compatibility of police and fire functional activity.

It is further suggested that the principle of budgeting on an annual basis should be reappraised in the light of changing community objectives. With the rapid growth of many urban centers, the annual budget often is insufficiently geared to changing program requirements. Frequent program review in such cases is essential, and the program budget is far more flexible and offers more opportunity for review than its less sophisticated cousin, the line-item budget.

CONCLUSION

Recognition of program budgeting by a growing number of cities stems from its superiority, first, as a more meaningful and effective tool in the hands of the legislative body for evaluating and controlling the direction of government; second, as an improved instrument for management at all levels of administration; and third, as a plan of governmental services and activities more comprehensible to the individual citizen. Adherence to traditional concepts of budgeting, undue concentration upon cost accounting dogma, and restrictive legislation have deterred the full realization of the advantages of program budgeting. The outer space of program budgeting has been penetrated—it has not yet been occupied.

51. The Place of Purchasing in State Government*

WILLIAM E. STEVENSON

As you may know, I am a charter member of the National Association of State Purchasing Officials, and have a deep and abiding respect for it. Through the years, I have been privileged to know and work with some of the finest men and minds that the public service has produced.

These men have handed down a great heritage, and much of the great progress which has been made in public procurement is directly the result of their contributions. In my remarks I hope to bring forward the spirit, the thought, and some of the contributions which these men, including many now passed from the scene, have provided for us and the future of our art.

We read at every turn today that democracy faces a challenge more critical, more immediate and more basic for the future of our civilization than ever in history. Not only is the supremacy of free democratic government on trial, but its very survival is threatened. This is not alone a problem of the image created around the world by the federal government, but is a tremendous responsibility for every public servant, and particularly for those of us representing the states and territories. We must prove our effectiveness at meeting the basic needs of our citizens, while at the same time solving problems created by changes thrust upon us in terms of a booming population, science, invention and technology, and expanding services.

STATE GOVERNMENT OF OLD

State government has moved far in a short time from the simple negative role of maintaining the peace to one of vast, complex and critical programs and services demanded by and essential to our citizens.

Many of you represent states whose governmental history predates that of my own. Others of you represent states the state governmental history of which is young in comparison. But if you will permit me to trade on our Minnesota experience, I should like to trace briefly the tremendous change brought about in the relatively short space of but 100 years.

In our territorial days, 1848 to 1858, we had a struggling young university facing horrible financial problems and at one time unable to provide for its thirty-two students. Aside from that, and a few elective officers who were paid token salaries for the honor of serving the citizens, the territorial government consisted of little more than a few provisions for the protection of its citizens, and governmental services meant little more than local enforcement of laws to maintain peace.

Even in the early days of statehood, there were no state colleges, no state mental hospitals, no children's institutions, and state employees numbered but a handful.

Late in the Nineteenth Century we had begun to provide for mentally ill, we incarcerated our criminals, and we were collecting taxes to pay these minimal bills. We had also become conscious of the need to provide for education, and a normal school system began to develop for the specific purpose of training teachers to man the facilities

* Reprinted with permission from *State Government,* Winter 1962.

—which, except in the cities which had begun to grow, were mostly log cabins and one or two room school houses dotted over the state—and to provide the essentials of reading, writing and arithmetic.

Even by the turn of the century there were no such things as state highways, insurance against industrial accident, statutes for the protection of labor or the regulation of industry and commerce. We either did not have or did not recognize the problem of the aging; and juvenile delinquency was a personal matter between the parent and the child, usually resolved in the woodshed and only rarely involving the local constable. The idea of fair employment practices had not yet developed, hunting and fishing were not sports to occupy leisure time, but were still a means of providing essential subsistence for survival. While a consciousness was beginning to develop, problems of mass sanitation, the spread of communicable disease, water conservation, mass transportation, sewage disposal, etc., were pretty much local matters.

THE CHANGE SINCE WORLD WAR I

The impact of World War I, and its sudden and great demand on natural and human resources, not only served to highlight the need for governmental regulation in many areas but brought about expanded state government in many fields. It was, parenthetically, this same period which gave birth to the idea and impetus to the development of a new specialty, organized industrial purchasing.

The events of the twenty years which followed, through boom and depression, further extended the authority of existing governmental agencies, and prompted the creation of new ones. Huge operations now have grown where once none existed. Today government administers insurance against unemployment; administers programs of retirement; regulates almost every segment of the professions, trades and commerce; provides for the health, education, welfare and relief of its citizens; constructs and maintains huge networks of modern highways; is concerned with the safety of its citizens, the management, preservation and utilization of its natural resources; engages in research in many areas, and provides guidance and counsel in many fields. With our rapidly expanding population, complicated by an increasing percentage of those under 20 and over 60, with more leisure, greater mobility, a higher standard of living and the shifting from farm to city and then to suburban areas, the problems of government continue to mount and demand resolution.

STATE PURCHASING GAINS STATURE

Where once it was possible to support evolving programs independently, events have demonstrated that *supply* has become as complex as the programs themselves.

This leads to the role of purchasing in state governments. I have mentioned that between 1900, roughly, and World War I, industrial purchasing began to evolve as a systematic function. World War I gave impetus, and between World Wars I and II progressive managements recognized its importance, and organized accordingly. The advent of World War II brought the purchasing function of age; and today we note a highly specialized management aspect, a status art which approaches professional service.

During this period also, although this was later chronologically and slower in development, state government moved in a similar direction. By the mid-1940's many of the states had moved toward centralized purchasing. Today, although there is recognition of the importance and the advantages of central purchasing and although most of the states have at least adopted that principle, it is by no means universal, and there is a long way to go before we can claim maximum efficiency.

Dr. Russell Forbes once wrote, centralized purchasing in government is the "sentry at the tax exit gate." Feeble in its beginning, and resisted in its development, centralized purchasing where adopted has grown into a way of life. "The delegating to one office the authority to purchase supplies, material and equipment needed for use by all of the several operating agencies of government, is neither a fad nor a theory, but a combination of sound logic and good economics. Any method which can be developed to reduce the cost of commodities, increases the mileage of the tax dollar. If this can be accomplished, then either the government secures more commodities for the same cash outlay, and thereby increases its services to its citizens, or else it can buy the same commodities for less money, thereby reducing the tax demand."

THE STAKES IN SAVINGS

It has been estimated by students of public procurement that moving from wholly decentralized or independent buying to centralized and organized buying has effected savings to as much as 25 per cent. Furthermore, since state purchasing is concerned with roughly 20 per cent of the total budget, on the average, we are confronted with a potential savings which no public administrator dares overlook for long; and it is a sum which I dare say the public would prefer not to underwrite.

How, then, can the purpose be accomplished?

SIX CORNERSTONES

While statutes help, I would emphasize at the outset that people—you, the purchasing officials—are essential to the notion. No laws, no rules, no codes—

desirable and important as they are— are worth the effort of their adoption unless you make them work.

Modern public procurement, as is true of its industrial counterpart, is built on sound cornerstones. It has no secret nor mystic properties and is within the reach of all. I have enjoyed comparing notes with my industrial colleagues, and while there are many areas of difference (for example we are generally consumers' goods buyers, there are no customer relationships, etc.) there are many principles which apply commonly. I would like to trade for a moment on some of the many basic notions which I have learned through this association, and particularly from the venerable George Cronin, Dean of Public Purchasing Officials, now retired in Massachusetts. He summarizes good procurement by defining six words:

Simplification: reducing the number of items designed to perform the same or similar function; *Specification:* reducing to writing clear, precise and concise description of the commodity; *Standardization:* the insuring of universal use of the specification once adopted; *Competition:* any method by which a broad list of responsible suppliers is encouraged to compete for the business; *Inspection:* the procedures and methods used to insure that we receive what we have specified and paid for; and finally, *Utilization:* the methods and procedures for insuring that what has been purchased is used to the ultimate.

From your own reviews of the proceedings of this organization, you know that each of these words alone is individually and properly the subject of a full presentation. Six words are easy to remember. Their processes are easy to describe. But it would be something less than candid if we were not to observe that, where human beings are involved, there are differences of opinion. A part of the challenge of building sound procurement on these six cornerstones is the *constant* process of review and updating, and the education that goes into a successful program. Here, the purchasing agent is first an avid student and then a competent teacher.

FURTHER REQUIREMENTS

Purchasing is not an end in itself but a vital service to an end. Therefore, on top of the cornerstones we need to know intimately, accurately and sympathetically the problems, needs, functions and personalities of those whom we serve. In addition to knowing when to buy, how to buy, what to buy, we also need to know negatively what not to buy, when not to buy, and from whom not to buy.

This suggests many things. It suggests technique and procedure; it suggests communication; it suggests constant study; knowledge of all operations; cooperation; good public relations; and it suggests flexibility; but above all else, it requires adherence to principles.

One of the many contributions of the National Association of State Purchasing Officials to public procurement was the adoption in 1949 of a committee report published as "Principles and Best Practices in State Purchasing." Adherence to those principles, in my view, will provide good procurement; and wherever one finds good procurement, one also tends to find good government. The corollaries are many!

Any attitude that diminishes the confidence and respect for government held by citizens in our democracy is serious. Any situation that gives rise to any contrary attitude must be investigated promptly and corrected. If we are to make properly the necessary decisions of these critical times, we cannot allow any taint or taunt of sloppy operation or unethical behavior. This aspect we explored together three years ago. Its importance is not diminished.

OPPORTUNITIES ABOUND

Efficiency, economy, and honesty in government are more important than ever before, if for no other reason than that government itself has become an important and decisive part of the everyday life of every citizen. The purchasing agent is a custodian of his state's status—a sub-image of the government he represents. He sits in the forefront in a highly sensitive function. He can mold attitude.

While I concede that the principal cost of government is in people, and that there are broad areas for improvement in organization, systems and procedures, it nonetheless remains a fact that purchasing is in a key spot, through its research, to (1) eliminate personal whim and prejudice, (2) recommend improvements and (3) assist in their implementation. Purchasing is generally considered a service function, and with this I do not quarrel. However, there is a growing understanding on the part of top management—both industrially and in government—that it is a profit function. The potential for profit in private enterprise and the potential for economy in government which exist through proper performance of the purchasing function no longer escapes the attention of top management; it is expected. The purchasing agent is an ex-officio "idea man" whose limits are extremely wide. He is a full-fledged member of the profit team.

Notwithstanding the fact that the ordinary citizen organized in his interest group—whether it be his profession, the Parent-Teacher Association, or his church group is inclined to ask for additional services, he will, when separated from that group as an individual, complain about the cost of government. This is a part of the inevitable cost of democratic freedom. However, whether his complaint is reasonable or otherwise, that same citizen has the right to expect that the government which his tax dollar supports will make the most prudent and economical use of his tax contribution. The purchasing agent is a manager of his state's purse, and prudence is his staff. He must perform accordingly.

We must be on the lookout constantly for ways and means of reducing costs. A new (but really very old) purchasing activity is "Value Analysis," and it applies to much more than materials or things. The purchasing department is and must be in the forefront of these activities. The purchasing agent sits in a unique position, for his activity touches upon every aspect of state governmental operation. So we come again to the theorem that purchasing is something more than to buy the right quality and the right quantity at the right time at the right price. A purchasing executive worth his salt is a prime counsel to the other operating heads of government. His knowledge of materials, supplies, equipment, trends, conditions; his knowledge of systems, equipment capacities, etc., provide him with vital tools for the influencing of management judgments, thus enabling greater savings, more economies and greater efficiency. The purchasing agent can and must lead and influence for good

In a very basic sense, the attitudes, abilities, knowledge and experience of the purchasing agent will have a distinct bearing on the attitudes held by suppliers and the public. It is important that there be close communication between this function and the public.

FOR THE FUTURE OF GOVERNMENT

Sound purchasing is concerned with safeguarding equities, with defining purpose, with the development and maintenance of adequate standards, and with providing and preserving an environment conducive to progress. The successful purchasing agent succeeds not by imposing his will, but by encouraging initiative and imagination in others. To this end, he is a coordinator, ad-man and salesman—selling a program for the common good.

In my view, a key to the future of democratic government, of its success or failure, is the place purchasing takes —the role it assumes, and the quality of its overall product. I think the founders of this Association would have said no less!

52. Public Personnel: Agenda for the Sixties*

FELIX NIGRO

AT the beginning, let me make clear that I do not plan to play the role of Messiah, leading my flock of personnel administrators to a happy decade of successes in the Sixties. My task is of another order. It is to report on the emerging goals in the public personnel field as I discern them from the many

* Reprinted from *Public Administration Review*, Autumn 1961, by permission of the American Society for Public Administration. Footnotes omitted.

reports, articles, and other materials the trade kindly makes available to the textbook writer.

We can't talk about the Sixties without taking a long look into the past. I suggest we look back as far as the Thirties, for this will give us valuable perspective. Young or old, we are prone to forget or under-rate what has been accomplished in the past. We groan about present difficulties and despair of ever being able to solve some of them.

Everyone could make a long list of important things, urgent things which still remain to be done in his jurisdiction and in the personnel field generally. A mountain of work looms ahead, but, if you think back on the past, you suddenly realize that this mountain is not as big as it used to be.

Before making this comparison, I want to refer to what Lawrence Appley refers to as "the frustration gap." By this he means the contrast between ideals and reality and how discouraging this gap is as we struggle in the present to narrow it. Personnel practitioners usually don't think of themselves as idealists, but I know few of them who don't feel deeply that certain improvements should be made in personnel programs. There's no use denying that there is a "frustration gap" in personnel work; indeed, the difficulty of pointing to tangible measurements of what the personnel office has accomplished adds to this sense of despair. But note Appley's wise words: "what is significant in life is not how far human practice is from the ideal, but how much nearer it is to the ideal than it was at some previous time."

PERSONNEL ADMINISTRATION IN THE THIRTIES

Important developments were taking shape by the late Thirties, particularly in the Federal government, but in general this is the picture of public personnel administration in the country as a whole at that time:

A preponderance of the daily working hours devoted to the routine aspects of appointments, records, and classification.

Centralization of most important personnel decisions in the Civil Service Commission and normal delays of several weeks in placing someone on the department payrolls.

Very little in-service training activity and, worse, the definite opinion of Congress, the General Accounting Office, and some personnel people themselves that the employee was responsible for his own training.

Only scattered evidence of interest in the improved personnel practices being developed in private industry, despite the obvious importance of some of these techniques and the possibility of using them in the government.

Very little career planning in the line departments, despite the rush of college graduates, attracted by the New Deal, to Washington.

Internships chiefly limited to those generously provided by the National Institute of Public Affairs (even though the NIPA paid the interns, even the legality of this program was questioned!).

Almost a complete neglect of the importance of good supervision and of the personnel responsibilities of line officials in general.

A fairly high percentage of supervisors whose basic conception of their role was "to get the work out of" their subordinates.

Very few personnel directors with any real voice in the management policies of their agencies.

Little attention to employee welfare and health, apart from some low-priced cafeterias, emergency rooms, bowling leagues, and softball.

Nagging restrictions (none of which could safely be questioned), such as no payment of moving of household effects, travel expenses of applicants called for interview, and, in general, a niggardly attitude towards payment of legitimate expenses of employees.

HOW FAR UP THE HILL?

Why is the picture so much better today? Most important of all, the whole concept of personnel administration has changed. Today there is far more recognition of the vital role that personnel management can play in accomplishing agency objectives. It no longer is considered as just an adjunct to the agency program. On the contrary, it is now accepted by many as an indispensable part of the management equipment for carrying out the agency program successfully.

To quote Appley again, management *is* personnel administration. Many more people now accept this, and this is true in government, not just in industry. This description may seem to exaggerate the current rating of the personnel function. On the other hand, its present position, speaking generally for the nation as a whole, is one of relative strength and should not be under-rated.

What are some of the noteworthy improvements? The examination process is much faster; delays of several months in preparing eligible lists are no longer common. No self-respecting personnel administrator could get away with this nowadays. Even more important, the examinations themselves are substantially improved. In fact, there is good reason to believe that government does a better job of selection than most private companies. Recruitment efforts are both more intensive and more effective. In fact, we may have gone so far in this direction that some possible candidates, for example college students, are given an exaggerated sense of their importance. But certainly it is better to woo them as a group than to make no appeal at all to any of them.

DECENTRALIZATION

Could the Civil Service Commission be persuaded to decentralize? This was a question many personnel people discussed anxiously before the outbreak of World War II. One personnel man present at a large meeting of Federal personnel workers during the War suggested that the Commission should allow the agencies to classify positions, subject to Commission standards and post-audit. Actually, to meet the war emergency the Commission had greatly speeded up approval of classification and appointment actions. Still the suggestion seemed utopian at the time. It was thought that the Commission would never agree to this. Yet just a few years afterwards in 1949, such decentralization was provided for by law, with the Commission concurring. Perhaps there should be even more decentralization than there is today, but no one can deny that, whereas the Commission insisted on many prior approvals before the War, today its keynote is decentralization and reliance on agency initiative and responsibility.

TRAINING

The contrast with the past is the greatest in the field of training. It is true that such astute observers as Gladys Kammerer have not found too much in the way of significant advance in training activities in many state governments. Yet some state and local jurisdictions have progressed greatly in this area. The increasing tendency of local government units to pay tuition and related expenses for the further eduction of their employees in colleges, universities, and other outside facilities definitely is a development which reflects the spirit of the public personnel administration of the postwar days. Even the less highly-rated state and local civil service agencies seem to find it necessary to do something, even if not very much, in the field of in-service training. They are at least conscious that this is a part of the personnel responsibility.

The biggest burst of training activity has taken place, of course, in the Federal government. What made this possible—the training legislation passed in 1958—was slow in coming, but, to illustrate the changed outlook, now the Commission is speaking of training as a continuing necessity for every employee. In other words, even the best workers never reach the point where they are in need of no improvement and therefore of no further training.

When he was Chairman of the Commission, Roger Jones expressed that philosophy, and apparently it has growing acceptance whereas once few dared advocate it.

We have even reached the point where orientation training of political, policy-making officials is a recognized responsibility of the personnel office. Few could have predicted this in the Thirties. Again, the personnel people now even have programs for briefing legislators and their staffs on the essential elements of the civil service system as it functions in the particular jurisdiction. Not too long ago many legislators would have been unreceptive to such briefing.

THE PUBLIC VIEW

Improvements are possible only when there is awareness of their need and desirability. So, understandably, at this point the emphasis shifts from an optimistic review of past gains to a sobering account of what still has to be done.

The key to further progress in public personnel administration, as in many other things, is the willingness of the public to invest more money in it. This obviously is not easy to achieve and it cannot, with justice, be said to be the total responsibility of the personnel administrator. Yet, more must be done in this vital area of public acceptance.

These are some of the questions which need to be asked:

How effective is our liaison with the legislative body in general and with individual legislators in particular?

What can be done to enlist and keep the support of the Chief Executive of the jurisdiction? How can he be persuaded to recommend more adequate funds for the personnel function?

Can it honestly be said that personnel people lobby with the legislative body as strenuously as is the traditional practice of other administrative agencies? Can the same be said for our contacts with the Chief Executive and other influential political policy-making officials?

Do personnel people try to build community support in the same thorough-going way, for example, as some public universities and colleges? (Agreed this comparison is unfair, but is it not at least suggestive?)

Do personnel people use every opportunity available to join forces with public employee organizations in obtaining legislation and public support? Or do they stand aloof or refuse to compromise minor differences with such organizations?

These are the real problems of public relations. Recruiting campaigns, posters, brochures—all of these are very useful, but by themselves they cannot create real public understanding and support. True, luck plays an important role in shaping community attitudes. The two sputniks spurred Congress and some state legislatures to vote bigger appropriations for the support of public education and related activities, *such as training of public employees.* Charles E. Johnson, Counsel for the House Post Office and Civil Service Committee, has said that the Government Employees Training Act of 1958 might not have been passed "if it had not been for Sputnik."

Well, luck or not, it is true that already in the Sixties there has been some about-face in traditional American ideas about what is practical and what isn't. Clearly, there is more willingness to spend money on, and devote time to, projects and activities which cannot be expected to produce results very quickly. It follows then, that a primary goal for the rest of this decade is to capitalize to the utmost on these stirrings of greater interest in improving the human resources of the country. Developing these human resources is the real business of personnel administration.

THE ROLE OF PERSONNEL RESEARCH

Lawrence Appley, in a fine essay entitled "Time Invested v. Time Spent," developed a very simple theme: we can either use up our time with little or nothing to show for it, or we can sacrifice on present pleasures and invest it in hard efforts which bring future rewards. Walter Lippmann and others have made the same point in referring to proposed additional public expenditures for schools, roads, and social security. Under one view, held by many taxpayers, this would be too expensive, but, as Lippmann points out, these are wise investments for the future. If a private company invests in future plant this is good American common sense. If the same is attempted in government, it is extravagance.

To the busy administrator, someone's talking of research may be as irritating as it is to some legislators. To many people, research means time lost in impractical theorizing. Besides, the personnel administrator is not supposed to give anyone the impression that he is interested in long-haired pursuits. He must show above all that he is interested in practical things and in people.

The fallacy here, of course, is that research can and does deal with practical things. It has also told us a good deal about people and their characteristics. Furthermore, no one expects any on personnel office to carry out more than a very small part of the total personnel research effort. Two recent publications bring out very well the tremendous dimensions of the unfinished business in this area: *Personnel Research Frontiers,* by Cecil E. Goode for the PPA, and *An Agenda for Research in Public Personnel Administration,* the latter prepared by Wallace S. Sayre and Frederick C. Mosher for the National Planning Association. . . .

Goode defines personnel research as all research efforts aimed at improving worker productivity, satisfaction, and service. His findings were far from encouraging. Although he did discover that some $25 to $55 million a year was being spent on personnel or human relations research, he found that very little of it had a direct application to the public service. . . . Goode puts it bluntly: "Practitioners do not have much understanding or knowledge of important new human research and insights." By practitioners he means practicing personnel people.

Now the purpose in quoting the words of Goode is certainly not to indulge in the favorite sport of some teachers—castigating the practitioner. It would, among other things, be poor research to do so, because Goode also concludes that "many political scientists and public administration people are not interested in studying personnel problems." Everyone shares the blame for the scant attention given to personnel research. . . .

The Sayre-Mosher "Agenda" is downright frightening. Under many different headings, the authors list hundreds of specific problems and issues about which there is insufficient information. Of course, it is true that in many cases what they seek is more adequate information than is now available; it is not that there is no information or real knowledge in many important areas. Yet this "Agenda" projects enough research to absorb us and many others for quite a few years. It is clear that it could not all be accomplished in the Sixties!

Much of this research, of course, can and should be carried out by private foundations, universities, and similar organizations. Most of the items on the Sayre-Mosher "Agenda" are of this character, for they do not deal with the technical operating problems of immediate concern to the personnel practitioner.

At this point, the work of the recently-formed Municipal Manpower Commission should be noted. This Commission was established by the Ford Foundation to make a detailed analysis of the needs of urban governments for administrative, technical, and professional personnel. When it has finished its fact-finding, it will then recommend means for the education, recruitment, and utilization of such personnel.

* * *

AGENDA FOR THE SIXTIES

Apart from more effective public relations and vastly expanded personnel research in general, what are some of the specific problems or issues that personnel administrators should be, and are, placing on their "Agenda" for solution in the Sixties? That is, some of the vexing operating problems that daily confront the personnel administrator and technicians. High on the "Agenda" would be the following.

Public Service Careers: Increased attention to career service planning, particularly in state and local governments. The Federal government has certainly not reached the millennium in this regard, but it has definitely improved its drawing power, largely through its success with the Federal Service Entrance Examination.

Of course, the Federal service can offer better pay, but I have found that there is nothing most states offer which is in any way comparable to the FSEE. Today most college students, no matter what their major, can be shown that there is a possible career for them in the Federal service. It is much more difficult to convince them of this in the case of state and local government.

Is it so very difficult to obtain the equivalent of the FSEE in state and local governments? There is no reason why this should be so, particularly in the larger and better-supported jurisdictions. Is enough attention being given to really intensive efforts to achieve the goal of career service? Some stock-taking here certainly is in order.

Merit versus Seniority: Improving the merit system by placing more emphasis on merit and less on seniority.

Of course, civil service law and regulations usually tie the personnel office's hands as far as seniority is concerned. It may be required, for example, to give additional points in promotional examinations for length of service. It may have to lay off a first-rate employee and keep a much inferior one because the latter has more "seniority."

This may be true, but personnel people themselves have been sometimes lulled into too much acceptance of the seniority cult. Is it not perturbing that in *merit* systems the practice of basing promotions largely on seniority should not only exist but frequently be accepted as correct? How can this be reconciled with strict application of the merit principle in original recruitment? Why is selection of the best-qualified persons desirable in the one case and not in the other? And is it not true that one of the biggest obstacles to a true career system has been this undue emphasis on seniority? Surely the line should be held, at least, and any further inroads of the seniority principle opposed.

Compensation Plans: More willingness to depart from traditional practices in establishing and administering pay plans. Here again administrative discretion is limited, but strong recommendations can be made to the legislative body and the Chief Executive.

A high-priority objective in the Sixties should be to obtain acceptance of the principle of paying prevailing wages to white, as well as blue, collar employees. It has been perfectly obvious for some times that it is illogical for government to meet industry competition for skilled and unskilled workers in the trade and labor fields but not to do so in the case of executives, specialists in the different professions, and clerical workers.

The U.S. Civil Service Commission now not only accepts the prevailing wage principle but recommends its adoption immediately. It still remains, of course, for the Congress to act, but previously a serious obstacle had been lack of initiative within the Executive Branch in obtaining this kind of change. The legislature cannot be expected to take the initiative, and personnel people can help greatly in getting the ball rolling. [*Editor's note: Congress did act in 1962 when it passed a pay bill based on the principle of comparability of Federal salaries with those in private enterprise.*]

It also seems that many jurisdictions still devote much more time to the classification, than they do to the compensation, plan. Both are important, but more consideration should be given to such possible innovations as longevity increases and salary premiums for critical occupations. Some of these ideas, like salary premiums, may prove neither practical nor sound, but some local jurisdictions have already pioneered with good results.

Combining merit with automatic salary increases is one example. Using progressive instead of "level" increments is still another. Other examples could be cited, but the question here is how many jurisdictions are really weighing the advantages of and testing these new ideas in practice? It seems apparent that not enough jurisdictions are critically reexamining the traditional concepts of wage and salary administration.

Performance Evaluation: Development of much more reliable and acceptable systems of evaluating employee performance. It is no secret that little progress has been made in this area. The problem is difficult, but certainly better results should be possible than are now being obtained. Should it not at least be possible before the end of the Sixties to so improve service ratings that people won't snicker as they do now at the mere mention of such ratings? Can we afford this continuing embarrassment of ratings which nobody takes seriously?

*   *   *

The trend in private industry is clearly away from trait rating schemes, with their inherent vagueness, to plans based on an accurate identification of the main elements in the particular job and an evaluation of how effectively the employee carries them out. This principle is solidly accepted by many public personnel technicians, but the tendency still is to stick with the system already in use or not to make any thoroughgoing changes in it.

It is obvious that really good service rating systems won't be developed unless legislative bodies and the public come to recognize that much more money is going to have to be allocated to this part of the personnel job than at present. Like tests, evaluation of employee performance requires a good deal of study and experimentation, all of which costs money. If this had been recognized a long time ago, certainly much better results would have been achieved in this area.

Probation: Making the probationary period effective, instead of allowing it to remain the dead letter it is in most jurisdictions. The law and regulations usually make it easy to dismiss unsatisfactory employees during the working test period.

Of course, the fault is that of the supervisors; they simply won't be tough enough to recommend separating even a non-permanent employee. Is that any responsibility of the personnel office? Yes, because, while human nature is difficult to change, the supervisor can be prodded to discharge his personnel responsibilities properly. If he can be told he can't hire someone, why can't he be told that he has the responsibility to drop any probationer with whose performance he is not satisfied?

Too often, the supervisor justifies his failure to act by convincing himself that the personnel office would only supply him with an even less satisfactory employee. Meanwhile, the personnel office hears rumors about, or even has direct evidence of, the inefficiency of the probationary employee. It, however, washes its hands of the matter by deciding that it is up to the supervisor to act and that there is nothing that it can do. The personnel office ought to be able to get into the picture at the right time and to try, at least, to induce the supervisor to carry out this important part of his responsibility.

The Back Door: Dismissing permanent employees if they are clearly unsatisfactory. Here, of course, the employee's rights of appeal and a hearing provide the supervisor with a ready excuse: it is all so much trouble.

Yet, union agreements complicate the dismissal process in industry as well. It takes courage to discharge someone both in industry and government. In government, it may also take the patience of Job. It is also true that it should not be made possible for a supervisor to fire anyone just because he doesn't like him. And, just as in the case of the probationary employee, it is the responsibility of the supervisor to initiate the dismissal action. But supervisors need to be educated and encouraged and the personnel office should have a positive program for doing so.

There is a definite technique to preparing dismissal cases for hearing before the Civil Service Commission or other reviewing agency. Is as much time spent on this as the desired results deserve? It is all very annoying, but in the end worth it.

Employee-Management Relations: Developing machinery for systematic employee-management cooperation in improving personnel practices and carrying out the work of the agency in general. In most jurisdictions, numerous safeguards and protections exist for the individual employee. What very often is missing, however, is a recognized channel for registering and making effective the viewpoints of the employees as a group.

Management stands to gain when it regularly seeks the suggestions of the employee groups and sounds them out on proposed policies. Labor-management cooperation in industry has proved its value. Frequently, misunderstandings and friction arise simply because adequate channels for communication do not exist. Certainly, this is a problem area which cannot be neglected in the Sixties as pressures for union recognition and collective bargaining rights increase. The wisest policy is to anticipate these pressures and for personnel administrators and management in general to take the initiative in developing this machinery for mutual cooperation.

These problems need much more intensive treatment to do them justice than has been possible in this brief paper. However, one thing seems clear from placing the development, achievements, and goals of the personnel administration field in perspective. The personnel profession is in good shape to meet the challenges of the Sixties and significant progress in personnel administration is in prospect.

53. Collective Bargaining in Public Employment: Form and Scope*

STERLING D. SPERO

LABOR management relations in the public service are moving toward the

* Reprinted from *Public Administration Review,* Winter 1962, by permission of the American Society for Public Administration.

patterns prevailing in private employment. The traditional methods of determining working conditions by legislation or unilateral decision by the employing authority are slowly giving way to systems of collective bargaining analogous to those outside the government services. This development has been most marked in municipal employment. Philadelphia has signed union contracts covering all of its employees outside the uniformed forces. New York City adopted collective bargaining a few years ago. Its Board of Education is now in the process of installing formal bargaining arrangements for its 44,000 employees. More than 400 local and state government agencies as well as scores of school and special districts now have collective agreements with their employees. The federal government is implementing the report of a Task Force recommending the formal recognition of employee organizations for collective bargaining on all personnel matters within the competence of the employing agency.

COLLECTIVE BARGAINING OR COLLECTIVE NEGOTIATION?

Yet opposition to determining the working conditions of government employees by negotiation and agreement between the employing authority and its organized workers is still strong in many quarters. The roots of this opposition lie in the theory of the sovereign state under which government as the custodian of ultimate authority in the community must exercise the right of final decision in all matters affecting its relations with its servants. The opponents of collective bargaining regard it as a process presupposing equality between the parties to the employment relationship which conflicts with the claims of the sovereign employer and runs counter to the "nature of the state."

This position was implied in President Franklin D. Roosevelt's statement in 1937:

. . . the process of collective bargaining as usually understood cannot be transplanted into the public service.

. . . The very nature and purposes of government make it impossible for administrative officers to represent fully or bind the employer in mutual discussions with government employee organizations. . . .

Many employing authorities have sought to justify their unwillingness to bargain collectively with employee organizations by seizing upon this statement as proof that it was "impossible" for them to do so. This attitude has persisted in spite of the fact that the President in dedicating the Chicamauga Dam of the Tennessee Valley Authority three years after he made this statement praised "the splendid new agreement between organized labor and the T.V.A.," which had just been consummated, declaring, "collective bargaining and efficiency have proceeded hand in hand."

It should be noted that President Roosevelt specifically used the term "collective bargaining." Public administrators and employee organizations which engage in collective negotiation and are fully aware of the differences between public and private employment believe that the term accurately describes the labor relations process in which they engage. Others, however, prefer such terms as "collective negotiation," "collective dealing," "joint consultation and agreement," on the ground that "collective bargaining" has legal connotations applicable only in private enterprise.

The primary distinction between public and private labor-management agreements is the fact that the former are made subject to the overriding power of the government. The T.V.A. agreements to which President Roosevelt referred declare:

The parties recognize that T.V.A. is an agency of and is accountable to the government of the United States of America. Therefore T.V.A. must operate within the limits of its legally delegated authority and responsibility.

Similarly the Constitution of Whitley Councils in Great Britain, which are highly formalized instruments for employee-management negotiations, provide that the agreements reached between the organized "staff side" and the government's representatives known as the "official side" shall become effective "subject to the overriding authority of Parliament and the responsibility of the minister."

While the legal differences between collective agreements in public and private employment are important, the tendency to regard collective bargaining in the public service as a question of law rather than as a matter of public policy has been a source of confusion. A central aspect of sovereign power is authority to make public policy decisions. A policy decision by government to establish collective bargaining procedures in its services is itself a sovereign act.

FORM AND SCOPE OF COLLECTIVE BARGAINING

Although the growth of public service collective bargaining moves consideration of the process from the realm of political and legal theory to the field of administrative policy and practice, the law continues to be a primary factor affecting the solution of practical problems.

Two such practical problems rooted in the law are the form and the scope of the public collective agreement. Both problems involve administrative discretion. In many instances courts or law officers have questioned the power of public authorities to enter into formal contracts either because they found no legal grant of power to do so or because they believed that a formal contract improperly delegated the authority of the employing agency and bound its freedom to administer. Although government in its dealings with business constantly enters into contracts which bind administrative discretion, courts and law officers have been reluctant to admit such contractual authority in personnel matters. In such circumstances when collective bargaining was desired by employing agencies the essence of the bargaining process has been sustained and the letter of the law preserved by publishing agreements in the form of unilateral statements of policy, executive directives, or memoranda of agreement. In some cities the results of collective bargaining agreements were published as resolutions or acts of the local legislative body.

The scope of collective bargaining likewise involves the issue of administrative discretion. Where an agency has a high degree of autonomy and fiscal independence, the scope of collective bargaining is virtually as wide as in private employment. Where, on the other hand, basic conditions of work are fixed by classification acts, time and leave laws, and statutory hiring and promotion procedures, the scope of collective bargaining is obviously far more limited. But even here the area of administrative discretion in the application of the laws is substantial. The manner in which the classification system is carried out, in which vacation dates are determined, in which assignments and promotions are made are all matters of deep employee concern. Employee-management agreements covering such matters in the postal service and government industrial works as well as in white collar agencies and public institutions on all governmental levels have been in effect for many years. As government services become larger and more complex, it becomes increasingly desirable to devolve discretion over personnel matters to administrators. Public employees want a voice in the exercise of this discretion for the same reasons as do employees in private industry.

NEED FOR AN EXCLUSIVE BARGAINING UNIT

No collective bargaining, whether of broad or more limited scope, can take place until there is a responsible employee bargaining agent with which to deal. Where the bargaining process concerns conditions of work, the recognition of a sole bargaining agent to represent all employees of a given category is clearly indicated. There can be only one system of working conditions in a jurisdiction. Objections have been raised to the recognition of exclusive bargaining agents on the ground that such recognition compels employees in an open employment system recruited on the basis of merit to be represented by an organization to which they may not wish to belong.

Negotiation between management and a multi-organization panel or committee has been suggested as an alternative. Such plans, however, have not proved satisfactory. They give rise to pulling and hauling among the competing groups within the negotiating panel. In the end, they tend to break down or to evolve into a system of sole representation. The experiences of the New York Transit System, where a plural representation plan established in the 1940's was eventually abandoned in favor of an exclusive bargaining unit, is a striking example. The Tennessee Valley Authority had a somewhat similar experience with its white-collar employees. The Report of the President's Task Force of Employee-Management Relations in the Federal Service endorses exclusive representation for purposes of negotiation and agreement on working conditions where a union has the support of a majority in an agency, but reserves "informal recognition" and access to management for the presentation of views to minority groups.

After all, the problem of bargaining representation is a practical one. Majority rule in politics may give rise to many individual dissatisfactions, but it is a practical device. An exclusive bargaining agent freely chosen representing a majority of the employees concerned is a manifestation of majority rule and representative industrial government. Supervision of the choice of

a bargaining agent can either be made the duty of the central personnel agency or another independent body.

The check-off of dues is usually regarded as a feature of exclusive bargaining. There are many unions in private employment in this country and abroad which prefer to have their agents circulate among their members and hear their gripes and learn their attitudes in the dues collecting process. However, the check-off has become a recognized practice in public employment. Sometimes the cost of the process is shared by the parties, sometimes it is borne by one or the other of them. The President's Task Force has recommended that Congress authorize a voluntary check-off in the Federal service.

Some employee organizations insist that the union shop under which all employees in the bargaining unit are required to join the union is the logical consequence of the recognition of an exclusive bargaining agent. The union shop, they hold, prevents "free riding" by individuals who receive the benefits of the union without paying dues or bearing the responsibilities of membership. The union shop is a device invented by the labor movement in private industry to prevent employers from weakening the union and undermining standards through the introduction of cheap non-union labor. Such tactics are possible in jurisdictions without merit systems, but highly unlikely, if not impossible, where recruitment is on a merit basis and standards are uniform and publicly declared. In such situations unions have generally been able to convince non-members to join by demonstrating the significance of their services. Although the union shop seems to be winning increasing acceptance in local governments and exists for practical purposes, without formal recognition, in some federal agencies, it is not an essential complement of collective bargaining in the public service.

It is essential, however, that procedures be available for the resolution of grievances and other disputes arising under the collective agreements. In industry labor-management contracts almost invariably provide for the settlement of disputes arising under them through final and binding arbitration by impartial third parties. Legal objections have at times been raised to such procedures in the public service on the ground that they permit outsiders to bind the administrative discretion of public officials. But ways have been found to overcome this obstacle by designating public officers of official bodies as arbitrators. Thus the Secretary of Labor serves as binding arbitrator on wages in the T.V.A. and the Joint Committee on Printing performs the same function in the Government Printing Office. The State Legislature has clothed an outside arbitrator with official status in the New York Transit System. Many other examples might be cited. Final and binding awards under such circumstances derogate administrative authority no more than rulings on appeal to central personnel agencies or boards of review on ratings, discipline, or dismissals.

In practice final and binding awards under agreements have not proved necessary. Awards in the form of advice to the agency head are all that are normally required. The publicity attached to them has given the parties ample protection while the legal authority of the agency has remained intact.

ANTI-STRIKE POLICY: A FACT IN THE PUBLIC SERVICE

The more difficult problem is that of resolving disputes regarding working conditions where the bargaining process results in an impasse. In private employment under such circumstances workers have recourse to the strike. In the public service strikes are outlawed either by legislation as in the case of the federal government and eleven states or by other sanctions such as the attitude of the public authorities, the courts, and the press. Many countries actually guarantee the right of their government employees to strike. The right has often been exercised and the governments concerned still stand. Yet, in the United States, the slogan "one cannot strike against the government" has become an article of faith to be accepted without question. This, despite the fact that strikes by many classes of workers in private industry could do far more damage to the community than strikes of certain classes of public employees. It is hardly logical for the government to guarantee the right to strike to transportation, communication and utility workers, and the handlers of perishable foods, who are private employees, and forbid it by law or practice to park attendants, charwomen in government buildings, or record office clerks, who are government employees. If it is not the convenience and welfare of the community but the continuous functioning of the public services which justifies anti-strike policy for public employees, then it should be noted that strikes by private utility or transport workers could interfere with the operations of government as directly as strikes by government employees.

However illogical anti-strike policy confined to public workers may be, it is nevertheless a fact. Equally important is the fact that, although strikes have occurred even in the face of drastic legislation, the strike is not a significant weapon in the American public service. All of the techniques for the settlement of disputes in private employment have been used in the course of public service negotiation. These have included mediation and conciliation, fact finding with and without recommendations, and advisory or final and binding voluntary arbitration.

Compulsory arbitration has been widely recommended as a socially desirable substitute for the strike. Private industry has generally rejected it. Many of the reasons given for such rejection are also applicable in the public service, particularly the objection that the compulsory process tends to discourage full and effective bargaining. Its very availability encourages the parties to dump their problems into the arbitrator's lap, relieving the principals from making difficult decisions and unpleasant concessions to be justified to their constituents. Compulsory arbitration has long been a feature of Australian and Canadian labor relations. It has been tried in the Canadian municipal services with so little success in some cases that the local governments concerned have recommended the recognition of the right to strike. This recommendation was based on the ground that the compulsory process not only discouraged effective bargaining pushing hard questions into arbitration, but also led employee organizations to make excessive demands in the belief that they could always be sure of getting a good part of what they asked from the arbitrators.

THE LEVER OF POLITICAL POWER

The most effective substitute for the strike in government service is the political power of the employees. The political environment in which public employee-management relations are carried on is quite different from the milieu of private labor relations. Pressure on the public official which ultimately might affect his job gives the public employee organization a leverage which is at least a partial substitute for the strike. Publicity by employee organizations through demonstrations, advertisements in the newspapers, broadcasts, and loud general screaming frequently provide the setting in which the process of bargaining takes place. The atmosphere thus created is intended not only to soften the administration but also to ease the way for deals with legislative and party leaders. Arrangements prior

to formal bargaining between unions and elected officials in which political support is exchanged for promises of concessions to the employees are hardly unknown even under the most meticulously correct merit systems. This sort of thing is more common in local and state jurisdictions than in the Federal government, but it has its counterparts, though somewhat less bizarre, even there.

Traditionally government employee unions on all governmental levels have used their political power to check or overrule the administration and to obtain legislation spelling out working conditions in detail. This greatly circumscribed the administrative discretion of operating officials, but it was exactly what the unions wished to do. They regarded the legislature as a buffer between themselves and their bosses, who with rare exceptions refused to recognize and deal with them, thus making recourse to the legislature their only alternative to accepting unchecked executive control over their working lives.

If civil service reform in this country had not begun at the wrong end, at the bottom with the clerks instead of at the top with the administrators (perhaps this was inevitable at the time) the country might long ago have developed a corps of government executives in whom the great body of employees had confidence. This now has begun to happen and the change is one of the reasons why employee negotiation with officials with broad administrative discretion can take the place of the traditional system of detailed legislative regulation.

Collective bargaining has had its best results in government employment in the agencies with a high degree of autonomy and broad discretionary authority. The test will henceforth be in the agencies which operate under tight personnel legislation. At the beginning the scope of possible negotiation will necessarily be limited. Success in this limited area can be expected to lead to the relaxation of legislative strictures and thus to widening the field open for employee-management agreement. This should give the employees greater influence over their working lives than they have under the legislative system and the administrator the freer hand in the operation of his agency that the complexity of modern public administration requires.

Part VIII

LOCAL GOVERNMENTS

ALTHOUGH dreamers from time to time have called for its abolition, the county continues to function as a vital unit of local government in most parts of the United States. Even though the county in many places functions primarily to provide services to rural areas, it is of growing importance to urban residents. In his brief article, Victor Jones calls attention to the variety of urban-type services provided by counties with a population in excess of 100,000. Although Mr. Jones' specific reference is to Alameda County, California, his observations provide insight into the changing nature of county government today.

It is a truism that cities everywhere face increasingly troublesome problems. The nature of the problems faced by individual cities and the manner in which they are handled are determined in part by the economic and social characteristics of their residents. Victor Jones, Richard Forstall, and Andrew Collver call attention to this basis for the classification of cities. The crucial question of "Who Runs Our Town?" is examined by John Yager; he stresses the importance of the nature of political leadership in a community—its "power structure"— and outlines the chief potential sources of such leadership. Also, the *form* of city government may well be affected by these same factors. Edgar L. Sherbenou develops the thesis that a relationship exists between the council-manager form of government and the class structure of the cities in which it is found. Mr. Sherbenou's findings are based on a study of 74 suburban cities around Chicago, and he concludes that when these cities "are ranked from top to bottom according to their median housing values, a definite coincidence of high housing values and the council-manager form of municipal government becomes apparent." In the top 20 cities, manager government exists in all but two, while in the bottom 31 communities, there is not a single instance of this form of government.

The difficulties often encountered in the efforts to apply the home rule concept to specific circumstances are illustrated in *Pipoly v. Benson* and *State ex rel. Heinig v. City of Milwaukee*. The nature of the problem of local tort liability is considered in *Muskopf v. Corning Hospital District*. The decision of the court in this case is in accord with the gradual trend toward reducing the area of governmental immunity.

A thorough examination and description of special districts, the "new dark continent of American politics," is found in *Special District Governments in the United States,* by John C. Bollens. In his examination of the "General Characteristics of Special Districts," Mr. Bollens provides the reader with an exceptionally clear and comprehensive understanding of the nature of these increasingly important units of local government. He defines them, examines the causes leading to their proliferation, describes the procedures followed in their creation, details the functions that they perform, notes their potentialities and handicaps, analyzes the nature of their governing bodies, and explains their finances.

The problems of large urban areas disregard the boundaries of local governmental jurisdictions, making action by larger governments imperative. The states cannot afford to disregard their responsibilities, since they are the only institutions now capable of meeting some of the problems generated by rapid urban growth; and the states have inaugurated numerous programs directed toward this objective. According to John Grumm, however, they have not met their responsibilities adequately. He argues that by concentrating their local services, research, and supervisory activities into one agency, the states could do a more effective job. A few states, including New Jersey, Pennsylvania, and Tennessee have taken steps in this direction.

54. The Changing Role of the Urban County in Local Government*

VICTOR JONES

THE Alameda County Board of Supervisors and other county officials, as well as the members of the Citizens' Charter

* Reprinted with permission from *Public Affairs Report,* Institute of Governmental Studies, Universityy of California, Berkeley, June 1963. Footnotes omitted.

Review Committee of Alameda County, are concerned with the County's ability to provide certain areawide services and to establish and maintain control over the physical development of the rapidly growing unincorporated portion of the county. An additional concern arises from changes in the role of urban counties in governing metropolitan areas. Alameda County has become an active partner with its own municipalities, with other counties and cities in the Bay Area, with metropolitan special districts, and with state and federal agencies in planning, formulating, and administering many important public policies.

I shall try to place these changes in county government, which have been under way in Alameda County and the Bay Area for at least a third of a century, in an historical perspective and in the contemporary context of national problems and responses. It is not only a comfort but it is enlightening to see that our immediate efforts and concerns are shared by other people in many other counties throughout the United States.

Traditionally, the county has been considered as a geographical subdivision of the state in which designated officials are elected or appointed to administer certain state laws. In this respect they have usually been contrasted with municipalities, which are said to be "created mainly for the interest, advantage, and convenience of the locality and its people." This quotation is taken from an opinion of the Ohio Supreme Court in 1857. The opinion is still cited frequently, but increasingly it is now qualified by statements that in the last 100 years urban counties have become more like municipal corporations.

Nevertheless, the full statement in *Commissioners of Hamilton County* v. *Mighels* (7 Ohio St. 109, 118-119 [1857]) can be taken as the classic concept of the role to be played by county government. It also serves as a bench mark from which to measure the extent to which county government has changed in the last century, at least in urban areas.

Municipal corporations proper are called into existence, either at the direct solicitation or by the free consent of the people who compose them.

Counties are local subdivisions of *a* state, created by the sovereign power of the state, of its own sovereign will, without the particular solicitation, consent, or concurrent action of the people who inhabit them. The former organization is asked for, or at least assented to by the people it embraces; the latter is superimposed by a sovereign and paramount authority.

A municipal corporation proper is created mainly for the interest, advantage, and convenience of the locality and its people; a county organization is created almost exclusively with a view to the policy of the state at large, for purposes of political organization and civil administration, in matters of finance, of education, of provision for the poor, of military organization, of the means of travel and transport, and especially for the general administration of justice. With scarcely an exception, all the powers and functions of the county organization have a direct and exclusive reference to the general policy of the state, and are, in fact, but a branch of the general administration of that policy.

There are still significant differences between cities and counties, but the differences emphasized in 1857 have become blurred. Since the early years of the 19th century, county officials have been locally selected, usually by popular election. The primary functions of counties may have been state functions but county government could never have been a "mere administrative agency" of the state when its officials were locally elected and locally accountable for their political tenure of office.

In the second place, cities have also been used as "agents" for the administration of state laws. And, thirdly, urban counties have engaged in activities for the convenience and benefit of local inhabitants.

These changes have been more extensive and rapid in metropolitan and urban areas than in the rest of the country. In 1960 there were 310 counties in metropolitan areas, or approximately 10 per cent of the . . . counties in the United States. Almost two thirds of the metropolitan counties had populations of 100,000 or more. Only 13 counties in the United States are larger than Alameda County.

As the metropolitan county feels the impact of rapid growth and reacts to the demands and needs of urban residents, it finds itself playing four different, yet interweaving, roles:

1. *The county is still the traditional local "administrative" agent of the state.* As I have already pointed out, other units of local government also share this function with the county. The state, either alone or in conjunction with the federal government, will rely increasingly upon local governments to carry out its programs for urban inhabitants.

Even in this traditional role, urban and metropolitan counties can no longer be correctly called "mere administrative agencies." They are local governments with political lines to local power structures and accountable to local constituencies.

2. *Urban and metropolitan counties have in different ways and in varying degrees become, or are becoming, the substitute for a municipal government in providing urban services to people who live outside municipal boundaries.* Los Angeles County has gone further in developing this role than any other county, although it is now acting through the Lakewood plan whereby it assists unincorporated municipalities to incorporate and contract with the county for the provision of most municipal services. Tables 1, 2, and 3 show how far urban and metropolitan counties in the United States have gone into "the municipal business."

Counties and cities have fought over the extent to which the financing of such services for a portion of the county residents should come from the general fund, raised by a levy upon all resi-

TABLE 1   *Number of Counties Over 100,000 Population Providing Urban Type Services to Unincorporated Urban Areas, 1961*

Service	Total	Over 1,000,000	500,000 to 1,000,000	250,000 to 500,000	100,000 to 250,000
Police	152	5	27	28	92
Fire	54	2	11	12	29
Street construction	112	7	26	24	55
Street lighting	39	1	12	10	16
Recreation	83	5	15	27	36
Parks	95	9	25	28	53
Garbage collection	28	0	8	6	14
Public housing	15	1	6	1	7
Libraries	100	5	17	23	55
None	9	0	2	1	6
Not reporting	15	0	0	3	12

TABLE 2   *Number of Counties Over 100,000 Population Providing Urban Type Services Throughout the County, 1961*

Service	Total	Over 1,000,000	500,000 to 1,000,000	250,000 to 500,000	100,000 to 250,000
Police	73	0	9	10	54
Fire	12	0	0	2	10
Street construction	45	0	9	10	26
Street lighting	3	0	0	0	3
Recreation	47	1	9	15	22
Parks	73	5	16	18	34
Garbage collection	5	0	1	0	4
Public housing	3	0	1	0	2
Libraries	64	3	7	16	38
None	52	3	12	11	26
Not reporting	42	1	3	9	29

TABLE 3   *Percentage of Counties Over 100,000 Population Providing Services to Entire County and to Unincorporated Areas, 1961*

	Per Cent of Counties Providing Services to	
	Entire County	Unincorporated Areas
Police	33.0	68.8
Fire	5.4	24.4
Street construction	20.4	50.7
Street lighting	1.4	17.6
Recreation	21.3	37.5
Parks	33.0	42.9
Garbage collection	2.3	12.7
Public housing	1.4	6.8
Libraries	28.9	45.2
None	23.5	4.1
Not reporting	19.0	6.8

dents. The issue is still unresolved, even in Miami or, for that matter, in Los Angeles under the Lakewood plan. The matter has recently been explored by the Alameda County Mayors' Conference and the Board of Supervisors.

One result of the search for a means of insuring that localized services are paid for by the immediate beneficiaries has been the multiplication of small special districts. This problem is now being studied by a committee of the Association of Bay Area Governments.

The problem of providing municipal services and land use controls in unincorporated areas is not shrinking in Alameda County. In 1960, there were 117,716 residents of the county living outside corporate boundaries. This is only 13 per cent of the population of the county, but it represents a sizable population to be governed and serviced. Only 135 cities in the United States have more inhabitants than the unincorporated population of Alameda County.

Furthermore, the number and perhaps the percentage of this group of county residents is likely to increase. Incorporations of new municipalities and extensive annexations to existing cities will undoubtedly reduce the pressure. If three new cities had not been incorporated in the southern part of the county between 1950 and 1960 and if older cities in the same part of the county had not annexed so widely, the unincorporated population would have been approximately 274,000 in 1960.

*   *   *

. . . we can expect demands for services to increase. Even more important is the need for the planning of urban expansion. At the present time, only the county can guide and control this development during the period while it is occurring and before incorporation and annexation. In the absence of adequate planning by the county and effective controls in the development and use of land, pressure for state controls will increase.

3. *At the same time that urban and metropolitan counties begin to look like suburban governments, they face demands that they act like regional governments.* The principal reason is that more of the metropolitan area lies within the jurisdiction of county government than any other general unit of government. In fact, in 120 of the 212 standard metropolitan statistical areas,

recognized by the U.S. Bureau of the Census, all of the metropolitan area is within a single county. Tables 2 and 3 indicate the services that urban and metropolitan counties provide throughout the county.

Alameda County covers only a portion of the Bay Area and cannot, therefore, be used to provide whatever services and controls may be desired on a regional basis. The Bay Area, however, is so large and complex that responsive counties can play an important role in providing selective services and controls on a level intermediate between municipalities and the entire Bay Area.

4. *As participants in intergovernmental programs,* counties and municipalities are beginning to collaborate in the formulation of intergovernmental urban programs, in the adaptation of such programs to a particular urban area, in regional planning, and in regional administration. In playing this role, the county is not acting as the local "administrative" agent of the state or the national government.

In fact, the role of equal partner can be played effectively only if local governments collaborate on a metropolitan basis for the purpose of understanding local and regional issues, arriving at a consensus or some other form of decision about desirable governmental policies, and participating from the strength of these positions in negotiations with state and federal agencies. Alameda County supervisors were among the leaders in organizing and developing the Association of Bay Area Governments. Similar regional organizations of elected local officials are to be found in the Detroit, New York, Philadelphia, Washington, D.C., and Puget Sound metropolitan areas.

County boards of supervisors, along with city selection committees in each county, either participate directly or indirectly in selecting members of the governing bodies of regional districts, e.g., Bay Area Air Pollution Control District and the San Francisco Bay Area Rapid Transit District. Supervisors would also serve as members of the policy committee of the proposed Bay Area comprehensive transportation study.

Despite the changing role of the urban county, no county in the United States is organized to play its modern role effectively and responsively. The drag of history, operating through weak county boards and many independently elected officials, has slowed the conversion of the county from a rural to an urban government. Significant changes have been made in a few cases. The metropolitan counties of California, operating under constitutional home rule, have gone farther than most. However, the following matters need to be reexamined to see if the officials and citizens of Alameda County wish to change the structure and procedures of county government.

1. *The policy-making role of the Board of Supervisors.* Should it be relieved of a multitude of detailed administrative tasks to enable it to consider and develop public policies and to participate more extensively in the intergovernmental relations of the Bay Area? Should additional elective offices be made appointive?

2. *Is the Board of Supervisors representative?* This question becomes more important as the county increases in population and becomes involved in urban and metropolitan affairs. The problem is not solely one of numerical equality among supervisorial districts. Is the Board large enough to be representative of the complex interests of residents in the county? Are boundaries of supervisorial districts drawn in a manner to preclude the election of supervisors to represent important though not predominant interests? Are questions such as these relevant in Alameda County in 1963?

3. *The County Administrator.* Should this office be strengthened in order to relieve the Board of Supervisors of the burden of detailed administrative direction of county affairs? What should be the formal relationship of the chief ad-

ministrator to the Board? Do county activities require the administrative supervision of a county manager?

4. *Planning and development.* How can provision be made for the development and continual revision of *long-range* county plans? How can county plans be tied in with state and federal plans and programs, with Bay Area plans, and with municipal plans? Is this function of the county so important today and for the future that it should be given special attention in revising the county charter?

5. *Intergovernmental relations.* Should the county charter specifically recognize that Alameda County is part of the San Francisco Bay Area? Are there provisions in the present charter that impede effective cooperation with federal, state, and other local governments? Can suggestions be made for facilitating and making Alameda County's participation in ABAG more effective?

6. *Civil service.* Can the county, under present or proposed provisions of the charter, recruit and retain an adequate corps of trained and competent specialists and administrators?

7. *Financing urban services.* Should the county Charter provide means whereby residents of unincorporated territory would pay for all urban-type services furnished them by the county? How are such services to be distinguished from general county services?

All four roles of urban and metropolitan counties—traditional, municipal-service, regional and intergovernmental—must be kept in mind as the Charter of Alameda County is reviewed. The first question to be answered is: What do we want the county to do? The second question follows from our answer to the first question: How can the county be organized to function effectively, efficiently, responsively, and responsibly as it discharges all four functions simultaneously?

Definitive answers to these questions cannot be written into a charter. The answers will have to be worked out over the years as the people of Alameda County and the Bay Area decide what they want local government, as well as the state and national governments, to do and not to do and as the active participants engage in planning, policy-making, and administration. What a citizens' charter review committee, or a board of freeholders, can do is to propose changes in organization and procedure that reasoning and experience indicate will enable elected and appointed officials to function more effectively, efficiently, responsively, *and* responsibly.

* * *

55. Economic and Social Classification of Cities*

VICTOR JONES, RICHARD L. FORSTALL, and ANDREW COLLVER

THE industrial development of the South and West, the rising level of urbanization, the movement of the population to the coastal areas, the migration of Negroes to the largest central cities, and the dispersion of metropolitan residents to widely scattered suburbs, have all produced marked differences in the characteristics of the nation's cities. These rapid shifts in the national economy and in the growth and distribution of the population are reflected in the social and economic characteristics of 1,762 cities listed in the classification of cities in the *1963 Municipal Year Book,* to be published in June.

The functional classifications, indices, ratios, and percentages presented in the *1963 Municipal Year Book,* Tables III and 1-10, while considered as raw data, will be enlightening and useful to users of other governmental data in the *Year Book,* enabling them to compare particular cities with other places possessing similar characteristics. Moreover, the raw classification data may be used by social scientists as a basis for grouping cities in order to study the relationship between communal types and political and other social behaviors.

Local governments face a wide vari-

ety of problems, both in kind and in magnitude. In some places parochial and private schools have taken the responsibility for a large portion of elementary teaching; in others this function is performed entirely by the public schools. Some communities are flooded by new residents for whom additional housing, utilities, and other services must be provided; others, confronted with population decline, are in need of some means to revitalize a sagging local economy. Many of the older cities with slowly growing populations have still another problem: that of an obsolete and deteriorating physical plant. Also of major importance as a measure of a city's ability to meet and solve its problems, as well as an index of demands made upon the city, is the composition of the population in terms of socio-economic status. Political participation and the focus of politics is likely to be different in cities with a high proportion of high-income, white-collar, home-owning, white residents.

While this article makes no attempt to explore the connections between social and economic characteristics, singly or in clusters, and political organization and behavior, it is interesting to note that such a connection exists. The purpose here is to summarize the economic classification and other data reproduced

* Reprinted with permission from *Public Management,* May 1963.

and calculated from the 1958 Censuses of Manufactures and Business and the 1960 Censuses of Population and Housing. A secondary purpose is to call attention to the distribution of characteristics by region, size of place, and metropolitan status.

MATERIAL REVISED AND UPDATED

The material on the economic classification of urban places of 10,000 inhabitants or more has been revised and updated since the last economic classification appeared in the *1960 Municipal Year Book*. This has made it possible to present a substantially greater number of urban places than in the past, partly because of expanded coverage, but principally because of the increase in the number of places or urban towns of 10,000 population or more. The number of urban places for which a classification by economic function may now be given has increased from the 1,222 included in the 1960 edition of the Year Book to 1,679 in the present edition.

Cities are classified in five major economic classifications and according to specialized activities. The five major classifications are manufacturing, industrial, diversified-manufacturing, diversified-retailing, and retailing. These classifications, which are based primarily on the balance between manufacturing and retail employment, embrace more than 90 per cent (1,557) of the 1,679 cities classified.

The small minority of 122 cities remaining are those in which some unusual economic activity forms the principal support of the community. These 122 cities are classified as follows: wholesaling, 13; mining, 11; transportation, 8; resort, 5; government, 8; armed forces, 17; professional, 1; hospital, 1; education, 45; and services, 13.

In classifying cities economically, important regional differences in the distributions of the different functional types become very evident. More than 80 per cent of the manufacturing cities are in the Northeast or North Central regions, where they account for more than 50 per cent and 35 per cent of the cities respectively. In contrast, the manufacturing cities and the industrial cities together constitute only 21 per cent of the Southern cities and a mere 13 per cent of Western cities.

The industrial group is found most frequently in the Midwest, while manufacturing cities show a very even distribution, accounting for between 10 per cent and 15 per cent of the cities in each of the four regions. Diversified-retailing and retailing cities are distributed regionally in inverse proportion to the manufacturing cities. However, diversified-retailing cities in which manufacturing plays a significant though secondary role are more common in the South, while the retailing cities are particularly frequent in the West.

SPECIALIZED CITIES COMMON IN WEST

Specialized cities are far more common in the West (14 per cent of all cities) than in the Northeast (only 3 per cent). Only three of the 45 education cities are in the Northeast; the many academic institutions of that region are either in large cities or in towns below 10,000.

There are surprising variations in the frequency with which given functional classifications occur in cities of different size groups. Most notable of these is the tendency of diversified-manufacturing cities to be very large. More than 50 per cent of the cities over 250,000 population are classed as diversified-manufacturing, but this drops to 21 per cent of those from 100,000 to 250,000, and about 11 per cent of the cities of less than 100,000 population. This suggests strongly that few cities grow very large without substantial manufacturing, and that very large cities may tend toward an approximate balance among the various economic activities—a balance less likely to be found in the smaller cities.

Manufacturing cities are common in the middle-sized groups, accounting for about 40 per cent of all cities between 50,000 and 250,000, but only about 30 per cent of those below 50,000 and only 20 per cent of those over 250,000. In part, this may reflect the strong representation of residential suburban cities (many in the retailing class) in the small size groups.

MOST INDUSTRIAL CITIES SMALL

The industrial cities are nearly all small with 90 per cent of them below 50,000. Diversified-retailing cities, characteristic particularly of the South, account for a consistent share of all size groups up to 500,000. Retailing cities, in contrast, are found in greater and greater proportions in successively lower size groups.

Most of the specialized cities are small, though Washington, D.C. (governmental), is a notable exception. Only 10 of the 122 specialized cities are over 50,000. Of the 45 education cities, 17 are over 25,000, but in most of the specialized categories the 10,000 to 25,000 category accounts for the large majority of cities.

Most of the variations found in the distribution of cities by metropolitan status run parallel to the differences in size. Central cities are far more likely to be diversified-manufacturing than are suburban or independent cities, but manufacturing is the most common classification of all three types. The specialized cities are mainly independent, but quite a number are suburbs; only 10 are central cities. Most education and mining cities are independent cities, while most cities classified government or service are suburbs. The

distribution of cities classified armed forces or wholesaling is about equal between the two groups.

EMPLOYMENT-RESIDENCE RATIO

The distribution of cities by employment-residence ratio shows that balanced and employing cities are found to have quite similar distributions by size group and by region, though employing cities are somewhat more significant in the Northeast.[1] This may reflect either a tendency for manufacturing cities to require more workers from a distance and hence to have higher employment-residence ratios, or a tendency for Northeastern cities to have relatively restricted city limits and large suburban areas supplying relatively large numbers of workers to employing centers. Dormitory cities, of course, are overwhelmingly (over 80 per cent) concentrated in the suburb class. As a result, they are more frequently found in the Northeast, North Central, and Western regions than in the South, where large incorporated suburbs are uncommon.

Among each of the metropolitan-status categories, employing cities are more common than balanced cities, and of course both are far more common than dormitory cities among both central cities and independent cities. Almost 60 per cent of suburbs are dormitory towns, but over 20 per cent of the suburbs are in the employing category. This compares with over 50 per cent

[1] The employment-residence ratio is derived from the number of persons employed in a community as compared to the number of employed persons residing in the community. Where the numbers are about equal, the community is classified as balanced, where the number employed exceeds the number of resident workers by 16 per cent or more, the community is placed in the employing class; where less than 85 per cent of the resident workers are employed in a community, the community is designated dormitory.

of the independent cities in the employing category, and with over 60 per cent of the central cities classed as employing.

POPULATION CHANGE

In compiling a social and economic classification of cities, it is interesting to note that the rate of population change from 1950 to 1960 varied from −30 per cent in Shenandoah, Pennsylvania, to +12,176 per cent in Warren, Michigan. Loss of population and low rates of growth were proportionately higher in the larger cities in the Northeast and North Central states and in the central cities. A much larger proportion of the suburbs were above the median rate of growth than either central cities or independent cities.

More than 14 per cent of the cities over 10,000 population lost population in the decade. The majority of these were in the Northeast and the least number in the West. The continuing significance of annexation in all regions except the Northeast is demonstrated by the fact that 182 additional cities would have lost population without annexation. More than 78 of these cities were in the North Central and Southern regions. Most cities in all regions, with the exception of the Northeast region, annexed some territory during the decade. Highest percentages of annexations occurred in the West and South where annexations occurred in almost 90 per cent and more than 87 per cent of the cities respectively. By contrast, the equivalent figures were 72 per cent in the North Central region and only 22 per cent in the Northeast. Even so, almost half of the annexing cities in the Northeast lost population.

Recently incorporated places, of which there were 71 during the decade of 1950 to 1960, contain a highly selected population. The indices of social and economic characteristics of these cities indicate a combination of wealth and youth. Only 6 per cent of them are above the national median in the percentage of families with incomes below $3,000 while 71 per cent are above the percentage of families with incomes of $10,000 and more. As to other national medians, 97 per cent of the gross family incomes are above the median of all cities of 10,000 population or more; 87 per cent are above the median for gross monthly rental; and 85 per cent are above the median for the percentage of nonwhites.

The population of recently incorporated places is young. In regard to median age, 92 per cent of the cities fall in the first or second quartiles and 96 per cent are among the cities with the highest percentage of the population under 18 years of age. Only 3 per cent of the newly incorporated cities are above the median with respect to the percentage of persons 65 years of age and over. Nevertheless, almost six out of 10 recently incorporated suburbs have predominantly blue-collar labor forces. The proportion of blue-collar suburbs is approximately reversed for the country as a whole.

OTHER CHARACTERISTICS

Social and economic classifications of the cities over 10,000 population are analyzed in the *1963 Municipal Year Book* by metropolitan status, geographic region, and population-size group. Because of space limitations, the balance of this article is limited to a brief review of the analysis by population groups.

Most cities in each population group, except those below 25,000 population, are multiunit residential cities. The percentages run progressively downward from 95 per cent in cities over 500,000. However, the only group in which a majority of cities are predominantly places of single-unit residences is that below 25,000. The residential structure of one-fourth of the cities over 500,000 is relatively new. Although the proportions of cities which are in the upper quartiles with respect to the percentage of housing units built between 1950 and 1960 is considerably higher in lower population groups, only one group, 25,000 to 50,000, has more than half of its cities in the upper quartiles.

Housing units rated "sound, with all plumbing facilities" constitute a sufficient proportion to place 38 per cent of the cities over 500,000 in the upper half of the national distribution. But the relative percentages drop to 14 per cent for cities between 250,000 and 500,000, and rise to only 31 per cent of the cities between 100,000 and 250,000. The two groups between 25,000 and 100,000 rise to 52 and 54 per cent respectively, but the proportion drops to below the mid-point again for the lowest population group (47 per cent).

Two-thirds of the cities in the two groups above 250,000 have higher-than-average percentages of family incomes under $3,000. The comparable proportions drop to 56 per cent for cities between 100,000 and 250,000 and sharply to 38 and 37 per cent respectively for the two groups between 25,000 and 100,000. For the group under 25,000,

the proportion of cities with low incomes rises again to 45 per cent. The group with the largest proportion of high family income is that between 250,000 and 500,000. The group over one-half million and the one of 50,000 to 100,000 have comparable percentages of 57 and 55 per cent respectively. However, in the intermediate group of 100,000 to 250,000 the percentage of high-income cities is down to 44 per cent. Only four out of 10 of the smallest cities, 10,000 to 25,000, fall in this category.

All cities in the two groups above 250,000 and 85 per cent of those between 100,000 and 250,000 are in the upper quartile with respect to the percentages of nonwhites. The proportions drop to 56 and 50 per cent in the next two population groups and to 39 per cent of cities between 10,000 and 25,000.

The difference between the proportion of cities over 500,000 and that for all other population groups in the per cent of elementary school children enrolled in private schools is very large. Eighty-six per cent of the largest cities are in the two upper quartiles.

56. Who Runs Our Town?*

JOHN W. YAGER

"WHO runs our town?"—that is, what persons or groups make the basic decisions in any community on the conduct of government on the local level? There can be a wide variety of answers to this question for at least two reasons.

First, communities differ as individuals do as a result of both heredity and environment. Municipal genes and environmental influences create unique communities with their own peculiar factors or factions of political leader-

* Reprinted with permission from *National Civic Review*, May 1963. Footnotes omitted.

ship. The sources of political leadership will be singularly different in every community.

Second, in each community these sources of political leadership are constantly changing. I doubt that the answer to our question as to any one community would be the same today as it would have been ten or twenty years ago and that it will be a different answer at a like period in the future. Communities change—they grow or decline. Political institutions change—new personalities and problems appear on the scene. No community is static and therefore political leadership is dynamic.

Without a comprehensive study of a community's "power structure" any answer or conclusion is probably a combination of opinion and speculation. A valid answer would require a study in depth such as was reported by Floyd Hunter in his *Community Power Structure* about the anonymous "Region City" or the survey of Knoxville by the Presbyterian Church.

Before examining the specifics of local political leadership at least one definition is necessary—that of "political." Although political leadership sources include the normal partisan connotations—referred to later—I am sure the planners of this workshop did not intend to limit us to this narrow scope. The term "political" should include consideration of the following:

1. Who are the elected (or appointed) public officials and how are they selected—actually even elected officials must first be selected, since they are either the sources of political leadership itself or the by-product of it, and

2. Who, if the public officials do not themselves constitute the sole source of political leadership, which I am sure few would argue they do, control—and to what degree do they control—the actions, either within or without the governmental structure, which result in a policy or program or law that affects the general public?

It might be noted that there is little that happens in a community that does not directly involve local government. Although local government exists for the broad purpose of providing for, protecting and promoting the general health, welfare and safety of the community, its functions and responsibilities have become so all encompassing that a contemporary of only ten or fifteen years ago would be shocked to learn just how much has become the concern of local government. All one needs to do is to look at the typical agenda of a city council—it will run the gamut from industrial development to massive federal programs which were unheard of only a few years ago. Whether this is good or bad, we will leave unanswered but certainly it means that local political leadership has become an increasingly important subject.

Theoretically, political leadership in a democracy originates or springs from the people—the governed. The voters elect responsible public officials and periodically have the opportunity to replace them. Governmental programs and policies are, theoretically, dependent upon the support or approval of the constituency and, to a certain degree, this is true. But in actual practice it is not the way things work, particularly in the area of sources of political leadership. I am not suggesting that we change any of our democratic framework but only that we recognize reality. In examining the sources of political leadership in local government, we find in every community what has come to be known as the "power structure"—the persons or groups who make the basic decisions in the community, both governmental and otherwise. The power structure is, or may be, involved in who runs for public office, who is elected to public office, what actions public officials take or don't take, what issues or programs are undertaken in the community—in other words it runs or attempts to run the community by influence or direct control. This may be done or attempted either within the framework of government or outside it. The power structure may or may not include the public officials themselves. It may be strong or weak, continuous or sporadic, evil or good—but in every community it is there most of the time.

There are those communities where there is a vacuum in local political leadership. Such a situation results in one of two things—either in no or an ineffectual power structure or one dominated by a partisan political factor or a special interest faction. Sometimes, where there is a vacuum, there can be such nearly equal conflicting interests that a stalemate for the community results. Leadership, such as it is, goes by default to those who will assume it. Of course, the cause of this type of leadership is individual and community apathy.

In addition to apathy being a cause of "vacuum leadership," I have heard the argument that government has become too big—even local government. That because it is so big and complex, the average person has no control over it. This grass roots concept that little government is closer to the people is not as infallible as it may seem, particularly if it is proposed that only through it will we get real political leadership. I submit that there are the same problems of political leadership, the source and conduct of political leadership, whether we are talking about a small township or village or school district or a large metropolitan city. Where there is a vacuum in political leadership, regardless of the cause, the caliber of the government is likely to suffer. Sometimes the best fitted citizens do not seek public office or will not accept appointive office. In such a community the concept that "politics" and "politician" are dirty words is prevalent. In such a community voter apathy is apparent on election day, problems remain unsolved, progress is merely the wish or goal of a few and the political or special interest clique remains entrenched.

Let us examine the traditional source of political leadership—the partisan political source. First, let me plead guilty to being strongly nonpartisan in so far as local government is concerned. The best local government—and political leadership—is nonpartisan. Municipal government involving basically the administration of local services is best served by nonpartisan elections and operation. I do not advocate the elimination of our traditional two-party system for my prejudice in this area does not extend to state or national government.

There are those, particularly in one element in the power structure in my city, who contend that responsible local government can be achieved only through the competing parties providing community political leadership.

Fortunately, partisan politics is disappearing from the local scene. Of course, there are exceptions, particularly in the very large cities, but even there the influence of the independent voter is on the increase. More and more people, although they are willing to identify themselves as either Republicans or Democrats for other purposes, act and vote nonpartisan on the local level. In turn the political leadership in our communities is becoming increasingly nonpartisan. If local partisan politics means only "profit, power and prestige —nothing else," then we are better off without it.

The decline of partisan political influence on the local level has resulted, from my observation, because of its failure to provide either adequate or progressive leadership in the form of candidates and programs. This is true of both parties. This does not mean that partisan politics is still not a factor in even a nonpartisan community or that it is not a part of the average community's power structure. Normally, even in nonpartisan municipal elections, each party will campaign for an endorsed slate and most of the candidates will identify themselves with one or the other of the national parties.

Perhaps there is nothing basically wrong with this even from a nonpartisan standpoint (assuming, of course, that the ballot is nonpartisan). If a political party wants to present a slate of candidates on the basis that these are qualified men who happen to belong to our party, I see no reason why it cannot do so any more than any other group. Even in strictly nonpartisan communities, political leadership must come from somewhere. And many groups, whether they be a good government league, a city manager league or a charter party, are really political parties operating exclusively on the local level. As such they become partisan influences if not special interest groups in the community's power structure.

What about special interest groups as sources of political leadership? In most communities, unless the political leadership comes from the traditional partisan political sources, it will be provided by one or more special interest sources. I do not use the term "special interest" group derogatively. We are all members of special interest groups—individuals who because of their mutual interests naturally seek special goals. Every community has many of these and every public official is subject to their pressures. I believe that a good public official should listen to the points of view of the special interest groups and then exercise his own personal judgment. Briefly, let me comment on four such potential sources of political leadership:

1. *Economic.* In a majority of communities, large and small, I would guess that the economic group is the predominant one. Although the group could be either—and is—the business-financial group or the labor group, I refer to the former in asserting that it provides the greatest political leadership. There are, of course, labor communities where organized labor is the dominant factor and in most industrialized communities labor is decidedly a factor. But I do not believe this economic group exerts the influence sometimes attributed to it. This is probably true because usually labor will function politically through existing political channels—and may exert considerable influence in this manner—and because labor has not been particularly effective in controlling its own members—perhaps because of the growing movement toward independent voting on the local level.

It is, however, the business-financial economic group that runs most communities. This was certainly proven conclusively by Mr. Hunter's study of a large metropolitan city. The political leadership in the community he studied was clearly established to be from the business - industrial - banking element, surprisingly with only minor contributions from the professions.

2. *The Press.* This category could include radio and television as well as newspapers and, with the trend to editorializing by radio and TV stations, perhaps their influence will increase. It is still primarily the newspapers, however, that provide political leadership in our communities. In some instances their influence is considerable and even may be dominant. I have the impression, however, that the power of the press is not what it used to be, but it cannot be underrated. Certainly a newspaper's support of or opposition to a candidate or a program—particularly in a monopoly newspaper situation—can make a crucial difference. This is especially so where most elections are decided by a difference of a few percentage points of the total vote cast.

It would be both interesting and revealing to any community to have a study done on the influence of its local press, as was done in Toledo by Reo M. Christenso. In many communities I predict that the press will be found to be a source of political leadership.

3. *Minorities.* Minorities by definition should not be considered as potential sources of political leadership. In fact, however, they are in many communities and will be to an increasing degree in the future. Of course, the minority that most readily comes to mind is the non-white group but there are also religious and racial minorities that are factors in many communities. As with the press, the most potent influence of minorities is found in the control they can exercise in close elections. Where a switch of only 2 or 3 per cent can decide a close election, a minority can become the "swing" vote that decides the result. Thus, their influence makes a substantial minority group, if not part of the community's power structure, at least an appendage to it.

4. *Mugwumps.* Under this category are included those independent, political, citizen-action groups that have been and are a source of political leadership in many communities. The term, of course, is from Lorin Peterson's most intriguing and interesting book, *The Day of the Mugwumps.* These organizations—a research bureau, a citizens league, a third political party or an exclusive leadership committee—become or are generating groups of political leadership. In some of the larger cities they are at times the dominant faction of the community's power structure. As such, they serve as a rallying point or a concentration of other traditional sources of political leadership.

Although, as Mr. Peterson points out, their main purpose from the turn of the century to recent years has been to combat corrupt government by partisan influence, their present and future function appears to be to join battle in the approaching status struggle and revitalization efforts of our metropolitan entities.

In conclusion, there are many other sources of political leadership used or available on the local level. The question of "Who Provides Local Political Leadership?" is one subject to different answers from different communities and also varying answers from time to time in each community. An equally puzzling question might be *how* is such political leadership asserted in our communities, if the *who* question is first answered.

57. Class, Participation, and the Council-Manager Plan*

EDGAR L. SHERBENOU

WHILE the council-manager form of municipal government continues to develop and expand, the argument concerning its nature and value continues unabated. Much of the formal discussion turns about the policy role of the manager, and the participation of councilmen and citizens in the initiation and determination of policy. There is little formal discussion of the relationship of the council-manager form of government to the class system of either the particular community or the nation. The absence of such formal discussion is consistent with historic reluctance to give overt recognition to social class as a fact or as an issue. However, council-manager adoption and abandonment campaigns and elections often turn, at least covertly, about social class as an issue, and about the relationship of the council-manager plan to the class issue.

Election at large and non-partisan election are ordinarily part of the council-manager approach, and it is in terms of these devices that the lower status person is most often able to objectify his apprehension that the council-manager form means government by and for the upper classes. It is ordinarily claimed, for example, that election at large produces a higher quality councilman. The most obvious dynamic of election at large is that the candidates who are known and respected by the whole city will be of upper middle or upper class position. Without the aid of partisan organization the lower status

* Reprinted from *Public Administration Review,* Summer 1961, by permission of the American Society for Public Administration. Footnotes omitted.

person will be at a severe disadvantage indeed. The term "quality" has several meanings in this country.

THE MANAGER
AND SOCIAL CLASS

It is possible to imagine that the council-manager form could be combined with ward elections or even with partisan elections. Such concessions, however, might not calm all the fears or nullify all the resistance of the plan's opponents. It is entirely probable that the systematic rationalization of administrative structure is bewildering and offensive to many persons, and perhaps especially to those who have been least effective in securing their social, economic, and political goals. To many persons such terms as "efficiency" and "management" are associated with insensitivity to human values. The adoption of the plan is usually associated with a drive to get "politics" out of city administration. This often means that the privatization of municipal offices is to be systematically reduced, and that purely personal fiefs are to be eradicated in the interest of the community. The interests of the upper status persons are protected by civilization's laws and customs while a sentiment of ownership in a municipal job may be the extent of the lower status person's attempt to protect his interests politically. Thus the rationalization of administrative organization may seem to injure only the poor and benefit only the wealthy.

In considering the relationship of the council-manager plan to social class it is important to remember that the plan does not create a class structure. The change from an aldermanic or commission form to a council-manager form is certainly important and significant, but as a revolution it is strictly minor. Class systems are much too deeply imbedded in the beliefs and practices of the society to be greatly modified by a relatively small change in local governmental structure. Thus if there is any causal relationship between the class system and the council-manager plan, the latter is the dependent variable.

STUDY SUBURBAN
CHICAGO CITIES

The suburban cities which surround the central city in a great metropolitan area offer a special opportunity to investigate certain phases of the relationship between classes and the council-manager plan. These suburban cities are more specialized in function than cities with comparatively greater independence. Several of the suburban cities have an entirely residential function, but some have commercial and industrial development of their own. However, all the suburban cities exist in a basically dependent relationship to the great metropolitan complex. In other words, each suburban city represents a very limited part of the total system and depends upon the other cities in the metropolitan area to perform the other functions essential to a complete social, economic, or political system. The specialization of the suburb may serve to isolate variables so that we are able to compare them with other variables.

The research to be reported here is a study of the suburban cities which surround the City of Chicago. During the first phase of the study the seventy-four suburban cities nearest to Chicago in Cook, Lake, and DuPage counties which had more than 2,500 people were arranged in the order of their median dwelling unit values as reported by the Housing Census of 1950. At a later stage in the study the forty-nine suburban cities with more than 5,000 population in 1950 were divided into two groups. The council-manager cities were placed in one group and the non-manager cities in a second group. This division made it possible to compare some of the over-all aspects of the expenditure, debt, and tax patterns in manager suburbs with the patterns in the non-manager suburban cities. It should be noted that the group of seventy-four cities and the group of forty-nine cities overlap. The forty-nine cities are merely the larger cities among the seventy-four cities.

HOUSING VALUE AS A PRIVATE MEASURE OF CLASS

The objective of arranging the seventy-four cities in the order of their median dwelling unit values is to compare their forms of government with a measure of socio-economic class. Precise measurement of class position may require combination of residence with other variables. W. Lloyd Warner and his associates developed measures of ethnicity, education, amount of income, source of income, dwelling area, house type, and occupation as parts of their measurement of social class. However, the purposes of this project require only a general measure of the socio-economic position of each suburb, and housing values reveal the social positions of neighborhoods in this general way.

The Chicago suburbs in Illinois describe an arc which begins on the lake shore north of the central city and continues around the city to the Indiana line on the South Side. When the seventy-four suburban cities are arranged from top to bottom according to their median dwelling unit values, the resultant pattern generally resembles the geographic pattern. With only a few exceptions the cities with very high residential values appear to the north of the central city near the lake in the area commonly known as the "North Shore." As one moves away from the lake and around to the west of the central city, the median values drop noticeably to distinctly middle class levels. River Forest on the West Side has one of the highest medians, but the other cities in the western area are definitely below the top residential values. With one or two exceptions the South Side is an area of lower median residential values.

When the seventy-four suburban cities are ranked from top to bottom according to their median housing values, a definite coincidence of high housing values and the council-manager form of municipal government becomes apparent. Council-manager governments are found in all but two of the top twenty cities. As the median value of the housing drops, a few more non-manager cities appear. About halfway down the list, manager and non-manager cities are in about the same proportion, but as we move past the middle of the scale of medians the manager cities cease to appear entirely. Oak Lawn, number forty-three on the list, is the last council-manager city. Above Oak Lawn there are twenty-nine manager cities and fourteen non-manager cities, while below Oak Lawn there are thirty-one non-manager cities and not a single manager city. The pattern is very striking. When we consider the generally close relationship between residential values and social class, the definite coincidence of the council-manager form with middle and upper class patterns is unmistakable.

MANAGER ADOPTION PATTERNS

The order in which the manager cities adopted the council-manager form suggests a further hypothesis. As measured by the median housing values of 1950, the council-manager plan was adopted by the top suburbs on the North Shore in 1914 and 1915. Riverside, on the West Side, but tenth in median housing value, chose the manager plan in 1925. Two more adoptions were made on the North Side in 1930 and 1931. Brookfield and Western Springs, neighbors to Riverside, adopted the plan in 1947 and 1948. From these beginnings several adoptions were made after more favorable legislation was passed by the legislature in 1951. The first interpretation suggested by this pattern is that once the council-manager is adopted by a city, it is more likely to be adopted by other cities in the same area. But more interesting yet, from the viewpoint of this paper, is the possibility that the plan spreads downward from the upper class suburbs into the middle class suburbs. The evidence is far from conclusive even for the Chicago area, but other suburban areas might be checked for the presence of such a relationship.

The second phase of the study involved a modification in method. The smaller cities were set aside, and only the forty-nine relatively larger suburban cities which had populations of 5,000 or more in 1950 were used. The forty-nine cities included twenty-four council-manager cities and twenty-five non-manager cities. The manager cities and non-manager cities were then compared by computing means of several variables for each group. For example, between 1950 and 1960 the manager cities averaged 89.9 per cent population growth as compared to 76.7 per cent in the non-manager cities.

Comparison of the housing values supplied by the Housing Census of 1950 for the manager and non-manager cities offers vivid evidence of the relatively affluent position of the residents of the manager cities. This comparison is set forth in Table 1. The Census

only a part of the total difference between the housing values of the two groups. Eight of the forty-nine cities were listed as having median dwelling unit values of more than $20 thousand. Seven of these eight employ the council-manager form of government.

PUBLIC MEASURES OF SOCIAL CLASS

Expenditure for housing is primarily a private matter. Since we Americans customarily satisfy our private wants before we seek public approaches to the common good, no measure of public affluence offers the same degree of contrast between the manager and non-manager cities as does the comparison of their mean housing values. However, comparison on the basis of arithmetic means of three important variables in public finance is offered in Table 2. Table 3 supplies the ranges of the same variables for the manager cities and for the non-manager cities. In Table 2 it is made clear that on the average the manager cities had a higher expenditure per capita, a lower net municipal debt per capita, and higher property taxes per capita.

TABLE 1 *Comparison of Housing Values for Selected Suburban Chicago Manager and Non-Manager Cities Over 5,000 Population in 1950*

	Twenty-four Manager Cities	Twenty-five Non-Manager Cities
Average of the median dwelling unit values	$16,972	$12,513
Median of the median dwelling unit values	$17,809	$12,114

Bureau lists high medians merely at $20,000 plus. Thus an average (arithmetic mean) of the medians expresses

TABLE 2 *Comparison of Per Capita Average Total Expenditures, Net Municipal Debt, and Average Municipal Property Tax for Selected Suburban Chicago Manager and Non-Manager Cities Over 5,000 Population in 1957*

	Twenty-four Manager Cities	Twenty-five Non-Manager Cities
Average total expenditure per capita	$68.42	$54.24
Average net municipal debt per capita	$26.43	$34.81
Average municipal property tax per capita	$18.84	$13.99

*   *   *

A few of the council-manager cities have lower expenditure and tax patterns than the majority of the non-manager cities in the sample. These cities demonstrate that the council-manager form may be used primarily for frugal purposes. However, the general pattern is definitely toward higher expenditures, higher property taxes, and a more conservative policy toward the incurrence of debt. The major variable in this pattern is undoubtedly the greater wealth of many of the suburban cities which have chosen the council-manager plan. Recalling the strikingly higher level of the housing in many of the manager cities, we infer that they have more money. Having more money, they spend more. Proponents of the plan argue that council-management tends to develop a public confidence in the efficiency and responsibility of municipal government. Greater public confidence leads naturally to demands for an expanded program of municipal services and an increased willingness to spend by way of the municipality. Such evidence as the present study affords tends to support this argument.

SIGNIFICANCE OF OCCUPATIONAL EXPENSE

The relative willingness of the middle and upper classes to try the council-manager government may be at least partly explained by their occupational experiences. Many members of these groups are executives in corporations or other business groups. Other middle and upper class persons may practice a profession or otherwise have acquaintance with professional approaches to organization. It is natural that such people find it relatively easy to visualize a professional approach to municipal administration. It should be noticed also that any particular middle or upper class suburb is more likely to exist in geographical proximity to suburbs currently using the council-manager plan. We might infer that they choose it because they know it and like it.

The counterpart of these logics is that

TABLE 3 *Comparison of the Range of Per Capita Total Expenditures, Municipal Debt, and Property Tax for Selected Suburban Chicago Manager and Non-Manager Cities Over 5,000 Population in 1957*

	Twenty-four Manager Cities	Twenty-five Non-Manager Cities
Range of total expenditure per capita	$ 21.75 to $167.57	$ 28.52 to $ 82.02
Range of municipal debt per capita	$113.63 debt to $115.38 surplus	$159.05 debt to $ 56.17 surplus
Range of property tax per capita	$ 7.02 to $ 70.48	$ 7.63 to $ 32.72

those further down the scale lack experience in executive or professional positions and thus do not have a ready-made basis for sympathetic vision of professional public management. Also, the further down the status scale, the less likely that neighboring cities will use the council-manager form. Thus, a clear impression of the plan is geographically less available.

PLANNING FOR CITIZEN PARTICIPATION

Proponents of the commission and mayor-council forms often claim that these forms offer relatively greater opportunities for citizen participation than does the council-manager plan. If this allegation is accurate, it seems strange that the council-manager form should appear primarily in those Chicago suburbs most likely to be inhabited by high participation groups. It is precisely the executive, business, and professional groups that achieve the most effective political representation of their interests. Those groups ordinarily most expert at achieving their political goals evidently favor the council-manager form. The argument, then, must be that lower status persons have more opportunity for participation in the commission or mayor-council forms than they have in the council-manager form. It is easy to demonstrate that lower status persons have less opportunity to hold municipal office where election at large is employed. In addition it is entirely probable that many persons in lower status groups have relatively more difficulty understanding how they can achieve representation in the council-manager system. With these considerations the argument becomes that we should keep the mayor-council system in order to encourage participation on the part of those who have thus far been rather ineffective in achieving participation.

This situation as a whole strongly suggests that those citizen groups which have an interest in the council-manager plan especially need to study the problem of communication with those members of the community of lower social rank. Perhaps the explanation of the council-manager form by analogy to the business or industrial corporation is a short cut which is rather easily too much used. Perhaps some of the difficulties of the plan can be overcome by more deliberate planning for representation of all major groups and areas on a common slate or ticket. The circumstances in which all the council members elected at large reside in the same small cluster of houses in an upper class ward is natural. However, it can be avoided with a little self-conscious planning. Certainly all major groups should be represented in the discussion of community goals and in the selection and development of public programs.

The council-manager plan offers no advantage or disadvantage to groups of equal political competence. The issue arises out of the political advantage which top ranking groups enjoy in our political systems. A small number of individuals and their relatives may derive satisfaction and public prominence from ward politics under the aldermanic form. But, the pattern of personal (or family) favors which ordinarily accompanies ward politics offers no realistic advantage to a group of significant size. The aura of representativeness which has sometimes emanated from such systems has often been deceptive. The distribution of personal favors, often petty, by ward leaders can have only a mild effect upon the basic power relations of our political system.

Effective political participation by large groups depends upon the development of program politics and majority coalitions of interest groups. These ingredients may be woefully lacking in our present version of a democratic system, but the council-manager plan is not to blame for this weakness. It is quite as amenable to program as any other system of representation. In fact, professional management is more likely than competitive forms to carry out such programs as are developed and selected by the community. Rationally speaking, we can certainly say that lower status groups have much to gain from the greater confidence in public instruments engendered by the elimination of personal favoritism, and by the systematic rationalization of administrative organization.

58. *Pipoly v. Benson*

125 P.2d 482 (1942)

THE decisive issue presented by this appeal, therefore, is whether the Los Angeles ordinance regulating the conduct of pedestrians at crosswalks is in conflict with the provisions of the Vehicle Code and is for that reason invalid. If so, the giving of conflicting instructions where one is based upon the provisions of an invalid ordinance clearly constitutes error. . . .

Where "municipal affairs" are concerned the Constitution gives authority to local governments to make and enforce laws and regulations subject only to the provisions of their charters. Const. art. XI, sec. 6. As to such matters local regulations are superior to the provisions of a state statute if there is conflict between the two. . . , The regulation of traffic upon the streets of a city, however, is not one of those municipal affairs over which the local authorities are given a power superior to that of the legislature. . . . In such a field as that presented in this case where the particular matter is outside the limited group of "municipal affairs," it is clear that local regulations upon the subject may be enforced only if they "are not in conflict with general laws." Const., art. XI, sec. 11. The applicable rule in these situations where state control is dominant has been stated as follows: "Where the Legislature has assumed to regulate a given course of conduct by prohibitory enactments, a municipality with subordinate power to act in the matter may make such new and additional regulations in aid and furtherance of the purpose of the general law as may seem fit and appropriate to the necessities of the particular locality, and which

are not in themselves unreasonable." . . .

This general rule permitting the adoption of additional local regulations supplementary to the state statutes is subject to an exception, however, which is important in the present case. Regardless of whether there is any actual grammatical conflict between an ordinance and a statute, the ordinance is invalid if it attempts to impose additional requirements in a field which is fully occupied by the statute. . . .

*   *   *

On this appeal plaintiffs urge that the ordinance involved is unconstitutional since it invades a field of traffic regulation which the legislature intended to occupy fully. We think this contention is correct. . . . The regulation of pedestrian traffic in its use of the public roadways, however, is not a matter concerning which express authorization has been given for local regulation. . . .

*   *   *

For the reasons set forth herein, we conclude that section 80.38 of the Municipal Code of Los Angeles must be held to be unconstitutional since it conflicts with the Vehicle Code by attempting to legislate upon a subject intended to be covered fully by an act of the legislature. The instruction given by the trial court which was based upon the provisions of the Los Angeles ordinance, therefore, was erroneous and since it conflicted with the instruction based upon the provisions of the Vehicle Code, the error requires a reversal of the judgment. . . .

59. *State ex rel. Heinig. v. City of Milwaukie*

373 P.2d 680 (1962)

THIS is a mandamus proceeding, commenced in the court below, through which plaintiff seeks to compel the city of Milwaukie [Oregon] and the members of the city council to establish a civil service commission in accordance with ORS 242.702 to 242.990 which provides for a civil service system for firemen.

* * *

Defendant city operates under a home rule charter. The city has made no provision for the establishment of a civil service system covering the employees of its fire department. Provisions relating to the employment and discharge of city personnel including firemen are, however, found in the city charter. . . .

The defendants contend that matters relating to the operation of the city fire department, including the employment and discharge of firemen, are matters of purely local municipal concern and, therefore, not subject to regulation or control by the legislative assembly. . . .

The two principal questions presented in this appeal are: (1) does the legislative assembly have the constitutional authority to enact a general law applicable to all cities when the enactment relates to a matter of local concern and in which there is no need for general regulation outside city boundaries; (2) is the establishment of a civil service system for city firemen a local matter or is it a matter of state-wide concern? These precise questions have been presented to this court in previous cases. Unfortunately, not all of these cases are in harmony with each other.

* * *

. . . we now expressly hold that the legislative assembly does not have the authority to enact a law relating to city government even though it is of general applicability to all cities in the state unless the subject matter of the enactment is of general concern to the state as a whole, that is to say that it is a matter of more than local concern to each of the municipalities purported to be regulated by the enactment. Borrowing the language from Branch v. Albee, 71 Or. 188, 142 p. 598, 599 (1914), we hold that the people of a city are not "subject to the will of the Legislature in the management of purely local, municipal business in which the state at large is not interested, and which is not of any interest to any outside the local municipality."

An enactment is not of state-wide interest simply because the legislaure decides that each of the cities in the state should be governed by the same law. In the appropriate case the need for uniformity in the operation of the law may be a sufficient basis for legislative preemption. But uniformity in itself is no virtue, and a municipality is entitled to shape its local law as it sees fit if there is no discernible pervading state interest involved.

* * *

We next consider the question of whether the statutes relied upon by plaintiffs deal with a matter of local or of more general concern. Here again we are met with confusion and conflict in the cases. As has been observed, "The courts have, generally speaking, been unable to devise any objective test whereby it can be determined with certainty what matters come within the term 'municipal affairs,' for the term has no fixed quantity, fluctuates with every change in the conditions upon which it operates, and has of necessity been determined by a slow process of judicial inclusion and exclusion."

Purely upon the basis of precedent our own decision in Branch v. Albee, 71 Or. 188, 142 P.2d 598 (1914) holding that the pensioning of city police is a municipal matter would, in our opinion, be conclusive in the present case. In relation to the question before us we can see no substantial difference between the establishemnt of a pension system for city police and the establishment of a civil service system for city firemen. But even if we were to consider the question as res integra we would still hold that the manner of employing and discharging the personnel of a municipal fire department is a matter of local rather than state concern. To be sure, it could be shown that the manner of dealing with personnel of local fire departments may have some relation to the affairs of the state outside of the city boundary—In a sense all events in life are related—but the question requiring our answer is whether the extramural effect is substantial or insignificant. "The real test is not whether the state or the city has an interest in the matter, for usually they both have, but whether the state's interest or that of the city is paramount."

The solution cannot be arrived at by a recitation of the definitions of "local" or "municipal" affairs. The question is, of course, one of degree, and the allocation of power between legislature and municipality must be made by us in accordance with the purpose, as we understand it, of the constitutional amendments which vested in the cities a part and an exclusive part of the power to legislate free from the control of the state legislative assembly.

*   *   *

The constitutional recognition that the municipality is to have exclusive authority to legislate on some matters presupposes that we are able to decide whether a function is predominantly local or predominantly state-wide. Not being aided by any evidence on the question, we must make the choice solely upon the basis of our knowledge of the manner in which local and state governments operate and the relative importance of the function in question to the cities and to the state as a whole. It has been said that "The question of which level of government should provide a given service is essentially a political one and should be determined by the political agencies of government." But under the theory of home rule which we have adopted there are involved two political agencies making conflicting claims . . . , and the resolution of that conflict must be made by the courts.

In our opinion the administrative machinery by which the employment and discharge of city firemen is to be determined is a matter of local concern. The principal function of a city fire department is to provide fire protection within the city. On occasion the department may be called upon to assist in the suppression of fires outside of its limits, or it may engage in other cooperative extramural activities but this interrelation between the city and those benefited outside is not of such frequency and importance as to warrant describing it as a matter of state-wide concern.

*   *   *

We are unable to see how the manner of the employment and discharge of the personnel of a city fire department is relevant in any substantial way to the function of the state in the field of fire protection. Granting that a compulsory civil service system for firemen would tend to improve the quality of the personnel in city fire departments throughout the state, it seems to us that considering the limited function which the city fireman performs outside the city there is not sufficient justification for depriving the city of control over this aspect of the operation of city government. If the legislative assembly has the power to deprive the people of municipalities of self-government in this respect, it would be difficult to imagine an area of activity engaged in by the city which could not be similarly controlled.

*   *   *

. . . Each case requires a weighing of the state's interest against the interest of the municipality. In some instances the need for uniformity, or the benefit of a widespread application of the law, or the recognition that the matter dealt with is interrelated with other functions of the state and similar considerations will require that the statute have preference over the charter; on the other hand the charter will prevail when the advantages of local autonomy are paramount.

*   *   *

Judgment reversed.

60. *Muskopf v. Corning Hospital District*

359 P.2d 457 (Calif., 1961)

PLAINTIFF was a paying patient in the Corning Memorial Hospital. She and her husband allege that because of the negligence of the hospital staff she fell and further injured the broken hip for which she was being treated. Defendant demurred on the ground that the Corning Hospital District is immune from liability for tort under the rule of Talley v. Northern San Diego Hospital District, 41 Cal.2d 33, 257 P.2d 22, which held that a hospital district was a state agency exercising a governmental function and as such was immune from tort liability. . . .

Plaintiffs contend that operating a hospital is a proprietary function of government and that in any event the rule of governmental immunity should be discarded.

After a re-evaluation of the rule of governmental immunity from tort liability we have concluded that it must be discarded as mistaken and unjust.

The rule of hospital district tort immunity was based on cases upholding county hospital immunity. . . . These cases rest on the grounds that a county, like the state, can act only in governmental capacity and that a hospital is protected by the rule of charitable im-

munity. The latter doctrine has been abolished in this state . . . and it is now settled that the state, like a municipality, can act in a proprietary capacity. . . .

The shifting fortune of the rule of governmental immunity as applied to hospitals is illustrative of the history of the rule itself. From the beginning there has been misstatement, confusion, and retraction. At the earliest common law the doctrine of "sovereign immunity" did not produce the harsh results it does today. It was a rule that allowed substantial relief. It began as the personal prerogative of the king, gained impetus from sixteenth century metaphysical concepts, may have been based on the misreading of an ancient maxim, and only rarely had the effect of completely denying compensation. How it became in the United States the basis for a rule that the federal and state governments did not have to answer for their torts has been called "one of the mysteries of legal evolution." . . .

The rule of county or local district immunity did not originate with the concept of sovereign immunity. The first case to hold that local government units were not liable for tort was Russell v. Men of Devon, 100 Eng. Rep. 359. The case involved an action in tort against an unincorporated county. The action was disallowed on two grounds: since the group was unincorporated there was no fund out of which the judgment could be paid; and "it is better that an individual should sustain an injury than that the public should suffer an inconvenience." . . . The rule of the Russell case was first brought into this country by Mower v. Inhabitants of Leicester, 9 Mass. 247, 249. There the county was incorporated, could sue and be sued, and there was a corporate fund out of which a judgment could be satisfied. Ignoring these differences, the Massachusetts court adopted the rule of the Russell case, which became the general American rule.

If the reasons for Russell v. Men of Devon and the rule of county or local district immunity ever had any substance they have none today. Public convenience does not outweigh individual compensation, and a suit against a county hospital or hospital district is against an entity legally and financially capable of satisfying a judgment. . . .

The rule of governmental immunity for tort is an anachronism, without rational basis, and has existed only by the force of inertia. . . .

None of the reasons for its continuance can withstand analysis. No one defends total governmental immunity. In fact, it does not exist. It has become riddled with exceptions, both legislative . . . and judicial . . . , and the exceptions operate so illogically as to cause serious inequality. Some who are injured by governmental agencies can recover, others cannot: one injured while attending a community theater in a public park may recover . . . , but one injured in a children's playground may not . . . ; for torts committed in the course of a "governmental function" there is no liability, unless the tort be classified as a nuisance. . . . The illogical and inequitable extreme is reached in this case: we are asked to affirm a rule that denies recovery to one injured in a county or hospital district hospital, although recovery may be had by one injured in a city and county hospital.

* * *

It is strenuously urged . . . that it is for the Legislature and not the courts to remove the existing governmental immunities. Two basic arguments are made to deny the court's power: first, that by enacting various statutes affecting immunity the Legislature has determined that no further change is to be made by the court; and second, that by the force of stare decisis the rule has become so firmly entrenched that only the Legislature can change it. Neither argument is persuasive.

* * *

We are not here faced with a situation in which the Legislature has adopted an established judicial interpretation by repeated re-enactment of a statute. . . . Nor are we faced with a comprehensive legislative enactment designed to cover a field. What is before us is a series of sporadic statutes, each operating on a separate area of governmental immunity where its evil was felt most. Defendant would have us say that because the Legislature has removed governmental immunity in these areas we are powerless to remove it in others. We read the statutes as meaning only what they say: that in the areas indicated there shall be no governmental immunity. They leave to the court whether it should adhere to its own rule of immunity in other areas.

Defendant also urges that even if the Legislature has not adopted the rule of governmental immunity in the areas in which it has not expressly abolished it, the rule has existed for so long that only the Legislature has the power to change it. The "rule" of governmental immunity, however, has not existed with the force that its repetition would imply. From its inception there has been constant judicial restriction, going hand in hand with accompanying legislative restriction. . . .

In formulating "rules" and "exceptions" we are apt to forget that when there is negligence, the rule is liability, immunity is the exception. This court implemented that policy when it overruled the doctrine of charitable immunity . . . , an immunity that was also claimed to be so firmly embedded that only the Legislature could change it.

* * *

Only the vestigial remains of such governmental immunity have survived;

its requiem has long been foreshadowed. For years the process of erosion of governmental immunity has gone on unabated. The Legislature has contributed mightily to that erosion. The courts, by distinction and extension, have removed much of the force of the rule. Thus, in holding that the doctrine of governmental immunity for torts for which its agents are liable has no place in our law we make no startling break with the past but merely take the final step that carries to its conclusion an established legislative and judicial trend.

The judgment is reversed.

61. General Characteristics of Special Districts*

JOHN C. BOLLENS

SPECIAL districts, a varied class of governmental units, have without much notice and concern become a significant part of the governmental pattern of the United States. They are furthermore becoming increasingly important despite a widespread lack of general understanding and knowledge about them. Only one kind of special districts, the school district, is reasonably well known, although subject to frequent misconceptions, and many nonschool districts are erroneously regarded as parts of other governments. Special districts, especially those in nonschool categories, constitute the "new dark continent of American politics," a phrase applied earlier in the century to counties.

What are special districts? Much of the analysis that follows seeks to answer this question fully, but a general

* Reprinted with permission from *Special District Governments in the United States,* by John C. Bollens, University of California Press, 1957. Footnotes omitted.

statement is appropriate here. In common with all other kinds of governmental units, special districts have certain essential characteristics. They are organized entities, possessing a structural form, an official name, perpetual succession, and the rights to sue and be sued, to make contracts, and to obtain and dispose of property. They have officers who are popularly elected or are chosen by other public officials. They have a high degree of public accountability. Moreover, they have considerable fiscal and administrative independence from other governments. The financial and administrative criteria distinguish special districts and other governments from all dependent or subordinate districts and from most authorities which, lacking one or both of these standards, are not governmental units. However, some entities legally identified as authorities, especially those in public housing, meet the requirements and are considered as special district governments. Special districts are also to be distinguished from the field offices or districts of national and state governments. Unlike most other governments, individual special districts usually provide only one or a few functions. In this respect they most closely resemble the townships in a number of Midwestern states, but it is not difficult to differentiate them. . . .

GENERAL EVIDENCE OF SIGNIFICANCE

NUMBERS AND GEOGRAPHICAL EXTENSIVENESS

One test of the significance of special districts is their number in relation to the over-all total for all governmental units . . . about thirteen of every twenty governments are special districts—eleven in the school category and two in the nonschool category. In addition, they are not only very numerous but also geographically widespread. There two characteristics are both evident in the fact that in thirty-five states special districts are more numerous than any other class of government. Even the school and nonschool categories separately often outrank numerically each of the other governmental classes. . . . Tens to thousands of special districts exist in every one of the states, and at least one such district is found in a large majority of the . . . counties in the country.

*　　*　　*

FINANCES AND PERSONNEL

Special districts are also consequential because of the extensiveness of their collective activity. In the fiscal year ending in 1955, school and nonschool districts spent $8.2 billion and $1.6 billion, respectively. This combined total of approximately $9.8 billion easily outranked the collective expenses of counties, townships, and towns, and stood close to the $10.5 billion figure for cities. At the same time the outstanding

debt of all special districts was more than $13 billion, more than two-fifths of which was owed by nonschool districts. The indebtedness of the school and nonschool groups of special districts each exceeded that of counties, townships, and towns combined, and the total district debt was more than that of all state governments together. Payrolls further illustrate the large amount of activity. The monthly payrolls for October, 1955, totaled $486 million for all special districts, more than nine-tenths of which went to school districts. The total for all district payrolls was thus larger than that for any other class of state and local governments. In the same month special districts also stood first among state and local governments in the number of persons employed. . . .

A POSSIBLE SYMPTOM

It is therefore evident that special districts are important in many aspects, including number, geographical extensiveness, finances, and personnel. Not so readily apparent but also of great possible significance is that the current number, the total operational extent, and particularly the sustained recent growth of various kinds of special districts may be symptomatic of weaknesses in other governments. The analysis of specific features of special districts, including their diversity, flexibility, and complexity, may furnish keys to a better comprehension and subsequent improvement of the governmental system of the United States.

CAUSES

Since special districts are expanding in over-all importance, the reasons prompting their establishment as part of the United States pattern of government are of growing consequence. As is true of many governmental institutions, there is no single all-inclusive cause. Instead, a series of factors is usually behind the formation of a particular district. Furthermore, the reasons are sometimes intertwined and interdependent, making it difficult to determine which is the controlling one and to separate it entirely from the others. The problem is further complicated by another difficulty. Because special districts have been so widely accepted in a relatively short period of time, or because it has been so quickly forgotten that they are separate governmental units, reports and individuals concerned with them do not usually analyze the causes bringing them into existence. Despite these difficulties, a number of reasons for the creation and continuance of most special districts can be identified.

UNSUITABILITY OF OTHER LOCAL UNITS: AREA

High-ranking among the reasons for special districts is the unsuitability of existing general local governments in terms of their area, financing, functions, or administration, or of the attitudes of those controlling them. There may be legal or operating inadequacies, or unwillingness by a government to perform a certain function. In many instances no general local government is permitted, equipped, or willing to undertake the service desired. Consideration of the inappropriateness of existing governments in these various respects will explain the establishment of numerous special districts.

Frequently the area appropriate to a particular function wanted by residents or property owners does not coincide with that of any existing general local government. The territory of the general unit may be smaller or larger. Thus the area of service need does not correspond to the boundaries of a local government presently in operation. Despite the post-World War II upsurge in annexation by cities, the limits of most governments are rigidly or relatively inflexible. Such inflexibility is a crucial problem when the area of the general

unit is smaller than the territory needing the service. In other circumstances, the functional need can encompass part or all of several existing units and cross over numerous boundaries, sometimes interstate or even international. Furthermore, long-term contracts between general governments to handle a functional need in an area larger than a single unit, although increasing in number, are not in general use. Therefore, when existing governments are smaller territorially than the area having a specific need, the district device is frequently utilized as a substitute for land absorption, consolidation of general units, or contractual agreements.

A comparable type of unsuitableness similarly develops when an operating government is larger territorially than the area wanting a service. Under these conditions area rigidity normally intervenes, because the general government performs functions and finances them with substantial uniformity throughout its entire territory. Here the factors of area and financing inadaptability are intermeshed, since many general governments are not permitted to make additional charges in one section in exchange for performing an extra service. Furthermore, the area unsuitability of general governments is frequently the outgrowth of such ecological factors as population shifts, technological changes, especially in transportation, and new knowledge and methods concerned with soil and water.

UNSUITABILITY OF OTHER LOCAL UNITS: FINANCES AND FUNCTIONS

Legal and operating limitations on financing the services of existing units are another heavy contributor to the formation of special districts. The legal obstacles usually take the form of state constitutional and legislative restrictions on the tax and debt limits of general governments. When these maximums are reached, no methods of performing added or more intensified functions are available unless the restrictions are liberalized or eliminated. Despite the unrealistic nature of many of them in relation to financial needs of general units, their modification is frequently difficult to accomplish. Consequently, a general government attaining its tax or debt limit is prevented from expanding functionally. However, residents of exactly or approximately the same area are not often legally prevented from organizing a special district possessing the power to levy taxes or to incur debt, or both. Thus, special districts are sometimes created as a direct means of circumventing financial restrictions placed on general governments. . . .

The district device is also utilized to pool the financial resources of an area that includes at least several governments which feel that their individual financing ability is inadequate to undertake a function. In addition to wanting a new governmental unit made responsible for financing the service, existing general units in these circumstances often favor the establishment of a district for another reason. They regard such an arrangement as having greater permanency or consistency of performance than an intergovernmental contract under which the function would be jointly handled by all general governments or undertaken by one of them on behalf of the others.

The financial unsuitability of a general government such as the county works in two additional ways to foster special districts. One, mentioned previously, is that often this unit cannot legally set up a taxing or assessment area in a part of its territory in order to finance additional service. The second is that, since financial costs must be spread uniformly throughout its area, other general governments within its borders, usually cities, oppose its assumption of a function that they are already performing for their residents. Arguing that their residents would be paying twice for the same service, they advocate the establishment of a special district made up of the territory of the county but excluding them. This is the

reason for the creation of most of the county library districts in Missouri.

The range of functions that can legally be performed by a general government does not always include a service that is desired by some people. This lack of functional authorization in existing units stimulates the creation of special districts. Numerous general governments show little disposition to seek additional functions but are at the same time reluctant to relinquish authority. . . .

UNSUITABILITY OF OTHER LOCAL UNITS:
ADMINISTRATION AND ATTITUDE

The status of the administrative structure and processes and the quality of the operational performance of an established general unit contribute to the formation of special districts. Some general governments, lacking modern administrative organization or procedures, or both, have not sufficiently matured to handle properly particular functions that are wanted. Administratively they are simply not capable of assuming new responsibilities. Sometimes the low caliber of present operations has decisive effect. There may be evidence or charges of inefficiency, mismanagement, or unsavory political behavior. Professionalized performance of public work may be absent or irregular. Unsatisfactory administrative structure or performance in an existing unit therefore works in two directions to encourage the growth of special districts. First, a function that could legally be handled by an existing general unit is entrusted instead to a special district. Second, a function already being performed by a general unit is transferred to a special district.

The attitude of a general government is sometimes the predominant factor accounting for the creation of special districts. A general government may have or could develop suitable area, financing, functions, and administrative organization and methods for a specific activity, and the interested people may want the general government to perform the service. Nevertheless, the general government's reaction, as reflected by its governing body members, is often negative. This attitude takes several forms. The general government may refuse to perform a function which is already legally authorized or which would be granted upon request to the legislature. It may be extremely slow and reluctant to assume a new activity. It may exercise the function but at a level below that desired by certain people. It may seek to stop rendering a present service.

*   *   *

THE DESIRE FOR INDEPENDENCE

The desire for independence is a further reason for the creation of special districts. People and groups possessing a major interest in one function frequently resist having that function allocated to an established general government or even to another special district. The desire to have an activity performed apart from any existing government sometimes grows out of an unfounded allegation or well-based conviction regarding the condition of the particular government. At other times it is rooted in great concern for a single function. Under any of these circumstances the advocacy of separate status is generally expressed in terms of keeping (or taking) the function "out of politics," which may simply mean protecting the function from the highly partisan approach and unprofessional administration of an existing unit. Administrative personnel desiring increased job protection are sometimes in the forefront in presenting this argument. The phrase "out of politics," however, has other connotations, which are less than often openly expressed and represent the feelings of many lay and professional functional specialists. It may mean keeping or placing a certain group in control of the function instead of transferring it to another organization where the influence of this group

may be substantially lessened. It may mean that individuals and groups with special interest feel that they have a better chance of obtaining public funds for a specific function if that function is separated from competing demands within a general government. It may mean that there is expectation of greater zeal and fervor for an activity when it is independent. In practice, these meanings are all included within the term of keeping or taking the function "out of politics."

The desire for independence is also advanced in support of a government that is smaller either in operations or in area, and often in both. In various localities throughout the United States there are strong feelings in favor of simple localism as well as of governmental separatism. The attitude is commonly expressed as "grassroots" government. Therefore, instead of making an existing government more complex through functional enlargement, a new more simplified unit is created. This action is often related to a primary interest in one function, but it is also an outcropping of the belief that government can be better observed and controlled if it is kept small. In this line of reasoning large numbers of governments are regarded as preferable to huge operations by fewer governments. The desire for independence, in any one of its various expressions, may be a forceful factor stimulating the use of special districts even when established general units do not have or can overcome legal inadequacies.

ADVOCACY BY EXISTING GOVERNMENTS

Existing governmental units at all levels sometimes advocate the creation of special districts. Rivalry between local governments may have this result. For example, a local government may not have legal authorization to provide a specific service which is desired. Instead of suggesting that the interested people seek to become part of a local government of another class and thus obtain the function, it recommends the establishment of a special district. A government follows this course when it is unwilling to see a neighboring government strengthened. Sometimes a district results as a compromise when two different local governents both want to perform the function. Another circumstance, mentioned earlier in connection with financial unsuitability of existing general units, occasionally develops when one local government is located within the territory of another and is subject to financial charges made by the latter for services rendered. Already performing the desired function, the first government advocates the creation of a special district that does not include its territory. Finally, when various local units have a common functional problem but refuse to merge territorially or to effect an intergovernmental contract, a special district is often strongly advocated and, as the need becomes more urgent, ultimately utilized.

The influence of the state and national governments on the establishment of special districts is exerted differently. One of the most important means is through the impact of professional functional specialists. Their primary objective is the enhancement of a single public activity and their promotional work may be undertaken with little consideration of its effect on existing governments. They look upon the special district as a convenient method of overcoming the functional deficiency, for their basic concern is the accomplishment of the job by government, regardless of the government involved. Even though not directly urging the circumvention of existing units, they frequently point out the difficulty of using them and suggest the special district as an alternative that will be immediately useful. Recommendations favoring special districts may be incorporated in officially published reports but appear more often in memoranda to regional offices and in communications sent to individuals in specific communities. The reputation of persons who are specialists in a governmental function but not necessarily specialists in governmental structure and procedure is frequently impressive in decisions about satisfying service needs.

Financial aid by state and national governments for certain functions also influences the development of special districts. Programs are sponsored by these levels of government to remove or lessen a functional shortcoming. Again, performance of the service is emphasized without much regard for its best location governmentally. In turn, at times in response to the availability of aid from other governments, the financial inability of general government units accelerates the creation of special districts under existing laws and the passage of legislation authorizing new types of districts. The legislature or people of a state could, however, make the existing general units adequate to accept responsibility for such programs. Instead, new districts are often legally authorized. . . .

EXPEDIENCY AND AREA CONDITION

Expediency is important among the reasons for the creation of special districts. Setting up such a district is an easy method of responding to a need, and can often be done quickly on the basis of existing enabling laws. People want immediate relief to satisfy a need that seems particularly compelling at the time. With some frequency, then, the motivation for utilizing special district governments is nothing more than the urgency of a service deficiency and the need for a quick answer. Although the possibility of using a general government, sometimes only after its reorganization, is not deliberately bypassed, neither is it consciously investigated. When general governments are considered as an alternative, expediency may still enter into the situation. Reluctance to wait until a long-range, possibly better solution can materialize influences the decision that supplementing existing governments is much easier than reorganizing or supplanting them. Additions to the governmental scene are usually accomplished with much greater facility than revisions or substitutions. Furthermore, additions are more likely to be supported by the governments that would otherwise be affected by reorganization.

The actual functional needs and the limited financial resources of an area are two of the underlying causes of some special districts, even when the area desires to utilize general governments. An area that is not substantially developed may really need only a few services. Yet it may be impossible to obtain limited functions from a general government. Thus, the reluctance or legal inability of a general unit to provide substantially different quantities of service prompts people who desire only limited functions to turn to special districts. Even when the legal means exist, a general government may refuse limited service because of the difficulty of determining an equitable charge for one or several of the many functions it performs. Then, too, an area may not contain financial resources sufficient to support a general array of functions. Despite a fairly extensive range of needs, a general government may not want the responsibility for providing services in an area that may become a heavy financial liability. Again, the answer is a special district, which can operate at a low financial level as well as on a restricted functional basis.

UNADORNED SELF-INTEREST

Many of the reasons for the establishment of special districts contain shadings of self-interest on the part of groups and individuals. Some actions in favor of special districts, however, are so baldly based on complete selfishness that they warrant brief separate consideration. One illustration relates to the actions of private concerns anxious to sell equipment and supplies. Judging that their business opportuni-ties will be enhanced, they sometimes provide the principal stimulus for the establishment of special districts. The organization of supporting "citizen groups," the payment of election fees, and the circulation of district formation petitions and nominating papers of sympathetic governing body candidates are all techniques that have been employed by businesses acting wholly in their own self-interest. The result in one instance was the creation of a sanitary district which laid sewer pipes far in excess of the needs of both the present and the foreseeable future population. Another example of self-interest is the desire of local residents to realize a return on tax money collected in their area. The self-centered attitude explains the establishment of a number of road districts in Missouri. Another far from altruistic reason for creating road districts is that they provide employment opportunities, in construction and maintenance, for governing body members and their relatives and friends.

CREATION

The creation of special districts is usually based on state enabling legislation that can be utilized anywhere in the state. Occasionally, however, a state legislature will pass a special act for the formation of a certain district in a certain locality. Sometimes, as in Rhode Island fire districts, the special act is passed after local approval is gained. Less often the legal basis of creation is a state constitutional section or amendment, an interstate compact, or an international agreement, but in most of these situations, too, action by the state legislature is part of the process. Local charters, common in many cities and some counties, are virtually unknown in special districts.

The state legislature therefore occupies the key initiating position in the establishment of practically all special districts. It generally authorizes their formation by enacting the procedure for bringing them into legal existence. Furthermore, in these enabling laws, the state legislature decides upon the major governmental characteristics of the districts, such as area, function, organization, and financial authority. It may require the area of the district to include or exclude certain other governments, although frequently no area stipulations are mentioned. It permits the performance of a specific function or functions. It authorizes financing, which may or may not include taxation, bond issuance, and service charges. It establishes the number of governing body members, the method of selecting them, and the length of their terms of office. The state legislature is thus the usual source of rules for the creation and operation of special districts, and has, moreover, the freedom to change the conditions of their continuance; it may even abolish them by rescinding the supporting laws. Most types of special districts are not protected from legislative action by state constitutional provisions or local charters, a fact that could be of major importance in a comprehensive reform movement.

* * *

The events leading to district formation frequently occur in this sequence. Many district formation laws, although general in application, originate through sponsorship by a few individuals or a group in a single area seeking a governmental solution to a local problem. The proposal is introduced and passed in the legislature, often without opposition because the matter is judged to be one of local concern. Other areas may subsequently decide to use the provisions of the enabling law. Sometimes, however, after the law has been enacted, a group with a similar problem elsewhere in the state objects to certain features of the legislation. It may then seek to amend the law, but will probably encounter opposition from persons who have formed districts under the law and who want no changes. Or, the dissatisfied group may immediately seek

a new law relating to the same function or functions but differing in some respects. Numerous legislators have concluded that it is easier, and more satisfactory to all interested parties, to pass a new district enabling law than to amend an old one. This practice, utilized much more extensively in connection with special districts than with any other class of governments, results in a number of functionally similar districts operating under different enabling laws, some of which show evidence of poor draftsmanship. It also increases the amount of district legislation and adds to the widespread confusion about special districts. The abundance of district formation acts also demonstrates the ease with which a matter of local option can pass the state legislature.

Legislative authorization for a proposed district can at times be obtained much more readily than public approval in the area. Consequently, some district formation laws have never been used. Others are no longer in use, either because their original legal unworkability was never rectified or because all districts organized under their provisions are currently inactive. Yet both categories remain legally in existence because there is no impetus for their repeal. In all likelihood there are more unused and no longer used enabling laws for special districts than for any other class of governmental units. These unrepealed acts serve as a warning about the unrealism of studying district formation laws alone and emphasize the necessity for ascertaining which laws are in operation in order to obtain an accurate picture of special districts in action.

FORMATION AND DISSOLUTION DIVERSITY

The profusion of district enabling laws causes a great diversity of formation procedures. Petitioning is the most common first step in creating a special district. Only occasionally is a resolution by one or more of the governing bodies of governments in the proposed district territory substituted for the petition. Voting registration and property ownership are the two most widespread requirements for signing petitions, and both are extensively utilized. . . . Occasionally petition signers must be both property owners and residents, or they may merely be residents without necessarily being registered voters or property owners.

The percentage or absolute number of required signatures varies widely with the different petitioning bases. As few as twenty electors or 3 per cent, or as many as 5,000 voters or a majority may be required. Among property owners from as few as one to as many as two-thirds of the total, or hundreds of individual owners possessing property valued at not less than $1,000 to $2,000, may be the stipulation. There is usually little uniformity of requirements within the same state. . . .

In addition to two major qualifications for petition signers, there are two principal classes of officials to whom most of the completed petitions are transmitted. They are the governing body of the county in which the district is to be located, and the presiding judge or the entire membership of an intermediate level of the courts whose jurisdiction embraces the contemplated boundaries of the district. A petition proposing an intercounty district is frequently sent to the governing body of the largest county or of the county in which the largest part of the district will be situated. A similar procedure is often followed when the court receives the petition and operates solely within one county. Less often the petition receiver is the governing body of a city, a county government board or official, or a state government board, committee, department, or official. For example, at the state level, typical examples are the state engineer, the irrigation board, the board of health, the state soil conservation committee or board, and the department of roads and irrigation.

There is considerable variance in the responsibilities of those receiving the petition. Many of the receivers are limited to determining the sufficiency and correctness of the petition, giving adequate publicity to these facts, and calling an election if one is required. Others can change proposed boundaries, usually by reducing them after public hearings. Still others can stop the formation attempt by deciding that the district is not necessary. This infrequent right is seldom used, however.

As there are two major qualifications for petition signing and two main groups for receiving petitions, there are also two widely practiced methods of completing the formation attempt. One is by election decision of the voters who in some instances must be property owners in the proposed district. The other is through exclusive legal action, often an order, by an agency or official of another government, generally the one that initially received the petition. A frequent combination of steps involving the first method consists of petition by less than a majority of voters or property owners, or by owners of less than a majority of the land, followed by a local election. . . .

The second method—exclusive legal action by another government—is the predominant or the only practice in some states and in some types of special districts, such as housing authorities. A common combination is petition by a majority of the property owners or by the owners of a majority of the land, followed by a non-election decision. Under some groupings of petition and non-election requirements, districts that are not supported, or at times openly opposed, by a majority of the people within the affected territory can be brought into existence. Furthermore, when a small number or proportion of signatures is required on the petition and the petition receiver makes the sole legal judgment on activation of the district, it is sometimes possible to bring a substantial amount of land into the district, especially for purposes of taxation, whose owners may have definite justification for staying out.

Many districts have a dissolution procedure that exactly duplicates the formation process. A district may automatically cease to exist when its area is brought within the territorial limits of a city. This is by no means a universal practice, however, for in numerous circumstances a district must have a city within its boundaries in order to be created. Occasionally a highly unusual dissolution procedure is in effect. Noxious weed eradication districts in Nebraska, for example, have a twenty-five-year time limit which becomes operative unless abolition action is completed sooner. Automatic dissolution after a defined period is unknown in other classes of governments in the United States. Dissolving a district can be legally more difficult than creating it. Many districts established by the legal action of another government must be dissolved by election. Moreover, some of them require an extraordinary vote for dissolution as compared to a majority vote for formation. Two examples are irrigation and library districts in California, which can be established through majority consent but which need a two-thirds vote to be abolished.

In numerous situations it is currently a legal impossibility to abolish certain types of districts, simply because no procedure for eliminating them has ever been enacted. As an illustration, there is no abolition process for many kinds of districts in Illinois, including fire protection, sanitary, hospital, tuberculosis sanitarium, street lighting, and water. Many districts become inactive without formally dissolving under an authorized procedure or seeking to obtain such a procedure when it does not exist. Numerous school districts as well as a number of other governmental units, such as cities, have become inoperative. This practice can lead to confusion and to mistaken impressions by the casual observer. The governmental landscape is cluttered with many ghosts.

FUNCTIONS AND TITLES

Although most special districts individually provide only one or a few functions, they collectively supply an extremely broad range of activities, some of which are not usually undertaken by government. In some states they perform in total more services than some of the classes of general governments, such as counties and townships in certain states, and a number of less populous cities and New England towns. Most special districts, however, separately furnish only one function or a narrowly limited number of services and are therefore unique among the principal classes of governments in the United States. In this respect they are most strikingly different from the national government, but are also very unlike states, counties, cities, and many New England towns. Even townships, which have been declining in functional importance, possess more functions than many types of special districts. Most districts provide one or two services, and those supplying more are exceptions to the usual pattern.

ELEVEN CATEGORIES

The functions performed by special districts are so numerous that they do not easily lend themselves to classification, but a helpful grouping into eleven categories is possible. They are health and sanitation; protection to persons and property; road transportation facilities and aids; nonroad transportation facilities and aids; utilities; housing; natural resources and agricultural assistance; education; parks and recreation; cemeteries; and miscellaneous. The following enumeration of functions under each category is substantially all-inclusive and was formulated only after detailed analysis of the district powers in use under the laws of each state. The practice of considering district powers actually in operation, employed throughout this study, provides a realistic approach because numerous district laws are no longer in use or have never been utilized, and far from all districts perform the full extent of the authority granted them.

In the health and sanitation category, special districts provide sewage, garbage, and refuse disposal; drainage; general and special hospitals; water pollution control; mosquito abatement; pest extermination; food inspection; and various other sanitary and health measures and activities. In the protective field they supply policing and fire fighting and prevention.

Districts that furnish transportation facilities construct and maintain streets, pleasure drives, highways, sidewalks, bridges, tunnels, and terminals. They provide street and highway lighting as well as parking facilities. They plant and care for roadside trees. They own and operate mass transit facilities, including those in such densely populated places as the Boston and Chicago areas. In the nonroad transportation field, special districts build, manage, and control airports, harbors and ports, and their facilities. They operate airplanes and boats, regulate navigation, and supply watercourse improvements.

In the utilities category special districts supply water, lighting, power, telephone, heat, ice, and fuel. In the housing category they build and operate low-rent public housing projects, clear slum areas, and engage in urban redevelopment. There are many districts that provide natural resource and agricultural assistance. Some of them are concerned with the use or control of water and engage in irrigation, flood control, water conservation, reclamation, drainage, diking, and levee construction. Others revitalize and preserve the quality of the soil, eradicate debilitating weeds, eliminate predatory animals, undertake forestation, abate pests,

and build fences and gates to protect agricultural holdings.

In education, special districts provide instruction and other educational services, and range from kindergarten to the collegiate level. In addition, they build and operate libraries. In the parks and recreation category, special districts acquire and manage both city and regional parks as well as playgrounds and other recreational facilities, prevent beach erosion, and erect community centers. The function of acquiring and administering cemeteries stands as a separate division of district activities because it is not readily classifiable elsewhere and represents a substantial numerical total. The remaining functions of special districts are classified as miscellaneous because of their great diversity. Among other matters, special districts construct and direct veterans' memorial buildings, provide planning and zoning, license vehicles and businesses, and acquire and maintain marketing facilities.

*   *   *

HELPFUL AND CONFUSING TITLES

Unlike other governments, a special district very often has the function it performs as part of its official title or designation. The national government of the United States, the state government of New Hampshire, Republic County (Kansas), West Bloomfield Township (Michigan), and the City of Magnolia (Arkansas) are all official designations of units in other classes of governments, but none contains a functional word in its title. The official names of most special districts offer a strong contrast. Frequently the name of the geographic location or region covered by the district is adopted as part, and often the first portion, of the official appellation. . . .

The function appearing as part of the official name of a district does not always accurately indicate the range of the district's activities. Instead, it sometimes reveals merely one activity in which the district may legally be involved but which it may not actually be exercising. Furthermore, the functional designation in the title is at times overgeneralized and therefore not very meaningful. Thus, protection districts in California could be thought of as performing any one of a number of protective functions, whereas they actually safeguard against overflow water.

Generally the insertion of a too limited or too nebulous functional word into the formal designation of a special district causes much less confusion than other difficulty involving titles. The word "district" is usually part of the official appellation, but not always. Some special district governments are legally known as authorities, although it should be stressed that not all authorities are special districts. In addition, other words such as board, commission, association, and area are employed in place of district. Again, terms that are more generally employed in other types of governments are sometimes used by districts; examples are village in Maryland, community in Oregon, and precinct in New Hampshire. Usually terms such as these have been used in some states to designate some kinds of districts, while at the same time the word "district" has been applied to other kinds.

AREAS

Compared with other governments, special districts often have highly unusual area characteristics. A major differentiation is one of location rather than territorial size. Special districts can nearly always occupy any part of the area of all other kinds of special districts; only occasionally are they specifically excluded from doing so. Furthermore, the area of a special district can in many instances cover a segment of or all the territory of other governments that are not special districts. Territorially, therefore, most kinds of special districts do not have to be mutually exclusive of one another or of other governments. The result is that many types of special districts pile upon one another and other governments in the same area.

In contrast, no city may be situated on any portion of the territory of another city. Counties are also territorially exclusive of one another, as are townships, towns, states, and nations. A general government of one class, however, does sometimes overlap at least one of another class. Counties overlie the boundaries of cities in most states and of townships in states that have township organization. Some townships also contain cities within their borders. Nevertheless, the more general area flexibility of special districts in relation to other types of districts and other classes of governments largely accounts for the overlapping of governments in the United States.

MANDATORY INCLUSION AND EXCLUSION

In addition to the optional right of most districts to overlie the area of other governmental units, the frequent initial requirement that another government must be part of the district territory also contributes to overlapping. At least one city must be included within the boundaries of numerous kinds of districts. Most often only one city is required, but the mandatory inclusion of two or more cities is not unknown. Even though the district and the city are sometimes coterminous (which adds to the confusion), they are separate and independent governments. In a similar but less frequent pattern an entire county must be included within the district borders, and often the district and the county occupy exactly the same total area. Furthermore, several types of districts must have all or parts of two and sometimes more counties within their area, which means that they not only occupy at least part of the area of other governments but also cross over their boundaries. Infrequently a district is required by its enabling law to have another district within its boundaries. As mentioned previously, the existence of one district in the territory of other districts is not unusual.

The most common legal restriction on the area of districts is that certain ones can be organized only in unincorporated territory. In a practical sense this requirement excludes cities from the district territory. Although appearing with only moderate frequency, such formal exclusion does reduce governmental overlapping to some extent; it is, however, inapplicable to other districts, counties, and, in states where they are functioning, townships. As an illustration, a district that may not have a city within its borders may still cross over county, district, and township lines. It may even be interstate or international under appropriate written agreements. Another restriction, used even less often, stipulates that the territory of a district must be entirely within one county.

*   *   *

EFFECT OF OTHER GOVERNMENTS

A few kinds of districts must possess a specific minimal number of inhabitants. This usually occurs when a city or sometimes a county, possessing not less than a stated number of inhabitants, must be included within the proposed district. At times, when a district must contain at least two cities, they must have a minimum aggregate population. Such districts therefore cannot have less than the population of the city (or cities) or the county that is to be within their territorial limits. Only rarely is an exact district population minimum directly stipulated, irrespective of the presence or absence of other governments within the district.

Several kinds of districts are limited to a maximum area. Some of these restrictions are determined by the area of a government functioning within the borders of the district. The boundaries of some districts required to have a city within their territory may extend only

a specified number of miles beyond the limits of the city. Housing authorities in North Carolina, for example, may not extend more than 10 miles beyond the corporate limits of the city that must be part of the district. The area of the city itself and the nature of its borders therefore directly affect the total territory that can be brought within the district. Other districts have their territorial size conditioned by the population size of the cities they adjoin. . . .

POTENTIALITIES AND HANDICAPS

This consideration of various aspects of the area of special districts illustrates that one of their outstanding characteristics is area flexibility. Many of them are legally empowered to contain a large amount of territory without regard to the boundaries of other governments that cover all or part of the same land. Quite often they cross city, township, town, and county lines (as well as other district boundaries), and include both urban and rural land. Such authorization furnishes them great latitude in both location and territorial extent. Fifteen special districts include area within more than one state as the result of the adoption of interstate compacts. A few functon under international agreements and are international in that the facility they operate, such as a bridge, has its terminal points in two different countries.

Despite their area potentialities, many special districts are actually small in comparison with cities. Some encompass only a fraction of a square mile. But others, often including some of the same types utilized in small areas (such as water districts), embrace the major portion of a state. In some states, usually in rural sections, one special district possesses the smallest area and another the largest of all governments functioning below the state level. An occasional district is territorially larger than some of the smaller states in other parts of the Union. Although many districts have small areas, collectively they include most of the territory of the United States, and in some sections of the country they themselves constitute two or more layers of government. Both school and soil conservation districts include a very large portion of the United States. Below the state level, the county is the only governmental unit that rivals the total amount of territory within special districts. Cities, towns, and townships contain far less of the total land of the nation.

Many types of special districts have additional area flexibilty through legal authorization to annex territory not originally part of the district. The existing boundaries of other governments are usually no obstacle in such annexation actions. At times the enlargement procedure is quite easy. Frequently annexation can be initiated within either the district or the territory under consideration, and a combined, over-all vote of both areas or a nonvoter action, such as a court order, decides the issue. Sometimes a very small percentage or number of individuals can start the proceedings.

Ease of annexing is not universal, however. A number of districts are legally unable to change their boundaries through annexation once they have been established. In some states no kind of district is able to annex, and in others there are many that cannot do so. There is some indication that occasionally this was a legislative oversight rather than a purposeful omission.

* * *

One final characteristic should be noted because of its distinguishing nature and importance. The general lack of information and knowledge about the location and limits of special districts after their establishment makes even their approximate boundaries largely unknown. Such a deficiency, fostered by the numerousness and the pyramiding of districts, prevails among many district residents and among practically all outside persons, a number of whom may indirectly be very much affected

by district activities. Incoming residents usually know in advance, or soon learn about, the other governmental areas within which they are locating, such as a state, county, township, or city. But many of them do not discover their special district areas until the tax and service bills arrive. Even this kind of revelation is not always forthcoming, for such charges sometimes appear in the consolidated bill of another government which is serving as the collection agency for the district. Many individuals think that one of the other governments to which they are contributing financially is furnishing a service that is actually being supplied by a special district.

In this sense many special districts are phantom governments. People who receive services from them often do not know that they exist or exactly where they function. Although most districts have definite areas and boundaries which limit their jurisdiction, there is seldom visible evidence of these facts. Districts often create a crazy-quilt pattern of governmental areas and boundaries with only very slight public knowledge that they do so. Their phantom-like quality does not diminish their collective and sometimes individual importance. It merely increases the difficulty of comprehending a class of governments which is of rising significance.

GOVERNING BODIES

The most noticeable feature of the governing bodies of special districts is the division between direct election and appointment in the selection of their members. The members are elected in the majority of districts, but the margin of difference over appointment is not overwhelming. Some types of district governing bodies, in school districts, for example, are predominantly elected throughout various sections of the nation. Others, such as those in housing authorities, are always appointed. Some districts, such as soil conservation districts, usually have both appointive and elective governing personnel. The diversity is also evident in comparisons between states. . . .

Whether elected or appointed, governing bodies have numerous characteristics in common. The official title of the members is usually director, commissioner, or trustee, with supervisor and board member appearing less frequently. Occasionally the collective designation is citizen committee or prudential committee. Total membership is almost always an odd number, usually three to five, though it may range from eleven to as many as thirty-six. Infrequently a single person governs the district. Many district governing bodies are therefore smaller than those of most other governments and, although some are unwieldy in size, none approaches the total membership of the governing bodies of certain counties. A few districts have an even number of board members, which at times results in deadlocked votes.

The terms of office generally range from two to six years but three- and four-year terms are most prevalent. Governing body members, however, sometimes hold office for five or six years, and occasionally for only one year; a frequent combination involves three members serving for three years. There is much less uniformity in the length of the term when there are five members. Occasionally members who are appointed serve indefinitely at the pleasure of the appointing authority. Staggered or overlapping terms are frequent for both elective and appointive offices. Election methods are few in number and well known in many other governments; election is either at large or on a district basis, but the former is the more general practice. Conversely, appointment procedures are much more diversified and are frequently complex.

APPOINTMENT METHODS

Most often a single group or individual from another government acts as the appointing authority. Many times the authority that receives the formation petition and creates the district also chooses the governing body. The most frequent selecting agent is the governing body of the county in which the district is situated. Another customary appointive authority is a court or the presiding judge of a court, usually at an intermediate level of the state judicial system within whose jurisdiction the district lies. Appearing less often in the role of appointer is the governing body of a city, the mayor of a city, or the governor of a state. The governor usually appoints when the district covers a large area and handles a function, such as port or airport, which may be judged to have state-wide effect. The governing bodies of a few types of districts are chosen at the state level by an administrative official, an administrative agency, a committee, or the legislature. Generally, when the legislature does the appointing, it accepts the recommendation of the legislative delegation from the area involved.

At times a joint appointing responsibility, either dual or triple, of different units, levels, or branches of government adds to the variety and complexity of selecting the members of district governing boards. Selection decisions by the governing body or chief executive of at least two governments at the local level may be required. The various combinations are two or more cities, one or more cities and counties, a town and a village, or any of these units plus special districts. Each government may appoint a specified number separately, or may agree jointly upon selections for the entire membership. Action by different levels of government may be necessary. Separate appointments by the governor, the county governing body, and the city governing body constitute one system currently in operation. Another consists of independent appointment action by the county governing body and the governor. Occasionally one unit of government recommends, another has the right to approve or disapprove, and other nominations must be submitted in the event of disapproval. . . .

Different branches of government and sometimes different levels of government are jointly concerned in the selection of the governing members of some districts. Under the most complex method, individual appointments to the board are made by the judges of two different levels of courts, the county governing body, and the mayor of the largest city within the district. The procedure may be interstate or even international, with selection by the governors of two states or by the governor of one state and the appropriate authority of another country. Occasionally most of the members of a district governing body, appointed in various ways, choose others to serve with them. Under some of these procedures there is serious doubt as to the degree of effective control that people residing within the district and influenced by its operations can exercise over the governing body.

*　　*　　*

The governing bodies of some special districts are selected partly by election and partly by appointment. The most prominent example of this hybrid arrangement is a board of five members, two appointed by a state soil conservation committee and three elected by the local district voters. It is also possible for the membership of housing authorities in certain Massachusetts localities to be a mixture of elected and appointed members. Four are elected at the town meeting and the fifth is appointed by a state housing board.

How can these many types of special districts, governed wholly or partly by appointed board members, still be independent units of government? It is because, like special districts with elected governing boards, they conduct their fiscal and administrative activities without substantial review or modification by other governments, including those appointing board members. Within the framework of state legislative and constitutional limits on their finances and

any general state supervision of governments, they determine their own budgets and financing programs and carry out policy and administrative decisions which they have formulated. Appointed board members are not legally subject to important control by the appointing authority. Most members are selected for definite terms and cannot be removed by the appointing agent except upon substantiation of serious charges. This tenure right also strengthens their autonomy. In actual practice appointees have wide freedom during their period of service.

But what about district governing bodies with ex officio members? Such a district is an independent unit of government when the ex officio representatives from one other government do not constitute a majority. If a district is governed directly by the governing body of another unit, such as a county or a city, it is not an independent government but a dependent district or adjunct of another government. There are many dependent districts but they are not special districts in the sense of being separate governmental units.

The key test of a special district as a separate unit of government is not whether its governing body is appointed or elected or even ex officio. Some districts have elected governing bodies which are under close administrative and fiscal surveillance by another government; they are therefore dependent districts. The basic determinant is whether the district possesses substantial freedom from other governments in its fiscal and administrative operations.

NUMEROUS INFLUENCES

The selection method and the number of members on the governing board sometimes depend upon the size of the district or the number of governmental units within the district territory which are participating members. The state legislation does not always provide for the selection method and a fixed number of members. Sometimes decisions about appointment or election of the governing body and the number of members are made by the district voters at the election to create the district or by the circulators of petitions to form the district. Election of members has usually been favored. Determination of the appointing authority depends at times on whether the district is in one or more counties. Under one method, the county governing board chooses the governing body when the district includes only unincorporated territory within one county, and the governor selects the members when the area is intercounty. Other times the number of governments within the district determines both the appointing authority and the number on the board. One variation of this procedure is to have the mayor appoint a council-determined number when the area of the district is entirely within one city, and to have the mayor of each city choose one member when the district includes more than one city.

*   *   *

ELIGIBILITY, SALARY, AND SERVICE

The most usual eligibility requirements for governing body membership are residence, voting registration, and property ownership in the territory of the district. Sometimes it is necessary to have all three, but ordinarily one or two are sufficient. Only occasionally is there a more specialized requirement, such as in California memorial districts where the governing body members must be veterans. In practice, however, the members of many special districts are drawn heavily from occupations on which district activities have a direct bearing. Water and port districts are two frequent cases in point.

Compensation is generally nominal or nonexistent. This is true of large as well as of small operations, as indicated by the highly important Port of New York Authority and the Hartford County (Connecticut) Metropolitan District, whose boards receive no salary. Only a few governing body members receive as much as $1,000 a year. In scattered instances members receive relatively high pay for their services. For example, the directors of the Chicago Transit Authority are each paid an annual salary of $15,000, and the chairman's salary is even higher. A very large number of district board members serve more than a single term of one to six years, for many of them are reappointed or reelected. Frequently their tenure is terminated only because of their own desires, poor health, or death. Many who are elected run for reelection without opposition.

A widespread practice has developed among board members who obtain office on an elective basis. A member who has decided not to seek reelection resigns before the election so that his successor, often selected by the remainder of the board membership, can run as the incumbent. This seems to dissuade some individuals who might otherwise become candidates. The technique is not completely unknown to other governments, but it is more common among special districts. Sometimes, however, the decision by a governing board member not to seek reelection has created a situation where there are more offices to be filled by election than people formally seeking them. In some district elections not a single name appears on the official ballot. Under such circumstances a limited number of write-in votes, often cast for a reluctant or perhaps unknowing person, is sufficient. This sequence of events is highly extraordinary in elections held by other governmental units.

*   *   *

BOARD ACTIVITIES AND ADMINISTRATION

There is considerable variation in the amount and nature of the work performed by district governing bodies. Most of them convene once or twice a month, a small number meet every week, and a few hold annual meetings. Many handle directly all policy considerations and most of the administrative details, especially in the smaller districts. Some boards confine themselves to setting broad policies, generally overseeing administration, and assigning administrative activities to district administrators and employees. Some provide little policy initiation or administrative guidance. Most district governing boards have complete freedom in shaping the administrative organization because state laws are generally silent on the matter. This power is often unused because of the limited amount or volunteer nature of the activity undertaken by many districts.

* * *

District officials and employees are almost always appointed directly by the governing body members or with their ultimate approval. Usually the board creates an administrative organization centering on an individual who handles details arising between board meetings, or who coordinates or manages administrative operations. This person is called the manager, executive secretary, executive director, engineer, clerk, or superintendent. The last title is the prevalent one in school districts. In some medium-sized and large special districts the governing body does not organize the administration around a single person. Instead, it employs coequal managers of business and technical affairs and has each report to the board. Other employees include technical, professional, clerical, and laboring personnel. In the larger district establishments there is often an elaborate administrative structure, with numerous departments and divisions, supervisory officials, and staff aides to the central administrator in financial preparation and control and administrative and physical planning. When a fairly detailed administrative structure exists, employees are often actually hired by the department or division chief upon approval by the central administrator,

unless the board expresses opposition to specific appointments.

* * *

In many types of districts none of the employees, including the central administrator, has any tenure rights. Many districts have no formal civil service procedure and grant no contract to the administrator. This might be expected in small districts but it also prevails in some larger ones. Most of the exceptions are found among school districts, many of whose employees have job tenure after a probationary period and many of whose superintendents and administrative staff have contracts for one to four years. . . .

The meetings of district governing bodies are usually attended only by the members and their aides. Although such meetings are open to anyone, they are not often attended by either newspaper reporters or private citizens. The voluntary absence of the two groups is interrelated, since citizens stay away because they are not sufficiently interested, and newspapers generally report only those public affairs in which there is a reasonable amount of public interest. Most newspapers simply cannot afford to have representatives watch the activities of all the governments operating in a specific area, especially those attracting a minimum of public interest. Also, citizens do not like to make such an investment of personal time unless controversial issues are going to be aired.

* * *

Complete lack of newspaper and public observance of district governing body meetings over a sustained period of time sometimes results in strange proceedings. A pertinent illustration is the procedure followed by the directors of a special district, important both territorially and functionally, in the western part of the United States. The directors first hold a closed meeting in one of the inner offices of the headquarters building at a regularly scheduled time preceding the official meeting. There they resolve their differences of opinion, if any exist, and then proceed to the official meeting place at the announced time. Up to this point the procedure has not been unlike that actually followed by the governing bodies of many local governments. But once the governing body of the district officially convenes, the board secretary merely reads off as official acts of the directors the decisions that were made in closed session. Neither the chairman nor any member makes a motion for adoption or generally utters any comment during the reading by the secretary. The closed session is thus followed by an almost silent meeting.

FINANCES

LIMITED REVENUE METHODS

The revenue sources legally available to special districts for financing their services are generally quite narrow. This is true of both school and nonschool special districts, although they differ markedly in the types of sources most important to them. School districts derive more than nine-tenths of their revenue from taxes on property and transfers of funds from other governmental units, largely state governments. Most of the small remainder is obtained from service charges and other miscellaneous nontax sources with only incidental amounts coming from other taxes. The principal direct source of revenue for school districts is therefore the property tax, with heavy supplementation by grants and subventions from other governments. Only occasionally, as in Pennsylvania in recent years, do other types of taxes, like those on income and sales, produce a significant amount of direct revenue. By contrast, property taxes and intergovernmental transfers account for only approximately one-fourth of the revenue of nonschool districts. Instead, nontax revenues such as service charges, special

assessments, rates, and rents constitute about three-fourths of the total. The extremely heavy reliance of special districts on a highly restricted revenue base contrasts strongly with the diversification permitted other classes of governments, including cities, states, and the national government.

Another prominent financial characteristic of many nonschool special districts is the lack of legal authorization to levy taxes. More than one-third of them have no taxing authority. Furthermore, when the taxing power exists it is usually limited to the right to levy taxes on property. Individual and corporate income, sales and gross receipts, death and gift, and motor vehicle taxes therefore bring them no revenue. More than half of the districts that do have the power to tax property are restricted in its use. This restriction is usually stated as a maximum number of mills (frequently 2 to 5 mills), a specific number of cents on each $100 of assessed valuation (often 10 cents), or a certain per cent of the value of taxable property in the district (often 1 per cent). The money so derived may be used only to pay the costs of organizing the district, the interest on the retirement of bonds, or the incidental administrative expenses necessary to the functional activity of the district.

NONTAX SOURCES AND BONDS

Since many districts lack the taxing power or can use it only in a circumscribed way, where do they acquire additional money to finance their operations? Nearly one-half of the types of nonschool districts and a large number of school districts are legally empowered to obtain revenue through charges for services rendered. This is an extremely important source of public funds for special districts, particularly for many nonschool districts that lack authority to levy property taxes. Many more school districts have both revenue possibilities, but service charges are much less significant to them than to nonschool districts. This nontax revenue source—service charges—is used in several ways by special districts. The diversity should not be interpreted as necessarily exemplifying uniformity of kind or function. Special assessments are exacted in proportion to the benefits derived from operation of the district. For example, districts levy assessments for draining excess water from land, transporting water to depleted soil for irrigation, or protecting an area from inundation. They impose tolls for the use of district property, such as crossing a bridge. They collect rates and charges for furnishing various services including power, transit, gas, and water. They obtain rents for housing they own and operate, and charge fees for the facilities and staff services of a hospital or sanitarium.

Districts obtain a major share of their money through borrowing, and thus incur indebtedness. Most special districts can legally issue bonds which are often retired by using income and other nontax sources rather than property taxation. Generally a bond proposal must gain the approval of voters eligible to participate in an election. A two-thirds popular majority is the most frequent stipulation, but a simple majority is often legally adequate; infrequently a three-fifths affirmative vote is necessary. Sometimes majorities must be obtained in different parts of the district, such as within and outside a city. The majority may vary with the nature of the bonds. For example, a two-thirds margin may be necessary for general obligation bonds and a simple majority may be sufficient for revenue bonds which are dependent for payment upon money collected by the district in performing its services. Occasionally bonds may be issued without submitting the question to the voters. This is done through action initiated and approved by the district governing body.

*　　*　　*

Nonschool districts rely most heavily upon bond issues and various types of service charges for income. Direct taxes and grants and subventions from other governments occupy subsidiary positions. Nonschool districts are thus the only governmental units in the United States that do not place heavy dependence upon direct taxation. Bonds are also important to the finances of school districts, but service charges are subordinate. In contrast, too, the transfer of revenue from other governments and direct tax levies, especially on property, are primary and almost equally productive sources of money to school districts. Special districts therefore derive their funds from various sources, but the relative importance of the sources differs for nonschool and school districts, and district financing is substantially unlike that of any other class of governments in the United States.

Because of the limited functional scope of most individual special districts, they collectively show a great diversity of types or kinds and a wide variety of characteristics, far exceeding those for any other class of governments. In turn, this has resulted in a greater over-all complexity of the nation's governmental pattern. . . .

62. Do We Need a State Agency for Local Affairs? *

JOHN G. GRUMM

THE steady growth of urban population has become an accepted fact of national life in the United States. The move to the cities has proceeded with virtually no interruption during the present century, and it would appear safe to anticipate a continued rising population in almost all major urban areas. Accompanying this has been a spreading out of urban population so that geographic expansion of urban areas also has shown a great increase.

One of the basic problems caused by the population movement is the absence of local governmental organizations broad enough geographically and functionally to cope with metropolitan matters. Instead, in most areas, there is a great multiplicity of governmental units which have not proven capable of making a concerted and coordinated attack on the pressing problems at hand. As a result, governmental services within the metropolitan region as a whole often present a chaotic picture. City streets, for example, may be laid down in an uncoordinated fashion with little relation to metropolitan traffic patterns. Within the same area, there may be great differences in the quality of services provided. The interests of the metropolitan area as a whole may easily be disregarded in the planning and zoning functions.

Still other problems are presented in the large unincorporated urban fringe areas surrounding the cities. In order to meet their needs, the unincorporated communities have either called upon the county to furnish services, or have set up a series of special districts for

* Reprinted with permission from *Public Management*, June 1961. Footnotes omitted.

that purpose, or both. Under these circumstances the resulting standards of service often tend to be lower than in the cities, and the aggregate local tax load tends to be higher.

VARIETY OF SOLUTIONS

To meet these complex problems, a variety of solutions has been devised and applied in metropolitan areas of the United States and Canada: city-county consolidation (New Orleans, Boston, Philadelphia), city-county separation (Baltimore, San Francisco, St. Louis), federation (Toronto), functional transfer (Dade County, Florida), and the metropolitan special district (Los Angeles, San Francisco Bay area). Annexation also has been used with varying success in a number of metropolitan areas. By and large these have provided only partial solutions.

In addition to the problems of the larger urban areas, small cities outside the major metropolitan regions are experiencing other problems because of their limited size and lack of resources. Many small and medium-sized cities have lost population in the rush to the larger urban centers. And even where there has been no loss, numerous incorporated places have remained very small in size and limited in their ability to finance governmental services.

These small cities need assistance of various types. Some cannot employ a full-time city attorney and need additional legal help. Many do not have adequate systems of personnel administration. Often small cities could use advice and assistance in budgeting, accounting, and debt management. Almost all of the smaller cities need help in city planning.

ROLE OF THE STATE

Although the problems of large metropolitan communities are vastly different from those of small municipalities, the state government has a vital role to play in the solution of both kinds of problems. Legally, the responsibility of the states in this regard cannot be ignored. From a practical standpoint, also, the state governments are the only institutions capable of handling some of these problems.

The activities of the state and of its local governments are, in essence, a joint endeavor, and many of the functions are shared functions. There are a few matters that can be considered *purely* local, but most of the activity of local government has an impact beyond local boundaries. Since the state is the more inclusive and legally superior entity, it is generally recognized that the state has primarily responsibility for a well-ordered system of state-local relations. The state also is superior to the localities in its ability to raise revenue. In the words of the Committee on State-Local Relations of the Council of State Governments, "This dual dominance of states—in law and finance—is an incontrovertible fact. It places a heavy obligation upon the states to create an orderly and effective system of state-local relations."

STATE-LOCAL RELATIONS

The role of the states in meeting urban problems would seem to be threefold. First they must provide the legal framework necessary for *effective* local government. This is a matter that might well be examined by most state legislatures. Second, the state's responsibility for the soundness and adequacy of local finances requires it to exercise

a degree of supervision over local fiscal procedures but at the same time avoid making limitations on local revenue sources too restrictive. Where local units cannot properly finance their operations from local sources, state money must be provided through grants-in-aid. Finally, the states need to improve local administrative practice through supervision, encouragement, and assistance. Many types of supervision and control are employed, but a more fruitful approach in many respects is the provision of expert advice, information, research, and technical services to local governments.

With a few notable exceptions, the states have not been meeting their responsibilities toward their local governments. A major difficulty is that the states have generally not sought to concentrate their local services, research, and supervisory activities in one agency. Characteristically almost every agency of state government is involved in relations with the local units in some way.

HOW CONCENTRATED?

A national authority on local government, Harold F. Alderfer, has argued that, since the responsibility for maintaining a sound system of local government constitutes a major state function, *all* of the activities related to this responsibility should be placed in one agency which would have departmental or cabinet status.

Another significant proposal, though less far-reaching, advocated a separate state *research and service agency* which would "aid in determining the present and changing needs of its metropolitan and non-metropolitan areas."

EXISTING STATE AGENCIES

A small number of states have established agencies primarily concerned with local government. The New Jersey

Division of Local Government is one. Its most important functions are examining municipal and county budgets and auditing municipal and county accounts. It also publishes guides and statistical reports for local units and is authorized to study the whole field of local government, to render advice to municipalities when requested, and to recommend plans for the improvement of local administration.

In Pennsylvania the Bureau of Municipal Affairs is responsible both for a wide range of services to localities and for some supervisory functions. In the breadth and variety of its activities, it is probably unique in the United States. Its activities are organized into four divisions which are responsible for: (1) research and information regarding local units, (2) the collection and dissemination of local government financial statistics, (3) providing assistance in city planning and landscape architecture to local public bodies, and (4) the approval of local bond issues and bond proceedings.

Another type of local government agency exists in Tennessee—the Municipal Technical Advisory Service. Attached to the University of Tennessee, it offers direct services in such areas as municipal management, finance and accounting, engineering and public works, fringe areas, municipal law, municipal information, and ordinance codification. In addition, its publication program includes directories, handbooks, statistical compilations, and analyses of state laws and constitutional amendments affecting local government.

The recently established New York Office for Local Government is primarily a staff agency to the governor, but a list of its powers suggests a potential of some magnitude. It is empowered to assist the governor in coordinating the activities and services of 20 state agencies having relationships with local governments, to provide advice and assistance to local units, to make studies of urban and metropolitan problems, to serve as a clearinghouse for information about local matters, and to encourage and assist cooperative efforts toward the solution of metropolitan problems.

A number of other states have agencies for local affairs that are somewhat more narrow in scope. The North Carolina Local Government Commission has the basic responsibility of controlling municipal borrowing. The Minnesota Municipal Commission and the Alaska Local Boundary Commission are concerned primarily with review and approval of municipal incorporations, annexations, and consolidations.

It should be noted also that most of the provincial governments of Canada have an agency concerned exclusively with local affairs. Some of their powers and responsibilities are quite comprehensive. A typical example is the Ontario Municipal Board, which has almost complete authority over local bond issues and boundary changes. The Ontario Department of Municipal Affairs, closely connected with the Board, offers a large number of services to local units. The Municipal Board took the initiative in establishing the well-known "Toronto Plan" which provided a workable system for federating the municipalities within the Toronto metropolitan area.

DESIRABILITY OF STATE AGENCY

Would the establishment of agencies responsible for the major state activities relating to its local government lessen the many problems which beset our urban communities? Agencies of this sort in Canada apparently have performed satisfactorily, and the few in the United States have done a good job within the limits of their authority. There are, however, a number of considerations that must be borne in mind before such a step is taken.

In listing the arguments in favor of a state agency for local affairs, one should first point out that the problems of urban areas are bound to increase and that only the state, by virtue of its superior legal position, can provide the positive measures that are needed. Therefore, a new state agency is advisable for the purpose of administering new local assistance and service programs and for coordinating some of the established local services that the state now provides.

Even without the addition of new functions, coordination of state-local relations is needed in most states. Generally a variety of agencies and officials administers existing aids and controls. This can lead to confusion and possibly to duplication of state efforts. From the standpoint of the city official, there is no central place where he can go in the state government to get information or help.

Second, it is argued that there should be a recognition of the central importance of state-local relations in the state system, and that creation of such an agency would achieve this. It is also consistent with this view that the agency should have departmental or "cabinet" status. Thus a focus would be created in the state government for policy leadership on local matters. Many urban states have "cabinet" level departments devoted to agriculture, but none has such a department devoted to urban matters. This is inequitable, it is argued, and puts the more populous urban areas at a disadvantage in relation to the rural sections. According to this view, cities need an effective representative of their interests in the executive branch of the state government.

One other factor is the increasing role of the federal government in urban matters. As one of the consequences of this trend, proposals for a federal department of urban affairs have been gaining increasing acceptance in the new administration. Undoubtedly the trend will not be reversed until the states become better organized to deal with their own local governments. According to this argument, the establishment of effective agencies for local affairs in most of the states, especially the heavily urbanized ones, would eliminate the need and pressures for a federal department and would reduce the influence of the federal government in local matters.

On the other side, there are generally three objections to a state agency for local affairs. First, it would introduce an incongruity into the state's administrative structure and might disrupt a well-established relationship. State programs affecting local governments cut across the jurisdiction of many existing agencies and departments (highways, social welfare and public health, for example). The *internal* coordination of each of these major functional programs by the existing agencies is probably more important than close coordination *among* all the agencies having contact with local government. In addition, many of the relationships between the functional departments and the local units have been built up over a long period of time, are well established, and would be difficult to change even if it were considered desirable to do so.

Second, it can be argued that a new state agency of this kind might tend to increase the dependence of the local units on the state. It is suggested that the cities and counties can solve their own financial and administrative problems and that at the present time the state need only give local governments sufficient leeway through enabling legislation to permit them to seek their own solutions.

Third, local governments already have many sources of outside help. In almost all states a league of municipalities can help with legal and technical advice and information. In some states local governments can rely on bureaus and institutes connected with state universities. In fact, it is argued that the existing services and aids offered by the various state agencies constitute, in the aggregate, an extensive program of assistance, research, and service for local units.

FUNCTIONS OF STATE AGENCY

Despite the objections raised, a properly constituted state agency for local affairs probably can play a significant role in many of the more urbanized states.

It would appear advisable, however, that the agency engage primarily in service and facilitative functions, rather than control or supervision, and that there be a minimum of interference with well-established programs of other departments dealing with local units.

Examples of some of the services that might be performed by the new agency would include planning assistance, personnel and civil service aids, assistance with budgeting and accounting procedures, aid in engineering and public works, and legal advice.

In addition the new agency almost certainly should be charged with conducting extensive research on urban problems. The research program would not seek to supplant those carried on by state leagues of municipalities or university bureaus of research but should be designed to complement them. General studies might be emphasized rather than studies of specific conditions in individual communities.

A final function of the new agency would be to assist the governor and legislature in coordinating state activities affecting local communities and in formulating policies with respect to urban areas. The agency could also serve as a central point of contact in the state government for local officials and representatives of municipal leagues and other local governmental associations.

The location of the agency within the state administrative structure is an important consideration. In many respects the best arrangement would be to establish it as a staff agency closely associated with or in the office of the governor. If it had no control functions, it would not have to be in the line structure of the executive branch. Close association with the governor's office would emphasize the agency's potential advantages as a source of information, research, and policy formulation in local affairs.

Part IX

METROPOLITAN AREAS

THE multiplication and aggravation of problems in metropolitan areas stimulate the need for reassessing the status quo and for determining appropriate action to meet the demands made upon government and society in general. The processes involved in community decision making are often complex, and the factors involved are frequently unclear. In recent years, considerable effort has been directed toward improving understanding in this area. In his article on "Community Decision Making," Peter Rossi outlines and evaluates the most significant investigations of this topic and presents some hypotheses regarding the manner in which such decisions are made.

Numerous proposals have been prepared and submitted to the public with the purpose of making individual metropolitan communities more desirable places in which to live. Charles R. Adrian notes that "The usual pattern is for metro proposals to be defeated almost before the game begins." Obviously, they have been unpopular with the voters in most instances. Mr. Adrian's study of public attitudes provides insight into the reasons why the majority of citizens have reacted unfavorably toward proposals for metropolitan reform.

In his examination of "The Political Implications of Metropolitan Growth," Edward Banfield compares and contrasts the American and British political systems with regard to meeting the burdens of metropolitan growth. He stresses the different environment in which local political institutions work in England as contrasted with the situation in the United States. One significant aspect of this difference is reflected in Mr. Banfield's observation that the British "believe it is the business of the government to govern. The voter may control the government by giving or withholding consent, but he may not participate in its affairs." Americans, on the other hand, stress the value of "grass-roots democracy," which means that the people demand the opportunity of participating directly in the process of government. This popular attitude is conducive to weakness on the part of government in attempting to cope with problems of metropolitan communities.

Among the most troublesome problems besetting local governments in metropolitan areas are those relating to efforts to obtain adequate funds. In his examination of "Some Fiscal Implications of Metropolitanism," Harvey Brazer considers "ideal" arrangements for financing adequate public services, the obstacles militating against the achievement of such arrangements, and means of minimizing these obstacles. Mr. Brazer stresses the fact that differences in the characteristics of metropolitan areas make very difficult any effort to generalize with regard to a single satisfactory approach to their fiscal problems. Especially significant are contrasts in the size and structure of tax bases relative to population.

The Advisory Commission on Intergovernmental Relations provides "Criteria for Appraising Different Approaches to Reorganization of Local Government in Metropolitan Areas." The Commission asserts that "local governments should serve the people effectively and efficiently, with active citizen participation and control, with an adequate and equitable revenue system, with a sufficient degree of local initiative and self-government for traditional or natural communities in the area, and with provisions for adaptation to growth and change." It then describes eight criteria for the purpose of evaluating various approaches to governmental reorganization in metropolitan areas.

In its study of "Voter Reaction to Metropolitan Reorganization," the Advisory Commission reviews eighteen proposals for metropolitan reorganization submitted to popular vote between 1950 and 1961. On the basis of information obtained from observers in the areas affected by these proposals, insight is provided into the rationale of proponents and opponents. Especially noteworthy is the Commission's examination of the role of various community elements whose position on the proposed reorganizations could be identified as well as those factors that apparently had an important bearing on the success or failure of individual reorganization efforts.

In spite of widespread gloom concerning the future of metropolitan communities, Scott Greer, in his look at "The Metropolity and Its Future," concludes that "The metropolis is in little danger of a breakdown." He notes that through voluntary cooperation, resort to the special district, and outside subsidy the governmental work of metropolitan areas gets done. Mr. Greer proceeds to analyze changes in the role of the central city and the suburbs that will be dictated by ongoing changes in the nature of the metropolis.

63. Community Decision Making*

PETER H. ROSSI

PERHAPS the most striking feature of contemporary communities is their ceaselessly changing nature. Within decades, demographic shifts have transformed hamlets into towns, towns into cities, and cities into metropolises. Physical appearances undergo transformations, often making painful experiences of our visits to the scenes of our childhood memories.

Less obvious, but equally important, are the structural changes in society which accompany the growth or decline measured in population and building-plant terms. On the institutional side, innovation after innovation in the forms of local government have been designed to catch up with the problems presented by the increasing complexity of our predominantly urban life. In the last few decades our public-school systems have increased their coverage of our youth tremendously, and in the same period they have been transformed from one form to a variety of forms. Private associations, such as community chests, chambers of commerce, and so forth, have arisen to fill the needs of "community organization" brought on by the urban transformation.

Many of the changes which appear so dramatic are the results of ecological processes. Individual citizens and private organizations, in the course of working out their individual destinies, make decisions which, when compounded in the mass, profoundly affect the physical and social structure of our communities. The market or location decisions of an industrial organization can bring relative prosperity or its op-

posite to the small community. Individual migration decisions may depopulate an area or flood a labor market, and so on. Such changes in the ecological order, while purposive from the point of view of the individual or subsystem of the community, are nonpurposive from the point of view of the community as such. It goes without saying, however, that the effect of such decisions may be considerable.

In contrast, some community changes may result from the self-conscious actions of individuals and organizations —actions directed at the transformation or maintenance of *status quo* of the community. It is to these actions that we must look for our understanding of much of the change in the formal social structure of the community, the local government, such community organizations as the community chest, the public-school system, and so on.

Our purpose in this paper is to review research on *community decisions* —choices among alternative lines of action directed at affecting community-wide institutions. We shall outline and evaluate the major approaches to empirical research on this topic and present a few hypotheses concerning how such decisions are made.

COMMUNITY DECISIONS: DEFINITION AND LOCATION OF A PROBLEM

First we must make clear what is to be meant in this paper by "community decisions." A community decision is a choice among several modes of action which is made by an authoritative person or group within the community institutions and of which the goals are the

* Reprinted with permission from *Administrative Science Quarterly*, March 1957. Footnotes omitted.

change or maintenance of community-wide institutions or facilities.

We shall not be concerned whether the motives of the actors involved are personal profit, power, or the general welfare of the community. If a decision undertaken by an authoritative group or person involves actions directed toward change or nonchange within the community as such, this is a community decision.

Note that this definition contains two specifications. To qualify as a community decision, a choice must be made by an authoritative person or group, that is, one which either by law or by custom has the legitimate and recognized right to make the decision in question. The second specification indicates that the decision must involve community-wide institutions such as local government, locally oriented private associations, and so on.

What sorts of decisions does this concept exclude? It excludes, first, the myriad decisions whose goals are not community oriented, for example, the market decisions of business organizations, migration decisions of individuals, and so on. Second, decisions made by "outside" agencies or persons, for example, the state and national governments, are not covered. Finally, it excludes decisions made by persons who are not in authoritative positions.

The range of decisions included is considerable. On the broadest level, the citizen casting his vote in a local election is an authoritative decision maker in his role as voter. A mayor acting in the capacity of his office makes community decisions of a wide variety. So do the members of the board of directors of community organizations such as the community chest.

Implicit in our concept of community decisions is the idea of "community issues," which may be defined as choices as to policy open to the authoritative decision makers. Thus the issue before the voters in a local election are choices among slates of candidates, approval or disapproval of referenda, and so forth.

The issues before a city council may involve decisions within each of a wide variety of sets of alternatives, ranging from budget allocation for the whole municipality to the repair of a sidewalk in front of a particular citizen's house. Note that the issue defines the relevant decision maker according to the rules laid down by law and customs.

Issues, of course, involve more persons and groups than just the decision makers to which they are ultimately referred. Other members and groups within the community express preferences to each other and to the decision makers, attempt to persuade or even coerce decision makers, and so on. Each issue thus has its partisans, a category which may include—depending on the issue involved—almost the entire community or just one or two individuals. A *partisan* is some one person or group who is concerned to see that one or another alternative is chosen by a decision maker.

The definitions offered are not as precise as might be desired. It is not always easy to locate the decision maker for a given issue, although this may be less of a problem *post factum*. Nor is it always clear whether an issue involves the community and its status or noncommunity matters. Our definitions are designed to make rough distinctions, and their utility can be judged in the discussion which follows.

Our objective is to review and evaluate research on community decisions. How are such decisions made? How are issues settled? What factors have been found to be crucial in affecting the outcomes of issues? What general statements may be made about the decision-making process? What are the research designs employed and the problems which they seem best suited to study?

There are, of course, approaches to decision making which we shall not consider here, either because they are not empirically oriented or because they are not concerned with decision making on the community level. For example, we shall not touch upon the attempts to construct mathematical models for rational decision making. Nor shall we consider in detail most studies of the decision processes conducted in psychological laboratories. We shall confine the dicussion to attempts to describe and generalize about the decision-making processes within local communities.

THREE APPROACHES TO THE STUDY OF COMMUNITY DECISIONS

The small number of empirical researches on community decisions displays a variety of approaches and research methods. Without doing too much violence to the significant differences among such studies, however, we can classify most empirical work on this topic according to the employment of one of three basic research designs. In some studies, several approaches have been employed, although for our present purposes we will treat each approach separately.

One basic approach to the study of decision making has been concerned with the characteristics of *decision makers,* attempting to relate the social and personal differences among decision makers to the kinds of decisions made. The research techniques employed have ranged from the analysis of detailed quasi-clinical case histories through the statistical analysis of official biographical notes.

A second approach has given central attention to the *partisans* of issues, seeking to find in their actions vis-a-vis the decision makers the "ultimate" determinants of the outcome of decisions. Studies which focus on "pressure groups," or propaganda, or which search for the "power structure" belong to this class of research designs.

A third approach employs *decisions* as its reference point, seeking to understand the choices of decision makers as the outcome of relatively complex proc-

esses. Studies of decision making in contrived groups within laboratory settings fall into this category as well as analyses of retrospective accounts of the decision-making process obtained from interviews with the decision makers.

The remainder of this section will be devoted to taking up each approach in turn, presenting a few examples of each, abstracting the major substantive findings, and evaluating each approach.

THE DECISION-MAKER APPROACH

In outline form, the typical design of research in this category is constructed along the following lines. Decision makers, usually of a particular type, for example, precinct captains, school board members, voters, and so on, are located, and certain of their characteristics are noted and compared with some sort of reference population. The technique furnishing the essential characteristics of the decision makers may range from extensive life histories, as in the case of John T. Salter's study of Philadelphia "bosses," to published official biographical notes, as in the case of Donald R. Matthews' study of national and state legislators. The characteristics studied may range from the relatively simple ones of age, occupation, and education to the more complex attitudinal data such as are supplied in detailed interviews.

From a consideration of the ways in which the decision makers differ from the general population or from some other norm, inferences are made concerning the types of decisions which they are thereby disposed to make. Thus from the finding that the age of city councilmen is higher than that of the voters, the conclusion might be drawn that city councils tend to be conservative and resistant to change. Several brief examples follow:

An early study by George S. Counts showed that school-board members throughout the nation are primarily recruited from among the business and professional occupations. Hence the essentially conservative and business-oriented character of the public schools.

As a part of a study of adolescent behavior in a small midwest community, August B. Hollingshead made a detailed study of the social-class membership of the community's school board and top school officials. Finding that school-board members and school officials were recruited entirely from among the upper strata of the community, he concluded that the character of the school system stemmed at least in part from this pattern of recruitment.

W. Lloyd Warner's now-classic study of "Yankee City" contains data showing that the higher the office held in the local government, the higher the social class of the officeholder. The "class character" of the local political system is inferred from this pattern of officeholding.

In a very recent study of attitudes toward political nonconformists, Samuel A. Stouffer found that "community leaders" (mayors, heads of library boards, an so on) were more tolerant toward nonconformists than the general population of their communities. He suggests that those responsible for important decisions concerning civil liberties on the local level are more tolerant in their actions than would be the average citizen.

Oliver Garceau's study of the compositions of library boards in a sample of American communities indicated that there was little relationship to be discerned between the composition of these boards and the excellence of the library's services. The members of library boards tended to be concentrated in the higher social and economic strata of their communities.

Practically every modern study of voting behavior has relied heavily on the analysis of the way in which classes and regional groups display different electoral choices. See Seymour Lipset et al. for a résumé of these studies.

The most strongly established finding of these studies of decision makers concerns their differential recruitment. Whether we are concerned with the electorate or with elected or appointed officials, as a group decision makers tend to be drawn disproportionately from the higher age categories, classes, and ethnic groups of higher status. Furthermore, the higher the authority level of the decision maker, the more marked are the differences between decision makers and ordinary citizens. In other words, the upper, as compared with the lower, status groups are somewhat more likely to hold public or semipublic offices.

Most of the studies cited above go beyond the fact of differential recruitment, however, to make inferences concerning how decision making is affected by this pattern. This approach has been most successful when applied to mass voting behavior as a decision-making process, where, for most national and local elections, clear divisions may be discerned in the electorate along class, ethnic, and regional lines.

When applied to decision makers on higher levels, the inferences drawn from the differential recruitment pattern are somewhat shaky. For example, to demonstrate that a school board composed of business and professional men is bound to show a "class bias," it is necessary first to demonstrate that the classes in the community hold different opinions on the issues confronting a school board. Is there, for example, a class position on education policy? Or on the alternative solutions to a community's traffic problems?

In other words, it is open to question whether for many issues there are clear and consistent differences among class groups, ethnic groups, age levels, and so on, which could manifest themselves in different decisions dependent on what kind of decision maker holds office. The substitution of sets of decision makers of radically different background need not necessarily result in groups holding radically different positions on many issues.

Secondly, there is an assumption of a close association between an individual's background and personal characteristics and the behavior which he will manifest in office. While it is true that *in the general population* class position correlates with opinion on a variety of issues (see Richard Centers and Bendix and Lipset), these correlations are low enough to ensure a rather large number of deviants from the majority opinion on every class level. *It is precisely to these deviants on the upper occupational levels that the popular support of the lower strata of the community may be attracted.* Among elected decision makers, at least, social background may be a very poor predictor of decisions made, particularly on class-related issues. In other, nonelected positions, for example, membership on library boards, the community chest, and so on, some decision makers may owe their appointments to the fact that they represent deviant views among the upper strata.

Thirdly, to look to social background and personal characteristics as the major explanation of a man's behavior in a decision-maker role is to deny that a given individual may act differently when placed in different roles. It is noteworthy that this approach has been most successful when applied to the decision-making role of voter, which is the least demanding of all such roles under discussion. The higher-level decision-maker roles with which we are mainly concerned here are ordinarily rather well defined in both law and custom, by virtue of the concern with which the community has regarded them. Each role involves its incumbents in a set of structured relationships to other roles and is accompanied by for-

mally and informally defined criteria for its proper performance. Thus a local bank executive on a local school board is pressured to come to grips with the organizational problems of his school system in a way that he would never do as just a private citizen. His actions on the school board are at least in part determined by the demands of his role as school-board member. Especially when the role is professionalized—as in the case of school officials, public health officials, social workers, and so forth—and incumbents are specially trained to fill their positions, role expectations will probably be particularly important determinants of decisions. A school superintendent trained in a teachers' college will have been exposed to a very self-conscious view of educational policy and of the way a superintendent should behave in his role.

Finally, the decision maker does not operate entirely within a social vacuum. On many issues, particularly those which intimately affect the interests of significant persons or groups, he is bombarded with communications from partisans of one or another policy alternative. Attempts are made to persuade, influence, or coerce him to support particular policies. He is supplied with information, presented with arguments, offered rewards extending from the intangibles of social acceptance to the hard reality of money, and threatened with reprisals either to himself or to his organization. Undoubtedly the actions of partisans play some part, over and above predisposition and role, in the outcome of many issues.

The evaluation given above of the decision-maker approach should not be taken as a denial that an individual's social and personal characteristics have an effect on the performance of a decision-maker role. Our criticisms are offered as a warning that, beyond the voter level, such characteristics will not be related to decision making in a simple and direct fashion and that the assumption of differences among decision makers corresponding to their social backgrounds must be tested empirically rather than asserted as fiat.

So dramatic have been the documented instances in which partisans have managed to affect the outcome of issues that we can hardly overlook their actions as an important set of determinants of community decisions. The dramatic quality of these incidents stems in large part from their semilegitimate status in the light of our democratic values. On the one hand, we recognize the right of citizens to advocate and defend their individual interests as against the individual interests of others. On the other hand, we demand that the decision maker should be above partisan views and should act in line with the interests of the community, without, however, specifying how one might identify in any particular issue what they may be. *Hence when we examine the outcome of an issue, it is easier to see which individual interests have been served than to judge whether the community interests as such have been upheld.*

The effects of partisan activity have been studied on many levels of decision making. Recent research on voting has documented the existence of informal opinion leaders, persons of more than ordinary concern with politics, who affect the behavior of those voters with whom they may be in personal contact. On higher levels of decision making, the concept of power has been used to describe how persons and organizations controlling significant amounts of wealth or solidarity employ their resources to affect the outcome of issues. Power and influence are both relational terms, concepts employed to describe relationships between persons and/or groups. When we say that a man is influential or powerful, we mean that his behavior has significance for some other persons. In the case of power, we

imply a relationship in which individual A affects the behavior of individual B because B wishes to avoid the sanctions which A would employ if B did not comply with his wishes. In the case of influence, B's behavior is affected in the absence of sanctions. Thus although the process in each case by which A affects B is different, the general form of the relationship is the same, and hence researches on power and influence tend to follow the same basic designs. Indeed, so close is the relationship between power and influence that it is difficult empirically to distinguish between the two.

Roughly, there are three basic research designs which have been employed in the study of power and influence. First, we have studies of the potentials for power and influence, inventories of persons and organizations in a community who are in positions to influence or apply power to decision makers. Second, we have studies of power or influence reputations, researches on what community members consider the influence or power structures to be. Finally, there are researches on actual influence or power, studies of particular issues in which influence or power have played a part in the determination of the outcome.

Power and influence as potential. Since social relationships are notoriously difficult to study directly, some researchers have centered their attention on producing inventories of those positions in the community which have the necessary attributes for the wielding of influence or power. In the case of power, these studies document who within a community controls significant amounts of economic resources. By virtue of their control over economic organizations—banks, industrial and commercial enterprises, public utilities, and so forth—such persons are in a position to wield sanctions of an economic sort over decision makers. In the case of influence studies, inventories are obtained of "leaders," persons at the heads of various private associations or occupying important public offices. By virtue of their position, leaders can influence the opinions of their followers on a variety of issues. A few examples of these researches follow:

In his study of Middletown, Robert Lynd devotes a chapter to the X family showing how this family group either owns or controls a large number of enterprises and has representation in most of the other significant enterprises in the community.

Advising students how they may undertake surveys of communities, Robert K. Lamb stresses the procedure of obtaining a list of the banking and industrial officials, newspaper editors, owners of large blocks of real estate, and so forth. Such lists may be used to outline the power structure of the community.

The community leaders studied by Samuel A. Stouffer in his research on attitudes toward political nonconformity were chosen in part because their positions made them the likely leaders of public opinion in their communities.

C. Wright Mills and Melville Ullmer, in a study of single- and diversified-industry cities, identify the real leaders of their communities as the industrial and mercantile elite within each community. See also Mills's latest work, *The Power Elite*, where he describes the power structure of the United States.

Implicit in this approach is the assumption that the potential for power or influence undoubtedly will be employed. Business leaders, in fact, exercise their power to affect the decisions made by formal authorities. Furthermore, the potential for power is often regarded as equally effective regardless of the point at which it is applied— whether within the community chest or within the city council—and results in decisions which are different from those which would occur in the absence of such power. Similarly, the potential for influence is often regarded as equally effective regardless of the topic involved —whether political opinions, attitudes toward mental disease, and so forth— and when employed, it results in a different distribution of opinion among the public than would have occurred in its absence.

The studies of power cited above also contain anecdotal examples of the exercise of power in specific situations. Mills and Ullmer quote from an interview with a former mayor who stated that he had to "clear" even such matters as sidewalk repairs with the head of the largest industrial plant in his community. Examples cited are generally ones in which economic powers have blocked or vetoed proposed changes in the community, for example, new legislation, public improvements, the entry of new industry, and so on.

Studies of power or influence reputation: The perceived power or influence structure. With the development of sociometric techniques, it was almost inevitable that these devices be applied to the study of both power and influence in the local community. These techniques allow the researcher literally to chart the interrelationships within a group of people. Obviously, except for communities of very small size, some modification of sociometry was necessary before this technique could be used in the study either of power or of influence. In the case of power-reputation studies, informants are asked whom they perceive to be powerful within the community. Persons receiving a large number of "votes" from informants are identified as constituting the power structure. Similarly, in the case of "influence-reputation" studies, informants are asked to designate whose opinion would influence them on a variety of topics. Several examples of research along these lines follow:

Floyd Hunter, in his study of the power structure of "Regional City," asked a sample of community-organization leaders to designate who were the "top" as "civic, governmental, business and status" leaders in the community. The persons receiving the highest number of "votes" were designated as comprising the power structure of the community.

Robert K. Merton asked a sample of "Rovere" citizens to designate to whom they would look for advice on a variety of topics, e.g., on educational problems, political matters, health problems, and so forth. Persons receiving more than a minimum number of designations were termed influentials. Their characteristics were studied in direct interviews.

My associates and I, in a study of "Bay City," a small Massachusetts industrial city, asked members of the community's elite to choose the most important persons on a prepared list of some twenty-five names culled from among industrial, political, religious, and civic leaders. Interviews were obtained from members of this group, and an analysis was made of the factors which led them to be highly chosen by their fellows.

Elihu Katz and Paul F. Lazarsfeld report on a study of women who were asked to designate persons whom they "could trust to let them know what was really going on." Designated persons were then interviewed in order to identify their characteristics as compared with the persons who designated them.

In a study of the public administrators in "Bay City," J. Leiper Freeman obtained ratings from each public official of the importance for their operations of other officials and various groups in the city, e.g., the city council, mayor, chamber of commerce, and so forth. Persons designated as important for an official were considered potential sources of influence upon him.

Note that the power or influence structure is defined in terms of the "reputations" accorded to individuals by a set of judges. While the "reputations" involved are probably deserved in the sense that these are persons who are likely to exercise power or influence, it is still open to question whether, on a variety, let alone a majority, of issues outcomes of issues are heavily affected by their actions.

For example, in the case of Hunter's study, the range of issues with which the power structure concerns itself is delimited by example. The instances cited in which members of the power "structure" undertook to provide the leadership for community projects covered considerable ground. The implication is left that there are few areas of community life in which the power structure does not take a hand. Yet the total set of issues is unspecified, and hence the impact of the power structure on the life of the community is hard to assess.

Similarly, Merton's study of influentials is also on a general plane. Influentials are persons who are regarded as potential sources of trusted advice by members of the community; we do not know how frequently, in fact, they are employed as sources. That this is a relevant issue to raise is demonstrated in Katz and Lazarsfeld, where it is shown that *the persons who actually influenced specific opinion changes are likely to be very different from persons designated as potential sources of influence.*

The same question may be raised about the power reputation studies. It seems likely that they specify one of the important ways in which the outcomes of issues are settled, but we are not confident that this represents either the *typical* way for every decision or for every decision-maker role.

What have these studies established? First, it is clear that some individuals by virtue of their economic strength can and, on occasion, do exercise more than ordinary influence over decision makers. Secondly, this control is especially effective over some rather than other decision makers. Civic associations dependent on voluntary financial contributions seem particularly vulnerable. Thirdly, informal opinion leaders exist on all levels of the community and on occasion affect the opinions of the mass of citizens. It can be shown, furthermore, that these opinion leaders do not entirely overlap with the official public and organizational leaders of the community. (See especially Frank A. Stewart.)

Nevertheless, there remain to be answered a number of questions:

Granted that power is wielded and influence exists, as we must concede from the number of examples which these researches have collected, the question still remains as to the *proportion* of all decisions affected in this way. The method of collecting examples probably emphasizes the efficacy of the power or influence structure, as compared, for example, with some of the researches cited below which focus on decisions rather than partisans. It seems obvious, furthermore, that for any urban community of any size, the number of decision makers and the decisions made is so great that complete monitoring by the power structure is impossible, especially since the persons involved are usually engaged in other enterprises as well.

Secondly, assuming that some decisions are heavily affected by the power or influence structure of a community, it is relevant to ask what are the kinds of decisions involved. Lynd and Mills cite examples which suggest that the powers primarily attempt to exercise control over issues which directly affect their economic well-being and social status—public taxation, labor-union organization, social-club membership, and so forth. The power employed is primarily in the form of an attempted veto, used to block changes which might adversely affect the status and class position of those in power positions. In contrast, Hunter emphasizes innovation as the characteristic concern of the power structure in Regional City. His "powers" are leaders in getting new projects under way, for example, deciding on a new plan for the community, building a municipal auditorium, getting new industry into town, and so on. Furthermore, many of the projects apparently involve raising considerable sums of money through voluntary contributions, a large proportion to be supplied by the leaders themselves. Parenthetically, it may be noted that it is hardly surprising that these persons pay such careful attention to the working out of the details of such community projects, since it is their financial backing which pays for them.

In this connection, we may raise the question of whether all decision makers are equally vulnerable to the actions of a power "structure." Our own research in Massachusetts indicates that the decision makers in the voluntary civic associations are particularly vulnerable to the power wielded by heavy contributors, but that the decision makers within the local government are more sensitive to sanctions wielded by the leaders of solidary groups. This last point further suggests that control over economic and financial resources does not exhaust bases for power. Leaders of solidary organizations—labor unions, business and professional associations, churches, and so forth—also derive some degree of strength from their positions as organizational leaders, presumably based on their reputed ability to affect the opinions and behavior of their memberships.

Finally, we may raise questions concerning what forms the exercise of power takes. We conceive of power as the wielding of sanctions over decision makers. How are sanctions wielded? The powerful individuals in Regional City, for example, are primarily men of wealth in control of large industrial or financial enterprises. How do they use their positions? Is wealth used directly or converted into other sanctions, perhaps centering around status? More generally, what are the sanctions employed, and what sanctions are effective for which decision makers?

STUDIES OF DECISIONS:
THE PROCESS APPROACH

Up to this point, none of the researches discussed have paid central attention to decisions as such except to illustrate the operations of power, influence, or the background characteristics of decision makers. Even the concept of decision itself has been used rather ambiguously in our treatment, copying in large part the use of the authors whose work we have reviewed.

The blame for the neglect of decisions as a major research focus must be placed to a large degree on the nature of the phenomenon itself. Most of the issues in which we are most interested ordinarily entail a settlement process in which complicated chains of choices are made by a large number of decision makers. A description of the events involved, for example, in the approval of a municipal budget by a city council would result in a large document, while more complicated issues would demand even more complicated descriptions.

Nor would our task be more manageable if we concentrated on the choices made by a decision maker rather than on issues. The work of a mayor or city councilman involves a large number of choices of a great variety. Few of the decisions would be comparable in content, and those which were would be likely to be relatively trivial, e.g., a councilman's votes on public-works maintenance orders.

For these reasons the study of decisions has ordinarily been carried out either within the controlled environment of the laboratory or, in the field, on decisions which are relatively simple and hence comparable. Only a few studies have attempted to follow a particular issue from start to settlement.

The controlled observation approach. Laboratory studies of decision making have been at the heart of researches in general psychology. Most of the work done in learning, perceptual discrimination, and so forth, might be viewed as studies of decision-making processes of a very elementary kind. Although basic to an eventual definitive theory of decision making, the contributions of the general psychologist have not been immediately useful.

More relevant has been the laboratory study of small groups at work in the cooperative solution of experimental tasks. Since much of the decision making on the community level takes place within a group context, small legislative or semilegislative bodies—as, for example, city councils, library boards, community chest boards, and so on—a study of the interaction processes which occur as people are brought together to solve given problems must to some extent illumine our understanding of the decision-making process in the natural setting.

The typical research design involves bringing together a small number of individuals, setting before them some simple task, and observing the interaction occurring between members of the group. The interaction ordinarily is classified according to some scheme of categories and analyzed quantitatively. In the large number of experiments which have been conducted in the last few years, tasks have been varied; the effects of group size have been systematically probed; and the structure of the group has been manipulated through the use of role players and fixed communications patterns. Examples of the more relevant researches follow:

Fred L. Strodtbeck is currently studying the decision-making processes of juries. Jurors are selected from official panels and are brought to a jury room to listen to recorded cases. The interaction among jurors is analyzed to provide data on how different elements of cases affect verdicts; on how the jurors affect each other; and on how the verdict is affected by the kinds of jurors involved. Note how in this research design the concerns of the previously discussed researches might be met: Strodtbeck is studying how kinds of *jurors,* acting in different interpersonal environments, come to decisions on different *issues* (cases).

The long series of studies conducted by Robert F. Bales has shown that groups engaged in the solution of simple tasks go through typical phases of activity, alternating attacks on the task with behavior designed to weld the group together into a solidary unit. He finds that often two types of leaders emerge: an "instrumental leader," who contributes much to the solution of the task, and an "integrative leader," who helps keep the group interpersonal tension level down.

The issue career approach. Outside of the laboratory the study of decisions has been most successful when confined to mass observations of simple issues, as in mass voting behavior. Observations are made of large numbers of decision makers, each of whom has to make much the same choice among a small number of alternatives. A small group of researchers have attempted to follow the career of more complicated issues, observing the decisions made with respect to them by a large number of decision makers acting in different capacities.

Typically, the researcher isolates a population which has either made a decision of a particular kind or will shortly be faced with the necessity for doing so. The decision makers are interviewed concerning their past decisions or they are questioned periodically as they come to a choice on an issue which faces them.

Vote decisions are particularly suited to this approach. The issues before each voter and the form of the decision are identical. Two of the most valuable accounts of vote behavior (Paul Lazarsfeld, Bernard Berelson, and Helen Gaudet and Berelson, Lazarsfeld, and William N. McPhee) studied the decisions made by samples of voters interviewed repeatedly during the presidential campaigns of 1940 and 1948. Voters who came to their choices or shifted their preferences during the period of the interviewing were asked to tell how they came to their decisions. Using the same research design, my associates and I have studied vote decisions in two local elections, finding much the same patterns.

Katz and Lazarsfeld report a study of changes in marketing habits, fashions, and political opinions. A sample of women were interviewed concerning the reasons for their shifts of preference and opinion, with particular emphasis on the roles of the mass media and interpersonal contacts.

Studies of more complicated issues have been relatively rare:

Perhaps the most elaborate study of the career of an issue is the description of how sites were selected in Chicago during 1949 and 1950 for new public housing. Martin Meyerson and Edward C. Banfield (the former Planning Director of the Chicago Housing Authority during the period under study) have provided a fascinating account of the way in which sites were finally selected after much pulling and hauling among the housing authority, the city council, the mayor, local neighborhood groups, and so on. Basic data for the study came from documents of the various groups involved and interviews with participants.

A number of the cases collected by the Inter-University Case Program bear on community decisions. Presented as descriptive accounts, the cases follow through controversies from their beginnings to their final settlements.

In our own study an attempt was made to account for the outcome of two local issues: the selection of a superintendent of schools by a local school board and the approval of a municipal budget by a city council. School-board members and councilmen were intensively interviewed concerning their relationships to each other, their contacts with persons outside the decision-making groups, and their reasons for their particular positions on the issues.

What of a general nature can be learned from these studies of the decision-making process? Concerning the findings of controlled observation studies, it is difficult to transfer easily their findings to the natural group situation. Yet several major conclusions do emerge. First of all, these studies highlight the effects of the internal organization on decision-making groups. In the course of pursuing a task, groups of individuals who had hitherto no enduring relationship to each other rapidly develop a social organization the nature of which affects the way in which they come to decisions and the sort of decisions they make. Out of the necessity for cooperation needs develop, the satisfaction of which becomes a pressing matter. Since in the natural world the decision maker is always found embedded in an organizational context and under some necessity of working out mutually satisfactory relationships with the persons within that context, these studies highlight the importance of this set of factors. For example, a legislative body like a city council or a school board or a housing authority develops its own social organization, with codes of behavior, sets of mutual obligations, and so forth. How this organization affects the outcome of decisions is documented heavily in Meyerson and Banfield.

Secondly, there are many natural situations confronted by decision makers which bear more than a superficial resemblance to the artificial situations studied in the laboratory. To the extent that we find such correspondences, generalizations may be more easily transferred from the one to the other context. For example, many experiments (see especially Solomon E. Asch) concern the effects of group contexts on the interpretation of ambiguous stimuli. Many of the issues faced by a decision maker lack clarity and definition, for example, the problem of the voter presented with a list of unknown candidates for equally unknown public offices. In the laboratory the subject accepts cues for interpretation offered by the group about him. In real life the voter is influenced heavily by his family, friends, coworkers, a precinct captain, and so on.

Of course students of decision making need not wait for the small-groups field to produce spontaneously the relevant researches. It seems profitable to expend ingenuity on contriving experimental work which can be directly transferred to our major problems. For example, it is conceivable that experimental city councils may be devised and studied.

At first glance it would appear that field studies of decisions would yield the most valuable information concerning decision making. And this is the case for studies of voting. The pioneer work done by Lazarsfeld and his associates has increased enormously our understanding of vote behavior. These studies have documented the group basis of voting, contributed the notion of opinion leadership, and shown how the mass media's effects are channeled through opinion leaders to the persons whom they influence.

The field studies of more complicated decisions, however, have not been very valuable. The very complexity and apparent uniqueness of the processes they have unveiled makes generalization going beyond the specific issues studied very hazardous. These studies provide fascinating reading (especially Meyerson and Banfield), but because they are primarily single cases, it is hard to draw upon them for general knowledge. Only through a comparative approach, studies of large numbers of decisions on comparable issues, will it be possible to go beyond the particular. It is to be hoped that the Inter-University Case Program may eventually provide the comparative materials that are called for.

Surprisingly, little attention has been paid to the intrinsic features of the issues involved in the decisions studied. Laboratory studies of decision making, of course, have been concerned about how the characteristics of the task set before the experimental animal affect the choices he may make. The decision-making models constructed by the mathematical economists also have been concerned with choices made among alternatives, each of which is considered in terms of its probable outcome. But the consideration of how an issue, or even issues, is viewed by decision makers has not been given much attention in the studies of the decision-making process within the community context. The decision maker is almost regarded as having no internal dynamics of his own but as ruled by his group affiliations and interaction patterns.

SOME CONCLUSIONS AND QUESTIONS FOR FURTHER RESEARCH

Each of the approaches outlined in the previous section has contributed important substantive knowledge to our understanding of how community decisions are made. Yet it cannot be said that the definitive account of the decision-making process can be constructed now through the results of any one study or a simple combination of studies.

The *studies of decision makers* have contributed an emphasis on what the decision maker brings to his role in the way of general social background, attitudes, and values. A person occupying an office retains the personality and attitudinal sets acquired during his life's experiences. Under some conditions these factors affect the choices he makes.

Studies of the decision process emphasize that the decision maker is embedded in a web of social relationships. The voter acts not as an individual so much as the resultant of his group memberships. The higher-level decision maker's role is embedded in an organization which has needs and demands of its own.

Again, *the study of partisans* and their actions highlight the effects of persons standing outside the organizational context of the decision maker. Under some conditions partisans are able to affect the outcome of issues. Furthermore, we know that this ability accrues heavily to the upper strata of our communities.

There is a sense, however, in which these studies tend to contradict each other. For any particular decision, it cannot be equally true that the decision was determined by the decision maker's background, the pressure put on him by the wealthier elements in his community, and the loyalties he might feel to his staff or coequals. Since each approach has been able to present convincing evidence of the importance of its findings for some decisions and for some decision makers, the important question appears to be not, for example, whether there is a structure of power or whether the social background of a decision affects the decision maker's choices, but *under what conditions does each type of explanation best fit the case?*

The three types of determinants (decision-maker qualities, partisan activities, and organizational contexts) are best thought of as latent possibilities inherent in any issue. Latency implies only some probability of a determinant manifesting itself in any particular situation. Thus not all issues engage the attention of the power "structure"; nor does the decision maker's organization care about all his decisions, and so on. Hence it seems reasonable that the search for the understanding of any particular decision is not likely to be as fruitful as looking for tendencies within classes of decisions and types of decision makers. It is only when we examine and compare a number of decisions that the tendencies character-izing different issues and decision mak-ers can be discerned.

In other words, *research on decision making should be extensive rather than intensive and comparative rather than the case-study technique.* Three levels of comparisons should be made: deci-sion makers of *different types,* operat-ing within *different community and institutional settings* should be com-pared as they come to the settlement of a *range of issues.* This approach im-plies a sampling of decision makers, of issues, and of communities.

Our identification of these dimen-sions as the major points of comparison to be made stems for the most part from the findings of the researches we have reviewed in this paper. Each has contributed knowledge about variations which should be taken into account in designing research. As a summary state-ment, these major findings and some of the questions they raise are recapit-ulated below.

CONCERNING DECISION MAKERS

It seems likely that the most impor-tant source of variation among decision makers lies in their roles rather than in the personal qualities which they bring to their offices. The more of the decision maker's total interests and ac-tivities are invested in the role itself, the more likely are role expectations to determine his decision-making behav-ior. Thus, at the one extreme, we would expect that the role of voter, being poorly defined and undemanding, would have little effect on the voter's choices; while at the other extreme, the professional social worker in charge of a community organization would be acting according to a well-defined con-ception of the best way he might fill the demands of his office.

At the higher level of decision mak-ing, roles vary widely in three respects, each of which seems likely to affect the vulnerability of the decision maker's role both to the demands of the would-be power wielder and to those of his organization. First, the higher the pres-tige of the office, the more the decision maker will be able to act independently. In this connection, we may note that Supreme Court Justice achieved the highest prestige rating of all the occu-pations studied by the National Opin-ion Research Center. Secondly, deci-sion-maker roles in organizations which have an independent financial base are less vulnerable than those in organiza-tions dependent on support controlled by other persons or organizations, thus the vulnerability of the civic associa-tions dependent on voluntary contribu-tions and the relatively greater inde-pendence of public officials whose or-ganizations are supported by taxing powers. Finally, decision makers may derive independence from their basis of tenure: tenured officials might be ex-pected to be more independent than elected officials, who in turn may be more independent than those who are removable at will.

CONCERNING VARIATIONS IN COMMUNITIES

Unfortunately, it is not possible to make clear statements about the varia-tions in decision-making processes which we might expect in diverse types of communities. The number of com-munities which have been studied is relatively small, and their points of difference and comparability are not clearly discernible. Yet several differ-ences seem pertinent.

At one extreme we have one-industry towns and at the other, the economi-cally diversified metropolis. It appears likely, as is suggested by Mills and Ull-mer, that the less diversified the eco-nomic base of the community, the more clustered is the potential for power. The political homogeneity of a com-munity also seems to be a contributing factor. In one-party Regional City, the power structure seems much more or-ganized than in two-party Bay City, where the political strength of the industrial workers acts as a check on the free exercise of power by the industrialists.

Other differences between communities suggest themselves. The cities studied have all been relatively self-contained. What would the decision-making process look like in the satellite suburb? What kind of power structure would arise in a community with no independent economic base and with a relatively homogeneous population?

Communities also vary in the extent to which their dynamics of growth and change raise issues which demand solution. A growing community faces a number of problems which the matured town has faced and solved to some extent in the past. At least part of the differences between Bay City, a stationary community, and Regional City, still in its stage of great growth, must be allocated to this factor. The issues in Bay City may be more trivial than those in Regional City, engaging the attention of but a few partisans.

CONCERNING ISSUES

None of the studies reviewed here have considered the full range of issues which come before a particular decision maker. The closest to such consideration is in the studies of voting, but there are few studies of electoral behavior in local elections, primaries, and so forth. The issues which have been subjected to study have been on the more dramatic side perhaps more properly labeled "controversies."

By and large, we can expect that most issues up for decision are settled without becoming controversies. The routine business of any office or legislative body consists mainly of noncontroversial issues. How are these settled? Is this the point at which we should look for the effects of the personal characteristics of the decision maker?

What makes an issue into a controversy? Of course, the content of an issue makes a major contribution here; for example, few controversies will arise in a school board over appointments to the lowest levels of the teaching staff, but appointments on the administrative level are more likely to engage the attention of board members and partisans. In addition, some issues are made into controversies, often as channels for the expression of cleavages which cannot be expressed more directly. The recent controversies over fluoridation, for example, are most profitably viewed not as content controversies but as issues expressing the malaise of the older residents in communities experiencing rapid growth. Parenthetically, we may note that the ability to raise issues into controversies is an important source of power.

64. Public Attitudes and Metropolitan Decision Making*

CHARLES R. ADRIAN

THE study of individual metropolitan areas in the United States has become a ritualistic activity to be repeated every few years. The folk rite is engaged in with deadly seriousness by a handful of persons who are told by the local newspaper that they are "civic leaders."

* Eighth Annual Wherrett Lecture on Local Government, copyright 1962 by the Institute of Local Government, University of Pittsburgh. Reprinted with permission. Footnotes omitted.

With but a few exceptions, most of them very recent, the studies that have resulted have been highly predictable as to the way in which the operation is structured, the method of study used, the kinds of people who participate, the findings that are made, the recommendations that follow upon them—and the fate of the action proposals. The fate they suffer is, of course, nearly always to be greeted by an enormous citizen yawn, followed by rejection of any proposal which dares to present itself at the polling booth. Without attempting to decide whether or not these proposals are deserving of acceptance, or even of serious consideration, we can wonder at the almost unbelievably low batting average of the players. If the civic leaders were major league ballplayers, they would quickly be sent down to the minors for so inept a series of performances. There is little reason to believe that they will suffer an equivalent fate, however, or that they are considering a change in their batting styles. Although there was a successful metro reform during the present year—in Nashville—this points to no trend. The usual pattern is for metro proposals to be defeated almost before the game begins. One wonders why the effort is even made. In 1962, the people of St. Louis and St. Louis County voted on a so-called "borough" plan. It got a majority of the votes in only four city wards and failed to carry in a single township. This year, too, in Memphis, a county charter plan was rejected in a majority of precincts in both the city and the county. Many other cases of rejection by the voters, sometimes even by those of the core city, have been reported by the staff of the Commission on Intergovernmental Relations.

Clearly, proposed structural changes in metropolitan areas are unpopular with rank-and-file voters. But why are they unpopular? The usual lame excuse that the plan was opposed by "selfish" interests explains little, if anything. The world is made up of selfish people —selfish, if their interests are viewed from the perspectives of others. The fact is that although most metropolitan-area studies and resulting action programs have been carried on in the Age of the Opinion Poll, when techniques have existed for determining the limits of tolerance within which people will accept proposals and for determining what people consider to be their problems, almost no use has been made of these tools in the development of substantive plans and the strategies to be used in putting them into effect.

ANTI-POLITICS AND METROPOLITICS

We might first look at the question of why leaders of metropolitan government reform have paid so little attention to citizen attitudes and the political environment within which metro leaders must do their politicking. The subject, like almost any subject, has not been completely ignored in the past, of course. Among others who have been concerned with it, Luther Gulick has long had an interest in fundamental American values and their relevance to metropolitan decision making. Victor Jones, the leading pioneer in seeking to relate the political environment to the metropolitan "problem," wrote an insightful article as long ago as 1940, an article that never received the attention it deserved. Robert Wood, in constructing a process model for suburban decision making, dealt extensively with attitudes. But each of these gentlemen found little empirical evidence upon which to write and their words have not had much impact upon the way metropolitan studies have been conducted. As a result, few of their prescriptive statements have been subjected to empirical test—at least that has been the picture until very recently. There is reason to believe that those who will study the metropolis in the future will approach the subject with more of the open mind of academic inquisitiveness than has been the case in the past.

Why have citizen attitudes received so little attention and why has so little been done to integrate them into a theory of decision making in the metropolitan area? Probably because of the attitudes and values of the upper-middle-class citizens who have been the prime movers and financers of metropolitan-area studies—for most of them, I hesitate to use the word "research," for the frame of reference within which the researchers have had to operate for the most part has been such that research within the social scientific meaning has been discouraged. Often, the researcher is expected only to lend his good name and status to conclusions that the civic leader regards as "self-evident," and therefore beyond question. With most areas of inquiry foreclosed, there has been no reason to look at attitudes.

What have been the principal values and attitudes of the civic leader-reformer? They have been those of the efficiency and economy movement, in which he was also in the van, and through which he brought about many changes in municipal government. The typical reformer has brought to the metropolitan problem a strong middle-class bias: he has favored honesty over expediency, efficiency over representativeness, order over convenience. Most importantly, he subscribed to two major fallacies which stem from his beliefs: the Efficiency and Economy Fallacy, and the Rational Man Fallacy. The former, I have already discussed elsewhere. In brief, it is the view that the typical citizen shares with the upper-middle-class community leader a concern for efficiency and economy, however defined, and that these twin objectives are highly valued by the *hoi polloi*. I think there is ample, if unsystematic, evidence to show that these are not goals for many citizens, indeed that the citizen is cynical about efficiency if it interests him at all, and that he therefore concentrates on what is, in any case, a higher order of values to him—access to decision makers, and a

sense of having councils and boards that are representative.

The Rational Man Fallacy, of course, has roots dating from the eighteenth century and before. The metro leader, probably in part by projecting his values upon the typical citizen when doing his planning, has seen metropolitan man much as John Locke saw the middle-class Englishman of his day. The voter is assumed to be a rational person who believes in his capacity to control his own destiny. The reformer has assumed that if you "give people the facts," they will act in favor of metropolitan-wide government and other objectives of the reformer. Of course, there is no reason why he should have ensnared himself with this delusion. The writings on the nature of the voter and how he makes up his mind have been outlined by a series of scholars, such as Paul Lazarsfeld and Angus Campbell, and they date from before World War II. Furthermore, the community leader, or his father, has spent many years fighting political machines and he well knows that the ordinary citizen, even after decades of universal public education, has a reaction to things political that is overwhelmingly visceral in character. Closely reasoned logic stemming from a normative or ideal model cannot compete, they should have known, with the symbols which trigger emotions when effectively used by the professional politicians who often oppose their action programs. Similarly, the assumption that the ordinary metropolitan man believes that he is the master of his fate has for many years been under suspicion, if it is not outrightly repudiated by psychological studies on alienation—on the widespread feeling among ordinary citizens that whatever they may do, they cannot much affect the forces that control government, especially large governments.

The metropolitan reform leader, then, has typically spent his years in constructing models which are unconcerned with belief systems other than his own, and he has built into his models assumptions about psychological motivation and rationality that are as unrealistic as were those of John Locke, Jean Jacques Rousseau, or Adam Smith. No wonder that he has so often gone around the day after an election muttering about "selfish, narrow-minded voters" and "self-seeking politicians."

THE INGREDIENTS OF A POLITICAL SYSTEM

The model builders might well have started with the work of a man who had considerable success at the craft: Aristotle. As interpreted by Norton Long, the Aristotelian mode would be to seek metropolitan government through finding "a potential metropolitan governing class, the institutions through which it can function and a set of ideal goals which it can embody and which will render its leadership legitimate in the eyes of the people." Here we see why it is that models to date have not provided the basis for a viable political system: The metropolitan area is a complex of persons pursuing a variety of economic and social goals. There is no image of the "good metropolitan life" outside of the writings of reformers and planners, none that stems from the grass roots, a latter-day Jacksonianism as a foundation upon which to build a political system. To the typical citizen, the metropolitan area is a place where his work is. It is not a community, but an aggregate of persons and places.

In addition to the absence of a metropolitan community with a collective set of goals, there is also no governing class which is viewed as the source of legitimate leadership, as is the case with the middle class of England. Furthermore, the metropolitan leaders are handicapped by the present patterns of business and industrial administration. The Mellons of Pittsburgh and the Upjohns of Kalamazoo are still on the scene, but in most communities, their

ilk has been replaced by the essentially rootless organization man who moves from job to job, but is generally viewed neither as the law-giver—a function that belongs to the mayor or manager—or the job-giver—a function that belongs to the Chamber of Commerce secretary and the state employment service or state industrial development department. Organization man leads, if he leads the community at all, because he chooses to do so, not because it is an obligation of his class. It need hardly be added that Aristotle's third requirement, the necessary institutions, do not exist.

In addition to being accorded legitimacy and a set of consensual goals, a political system must, if it is to be democratic, be one in which people feel secure in the possession of a psychological sense of having access to the decision makers and of having decision makres who are representative of their interests and protective of their preferred life styles. I emphasize that this is a psychological matter—the question of whether the person does have access and whether his interests are, in fact, protected is largely irrelevant. We need only recall the old-fashioned political machines in which the function of the block worker was, among other things, to shortstop citizen complaints before they got to city hall by promises that the matter "will be looked into." Similarly, the machine leaders sometimes took enormous advantage of the trust placed in them by the *hoi polloi* by stealing their money and selling out their interests in some agreement convenient to the boss. Many an indignant reformer could not understand that these *de facto* breaches of trust were often unimportant to the ordinary slum dweller if his confidence in this leadership class remained undimmed and his feeling of security was unchanged. The facts, in politics, are never as important in determining loyalty and legitimacy as is the perception of reality—the picture in men's minds that Walter Lippmann long ago talked about.

If we so clearly lack the ingredients of a political system which can serve as the principal decision-making arena for the metropolis, how do we manage to get along? Had we taken literally the somber warnings concerning the consequences of our alleged folly as they have appeared over several decades, we would long ago have created metropolitan governments, believing it a necessary step for survival. And if the warnings had been accurate, the nation's population centers would today be in shambles. But they have not done so. Despite our resistance to advance planning, to the rational use of land, to the assumption of responsibility for preserving water supplies and keeping them unpolluted, and to dozens of other matters that are important to professional administrators in many fields of activity, the metropolis does not quite collapse of its own weight, or choke in its traffic or its non-abated smoke, or poison itself with its own sewage. Why not?

The present system of Balkanization never ceases to amaze observers who believe that it ought not to work, but somehow seems to fit surprisingly well American values, life styles, and aesthetics. It does this because of elaborate procedures and rituals for consultation and negotiation. In fact, some of the more imaginative work in the conceptualization of metropolitan areas has been through the use of analogies with the biological concept of ecology, the international relations concepts involved in diplomatic negotiations, and the economic concept of the market. Just as independence-interdependence, confusion, and occasionally terror and violence are a part of a natural ecology, yet it is a system that "works," so the metropolitan area is not ideal, yet to a degree it "works." Diplomacy is not the most efficient decision-making process, but most of the time it makes possible compromise agreements upon critical issues. Some person's sense of equity will sometimes be violated, but seldom to the extent that he would prefer no negotiation to negotiation. The market place possesses a mechanism that is functional, though its results again strain the values of those who feel that its laws favor those who are already privileged.

In addition to negotiation, compromise, and exchange among the many units of the metropolis—the present system of muddling through—state governments are available as institutions for metropolitan government. Although state boundaries are arbitrarily drawn and sometimes divide in two a metropolitan area, state government is often a viable decision-making unit and is certainly more appropriate than are the strip cities and continuous urban areas extending for hundreds of miles that seem to be the metropolitan areas of the future.

CITIZEN ATTITUDES AND METROPOLITAN MODELS

Let us turn to the information we have concerning citizen attitudes and see how it fits or may be fitted into a model for metropolitan government. We shall see at once that many of the items in popular belief systems are not what those who have in the past assumed responsibility for model building want. Furthermore, in spite of their implicit assumption that goals are shared, we shall see that there is much conflict among the values relevant to the building of a metropolitan model.

Legitimacy: The Proper Function of Local Government. There is, first of all, no agreement among urban residents as to why local governments exist at all. Some want these governments to serve primarily in order to provide for life's amenities; others see them as something of an arm of the local Chamber of Commerce, with the task of doing what is necessary in order to attract more business and industry to the area; a third group wants to keep down the cost of government at all levels and wants local government to restrict its activities to that which has been traditionally regarded as necessary; a fourth group, often consisting of self-conscious minorities, sees local government as an arbiter among many forces and a device whereby each minority gets at least some slice of the pie. These four images of local government contain within themselves many conflicts. Even the concept of amenities varies by class: the notion is quite different in the mind's eye of the middle-class suburbanite and of the welfare-oriented marginal worker in the slum. Furthermore, there is a considerable difference between the parochial or localite views of most members of the working class and the area-wide or cosmopolite views of the upper-middle-class. The laborer, preoccupied with a chronically tight family budget and hopeful of accumulating a few "luxuries" during his years of gainful employment, has neither the inclination nor the indoctrination which would cause him to be concerned about boosterism, the city beautiful, or the future of Zilchville. He has, as it were, a culturally imposed trained incapacity to react to generalities or to considerations that are unrelated to pocketbook or stomach. Personally, I do not blame him or expect much else from him. But the model builders have expected much more from him, and they have expected it without asking the question: how can people be led to believe that there is a causal relationship between an integrated governmental structure and their *personal* hopes for the future?

Legitimacy: That Government that Governs Most Blandly Governs Best. Between the working man and his concerns with neighborhood and family and the upper-middle-class do-gooder lies the vast area of the more typical middle class—the white-collar organization man and conformist *par excellence*. To him, the model of the reformer is unacceptable because it seeks to engulf him in political conflict. The reformer, of course, has no such intent, but there is little doubt in the mind of the $10,000 a year junior executive what an integrated government will mean. Has not the core city government been conflict ridden for years? Would not such conflict be transferred to a metropolitan government? Did he not move to the suburbs to gain what Robert Wood has called "fraternity" and to escape the duties and battles imposed by democracy as a mediating force? He, in other words, rejects the idea of government as arbiter. Indeed, in his problem-filled life at the office and home, he has enough of conflict. His government in his suburb can give him some peace by operating on the basis of consensus, just as did grandfather's small town. The middle-class suburbanite wants his politics bland. Even in state and national politics, he deplores conflict, and his image of the ideal is to take the politics out of politics.

The typical middle-class metropolitanite probably wants a government that has a minimal anxiety-producing potential. One that threatens, by area-wide control, to break down class, ethnic, and racial barriers is not a government that furthers his goals. Furthermore, a government is least anxiety-producing when its actions are highly predictable. The more consensus that exists within the governmental unit, the more predictable it is, the more conflict, the less predictable—another reason for the middle-class suburbanite to oppose metro government. From the surburbanite's point of view, the functions of government that are most important to him and that he therefore most wants to keep local control over, are those of land-use controls and public school policy. The former represent the only effective devices by which to shape the life styles of the suburb and to exclude those who do not fit it; the latter is important either because the bulk of those in a given suburban area do not use the public schools, or because they do want them and consider them important in establishing the image of the community and in preparing the children for preferred social roles.

Legitimacy: Access and Representativeness. The high-status model builders have never seemed to be concerned about access or representation as considerations in a model. This has probably been the case because these prestigeful persons have had no doubts about their personal ability to influence government at the metropolitan level. They had, of course, once been cognizant of the problem—they had strongly supported municipal home rule and opposed "interference" by the state legislature back in the salad days of the reform movement. In those days, they had been aware of the unpredictability of state decision-makers and the sense of lack of control over the situation that this had produced. As a result, they argued strongly for the independence of the local community in matters of local concern. But, once they had passed this phase, they forgot, apparently, that others might also be concerned about having a governmental structure over which they could have control.

Today, the upper-middle-class still has no doubt of its ability to secure a hearing and to influence the governing board or the executives of either local or metropolitan governments. But other metropolitan citizens are by no means so confident that they can preserve access once the established—and predictable—pattern has been abandoned. The core-city dweller, with his concern for a voice through his ward alderman, and the suburbanite, with his confidence in councilmen who share his income level and life style, see only a threat in any new and untried method of representation.

One of the greatest fears of the metropolitanite today is that he will lose access to, or influence over, government at all levels. He is confronted with a sense of alienation, or the feeling that no matter what he does, his actions will not influence decisions which are important to him. Proposals for metropolitan-wide government add fuel to his anxieties. Incipient alienation is to be seen, in addition to attitudes toward core city governments, in the belief that the suburbanite fight is a losing one—that eventually their area will become part of the core city or of a metropolitan super-government. In at least two empirical studies, these attitudes have been uncovered.

Despite this feeling of pessimism, the suburbanite wants to continue to have a separate local government. Some critics have argued that suburbanites do not value independence. The argument is that if they really valued it, they would be better informed about the identity of their leaders and about policy issues and conflicts than are residents of the core city. Several studies have shown that they are not, however. Yet, this criticism is almost certainly invalid, for what the suburbanite is interested in is a psychological sense of access to be used *when he needs it,* not something to be availed of every day of the year. He also wants to have the feeling that those who sit on the governing body think and act as he does. If he believes that they do so, and if government is through consensus rather than compromise, it is not necessary to know the actual names of the actors; indeed, it is a waste of time to learn them—they are interchangeable parts, any combination of which will produce essentially the same policies. The figures which show that suburbanites commonly cannot identify their local officials and that core city residents can do so more readily, probably do nothing more than demonstrate that core city officials and area-wide "civic leaders" get better publicity than do suburban officials.

Functionality. Despite frenetic insistence by reformers that the Balkanized approach to the metropolis leads only to chaos, there is evidence that the typical citizen of the area does not consider the problem to be serious. Indeed, he is likely to see the present arrangement as generally adequate. He does not even deign to take notice of metropolitan area studies—in Dayton, less than a majority even of the well-informed, or politically active citizens, knew that a major study of the area was being conducted. And in St. Louis, only one person in ten among the politically active could explain the three major provisions of the so-called borough plan that was voted upon in that area. But 20 per cent could even name one provision—and these were not among the typical, apathetic, apolitical citizens, but among the supposed leading citizens of the suburbs. As Scott Greer has noted, "the ordinary voters were not even voting on the plan: nobody knows what they *were* voting on." In many other circumstances, the voter turnout level has been very low, and this despite generous publicity by local newspapers and a frenetic effort by leaders of the cause.

Apathy is not the only indication of satisfaction with the status quo, or alternatively, of the lack of awareness on the part of the typical citizen. A study of farmers on the outer fringe of the Lansing metropolitan area indicated not only that most of them did not understand that they were farming directly in the path of future urban expansion, but did not even understand who were their political supporters or enemies. Not only does the typical American citizen grossly discount the future, he is incurably optimistic concerning the possibility of solving his problems—whenever he feels the time has come to face up to them.

Manageable Area. Each year the old idea of the reformers that a single metropolitan area should have a single government becomes less realistic. With strip cities and metropolises blending into metropolises, the prospects for a single government for such areas is about as likely as having a Rorschach blot come up as a rectangle. In addition, the typical citizen almost certainly does not view the metropolis as a manageable area for *local* government. No matter what reformers may argue, the citizen does not see metropolitan-wide structures as forms of local government. Furthermore, suburbanites tend to reject any conflict-ridden structure as being unacceptable—and all metropolitan-wide governments are institutions for the management of conflict. We need look only at the history of the Miami-Dade County plan to see that the ordinary citizen is realistic in his assumption that area-wide government is conflict-ridden. Robert Wood has made the point that such conflict is a part of democracy, but the ordinary citizen would rather avoid this part of his social responsibility whenever he can.

Effective Machinery. What of the views of the ordinary citizen as to the acceptable way of handling critical issues? He no doubt does recognize some issues as of importance from time to time. There is as yet no study that I know of, which has asked a sample of metropolitanites how serious problems should be handled, but there is evidence to indicate that most citizens either overtly prefer or tacitly accept three kinds of solutions, only one of them of the sort carried in the medicine bag of conventional reform. The three are: (1) use of the special districts; (2) use of the county; and (3) reliance on the state government to one degree or another.

The special district has been discussed so much I will not attempt to comment further on it here. The criticisms of it are well known, as are the reasons why both ordinary citizens and many professional and technical personnel favor it. The county has some serious built-in limitations as to its effectiveness. These are greater in some states than in others, but in all, urban counties are increasingly being turned to for the performance of municipal functions. Since about 75 per cent of all Standard Metropolitan Statistical Areas are contained within a single county, this approach often makes sense, though not necessarily to the farmers in the distant corners of the country. But this unit of government is well known to all except the most apolitical of citizens, it is deeply imbedded in the traditions of America and hence its proposed use for new functions creates much less uncertainty in the minds of voters than do proposals involving untried and unknown federated, district, or borough plans, or even city-county consolidation which, for all the innocence of its title, sounds like a new breed of animal to the uneasy, confused citizen.

The state has the same advantages as the county: familiarity and legitimacy. Despite ideological lessons about self-reliance and doing for ourselves at home whatever we can, the fact is that the typical metropolitanite probably does not see state government as any more distant or less responsive than a metropolitan-wide government. Furthermore, the state enjoys the advantage of being familiar and traditional, of having a substantial tax base, a sounder one than any local government, and probably sounder than any metropolitan government that might be created. In addition, the state has the legal powers to cope with the problems of most metropolitan areas.

Both state and Federal governments possess a sense of legitimacy when they enter a new metropolitan functional area that cannot be claimed by any new forms of government or even by the county. Furthermore, people turn to these levels of government because the marginal sacrifice in raising additional dollars is less there than at other levels, and the burdens is less visible. To this is added the great psychological advantage to the local politician of being able to step off the airplane from Harrisburg or Washington and announce to assembled reporters that Zilchville has just been qualified for a new grant-in-aid, or for a special one for a sewage-disposal plant, or that the state is about to adopt a new shared tax system. All of these allow him to say that he is bringing money into the community and relieving the "overburdened" local property tax—a task that is quite a bit easier for him than to have to say, "Well, folks, in order to provide the urban services you want, we will have to increase the property tax rate again next year; there just is no other way out." Today, there is, in fact, another way out. Furthermore, the state is increasingly assuming responsibility as an umpire among local units of government, and as the agency that applies sanctions on behalf of society when local units do not assume responsibility or cannot work out their differences. People object to "bureaucracy" or "red tape," to be sure, but they generally accept the increasingly good job that state governments are doing in such areas as pollution control and the planning and routing of freeways.

What of the Future? Despite evidence of pessimism by suburbanites concerning the future viability of their independent municipalities, prospects for the future would appear to imply conservatism in the making of readjustments. The projection of current trends a decade or two into the future indicates that both the size and number of metropolitan areas will increase. These areas will not usually be governed by area-wide governments, except for a few adoptions of city-county consolidation plans, and for the expanded function of the traditional county—whose boundaries will in only rare cases be changed to fit the urbanizing pattern.

In the meanwhile, the social service state will grow by slow evolution with additional domestic policy responsibilities being assumed by the Federal government and greater concern being shown for metropolitan public policy matters by the state. The consequences of having the courts assume jurisdiction over the determination of fair representation in state legislatures will almost surely have the eventual effect of making state governments more responsive to the wants of urban areas. The very fact of greater state awareness will diminish the demand for metropolitan-wide governments and with the greater weighting of urban areas in the legislatures, the confidence of urbanites in state government will probably increase. I think it a good guess, therefore, that the state will play an increasing role in the future, not just in connection with such high-expense items as highways, public schools, welfare, renewal, and pollution control, but also in the somewhat less expensive areas of physical planning, capital-outlay planning, and land-use controls. The economic and psychological advantages that ride with greater use of state and Federal financing will add to the pressures for making these units, and perhaps especially the state government, the true metropolitan-wide governments of the future. This is not to say that there will not continue to be financial problems in metropolitan areas. State and Federal grants will only soften the impact of increasing urbanization accompanied by increasing service level expectations. Yet, the projected expansion of the gross national product leads us to believe that the financial strain on the citizen will probably not be much greater in the future than it has been in the last decade. Probably no system for governing the metropolis could do much about reducing these costs or to prevent service supply from lagging somewhat behind demand. The rapid growth of our urban areas will keep "metropolitan area problems" constantly on the pages of the newspapers. Even if the rate of family formation declines, the professionals in various service areas will keep right on raising standards—there is no likelihood that we will ever catch them.

Problems will face the metropolis in the future, of course. Henrik Ibsen once noted that "life is cruel, life is earnest." And so it is, even in the affluent society. In addition to the ideological conflicts that will accompany the increasing role of the state and Federal governments, and in addition to the financial ques-

tions, here are a few items we will have to concern ourselves with:

1. The reluctance to face up to democratic responsibilities at the local level. The ghettoization of the suburbs has made it possible to put aside temporarily an issue that eventually must be faced. It is slowly being faced, however, it seems to me. Current trends, I think, will within a generation put our most successful Negro lawyers and physicians into homes in the most fashionable suburbs not as an occasional exception but as a matter of course. The rough cutting edge of status striving will hurt the lower middle class much more than the well-to-do, of course; this group will continue to see all kinds of threats to itself—and it will be the last to be reconciled to policies of open occupancy, desegregation of recreational facilities, and equal job opportunities. But the problems do not appear to be insurmountable.

2. Alienation. We today know too little about the sense of alienation in the urbanite. Some studies of the phenomenon have been made, however, and there is at least some reason to be concerned that the increasing size of urban places is correlated with increasing feelings of alienation. There are probably several ways by which this sense, which appears to be a side effect or withdrawal symptom related to the disappearance of grass-roots government, may be managed. Some possibly effective methods may not even have been conceived, as yet. But alienation probably can be reduced if we can find ways of creating in the typical citizen a sense of legitimacy for a leadership group. To some extent this sense is appearing in the form of deference to or at least acceptance of professional administrators in the crucial policy innovation and decision making roles. It could also be reduced if we modified the traditional American belief in the cult of the common man, the notion that any man can be a decision maker. A return to the traditional concept of

democracy would help; if we could re-learn the ancient lesson that democracy is a system of government in which the *hoi polloi* chooses the rulers but does not itself rule. If we could get some acceptance of this idea—a common one in Great Britain—we would see fewer parochial vetoes of bond issues and tax levies, and we could get greater acceptance of the role of the state as the guardian which steps in to the decision-making process when local governments do not do what is generally expected of them by the prevailing values of society. We might also seek to increase the sense of legitimacy and representativeness of state governments—but as this sense increases for members of the working classes, it may decline for members of the lower middle classes. There is also some doubt as to what would happen to the confidence levels of upper-middle-class reformers if state legislatures are drastically reapportioned, even though these are the persons who have been in the forefront of the campaign for stronger urban representation at the state capitals.

3. The Reuse of Urban Land. As a frontier nation, Americans found it convenient to despoil the land and then move on; clearing urban structures for rebuilding has long been viewed as uneconomic. The problems of the declining core-city tax base, the expansion of surburban slums, the increasing differences between the low-status core-city residents and the surburbanites, the penalizing effects of the property tax when land owners seek to improve their properties, are all too well known for me to discuss here. But if we ever do decide to take seriously the planned reuse of land—and this seems to be something I see in my crystal ball—it will probably be done largely with state and Federal subsidies and with direct state and Federal administrative participation. I see this as the trend despite the fact that actual experience in cities such as Pittsburgh indicate that it need not be the case. Of course, America has the wealth which would permit us to clean away all slums within a few years, if our citizens saw that as a truly worthwhile objective. So far, there is little evidence that attitudes of apathy and acceptance are changing. But the problem cannot be ignored, and to the extent action is demanded, the high cost makes it seem natural for the typical citizen to accept the expanding state and Federal role in the usual pattern of cooperative federalism.

4. Rational Land Use. I once described the metropolitan-area planner as a kind of group therapist, a community hand holder, and verbalizer of our ideals. Most Americans do not want those ideals denounced, but to date they do not want them acted upon with vigor, either. My interpretation of the planner does not imply that his task is futile or unimportant, of course. To the contrary, a psychiatrist is one with whom we often develop a dependency relationship—he becomes enormously important to us. He will become even more important in future years, for both economic and social pressures will demand a more rational approach to land use than has been the case in the past. In some instances, metropolitan planning agencies will be given effective powers to carry out planning decisions, but there is reason to believe that in many states this metropolitan task will be shared by the local units and the state government. In matters of great urgency involving area-wide services, we already turn to the state, as in connection with highway and water matters, for example. We will probably do so even more in the future. The state is a viable unit of government. It possesses effective jurisdiction and an adequate degree of legitimacy. The practical-minded American will turn to it. He will turn to it only when he thinks the time has come, however, and when he feels that he can no longer avoid doing so.

Closing note. My effort in this paper has been to show that activists and writers and scholars in the area of metropolitan-area problems have followed a line of endeavor that has borne relatively little fruit over a couple of generations and that this has been so because the implicit assumptions concerning the nature of the political process or the ingredients of a political system, have been unreal. I have also noted that plans for metropolitan-area government have often been made with no consideration for the values, goals, and limits of believability possessed by the ordinary citizen. I have tried to compare the requirements of a political system for the metropolis with what is popularly acceptable and I have suggested that the future metropolis will probably be governed through the process of cooperative federalism which has become so typical a part of the American political system. In particular, I have indicated that suburban governments will survive and urban counties will expand their functions somewhat,

but that the greatest future changes will be in the increased financial and administrative role of the state and Federal governments. Finally, I have indicated that the greatest future changes in role will take place at the state level. As legislatures become more representative, citizen acceptance of the role of the state as a legitimate one will expand. Its already ample legal powers and reasonably adequate financial powers will, in the future, make it the closest facsimile of a metropolitan-wide government in most urban areas. Whether the trend I anticipate is desirable or not, I would not be so arrogant as to claim to know. But I will say that democratic policy-making, like a biological infection, tends to follow the path of least resistance. And so far as I can tell, what I have been describing is that path. Persons interested in the problems of the metropolis might well give appropriate consideration as they make their plans for future action.

65. The Political Implications of Metropolitan Growth*

EDWARD C. BANFIELD

THE rapid growth of the metropolitan populations will not necessarily have much political effect. To be sure, many new facilities, especially schools, highways, and water suply and sewage disposal systems, will have to be built and much private activity will have to be regulated. But such things do not necessarily have anything to do with politics: the laying of a sewer pipe by a "public" body may involve the same kinds of behavior as the manufacture of the pipe by a "private" one. Difficulties that are "political" arise (and they may arise in "private" as well as in "public" un-

dertakings) only in so far as there is conflict—conflict over what the common good requires or between what it requires and what private interests want. The general political situation is affected, therefore, not by changes in population density or in the number and complexity of the needs that government serves ("persons," the human organisms whose noses are counted by census-takers, are not necessarily "political actors") but rather by actions which increase conflict in matters of public importance or make the management of it more difficult. In what follows, such actions will be called "burdens" upon the political system.

* Reprinted with permission from *Daedalus*, Winter 1960. Footnotes omitted.

In judging how a political system will work over time, increases and decreases in the burdens upon it are obviously extremely relevant. They are not all that must be considered, however. Changes in the "capability" of a system, that is, in its ability to manage conflict and to impose settlements, are equally relevant. The "effectiveness" of a political system is a ratio between burdens and capability. Even though the burdens upon it increase, the effectiveness of a system will also increase if there is a sufficient accompanying increase in its capability. Similarly, even though there is an increase in capability, the effectiveness of a system will decrease if there is a more than commensurate increase in burdens.

In this article an impressionistic account will be given with respect to two contrasting political systems, the British and the American, of the burdens metropolitan affairs place upon them and of their changing capabilities. Naturally, the focus of attention will be upon ratios of burdens to capabilities and upon the significance of these ratios for metropolitan affairs.

THE TASKS OF BRITISH LOCAL GOVERNMENT

Until recently British local government (meaning not only government that is locally controlled but all government that deals with local affairs) had, by American standards, very little to do. Until three or four years ago there was little traffic regulation in Britain because there were few cars (the first few parking meters, all set for two hours, were installed in London in the summer of 1958). Now all of a sudden there are 5,500,000 cars—more per mile of road than in any other country—and the number is increasing by a net of 1,500 per day; by 1975 there are expected to be 13,500,000. Obviously, the need for roads and parking places will be enormous. But the automobile will create other and graver problems for local government. When there are enough cars and highways, there will doubtless be a "flight to the suburbs." The central business districts will be damaged, and so will mass transit (94 percent of those who now enter London do so by public transportation) and the green belts.

Law enforcement has been relatively easy in Britain up to now. The British have not been culturally disposed toward violence or toward the kinds of vice that lead to major crimes. (There are only 450 dope addicts in all of Britain, whereas in Chicago alone there are from 12,000 to 15,000.) British opinion, moreover, has not demanded that some form of vice be made illegal, much less that vice in general be suppressed. In England adultery is not illegal, and neither is prostitution, although it is illegal to create a nuisance by soliciting. Physicians in England may prescribe dope to addicts. (In the United States, where this is illegal, black-market prices prevail and the addict must usually resort to crime to support his habit. In Chicago a week's supply of heroin costs at least $105; to realize this much, the addict must steal goods worth about $315. According to the estimate of a criminal court judge, about $50 million worth of goods is shoplifted every year in the central business district of Chicago by addicts.) Never having tried to suppress drinking, gambling, or prostitution, the British have no organized crime.

The task of law enforcement is also becoming more difficult, however. Dope addiction, and consequently crimes of violence, will increase with the number of West Indians and others who are not culturally at home in England. In the past year the horde of London prostitutes has been driven underground, where they may prove a powerful force tending toward the corruption of the police. As traffic fines increase in number and amount, the bribery of the police by motorists will also increase. "All Britain's big cities," an *Observer* writer recently said, "now have enclaves of crime where the major masculine trades appear to be pimping and dealing in dubious secondhand cars."

Even if motorists, dope addicts, and prostitutes do not seriously corrupt it, the police force is bound to deteriorate. The British have had extraordinarily fine policemen, partly because their social system has hitherto offered the working class few better opportunities. As it becomes easier to rise out of the working class, the police force will have to get along with less desirable types. It is significant that the Metropolitan Police are now 3,000 men short.

State-supported schooling, one of the heaviest tasks of local government in the United States, has been a comparatively easy one in Britain. Four out of five British children leave school before the age of 16. The British, it is said, are not likely to develop a taste for mass education. They are demanding more and better state-supported schools, however, and no doubt the government will have to do more in this field.

It would be wrong to infer that because of these changes the burden upon the British political system will henceforth be comparable to that upon our own or, indeed, that it will increase at all. Conceivably, the new tasks of local government will have no more political significance than would, say, a doubling of the volume of mail to be carried by the post office. One can imagine, for example, two opposite treatments of the London traffic problem, one of which would solve the problem without creating any burden upon the political system and the other of which would leave the problem unsolved while creating a considerable burden.

Possibility 1. The Ministry of Transport takes jurisdiction over London traffic. Acting on the recommendations of a Royal Commission, the Minister declares that the central city will be closed to private automobiles. His decision is acclaimed as wise and fair— "the only thing to do"—by everyone who matters.

Possibility 2. The boroughs retain their control over traffic because the minister is mindful of organized motorists. People feel that it is an outrageous infringement of the rights of Englishmen to charge for parking on the Queen's highway or to fine a motorist without having first served a summons upon him in the traditional manner. Traffic is unregulated, and everyone complains bitterly.

As this suggests, "governmental tasks" are "political burdens" only if public opinion makes them so. What would be an overwhelming burden in one society may not be any burden at all in another. What would not be a burden upon a particular political system at one time may become one at another. It is essential to inquire, therefore, what changes are occurring in the way such matters are usually viewed in Great Britain and in the United States. The factors that are particularly relevant in this connection include: the intensity with which ends are held and asserted; the willingness of actors to make concessions, to subordinate private to public interests, and to accept arbitration; and, finally, the readiness of the voters to back the government in imposing settlements.

THE RELATION OF CITIZEN TO GOVERNMENT

The British have a very different idea from ours of the proper relation between government and citizens. They believe that it is the business of the government to govern. The voter may control the government by giving or withholding consent, but he may not participate in its affairs. The leader of the majority in the London County Council, for example, has ample power to carry into effect what he and his policy committe decide upon; it is taken for granted that he will make use of his power (no one will call him a boss for doing so) and that he will not take advice or tolerate interference from outsiders.

Locally as well as nationally, British government has been in the hands of the middle and upper classes. Civil servants, drawn of course entirely from the middle class, have played leading and sometimes dominant roles. Most elected representatives have been middle or upper class. The lower class has not demanded, and apparently has not wanted, to be governed by its own kind or to have what in the United States is called "recognition." Although Labour has controlled the London County Council since 1934, there have never been in the Council any such gaudy representatives of the gutter as, for example, Alderman "Paddy" Bauler of Chicago. The unions have kept people with lower-class attributes, and sometimes people of lower-class origins as well, off the ballot. They would not have done so, of course, if the lower class had had a powerful itch to have its own kind in office. (In that case the unions would themselves have been taken over by the lower class.) As Bagehot said in explaining "deferential democracy," "the numerical majority is ready, is eager to delegate its power of choosing its ruler to a certain select minority."

The ordinary man's contact with government inspires him with awe and respect. (Is government respected because it pertains to the upper classes, or does casuality run the other way, the upper classes being respected because of their association with government?) "The English workingman," an Englishman who read an earlier draft of this article said, "seems to think that the assumption of governmental responsibilities calls for the solemnest of blue suits. They tend to be so overawed by their position as to be silenced by it."

The ethos of governing bodies, then, has been middle or upper class, even when most of their members have been lower class. So has that of the ordinary citizen when, literally or figuratively,

he has put on his blue suit to discharge his "governmental responsibilities" at the polls.

Consequently the standards of government have been exclusively those of the middle and upper classes. There has been great concern for fair play, great respect for civil rights, and great attention to public amenities—all matters dear to middle- and upper-class hearts. At the same time there has been entire disregard for the convenience and tastes of the working man. London pubs, for example, are required by law to close from two until six in the afternoon, not, presumably, because no one gets thirsty between those hours or because drinking then creates a special social problem, but merely because the convenience of pub keepers (who would have to remain open if competition were allowed to operate) is placed above that of their customers. Similarly, trains and buses do not leave the center of London after eleven at night, not, presumably, because no one wants to go home later, but because the people who make the rules deem it best for those who cannot afford taxis to get to bed early.

It is not simply class prejudice that accounts for these things. By common consent of the whole society the tastes of the individual count for little against prescriptive rights. When these rights pertain to the body politic—to the Crown, in the mystique—then the tastes of the individual may be disregarded entirely. Public convenience becomes everything, private convenience nothing.

As heirs of this tradition, the British town planners are in a fortunate position. They do not have to justify their schemes by consumers' preferences. It is enough for them to show that "public values" are served, for by common consent any gain in a public value, however small, outweighs any loss of consumers' satisfaction, however large. Millions of acres of land outside of London were taken to make a green belt without anyone's pointing out that workingmen are thus prevented from having small places in the country and that rents in the central city are forced up by the reduction in the supply of land. It is enough that a public amenity is being created (an amenity, incidentally, which can be enjoyed only by those having time and money to go out of London). The planning authorities of the London County Council, to cite another example of the general disregard for consumers' tastes, consider the following questions, among others, when they pass upon an application to erect a structure more than 100 feet in height:

> Would it spoil the skyline of architectural groups or landscapes? Would it have a positive visual or civic significance? Would it relate satisfactorily to open spaces and the Thames? Would its illuminations at night detract from London's night scene?

It is safe to say that the planners do not weigh the value of a gain in "visual significance" against the value of a loss in "consumer satisfaction." In all probability they do not try to discover what preferences the consumer actually has in the matter. Certainly they do not make elaborate market analyses such as are customarily used in the United States in planning not only shopping places but even public buildings.

Green belts and control of the use of land are only part of a plan of development which includes the creation of a dozen satellite towns, "decanting" the population of the metropolis, and much else. Where these sweeping plans have not been realized, it has not been because of political opposition. There has been virtually no opposition to any of these undertakings. The real estate, mercantile, banking, taxpayer, and labor union interests, which in any American city would kill such schemes before they were started, have not even made gestures of protest. The reason is not that none of them is adversely affected. It is that opposition would be futile.

THE DIRECTION OF CHANGE

Obviously, a political system that can do these things can do much else besides. If the relation between government and citizen in the next half century is as it has been in the past, the "governmental tasks" that were spoken of above will not prove to be "political burdens" of much weight. One can hardly doubt, for example, which of the two ways of handling London traffic would, on this assumption, be more probable.

There is reason to think, however, that fundamental changes are occurring in the relations between government and citizen. Ordinary people in Britain are entering more into politics, and public opinion is becoming more ebullient, restive, and assertive. The lower class no longer feels exaggerated respect for its betters, and if, as seems reasonable to assume, respect for public institutions and for political things has been in some way causally connected with respects for the governing classes, the ordinary man's attachment to his society may be changing in a very fundamental way. British democracy is still deferential, but it is less so than a generation ago, and before long it may be very little so.

It would not be surprising if the lower class were soon to begin wanting to have its own kind in office. Lower-class leaders would not necessarily be less mindful of the common good and of the principles of fair play than are the present middle and upper class ones, however. The ethos of the British lower class may not be as different from that of the other classes as we in America, judging others by ourselves, are likely to imagine.

There is in Britain a tendency to bring the citizen closer to the process of government. Witness, for example, a novel experiment (as the *Times* described it) tried recently by an urban district council. At the conclusion of its monthly meeting, the council invited the members of the public present (there were about twenty) to ask questions. According to the *Times*:

> The Council, having decided to cast themselves into the arms of the electorate, had obviously given some thought to how they could extricate themselves if the hug became an uncomfortable squeeze. The chairman, after expressing the hope that the experiment would be successful, suggested a few rules. It was undesirable, he said, that such a meeting should become an ordinary debate with members of the public debating with members of the council and perhaps members of the council debating with each other. He decreed that the public should be restricted to questions on policy or factual information. He finished the preliminaries by saying that if things got out of hand he would rise and would then expect all further discussion to cease.
>
> This last precaution proved to be unnecessary. The public were pertinent, probing, and shrewd in their questions, but content to observe the proprieties. The more vexed of domestic questions of Nantwich (the demolition of old property, road repairs, housing, and the like) were thrown down quickly and in every case received reasoned replies. The atmosphere of the chamber continued to be one of high good humor.

Carried far enough, this kind of thing would lead to the radical weakening of government. (There is no use giving people information unless you are going to listen to their opinions. And if you do that, you are in trouble, for their opinions are not likely to be on public grounds, and they are virtually certain to conflict.) The British are not likely to develop a taste for what in American cant is called "grass-roots democracy," however; the habit of leaving things to the government and of holding the government responsible is too deeply ingrained for that. What the public wants is not the privilege of participating in the process of government but, as the Franks Committee said, "openness, fairness, and impartiality" in official proceedings.

The tastes of the ordinary man (consumers' preferences) will be taken more into account in the future than they have been in the past, not because the ordinary man will demand it (he may in time, but he is far from doing so now) but because the ruling elite—an elite that will be more sophisticated in such things than formerly—will think it necessary and desirable. The efforts of the Conservative government to let the market allocate housing are a case in point. These have been motivated, not by desire to deprive the workingman of advantages he has had for half a century (that would be out of the question), but by awareness that people's tastes may be best served in a market. The cherished green belts are now being scrutinized by people who are aware of consumer demand for living space, and some planners are even beginning to wonder if there is not something to be said for the American system of zoning. It is not beyond the bounds of possibility that the British will exchange their system of controls of the use of land, which as it stands allows the planner to impose a positive conception, for something resembling ours, which permits the user of land to do as he pleases so long as he does not violate a rule of law.

The conclusion seems warranted that twenty or thirty years from now, when today's children have become political figures, governmental tasks which would not place much of a burden on the political system may then place a considerable one on it. Governmental tasks like traffic regulation will be more burdensome politically both because there will be insistent pressure to take a wider range of views and interests into account, but also, and perhaps primarily, because the ruling group will have become convinced that the preferences of ordinary people ought to count for a great deal even when "public values" are involved. It is not impossible that the elite may come to attach more importance to the preferences of ordinary people than will the ordinary people themselves.

THE CONTRASTING AMERICAN TRADITION

Local government in the United States presents a sharply contrasting picture. It has been required to do a great deal, and the nature of American institutions and culture has made almost all of its tasks into political burdens.

Although there have always been among us believers in strong central government, our governmental system, as compared to the British, has been extraordinarily weak and decentralized. This has been particularly true of state and local government. The general idea seems to have been that no one should govern, or failing that, that everyone should govern together. The principle of checks and balances and the division of power, mitigated in the Federal government by the great powers of the presidency, were carried to extreme lengths in the cities and states. As little as fifty years ago, most cities were governed by large councils, some of them bicameral, and by mayors who could do little but preside over the councils. There was no such thing as a state administration. Governors were ceremonial figures only, and state governments were mere congeries of independent boards and commissions. Before anything could be done, there had to occur a most elaborate process of give and take (often, alas, in the most literal sense) by which bits and pieces of power were gathered up temporarily, almost momentarily.

It was taken for granted that the ordinary citizen had a right—indeed, a sacred duty—to interfere in the day-to-day conduct of public affairs. Whereas in Britain the press and public have been excluded from the deliberations of official bodies, in the United States it has been common practice to require by law that all deliberations take place in meetings open to the public. Whereas in Britain the electorate is never given an opportunity to pass upon particular projects by vote, in the United States it usually is. In Los Angeles, according to James Q. Wilson, "The strategy of political conflict is more often than not based upon the assumption that the crucial decision will be made not by the City Council of Los Angeles, the Board of Supervisors of the county, or the legislature of the state, but by the voters in a referendum election."

Los Angeles is an extreme case, but the general practice of American cities, a practice required by law in many of them, is to get the voters' approval of major expenditures. The New York City government, one of the strongest, is now having to choose between building schools and making other necessary capital expenditures; it cannot do both because the voters of the state have refused to lift the constitutional limit on debt. Such a thing could not happen in London; there all such decisions are made by the authorities, *none of whom is elected at large.*

The government of American cities has for a century been almost entirely in the hands of the working class. This class, moreover, has had as its conception of a desirable political system one in which people are "taken care of" with jobs, favors, and protection, and in which class and ethnic attributes get "recognition." The idea that there are values, such as efficiency, which pertain to the community as a whole and to which the private interests of individuals ought to be subordinated has never impressed the working-class voter.

The right of the citizen to have his wishes, whether for favors, "recognition," or something else, served by local government, has beeen an aspect of the generally privileged position of the consumer. If the British theory has been that any gain in public amenity, however small, is worth any cost in consumer satisfaction, however large, ours has been the opposite: with us, any gain to the consumer is worth any cost to the public. What the consumer is not willing to pay for is not of much value in our eyes. Probably most Americans believe that if the consumer prefers his automobile to public transportation his taste ought to be respected, even if it means the destruction of the cities.

We have, indeed, gone far beyond the ideal of admitting everyone to participation in government and of serving everyone's tastes. We have made public affairs a game which anyone may play by acting "as if" he has something at stake, and these make-believe interests become subjects of political struggle just as if they were real. "The great game of politics" has for many people a significance of the same sort as, say, the game of business or the game of social mobility. All, in fact, are parts of one big game. The local community, as Norton E. Long has maintained in a brilliant article, may be viewed as an ecology of games: the games serve certain social functions (they provide determinate goals and calculable strategies, for example, and this gives an element of coordination to what would otherwise be a chaotic pull and haul), but the real satisfaction is in "playing the game."

Since the American political arena is more a playground than a forum, it is not surprising that, despite the expenditure of vast amounts of energy, problems often remain unsolved—after all, what is really wanted is not solutions but the fun of the game. Still less is it surprising that those in authority seldom try to make or impose comprehensive solutions. The mayor of an American city does not think it appropriate for him to do much more than ratify agreements reached by competing interest groups. For example, the mayor of Minneapolis does not, according to a recent report, "actively sponsor anything. He waits for private groups to

agree on a project. If he likes it, he endorses it. Since he has no formal power with which to pressure the Council himself, he feels that the private groups must take the responsibility for getting their plan accepted."

American cities, accordingly, seldom make and never carry out comprehensive plans. Plan making is with us an idle exercise, for we neither agree upon the content of a "public interest" that ought to override private ones nor permit the centralization of authority needed to carry a plan into effect if one were made. There is much talk of the need for metropolitan-area planning, but the talk can lead to nothing practical because there is no possibility of agreement on what the "general interest" of such an area requires concretely (whether, for example, it requires keeping the Negroes concentrated in the central city or spreading them out in the suburbs) and because, anyway, there does not exist in any area a government that could carry such plans into effect.

CHANGE IN THE UNITED STATES

The relation of the citizen to the government is changing in the United States as it is in Britain. But the direction of our development is opposite to that of the British: whereas their government is becoming more responsive to popular opinion and therefore weaker, ours is becoming less responsive and therefore stronger. In state and local government this trend has been under way for more than a generation and it has carried far. Two-thirds of our smaller cities are now run by professional managers, who, in routine matters at least, act without much interference. In the large central cities, mayors have wider spheres of authority than they did a generation ago, much more and much better staff assistance (most of them have deputies for administrative management), and greater freedom from the electorate. These gains are in most cases partly offset, and in some perhaps more than partly, by the decay of party machines, which could turn graft, patronage, and other "gravy" into political power, albeit power that was seldom used to public advantage.

Reformers in America have struggled persistently to strengthen government by overcoming the fragmentation of formal authority which has afflicted it from the beginning. The council manager system, the executive budget, metropolitan area organization—these have been intended more to increase the ability of government to get things done (its capability, in the terminology used above) than to make it less costly or less corrupt.

One of the devices by which power has been centralized and the capability of government increased is the special function district or authority. We now commonly use authorities to build and manage turnpikes, airports and ports, redevelopment projects and much else. They generally come into being because the jurisdictions of existing general-purpose governments do not coincide with the areas for which particular functions must be administered. But if this reason for them did not exist, they would have to be created anyway, for they provide a way of escaping to a considerable extent the controls and interferences under which government normally labors. The authority, as a rule, does not go before the electorate or even the legislature; it is exempt from the usual civil-service requirements, budget controls, and auditing, and it is privileged to conduct its affairs out of sight of the public.

The success of all these measures to strengthen government is to be explained by the changing class character of the urban electorate. The lower-class ideal of government, which recognized no community larger than the ward and measured advantages only in favors, "gravy," and nationality "recogni-

tion," has almost everywhere gone out of fashion. To be a Protestant and a Yankee is still a political handicap in every large Northern city, but to be thought honest, public-spirited, and in some degree statesmanlike is now essential. (John E. Powers, the candidate expected by everyone to win the 1959 Boston mayoralty election, lost apparently because he fitted too well an image of the Irish politician that the Irish electorate found embarrassing and wanted to repudiate.) Many voters still want "nationality recognition," it has been remarked, but they want a kind that is flattering. It appears to follow from this that the nationality-minded voter prefers a candidate who has the attributes of his group but has them in association with those of the admired Anglo-Saxon model. The perfect candidate is of Irish, Polish, Italian, or Jewish extraction, but has the speech, dress, and manner and also the public virtues (honesty, impartiality, devotion to the public good) that belong in the public mind to the upper class Anglo-Saxon.

The ascendant middle-class ideal of government emphasizes "public values," especially impartiality, consistency, and efficiency. The spread of the council-manager system and of nonpartisanship, the short ballot, at-large voting, and the merit system testify to the change.

Middle-class insistence upon honesty and efficiency has raised the influence and prestige of professionals in the civil service and in civic associations. These are in a position nowadays to give or withhold a good government "seal of approval" which the politician must display on his product.

The impartial expert who "gets things done" in spite of "politicians" and "pressure groups" has become a familiar figure on the urban scene and even something of a folk hero, especially among the builders, contractors, realtors, and bankers who fatten from vast construction projects. Robert Moses is the outstanding example, but there are many others in smaller bailiwicks. The special function district or authority is, of course, their natural habitat; without the protection it affords from the electorate they could not survive.

The professionals, of course, favor higher levels of spending for public amenities. Their enlarged influence might in itself lead to improvements in the quality and quantity of goods and services provided publicly. But the same public opinion that has elevated the professional has also elevated the importance of these publicly supplied goods and services. It is the upper middle- and the lower-class voters who support public expenditure proposals (the upper middle-class voters because they are mindful of "the good of the community" and the lower-class ones because they have everything to gain and nothing to lose by public expenditures); lower middle-class voters, who are worried about mortgage payments, hostile toward the lower class (which threatens to engulf them physically and otherwise), and indifferent to community-regarding values, constitute most of the opposition to public improvements of all kinds.

Thus it happens that as Britain begins to entertain doubts about green belts, about controls of the use of land that make much depend upon the taste of planners, and about treating public amenity as everything and consumer satisfaction as nothing, we are moving in the opposite direction. There is a lively demand in the United States for green belts (the *New York Times* recently called "self-evident truth" the astonishing statement of an economist that "it is greatly to be doubted if any unit of government under any circumstances has ever bought or can ever buy too much recreation land"); the courts are finding that zoning to secure aesthetic values is a justifiable exercise of the police power; performance zoning, which leaves a great deal to the discretion of the planner, is becoming fashionable, and J. K. Galbraith has made it a part of conventional wisdom to believe that much more of the national income should be spent for public amenities.

Perhaps in the next twenty or thirty years municipal affairs will pass entirely into the hands of honest, impartial, and nonpolitical "experts"; at any rate, this seems to be the logical fulfillment of the middle-class ideal. If the ideal is achieved, the voters will accept, from a sense of duty to the common good, whatever the experts say is required. We may see in the present willingness of business and civic leaders to take at face value the proposals being made by professionals for master planning, metropolitan organization, and the like, and, in the exalted position of Robert Moses of New York, portents of what is to come.

The presence in the central cities of large numbers of Negroes, Puerto Ricans, and white hillbillies creates a crosscurrent of some importance. For a generation, at least, these newcomers will prefer the old style politics of the ward boss and his "gravy train." How this anomaly will fit into the larger pattern of middle-class politics is hard to imagine. Possibly the lower class will simply be denied representation. And possibly the rate of increase of per capita income being what it is, the assimilation of these people into the middle class will take place faster than anyone now imagines.

SUMMARY AND CONCLUSIONS

It has been argued in this paper that the tasks a government must perform (the number and complexity of goods and services it must supply) have no necessary relation to political matters. Tasks may increase without accompanying increase in the burden placed upon a political system. The important questions for political analysis, therefore, concern not population density or other indicators of the demand for goods and services, but rather the amount and intensity of conflict and the capacity of the government for managing it. Looked at from this standpoint, it appears that the effectiveness of British government in matters of local concern will probably decrease somewhat over the long run. The demands that will be made upon it in the next generation will be vastly more burdensome than those of the recent past (although also vastly less burdensome than the same demands would be in America), and the capacity of the government will be somewhat less. The effectiveness of local government in the United States, on the other hand, will probably increase somewhat. Local government has had more tasks to perform here than in Britain, and these have imposed enormously greater burdens. The tasks of local government will doubtless increase here too in the next generation, but the burdens they impose will probably decline. American local government is becoming stronger and readier to assert the paramountcy of the public interest, real or alleged.

Although each system has moved a considerable distance in the direction of the other, they remain far apart and each retains its original character. The British, although more sensitive to public opinion, still believe that the government should govern. And we, although acknowledging that the development of metropolitan areas should be planned, still believe that everyone has a right to "get in on the act" and to make his influence felt. Obviously, the differences are crucial, and although the trend seems to be toward greater effectiveness here and toward reduced effectiveness in Britain, there can be no doubt that in absolute terms the effectiveness of the British system is and will remain far greater than that of ours. Despite the increase in the tasks it must perform, the burden upon it will remain low by American standards, and its capability will remain high. Matters which would cause great political difficulty here will probably be easily settled there.

The basic dynamic principle in both systems has not been change in population density but rather change in class structure. It is the relaxation of the bonds of status that has caused the British workingman to enter more into politics, that has made his tastes and views count for more, and that has raised questions about the right of an elite to decide matters. In America the assimilation of the lower class to the middle class and the consequent spread of an ideal of government which stresses honesty, impartiality, efficiency, and regard for public as well as private interest have encouraged the general strengthening of government.

The mere absence of dispute, acrimony, unworkable compromise, and stalemate (this, after all, is essentially what the concept "effectiveness" refers to in this connection) ought not, of course, to be taken as constituting a "good" political order. Arrogant officials may ignore the needs and wishes of ordinary citizens, and the ordinary citizens may respectfully acquiesce in their doing so, either because they think (as the British lower class does) that the gentleman knows best or (as the American middle class does) that the expert knows best. In such cases there may be great effectiveness—no dispute, no acrimony, no unworkable compromise, no stalemate—but far from signifying that the general welfare is being served, such a state of affairs signifies instead that the needs and wishes with which welfare under ordinary circumstances, especially in matters of local concern, is largely concerned are not being taken into account. To say, then, that our system is becoming somewhat more and the British system somewhat less effective does not by any means imply "improvement" for us and the opposite for them. It is quite conceivable that dispute, acrimony, unworkable compromise, and stalemate may be conspicuous features of any situation that approximates the idea of general welfare.

Such conclusions, resting as they do on rough and, at best, common-sense assessments, amply illustrate the difficulty of prediction, and—since the causal principles lie deep in social structure and in culture—the utter impossibility within a free society of a foresighted control of such matters.

66. Some Fiscal Implications of Metropolitanism*

HARVEY E. BRAZER

THIS paper is concerned with some of the major problems that arise in connection with our efforts to provide and finance public services for nearly two-thirds of the American population which currently lives in areas designated by the Census Bureau as "Standard Metropolitan Statistical Areas." Heterogeneity, in terms of economic function, income levels, social and political preferences, dominant ethnic origins, and so forth, typically characterizes the constituent parts of the metropolitan community, at least in the larger ones. And yet all residents, business units and families, as well as governing bodies, have a common stake in the performance of public services and the levying of taxes in all parts of the area. If a single central problem can be identified, therefore, it must be defined as *the problem of achieving efficiency in meeting common needs and reaching common goals within a framework of action that gives appropriate cognizance to the diversity in tastes and needs that exists.*

The general plan of this paper entails our taking up, in turn, the attempt to establish norms or "ideal" arrangements for supplying and financing public services in the metropolitan area, the obstacles in the way of achieving these norms, and the question of how we can most effectively live with or minimize these obstacles.

NORMATIVE GOALS FOR FISCAL ARRANGEMENTS

The establishment of norms of fiscal behavior for government requires that we define the roles we expect it to play. For government in general it is convenient to follow Musgrave's "multiple theory of the public household" which involves, for analytical purposes, separate treatment of public want satisfaction (his "allocation branch"), income redistribution through taxes and transfers (the distribution branch), and stabilization of the economy (the stabilization branch). Where government is expected to assume responsibility for all three, no one role or branch of the budget is, in practice, fully separable from the others; virtually all fiscal actions will have some repercussions of significance for allocation, distribution, and stabilization. And this remains true even if public want satisfaction is regarded as the sole overt objective of government, as, in my view, it must be in the case of local, as opposed to national government. Nevertheless, we may, in this instance, regard effects on

* Reprinted with permission from Guthrie S. Birkhead (ed.), *Metropolitan Issues: Social, Governmental, Fiscal,* The Maxwell Graduate School of Citizenship and Public Affairs, Syracuse University, 1962. Footnotes omitted.

income distribution and stabilization as being incidental and unsought, to be avoided as much as possible. Thus the role assumed for local governments in the metropolitan community is that of providing public goods and services under circumstances in which the national government is presumed to have succeeded in achieving its goals with respect to income distribution and economic stability at high and rising levels of employment with stable prices.

Local neutrality with respect to income distribution is suggested because of the obvious impossibility of achieving any specified goal in this area if thousands of state and local units of government attempt either to offset or supplement national action. Neutrality with respect to the stabilization function appears to be either desirable or unavoidable for a number of reasons. Local needs tend to be inflexible over short periods of time, being geared largely to changes in the size and character of the population or requiring continuity for their effective satisfaction. Stabilization measures pursued at the local level involve tremendous geographic leakages which give rise, among other things, to serious questions of inter-regional equity. The lack of monetary powers and existence of stringent debt limits, which frequently fluctuate countercyclically, impose major constraints upon policy. And, finally, mobility of resources in the national economy as a whole may be impaired through local efforts to increase employment by means of public action if such action is pursued at a time when employment is high locally but low nationally.

Most specifically relevant to our discussion of fiscal aspects of metropolitanism is the problem of allocating responsibility for public want satisfaction and its financing among the governmental units that operate within the metropolitan community. Our solution hinges primarily on externalities in consumption. At one extreme, if all of the

benefits derived from consumption of a good are appropriable by a single individual, so that there are no external economies of consumption, or spillover effects, there are no public aspects of consumption involved and neither must we face an allocation problem. But assuming that there are substantial external economies of consumption, and that we are therefore concerned with public want satisfaction, the interjurisdictional allocation problem involves the question of how far from the point of consumption, if one is identifiable, benefits extend. Conceptually, one may distinguish collective goods involving externalities that extend only to neighborhood or municipal boundaries, to county lines, to multi-county regions, to state lines, and finally those that extend to the nation as a whole or even to the community of nations.

The spelling out of a general rule that will provide the specific answer for each governmental function is obviously extremely difficult, if not impossible. However, we can obtain some guide-lines for action within metropolitan areas with respect, at least, to some functions. Thus air and stream pollution control obviously involve important externalities that demand their being undertaken on an area-wide basis, without regard to municipal boundary lines; the same may be said of arterial urban highways, mass transit, and water supply, with economies of scale adding weight to the argument for multi-unit action. Not quite so clear is the position of recreational facilities, public libraries, museums, and police protection. In each of these cases benefits cannot be confined to the boundaries of individual municipal jurisdictions; nor, on the other hand, are they uniformly distributed within the metropolitan area. Complicating the problem is the fact that a function such as police protection encompasses many sub-functions, some of which are purely local, with no spillovers to neighboring communities, while others either involve substantial spillovers or indivisibilities and major economies of scale.

The question of whether a given collective good should be provided by the sub-metropolitan jurisdiction or by some agency with broader geographical powers is further complicated by the fact that the issues involved cannot be regarded as being purely economic. We are necessarily concerned with something more than economic efficiency. The heterogeneity found among municipalities in a metropolitan area involves wide variations in tastes and preferences, the pursuit of which must be accorded a positive value. Thus the solution in terms of efficiency in an engineering sense, that is, the most product at the least cost, is inappropriate by itself. The problem may be fruitfully approached, perhaps, by drawing a distinction between those public services with respect to which taste differentials may be expected to be relatively unimportant, and for which narrowly construed economic efficiency criteria may be allowed to predominate, and those with respect to which purely local preferences will exhibit wide variations, with only minor spillover effects. What is wanted, of course, is a voluntary solution that can be achieved through voting or the political process. A solution that may be called for on grounds of economic efficiency may be rejected if members of local communities place a high value upon their ability to influence policy in the functional area involved. And, contrary to the views of those who are among the more extreme advocates of consolidation in metropolitan areas, there is no *prima facie* reason for insisting that the "efficient" solution be pursued.

In the attempt to define normative fiscal goals for the metropolitan area attention must also be directed toward the revenue side of the budget. If redistribution of income through the operation of the local public fisc is to be avoided and an optimal allocation of resources achieved, public service benefits must be paid for by those who enjoy such benefits. The problem is extremely complex, even in a purely general setting, because collective consumption, by its very nature, involves benefits inappropriable by the individual, to which the private-market exclusion principle cannot be applied. A tax system under which liabilities are determined by the individual's preferences for public goods is inoperative, because failure or refusal to reveal one's preferences would reduce tax liability while not denying the opportunity to consume.

Within the setting of metropolitan area finances the problem is even more intricate. Here we are concerned not only with the relationship between the individual and *the* government, but with the additional problems that arise because any one government may be expected to supply services the benefits from which accrue to its own residents *and* to residents of other jurisdictions. Thus even if it were possible for a municipality within the metropolitan area to finance its services by means of appropriate user charges and benefit levies upon its residents, spillover effects and consumptions by non-residents would ordinarily prevent an equation of benefits and charges at the margin. Ideally, benefits must be paid for by those who enjoy them, and all who enjoy public service benefits should participate in the decision-making process through which it is determined which goods and services are to be supplied and the quantities to be offered. Such an ideal solution is ruled out by spillover or neighborhood effects of local public services and non-resident collective consumption within the supplying jurisdiction, even if it were otherwise conceptually attainable. In setting out fiscal goals for metropolitan areas perhaps all that can be suggested is that the repercussions of these considerations should be minimized. This may be achieved through the appropriate allocation of functional responsibilities, coupled with the extension of taxing powers to overlapping jurisdictions and the employment, wherever feasible, of user charges.

OBSTACLES TO THE ACHIEVEMENT OF NORMATIVE GOALS

One of the more sanguine and interesting approaches to the theory of local finance in the metropolitan area is that of Professor Tiebout. In it, "The consumer-voter may be viewed as picking that community which best satisfies his preference pattern for public goods," having been offered a range of choices among jurisdictions, each of which has its "revenue and expenditure patterns more or less set." Thus the problem of getting individuals to reveal their preferences is solved, much as it is in the private-market sector, provided that there are enough communities from which to choose and the other assumptions of Tiebout's model hold. These other assumptions are: full mobility, including the absence of restraints associated with employment opportunities; full knowledge on the part of "consumer-voters"; no inter-community external economies or diseconomies are associated with local public services; some factor limits the optimum size (the size at which its services can be provided at lowest average cost) of each community, given its set pattern of services; and communities are constantly seeking to reach or maintain this optimum size. If we add to this list of assumptions the insistence that residents of each community are not only concerned with employment opportunities but also refrain from venturing into other communities for shopping, recreation, or any other purpose, except when involved in a change in their places of residence, we may, indeed, have a "conceptual solution" to the problem of determining optimal levels of consumption for a substantial portion of collective goods. And as an exercise in abstraction it may be a solution, as useful, perhaps, as many of the economist's abstractions.

Unfortunately, however, Tiebout's model cannot be said to be even a rough first approximation of the real world. The most pressing fiscal problems of metropolitanism arise precisely because of the very factors he denies in his assumptions. Even if individuals had full knowledge of differences among communities in revenue and service patterns and were willing to move in response to them and their own tastes, income, zoning, racial and religious discrimination, and other barriers to entry to various communities would restrict their mobility. (A low-income non-Caucasian family does not move from Detroit to Grosse Pointe because it prefers the latter's tax and expenditure pattern!) Families and individuals do extend their activities, in working, shopping and playing, across community lines, so that there is no clear-cut coincidence between one's place of residence and the place in which services are consumed and taxes paid. Employment opportunities do condition the choice of community of residence, particularly for lower-income families, and for all families commuting costs, like all transport costs, restrict choices. And when the existence of external economies and diseconomies between communities associated with public services (or their nonperformance) is assumed away we have not only thrown the baby out with the bath water, we have thrown away the bath.

DIFFERENCES IN COMMUNITY CHARACTERISTICS

A major source of fiscal difficulty in the metropolitan areas arises as a consequence of differences among local communities in the characteristics of their populations. As the Advisory Commission on Intergovernmental Relations noted recently "Population is tending to be increasingly distributed within metropolitan areas along economic and racial lines. Unless present trends are altered, the central cities may become increasingly the place of residence of new arrivals in the metropolitan areas, of non-whites, lower-income workers, younger couples, and the elderly." Thus while the total populations of five of the six largest central cities declined between 1950 and 1960, this decline was the product of a reduction in the white population, ranging from 6.7 per cent in New York to 23.5 per cent in Detroit, and an increase in non-white population which ranged from 45.3 per cent in Baltimore to 64.4 per cent in Chicago. Looking back over a longer period, 1930 to 1960, we find that for the 12 largest SMSA's combined the white population declined from 94 to 87 per cent of total population. But *all* of this decline took place in the central cities, where the white population declined from 92 to 79 per cent of the total.

The Detroit Area Study's findings on the income experience of whites and non-whites and residents of the suburbs and the central city, for the period 1951 to 1959, reveal some startling contrasts. Median family income rose from $4,400 to $4,800, by nine per cent, in the central city (including Highland Park and Hamtramck, which are encircled by Detroit), and from $4,900 to $7,200, or by 47 per cent, in the suburbs. At the same time the median income of white families increased by 33 per cent, for the area as a whole, compared to only eight per cent for non-whites. The movement of white, higher income families to Detroit's suburbs, coupled with their replacement in the central city by low-income newcomers, has increased the median family income differential from 11 per cent in 1951 to 50 per cent in 1959.

For Detroit and, one would expect, for other major central cities as well, developments of the kind described have had substantial fiscal repercussions. They have brought a high concentration to the central city of those who are most vulnerable to unemployment in recession and to loss of employment consequent upon technological change, and who tend to bring heavy demands upon welfare, health, and other public services. At the same time the value of residential property occupied per family declines, thus completing the fiscal squeeze.

None of this is new. It has been going on as long as newcomers of lower income and social or cultural values different from those predominating have concentrated in the central cities of our metropolitan communities. A growing difference between present and past experience arises, however, from the dispersion of industry to suburban locations. No longer is the core of the area necessarily the residential location that minimizes the costs of going to and from the job. Thus strong pressures have developed which have resulted in the growth in suburban communities of conditions once confined to low-income central city residential sections. In some of these fiscal problems that exist are even more intense than those experienced by the central city because the suburban community which houses the low-income worker is frequently not the location of the industrial plant employing him. Lower-income families no longer necessarily occupy with increasing density the older residential sections of the central city. They are found concentrated as well in development tracts in suburban communities where the tax base represented by their houses is far too low to permit the financing of an acceptable level of public services.

On the other hand, the suburb may constitute either an industrial enclave, with a very large tax base and few people, or a tightly restricted area of high-value houses. In neither of these cases do fiscal problems of major magnitude arise.

The resulting contrasts in the size of tax bases relative to population may be dramatically illustrated with data from the Cleveland metropolitan area within

Cuyahoga County. The range of assessed valuation per capita for 1956 extends from $122,237 in the Village of Cuyahoga Heights, an industrial enclave of less than three square miles with a population of 785, to $837 in the one-half square mile area that remains of Riveredge Township. Among the larger communities the assessed value per capita ranges from $1,858 in Garfield Heights to $4,256 in Shaker Heights, with the City of Cleveland at $2,852.

Similarly sharp contrasts, emphasizing the diversity among municipalities in structure rather than size of tax bases, may be seen in the Detroit area. In 1958 the assessed value of residential property in 34 cities, villages, and townships comprised 42 per cent of total assessed valuations in these communities. For the City of Detroit the ratio was 40 per cent, whereas for such industrial enclaves as River Rouge, Trenton, Hamtramck, Highland Park, and Warren, it was less than 20 per cent, while at the other end of the spectrum, in the Grosse Pointe communities, and Dearborn Township, the ratio was 85 per cent or higher.

Such extreme inequalities as those in the distribution within metropolitan areas of socio-economic groups of population and the property tax base give rise to wide differences in expenditures and tax rates. Tax rates and per capita expenditures both tend to be highest in central cities, but ranks with respect to tax rates and expenditures diverge for communities outside of the central city. Margolis found that industrial enclaves spend most while levying the lowest tax rates, "balanced" cities rank next on both counts, followed by "dormitory" cities. However, the omission from his data of school district taxes and expenditures results in a rather incomplete and, in substantial degree, misleading picture. It permits, among other things, the conclusion that balanced cities, relative to dormitory cities, fail "to derive fiscal advantage from their commercial and industrial prop-

erties." This conclusion is not supported by data drawn from the Detroit area. Here we find (Table 1) that com-

TABLE 1 *Effective Tax Rates in the Detroit Area, 1958, by Type of City*

Type of City[a]	Tax Rate[b] (per cent)
Central city	1.7
Low-income residential	1.6
High-income residential	1.6
Balanced city	1.3
Industrial city	1.0

[a] Detroit is the central city; residential cities are cities in which the assessed value of residential property exceeds 60 per cent of total assessed valuation in 1958; balanced cities are cities for which this ratio lies between 40 and 60 per cent; and industrial cities are those for which it is below 40 per cent.

[b] The effective tax rate is the mean of the ratios of property tax billed, according to local official records, to the owner's estimate of the value of his owner-occupied residential property, based on a total of 515 observations. Validity checks indicate a very close correspondence between owner's estimates and actual market values.

Source: Unpublished data compiled for the Detroit Area Study, 1958-59, Survey Research Center, The University of Michigan.

bined tax rates, including municipal, school, and county levies, are about the same for the central city and the residential cities, lower for the balanced cities, and, again, lowest for the industrial cities. The evidence suggests that residential or dormitory suburbs spend comparatively little for municipal functions, but bear a relatively heavy burden in school expenditures and taxes.

Thus, the Detroit Area data support the conclusion that addition to a community of industrial and commercial property does tend to reduce effective tax rates. But broad generalizations can easily be misleading. New industry entering a community may or may not relieve fiscal pressures. The answer in specific circumstances must depend on such things as the capital-labor ratio involved in production, the level of wage rates paid, the demand for the output of the community's economy that emanates from the plant's operation, the extent to which the labor force lives in or outside of the community in which the plant is located, and so on.

EQUITY AND EFFICIENCY

If there were no limitations upon the mobility of families and individuals between communities, one might contend that neither efficiency nor equity considerations need enter the discussion. If people chose their place of residence freely, it could then be argued that the price paid for living in one community rather than another, in terms of higher taxes paid for a given level of services or a given tax rate paid for a lower level of services, was voluntarily assumed. It might even be reflected in land values in such fashion as to be approximately offsetting in effect. But as long as barriers to mobility exist, through zoning regulations, racial discrimination, and so forth, such offsetting will not occur and neither equity nor efficiency can be achieved.

Equity, in the sense of equal treatment of equals vis-à-vis the local fisc, may not obtain as between equal individuals resident in different communities simply because of differences in the distribution of income and wealth between communities. Thus individual "A," resident in wealthy community "X," may be expected to enjoy a larger flow of public service benefits at a given tax cost to him than individual "B," "A"'s "equal," however defined, a resident of poor community "Y." In the absence of barriers to mobility between communities, we should expect B to remain in Y only if wage rates were higher and/or prices, including land values, were lower in Y than in X by amounts sufficient to offset the fiscal disadvantage. If wage rates were not higher or prices lower initially, the movement of people from Y to X

should lead to their adjustment in equilibrium at levels that will just compensate for the fiscal disadvantage of living in Y. However, if B, for reason, say, of color, is barred from community X, the adjustment cannot take place.

The analysis is complicated, of course, by recognition of the fact that individuals may live in one community, work in another, and shop in a third. In this case wage rates and prices of goods and services in the place of residence may be unaffected (at the extreme the community may be a "pure" bedroom suburb) and the burden of adjustment would fall entirely on land values, directly or through land rents, and, at least in the short run, on housing values and rents.

Thus far we have ignored the influence on inter-personal equity of differences among communities in the value of commercial and industrial property. If the cost of providing services to such property is equal to its tax contribution this influence is zero, but such cost-tax equality is extremely unlikely. If industry or commerce brings a net fiscal gain to the community its residents can enjoy a higher public service to tax cost ratio than can be enjoyed without it (all other things being equal). Again, with full mobility equity can be achieved, but not otherwise. The same conclusion holds, with opposite signs being attached to relative gains and losses, where the industrial or commercial property entails a net fiscal loss.

Efficiency in the allocation of resources, including those flowing through the public budget, requires a matching of benefits and costs at the margin, from the point of view of the consumer-voter, directly or on his behalf by "best-guessing" political representatives. On the assumption that the principal or only tax employed locally is the more or less uniformly applicable property tax, if the costs providing public services to non-residential property are regarded as given, a vote by individuals for a higher tax rate necessarily means that the increase in property tax receipts available for financing services for individuals will exceed the increment in taxes paid by them. This should bring an excessive allocation of resources to the local public sector, since expenditure benefits will have been underpriced to the individual taxpayer. Inefficiency arises as well from the firm's point of view, because taxes paid under these circumstances exceed the cost of providing services to it.

All of this suggests initially that the property tax as we know it is an inefficient tax instrument. Combined with differences among communities in the metropolitan area in relative size of industrial and commercial tax bases, it produces cost-benefit ratios for business and industry with respect to their inputs in the form of public services that may be expected to vary widely among communities. If individuals as voters act freely and fully in their own self-interest, we should expect the cost per unit of service received by industry to vary directly (if not proportionally) with the local ratio of non-residential to residential property. To the extent that this expectation is fulfilled, its influence should lead to a spatial distribution of industry and trade that is different from that which we should expect in its absence. Within any region firms will be induced to locate at less economically attractive points than they would otherwise choose because at more attractive points, where industry and commerce already exist, the cost of public service inputs will have been pushed to levels higher than those obtaining elsewhere.

This reasoning, plausible as it seems, is not consonant with the fact that industrial suburbs appear to levy lower tax rates than other satellite communities. It seems safe to hazard the guess that these lower tax rates are the product of political pressures brought to bear by industry and by the threat that industry will leave, or efforts to attract new industry, coupled with imperfections in the political process which may be expected to dilute the effective expression of voter self-interest.

The fact that many people live in one community and work in another substantially complicates the decision-making process in the local public sector. It means that individuals live and pay taxes—property taxes and, in some jurisdictions, income taxes—in one municipality while consuming public services in at least two. What does this imply for fiscal policy and efficiency in the allocation of resources to the local public sector in the metropolitan area? Is the jurisdiction in which the individual works "subsidizing" the one in which he lives? This question has generally been asked in the context of central city versus suburb, but it seems equally applicable as between suburbs.

Since part of their consumption occurs in a jurisdiction other than their place of residence, some consumers of public services are not consumer-voters. This renders the decision-making process with respect to local budgets in the metropolitan area far more difficult to cope with, even in conceptual terms. The usual benefit approach to budget theory requires that the consumer of public goods has either a direct or an indirect voice or vote in decisions as to what kinds and quantities of such goods are to be supplied and financed. But he is not permitted to vote when he is a commuter-consumer, unless the service is financed by means of user-charges, in which case there is no budget problem, for either the resident or the commuter. Suppose we consider traffic control on arterial streets providing ingress to and egress from the central business district of the core city. Here, presumably, the commuter-consumer has no choice but to accept what he is offered, and he is offered such services as the resident-consumer voters determine shall be offered. From the point of view of all consumers of the specific service we are bound to get under-allocation of resources to its supply, because the resident-consumer-voter can be expected to be willing to pay only for the quantity and quality he wishes to purchase, the demand emanating from the commuter being ignored. Alternatively, the commuter may be viewed as reducing, through his consumption, the product available to the resident per dollar's worth of input. This, again, would lead to less resources being allocated to traffic control than would be optimal were the demand of all consumers taken into account.

This line of argument offers one plausible explanation for the frequently stated observation that municipal services are undersupplied, in the sense, for example, that traffic control is inadequate to prevent heavy congestion in the metropolis. The illustration may readily be extended, with similar results, to a variety of other services, including recreation facilities, police protection, and so forth. The problem would not arise if Samuelson were correct in characterizing public goods as those the consumption of which by one person "leads to no subtraction from any other individual's consumption of that good. . . ." Unfortunately, however, this characterization applies, if at all, only to a very small proportion of collective or public goods supplied by municipalities.

The central cities of metropolitan areas and industrial suburbs have been shown to spend more per capita, in total and for major municipal functions (exclusive of education), than all local governments outside of the central city in the metropolitan area, residential suburbs, and cities located outside the standard metropolitan areas. Moreover, two studies of city expenditures have found that the proportion of the metropolitan area's population that lies outside of the central city is closely associated with the per capita expenditures of the central city. Both sets of findings reflect the fact that the number of people for whom the city must provide services is the sum of its resident population and the non-resident or contact population which spends time in the city in the course of the working day, shopping, pursuing recreation, and so forth. Margolis' data on tax rates in the San Francisco-Oakland area add further evidence in support of the suburban-exploitation-of-the-metropolis hypothesis.

Central cities may, in fact, provide more public services than surrounding communities, but it may be argued that this is a consequence not of differences in tastes, but of differences in needs, some of which are imposed on the central city by the behavior of suburban cities and socio-economic forces beyond the control of municipal governments. Irrespective of whether or not the commuter "pays his way" through adding to property values in the central city, he cannot be said to share in the high costs of services engendered by the increasing concentration there of lower-income newcomers, including the non white population. The latter, as we suggested earlier, tend to be less educated, more vulnerable to unemployment, and disorganized by moving from one cultural milieu to another that is totally unfamiliar and disruptive of traditional ties and mores. All of these factors give rise to expenditure demands to which the suburban community is subject, typically, with far less intensity—expenditures in such fields as welfare, police protection, public health, public housing and others. To the extent that suburban communities, through zoning regulations and discriminatory practices in rentals and real estate transactions, contribute directly to the concentration in the central city of socio-economic groups which impose heavy demands upon local government services, they are, in fact, exploiting the central city.

One consequence of the multiplicity of governmental units within the metropolitan area is that the provision of public services (or failure to provide them) in one community has neighborhood or spillover effects associated with it for other communities in the area. A high quality of police protection in City A, for example, will be reflected in a lower incidence of crime in neighboring City B, or efficient sewage treatment by A will benefit its down-river neighbor B, and so forth. Obviously each jurisdiction will be both the source and beneficiary or victim of such spillovers. But even if all jurisdictions "come out even," getting as much as they give, the existence of these neighborhood effects will have important repercussions upon efficiency in the allocation of resources to the local public sector.

In arriving at their decision as to how much to spend for sewage treatment, for example, the resident-voters of a given community can not be expected to take into account the repercussions of their decision on a neighboring community. To conclude otherwise is to assume that they are willing to engage in a form of public philanthropy. Nor can the fact that the first community enjoys some benefits emanating from the public services of another be expected to influence the voluntary decisions of its residents with respect to expenditures for collective consumption. The result, therefore, must be, again, an allocation of resources to collective consumption that is below the optimum level that would be indicated if all benefits of such consumption were appropriate in the spending community. At the extreme, public services that all residents of the congeries of jurisdictions want and are willing to pay for will not be supplied at all, because the proportion of the benefits appropriable by any one community's residents is so small as to make the expenditure less than worthwhile from their point of view.

Finally, if we turn the coin of Tiebout's complex of municipalities from which individuals may choose places of residence, we find that business firms are offered a similar set of alternatives in the metropolitan area. And this side of the coin may and does display some very troublesome difficulties stemming from inter-local competition for industry. Efficiency in the allocation of resources requires that the costs of production of industrial firms reflect the costs of supplying them with inputs in the form of public services and the social costs they impose upon the community, such as through pollution of air and water. But if differences in local tax costs can be employed as an effective means of inducing firms to select one jurisdiction rather than another, competition for industry will force local industrial taxes below the level suggested by our criterion. Similarly, if the costs of adequate treatment of the plant's effluents into the air, streams, rivers, and lakes are substantial and can be avoided by location in one part of the metropolitan area rather than another, no one jurisdiction, acting alone, can be expected to be able to enforce adequate control. Thus it is hardly surprising that rivers become open sewers and air pollution occurs.

APPROACHES TO RATIONAL ACTION

The main burden of the foregoing discussion rests on the divisive, constraining, and conflicting interests and forces which emanate from the fact that our larger urban communities are served by aggregations of uncoordinated governmental units. The inefficiencies, in terms of underallocation of resources to the public sector, and the accompanying inequities, go a long way toward providing some understanding, if not explanation, of the major problems confronting metropolitan America. Even if the forces discussed here could be eliminated others would remain. So-called "land pollution," for example, may be simply an unavoidable consequence of our unwillingness to restrict private rights in property to the point necessary to eliminate it, and there is not in sight a means of relieving the choking congestion brought by the automobile, short of prohibiting its use in certain areas or drastically curtailing the freedom of the auto-owner to decide when and where he will drive. However, achieving a framework in which voter-choice is better enabled to satisfy the collective consumption wants of urban dwellers will provide a more efficient allocation of resources and reduce inter-personal inequities.

One approach is governmental consolidation. The further consolidation is carried the greater is the extent to which spillover effects are reduced to appropriable benefits enjoyed by voter-consumers, that is, externalities are eliminated, as are inter-personal inequities. This can never be an entirely satisfactory solution, since border areas always remain. But more important is the fact that as the area covered by consolidation is extended the greater is the extent to which divergent interests and tastes are subordinated to the will of a more distant political majority. Thus efficiency, in an economic welfare sense, may or may not be improved, and the further dilution of the individual's ability to influence or participate directly in political decisions may be viewed as a major cost.

However, no one approach is likely to prove even conceptually satisfactory, whether or not it is politically feasible. Solutions to metropolitan area fiscal problems can, at best, only be compromises. The fact is that we cannot achieve desirable goals or objectives in a manner that permits the exercise of full freedom of individual choice. Rather, a modified objective appears necessary, one that will minimize the loss of consumer sovereignty in the local public sphere while avoiding a maximum of the inefficiencies and inter-personal inequities that arise under existing arrangements.

Perhaps a first requisite is the recognition and acceptance by the states, and to a lesser extent, the federal government, of their fiscal responsibilities in this area. The states can take several kinds of action. These might include

establishment of minimum standards of performance with respect to those functions which involve strong neighborhood effects or which are subject to curtailment through inter-local competition. Such functions would certainly include area-wide planning and air and water pollution control. In the case of these functions the neighborhood or spillover effects are of such overwhelming importance that their effective pursuit appears to be incompatible with freedom to establish purely local standards of performance and objectives. These appear to be cases which clearly justify the assertion that the primary obligation of people and individual municipal governments "is that of acceptance of some limitation of freedom of action in the interest of the greater good."

A second role that may properly be assumed by the states is the reduction of local differences in fiscal capacity and inter-local competition based on tax inducements to industry and commerce. This objective may be achieved by expansion of state aid, essentially substituting states taxes for locally levied taxes. This approach need not impinge upon budgetary efficiency. If it is well designed, relationships at the margin, particularly in the choice among alternatives in the allocation of resources within the public sector, need not be disturbed.

State assumption of responsibility for certain functions, directly or through grants-in-aid, seems indicated as well, particularly in the fields of welfare, public health, public housing, and urban renewal, functions whose costs impinge with great unevenness among communities in the metropolitan area. Problems in urban transportation, including both mass transit and arterial streets and highways, may be met by the states through a combination of devices, including grants-in-aid, establishment of minimum standards of performance, and direct assumption of responsibility. Justification for such action by the states may be found in the fact that functions such as those mentioned must be performed because of socio-economic forces that have their origin not in any one municipality but in the area, the state, or even the nation as a whole. They are a response to problems given by the social and technological environment in which we live. If that response is a purely local one, some members of society, those living in municipalities in which such problems may be avoided, are permitted to escape what may be regarded as a universal obligation.

Keeping in mind the fact that our primary objective is to achieve freedom of choice for individual consumer-voters while avoiding the costs emanating from uncoordinated local operations, what approaches seem indicated at the local level? If the states act in the manner suggested, some of the most pressing existing difficulties will have been eliminated or substantially reduced. One non-fiscal requirement would appear to be the elimination of barriers to mobility within the metropolitan community. Differences in zoning regulations will persist, and this may even be desirable, but other barriers are not tolerable, from the point of view of moral rectitude, efficiency or equity. The more immediately fiscal issues involve traditionally local functions with substantial spillover effects or important economies of scale. Proliferation of special-function agencies or districts which are not directly politically responsible has little to commend it, but some form of politically responsible federalism has much appeal. Alternatively, in some instances, the county government, with broadened powers, may be the appropriate instrument.

The function of either of these governmental forms can only be defined within the context of broader objectives sought in the metropolitan community. As was suggested above, economies of scale and spillover effects may be the forces upon which this definition may rest. Thus a federation of municipalities may assume responsibility for planning, water supply, sewage disposal, arterial highways, and mass transit, all of which involve economies of scale as well as spillover effects. Area-wide recreation facilities may also be delegated to the federal body, while neighborhood parks and playgrounds remain purely local responsibilities; the federation may provide central police services in specialized fields of police work, while basic police protection remains a local function; the same approach may be taken with respect to fire protection, education, property assessment, and certain other functions. Financing may be accomplished by delegation of taxing powers, contractual arrangements, and, wherever appropriate, user charges.

The problems related to the fact that many people live in one jurisdiction and work in another would be much abated under the kind of programs envisaged here. They would be further reduced through the extension of user charge financing and the use of non-property taxes. Particularly appealing among the latter is the income tax under which, as in the Toledo area, partial credit is provided for income taxes paid to the employee's place of residence.

More intensive employment of user charges and non-property taxes, coupled with the suggested expansion of state aid and/or state assumption of responsibility for some functions, should do much to alleviate existing local fiscal pressures. The deficiencies of the property tax, especially when it is levied at effective rates of 2 per cent or higher, are so manifest as to require that alternatives be sought. Very little is actually known about the effects of the property tax on land use in the metropolitan area, but as a tax that imposes substantial penalties upon improvement, rewards decay, and encourages land speculation that may have high social costs, it would appear to be a major contributor to the economic and fiscal ills of urban areas.

The very nature of collective consumption and the problems involved in attempting to achieve an approximation of maximum consumer-voter satisfaction in a local public sector operating within a predominantly free private economy are such as to defy conceptual, let alone actual, solution. But even conceptual models of the operation of the private market economy are satisfactory only within the framework of first approximation assumptions that take us a long way from the real world—some would say too far away to be very useful. Perhaps the economist still knows too little about either the private or the

public sector to permit him to do more than attempt to point up deficiencies relative to some commonly accepted criteria and, further, to indicate the kinds of actions that may minimize such deficiencies. With respect to one increasingly important part of the public sector, the urban complex known as the metropolitan area, a great deal more fruitful speculation and empirical investigation are needed before we can conclude that the economist can provide the needed guideposts to the policy maker.

67. Criteria for Appraising Different Approaches to Reorganization of Local Government in Metropolitan Areas*

ADVISORY COMMISSION ON INTERGOVERNMENTAL RELATIONS

THE principal objective of reorganization [*of local government in metropolitan areas*] . . . is to change local governments to improve their ability to handle functions of an area-wide nature. Such changes may affect objectives of local governments other than those of dealing adequately with area-wide problems. In establishing criteria for evaluating the approaches to reorganization, therefore, it is necessary to take into account the total objectives of local government.

Adequate consideration of these objectives would require extended treatment that is beyond the scope of this study. However, a general statement likely to represent broad consensus is that local governments should serve the people effectively and efficiently, with active citizen participation and

* Reprinted from *Alternative Approaches to Governmental Reorganization in Metropolitan Areas,* Advisory Commission on Intergovernmental Relations, June 1962. Footnotes omitted.

control, with an adequate and equitable revenue system, with a sufficient degree of local initiative and self-government for traditional or natural communities in the area, and with provisions for adaptation to growth and change.

From this statement a number of criteria can be derived which have a particular bearing on the geographical jurisdictions and powers of local governments, and therefore shall be used in evaluating the various alternative approaches to government reorganization in metropolitan areas. These criteria are: (1) Local governments should have broad enough area to cope adequately with the forces that create the problems which the citizens expect them to handle. (2) They should be able to raise adequate revenues, and do it equitably. (3) There should be flexibility to adjust governmental boundaries. (4) Local governments should be organized as general-purpose rather than single-purpose units. (5) Their areas should permit taking advantage of the economies of scale. (6) They should be accessible to and controllable by the citizens. (7) They should provide the conditions for active citizen participation.

One other criterion is used in making the appraisal—(8) political feasibility. This criterion involves factors, other than those contained in the other criteria, which have a bearing on the likelihood that the respective approach can be adopted.

A. EXPLANATION OF CRITERIA USED

The order of the listing of the criteria in the following elaboration is not intended to represent any sequence of relative importance.

(1) *Local governments should have broad enough jurisdiction to cope adequately with the forces that create the problems which the citizens expect them to handle.* "Coping adequately" means effective planning, decision, and execution. Effective planning means being able to embrace much or all of the area within which the major local forces producing the governmental problem have their effect. Effective decision means decision on the basis of a debate among a full range of interests having influence on these problems. Effective execution means being able to marshal adequate human and other resources to carry out the public decision. This criterion thus is closely related to that of adequate financing. It is also closely related to the criteria of citizen accessibility and participation to the extent that these stimulate citizen loyalty, since loyalty and respect have an important effect on citizen support for carrying out governmental policies and programs.

(2) *Local governments should be able to raise adequate revenues, and do it equitably.* As indicated, this criterion supports the first criterion of jurisdictional adequacy. It also contains the separate important idea of equitability of the revenue system. It means the reduction of disparities between tax and service boundaries.

(3) *There should be flexibility to adjust governmental boundaries.* The social, economic, political and demographic forces that make existing local government boundaries inadequate for many purposes are likely to accelerate rather than diminish in the future, increasing the need for flexibility in boundary adjustments.

(4) *Local governments should be organized as general-purpose rather than single-purpose governments.* Assignment of functions to general-purpose governments is more likely to produce proper balancing of total local needs and resources, a condition for effective decision-making and political responsibility. It is likely to produce more efficient administration through better coordination among functions and the reduction of overhead costs. It can sharpen citizen control by enabling the citizen to concentrate, rather than diffuse his attention on those organizations and officials with the power to make decisions. Adherence to this criterion means minimizing the overlapping among units of government.

(5) *Local government areas should be such as to permit taking advantage of the economies of scale.* Studies have shown that there is a relationship between the size of a governmental unit and the cost of performing its functions. The optimum size, i.e., the size at which unit cost is lowest, is not the same for all services. Local governmental units should have areas which minimize the unit cost of the services they provide.

(6) *Local governments should be accessible to and controllable by the people.* Accessibility and controllability of local government are determined to a significant degree by factors that have little relationship to the size of the governments. These factors, which concern structural and procedural features of government, include the number and nature of elective officials, the manner of their election (by district or at large),

their terms, the distribution of powers among them and the appointive personnel, provisions for notice and hearings on proposed policy changes, administrative provisions for receiving and acting on complaints, provisions for initiative and referendum, and recourse to the courts.

To the extent that the size of the governmental units does affect accessibility and control, however, arguments can be made for both smaller and larger size. Widespread popular sentiment seems to favor units as being "closer to the people." To some degree this is legitimately based on history and tradition, and the fear of overconcentration of power. On the other hand, as James Madison argued in *The Federalist,* the larger the area of government, the less the likelihood that any one special group will dominate the government, and thus the greater the likelihood that the many diverse groups of the community will have their interests respected. In terms of effective control and accessibility, therefore, the unit of government should be large enough to make it unlikely that any single interest can dominate it.

So far as the assignment of powers is concerned, as indicated under criterion (4), general-purpose government seems more conducive to effective citizen control than a multitude of special-purpose governmental units.

(7) *Local governments should provide the conditions for active citizen participation.* Citizen participation is also affected significantly by factors other than the area and powers of local government. The structural and procedural features cited under criterion (6), many of which depend on the form of government, are examples. Aside from such factors, however, participation is more likely to be stimulated by small governments than large ones, if for no other reason than that smallness makes for greater numbers. As one observer notes:

If all local government in America were suddenly abolished, the range of public decisions over which private citizens could exercise maximum control would be materially diminished in number if not in importance . . . Our democratic institutions . . . thrive on popular participation in the business of government. Perhaps the only area in which those decisions are straightforward enough to permit direct citizen participation is in the local government field . . .

*   *   *

(8) *Approaches to reorganization of local government conforming to any or all of the foregoing criteria should have political feasibility—the potential for receiving the approval required by the State constitution, statutes, or local government charter.* Political feasibility seems to depend on a number of interdependent factors, including:

(a) The potential of the proposal to advance the objectives of the governments affected in the metropolitan area. Thus, the reorganization is presumed to have political feasibility to the extent that it has the potential for fostering changes incorporating the first seven criteria. Some may argue that the merit of a proposal has nothing to do with its political acceptability. This argument would be quickly refuted by those who have had the difficult experience of trying to "sell" a weak or ill-conceived reorganization proposal.

(b) The desire to adopt the proposal on the part of those with the authority to act. These may be one or more legislatures, one or more local governing bodies, the electorate of one or more local governmental units, or a combination of some of these. Appraisal of this factor involves to some extent a judgment of the merits of the proposal. It also involves a judgment of the status of political resources of those who are anxious to "sell" the proposal to the groups in the position of authority. Such resources include the energy and skill necessary to plan, organize, and carry out a program of political educa-

tion. The nature of the political resources is not very directly related to
the major theme of this study, namely,
the different approaches to reorganization of local government in metropolitan areas. Therefore, an evaluation of
these resources is considered outside the
scope of this study.

(c) The status of constitutional,
legislative, and charter authority to
make the change.

(d) The nature of the legal procedure required to make the change,
that is, the legal provisions as to (1)
who needs to act (one or more legislatures, one or more local governmental
units, or a combination of some of
these); and (2) the kind of majority
action required (e.g., simple or two-
thirds; of all the governing bodies
affected or of only a simple majority).

These last two factors of political
feasibility—the legal permission to
make the change and the legal procedure actually to make it—are applied in this analysis. One additional
factor of political feasibility is applied:
the threat of the reorganization approach to the tenure and powers of
people in office. This is a part of the
complex of considerations in factor (b),
but is singled out because experience
with reorganization efforts over many
years indicates that it is a significant
and fairly predictable force.

In brief, therefore, reorganization approaches are regarded as having political feasibility to the degree that adequate permissive authority exists for
the adoption of the approach, that the
action of adoption is simple, and that
the approach can be accommodated to
the existing political power structure.

B. LIMITATION OF CRITERIA AND APPRAISAL

In applying the criteria to the alternative approaches to the reorganization
of local government in metropolitan
areas, several limitations must be clearly
recognized:

*First, an appraisal of this kind, as any
appraisal in the subject matter and
methodology of the social sciences, can
only suggest tendencies and "likeli-
hoods."* Much of the appraisal is a matter of judgment. Different individuals
would have different ideas of what
weights to give to different criteria,
and even "ideal" solutions would vary
among the 50 States and the 212 metropolitan areas.

*Second, all the criteria are compati-
ble, but only if each is moderated, not
maximized.* Balance is necessary, for
some of the criteria pull in different
directions, reflecting contradictory values which the different criteria are
presumed to secure. Generally speaking,
criterion (7), concerning citizen participation, and criterion (8), concerning political feasibility, tend to move
in the opposite direction from the first
six criteria. That is, they tend to favor smaller, numerous governments,
whereas the first six tend to favor
larger, fewer governments.

68. Voter Reaction to Metropolitan Reorganization*

ADVISORY COMMISSION ON INTERGOVERNMENTAL RELATIONS

In this study the Advisory Commission on Intergovernmental Relations reviewed eighteen proposals for metropolitan reorganization submitted to the voters between 1950 and 1961. The commission studied only those proposals which "aimed at significant change in the structure or powers of local government" in one of the 212 standard metropolitan statistical areas in the United States. Specifically, the study concerned reorganization efforts in these areas:

Albuquerque-Bernalillo County Consolidation, 1959. Defeated.

Atlanta-Fulton County "Plan of Improvement," 1950. Adopted.

Cuyahoga County (Cleveland) Home Rule Charter, 1959. Defeated.

Denver Metropolitan Capital Improvements District, 1961. Adopted. (Declared unconstitutional by Colorado Supreme Court in 1962.)

Durham - Durham County — "Durham County Unified," 1961. Defeated.

Erie County (Buffalo) Home Rule Charter, 1959. Adopted.

Knoxville-Knox County Metropolitan Charter—Consolidation, 1959, Defeated.

Louisville, Kentucky, "Plan for Improvement," 1956. Defeated.

Lucas County (Toledo) Home Rule Charter, 1959. Defeated.

Macon-Bibb County Consolidation, 1960. Defeated.

* Reprinted from *Factors Affecting Voter Reaction to Governmental Reorganization in Metropolitan Areas,* Advisory Commission on Intergovernmental Relations, May 1962. Footnotes omitted.

Miami-Dade County Metropolitan Federation, 1957. Adopted.

Nashville-Davidson County Metropolitan Charter — Consolidation. Defeated in 1958; adopted in 1962.

Newport News-Warwick Consolidation, 1957. Adopted.

Oneida County (Utica) Home Rule Charter, 1961. Adopted.

Onondaga County (Syracuse) Home Rule Charter, 1961. Adopted.

Richmond City-Henrico County Merger, 1961. Defeated.

St. Louis "Greater St. Louis City-County District," 1959. Defeated.

Seattle Special Purpose District, "Municipality of Metropolitan Seattle," 1959. Adopted.

In the words of the Commission's report:

Local observers were asked to indicate, from a detailed listing, the "issues or considerations that were of major importance in this reorganization effort." In spite of the diversity of proposals, . . . the issues raised for and against them show much similarity among the several areas.

In nearly every instance, the proponents of reorganization are reported to have focused strongly on two topics —the faultiness of existing local government structure or operations, and the need for urban-type services in outlying areas. The latter issue often specially involved particular functions, most commonly sewers and water supply, but with fire protection, rural zoning, police protection, and traffic control also mentioned. Financial implications are reported as important "pro-reorganization" factors for 10 of the 18 areas, with emphasis in some instances upon area wide totals of local government costs or taxes, and in other instances upon the geographic allocation of governmental costs. Few other main issues are reported on the "pro-reorganization" side for more than one or two areas. However, observers referred in varying ways to a common attitude which apparently encouraged several reorganization efforts: "The need for area leadership"; "A desire for more unity of purpose by the area as a whole"; "The need for a more cohesive and harmonious community"; "Desire to make more and better use of the 'leadership' available to the metropolitan area as a whole."

Opposition to reorganization proposals also concentrated heavily on a few key points. Financial implications are cited as an important basis for "anti" arguments in all but two of the 18 areas, with concern for geographic allocation of costs at least partly involved in most instances. In two-thirds of the 18 areas, opponents urged that the proposal was "too drastic or too sweeping." (Interestingly, this charge was encountered by most of the modest-effect county charters as well as by the other more drastic reorganization plans.) In about half of the 18 areas, observers considered that the prospective effect of reorganization upon local government employees or present elective officials was a major opposition factor. In five instances, the possible implication of the reorganization proposal for a colored racial minority concentrated mainly in the central city is cited as an important negative factor. In at least two or three areas, opponents argued against the particular plan proposed on the ground that some particular alternative approach would be a better way for meeting the local situation.

One of the issues listed on the survey worksheet was "The importance of independence for small communities in the area." However, observers reported this as a major issue against the reor-

ganization plan in only 7 of the 18 areas. This seems rather surprising in view of the emphasis which scholarly studies and casual observers alike have placed upon the desire for autonomy for existing units of government as a barrier to structural change in metropolitan areas. Much more explicit evidence than this limited set of observations would be needed to discount the presumption that such is the case. Perhaps the reported observations may be explained on the ground that the opponents' concern for localized autonomy was put before the voters mainly in terms of the possible effect of the reorganization proposal on governmental costs and their geographic allocation—issues which as noted above, were of major importance in most of the areas subject to survey.

THE ROLE OF VARIOUS COMMUNITY
ELEMENTS

Observers of these reorganization efforts were asked to indicate, from a detailed listing, those community elements whose position on the proposed reorganization could be identified, and to describe the role of each interested element in terms of a numbering system ranging from "Plus 3—a leading, active, united element for the plan" to minus 3, at the other end of the spectrum. Following is a summary of the observations reported concerning the 38 community elements listed on the survey worksheet. . . .

Interest in reorganization proposals may be roughly gauged by the number of areas where particular elements reportedly had any kind of role or attitude. As would be expected, such evidence appears for "metropolitan newspapers" in every instance. Nearly as widespread, being reported in all but one or two of the 18 areas, is interest of the following community elements:

Central city officials
County officials
League of Women Voters

Suburban newspapers
Central city commercial interests
Suburban commercial interests
Central city Chamber of Commerce
Central city real estate interests

At the other extreme, only limited or scattered evidence of interest appears for certain community elements. In fewer than 6 areas was any attitude or role reported for:

Parent-Teachers Association
Church groups or leaders
State political leaders
Government suppliers

Others of the 38 listed elements fall between these two extremes in frequency of mention. Surprisingly near the bottom of the range, being reported for only 6 to 8 of the 18 areas, are the following:

Central city neighborhood improvement groups
Suburban neighborhood improvement groups
Taxpayer group(s)
Civic research agency
Suburban Chambers of Commerce
Employees of fringe local governments

The *activity* of various community elements with regard to these reorganization efforts can also be roughly gauged from observers' reports. For 16 of the 18 areas, metropolitan newspapers appear as "A leading, active, united element *for* the plan." A similar role is indicated for the League of Women Voters in 11 of the 18 areas, and for the central city Chamber of Commerce in 8 of the 18 areas. Also cited as leading reorganization proponents in 5 or 6 areas each are the following:

Central city commercial interests
Radio and TV stations
Civic research agency
Banks
Central city officials

Active leadership of the opposition to the reorganization efforts was relatively scattered. Only two community elements are classed as "A leading active, united element *against* the plan" in as many as 5 of the 18 areas—namely, suburban newspapers and county government employees.

The *attitude or position* of various community elements toward local government reorganization in metropolitan areas is likely to depend, of course, upon the kind of change being proposed, and the nature of the original conditions sought to be altered. There was enough diversity among the 18 proposals surveyed that certain groups found in opposition in some particular areas were reportedly backing the prospective change in other areas. Nonetheless, the various proposals had one important common characteristic, in that each contemplated in one way or another the development or strengthening of a local government entity concerned with a relatively large geographic area —in most instances, an entire metropolitan county. It has therefore seemed worthwhile to construct a sort of composit index to measure the "typical" position of various community elements regarding these 18 reorganization efforts, which would give weight to the intensity and unanimity of their attitudes as well as to the number of areas where they played some role. A relatively crude index was therefore developed from observers' reports, with findings as summarized below.

Predominantly favoring these reorganization efforts were the following community elements, which are listed in descending order of the attitude index:

Metropolitan newspapers
League of Women Voters
Central city Chamber of Commerce
Central city commercial interests
Central city real estate interests
Radio and TV stations
Banks
Central city officials
Academic groups or spokesmen

Manufacturing industry
Utilities
Civic research agency
Central city homeowners

A smaller number of elements appear as having been commonly and strongly opposed to the reorganization proposal. In rank order, beginning with the most commonly opposed element, they were:

Farmers
Rural homeowners
County government employees
Suburban newspapers
Employees of fringe local governments
Farm organizations
Officials of fringe local governments
Suburban commercial interests

The other 17 of the 38 listed community elements ranged closely around the "zero" position, indicating considerable variation or splitting of attitude, or their inactivity or lack of interest in most areas. No doubt this finding partly reflects the range in kinds of reorganization being sought in various areas. For example, in 17 of the 18 areas there is some attitude reported for "county government officials" (as distinct from county government employees, mentioned above)—in 6 instances favoring, in 6 against, and in 5 a mixed or divergent position, altogether yielding a summary index figure of minus 2. It seems likely also, however, that some opposition elements were less evident or openly "visible," at least to the observers reporting on these reorganization efforts, than were community elements which took a favoring attitude. Subject to these important reservations, it may still be worthwhile to note that *no widespread, strong, and generally consistent position appears,* either for or against these reorganization proposals, for such potentially important elements as labor unions, taxpayer groups, neighborhood improvement groups, or minority racial elements.

PROMOTIONAL METHODS AND MEDIA

In most of these 18 areas, as has been indicated earlier, the proponents of reorganization had the potential advantage of an interested and "favorable" metropolitan press, while opponents generally had the backing of suburban newspapers. An effort has been made to ascertain what other media for information and promotion were used for and against these reorganization plans. . . .

*   *   *

The . . . record seems to indicate:

Greater formal organization and use of "mass media" by the proponents of reorganization than by opponents;
Only a limited number of areas where either proponents or opponents managed extensive face-to-face promotional efforts;
Extensive use by anti-reorganization forces of slogans and rumors, as distinct from more formal and detailed argumentation.

This record is supplemented by observers' replies to another set of questions, specifically asking whether a *localized* get-out-the-vote effort was waged widely and effectively on either or both sides of the referendum campaign. The answers are no doubt influenced by differing interpretations of the word "effectively," and perhaps to some degree by the observers' after-the-fact knowledge of the referendum outcome in various areas. Nonetheless, the findings seem to indicate the crucial importance of this phase of reorganization efforts:

A strong, localized get-out-the-vote effort by plan proponents is reported for six areas—Atlanta, Denver, Louisville, Newport News, Richmond, and Seattle. Four of these referendum efforts were successful, and the other two (Louisville and Richmond) received an overall majority though not the concurrent majorities required.

For the other four areas where reorganization proposals obtained a favorable majority vote (Miami, Erie, Oneida, and Onondaga), observers' comments indicate less intensive vote-getting efforts by proponents than in the six areas mentioned above. In each of these instances, however, the opposition effort was reportedly even less fully organized.

Of the eight areas where reorganization plans failed to receive a favorable majority, there were four (Durham, Macon, Nashville, and Lucas County, Ohio) where localized vote-getting efforts by the opposition were regarded by observers as being clearly more vigorous and widespread than those of the plan supporters.

In the four other "losing" areas (Albuquerque, Cuyahoga, Knoxville, and St. Louis), according to observers, neither proponents nor opponents mounted a vigorous localized vote-getting effort.

INFLUENTIAL FACTORS

From observers' comments and other sources, it is possible to identify a number of factors which apparently had an important bearing upon the success or failure of these various efforts at reorganization. Some of these are briefly listed below. . . .

It might go without saying, of course, that all of the reorganization efforts studied had the benefit of concern, interest, and effort by some important community leaders and elements. Following are certain other *favorable* factors observable only in some of the areas:

1. A sympathetic and cooperative attitude by State legislators from the area.

*   *   *

2. The use of locally knowledgeable individuals as staff to conduct background research and to develop recommendations.

*   *   *

3. The conduct of extensive public hearings by the responsible plan-preparing group.

*   *   *

4. Careful concern, in the design of the reorganization proposal, for problems involving representation of various districts and population elements.

*   *   *

Following are some of the *unfavorable* factors emphasized by observers, and which probably were of telling influence in several areas:

1. Absence of a critical situation to be remedied—or of widespread popular recognition of such a situation.

*   *   *

2. Vagueness of specification as to some important aspects or implications of the reorganization proposal.

*   *   *

3. Active or covert opposition by some leading political figures in the area.

*   *   *

4. Discontinuity or lack of vigor in promotion of the reorganization proposal.

*   *   *

5. Popular suspicion of the substantial unanimity expressed for the proposal by metropolitan mass media (newspapers, TV, and radio).

*   *   *

6. Inability of the proponents to allay popular fear of the effects of the proposed reorganization upon local taxes.

*   *   *

7. Failure by the plan proponents to communicate broadly, in a manner to reach relatively unsophisticated voters as well as others.

*   *   *

8. Failure by the proponents to anticipate and prepare for late-stage opposition efforts in the referendum campaign.

CONCLUSIONS AND INFERENCES

A number of generalizations with regard to problems of governmental reorganization in metropolitan areas seem to be justified by the record of the 18 area efforts which have been subject to review.

1. *Proposals for governmental reorganization in metropolitan areas have faced a largely apathetic public.*

Typically, within the 18 areas studied, only one in four persons of voting age bothered to cast a vote on the reorganization proposal. In only two instances was there voting participation by as much as one-third of the adult population. The 18 areas were distributed as follows:

Total referendum vote as per cent of voting-age population	Number of areas
40 to 45%	2
30 to 35%	2
25 to 29%	5
20 to 24%	4
15 to 19%	3
10 to 14%	2

In any sizable community, of course, the total population of voting age includes some persons not entitled to vote —for example, through lack of citizenship, recency of moving into the area, or (generally most important) failure to register. . . .

*   *   *

It is not being suggested, of course, that an increased turnout at the polls would automatically assure adoption of any particular reorganization proposal.

In fact, the 18 efforts studied offer no clear evidence on this score: some obtained a favorable majority with a rather limited turnout of voters, and some lost in spite of a relatively high percentage of voter participation. . . .

*   *   *

However, a big turnout at the polls at least provides an *opportunity* to overcome relatively limited elements opposing change in the status quo. And whatever the outcome, the expression of the "consent of the governed" by a considerable fraction rather than by only a minor part of the electorate is likely to have clear advantages. If reorganization is thus authorized, the new arrangements start with a better chance of general community acceptance than if they could be "blamed" upon a limited, though active and effective, minority of the electorate. Furthermore, even though defeat of a particular proposal will generally leave unsolved the problems that led to its development, widespread popular participation in the action is more likely than a sparsely shared referendum to "clear the air" and perhaps to suggest what alternative kinds of change might be more likely to obtain popular approval.

2. *Reorganization efforts should not be undertaken lightly, but with full recognition of obstacles to their success.*

One kind of problem has been widely noted—the difficulty of obtaining concurrents on desirable change from a majority of voters in various parts of the entire area concerned. The requirement of concurrent majorities has been cited as a major barrier to local government reorganization.

It is frequently averred that proposals for local government reorganization in metropolitan areas are likely to carry in the central city but lose in the suburbs, giving rise to arguments against requirements for "concurrent majorities." The following tabulation shows how each plan fared in this respect:

Proposal	Area-wide	Central City	Outside C. C.	Net Result
Albuquerque-Bernalillo Co.	Lost	Lost	Lost	Defeated
Atlanta-Fulton Co.	Won	Won	Won	Adopted
Cuyahoga Co. (Cleveland)	Lost	Lost	Lost	Defeated
Denver Metropolitan Area	Won	Won	Lost	Adopted
Durham-Durham Co.	Lost	Lost	Lost	Defeated
Erie Co. (Buffalo), N.Y.	Won	Won	Won	Adopted
Knoxville-Knox Co.	Lost	Lost	Lost	Defeated
Louisville, Ky.	Won	Won	Lost	Defeated
Lucas Co. (Toledo)	Lost	Lost	Lost	Defeated
Macon-Bibb Co.	Lost	Won	Lost	Defeated
Miami-Dade Co.	Won	Won	Lost	Adopted
Nashville-Davidson Co.	Lost	Won	Lost	Defeated [*Editor's note: Adopted 1962*]
Newport News-Warwick	Won	Won	Won	Adopted
Oneida Co., N.Y.	Won	Won	Won	Adopted
Onondaga Co., N.Y.	Won	Won	Won	Adopted
Richmond-Henrico Co.	Won	Won	Lost	Defeated
St. Louis Metropolitan Area	Lost	Lost	Lost	Defeated
Seattle Metropolitan Area	Won	Won	Won	Adopted

Of the 18 proposals surveyed here, only 2 of the 10 which failed of adoption owed their defeat directly to the demand for concurrent majorities—i.e., the Louisville "Plan for Improvement," and the Richmond-Henrico merger proposal. Of the reorganization efforts adopted, there were two, Denver and Miami, which depended only upon an areawide majority and would have lost if concurrent majorities within subareas had also been legally necessary. And there were two defeated plans which received a favorable majority in a central city but lost in outlying territory as well as in total (Macon-Bibb County, and Nashville-Davidson County). In the other 12 of the 18 reorganization efforts studied, pluralities ran parallel in the central and outlying parts of the area concerned, favorably in six instances and unfavorably in the other six. Altogether, this record suggests a somewhat less forbidding cleavage of public attitudes geographically, than some discussions of metropolitan problems might suggest. Nonetheless, the common requirement for multiple majorities for adoption of a large-area reorganization proposal must be recognized as a difficult hurdle to surmount.

But there is an even more troublesome problem which has not been widely emphasized. Any particular reorganization plan submitted to referendum is typically competing for public favor not merely against the status quo ("this particular change against no change at all"), but potentially also against alternative ways of dealing with the problems that gave rise to the proposal. The difficulty of this assignment may be suggested by analogy: it is as if, in order to replace the incumbent of an elective office, some one opposing candidate had to obtain more votes than the total cast for the incumbent *and* all other candidates combined, in a single election open to any number of candidates and without any primary or run-off arrangement.

In several of the reorganization efforts surveyed, some of the most effective and telling opposition emphasized the limitations of the change that was being urged as compared with a different kind of structural adjustment. For example, the St. Louis proposal was attacked on the ground that it contemplated the creation of an additional layer of local government, which might be avoided by another kind of change; and some of the proposals elsewhere for city-county combination met the charge that the fixity of county boundaries made this a less desirable reform than extensive use of the municipal annexation approach. Perhaps in certain instances the preference expressed for "something else" is not entirely sincere, but the variety of problems commonly involved in a restructuring of local government in metropolitan areas makes this a plausible basis for opposing any particular proposition.

Thus, the task of the would-be reorganizer is not merely to arouse public concern with existing conditions that are undesirable, nor even besides this to provide a convincing case that his particular plan would provide a reasonable remedy, but also to be prepared to demonstrate that his proposal is better than any available alternative.

3. *Any consequential local government reorganization in a metropolitan area will inevitably involve "political" issues.*

It is folly to expect that some proposal or approach will have such overwhelming logic from the standpoint of equity or "economy and efficiency" that it can avoid or readily withstand attack from individuals, groups, neighborhoods, or population elements whose position in the area it may seem to jeopardize. Herein, perhaps, lies the most serious limitation of the "outside" adviser, however technically knowledgeable he may be, in developing a reorganization proposal sufficiently oriented to the political facts of life of a particular area that popular acceptability may reasonably be expected.

The 18 efforts which have been reviewed for this study offer numerous illustrations of various kinds of political issues likely to be encountered. For example:

1. The status of individual elective officials and other communities is usually involved. This is obvious where two or more independent governments are proposed to be consolidated, but it is inherent even in a proposal to change the size of a governing body, to eliminate or combine existing offices, or to subordinate some officials or agencies more fully to a governing body or a chief executive, as may be sought in a single-government charter plan. The incumbents affected and at least some of their subordinates are understandably likely to have reservations about such proposed changes.

2. Another difficult political problem pertains to the size and nature of constituencies for members of governing bodies, and for other elective officers. In general, metropolitan reorganization looks toward the development or strengthening of some large-area instrumentality. If the governing body is to be reasonably limited in size, the issue of its members' remoteness or limited accessibility to the public automatically arises. Where the proposed change involves some shift of responsibility from other bodies which have previously served areas of differing population characteristics, an especially difficult problem may exist. Some of the reorganization plans reviewed took explicit account of this kind of situation, and included provisions that were designed to safeguard the future representation interests of diverse subareas.

3. Numerous other groups in the area are likely to have some attachment to existing arrangements which might be affected by the proposed change in the status quo—local government employees, contractors, suppliers, and the like. Several of the reorganization plans reviewed had certain provisions to minimize this prospective issue insofar as local government personnel were concerned— for example, explicit protection of

their employment and retirement rights, in the event of intergovernmental or interagency transfers. Defeat of at least one or two of the proposals studied has been attributed by observers to the vigorous opposition of firms and organizations supplying certain urban-type services (such as refuse collection) on a contract basis in suburban areas.

As the foregoing paragraphs may suggest, the reference here to "political" issues does not mainly involve partisan politics. Among the 18 reorganization efforts reviewed, there was only one (Lucas County, Ohio) where, according to observers, opposing positions by the major political parties played a highly significant part in the referendum campaign. It should be noted, however, that 9 of the 18 areas involved are in the South, where major controversial issues are often fought out within a dominant party rather than between two closely matched parties. Where there is strong divergence in prevailing party loyalty, among various portions of the total area involved in a particular reorganization effort (for example, between a central city and outlying areas), the chance is increased that pro and con attitudes may be taken locally by the opposing parties, or at least by certain of their recognized leaders.

4. *One condition for success in metropolitan reorganization is an intensive and deliberate effort to develop a broad consensus on the best attainable alternative to the status quo.*

This point follows obviously from those stated above, concerning the many barriers to accomplishment of change. It points toward the application of time and effort not only to assemble information about problems which need solution but also to develop a particular plan which has some reasonable prospect of predominant area support. This does not necessarily dictate a willingness to settle for such a low common denominator approach that most of the problems involved are left untouched, although there undoubtedly are situations where a realistic preliminary appraisal will suggest that efforts at desirable change should be postponed.

The record reviewed here tends to support the understandable presumption that a proposal for major structural change has less chance of popular acceptance than would something less extensive . . . only 1 of the 5 least drastic reorganization proposals subject to survey was defeated, as compared with . . . 6 of the 7 proposals involving the greatest structural change. On the other hand, some proposals were attacked in local referendum campaigns on the ground that they were inadequate or palliative in nature. Perhaps one important consideration as to a "best" approach involves looking beyond immediate effects to consider the question: Would the accomplishment of this particular change tend to facilitate—or, on the other hand, to prevent or hamper—adaptations likely to be needed in the future?

It is not to be expected that all elements of potential opposition to reorganization can be avoided or mollified. But it is important: that there be an early, realistic, and hard-headed consideration of the implications of structural change for key groups and leaders in the area; that these implications enter into the choice among possible alternatives in the development of a particular reorganization proposal; and that the process by which a specific proposal is developed be such as to enlist the interest and expression of views by a diverse range of community elements.

* * *

At least three important purposes may be served by a deliberate effort, through hearings or otherwise, to enlist the views of potential opponents as well as probable supporters of metropolitan reorganization: this should provide further insight on the political feasibility of alternative kinds of structural change; it is likely to develop certain of the arguments that will arise in the subsequent referendum campaign, on issues not subject to compromise or adjustment in the proposal as finally developed; and it may serve to win potential backing or at least neutrality from some individuals and groups that might otherwise be hostile through lack of information or through suspicion of the motives of the plan-preparing body.

An alternative point of view might be urged—that the development of a particular reorganization proposal should be handled "close to the chest," to avoid "advance warning" to prospective opponents—if it appeared that the attitudes of various elements are fixed in a rigid and predictable pattern. Fortunately, the record of the various reorganization efforts which have been surveyed tend to discount such a presumption. . . .

* * *

5. *Enlistment of popular support for governmental change in a metropolitan area calls for the use of variety of promotional methods, suited to the diverse composition of the electorate.*

This point sounds like a truism, but failure to take it adequately into account was apparently a major limiting factor in several of the reorganization efforts which have been reviewed. Findings which have been reported in detail about the referendum campaign in

Nashville-Davidson County, Tennessee resemble the impression one may gather for various other areas. In Davidson County . . . the reorganization plan was developed and promoted by individuals with a strong areawide identification—"cosmopolitans"—who did not manage to communicate effectively with that large part of the population lacking such an identification.

Facts . . . suggest that a similar story might commonly be told about the proponents of reorganization in other areas: overconfidence due to predominantly favorable press coverage; heavy reliance upon mass media of communication; little or no development of a precinct or neighborhood system for enlisting popular interest and backing; and only limited use of other face-to-face methods of recruiting voter support.

* * *

This suggests . . . how important it is for efforts at metropolitan reorganization to have the active participation of experienced politicians. Less generally than civic "amateurs" are such individuals likely to underestimate the need to summarize issues simply for many voters; to fall into the error of overconfidence; or to overlook the importance of localized and face-to-face methods of enlisting popular support.

69. The Metropolity and Its Future*

SCOTT GREER

GALBRAITH has remarked that, according to the laws of aerodynamics, it is impossible for the bumblebee to fly. And according to the rules of some political theorists, it is impossible for anything resembling a metropolitan

* Reprinted with permission from *Governing the Metropolis,* by Scott Greer, John Wiley and Sons, 1962. Footnotes omitted.

polity to function. Yet the bumblebee flies, and the metropolis meets, in some fashion, the consequences of massive change. The millions are housed, fed, transported, and policed, and the metropolitan region still maintains its attraction for the migrant. Smog and traffic and farcical contradictions in land use are commonplace in Los Angeles, yet it moves rapidly towards the status of second city in the nation. None of the urban ills of St. Louis prevents its continued growth and increasing prosperity.

SUBSTITUTES FOR METROPOLITAN GOVERNMENT

The metropolis is in little danger of a breakdown. The reason is partly that within the straitjacket of the democratic ideology and the constitutions, there *is* room to maneuver. Coordination takes place at the municipality level. There is a continuum, from voluntary consultation and joint planning among suburbs to those contractual arrangements which house the prisoners of many places in one suburb's jail or draw upon the county government for many basic services. Such consultation and cooperation is in fact the alternative to metropolitan merger proposed by the defenders of little governments. But voluntary cooperation requires an obvious interdependence, a nearly equal cost and benefit ratio, and a rational view of collective needs. It also depends upon an adequate public treasury. It suffers all the political weakness of confederations, and many major services are not possible through such arrangements. In these cases, two subterfuges have been widely adopted: the special district and outside subsidy.

The special district government emerged as an expedient solution for the problems of jurisdictional fragmentation. Created as a new governmental entity, the special district government has access to taxes and borrowing powers outside those granted the municipality. Bypassing the municipal government, it escapes both the jealous particularism of the elected council and the niggardliness of the citizens. Defined as outside the political process, it can apply the rules of thumb appropriate to a business enterprise. At the extreme, as in the case of the New York Port Authority, it can commandeer the

most profitable tasks of government (toll bridges and tunnels and the like), pay its way, and have money to invest.

If we compile a rough check list of the special district governments in the United States today, the total is staggering. School districts, water districts, fire districts, port districts, sanitation districts, park districts—the variety is almost as great as the tasks that local government can perform. Created on an *ad hoc* basis, as needs arise and the local fisc and powers prove inadequate, such districts are frequently the basis for the only adequate services in many suburbs. They are also, in many urban areas, the only metropolitan governmental unit in being. Such metropolitan giants as the New York Port Authority, the Metropolitan St. Louis Sewer District, the Chicago Park District, are partial solutions to some of the problems of metropolitan growth.

However, there are narrow limits to their utility. The services that are their basis must be in wide demand. Many needed services are not considered by the voters. Furthermore, only a few governmental services can be made profitable: most of them are "losers" and remain the prerogative of existing municipal governments. And the losers, whether organized in a special district or not, continue to demand a share of the limited fiscal powers of the jurisdiction. As the local resources (or those the voters will make available within the limits of the state's constitutional provisions) are exhausted in the existing functions of government, the pressure mounts for subsidy from elsewhere. The State government and the federal agencies are the chief sources of outside funds.

Through these channels come supports for the expenses of both central city and suburbs. The welfare burdens of the central city, such as aid to dependent children, aid to the handicapped, preventive medicine, clinics, hospitals, school lunches, and the like are greatly lightened by funds from elsewhere. The problems involved in rebuilding the obsolescent plant at the center of the city are turned over to the Urban Renewal Authority, a local recipient of massive federal grants. In the suburbs also the cost of plant expansion is lightened greatly by what Wood has called "the new Federalism." The Federal Highway Program, in building great new arterials and circumferential highways, solves many fiscal problems of the suburbs, and any aid to schools (especially that earmarked for buildings) will be disproportionately distributed in suburbia, for the central city's educational plant is nearly complete. In suburbia, too, welfare costs are passed upwards.

CONSEQUENCES OF USING SUBSTITUTES

These expedients have consequences for the situation which brought them about. They are, for one thing, removed from the surveillance and control of the local voters, and may be largely inaccessible to the politician and governmental official. Thus they violate the norm of local self-rule and responsiility to the local voters. This is the very reason for their creation: they bypass the local political process. Money and powers guarded jealously from the central city and suburban municipalities are passed upwards to Washington, from which they return free of the political blame that local officials would have to bear. Ironically, the net result of the system which keeps government "close to the people" is its removal as far as possible from the people—to the United States Congress, a State agency, or a Federal agency. Or, as with special districts, the power is handed to agencies whose decisions are rarely ever known to their clients, much less controlled by them, agencies which have been dubbed "ghost governments."

Another important aspect of these expedients is their segmental nature. Each task of government is handled without reference to others, even though their interaction is crucial for the developing shape of the city and its welfare. (It is not, at present, even possible to learn the total resources and powers of the federal government engaged in any given metropolis. Apparently *nobody* knows.) But the increasing network of speedy trafficways continues, blindly, the change in space-time ratio which produces the suburban dispersion. As the arterials multiply, as the circumferential highways tie suburb to suburb, as the center hub becomes a five-level interchange, the result can only be a continual stimulus to further centrifugal development. At the same time, however, the urban redevelopment program is investing billions of dollars in rebuilding the central city for its old uses—commercial, industrial, residential. Thus two massive programs are under way, each largely financed outside the metropolis, each the *raison d'etre* for huge bureaucracies—and each directly contradicting the purposes of the other. The central city is declining as a useful site for activity precisely because of the land accessible in the suburbs; to renovate downtown sites while increasing the ease of movement outwards is to give with one hand and take away with the other.

In fact, the strongest argument for local determination of the crucial decisions in public capital expansion is based upon the effects of partial and unplanned action from above. Those who are neighbors, committed to the same metropolitan site and social system, *must live with the consequences of these decisions.* The shape of the city, the quality of services, the cost-benefit ratio, the nature of the public order, all of these aspects of urban government are peculiarly the burden of the population living in the area. Frequently there is no technical rule for a decision: when a freeway is located, some people will benefit at little cost, others will lose. Somebody's ox is always gored, and the democratic polity is in theory supposed to allow that person his day in court. This is not possible when autonomous agencies, local or federal, move without the consent of the governed.

To be sure, combining all functions and powers of government in the metropolitan area would not guarantee an integrated polity. There is ample evidence of lack of planning among the agencies of any central city government: the struggles of the great bureaucracies for survival and growth frequently resemble those of giant lizards in the jungles of the Jurassic Era. It is certain, however, that little coordination can come about in the present ecology of political orders: the power of legal autonomy is a strong shield against forced confrontation. Thus the planning agencies in a great city may live their lives in complete ignorance of each other; traffic engineers and urban renewal agency heads may be complete strangers. Nobody is accountable beyond the narrow limits of his designated task. The metropolitan polity is a net result: a continuous, cumulative total of the decisions made is suburban municipality, fire districts, metropolitan district, central city bureaucracy, county government, federal agency, and state bureau.

THE FUTURE COURSE
OF THE METROPOLIS

The metropolis in being is, in many respects, a museum of the urban past. Because dense areas were built up for the City of Steam, because they represent social value derived from the funded energy of the past, we have today the near-obsolescence of much of the downtown. Because the suburbs developed outside the central city's jurisdiction we have today the patchwork quilt of jurisdictions on the outskirts. In short, we inherit our given conditions from the past, and they are largely unforeseen results of expediential decisions. It is fairly certain that the people of the metropolis are not concerned with governmental change that

would allow more foresight in the future. What, then, can we expect to emerge from the present course of development?

Returning to basic considerations, we must remember that the process of increase in scale continues. History, the unfolding of consequences through time, does not stand still to be photographed. We may confidently predict a further increase in the societal surplus, a further decline in the time and money cost of movement, a further extension of the organizational networks. From these we certainly expect a continuing increase in the absolute and relative size of the United States' population living in metropolitan areas.

Increase in the societal surplus will result in a continuing upward movement in social rank for the entire population. Mechanization and the use of nonhuman energy sources will make unskilled labor obsolete; the increasing demand for rationality will increase the workforce in the areas of organizational control—those workers who manipulate symbols and persons. But mechanization will invade these areas also: electronic computers can store and process information much more rapidly and cheaply than their present day substitutes, the white-collar girls. Thus we will continue to experience a decline in routine jobs and an increase in those demanding specialized skills. The professional and semi-professional worker, the technician and the manager will increase at the expense of unskilled and semiskilled labor. To prepare for the former jobs, however, individuals will be forced to increase their formal education. Thus occupational and educational levels will go upwards together. The net effect of such a workforce, with its machines and sources of energy, will be a continuous increase in the social surplus: real income will rise concomitantly.

As this occurs, the range of social choice will also increase and will be available to more people. The choice between an urban and familistic way of life will become a constant differentiator, as families at all levels of social rank have enough "elbow room" to choose how and, within limits, where they will live. With so many opportunities for advancement open, we may expect acculturation to progress further: most ethnic minorities should become largely invisible in a few decades. Thus the total population of the metropolis should approximate more and more closely the social class range of those now in suburbia.

The space-time ratio will continue to affect, drastically, the layout and population distribution of the metropolitan area. As highways reach further into the countryside, as the automobile-owning population becomes well-nigh universal, the spaces between arterials will fill in. Residential expansion on the fringes will accommodate millions of new urban residents in the immediate future. Urban redevelopment programs may try to attract them to the central city, but as Raymond Vernon has recently stated, "it is one of the paradoxes of urban growth today that the increase in the supply of urban land is probably outstripping the demand." Automobile and roadway continually recapture new domains for the metropolitan complex.

Changes in the space-time ratio for transport and communication will also allow continual decentralization of work. The further dispersion of work sites requires no decrease of effective centralized control, in the day of two-way telecommunication and jet travel. The sites for work and commerce will also move rapidly away from the center insofar as truck transport can take the place of rail and water. Leon Moses has recently documented the shift of truck terminals outwards in Chicago. They follow either the warehouses which follow the retail outlets, or the industrial plants which follow the most desirable labor force. The economic map of the metropolis moves from a city with hinterland to a larger unit, in Vernon's terms a "region."

THE CHANGING TASKS OF THE CENTRAL CITY

Let us turn, then, to the consequences of these ongoing changes for the social structure of the metropolis. The central city's role, in a drama already different from one in which it played the lead and most of the characters, can be expected to alter further. As the nonsegregated and familistic populations move outward the city becomes increasingly the municipality of the ethnic and the working class. The remnants of the traditional urban working class, familistic, and usually first or second generation ethnic, will recede slowly from the neighborhoods that are their urban home. The colored populations will continue to increase at a steady rate. The continued upgrading of social rank will have a differential effect for these, most segregated and disprivileged segments of the society. Negroes, Puerto Ricans, and Mexicans, last in the urban labor force from the rural hinterlands, are concentrated in precisely the kinds of jobs most likely to be abolished by mechanization. They are also segregated within the wards of the central city. Thus the population of the center will shoulder a disproportionately heavy share of the social burdens produced by automation.

The center's residential function will be, then, more consistently biased towards the lower half of the job distribution. Its other functions can be expected to change slowly through time. As those activities that are more conveniently located in the suburbs depart, those that are best suited to the center will stand out in sharper relief. One obvious use for the center is the interchange, the crossroads for superhighways knitting the metropolitan map together. Another is that of exchange center for those items which require an areawide market. Still another use is that of a site for activities which require personal confrontation, those negotiations between firms and consultations with experts that must be conducted face to face. Nobody knows just how large these uses will bulk, in the aggregate.

Nor does anybody know how large the demand will be for the urbane living conditions of the center. We can expect those whose life-style fits the apartment-house districts to continue their residency; we do not know how large a proportion of the total they will be. We can also expect the wealthy to continue part-time residence in such places as Beacon Hill, Nob Hill, and Executive House. As many have pointed out, for the aged also a safe downtown apartment-house neighborhood may be preferable to the dispersed areas of suburbia. But factors of cost and budget, as well as the rarity of safe neighborhoods in many parts of center, will probably limit the return of the "post-child" family to the urban center.

THE DEVELOPING SUBURBS

The suburbs should be, increasingly, a world inhabited by the lower-middle to upper social ranks of the metropolis. The raw, new neighborhoods will slowly settle in, with public facilities developed and horticulture softening the angles of the tract development. Though some persons have looked at the cheap neighborhoods built for craftsmen and operatives and predicted the slums of the future, this seems unlikely. Instead, the continuous input of time and energy and money by the suburban home owner, the do-it-yourself movement, can be expected to upgrade or at least stabilize these neighborhoods for many years. The decay of neighborhoods is a social phenomenon; as we have seen, suburban neighborhoods develop very powerful communication flows and a normative structure capable of educating the new neighbors. This in turn results in that regular input of energy which prevents age of structure from being synonymous with decay of structure.

Since the suburbs will include the richest markets for household consumables, the movement of convenience shopping outward will continue in full force. From neighborhood store to shopping center to the giant commercial subnucleus with its shopping malls, meeting rooms, and branches of downtown stores and banks, a regular system of retail dominance will develop. In large segments of the suburbs we can expect a partial reintegration of the lives of suburbanites; the giant subnucleus can produce a concentration of work places and contain the essential folk institutions of church, school, government, recreation, and the like. Since they will also contain a large proportion of friends and relatives, as well as the omnipresent neighbors, they may become self-contained social worlds for many of their inhabitants.

It is even possible that many activities now universally conceived of as best located in the downtown area may also move towards suburbia. The public arts, for example, music and theatre, ballet and the museums might well be decentralized. Their chief markets are, after all, the suburban populations. And with the development of convenient transport within the giant subnuclei, a touring company or a traveling exhibit could easily move from one area to another.

At the level of economic and social functions, the central city will continue to recede as the overwhelming force of the metropolis. Though for many it still maintains its magic as hub and symbolic center of the metropolitan community, it is in many respects simply one differentiated area of residence and work, equal among equals in the cluster of great subnuclei which make up the metropolis. Its proportionate size does not stand for a proportionate representation of the total urban population, and its polity is not that of the metropolitan region. Nor, given its biased sample urbanites, could it be. Let us turn then to the probable developments of the polity in each half of the urban region.

THE FUTURE POLITY

For each half of the metropolis we will ask: how does its nature condition the burdens of government, and what are its resources for handling those tasks?

The central city is the inheritor of the aged neighborhoods and the obsolete workplaces of a Paleotechnic city. Two movements are afoot to change this social heritage: the metropolitan government movement, and the urban redevelopment program. The first aims to solve the problem by reincorporating the center with all its sprawling suburbs into a new unity; we have already considered the problems and prospects of such an enterprise. The urban redevelopment program would appear almost equally hopeless, *if* one accepts the enthusiastic plans of some of its backers to remake the central city.

The central city of even a moderate-sized metropolis is an enormous plant. There are mile upon mile of neighborhoods built in another day, for other lifestyles, and therefore depopulated by the kinds of people who once built them and lived in them. These are street after street of tall loft buildings, high rise elevator warehouses. These are now hopelessly obsolete in competition with suburban warehouses, whose horizontal floors allow the use of new and more efficient equipment (moving belts, fork lifts, and the like). There are hundred of acres of neighborhoods whose street space, already far too narrow for contemporary vehicular traffic, must also provide parking, for the automobile was not envisaged when they were built. Though this plant has a social value (for the structures are often sound) it is not attractive to enterprises that are better situated in suburbia's new acres. It still has a market value, because it has uses: and those who wish to rebuild the city must confront these uses as reflected in market value. (The American norms of local government do not easily permit simple confiscation.) The price for purchase and demolition in most central cities has been estimated at $160,000,000 and up per square mile: at the end of these processes one would have only a bare plot of ground. Such a site might or might not be valuable to private enterprise; to "write it down" to prices competitive with new land on the outskirts, however, would result in monstrous public costs.

Robert Wood has called the New York City Urban Renewal Program probably the most vigorously developed and certainly the largest in the United States. Yet if one includes work complete, in progress, or definitely planned for the future, only 1,000 acres will be affected. His estimate is that 5,000 acres of New York City are already so far gone that they demand rebuilding—and by the time the work on the 1,000 is complete, there is every likelihood that the 5,000 total will remain approximately the same. Furthermore, Vernon has called attention to what he calls the grey areas, those far outside the central location (which he believes *does* have use value) and far gone in their obsolescence. For such areas he can foresee little demand, either as commercial or residential building sites. One might, in fact, wonder if urban redevelopment does not require eventually rebuilding the entire older city. Against such problems the present program, massive as it appears in isolation, is a drop in the bucket.

POLICY FOR THE
CENTRAL CITY

The central city is not apt to change radically in its composition. Its people will be working class, ethnic, residents of neighborhoods ranging from the slums to the shabby genteel hand-me-downs of the past middle classes. If this is so, it will probably call forth specific kinds of governmental action. Instead of pouring public wealth into new building, hoping that a neighborhood will attract private investors, it will seem more relevant to spend money on the conservation of existing neighborhoods, working to protect existing homes through improvement, better public services, and most of all support of the existing communication and normative structures that lead to reinvestment in their maintenance.

If the central city is to be the workingman's municipality, its governors will eventually come to assess its programs with this fact in mind, rather than evoking its lost role of center and symbol to a region. Thus its educational needs will be defined as different from those of suburbia. Such institutions as the University of Pennsylvania, the University of Chicago, or the University of Southern California, private universities which service the suburbs and the nation, will be considered less relevant to the sons of workers and therefore to the city's polity than the "open door colleges." These publicly supported institutions must accommodate the increasingly large percentage of high school graduates who can and must go to college if they are to be useful members of the labor force. The educational system of the central city will also be forced to concern itself with the problem of retraining the technologically displaced, for the central city will inherit a large share of the social costs involved in such displacement.

The government of the central city can also be expected to accept the responsibility of housing, policing, educating, and servicing the neighborhoods of nonwhite minorities, rapidly becoming its single largest voting bloc. Segregation in housing and schools, and differential treatment by the agencies of government (particularly by the police) is becoming politically inexpedient in the short run, foolhardy in the long run. While new land uses and new industry are important for the declining fiscal prowess of the city government, such new uses, as far as they further shorten the supply of housing available to nonwhites, are gift horses which will be subject to increasingly sharp inspec-

tion as nonwhites respond at the polls.

The resources available to the central city government in responding to its status and problems as a working-class municipality are changing rapidly. While the property tax base is slowly declining, a result of changing population and the increase in public facilities, new taxes are being invented. The earnings tax which applies to all who work in the city, suburbanite and city resident alike, amounts to a radical readjustment of equity. Departing from property as an index of use and ability to pay, the earnings tax is based upon the chief source of wealth in our society, income. The suburbanite, who uses the city for his livelihood, pays a share of the maintenance.

The suburbanite also pays as the federal government accepts more fiscal responsibility for the central city. The suburban personal income tax far outweighs that of the city. And we have already noted the present importance of federal funds for the metropolis. With the increasingly important role of urban affairs in the federal government, we can expect more subsidy, for renewal, conservation, education, and the like. Such funds can be used to adjust the present limits upon the life space of the nonwhite population: the conservation of neighborhoods and the broadened base for higher education would do much to level the present distinctions by color. As for the grey areas, as well as the miles of shabby genteel housing outside them, they may find their most suitable use as areas of open occupancy for those now crowded into the Negro ghettoes. The declining neighborhoods of the central city may be seen as a major resource for increasing the housing available to the segregated. Open occupancy combined with a sophisticated and well-financed program of neighborhood organization, rebuilding, and conservation may solve several problems at once.

In short, if the central city is viewed in its new role as a specialized area in the metropolitan complex, a home for the working class and the ethnics, its situation is not so desperate. If it is viewed as still the major and most valuable part of the metropolis, one which should be inclusive of the total population, the symbol and hub of central tendencies in the entire urban complex, its future is dark. The arterials move outward month by month, the circumferentials circle the area in concentric rings, and the automobile becomes standard equipment. The fifty million new urbanites of the next few decades provide a long-run and lucrative market for continuous new development on the fringes. It is unlikely that the center can compete as the site for much of this new growth.

POLICY FOR SUBURBIA

In the suburbs the limiting conditions are also a result of past commitments. The dozens or hundreds of small jurisdictions also result from the governmental "freeze." Many of them have little or no space for industry, inadequate commercial districts, and no room for parks, playgrounds, and educational facilities, and they are landlocked by neighboring domains. Each enjoys a degree of autonomy, and the price is that of the isolated peasant village—it is alone with its fiscal and governmental problems. For the fortunate few in Valhalla, this is no problem; for many others it is a basic and continuing one.

The problems in the life-cycle of a suburb are as follows. First, the determination of land use, then the provisions of governmental facilities and resources, then the maintenance of the area's character, and finally the adjustment to change in the population. As the neighborhoods grow older they lose their competitive attraction for the social rank which built them, and are slowly invaded and eventually populated by a different class. Such change may be agonizing for the older inhabitants, committed financially and emotionally to their old image of the suburban country town with a pretty name. It will not be so agonizing, however, for most of those who might lead a fight to repulse the invaders, for they will already have moved outward.

The resources available to the suburbs have been detailed. Massive and probably increasing federal aid for schools, roads, sanitation, and the like, augmented by such fiscal dodges as the special district, supplement the *ad hoc* cooperation among municipalities. To be sure, as the burdens of government press heavier on the fisc, there may be efforts to solve the problem by changing land use, attracting industry and other high tax-yield activities. However, such efforts are usually hamstrung by the very conditions which stimulate them; awareness of serious fiscal problems typically follows the building up of available sites. The time lag between public act and consequence (and the magic phrase "a city of homes") limits the political appeal of such efforts when they are still practical. But above all, the location of activities tends to result from position in the space-time grid of the city, not from the blandishments of local councilmen. . . .

As for the problems created by the slow change, the movement of a suburb downhill in the scale of housing values, there seems to be no real solution possible for any given unit. What occurs instead is the dispersion of the population to new areas now preferable to the old neighborhood. The continual increase in land resulting from the changing space-time ratio solves most of the problems of invasion by the same mechanism which brings them about in the first place, movement to new locales.

In summary, then, there is no polity which sees the metropolitan complex as a whole, continuous in time and interdependent in the present. The basic and pressing needs of the metropolitan population, as they can be translated into political pressure, result in new burdens for government. Thus the public sector of the economy, like the private sector, responds to those who can and will pay. The metropolitan citizen does not appear willing to pay in money or loss of local self-rule for a metropolitan government. He is willing to pay for special districts, area-wide in scope, to solve his most pressing problems. Sewage disposal can be such a pressing problem. Traffic and transport may well become another interest which causes the electoral turnstiles to ring. If so, there will be metropolitan transportation systems under coordinated management. But transport, crucial as it is to many other public tasks and basic to the emerging shape of the city, will then function even more freely outside the pressures of other competing and legitimate interests. As Wood puts it:

> The highway transportation agencies, the mortgage programs of the Federal Housing Administration and Veterans Administration proceed on the same philosophy of supply and demand that governs the behavior of private firms. . . . The final result is that a public sector committed to this ideology by financing and structure offers no countervailing influence against the trends generated in the private sector. . . . They underwrite and accelerate the process of scatteration.

This scatteration is more than physical. It is also a scatteration in social and political space, a separation of control and planning centers, and therefore a forswearing of the possibility of politically or technically rational policy. The conservative, steady state governments of the central cities drift towards a polyarchy or great bureaucracies largely moved and shaken by programs generated elsewhere. The patchwork governments of suburbia fight for their place in the sun of federal aid, hoping someone, somewhere else, will solve the problems of their collective destiny for them. Businessmen expect action from governmental officials: the politicians wait to bless any decision upon which interested parties can agree. As Morris Janowitz has put it: "The issue is not the manipulation of the citizenry by a small elite, but rather the inability of elites to create the conditions required for making decisions."

The metropolitan area is the dominant form of spatial community in the present society of large and increasing scale. It is also a new form: the wide and variegated pattern of settlement reflects the consequences of changes in the space-time ratio, increase in the surplus, and the extension of networks of interdependence, communication, and control. The changes have far outrun the older models of local government, and the specific form of the generalized norms which provided their legitimation. We harvest the results in a weak and passive governmental response to ongoing change. As our world is transformed these older forms change their meaning—become, in fact, caricatures of themselves. In many cases defenses against any government at all, the multiplying suburbs cause a drift of power upwards to the highest level, the federal bureaucracies.

As problems press and action results, we do see a form of social invention taking place in the metropolis. Special district agencies, government by contract and subcontract, earnings taxes and public corporate enterprise, are ingenious and remarkable stopgaps. They allow us to retain our pieties, while getting on somehow with the job at hand. People get what they want to pay for, within the limts of their inherited folklore and sacred constitutions. Of course, they get many other things in the bargain, some of which they do not want. But the development of large-scale society has been in no respect planned from the present into the future. Nor are we certain of our abilities to do so: the sheer complexity of knowledge required is staggering, while the choice points are really political issues —basic, moral, and not to be solved through scientific argument. For a choice point, in political life, is no simple decision between right and wrong: it is a forced choice between two mutually contradictory values, *both* of which are sacred and precious to someone. Thus it is just as well that the social scientist cannot assume the position of the philosopher-king.

We cannot believe in a wide distribution of power, and therefore of freedom, and at the same time insist upon a rigorous control of the future. To be sure, this frequently means that we all cooperate in producing something that nobody wants. Such a result may not be simply due to ignorance or clumsiness, however; it may mirror the plural interests of a pluralistic society. The loose system allows some room for variation and innovation (though implementing them is difficult); while it greatly overweighs the experiences of the past, it allows for some continuity. Change *is* accomplished; order *is* maintained. There are even unique values in the present system. How else can the polity of a village be reproduced in large-scale society, save in residential municipalities? Furthermore, where else in our society are the segregated, the insulted and injured, as fairly represented as in *their* municipality, the central city? Such results were not planned. "The metropolitan community is continuously improvised: its evolution is organic, not rational; change is crescive, not revolutionary; problems are solved by trial and error rather than by fiat."

Part X

PROGRAMS AND POLICIES

A MAJOR function of the law is to impose a ban on certain actions that are considered to be inimical to public health, safety, welfare, or morals. Primary responsibility for the enforcement of these laws rests with police agencies of various types—national, state, and local. Effective police work is essential, but many different notions exist as to the type of law enforcement that is most desirable. As Herman Goldstein notes in his consideration of the exercise of discretion by police, a tacit assumption exists in some quarters that all laws should be fully enforced at all times. Such a policy of "full enforcement" implies that the police cannot exercise any discretion. Obviously, this viewpoint is entirely unrealistic because, if for no other reason, sufficient resources are never available to permit constant, complete enforcement of all laws. Mr. Goldstein presents an informative analysis of the dilemma faced by the police in their effort to decide just how the laws shall be enforced.

The proportion of our population over 65 years of age is increasing. Many older people lack adequate resources to maintain for themselves a decent standard of living. Elias Cohen describes the impact of an aging population on state governments and outlines some of the things the states have done and may do in an effort to meet the needs of this increasingly large segment of our people.

Urban renewal is a controversial technique employed in recent years by local governments, under the stimulation of federal aid, to combat blight and slums. George Duggar relates some current attacks on urban renewal and demonstrates the need for better public understanding of its purposes and methods.

Almost everyone accepts the proposition that opportunities for the unskilled, the untrained, and the uneducated are constantly decreasing in our technological society. The importance of this proposition to education, particularly higher education, is often not appreciated. Its significance is sometimes overlooked by educators as well as laymen. Alonzo G. Grace calls attention to the need for a re-evaluation of policies with regard to higher education in light of the two chief goals of education: (1) to provide the kind and amount of education that will enable each individual to develop to the limit of his potentiality, and (2) to insure national security. John A. Perkins examines the crucial problem of the professor's teaching load, the faculty-student ratio, as it relates to quality and efficiency in higher education. He stresses the need for better understanding of the factors that determine "reasonable" teaching loads.

The results of agricultural research have been most directly beneficial to the farmer. They have, indeed, changed his way of life in recent times. L. L. Rummell points to the benefits of farm research to all the people, not just to farmers. The work of agricultural experiment stations, operating in every state, affects the lives of city people as well as rural dwellers.

Planning in the sense of doing a comprehensive job of forecasting needs on a statewide basis and projecting programs to meet such needs is not generally considered to be a major responsibility of state governments. In another sense, planning permeates state and local governments. In order that it may be prepared to meet future demands, even those of the immediate future, each agency must plan so as to maintain its physical plant, expand its institutional facilities, articulate land use with other public or private developments, and coordinate its work with related activities. Indeed, according to James W. Martin, there is much more of this somewhat limited type of planning than is generally realized.

Among the most controversial kinds of legislation recently enacted by some states is the right to work law, which prohibits the imposition of union membership as a condition of employment. Proponents of such laws maintain that they protect freedom of individual choice, i.e., freedom on the part of the worker not to join a union if he chooses not to do so. Opponents, particularly organized labor, contend that right to work laws weaken unions and encourage workers to enjoy the benefits obtained by the unions without their support. J. C. Gibson examines "The Legal and Moral Basis of Right to Work Laws" and concludes that the advocates of this type of limitation on union activity have the better case.

In an effort to avoid the consequences of outlawing the closed and union shop, unions in some instances resorted to the agency shop whereby employees covered by a negotiated agreement who chose not to join the union were required, as a condition of employment, to pay "service fees" to the union—membership dues by another name. This practice was challenged by nonunion employees under Florida's right to work law, and the Florida Supreme Court held it to be illegal. This action was upheld by the United States Supreme Court in *Retail Clerks International Association, Local 1625 v. Alberta Schermerhorn*.

70. Police Discretion: The Ideal Versus the Real*

HERMAN GOLDSTEIN

PARKING meters are a common source of irritation to both the public and the police. They were a particular source of annoyance to a city manager-friend of mine whose council membership included one man whose sole concern in life appeared to be those vehicles parked alongside meters on which the time had expired. After repeated criticism of the police department for its failure to achieve a greater degree of compliance and enforcement, the city manager was moved to speak on the issue. He offered the councilman a choice from among what he referred to as levels of enforcement. He suggested that the city could assign one police officer to enforcing all of the meters throughout the city. If this was done, he anticipated that the frequency of checks would be low and the number of overtime violations and red flags would increase. On the other hand, he could assign one police officer to each parking meter in the city. With such extensive coverage, there would be reasonable assurance that a summons would be issued at the moment the meter expired. The city manager then suggested that the council determine

* Reprinted from *Public Administration Review*, September 1963, by permission of the American Society for Public Administration. Footnotes omitted.

through its appropriation, just how many police officers were to be provided and what level of enforcement was desired as between the two extremes. The point was well made.

Without full recognition on his part, the city manager was addressing himself to one of the very basic problems in law enforcement today. We need only substitute people for parking meters and the broader categories of crime for red overtime flags. Given the total amount of criminality in a community and the resources with which to cope with it, what is the position or policy of the local law enforcement agency? Is the agency committed to a concept of "full enforcement" of all laws, or is it committed to something less than full enforcement?

A policy of "full enforcement" implies that the police are required and expected to enforce all criminal statutes and city ordinances at all times against all offenders. It suggests that the police are without authority to ignore violations, to warn offenders when a violation has in fact occurred, or to do anything short of arresting the offender and placing a charge against him for the specific crime committed. It views the police function to be that of relating the provisions of the law to a fine measurement of the quantum of evidence. Out of this cold and somewhat mechanical calculation evolves an answer which provides the basis for police action.

The exercise of discretion, on the other hand, suggests that the police are required, because of a variety of factors, to decide overtly how much of an effort is to be made to enforce specific laws. It recognizes that actions short of arrest may achieve the desired goal. It implies that a police officer may decide not to make an arrest even in those situations in which an offense has been committed and both the offender and the evidence are at hand. It tends to portray police officers as something other than automatons—as reasonable men whose judgment is essential in determining whether or not to invoke the criminal process.

To date, this dilemma has been of principal concern to those interested in the total system for the administration of criminal justice—those interested in the workings of the prosecution, the courts, and the correctional agencies as well as the police. To understand how the system functions in its entirety, these students of criminal law necessarily focused their attention at that point where it is most commonly determined whether or not a person is to be subject to the system—on the initial screening function performed by the police. If a person is arrested, he enters the system and the path which he takes, in large measure, is established. If he is not arrested, the action of the police terminates the case before the person enters the system and the action is not subject to further review.

The bibliography of thinking on this subject is rapidly increasing. This body of thought and analysis is of more than academic interest to the police. It has some very practical implications.

What is the position of the average police administrator in these deliberations? He is most likely to support the view—somewhat hesitatingly—that he is committed to a policy of full enforcement. It is, after all, the policy most commonly enunciated by police agencies. In contrast, the mere suggestion that a police administrator exercises discretion in fulfilling his job may be taken as an affront—an attack upon the objective and sacrosanct nature of his job—that of enforcing the law without fear or favor. Here too, there is a little hesitation—an awareness that discretion must be and is exercised. But like planned parenthood, it may be something you practice; it is not something you admit or even discuss.

This awkward position, in my opinion, places the average police official in a most embarrassing situation. What are the facts?

Do we have full enforcement, as the term is defined here? Obviously, we do not. How often have law enforcement personnel released a drunk and disorderly person without charging him? released a juvenile offender to his parents? warned a driver who had clearly committed a violation? ignored the enforcement of some city ordinance? arrested an individual known to have committed fornication or adultery? arranged for the release of a narcotic addict in exchange for information? dropped charges against an assailant when the victim failed to cooperate in the prosecution? ignored Sunday blue laws or simply been instructed not to enforce a specific law?

And yet, in acknowledging that some or all of these practices exist, police officials feel a sense of guilt; that these actions were not quite proper; and that they had no basis in law. Why, then, do police officials do these things? Because they are, consciously or unconsciously, acknowledging what they do not wish to proclaim—that the police must exercise discretion.

THE EXERCISE OF DISCRETION

Why must discretion be exercised? Let us take a look at some of the laws under which the police operate, some of the procedures which must be followed, and some of the pressures which exist in the typical community which the police serve.

Examine, for example, the criminal code of any one of our states. By its action, the legislature has attempted to establish those forms of conduct which its members desire to be declared criminal. But this action, as reflected in the statement of the criminal law, is often expressed in such broad terms as to render a clear interpretation of the legislature's intentions most difficult. Ambiguity may be intentional so as to provide greater flexibility in enforcement; it may result from a failure to envisage the day-to-day problems encountered by the police; or it may simply be a result of language limitations. Whatever the basis for the broad statement of the law, the need for resolving these ambiguities frequently places the police in the position of having to determine the forms of conduct which are to be subject to the criminal process.

The State of Illinois has a typically broad statute defining gambling. Under its provisions, the flip of a coin to determine who shall purchase coffee or the playing of penny-ante poker must be considered a violation. As a general policy, the Chicago Police Department devotes its efforts to seeking out gambling activities which are part of an organized operation. We do not devote manpower to ferreting out social card games conducted in the privacy of a home. But, upon complaint, we have an obligation to conduct an investigation of any alleged gambling activity.

In March of this year, the department received a complaint of gambling in the basement of an American Legion Post. Three police officers were sent to investigate. They quickly established that the affair was being run by the post auxiliary as a benefit and that a variation of bingo was to be played with proceeds going to the men at a veterans' hospital. The officers politely warned against any activity which would be considered gambling and

left. The patrons of the social, however, got panicky, grabbed their hats and coats and fled. The expected flurry of letters and newspaper articles followed. One such article concluded with this statement addressed to the Superintendent: "Most of the people of Chicago don't want you or your men to raid a women's social. They want you to go chase some crooks and leave the good people alone."

Both state statutes and city ordinances may be explicit in defining conduct to be considered criminal, but there may be little expectation on the part of those who enacted the laws that they be enforced to the letter. The statute or ordinance may be stating the ideals of the community; that adulterous activity, for example, will not be tolerated. Through this action, the community is placed on record as opposing a form of conduct considered morally wrong. Lawmakers and citizens alike derive a certain degree of comfort from having legislated against such activity. Should this false sense of comfort be a source of concern to the legislator, he is faced with a dilemma: he might more easily choose to seek full enforcement than to be caught supporting the repeal of such a prohibition. Since few legislative consciences are upset, it falls to the police agency to live with the law without enforcing it.

The problem does not always stem from a double standard in matters of morality. Often it stems from mere obsolescence. Earlier this year, the Chicago Police Department was subject to the wrath of the community for having arrested a driver of a jeep, equipped with a snow plow, which was used in the plowing of neighborhood sidewalks as a friendly gesture and without charge. The young officer who made the arrest had been confronted with a complaint. The benevolent driver had piled snow in a driveway to the displeasure of its owner. The officer was unable to find an ordinance that prohibited piling snow in driveways, but he did find an ordinance which prohibited four-wheeled vehicles from being driven on sidewalks. The public became enraged as news of this action spread and we were once again asked if we had run out of honest-to-goodness crooks in need of apprehension. Members of the department no longer arrest the drivers of four-wheeled sidewalk plows; the ordinance, however, remains on the books. We have just decided not to enforce it.

Another major factor which forces the exercise of discretion is the limitation on manpower and other resources —a factor to which previous reference was made. Few police agencies have the number of personnel that would be required to detect the total amount of criminality which exists in a community and to prosecute all offenders. Rarely is consideration given to the relationship between the volume of what can be termed criminal acts and the resources available to deal with them. New legislation declaring a form of conduct to be criminal is rarely accompanied by an appropriation to support the resources for its enforcement. The average municipal administrator who has budget responsibilities brings a different orientation to the problem than does the police chief: his determination as to the size of the police force is based more directly upon a value judgment as to what the tax structure can afford rather than upon a determination of the degree to which the community wishes to enforce the criminal laws; he is more concerned with efficiency, production, and quality of services in handling the routine tasks which accrue to the police and which are so important to the citizenry; he has only a slight interest in or knowledge of the provisions of the criminal law.

Since there are no established priorities for the enforcement of laws prohibiting one type of conduct as against another, the police official must determine the manner in which available manpower and equipment will be used. The daily assignment of manpower is, therefore, perhaps the most easily iden-

tifiable exercise of discretion on the part of the police.

*   *   *

In establishing priorities of enforcement, greater attention is ordinarily given to more serious crimes. A determination not to arrest is most common at the level of the petty offender—and especially if the offender is an otherwise law-abiding citizen. Policies—albeit unwritten—begin to evolve. Just as social gamblers may be arrested only if their activities become organized and move into public places, so drunkards may be arrested only if they are belligerent and homeless as distinct from those who are cooperative and long-established residents.

Discretion may be exercised on the basis of a police officer's particular assignment. Many police agencies have officers assigned to specific types of investigations, such as those relating to homicides, burglaries, or narcotics. Officers so assigned understandably consider their respective specialized function as being of greatest importance to the department. The generalization can be made that police officers frequently refrain from invoking the criminal process for conduct which is considered of less seriousness than that which they are primarily responsible for investigating. A group of officers, intent on solving a homicide, for example, will complain bitterly of the lack of prostitutes on the streets from whom they may obtain information. Narcotic detectives will likewise make frequent use of gamblers and may even tolerate petty larcenies and minor drug violations on the part of their informants. Whatever the merits of the practice, the goal is an acceptable one: that of solving the more serious crime.

Where the volume of criminal activity is high, it is common to observe police policies which result in the dropping of charges against minor assailants when the victim is unwilling to testify. Without a complainant, the case cannot usually be prosecuted successfully. While an effort can be made to prosecute in the name of the state, the mere volume of work demanding attention ordinarily rules out a decision to do so. The determination not to proceed is clearly an exercise of discretion and terminates at this early stage in the process a case in which an offense has clearly occurred and an offender was identified and apprehended.

Discretion is often exercised by the police in a sincere effort to accomplish a social good. This is a sort of humanitarian gesture in which the police achieve the desired objective without full imposition of the coldness and harshness of the criminal process. The drunk may be ushered home; the juveniles turned over to their parents; the new woman driver warned of being found headed in the wrong direction on a one-way street. It is the exercise of discretion such as this to accomplish a desired goal to which others refer when they exhort the police to enforce the "spirit" rather than the "letter" of the law.

These are some of the reasons why the police do, in fact, exercise discretion not to invoke the criminal process in many cases. These same considerations provide ample indication that the police do not, in fact, engage in full enforcement. Why then are the police so reluctant to acknowledge that discretion is exercised?

REASONS FOR NOT ACKNOWLEDGING THE EXERCISE OF DISCRETION

To acknowledge that law enforcement officials do exercise discretion requires an overt act—the articulation of a position—an action which is rare among those in the police field. Most law enforcement officials long ago resigned themselves to the role of the underdog upon whom the unsolved problems of society were piled high. Having developed what might best be termed a defensive posture, the police have, for example, widely accepted responsibility for all that is criminal despite the fact that crimes are not committed by the police, but rather by the citizens of the community they serve. How often do we hear a police official admonish a community for a rise in crime? How often does a police official point an accusing finger at conditions which produce crime and criminals? Instead, whenever the publication of crime statistics indicates a rise in crime, he feels that he has in some way failed and that his department has failed. In carrying such a burden, the average police official sees nothing especially strange about having to carry responsibility for a type of enforcement he is unable to fulfill. He has learned two characteristics of his job: he must bear this burden well and he must refrain from discussing it lest it be a source of embarrassment to him and the community.

If he should have the urge to discuss his problem of achieving full enforcement, the average police official would not wish to do so in public. To acknowledge the exercise of discretion belies the very image in which he takes such pride and which he strives so hard to achieve. This is the image of total objectivity—of impartiality—and of enforcement without fear or favor. A cursory examination of the typical oath of office administered to police officers, the rules and regulations of police departments, and the several codes of governing police conduct give the general impression that strict adherence to the "letter of the law" has come to be the ideal toward which all well-intentioned police officers should strive. There is great difficulty in recognizing that discretion can be exercised without being partial. It is, of course, extremely important that police officers be impartial in their enforcement policies, but it is possible for them to be so and still exercise discretion.

Impartiality requires the establishment of criteria for uniform action— a difficult task and one which perhaps constitutes the most valid objection to acknowledging discretionary powers. It is easy, from an administrative standpoint, to support a program of full enforcement. Instructions and training are simple. One need only teach the difference between black and white. If discretion is to be exercised, criteria become essential. And here the problems begin: (1) there is a general reluctance to spell out criteria as to those conditions under which an arrest is to take place lest this written modification of existing laws be attacked as presumptuous on the part of an administrative agency and contemptuous of the legislative body; (2) in the absence of written instructions, it is extremely difficult to communicate to large numbers of policemen the bounds of the discretion to be exercised; (3) an officer cannot be forced to exercise discretion, since the broad oath which he takes places him under obligation to enforce all laws and he can maintain that he is adhering to this higher authority; and (4) if a written document is desired, the preparation of criteria for the exercise of discretion requires an expert draftsman—one more skilled than the legislative draftsman who may have tried and failed. Is it any wonder that the typical reaction of the police administrator to the mere suggestion that discretion be acknowledged is likely to be: "It isn't worth the trouble!"?

Broadly-stated laws are, after all, one of the lesser concerns of the police. Most attention of law enforcement officers in recent years has focused upon legal provisions which are too narrow. The average police official is not very concerned about having the authority to enforce adultery statutes and not having the manpower or the community support necessary to do so. He is much more concerned because of his inability to attack organized crime effectively. And there may be an occasion upon which he can use an obscure or otherwise unenforced law to launch an oblique attack against a situation or activity which he feels warrants action on his part. His attitude is often that the law should be left on the books; it may come in handy sometime. Why impose self-limitations on police authority beyond those established by the legislature?

Another contention is that discretion breeds corruption and for this reason should be denied. This constitutes another strong administrative argument against acknowledging its existence. The average police administrator spends a considerable portion of his time worrying about the integrity of his force. Corruption, when it does exist, usually stems from the misuse of authority in order to attain selfish ends or from restraint from exerting authority in exchange for personal gain. It is always difficult to investigate. But, it is easier to do so, if policemen are expected to function on a black or white basis. If regulations require that an officer make an arrest when a violation occurs, the officer who does not do so is suspect. If, on the other hand, an officer is told that his decision to arrest should weigh a number of factors, it is difficult to determine if his failure to act was an exercise of good judgment or in exchange for a favor or a bribe. If the exercise of discretion is sanctioned by a department's administration, it becomes known both to the violator and the officer and creates the atmosphere and bargaining power for a corrupt act. It is the fear of this possible consequence that constitutes another strong reason that open acknowledgment of discretionary authority is frowned upon by most police administrators.

To the several arguments already stated, the police will usually add the contention that whatever their practice, they are required by law to subscribe to full enforcement. Indeed, in response to a suggestion that discretion in the area of traffic enforcement be acknowledged, the objection was raised that such an assumption on the part of a police department would be "unconstitutional." Some jurisdictions do go so far as to impose a penalty upon police officers who fail to take action upon learning of a crime, but there is no indication that such jurisdictions provide a higher level of enforcement than do those without such provisions.

There is, among police officers, a healthy respect for "the law" in its generic form whatever the attitude may be toward specific provisions of either the substantive or procedural codes. It is one thing to ignore a law; it is much more serious to acknowledge publicly that it is being ignored.

One of the factors that results in a healthy respect for the law is the knowledge on the part of every police officer that he may personally be held accountable in a legal suit for actions which he takes as a police officer. Should he be subject to legal action, he knows that a literal interpretation of his authority and his actions will determine the outcome; and that any exercise of discretion on his part is, in the eyes of the court, clearly outside the law. Concern for legal actions fosters support for a concept of full enforcement.

There is some basis to share the concern expressed for the legal obligation to enforce all laws without the exercise of discretion. In 1960, the then Police Commissioner of Philadelphia asserted that for lack of funds and personnel, he would limit initial enforcement of the Sunday closing law to large retail establishments. When a Pennsylvania court reviewed this action, they ruled in favor of one of the large retail merchants and stated that

"The admitted discrimination in enforcement is a calculated result of a definite policy on the part of a public official and thus results in a denial to the plaintiff of the equal protection of the law to which it is entitled by virtue of the fourteenth amendment of the United States Constitution."

Strong as is the fear of legal entanglements, the fear of public reaction to an announced policy of selective enforce-

ment is even greater. Since the police know how difficult it is to meet accusations of nonenforcement when they profess full enforcement, they fear that acknowledging a policy of nonenforcement is even less defensible. The average police official recognizes that no amount of explanation will placate the citizen who, for example, is obsessed with the need for strict enforcement of an ordinance requiring that bicycles not be ridden on sidewalks. He must simply be politely "brushed off." But, what does one tell the citizen who feels that too much effort is going into traffic enforcement and not enough into apprehending burglars; what is said to the citizen who demands additional manpower to apprehend disorderly youths congregating in park areas; and what does one tell the citizen who argues in favor of tripling the effort presently directed toward apprehending narcotic peddlers?

To answer such questions intelligently, the police official must have a defensible formula for the distribution of his manpower. Such a formula rarely exists because of the reluctance of the average police official to make value judgments. He, understandably, is unwilling to decide what should be of greatest concern to the community. The whole thought of trying to defend a policy of selective enforcement is a bit frightening. It is asking for trouble. So, he often concludes that it is, in his opinion, much safer to maintain he has no discretion in these matters.

THE ADVANTAGES INHERENT IN A POLICY OF RECOGNIZING THE EXERCISE OF DISCRETION

Some of the arguments in behalf of a denial of discretion are convincing arguments. They lend strong support to those who advocate a policy of full enforcement. If there was any indication that the breach between actual practice and the concept of full enforcement was narrowing, one might be encouraged to lean even more strongly in the direction of supporting a policy of full enforcement. The opposite, however, is true. The gulf between the ideal and reality in criminal law enforcement is growing wider. Every police official is keenly aware that the demands for his services are constantly increasing and that he is not given a proportionate increase in the resources with which to meet these demands. Crime is on the increase and gives no sign of leveling off. But, beyond this, there is evidence of a growing concern on the part of the public for a problem toward which there has more commonly been an attitude of complete apathy. The public no longer tolerates mental illness, unemployment, poor housing, or dropouts from high school. They do something about these social problems and there is an increasing indication that they intend to do more about crime. As this concern increases, the demands on law enforcement agencies will similarly increase.

How, then, does the dilemma posed here relate to improved law enforcement? How would its resolution better enable us to cope with present problems and those which develop in the future?

Law enforcement agencies cannot make progress so long as they remain on the defensive. They cannot win public support if they fail to level with the public. They cannot solve their problems if they fail to identify these problems.

There are a number of advantages to be gained by the police by being forthright in acknowledging the role which the police play in determining whether or not to invoke the criminal process. Let us examine the major ones.

Once and for all, acknowledging discretion would enable the police to climb out from underneath the impossible burden which has been placed upon them and which has placed them on the defensive in dealing with the public. And they would be doing so, not by abdicating their legal responsibilities, but by simply acknowledging the true magnitude of their responsibilities. It

is the function of the police to demonstrate the impossibility of full enforcement to the community—making citizens aware that the enactment of laws does not cure a problem unless consideration is given to the means of enforcement. An appeal must be made to the public to accept the best judgment and efforts of the police in their approach to the total problem of criminal law enforcement. The community can be given the alternatives of providing additional funds for a level of enforcement closer to full enforcement, of relieving the police of non-police functions which deplete the effort devoted to criminal law enforcement, or of providing the police with more realistic legal guidance in how to fulfill their broad responsibilities. Citizens will choose a level of enforcement, if it is put to them in terms of cost. Somewhere between the extremes of having a police officer for each citizen and having none, a determination must be made as to the number of officers to be employed. Placed in these terms, the degree to which full enforcement can be achieved is a matter known not only to the police agency, but to the community as a whole.

In the administration of governmental affairs, respect for the law takes a second place only to the need for honesty in dealing with the public. Because police officials have been placed in so awkward a position for so long and have felt compelled to deny the obvious, the public typically reacts with initial shock and subsequent pleasure when a police official is refreshingly forthright in his public pronouncements. Keeping the public well informed on police problems, including police shortcomings, clearly develops support for good law enforcement—and public support is the key to the solution of most police problems.

What are some of the specific implications of a policy which recognizes the discretion exercised by the police? At the present time, new legislation is enacted without regard to its enforceability. The assumption is that the police will, as always, assume responsibility for the new task much as a sponge absorbs water. Rarely is consideration given to possible problems of enforcement—or to the manpower which may be required. If the police are articulate on such occasions, legislative groups may be less likely to act without regard to considering enforcement.

It is not, in the long run, to the advantage of law enforcement agencies to have laws on the books which are widely ignored. The police have an obligation to help build respect among all citizens for law and order. A law which is known to exist and which is honored more in the breach than by compliance, tends to breed contempt for law enforcement—and usually among the very element in whom there is the greatest need for building respect. Knowledgeable in the techniques of enforcement, the police are probably in a better position to seek repeal of an obsolete or unenforceable law than any other element in the community. Their position need not be based on whether the conduct ought to be criminal, but rather on what are the practical aspects of enforcement.

The unworkability or inappropriateness of a legislative provision becomes apparent to a law enforcement agency more rapidly than it does to a legislative body. To persist in adhering to these legal requirements is nonsensical; such a policy tends only to harass citizens and lessen respect for the police. Applause will greet the police administrator who takes what the community terms an enlightened approach to such problems—publicly acknowledging the inappropriateness of the legislative provision.

Until this past year, members of the Chicago Police Department issued a summons to any motorist having a faulty headlight. This policy had been followed for years. It was, after all, the law. Had an effort been made, it is doubtful if one could have devised a more effective way of antagonizing the public. The violator rarely was aware of his violation.

A department memorandum was issued. It said, in clear language, that a police officer need not arrest a motorist with a defective light when the police officer was of the belief that the light would be repaired immediately. And further criteria were set forth:

"Where more than one lighting fixture is inoperative, or where one is in such a state of disrepair as to indicate that it was not a recent, temporary malfunction, or where the lighting violation was the cause of an accident, or is only one of several violations, the operator will be cited." (Chicago Police Department, Department Memorandum No. 63-35)

The reaction on the part of the press was that the public had cause to rejoice, that the department was "thinking big," that the policy was fair, and that the motorist who purposely breaks the law deserves to be punished. The police, they declared, were finally sensible about faulty car lights.

Taking the initiative in these matters has another advantage. A person who is unnecessarily aggrieved is not only critical of the procedure which was particularly offensive to him. He tends to broaden his interest and attack the whole range of police procedures which suddenly appear to him to be unusually oppressive; he may consider the police devoid of concern for civil rights; and perhaps, in moments of extreme delirium, he may even accuse them of fascistic or communistic tendencies. Regrettably, such a person usually resorts to the therapy of letterwriting to vent his emotions, with carbon copies clearly labeled and sent in all directions. The pattern is a familiar one.

Police officials too often fail to recognize that there are many in the communities which they serve who have an inherent distaste for authority—and especially police authority. Joining with others of the same view and those whose beliefs are more firmly grounded in a support for our democratic processes, these people closely guard against the improper use of authority by the police. It behooves law enforcement officials to refrain from unnecessarily creating a situation which annoys such individuals. Such situations can often be avoided through the exercise of proper discretion.

One of the greatest needs in law enforcement is effective leadership. Presently, because of its defensive posture, law enforcement agencies have too often cultivated a form of defensive leadership. Many law enforcement officials today fulfill the need for defensive leadership in their respective organizations, but are not equal to the challenge of the times. Unfortunately, this type of need places a premium on the police administrator who can successfully dodge the issue of why he fails to provide full enforcement, who can create the impression that he is endeavoring to enforce all of the laws of the time, who can take repeated attacks and onslaughts of public criticism, and who can be devious and less than forthright in his dealings with the public. While such leadership may have served some purpose in the past, it has not given law enforcement the type of guidance and impetus which is required to meet the problems of the 1960's.

Open recognition of basic police problems gives the police leader a clean atmosphere in which to operate. He becomes a leader rather than a defender. Police service today demands a bolder, more aggressive individual who is adept at articulating police problems in a forthright manner and developing community support for their solution.

The police have sought professional status. But, professional status does not normally accrue to individuals performing ministerial functions. One of the marks of a true profession is the inherent need for making value judgments and for exercising discretion based upon professional competence. To deny that discretion is exercised gives support to those citizens who maintain that the job of a police officer is a simple one, that it requires little judgment, and that it is not worthy of professional status. By acknowledging the discretionary role the police do fulfill, the drive toward a higher degree of respect and recognition for law enforcement personnel is given impetus.

THE CHOICE AND THE TASK

The real choice for a police administrator is not between "full enforcement" and "discretion" but rather more precisely between the ideal and reality. As the public becomes increasingly intolerant of crime, pressures will develop to improve and streamline not only our police organizations, but the laws and procedures under which they operate. An essential first step will then be to inform the public, to challenge some of our basic concepts, to take stock of the total responsibilities of the police, to recognize the limitations under which the police operate, and to acknowledge the need for the exercise of discretion. It is then likely that a new atmosphere will be created which will foster some new thinking and some new developments to aid in the improvement of the total system for the administration of criminal justice.

This is a big task. It is not a function for the police alone. Law—and the enforcement of law—is a vital element in our form of government. In law enforcement, one comes to grips with some of the basic legal, political and social concerns and issues of our time. Clearly, it warrants more than it has received in attention from not only the public, but from our universities and colleges as well. There is need for a much greater body of knowledge and understanding of our present operations. Such knowledge and understanding is essential if we are to develop intelligent solutions to our present and future problems.

71. An Aging Population and State Government*

ELIAS S. COHEN

CAUGHT between the Scylla of conscience over a segment of the population too long neglected by society and the Charybdis of a rapidly growing number of senior citizens, the states are searching out and reviewing a wide variety of services for the aging.

Oddly, the field of aging is being viewed as something new for state activity. In actual fact, the states have been spending large sums for their aged populations—perhaps not enough to meet real needs, but in a substantial commitment. This article will attempt to view state measures and potential measures for the aging in the following terms:

(1) What impact have the needs of an aging population had on major state government programs?

(2) What special problems and factors are presented by the federal government system of grants-in-aid concerning the aged?

(3) What are the most important steps for the states to take in approaching realistic plans for services to meet needs of this rapidly growing group of citizens?

*   *   *

I. THE IMPACT OF AN AGING POPULATION ON STATE GOVERNMENT FUNCTIONS

What has been the impact of the aging population on major state government functions?

Certain of these functions have been largely unaffected by the rising num-

* Reprinted with permission from *State Government*, Summer 1962. Footnotes omitted.

bers of older people; highways, corrections and natural resources are notable examples. Others may have experienced slight collateral effect, as in the case of civil defense and public protection. Two affected areas stand out, however: income maintenance and health care. Following, in order of diminishing fiscal investment, if not in importance, are housing, adult education, and the state's role in community organization.

INCOME MAINTENANCE

Public Assistance. In December 1961, 2,267,670 aged persons in the United States received old age assistance; seven years earlier, despite a smaller aged population, 2,564,686 persons took advantage of OAA. However, the impact of inflation, and some pressures to increase levels of grants, increased expenditures during the period from $133,103,960 in December 1954 to $155,964,054 in December 1961. Some of the impact of the population and of the pressures presented may be seen more readily from figures concerning medical assistance for the aged for December 1961, when $13,959,808 was spent by eighteen states in behalf of 72,159 persons under the new program, initiated in October 1960.

A key factor operating in the public assistance field is the growth of old age and survivors insurance coverage and the improvements in benefits under it. The problem is less one of numbers of people than of inflation, and a higher level of community conscience. Increasing numbers of older people and decreasing mortality rates (accompanied by increased morbidity), however, can

382 PROGRAMS AND POLICIES

be expected to raise the level of demands for medical assistance for the aged.

Older Worker Programs. Another area of income maintenance lies in job retention and employment for older workers. A variety of factors combine to make these a relatively unlikely area of success for state action: These factors include the rapid technological changes in industries looking toward automated processes; a level of general unemployment which poses especially large obstacles for the older worker regarded as marginal; the higher pension costs assumed when significant numbers of older workers are hired; and pressures within the labor movement to make way for young men with families.

HEALTH

The growth of our aging population has probably had its greatest visible impact, so far as state programs are concerned, in the health fields. Three major areas are involved: (1) mental health; (2) hospital and medical facilities construction; and (3) nursing home supervision.

Mental Health. Approximately a third of our mental hospital beds are occupied by people 65 or over—165,000 of them, representing an increase of 95,000 in twenty years. Moreover, the rate of first admissions of the aging substantially exceeds that of younger age groups. . . .

Hospital and Medical Facilities Construction. Administration of funds under the Hill-Burton Hospital Survey and Construction Act has had considerable effect in the states on development of satisfactory nursing home and chronic disease facilities. However, the federal grant program is dependent upon congressional appropriations; measured against the magnitude of the problem, the construction undertaken represents a relatively small part of total facilities. . . .

Recent surveys have not been undertaken, but it is estimated that there are well over 400,000 nursing home beds in the United States today, at least one-half of which are unsuitable from the standpoint of programming, staffing or construction.

Nursing Home Supervision. Scarcely a state in the Union, other than states with so few nursing homes that supervision presents only minor problems, has developed a program of licensure and supervision which can assure in virtually all homes a standard of safety and a level of care consonant with Mid-Twentieth Century knowledge. The growth of the aged population, and the growing numbers of chronically ill, indigent persons, place greater and greater pressure on public assistance agencies. Typically, rates for nursing home care paid by public assistance do not meet costs of proper programs. This, in turn, holds down the development of nursing home facilities. The implications for the states lie in adequate financing through public assistance, a search for methods of developing nonprofit and public facilities as the basis for nursing home care, and development of licensing and supervision programs at least as effective as those now governing barber shops.

HOUSING

The growing population of elderly persons has had little effect on state programs of housing for the elderly. The programs appear to be more and more characterized by federal leadership and local participation. . . .

* * *

Another important, but too frequently overlooked, factor in state programming for housing the elderly lies in public assistance. Low grant levels are a major consideration in the continued existence of urban and rural slums. It appears that building inspection agencies are ineffective in breaking the slum patterns in too many areas.

State expenditures for education in 1960 comprised $8.85 billion, or 32.5 per cent of all general expenditures by the several states. Of this amount, one can only guess that an infinitesimal amount was spent on account of older persons. Despite some notable examples of state university gerontological institutes, and progressive adult education programs in a few states, the increasing aged population is having little significant effect upon the largest state program so far as financial outlay is concerned.

While it cannot be properly classified as an expenditure in behalf of the present aged population, a major impact has been made upon state government through the Social Security Act amendments which permit public employees and their employers to participate in the old age survivors and disability insurance program. State participation in this program may be said to represent the state's investment in its own employees' retirement years.

In 1960, state government contributions to state-administered public employee retirement systems alone amounted to $659 million. This does not include contributions to the OASI trust fund. . . . This single activity probably represents the most massive investment for a relatively small number of people that the state makes by way of preventive service for problems of old age.

One manifestation of state government concern not present a decade ago is the state unit on aging. With varying degrees of effectiveness, the state unit —often a Governor's commission or committee—has undertaken a major effort in the field of community organization of local forces to achieve given service objectives. More often than not it has served as the instrument to give visibility to the concern of the state administration for the older persons in the state.

The massive nature of the problems of income maintenance (including the problems produced by inflation), health care, and housing, in many ways precludes effective attack by states. Not the least of these problems is the dilemma the states face in financing.

Thus the states, faced with massive problems demanding massive solutions, must look to activities where the greatest effect can be secured for the senior citizens *within the capacity of the state government.*

II. IMPACT OF FEDERAL PROGRAMS ON THE STATES

A major factor that cannot be overlooked is the impact of federal programs upon state activities. The federal government has moved on a wide variety of fronts in the field of aging. George Leader, Former Governor of Pennsylvania, has commented rather sharply that "The approach in planning for older people at the federal level, as well as elsewhere, has been insular in nature. Agencies have set up programs which deal with particular problems but which are unrelated in any way either programmatically or administratively. If this is competitive at the federal level, it is confusing at the state level and utterly chaotic at the point of consumption." Referring to the problem of nursing home care for the elderly, he cites six federal programs which have been developed over a period of time. They include the Hill-Burton grants for nursing homes; Federal Housing Administration mortgage insurance for proprietary nursing homes; the medical assistance for the aged program; the regular public assistance program, which may include participation in the cost of medical institutional care; the Public Health Service program, designed to improve the quality of nursing home care; and some aspects of the new Community Health Facilities Act project grant program.

To those which former Governor Leader has enumerated, one might add the Public Health Service chronic disease program and the direct loan program of the Community Health Facilities Act in connection with infirmaries in homes for the aged.

Few of these programs carry any relationship to one another. The situation is difficult to say the least. The flow of federal monies too often determines how state programs must be organized. As Governor Leader pointed out: "This leads the states to establish programs and structures in ways that will yield the greatest administrative convenience and the easiest flow of federal monies, rather than in ways which help people solve their problems."

It is important to recognize that the increasing reliance, necessary as it may be, upon the federal government, has produced for the states a variety of problems in coordinating services, in many ways beyond their control. Except as they can exercise concerted influence upon the federal agencies, and particularly upon the Office of the President, to abandon a rigid categorical approach and program orientation, and develop new techniques for grant-in-aid programs to serve older people, they will have to cope with an insular structure reinforced by a baronial approach from federal departments.

III. STATE PROGRAM DEVELOPMENT FOR THE AGING POPULATION

The 1955 report by the Council of State Governments indicated that twenty states had at that time already established some kind of special unit or commission to deal with the problems the aged population seemed to present. In addition, at least five Governors had called statewide conferences on aging, all of which adopted resolutions for action. Within the next two years more than thirty states had some form of organization in operation.

While the 1961 White House Conference on Aging created tremendous

interest, and it appears that commissions and committees are being organized with considerable enthusiasm, it is worth noting that nearly a dozen states have no state organization on aging. A dozen more have temporary state structures, the average appropriation for which is $1,500. Thus it appears that, in terms of organization, approximately half of the states either have no state unit on aging or one which is predicated almost entirely on volunteer activity.

FUNCTIONS OF STATE UNITS

The recent Federal Conference of State Executives in the Field of Aging produced a thoughtful analysis of functions of state units. The functions were described in the following terms:

(1) Policy setting and program planning.
(2) Coordinating existing structures.
(3) Organizing new structures.
(4) Research and distribution of results.
(5) Referral, information and publicity.
(6) Training of personnel.

The evaluation of these functions and of the effectiveness of state units on aging was disturbing. Dr. Morton Leeds, Secretary of the Indiana Commission on the Aging and Aged, pointed out with candor and perception that state units on aging have been less than clear in their purpose. He indicated that state units have fallen down especially in priority setting as regards the policy and program development function. "A great many projects," he said, "are begun simply because someone was interested in a special problem, rather than in response to urgent state or local need. . . . The attack on problems has been spasmodic, not consistent; . . . emotional rather than rational. The need, on the other hand, is for a systematic attack, one that achieves goal after goal. . . ."

Dr. Leeds pointed to the difficulties

that many independent commissions have in coordinating the several departments involved. He implied that interdepartmental committees and interdepartmental projects, where there is genuine interest not only by the cabinet officers but by the chief executive as well, produce the best results.

It is in the organization of new structures, particularly at the local level, that state units on aging have devoted their greatest energies and in some ways have achieved their most notable successes. The organization of county committees, city committees, special units attached to local health and welfare councils, Mayors' offices and similar bodies have been much in evidence. In a few states (including Arkansas, Indiana, Tennessee and Texas) regional groups have been established. Massachusetts was the first state to make grants to local councils for support of local activities. However, only three states thus far have provided sizable grant programs to help develop local services outside of the more traditional spheres of public assistance and mental health. California, through its Department of Social Welfare, has $150,000 set aside for home finding, information and referral services, senior citizen centers, voluntary training programs, friendly visiting, casework and group work services, and visiting nurses.

Pennsylvania's grant program of $200,000 per year is designed to strengthen local public welfare services, including establishment of an adult welfare worker at the county level and development of homemaker services, foster care placement programs for adults, day care centers, and casework and counselling.

New Jersey is providing funds for a series of experimental grants for study purposes.

Programs like these, which, through the use of the grant-in-aid mechanism, can shake loose local, public and private money, can also lead to the development of coherent, overall planning at the local level. The dangers, however, in developing a system of grants for aging, lie in the creation of still another "category" which may impede the development of comprehensive welfare services for many of our population who are neglected, dependent, and cannot care and provide for their own basic needs. This may represent a necessary step in order to secure recognition for the aged. However, a long-term, broad approach to the role of government in meeting human needs must necessarily look to the day when truly comprehensive welfare planning can take place.

Research in this field is spotty and sparse. Very few state units on aging conduct research themselves, and only a few have funds to subsidize other organizations to conduct research. There is little coordination in research, and the state units on aging are little involved in it.

The meager budgets and staffs of state units on aging have not been sufficient to develop adequate programs of referral, information and publicity. Dr. Leeds points out that "Less than a half dozen commissions today have a current up-to-date directory of resources useful to the aged." Indiana, Maryland, New York, Pennsylvania and Washington are cited as examples of states which have developed series of publications including listings and directories of clubs, committees, institutions, "how-to" manuals, and similar documents.

Direct responsibility for the conduct of training programs for persons working with older individuals has been taken up largely by the operating departments. This is probably as it should be. The grants of the United States Public Health Service to the states for the improvement of quality of nursing home care has led to a variety of institutes, workshops and training courses for nursing home personnel throughout the states. Public assistance has undertaken a variety of techniques and methods to train its own personnel. Health departments have been very active in this area for individuals working with nursing homes and in the field of chronic diseases.

The state units on aging, however, have had relatively little impact on the universities, particularly as regards social work and medicine, areas in which there is some feeling that special emphasis should be given to the needs of older persons.

Thus one must conclude that generally the state units on aging, while sincere in their efforts, have not lived up to the functions which the section on State Organization of the 1961 White House Conference on Aging set for them.

ADMINISTRATIVE STRUCTURE

While there is a tendency to overemphasize the importance of structure in programming, it may be worth while to view the current picture in the states. The vast majority of states with units on aging have established independent commissions which operate outside of the ordinary departmental structure. This has been done to achieve independence and, theoretically, to enable the units to cut across many departmental lines. This arrangement secured overwhelming approval by the Section on State Organization at the White House Conference. Yet Dr. Leeds points out that some of the most successful programs are taking place in Minnesota, North Carolina and Pennsylvania, where primary responsibility for the state unit on aging lies within an operating state department. To this list one might add New Jersey, and to some extent New York, in which the unit operates out of the Governor's office but is attached to the Department of Social Welfare.

This writer would submit that the field of aging, in its present stage, is an inappropriate function for an independent commission. The success of units on aging will be measured in the services they produce for older people, not in the reports that are written or

the conferences conducted. A unit on aging placed within a department does not preclude the operation of an advisory committee or the utilization of an interdepartmental committee. In many ways, coordination among sister departments, with one taking primary staff responsibilities, can be accomplished more easily than through an "out-of-town cousin" commission, respectfully treated but seldom getting the deciding vote. Effective coordination from the Governor's office can also proceed better under a unit located within a department. In the absence of strong and enthusiastic gubernatorial support for improving operating programs for older people, however, neither a commission nor a departmental unit can be too effective.

IV. PRESENT PROBLEMS AND FUTURE ACTION

Beset as they are by major fiscal problems, the states must view realistically what they can do in the field of aging. In fact, adequate improvements in aspects such as public assistance, housing, mental health, and other direct health services, will not come about in the absence of additional infusions of federal money or the further development of social insurance to relieve the financial strain.

Thus the states must look, it seems, to other basic areas: (1) improvement of the present machinery of state government so that current state efforts are maximized; (2) development of techniques of planning and evaluation of the social problems of the aged, so that adequate allocation of resources can be made for the future; (3) stimulation of other social resources such as the church, voluntary groups, private agencies and local government to accommodate some of the problems of the aged; and (4) a search for new, different and better ways of handling current problems.

Policy on major problem areas should

flow from the office of the Governor. However, Governors' offices usually are understaffed and underbudgeted. Under such conditions they cannot adequately collect and assimilate the information and recommendations of the several departments. Significant and effective state policy making requires major improvements in the executive office.

If this is true at the executive level, it is certainly true at the legislative level. To expect a legislative committee without staff and without sufficient time to consider vast new programs for the aged at the state level, in times when the competition for the tax dollar is keen, is neither reasonable nor desirable. Thus it appears that a necessary prelude to major state action in this field is the equipping of the centers of executive and legislative power with the wherewithal to consider the problem, ponder the solutions, and develop broad, statewide legislative and executive policies.

Secondly, there must be a careful examination of state-federal relationships in programs affecting older people. If we find that federal programs as currently organized and administered fail to promote or if they impede coordination among programs at the state level, it behooves the Governors to seek and effect change, be it through their delegations to Congress or by virtue of their special relationship to the President as chief executives of the several states.

Moreover, the role of the state unit on aging must be reevaluated in terms of its real capacities and its greatest usefulness. Public programs should fall within some overall plan, and point toward some set of goals concerned with service to the public and the relief of need, neglect and suffering. At least two lines of action appear essential in this connection: (1) activities concerned with planning and policy development for executive and legislative consideration; and (2) active leadership and participation in the process of community organization at the local level, to promote and develop services for the aged which can and should be carried forth in the locality by public, voluntary and private resources.

In the area of planning and policy development, the state unit should undertake the orderly collection and analysis of data concerning the aged and the programs serving them. The state unit can provide some of the basic staff service for the Governor's office and for an interdepartmental committee (if there is one) on the development of program proposals or on improvements and innovations in the current governmental machinery. The state unit also should serve the administration in the capacity of gadfly in the development of new ideas and new ways to serve older people more effectively.

In the area of community organization activity, the program should be self-liquidating. The basic services must ultimately be undertaken by the program agencies themselves. If the states are truly successful in meeting human needs, it will be on the basis of solving people's problems without resort to categorical approaches. Community organization activity will move forward to mobilize men, materials and money for the general welfare, and the role of community organization *for the aging per se* will wither away, and properly so.

In the meantime, however zealous we are, we must be ever mindful of the responsibility to maintain balance among services of a wide variety. The field of aging offers a unique opportunity to state government as a demonstration of responsible development in an emerging area. The alternative may be the ugly growth of another bureau advocating its own constituency to the exclusion of the larger welfare.

72. Urban Renewal: Current Criticism and the Search for a Rationale*

GEORGE S. DUGGAR

ONE E. W. Dykes, in an article reprinted by the *American Mercury,* describes the "chain letter fraud" and then sets forth his version of the procedure to obtain federal aid for urban renewal. The inference that the latter is "Worse Than Chain Letters" is followed with the conclusion that "One form of slopping at the public trough that is now coming into vogue is *urban renewal.*"

THE OPPOSITION

In the famous last words before the riot, that is an interesting topic for discussion. More interesting, but less discussable, is an article by Jane Jacobs in *Architectural Forum* where, in a series of flashbacks, she describes alternately a pair of conversations, one rather sweet among neighborhood leaders, and the other a dastardly scene, apparently among villainous urban renewal officials and their advisers in a Machiavellian city hall session.

And then there are the local, life-and-death struggles over urban renewal such as have occurred recently in Phoenix, Arizona; Spokane, Washington; and Springfield, Oregon, where in floods of vocal opposition the local renewal programs were swept away. These surging floods of local opposition make little use of the vitriol supplied by Dykes and Co., and even Jane Jacobs touches only on the edges of the issues.

It may be that those who organize the phalanxes of little old ladies to deluge city hall with telephone calls have Dykesian or Jacobsian ideas. Perhaps the leaders, with Dykes, object to a high level of federal expenditures, but Dykes does not seem much interested in urban renewal. Indeed, he soon notes that blight is "only one of the problems that cities are reputed to be unable to solve with their own means," and he goes on to question aid to farmers, highways, power, rural electrification, education, foreign economic development, "and so on."

THE ARGUMENTS

Perhaps the leadership of renewal opposition fears, with Dykes, that as in chain letters federal aid money flows "from all" to a "few who get in early" and that "the money is bound to run out." But this fear may not be widely shared. It is obvious that the federal program is growing rapidly and that new federal-aid programs are appearing from time to time. Maybe leaders of renewal opposition are as likely to fear that the federal source will *not* dry up and instead continue to add to the federal tax burden.

Perhaps the local leadership believes that the burden of the federal tax structure is distributed less to their liking than state and local taxes. But this seems a tenuous argument. If one looks, for instance, at the "progressivity" of the federal income tax one would conclude that people of higher income will absorb more of the burden than if state and local taxes supported a function. But one gets a different impression if one looks at the huge federal

* Reprinted with permission from *Public Management*, September 1962.

corporate income tax and notes that economists have not been able to determine who really bears its burden.

But all these are mere suppositions. The financial questions are not clearly important in the local attacks on urban renewal. Nor is it even clear that the attacks are made under Jane Jacobs' banner. The arguments do not stress so much, as she does, the preservation of neighborhood life and the possibilities of unslumming through encouraging local owners. Rather, the emphasis is on the right of property owners to utilize their properties as they see fit. Only within the context of this major issue and its overtones of fundamental Americanism are other arguments brought to bear. Perhaps the underlying problem for the renewal program is that there is so little understanding of the issues that people who object to one aspect of the urban renewal program can use, without successful contradiction, almost any argument.

THE KNOWLEDGE GAP

The large number of speeches being made these days by officials of the Housing and Home Finance Agency and its Urban Renewal Administration seem to be bucket brigades to fill this knowledge gap. But the Agency is beset by an accumulated popular ignorance which seems to have its origin in the decade, only recently ended, when the Agency had no real research arm to clarify urban issues and its own policies. While programs have survived lack of widespread public understanding before, it is necessary to the political health of the program that at least the supporters of urban renewal understand two concepts fundamental to the renewal endeavor—how the city "works" physically and how both public and private participation is possible in a common urban enterprise.

First, there must be understanding of how a city works physically in respect to the processes of deterioration, relocation, and renewal. The fallout from Jane Jacobs' remarks is so great as almost to obscure her insights, but among the contributions of her book, *The Death and Life of Great American Cities,* is the profound common sense that one should think first not of what to "clear" in a blighted area but of what to *add*. And she urges that we must cultivate the process of "unslumming" by which she means that families and enterprises making their ways in the world tend to rise in income, status, and well-being, and that this upward striving can be channeled into area improvement if, instead of moving them out during the impecunious phase, they are encouraged to stay and invest.

Jane Jacobs' observations refer specifically to the near-in portions of very large cities, and her references to experience are exceedingly parochial. It is ironic that while she generally attacks urban renewal, she has really supplied a needed rationale for it, particularly for the shift in federal policy, made half a dozen years before she published her book. Perhaps this reflects the slowness of her home city, New York, to make the changes intended under the Housing Act of 1954, and its failure, alone in the country, to made relocation a public function, leaving site families and businesses instead to the tender mercies of the corporations doing the redeveloping.

RELOCATION AND MOBILITY

Once it is accepted that the task of urban renewal is to stimulate the process of unslumming, it is necessary to take account of what those with wide knowledge of renewal have concluded —that in many areas unslumming through conservation and rehabilitation will not work. Apparently these are areas which are not sufficiently attractive to hold any large proportion of the striving families and firms. It is important to note that we are only beginning to understand how to stimulate conservation and rehabilitation even in the areas which lend themselves to it.

And it is not too unfair to retort to Jane Jacobs, "That's fine, but what do we do where your program of faith healing doesn't work?" Here we refer to the gray area, a meaningless phrase except that it indicates that we are hazy about some areas and what to do about them. Neither Jane Jacobs nor the champions of clearance and redevelopment offer the illumination that will clear the haze. But our failure to deal with the gray areas does not lead to political failure. The local political struggles center on what *is* done.

Relocation alone may not be the decisive issue in many cities, but the strength of the program is sapped by the low level of popular understanding. In the first place, most of the local problems of relocation until recently were associated more with highway clearance than with urban renewal. Even as urban renewal gets into high gear it will rank far below miscellaneous market forces, public programs, and fire and flood as a source of net dwelling losses through demolition.

More important, mobility of urban families and changes in family status are rapid, and mortality of small business is high. The movement and closings accompanying renewal may represent only a slight speed-up in what would have happened anyway. Throughout much of the urban area, families move once a year on the average, and an annual turnover of several hundred per cent is reported in some school classes in slum areas. The relevant question may be whether the aided relocation in connection with urban renewal works more advantageously for the families, especially the multiproblem families.

For years, enforcement of the federal relocation requirement took the form of detailed and partly meaningless bookkeeping, where it was more important to know afterward where each site family had moved than to assure ahead of time that the available supply of housing was adequate in the appropriate rent ranges and locations. The development of the art of relocating families awaits better technical knowledge of the swirls and currents of urban mobility.

PRIORITIES

It is necessary to make clear the various time processes in which renewal occurs. A community may usually buy an easier task of relocation at the expense of delay in site clearance or comprehensive code enforcement (and it is necessary to make clear that effective code enforcement as well as clearance displaces families). Urban renewal programs have been characterized by wildly faulty time perspectives. "No slums in ten years," though a catchy slogan, is not only impractical but wrongly implies that slum formation can be completely arrested. But slum and blight formation may result from the very process of urban growth, as the demands made upon the urban hub grow and change with growth in the total area.

Indeed, the mistaken conception that the blighted area is itself the source of the problem, and not just an undesirable symptom, is so widely held as to undermine the case for central-city renewal, which then appears as somehow a perversion of the purpose of renewal. Yet there is ample reason to believe that changes, such as the unplanned growth of the vehicle-handling capacity of the central area, are important causes of blight through the surrounding areas through which the vehicles pass and park.

Faulty, static habits of thought even present the danger that the federally aided local "community renewal programs" will now be deflected from the problem of identifying the most critical points for speed-up in renewal and become mere benefit-cost analyses. Communities which continue with renewal are likely to find ways to produce benefits surpassing costs, and with a fine sense of the local cost immeasurables. But the communities may need sizable renewal grants to determine the actions on which the speed of the whole process chiefly depends and the sequences which are most necessary. The large local research programs are politically vulnerable at best. The charge that the computer jockeys and the whiz kids are feeding us all to the machines had better be countered by improving the process rather than by a search for the holy grail of measured costs and benefits.

BETTER UNDERSTANDING

Not only is it necessary that many more people quickly learn how a city works physically, but it is also essential that they learn how public and private organizations can participate in a common urban enterprise. William Slayton, Commissioner of the Urban Renewal Administration, in a recent speech to the Practicing Law Institute, made this point as it applies to the relation between the private developer and the city government. But it is critically important, particularly in the local political arena, that code enforcement also be widely understood in a similar context.

Slayton helps to slay the dragon inherited from our muckraking past, a mythical monster who scares little children and nice old ladies with the flames of scandal whenever private and public agencies work together. With the dragon slain, we can assess the real dangers of corruption while drawing conclusions concerning the ways local and federal governments and local redevelopment and housing authorities work with redevelopers, citizens associations, newspapers, property owners, highway and transportation agencies, designers, city planners, and social agencies to produce effective urban renewal.

Unfortunately classic administrative theory does not help much to illuminate this process. Administrative structure has been seen as existing within one formal organization, together with those who cluster about it as participants. Urban renewal, on the contrary, is a more or less free association of several organizations, no one of which accepts continuing subordination to the others. The renewal enterprise is a structure of relationships such that the varied interests of the several participants holds them together long enough for a cumulative process to be set up. In this process the commitment of each grows as the project itself becomes clarified, as the uncertainties are reduced, and as the costs of planning and preparation mount.

In the early stages of local renewal very little, if any, formal structure holds this association of participants together in a forward-looking and venturesome effort to weigh prospects and develop a strategy. Gradually a network of contractual rights and obligations begins to formalize the relation of the federal to local government, both to the redevelopment and housing authority, it to designers, property owners and redevelopers, and all to a public which begins to entertain firm expectations. Cities that have attempted a whole series of renewal projects tend to develop a structure for planning and control to regularize these relationships and to increase efficiency. Then a hierarchy emerges.

Code enforcement appears necessary in this context, not just as a part of the workable program required by the federal government, but as a formal device which enables members of the enterprise to do together what the property owners could not do separately. The enterprise itself produces a profit of sorts, a money profit to those who demand it as the price of participation, and an additional social profit which justifies the sacrifice, in the public interest, demanded of some of the property owners and of the federal and local taxpayers.

The current attacks on urban renewal, while they should not be overemphasized, provide evidence of the need for a rationale such as this, clarified of course and made specific. Urban renewal in the United States is in the peculiar position where great progress has been made, but the rationale has lagged behind. The friends of urban renewal have not sufficiently developed theirs and have not imparted enough of it widely to assure the political health of the program. With such spread of renewal rationale the attacks which now appear as destructive and threatening can recede to their proper role as vigilant but essentially constructive criticism.

73. Ratios, Teaching Loads and Efficiency in Higher Education*

JOHN A. PERKINS

THROUGHOUT higher education, particularly public higher education, there has been a felt need for standard data relative to faculty, students and the credit hours of work offered. Inevitably, in their efforts to understand more fully the financial requirements of the colleges and universities for which they must appropriate funds, legislators, budget officers and other state officers also have been eager for these statistics. One aspect in particular, that of faculty-student ratios, has received much attention in many quarters, including state governments.

Unfortunately, of all the available measures of quality and efficiency, the faculty-student ratio is the least reliable and the most difficult to determine and make meaningful. It is interrelated to many complex educational factors: learning theory, class size, levels of instruction (freshmen, upper class, and graduate), and the nature of the subjects being taught (Shakespeare's plays, for example, in contrast to ward-round clinical instruction in medical schools). Such factors and their full significance must be understood by those who would use the faculty-student ratio.

Interest in faculty-student ratios arises at this time for several reasons.

Enrollments have been rising. In the immediate future they will climb much faster. Money to hire more instructors is being requested by responsible college and university administrators. To add faculty needed for growing enrollments will necessitate increases in the budgets of all institutions, whether public or private. Admittedly, it is primarily the public institutions that will be expected to grow. To substantiate requests for more faculty, educators understandably indicate a vital relationship between the number of students and number of instructors on the payroll. It is even implied that if the two are not reasonably related, accreditation may be jeopardized. Most accrediting agencies have not established arbitrary norms relative to faculty-student ratios. Those that do have norms apply them with considerable flexibility. Obviously, however, accreditation might be withheld if an institution were instructing with so few teachers that the curricula offered were not properly taught to the larger numbers enrolled.

REASONABLE TEACHING LOADS

In any case, the ratio of faculty to students needs to be better understood.

* Reprinted with permission from *State Government*, Winter 1961. Footnotes omitted.

It relates directly to instructional costs, and indirectly to the quality of instruction offered. The prestigious colleges and universities understandably boast of their large numbers of faculty relative to their modest enrollments. The president and deans of every institution want to hire the best young men emerging from the graduate schools and retain the most competent professors. They realize, and so should the citizenry, that quite as important as salary to both is assurance of "reasonable" teaching responsibilities. This may mean few hours of teaching per week, few students in each class, or few different course preparations, or a combination of these. For good reason these advantages are especially expected in institutions purporting to be universities or even first-class colleges.

There is still another reason why first-rate faculty want "reasonable" teaching loads. In our strongest institutions of higher learning research is a coordinate function, along with teaching. It must be. Such a differentiation between what is a true university or first-rate college and a run-of-the-mill school has often been overlooked by citizen supporters, alumni and legislators. Successive actions are sanctioned changing teachers colleges first to liberal arts colleges and then to universities without appreciation of the implications. Such name-changing, if the traditional designations of institutions of higher learning are to retain valid meaning and if higher education is to maintain respectability, requires commensurate adaptations in institutional function and in the level of financial support. The only way a place can be a university, whatever its name, is to have intellectual interaction on the forefront of knowledge between teachers of high quality and students of high quality. In our age of scientific revolution, a man who just teaches may soon be as out of date in the university classroom as a buggy whip in the garage. J. Robert Oppenheimer, the A-Bomb physicist, suggests that scientific knowledge has essentially doubled every ten years.

Furthermore, for scholar-teachers who are up to date, university administrators cannot freely set all the terms of employment. Scientific and highly specialized personnel, owing to the low birthrate of the thirties, is not coming into the academic market place in anything like the numbers needed. It is estimated that by 1970 we may have 250,000 fewer fully qualified college teachers than we shall need. The small group who are about to enter teaching are in a seller's market. They can, if they are first-rate in ability and have a good measure of common sense, judgment and acceptable personality, virtually write their own ticket. The dilemma is that, because of the flood of students, higher education needs more teaching done by the competent few who are available, but is in a difficult position to push far in this direction. The institutions that are too aggressive in increasing teaching productivity may lose the best of the faculty they have.

*   *   *

THE PROFESSORS' RESPONSIBILITIES

What are the professors' total responsibilities? There are many mistaken notions abroad concerning the life and work of the college and especially the university teacher.

First, the hours spent in teaching students are erroneously considered to be the job in its entirety. Actually, if the professor meets the expectations that first-rate universities set for faculty, industry's forty-hour week looks easy. When he is not in the classroom or preparing for it, he is expected to spend his time in research or other creative activity such as writing, musical composition, inventing or painting. The truly devoted scholar never finds enough time for these activities. As often as not, they consume his Saturdays and sometimes Sundays. Admittedly, there are college teachers who don't have the creative ability or the self-discipline to do these things. Those who can't may merely make pretense of doing so. But in this respect those on higher education's payrolls are no worse than people in business. One head of a giant industry was asked, "How many people work for you?" He purportedly replied; "About 50 per cent of them."

Secondly, today very few outstanding faculty members serve full time as teachers. Many have half or more of their time in effect bought from teaching by industry, governments and foundations, for research, consultancies, travel and other services seemingly required by our society. The institution which denies faculty such opportunity to advance their personal careers soon loses its better people. These activities give some advantage to the universities themselves. When outside subsidy is not forthcoming (and such fields as art and history are not readily subsidized by government or industry) the university or college budget often is expected to bear the cost. Released time from teaching must be provided if the faculty is to be kept reasonably satisfied; the developing teacher-scholar must be enabled to finish writing a book, go on an expedition, staff an overseas project, or visit libraries and museums at distant places. In great likelihood, faculty who do not demand such special privileges are not capable of providing up-to-date, first-rate higher learning. And, with today's shortages, let it be remembered, the faculty can be choosers.

Thirdly, the teaching assignment of college teachers is often mistakenly viewed in terms of the number of hours spent *in* the classroom. Actually, for every hour before students the teacher at the collegiate level should spend several hours beforehand in his office or the library, bringing his lectures up to date or replenishing his store of knowledge. The preparation of stimulating assignments and examinations and the reading and grading of them are another out-of-class aspect. Charles T. Copeland, the great Harvard teacher of English composition and literature, gave almost every Friday evening of his teaching life to informal sessions with undergraduate students, who were invited to his apartment where he read to them or had outstanding personalities as guests. The professor, moreover, usually should and does devote hours to counseling students, on both academic and personal matters. The truly great professor must be as willing to spend hours with a student as to write an essay whose publication might immortalize him. And the community, whether it be a locality, or the nation, calls upon the professor to give speeches, appear on panels, television and radio, usually without extra compensation. Twelve or nine hours a week in a classroom certainly is not all there is to the work of a conscientious professor.

RATIOS ARE A FAULTY APPROACH

Now to return to the faculty-student ratio.

Knowledgeable people in higher education do not accept this ratio as a *good* measure of teaching productivity. Its weaknesses are these: There is no uniformity of agreement among colleges and universities as to who is to be counted as a faculty member, or, indeed, as a student, in the computing of such ratios. Some institutions give academic appointments to professional personnel who work in the libraries, the museums and art galleries, and in counseling and guidance work. Others do not. Such appointment policies, conceived without any concern for teacher-student ratios, nevertheless greatly affect the ratios. Moreover, there is the research professor who may not regularly teach, except to associate with a few graduate students who are more like colleagues in his research than course enrollees. In addition, some graduate students teach. There is no agreement as to how they are to be figured into ratios. In fairness to an accurate ratio in any given year, the numerous faculty who are on full or part-time leaves, sabbatical or otherwise, cannot be counted. But they often are.

As for students, some colleges count only full-time campus students; others count full and part-time students with equal weight; still others, with more accuracy, use "full-time equivalent" student figures. Because of these variations, my own university and any other can, with complete integrity, cite ratios of faculty to students which can vary by as much as 50 per cent.

MEASURING THE LOAD

There are better methods than ratios to ascertain how many teachers are required. These are related to teaching loads. It should be reemphasized that they do not measure the professor's total responsibilities on the campus of a first-rate institution. Nor do they give a clue as to how effectively a man teaches, or how much students may learn owing to his efforts. And these are the truly important aspects of teaching.

The most widely used but not the best way of quantifying a college professor's teaching load is not difficult. Simply divide that part of a professor's time assigned to instruction ($\frac{1}{2}$, $\frac{3}{4}$ or $\frac{2}{3}$) into either the number of credit hours or even clock hours taught weekly. The resultant hour load per full-time teacher will commonly vary in respectable institutions between six and fifteen hours in the classroom per week.

A much more important measure of load is the number of students taught during these so-called weekly hour loads. A professor, for example, may teach only six hours a week, but if his classes enroll seventy-five to one hundred students his productivity may be greater than that of a colleague who is in the classroom twelve or fifteen hours a week but whose classes average only ten to twelve students. When teaching productivity is approached in terms of students taught, a truly meaningful measure of productivity is found by multiplying the number of students taught by the number of credit hours taught weekly. The resulting product is known in the jargon of academic cost accounting as "student credit hours."

The student credit hour load cannot and should not be the same for every teacher, every department, each school within a given university, or among a number of institutions. The student credit hour load will necessarily vary among teachers depending upon the subject taught and whether the course is elementary, intermediate, or advanced, laboratory or non-laboratory, required or elective. For example, with respect to required courses, in order to give a complete curriculum in a given field, a minimum number of advanced courses must be offered annually whether or not there are sufficient enrollments to justify them on a purely cost basis. Given traditional teaching techniques, certain elementary courses, owing to the very nature of instruction called for, must have limited enrollments. In freshman English, if enough themes are required and carefully corrected so that students gain a true experience in writing, modest-sized classes are necessary. Students often have not learned to write good English in high school simply because the classes were too large for intensive writing practice and the correction of papers. For administrative and budget purposes, more important than consideration of the load of each staff member is the total productivity of a department or school in a university. Even so, appropriations for higher education cannot be *strictly* on the basis of formulas, no matter how accurate or well-conceived they may be.

WHAT EDUCATION IS FOR

Right here it is appropriate to add a note of warning about our American attitude toward education at all levels. In general, parents and students alike are after the diploma rather than the mastery of skills and the gaining of knowledge and deep insights. The latter are the very stuff of education. They are more important than the high school diploma or the baccalaureate degree. Americans should not go on deluding themselves by providing buildings, equipment and courses without regard to whether they are accomplishing education's real mission, which is learning, and not just passing courses.

A college or a university is not created by naming it or even by chartering it. Only through offering high quality instruction to students who have a sincere desire to learn is it truly built. There are empire builders among the educational fraternity who in their zeal to start new junior and even four-year colleges won't face these facts any more than laymen do.

*   *   *

A TASK FOR EDUCATORS

Certainly studies of teaching loads and ratios, if they are to be more a help than a hindrance, should be done by the educational institutions themselves. There the presidents, deans and other authorities who are cognizant of the many complexities can apply them sensibly.

Some necessary variables have already been discussed. Here are a few others. First, in this age of extreme specialization a professor may be qualified to offer courses only in his specialty. His teaching talents cannot be used more broadly in his department even if a dean or department chairman would like to do so. All the courses of such highly specialized men may have small enrollments and appear to be unnecessarily overlapping. Secondly, some professors can lecture effectively to large numbers, others cannot. Thirdly, some colleges are short on classrooms to accommodate large numbers of students; therefore more teachers are necessary to meet large numbers of small groups. Fourthly, institutions with unusually heavy enrollments in the sciences may need to have lighter teaching loads than those in which students are enrolled more heavily in the humanities and the social sciences. Fifthly, graduate work, necessarily very costly because instruction is so highly individualized, cannot be evaluated cost-wise or ratio-wise to much advantage except within a single institution. It may be that graduate work provides a good supply of part-time teachers, thereby greatly reducing the cost of instruction of undergraduates, especially freshmen. On balance, what seems like very expensive graduate work may even save the institution money.

In spite of all the variables and the delicacy called for, particularly in making decisions on the basis of teaching load analysis, such studies must be made. Moreover, studies along the lines suggested should enable and prompt colleges and universities to exchange new-found, meaningful data among themselves. Sound reason suggests that the responsibility for doing so rests within the individual institutions. But if such studies are not made voluntarily, governing boards should see to it that they are made; the boards may need to be prompted to this by Governors and legislators.

The design of research and the interpretation of the data uncovered is the proper life work of seasoned academic administrators. They know thoroughly the individual institutions analyzed and the world of scholarship generally. For those unskilled in all the intricacies of higher education to make quite possibly superficial studies, and arbitrarily to apply teaching load and other formulas, could be as hazardous as making a surgeon out of a butcher. To interchange the budget officer, legislator, or Governor for a skilled university administrator could ultimately contribute to destroying a nation, even a civilization. This is a day when quality higher education in the United States is essential to our national defense, to an upward curve in our national economic growth, and to our winning the tight race between capitalism and communism.

State officials, of course, *could* make such studies. They might even come to know the particular circumstances within each of their state colleges and universities to an extent that would enable them to apply their findings to create efficiency. But the probability is that they would weaken quality. It would be hazardous if such studies were to set back for a generation a fine university, when we already have far too few first-rate ones. Moreover, would such studies be a wise use of official time? To enter into highway department matters with comparable thoroughness would be to undertake studies of the proper cement mix and reenforcement for concrete roads; with respect to conservation, it would mean determining the proper planting stock in view of soil, climate and parasites. Entering upon such detailed work, which when compared with a complex university is quite simple, is obviously the work of the line departments. If such study is not reserved to the experts within departments or, in this case, the universities and colleges, the states will be beset with duplicated effort. If it is done in staff agencies, such as budget bureaus or legislative audit

offices, not only will there be duplicate effort but possibly confusion of responsibility. Fortunately, in my experience in Michigan and Delaware, I have not personally confronted such hazardous developments, but I understand they are not unknown elsewhere.

FOUR NEEDED STEPS

All need for such unsatisfactory circumstances can be avoided, and efficiency served as well, if several steps are taken. First, good faith, respect and understanding of the other fellow's job must exist both in the educational world and among the citizens, especially those in the state capitols. Second, the colleges and universities must make the studies in question with all possible thoroughness. Third, the findings and their implications should be discussed with appropriate state officers who indicate interest in them and are willing to give the time to listen and learn. Fourth, state officials should find such time, but not amidst the hurly-burly of budget making. Otherwise, their decision-making may be arbitrary and ill-informed relative to higher education. This could break confidence in democratic government at the most vital point for the dissemination of respect for it—the nation's colleges. More important, in view of the indispensability of higher learning, decisions with respect to public higher education will not be as intelligently made as the times demand.

74. Needed: A Re-evaluation of Policies for Higher Education*

ALONZO G. GRACE

THE United States continues to face a staggering task in providing the teachers and classroom facilities required for the formal education of our children and youth. Equally staggering, however, are the financial implications both for public and non-public education. We shall not be able to resolve the problem by considering annual or even biennial budgets isolated from the future. We should be facing now the implications ten years hence and should evolve policy accordingly. The real education crisis confronting the people of the United States, however, is with respect to policy.

It should not take a crisis to initiate the educational policies required to advance our culture and to preserve and improve our way of life. Unfortunately, however, this appears to be the case. Soviet penetration of outer space, irrespective of our delayed effort in this direction, had an immediate effect on the people of the United States. The educational system did not escape the impact of this accomplishment.

The need for greater emphasis on languages, science, mathematics and technology hardly is a matter of dispute in view of the age in which we live. And in spite of the educational view of a minority in our country, the adoption of a policy concerned largely with the identification and education of the intellectually elite would be completely foreign to our culture.

The kind of genius we need, however, will not be uncovered overnight by crash programs. The derivation of policy must not result in legislation by

* Reprinted with permission from *State Government,* Winter 1960. Footnotes omitted.

hysteria, unfounded criticism of men and institutions, disunity through rumor. We are doing irreparable damage to ourselves without the aid of those who would destroy us. This also is an era of great hope and challenge. If we have the will to look beyond the horizon, education in the United States will emerge with new missions and enhanced values. But this will not be accomplished by selfishly clinging to old patterns, by protecting vested interests or by resistance to needed adjustments in policy, organization and program. We need to keep our educational feet on the ground.

. . . New institutions and expanded educational programs in established universities and colleges are contemplated in practically every state. However, growing like Topsy without intelligent consideration of policy is likely to have one primary result, educational chaos. In this paper five areas are suggested for study and the derivation of policy: (1) the organization of higher education, (2) the expanding curriculum, (3) use of the educational plant, (4) competitive programs and regional planning, and (5) the principles involved.

ORGANIZATION

Within the past five years the organization of higher education has changed substantially. The one, two, or even three-year normal school, once common in the educational structure, has been replaced in most states by the four-year teachers college. The teachers college in turn is now disappearing. In many states these institutions have become "state colleges" serving regional educational demands for higher education while retaining the original responsibility for educating teachers. In several states teachers colleges have been designated as "state universities." Meantime state agricultural colleges, or state colleges as many are called, are becoming universities.

Few states can afford the luxury of several real state universities. Equally illogical is the legal transition of teachers colleges to state colleges completely unrelated to the state university. Wise educational and financial planning requires that higher education in the state be coordinated in a more effective manner than the present trend indicates.

The pressures brought to bear on a legislature or Governor to prevent the consolidation of boards, secure more effective financial planning and control or alter the educational structure in any important way are not unfamiliar problems. Following are examples of a few areas in which sound judgment and common sense indicate the need for a sound policy.

1. The presence of several state universities in a single state will lead only to educational and financial confusion. Few states will be able to maintain several higher educational institutions of high quality unless a division of labor can be secured. A university system having a single board of higher education with a chief administrative officer should coordinate the entire system; each state, however should of course adopt an organization pattern adapted to its own needs.

2. Teachers colleges which become state colleges with an expanded program should be an integral part of the university system and in many instances regional branches of the state university.

3. The establishment of community colleges, many formerly known as junior colleges, represents another important trend. It will be important to retain them, as a rule, on a two-year basis, though it is entirely possible that many ultimately will extend programs to include full four year programs. The two-year colleges, however, present an opportunity for many universities to select students from those in the two-year programs, and possibly to eliminate at the university level the freshman and sophomore programs. In many cases today, students are admitted to a university because the law specifies that any graduate of an accredited high school has a right to enter. In many cases a substantial percentage of the freshman class then is dropped before reaching the second year.

4. The secondary school is not the subject of this consideration. The present policy of four years to complete the high school program, however, should be modified to permit qualified students to enter higher education directly from the third year in high school.

5. State departments of education, in general, need not expand if a more effective relationship with state educational institutions is developed.

6. Many states have authorized or completed surveys of higher education. Such a survey should be continuous. It should be developed cooperatively. In general, it should be a self-survey, for each state has its full share of competent experts and interested citizens who are fully able to study and evaluate educational policy and program. Too frequently in the past, however, surveys have resulted primarily in the production of a number of volumes which repose safely in the archives of the library.

THE EXPANDING CURRICULUM

The courses approved and offered by an institution naturally require teaching personnel and this involves, as it should, a major part of the budget. However, examination of most university or college catalogs will reveal a multiplicity of courses. In many cases, courses have been divided and subdivided to form new courses, to the point that in some instances hardly a good idea is left. Many courses could be eliminated, consolidated, or arranged in larger areas, without depreciating the intellectual curiosity of the individual or contributing to the decadence of the democratic ideal. An evaluation of course offerings in most institutions would reveal much unnecessary duplication and marginal educational offering.

Departmental lines and the walls between schools, colleges and divisions within a university are difficult to penetrate. Few educators would be willing to return to the era of the fixed curriculum in the light of the evolution of our social system and the world situation, and this would not be desirable. On the other hand, our educational cafeteria has been the end result of an uncontrolled elective system which now has reached a point that makes it entirely possible for the individual to elect himself out of an education. Few would dispute the value of developing the kinds of educational experience that will contribute to the security of our constitutional government and develop the individual to the fullest extent of his endowment; but these goals are not attained by fragmenting courses.

The elective principle was accepted as a result of early experimentation on a small scale by President Elliot of Harvard in 1869. It was not until the middle of the 1880's, however, that the elective system was put into full operation. The academic environment then, in many aspects, was little different from what it is at the present time. Less serious students would pick courses in terms of their personal comfort; the more serious minded would begin intensive specialization early in their university careers. Professors, in many cases, were teaching introductory courses in most subjects as if the students were planning to become specialists in the subject, and this growing emphasis on specialization resulted in

an extensive system of prerequisites for it.

*   *   *

Institutions also should consider, at the upper levels of collegiate education and especially the graduate school level, the value of independent study on the part of candidates for degrees. The student who undertakes to pursue a course voluntarily and on his own initiative would relieve the necessity of adding courses. This would recognize the intellectual maturity and more nearly meet the objectives of many serious minded students.

USE OF THE EDUCATIONAL PLANT

Several factors should be considered in a thorough study of the use of the educational plant. Only two such factors are presented here: the academic calendar and schedule of classes, and class size.

THE SCHEDULE

Each institution of higher education should provide for a continuous study of plant utilization. The institution may find that it does not provide for an academic program that makes full use of available classroom space. Classrooms in many institutions are unused during the period between the annual commencement and the opening for the fall semester. In other instances classrooms, laboratories, and other facilities are unused during the late afternoons and evenings. Frequently, under the autonomous organization of the several schools and divisions in institutions of higher education, the presence of unused rooms in one school or college may be unknown to another part of the university that needs them. These are not easy matters to solve, but continuous study of the use of facilities—including classrooms, laboratories and special facilities—would result in more efficient use of the plant and, in many instances, in better planning when new classroom buildings are requested.

* * *

SIZE OF CLASSES

A trend toward experimentation with large classes has continued for some time. In recent years the introduction of mass media—notably television, radio and other audio-visual aids—has resulted in important experimental developments. It is not the purpose of this presentation to evaluate television as an instructional device, either as supplementary to classroom teaching or as a substitute for it, but rather to consider class size as an essential factor in wise educational and financial planning.

Considerable confusion exists with respect to what constitutes class size. In many cases, a ratio is obtained by dividing the total enrollment by the total educational personnel, including administrators, supervisors, non-teaching department heads and other special personnel. Many institutions will reflect a small student-teacher ratio because of this practice. The most important way of computing the actual size of classes in any institution is to know the number of students each teacher actually has under his supervision in each course. The defense of administrative, supervisory or other positions must be made on some other basis than the number of students enrolled per class.

There is no question that the proliferation of the curriculum through the introduction of many courses may result in a number of exceedingly small classes. In many cases this is not defensible. The results of studies of small classes will not reveal more effective acquisition of knowledge or a better quality of education, if these be the only criteria of individual educational progress. Certainly a small class should not be regarded as a device to insure good teaching. Mediocrity in teaching will remain mediocrity irrespective of class size.

There is no standard formula to guide administrators in preparing a schedule of courses that will result in the elimination of small classes. Many small classes continue primarily because the teacher is available. However, a combination of classes or alternating of certain offerings is entirely possible in many cases. There is little validity in attempting to arrange a schedule on the basis of so many students per teacher. Classes in many disciplines that have as few as ten or fifteen students could be increased substantially without impeding the diffusion of knowledge or the educational future of the individual. The class size policy should be a matter of continuous study in each institution. And in the records of the institution there should be a breakdown showing the actual registration in each course.

To defend a small class on the basis of the nature of the discipline, or the requirement for personalized attention, is to do so on no grounds at all. At the advanced graduate level small seminars frequently are entirely justified. But even at the graduate level, where a student is working on a research proposal, one teacher per fifteen students is adequate if the teachers will recognize the maturity of the individual, his intellectual competency and his capacity to work independently. In fact, higher education in this country includes a great deal of "wet nursing," so to speak, that ought to be discouraged early in the graduate student's career.

In many disciplines, thirty-five students per teacher is not excessive. For some, in which the lecture is the primary method of instruction, 100 to 200 students per teacher would not be excessive—provided that the teacher is a master and his load is adjusted to the many personal conferences that represent an important part of the educational process.

COMPETITIVE PROGRAMS AND REGIONAL PLANNING

A loose structural organization frequently results in the development of competitive programs. This problem will become more complex as more universities are authorized. Care should be exercised so that in most instances institutions with excellent programs, designed to meet their original objective, are not permitted to expand without reference to the other higher educational resources in the state.

* * *

It also may be that within an institution of higher education, particularly at the graduate level, specialization in a given field is not available, and the development of a separate department would lead to considerable expenditure of funds. Barriers between institutions should be removed so that a student in one institution may spend a portion of a year or a year in another institution, where he can secure the benefit of the specialization with which he is concerned—thus making it unnecessary for the home institution to establish some new school, college or division.

A BASIC PRINCIPLE AND SUGGESTED NATIONAL GOALS

Affecting all these considerations are two basic elements in the evolution of our system of education: viz., basic educational principles and our national goals in education.

PRINCIPLE OF UNIVERSALITY

Only one major principle of education in the United States is considered here —that of universality. Our citizens soon will have to ask the questions: How much formal schooling is necessary for all? Shall it be universal higher education for everyone? Are we confusing equality of educational opportunity with equal education for all? We must

soon realize that every individual is important in our society, irrespective of the honest labor in which he is engaged. But does this importance require universal higher education?

Education for all the children of all the people does not imply higher education for everyone irrespective of his capacity. We cannot, on the other hand, afford to develop an educational system limited to the intellectually elite in the United States. I have observed that policy and the results in Germany. But I would plead for a system that contributes to the advancement of our culture.

We are agreed that no one asks how much education one has or what his I.Q. is when he casts his vote. These are not requirements if one runs for office, or serves on a jury, or buys goods. The security of this country *is* vested in an educated citizenship. Our first line of defense is a citizenship prepared to protect and improve our way of life and to defend the principles for which our country stands. But this does not require equal education for all. Nor should it prevent the development of a scholarship program to enable many of the talented youth who today never enter college to secure a college education.

SUGGESTED NATIONAL GOALS

The primary aim of education under totalitarian auspices is indoctrination in the ideology of the party. The principal goal is the creation of the national, political human being. In the case of the Nazis it was the creation of the National Socialist human being; in the case of the Communists it is the creation of the National Communist human being. Freedom, the right to private judgment, the dignity of the individual, the search for and the dissemination of truth, no longer are the possessions of the individual in such systems, for the individual is a servant of the state, and the state is master of the individual.

"The first aim of education," commented a London newspaper a few years ago, "is to get our values right. We must understand from the start that we have to develop not more machine-like aptitudes but the whole worth of human beings. Intelligence needs to be directed by such qualities of character as goodness, kindness, and courage. If not, we might produce a Dr. Goebbels, but we would have forgotten our civilization." This probably is a fair statement of the aims of education as conceived by nations interested in free men interested in a free society.

Over the years the aims of education in the United States have been derived from the deliberation of voluntary, national educational associations, or committees of educators, or individual educators. These represent a somewhat extensive statement of what the educational system, in large measure, is expected to accomplish. But we have done little to ascertain whether or not these aims are translated into actuality in the classroom.

It would seem that we have decentralized our educational system to such an extent that the accomplishment of our aims remains largely a pious hope. The aim and spirit of education in the United States could be expressed in the following manner: (1) to provide the kind and amount of education that will develop the individual to the highest point of his potentiality or within the limit of his ability; (2) to insure the national security. The latter would involve a constant inventory of our manpower needs and the training and education required to meet these needs.

This is an era of re-evaluation. Educators in partnership with citizens should be concerned with the elements that will lead to quality on a mass education basis; with the distinction between equal education for all and equality of opportunity; with the more effective identification and education of talent; with the development of the ability to think independently and constructively; with the dignity of work, and the usefulness of each of us in this constitutional government; with devotion to the continuance and the improvement of our freedom and our way of life. There are sufficient issues and problems involved in deriving a policy of quality in American education that citizens and educators well can afford to devote their constructive, joint efforts constantly to the problem.

We need to resolve the issues. But we first must face them realistically.

75. Farm Research—Its Benefits for America*

L. L. RUMMELL

*   *   *

WHEN Abraham Lincoln signed the Morrill Act in 1862 to establish land grant colleges, embracing agriculture and the mechanic arts, he did not foresee that research would be needed to keep the agricultural colleges refreshed

* Reprinted with permission from *State Government*, November 1957.

with new ideas. It took twenty-five years for this need to become evident. Then in 1877 the Congress passed the Hatch Act authorizing grants to states to establish and maintain agricultural experiment stations in every state, correlated with the agricultural colleges. In another quarter century extension was added to take these research findings out to the farmers to use them.

Within the last decade more attention has been given to increased support for research and extension than in any like previous period. Despite farm surpluses the Congress has recognized that research and extension must receive increased attention. The approach in research has been to improve efficiency of farm operation, to improve marketing relations, to study farm and home problems in a new economy, and to find new uses for farm products.

With declining numbers of farms, fewer acres to raise foods and fiber, and with constantly increasing population, there can logically be expected a day before many years when surpluses disappear. One unfavorable crop season nationally right now would make us conscious of the small reserve the United States holds.

Now let us come back to that question Mr. Average Citizen raises: What do I get out of my tax dollar in all this?

May I set forth some considerations here from the standpoint of the urban citizen, what benefits he receives from farm research? I got a cue one time from a remark of Charles F. Kettering of General Motors, who sits on our Board of Trustees at the Ohio State University. He made it after I had offered a rather comprehensive report of the year's activities in our state agricultural experiment station. He listened intently, and then remarked: "What you need is a book that will tell the public what research means to them. Research is an investment. It does not cost. It pays. And it pays the city consumer. You must deal with city consumers because they are in the majority."

FARM INTEREST—
CITY INTEREST

Let us look at "Boss Ket's" contention: Today only about 13 per cent of our population live on farms. There are twenty states that have fewer than 20 per cent farm population. We in Ohio have 10 per cent, with the farm population constantly declining. You do not need to tell these farmers that research makes them more efficient, more proserous farmers. They visit the colleges of agriculture and the experiment stations. They read the bulletins from these stations and from the U.S. Department of Agriculture. They know their county agents, read farm papers and newspapers, listen to radio and TV, or they copy their neighbor's practices frequently when they see him doing a better job of farming.

But how about the 87 per cent who live in the city? Do they feel that agricultural research influences them, makes them better nourished? With each decade, feeding this city population becomes more acute. Three million more mouths are added anually here at home, and we have been helping under-privileged nations as well. It may be a real challenge to the land grant colleges and experiment stations to find the means of feeding these increased millions by, say 1975, on fewer acres. We must step up technological "know how" to increase vertically—that is, to make each acre, each animal, produce more. There are but few acres in America still to be brought under the plow.

*   *   *

HOW THE CITIES GAIN

At a Senate appropriations hearing in our state Assembly a few years ago, after a presentation of the experiment station needs for the biennium, one shrewd Senator shot a comment at me: "Why do we have an agricultural experiment station anyhow at taxpayers' expense? It just looks to me like another farm subsidy."

Our answer to him was that he had a knife and fork interest in this appropriation, and so did all his constituents in the metropolitan area where he lived. Three times a day he sits down at the table with his family with an abundance of food of highest quality and at an economical cost. Nowhere else in the world can he do this. He need not question whether there will be sufficient food or raiment, and he can always look for excellence in quality.

How many more representatives of the people feel as the Senator did? We have some research that directly affects them, as testing fibers and clothing, nutrition of school children, care of lawns, control of diseases—as in their elm and oak trees, or culture of flowers and shrubs. We have rather extensive experiments in all these areas. About 400 people, nearly all city folks, just came to our Ohio Agricultural Experiment Station field day recently on lawns and ornamentals.

Again, we have certain farm research that is of keen interest to city businessmen. We have field days with machinery, rural electrification, drainage, credit and banking, retail marketing, household appliances, hatcherymen and the like. They are all city interests that spring from farming operations. Hence we cater to them. They are vital to that 87 per cent of our population who live off the farm.

* * *

THE WIDER PURPOSES

Still, there is a greater underlying philosophy in farm research and how it pays for all citizens. This is the story of foods and fibers, of production efficiency, of greater nutrition, wonder drugs, medicines, atomic energy—all related to farm research and of vital importance in everyday living to all citizens. Many of these stories read like fairy tales, beyond the imagination of a Horatio Alger.

Look for instance at an immigrant boy who came to New Jersey. For years Selman Waksman was looking through a microscope at biological life in the soil. One day he found something he had never recognized before—streptomycin. We know of the wonder drugs in use today by the human family—

how they have saved lives, prolonged our lives, improved our efficiency, added to human happiness. The experimental work was done not on human guinea pigs but with farm animals and in agricultural experiment stations. Streptomycin and aureomycin are familiar words today in every household. They came from the work of a then obscure scientist at Rutgers, New Jersey, working in soils.

Earlier the research work with minerals and vitamins was likewise done with agricultural experiment stations. We learned, for example, that minerals are needed for growing pigs and that vitamins are essential for health and growth in pigs and chicks and calves. Then we took this new knowledge and applied it to human nutrition. Our home economists revised their menus so that today more dependence is placed on green, leafy and yellow vegetables, on tomatoes and fruits, on dairy products and other foods rich in vitamins and minerals. A multi-million dollar business has grown up in drug stores for supplementary products in pill form.

The antibiotics play an important role in agriculture, in animal feeding, in plant pathology and even in food processing. Farm magazines carry display advertisements for such products as aureomycin and terramycin for livestock feeding, because they promote growth in young animals and chicks. Streptomycin and aureomycin have been miraculous in control of fire blight in pears and aples. A pear industry that seemed doomed to extinction was saved. Cheaper meats are another result.

* * *

EFFECTS ON COMMON FOODS

Let us look at a few of our common foods and see what research has done to make them cheaper and of better quality.

It has not been uncommon for the homemaker to go to the supermarket for her pork roast or chops for dinner and find that the red meat was a tiny eye of a couple bites, while all about it was fat which had to be discarded. On the other hand, she might have been able to find a roast with a high percentage of red meat and little fat. It all depended upon the type of hog.

We have a swine evaluation station where annually hundreds of pigs are tested side by side. Everything is the same except heredity. Thus we find certain families that breed the "meat type." Farmers find they feed out with more profit; the market pays a premium of 50 cents to $1.00 a hundredweight, and best of all the city housewife is better satisfied with the meat for her family.

We have likewise been testing certain bovine families or strains. Here, again, there are marked variations in type of meat. At one of the experiment stations we found that silage has a high value in producing cheap beef, and that corncobs have half the feeding value of the shelled corn. This spells cheaper beef for the shopper at the supermarket.

Now the latest research shows even a greater gain on cattle to lower feed costs. This comes from a small amount of hormone called diethyl stilbestrol. Bulls make about a quarter of a pound daily faster gain, and steers will also step up rate of gain.

Nearly all cattle feeds today carry stilbestrol. We implant a small dose in the base of the ear. It has no deleterious effect on the animal; it does not carry over into the meat to concern the consumer; but it does mean a faster gain, and therefore cheaper meat for the consumer.

HYBRID CORN—MORE MILK

Probably the most sensational research of recent years to step up production has been with hybrid corn. We expect about a 20 per cent increase in yield over the old open pollinated varieties of grandfather's day. In a state like Ohio, with 200 million bushels of corn production, that can add to the farmers' income at least $40 million annually—more than has been spent by the state on the experiment station in 75 years!

On the same acreage, with the same fertilizer and cultivation, the farmer harvests 100 bushels where he used to get 80 to 85 bushels. This means cheaper grain. And it means cheaper meat from hogs and cattle consuming it, cheaper milk from cows fed this corn, cheaper eggs from the poultry flock. Increased yields therefore benefit not just the farmer alone but every person who eats the foods produced by that farmer.

In my boyhood dairy cows averaged about 3,500 pounds of milk a year. Today the Ohio average is 6,500 pounds, and our dairy herd improvement associations report an average of 9,200 pounds a year from cows on test. We have an experimental herd of about thirty Holsteins that average 14,000 pounds a year. This herd is 100 per cent the result of artificial breeding, and all these cows have been bred artificially to bulls of known high production. It is the greatest improvement of recent years for the dairy industry—this artificial insemination from bulls that have proved they will transmit high milk production to their offspring.

Not only is the city consumer getting more and cheaper milk, but she knows it is safe—no disease, thanks to control programs in herds and to pasteurization, and she gets it in a more convenient, cheaper container, likely in paper. It is one of her cheapest foods from a nutrition standpoint—again a strike for research.

A RICHER VEGETABLE KINGDOM

A quick look at the vegetable kingdom can round out this picture. The first bulletin from our Ohio station was on potatoes. There has been a vast improvement in this crop, with yields three or four times as great—600 bushels per acre in many cases. And the potatoes are of better quality—white, smooth, with few eyes, good for baking, french fries or potato chips. A by-product of the second world war, DDT, has added about 100 bushels per acre to the potato yield just by control of insects that defied the earlier sprays. Modern machinery, better spraying, heavy fertilization, newer varieties have all contributed to give us potatoes of higher quality and lower cost.

* * *

Johnny Appleseed is a romantic, historic character that roamed across the state toward Lake Erie, planting thousands of apple seeds in the wilderness. Monuments have been erected to his memory, and recently a state highway was named in his honor. Yet not a single commercial apple traces to him. The quality fruit in the supermarket is the result of years of patient breeding to get a fruit of supreme quality. In twenty-five years at the Ohio station three new varieties—Melrose, Franklin and Ruby—have been developed. All yield well, and the fruit has good eating and culinary quality.

In this story of research, I have selected examples of a few common, everyday foods—meat, potatoes, milk, cereal, tomatoes for salad and apples for dessert. We might well have used dozens of other examples, for nearly every food is an object of research in some state agricultural experiment station in America.

We could finish the illustrations with the decorations upon the dinner table. Flowers, too, are constant objects of research, along with other ornamentals. They are selected for greater beauty and hardiness, protected from pests, even studied for most efficient marketing. Here again is an example of agricultural research at work to make life more enjoyable, whether you live in the country or in a metropolitan center.

Home economics is a study of research today in all agricultural experiment stations. Foods and nutrition, textiles, household appliances, wall coverings, menus for school children, economics and community activities are all studied in research, and form a part of the program of agricultural college instruction and extension. Farming is a family business. The research has a wider application to families everywhere.

RESEARCH AND THE FUTURE

Research, then, is not accented today for greater production. Rather it is designed to find ways to cut costs all along the line—in production, in processing and in marketing. Control of diseases in plants and animals, checking insect attacks, reducing weeds, all affect the nation's food supply in costs as well as in quantity. Conservation of water and soil resources may affect production costs today, but it is a means to insure the future resources of the land.

In recent years 20 per cent of increased federal funds for agricultural research have been tagged for research in marketing. This is double edged, benefiting both farmer and consumer. Much of this new research has been aimed at consumer desires and economies. Extension has further aided by consumer information service.

Examples of further research in experiment stations are legion. Far more research will be essential in years ahead if we are to keep ahead of the procession in population growth and maintain the standards of nutrition we enjoy today.

May we daily, as we sit down to our three square meals, thank God that we live in an America where food is abundant, where it has highest quality, and where it comes at economical cost. Thank God we have an educated farmer, and back of him the land grant college with its experiment station and its extension. All three are keys to our national security.

76. The States Must Plan*

JAMES W. MARTIN

ONE general reaction to the question as to whether a state needs planning is that every service the commonwealth operates must be carefully planned and continually replanned if it is to be economically rendered. Even so it should perhaps be accepted as a matter of course that the question is intended to raise issues which are distinctly more complex.

Let me answer the basic question affirmatively. Speaking as a citizen who has no technical background in planning, I believe each state generally, and Kentucky specifically, ought to have solid planning facilities. I suggest we examine two or three of the functions which seem to be inadequately worked out in most states and thereby lay the groundwork for an answer to the basic query.

There are at least three major phases of the state's problem of looking after its physical plant that are inadequately provided in most cases: (1) Maintenance of existing resources, (2) aesthetic and economical development of institutions and other land-using facilities, and (3) tying state enterprises into communities in such a way as to aid rather than to hinder efficient local growth. In general, professional planners have relatively little experience in the first of these areas, much more in the second and most of all in the third.

MAINTENANCE

As Kentucky commissioner of finance and later as commissioner of highways, I had to learn the hard way of the need for planning systematically

* Reprinted with permission from *National Civic Review*, July 1962.

for state property maintenance. Fairly early in my service in the Kentucky Department of Finance, the director of the Division of Purchases reported uncertainty as to the best quality of coal to buy for certain state institutions. To aid in the solution of this straightforward specification problem, we sought suitable professional aid in a special study of state coal-burning equipment. It soon became apparent that this purchasing issue was thoroughly mixed up with matters of institutional and state management, with the caliber of particular classes of employees, with water treatment practices, with heating installations aside from the furnace itself, and with the physical facilities for handling coal and housing furnaces—to mention only a few of the variables.

In short, it became obvious that, if the state were to use coal effectively, it must deal with a complex of factors in such a manner as to reverse the prevailing philosophy of management. It must focus on prevention rather than repair in the conduct of its maintenance program.

From the point of view of this discussion two phases of this preventive maintenance policy are important: (1) The action program, to be effective at low cost, had to be based on a carefully defined policy in terms of a philosophy of maintenance; (2) the implementation of the policy required comprehensive planning in the context of an involved situation.

The planners needed to recognize that the state's plant was employed for educational, hospital, welfare, correctional, general office and numerous other purposes. They had to keep in mind the fact that the Department of Finance directly managed some plants, that another central agency managed other facilities and that localized institutions managed still other property. They were required to take into account the fact that some plant administrators were cooperative, some were not. And they were constrained to envisage a program not only affecting the use of fuel but broad enough to provide for preventing leaking roofs, undue deterioration of building woodwork, fire hazards from rubbish piles or breakdowns in laundry, refrigerating, air conditioning, dairy, farm, kitchen, or elevator equipment.

To plan such activity in the complicated maze of relationships, then, the state must have technical aid from diverse personnel in addition to those employees with a planning outlook, such as all types of engineers, architects, managers and specialists having knowledge of all the programs concerned. It must secure something like a consensus among diverse officials and employees in some manner involving little or no compulsion.

In its complexity the situation presented a characteristic planning problem; but in its particular focus, it exhibited aspects scarcely typical of the settings in which the professional planner usually works.

INSTITUTIONAL PLANNING

Another setting in which the state may find its planning inadequate has to do with intra-institutional development. As particular localized educational, welfare, correctional, public construction and other plants expand to service enlarged programs, there is historical precedent for confining growth plans to telling an architect he is to design a school for a specified vacant space which will cost $400,000 or $4,000,000 as the case may be. Too often inadequate prior professional consideration has been given as to how the proposed building is related in function or appearance to the previ-

ously constructed facilities or to those to be provided in the future. Much less, in some cases, is full professional attention devoted to the relationship of the plant facilities and their objectives to the terrain, the soil, the subsoil and the economy in which the institution functions.

Part of this absence of adequate planning is related to the lack of foresight —and of appropriate professional advice—on the part of public leadership when particular institutions were begun in the 1830s, the 1880s, or the 1920s. Such deficiencies have often meant absolutely inadequate land acreage for the long pull. This situation is eloquently exemplified by many present-day universities. . . .

Incidentally, it is important to perspective that blame for this situation be distributed parsimoniously. To illustrate the point, I mention a new urban bypass which, according to a planning consultant's 1947 estimate, would have to accommodate 10,000 vehicles a day by 1960 but which the city found to be handling 12,000 vehicles a day in the latter part of 1949—only two years following the estimate. . . .

The inadequacies of institutional planning for the long run can be greatly reduced in most states by rather simple expedients, even though the existing disharmonies of appearance, the inept functional arrangements and the inefficient land utilization cannot be entirely corrected. . . .

ARTICULATING STATE LAND USE WITH THE ENVIRONMENT

The problem of so planning the use of state lands that facilities and their arrangement not only function efficiently within the institutional unit itself but also conform with the surroundings—physical, aesthetic and social—claims planning attention. Many states have made marked progress in this area or in phases of it, but others have made none except by chance.

There are various possible explanations of failure to coordinate with other public or private developments or plans. In some cases there are state government deficiencies; in others there are not. For example, a state may be prepared to locate and design highways in such a manner as to facilitate the implementation of local master plans. If the local government has no master plan, however, there are difficulties. North Carolina makes construction of certain highway facilities contingent on the existence of such a local master plan. In particular cases, the State Highway Department makes assistance available if the locality lacks and requests technical aid.

A more usual situation, however, is one in which state construction goes forward without being deliberately planned in consonance with the local or sectional outlook or even with obvious local or state growth trends. Indeed, conflicts among state agencies themselves are far too usual.

One example of the latter is the expansion decision in an urban or suburban setting which assumes the availability of nonexistent local resources. The state's location of a stadium, hospital or traffic generating plant or plant extension in a downtown area which lacks street or parking facilities can preclude the execution of the most carefully conceived city master plan. In some settings such a project can even interrupt obvious and entirely wholesome growth trends.

With adequate state planning, the unilateral prevention of tragedies such as these is usually easy and economical. That the opportunity for a decision in the interest of long-range community development, and of efficient use of the plant or plant extension itself, is not apparent to each state institutional management strongly suggests that every major land-use development or other change ought to involve the talents of specialists. Moreover, the planning assignment should extend not only to intra-institutional efficiencies but also to the aesthetic, social, physical and functional tie with the whole community.

The state government, in brief, requires planning incident to three basic functions in relation to its physical resources:

(1) The efficient preservation and use of the existing plant necessitate comprehensive planning for preventive maintenance;

(2) The satisfactory expansion of existing land-using facilities and the development of new institutional establishments, if they are to perform their functions at low unit cost, must benefit not only from the skills of program management specialists but also from those of architects, various classes of engineers and professional planners conscious of institutional objectives;

(3) If the state institutional plant is to net an addition, rather than an impediment, to the growth of the city in or near which it is situated and to serve the state efficiently, its management must have the most sophisticated community planning skill available brought to bear on locational and other developmental decisions.

Perhaps this summary of the need for state planning in relation to physical plant is incomplete without emphasis on the highway as an urgent point of focus at the present time. From all three of the angles presented above the need for better state highway planning is acute in many states.

THE SERVICE PROGRAM

Every state government seems to want specialized operations planning to ensure efficient service programs. In a well managed state, the budget staff seeks to perform this function from the viewpoint of agency-by-agency efficiency and from that of balancing support among various services. But in most states—including even those which have good budgeting—there is inadequate attention to program coordination in the total administrative process.

Let us first take a look at state natural resource administrative functions, not because they are most important but because they may well be closest to the professional planner's area of interest. In many states there is at least one agency concerned with soil conservation. There are administrators having to do with water resources. There is separate attention to forests. And of course there is usually an entirely independent department—or more than one department—concerned with wild life in the forest and with that in the water. These and other governmental departments, bureaus, divisions or institution often operate with no planning coordination to assure that uneconomical duplication is eliminated and that disastrous omission of service areas is discovered and corrected. This lack is complicated by the fact that some of the agencies involved, such as the agricultural extension service, are typically not directly, if at all, subordinate to the governor.

Particular states have sought to deal with this coordination problem by setting up an over-all department of conservation. Such action may alleviate the difficulty. In practice, however, this kind of solution is partial in coverage and may be incomplete even as to the services brought together within the departmental structure. Thus the states which have maximum management structural integration may possibly lack facilities for planning functional attacks on all fronts in the natural resources administration area.

A second kindred problem presents itself in the field of business regulation. In the broader sense regulatory functions include the licensing of professions and other callings similarly treated under the policing authority. They also include the regulation of transactions in certain commodities such as alcohol, feed, seeds and fertilizers. And they are especially concerned with public utility supervision to assure reasonable rates and services. State arrangements for administering these functions are frequently affected in much the same way as natural resource administration. There may also be a business regulation problem of securing consistency of policy.

Some states have tackled the regulation difficulty by structural rearrangement. For example, this attack has aided greatly as to regulation of the public service corporations. Apparently, however, the reorganization approach is inapplicable to the solution of the entire problem without causing more trouble than it cures.

Then, there is difficulty as to the coordination of state educational programs. One phase concerns the consideration of elementary, secondary, collegiate and special programs, some of which the state conducts directly and some of which it administers through counties, towns (or townships), cities or independent school districts. There may even be problems of coordination with privately conducted schools or colleges. Another dimension of the educational problem has to do with the intergovernmental relationships implicit in the usual decentralized approach to common school administration. The state, as the party having the dominant legal function, finds practical human relations even more troublesome than the disagreements regarding prerogatives among federal, state and local governments.

In a number of states, educational administration is even more disintegrated structurally at the state level than is natural resource management. In Kentucky, the School for the Deaf, the University of Kentucky and each state college operates under a separate governing authority. The Department of Education, unlike the other boards, has tenuous ties with the governor. It operates Lincoln Institute, the School for the Blind, the three vocational schools and the several vocational secondary school centers largely independently of each other. And none of them is completely integrated with the common school education program conducted through independent school districts.

To deal with these and kindred difficulties, states may find a variety of approaches. Whatever the frontal attack on the problem of securing coordination, the common ingredient, it would seem, is systematic, long-range but flexible-minded planning. Planning must be democratic in the sense that numerous interested agency representatives must be directly involved. There is good reason, however, why states should utilize planning leadership independent of the operating or line agencies directly concerned—as such an arrangement appears to be essential in local government—if satisfactory results are to ensue. Even to a greater extent than in local government this staff task needs to be closely linked with budget administration.

Such planning requires the highest caliber of manpower. This particular prescription seems to have been met when a few years ago Pennsylvania set up apparatus to do a part of the planning which in the present discussion is envisaged as the element that must be present in any onslaught on the problem of securing functional coordination among the agencies and subagencies of state government.

CONCLUSION

To return to the fundamental question as to whether there is need for state planning, it is appropriate to conclude that there *is* such a need:

(1) The state, like the city, must plan the preservation and development of its own property both for efficient use and for effective relationships with the community. The maintenance element, for various reasons, may bulk larger in states than in cities.

(2) The state needs planning for its own service programs in ways which in part are usually reasonably well handled and in part are rarely, if ever, looked after effectively. In particular, the state requires careful, cooperative planning for programs which involve multi-agency execution.

77. The Legal and Moral Basis of Right to Work Laws*

J. C. GIBSON

THE subject we discuss here today is legislative restrictions on union security agreements. The union security agreement we are talking about is a contract providing for compulsory union membership, and the issue is whether compulsory membership should be authorized and fostered, or banned in the interest of personal liberty.

* Address before the Section of Labor Relations Law, American Bar Association, Philadelphia, Pa., August 23, 1955.

THE RIGHT TO WORK LAWS

The laws restricting compulsory union membership agreements are commonly and quite accurately called right to work laws. The appellation is derived from one of the two fundamental principles of American constitutional law which the right to work statutes implement in this field. The first of these principles is the right to work, and the second is the right of association.

The core of the typical right to work statute consists of two simple provisions; *first*, that the right to work shall not be denied by reason either of membership or non-membership in a labor union; and *second*, that any agreement or understanding which conditions the right to work in any occupation upon membership or non-membership in a labor union is illegal and void.

Eighteen states in the south, middle west and west have right to work laws of this kind. Some of them are found in constitutional provisions, but the majority take the form of statutes.

These laws have been upheld as consistent with federal and state constitutions. The Supreme Court of the United States rejected a constitutional attack on them in *Lincoln Union* v. *Northwestern Co.*, 335 U.S. 525, 531 (1949).

But there would seem to be other kinds of right to work laws in the states which are not always recognized as such. For instance, there are the little Norris-LaGuardia acts, about 29 of them, pretty largely copied after the Federal statute. These statutes contain a declaration of public policy which says that the worker "Though he should be free to decline to associate with his fellows it is necessary that he have full freedom of association, self-organization and designation of representatives of his own choosing* * *." 29 USC Section 102. On its face this language sets forth a public policy in favor of giving the worker complete freedom of choice as to whether he will join or decline to join a union. The courts of some states have so held in cases where picketing to force employer acceptance of a union shop agreement has been enjoined. *Roth* v. *Retail Clerks Union*, 216 Ind. 363, 24 N. E. 2d 280 (1939), *Bartenders Union* v. *Clark Restaurants, Inc.*, 122 Ind. Ap. 165, 102 N. E. 2d 220 (1951), *Building Service Union* v. *Gazzam*, 29 Wash. 2d 488, 188 P. 2d 97 (1948). Other courts, however, have held that to attach such significance to the declaration

of policy would contravene the major purpose of the statutes. *Denver Local Union No. 13* v. *Perry Truck Lines*, 106 Colo. 25, 101 P. 2d 436 (1940). . . .

The ultimate case for these laws rests primarily on the proposition that they implement and extend specific statutory protection to fundamental constitutional rights, among them the right to work and the freedom of association, and this protection is accorded without impairing the effectiveness or welfare of labor unions.

THE INHERENT RIGHT TO WORK

What then is the concept of this right to work?

The right to work is coextensive with the right of life itself, for all save a small fraction of mankind must work for a living, and a denial of the basic means of survival imperils life itself. This utter dependence of man upon freedom of opportunity to engage in the common occupations of life has been brought home to members of minority groups time after time in country after country. . . .

What we are talking about is of course the right to work in the American and not in the Marxian sense of the term. In the Marxian sense the right to work is interpreted as embracing a guaranty of employment by a paternalistic state controlling all of the means of production. In its American sense the term signifies the inherent right of every man to an opportunity to seek and retain the gainful employment which he desires, for which he may be fitted, and which is available in our economy. The right to work demands that this opportunity be unfettered by artificial and unnecessary restrictions or the imposition of unreasonable or arbitrary conditions, such as a requirement of union membership. . . .

There is no right to work in the sense of a right to march up to an employer and to demand a particular job as, say, a machinist or a pattern maker, and there is no right to work which can prevent an employer from discharging a man for cause, or because there is just no more work for him to do.

Right to work laws do not purport to create new rights but only to protect fundamental rights from invasion through imposition of compulsory unionism as a condition of employment. They do not directly create any jobs, but by helping to keep the economy free and by keeping opportunities open, they inevitably in the long run lead to more and more chances for employment.

The fundamental nature of the right to work was first proclaimed by the Supreme Court of the United States in decisions invalidating post-Civil War legislation depriving those who had supported the Confederacy in the Civil War of the right to engage in the professions. Thereafter, it was successfully invoked to protect Chinese laundrymen in San Francisco who were being run out of business by discriminatory enforcement of a municipal ordinance; to protect alien restaurant workers from a state quota law in Arizona; to protect railroad men in Texas who, while possessing long experience and ample competence, yet could not qualify under a statutory test cunningly devised to channel employment exclusively to a special group; to protect owners of private employment agencies from statutes contrived to drive them out of business. It was used as a shield against attempts to drive out of employment teachers of foreign languages in the hysteria engendered by World War I. After World War II it was successfully invoked against a California statute which would have denied Japanese fishermen the right to resume their long standing occupation off the Pacific Coast.

The right to work was declared to be a plain and self-evident principle of American constitutional law by Justice Charles Evans Hughes when, forty years ago, he declared in *Truax* v. *Raich,* 239 U.S. 33 (1915):

"It requires no argument to show that *the right to work for a living in the common occupations of the community* is of the very essence of the personal freedom and opportunity that it was the purpose of the Amendment to secure." (Emphasis supplied)

The amendment of which he spoke was the Fourteenth which, like the Fifth Amendment to the Federal Constitution, forbids the government to deprive any person of life, liberty or property without due process of law.

The right to work has never been more eloquently delineated than by Mr. Justice Douglas in *Barsky* v. *Board of Regents,* 347 U.S. 442, 472 (1954), in dissenting in a border line case from the view that the State of New York could suspend a physician from the practice of his profession because he had been convicted of contempt of a Congressional committee:

"The right to work, I had assumed, was the most precious liberty that man possesses. Man has indeed as much right to work as he has to live, to be free, to own property. The American ideal was stated by Emerson in his essay on Politics, 'A man has a right to be employed, to be trusted, to be loved, to be revered.' It does many men little good to stay alive and free and propertied, if they cannot work. To work means to eat. It also means to live. For many it would be better to work in jail, than to sit idle on the curb. The great values of freedom are in the opportunities afforded man to press to new horizons, to pit his strength against the forces of nature, to match skills with his fellow man."

*   *   *

FREEDOM OF ASSOCIATION IS A CONSTITUTIONAL RIGHT

The second fundamental right guaranteed by the Constitution and protected by right to work laws is the free-

dom of association. This freedom necessarily has both an affirmative and a negative side—it guarantees the right not only to join but *to refrain from joining* any private organization or association.

The freedom of association springs from the liberty of the individual to order his life as he sees fit, to choose where he will work, and what, if any, church, political party, fraternity, lodge, society, league, club or other private organization he will join and support.

Some working men and women want to join a union. Others do not. In either event their choice should be respected whether the reasons are good or bad or indifferent. A union, after all, is seldom merely a collective bargaining representative. It is always partly that, but it is often also partly a political organization, partly a fraternal order, partly a social club, and partly an insurance concern. Even more often it aspires to be a state within a state and to exercise a high degree of discipline and control over its members. All of these things may not be objectionable where membership is on a voluntary basis, but it violates fundamental American principles to force a man into a private organization against his will. . . .

The right of association has been upheld time after time by the Supreme Court of the United States as one of the fundamental rights protected by the Constitution. It is the principal basis for the recognition of the right to organize labor unions, forming one of the grounds upon which Chief Justice Hughes upheld the National Labor Relations Act as constitutional in *Labor Board* v. *Jones & Laughlin Steel Corp.*, 301 U.S. 1, 33, 34 (1937). It is a strange spectacle to see labor unions set out to destroy or to limit and qualify a fundamental constitutional liberty when it is the principle upon which their very existence is founded. Yet that is precisely what they are doing when they deny a man the right not to join a union.

*   *   *

The right not to join is a necessary corollary of the right to join, for without a right not to join there can be no such thing as a right to join. Freedom rests on choice, and where choice is denied freedom is destroyed as well.

Thus it is that the Supreme Court has recognized the affirmative and negative sides of constitutional liberties—in *Board of Education* v. *Barnette,* 319 U.S. 624, 633 (1943), it specifically pointed out that freedom of speech carries with it a freedom to remain silent. And in *Santa Fe* v. *Brown,* 80 Kan. 312, 101 P. 459, 460 (1909), the Supreme Court of Kansas said:

"It would seem that the liberty to remain silent is correlative to the freedom to speak. If one must speak, he cannot be said to freely speak."

If men are to be free to join unions they must also be free not to join, for otherwise they will be burdened with a duty or obligation to join an organization selected, not by themselves but by others—which is the coercion of the slave state and the very antithesis of the freedom of choice of the individual which is the core of American constitutional liberty.

*   *   *

ATTEMPTED JUSTIFICATION OF COMPULSORY UNIONISM

These concepts are tied in with the grounds which are commonly brought forward to justify compulsory unionism. The most important of these are to the effect (1) that the arrangement grows out of a voluntary agreement between employer and union which should be respected; (2) that it is justified by the necessity for union security; (3) that it is only fair to require all workers to pay for union services; (4) that the principle of majority rule requires all workers to belong to a union when a majority are members; and (5) that the arrangement makes a valuable contribution to labor peace and productivity. None of these grounds nor all of them together furnish sufficient justification for compulsory union membership. But even if the reasons were much stronger than they actually are, they could not possibly justify adoption of an arrangement so utterly alien to our free institutions.

COMPULSORY UNIONISM NOT JUSTIFIED UNDER FREEDOM OF CONTRACT

The plea that the arrangement is merely a voluntary agreement between private parties is not only specious but is an unworthy attempt to avoid the application of constitutional principles.

It is fallacious to characterize a union shop as a voluntary arrangement. Ordinarily it is not voluntary in any true sense. It is usually brought into existence by some form of pressure, some form of coercion exercised against the employer. It therefore may properly be regarded as coercive not only against employees who do not desire union affiliation but also as coercive against the employer.

Actually there is no such thing in this country as freedom of contract with respect to union membership. There once was, but that day is no more. The freedom advocated by the proponents of compulsory unionism is distinctly a one-sided affair. They are not advocating full freedom of contract with respect to the matter of union membership, but only so much of that freedom as is consistent with their objectives. They would not have the employer free to contract with employees that they will not join a union; rather the freedom of contract they seek is only a freedom of the employer to contract with union leaders that all employees must join a union.

The overwhelming majority of employers in the country are opposed to any form of compulsory union membership. Many of them have nevertheless agreed to the union shop because of the coercion of labor leaders by strikes or threats of strikes. In any field where the ruling influence is coercion, freedom of contract is a mockery. What the proponents of the closed shop and the union shop desire is preservation not of freedom of contract but of freedom of coercion.

The first ten amendments and the Fourteenth Amendment to the Federal Constitution do not apply to purely private action but instead serve only to check assertions of governmental power. But labor relations are so regulated by law today that compulsory union membership is ordinarily possible only by governmental permission, and it is usually imposed by union leaders using as a weapon the great complex of powers placed in their hands by modern labor law. To suppose that agreements for compulsory union membership made under these conditions represent purely private action is to substitute fiction for reality.

President Roosevelt in 1941 declared that under his leadership the government would never compel employees to join a union by government decree. "That," he said, "would be too much like the Hitler methods toward labor."

But actually these are the methods which are in substance and effect being employed today when compulsory union membership is authorized by law and put in force by unions in the exercise of tremendous powers granted them by law.

*   *   *

There was a day when many employers, reacting to what they considered union abuses, required their workmen to agree not to join a labor union. Labor leaders found this type of agreement a serious obstacle to their organizing drives. They objected to it as a violation of every principle of American liberty. They enlisted the sympathetic support of liberals and together they succeeded in persuading Congress as well as the legislatures of many states to enact statutes outlawing it and guaranteeing to every workman complete freedom of choice to belong to a labor union.

The Supreme Court in *Adair* v. *United States*, 208 U.S. 161 (1908), and *Coppage* v. *Kansas*, 236 U.S. 1 (1915), struck down these statutes as unconstitutional invasions of liberty of contract.

In 1932 the alliance of liberals and union leaders tried again. They persuaded Congress to pass the Norris-LaGuardia Act which not only curbed the use of injunctions in labor disputes but also expressly declared a public policy of giving protection to the right to join as well as the right not to join a labor union. It became law with the signature of President Hoover. The right to join a labor union was reaffirmed in the Wagner Act of 1935, 29 U.S.C. (1946 ed) Sec. 157, which was upheld as constitutional in *National Labor Relations Board* v. *Jones & Laughlin Steel Corp.*, 301 U.S. 1, 33, 34 (1937). The doctrine of freedom of contract of the *Adair* and *Coppage* cases was expressly overruled in *Phelps Dodge Corp.* v. *National Labor Relations Board*, 313 U.S. 177, 187 (1941).

Thus the freedom of contract which once existed in this field has been stricken down by Congress and the Supreme Court at the instance of the labor leaders who invoked the right to work and the right of association as constitutional rights which on balance outweigh freedom of contract.

But after having played a leading role in the destruction of this freedom of contract the labor leaders then attempted to revive it as a vehicle for compulsory union membership. They failed when they used it to attack the constitutionality of right to work laws in *Lincoln Union* v. *Northwestern Co.*, 335 U.S. 525 (1949), but they still use the argument in their appeals to public opinion and to law-making bodies.

Thus although labor leaders were bitterly opposed to the first type of restrictive contract forbidding workers to join a labor union, they fervently espouse the second type requiring the workman to join a union, even though against his will. They vehemently oppose all legislative attempts to give the working man and woman freedom of choice regarding union membership. Where once they championed the freedom of the individual, they now clamor for the right to force and coerce him into union membership. Compulsory union membership is a device they employ to acquire more power over their own union members as well as over the employer. It is one of the principal symptoms of the emergence of the union as a separate institution with interests and policies different from and sometimes hostile to those of its members.

COMPULSORY UNIONISM UNNECESSARY FOR UNION SECURITY

Union leaders reason that they must have the maximum bargaining power, and since this power requires compulsory membership, it is the moral and legal duty of every worker to belong to the union.

The validity of this proposition depends upon the soundness of its premises, and particularly upon the premise that compulsory membership is necessary for union security.

The fact is that this premise is unsound, for organized labor today has more security than any other type of private association or business organization. The Norris-LaGuardia Act, the National Labor Relations Act, the Railway Labor Act, and the exemptions from the antitrust statutes, not to mention comparable state laws, give unions a full measure of security.

These statutory protections render the union plea for further security through compulsory unionism very hollow indeed. Employees are guaranteed the right to organize and bargain collectively through a representative of their own choosing and the employer is forbidden to interfere. When a union is selected by a majority of employees, the employer must bargain with that union. The union is vested with the power to represent and bind not only its own members but also all other employees in the bargaining unit whether they be members of a different union or are non-union men.

That no well managed union needs whatever degree of security compulsory membership may give it has been demonstrated by actual experience in the railroad industry. From 1934 to 1951 there was a right to work provision in the Railway Labor Act which forbade compulsory unionism in any form. Yet during the seventeen years this provision was in effect the non-operating unions trebled their membership, registered great gains in their financial positions, and extended their jurisdiction to cover for practical purposes all railroad mileage in the United States.

In 1942 some of the railway unions demanded compulsory union membership. The resulting dispute was referred by President Roosevelt to the Sharfman Board which not only held that the demand could not be granted consistently with the law as it then stood but found that the arrangement was not necessary for the security of the unions. . . .

When the leaders of the same railroad unions went before Congress in their successful attempt to secure legislation legalizing the union shop, their chief spokesman frankly admitted that compulsory union membership was not necessary to strengthen the unions in their industry-wide bargaining. He said, "If I get a majority of employees to vote for my union as a bargaining agent, I have got as much economic power at that stage of the development as I will ever have." (Hearings before House Committee on Interstate and Foreign Commerce, H. R. 7789, Eighty-First Congress, Second Session, May 9, 1950, pp. 20-21.)

All over the free world unions have grown strong and prospered without the aid of compulsory union membership. In this country union after union has been organized and has grown great as a voluntary association. In fact they have commonly been unable to impose the compulsory membership requirement until after they have grown well-nigh impregnably strong. An economist friendly to labor recently made a study of union growth in Texas, where there is a right to work law. He found that in the last fifteen years union membership has made great strides and its progress was not even slowed down by the passage of the right to work law in 1947.

*   *   *

Some of the advocates of compulsory unionism devote a great deal of time to assailing the motives of those who favor right to work laws, asserting that their objective is destruction of all labor organizations and the whole process of collective bargaining. To their mind, one who supports right to work laws is by that token alone anti-union and hostile to everything labor organizations stand for.

But there are a great mass of people, in and out of labor organizations, who favor unions and collective bargaining but are strenuously opposed to compulsory unionism with its impairment of fundamental individual rights.

Public opinion polls indicate that the majority of the people favor unions. But these polls show that a sizeable majority of the people in every section of the country—north, south, east and west—disapprove of compulsory union membership and favor state right to work laws. The number of states with these statutes on the books has increased despite the often effective opposition of the unions who have used their power as a minority pressure group to thwart the popular will.

Some union leaders have recognized the value of voluntarism in the matter of union membership and the dangers inherent in compulsion. Warren S. Stone, for many years Grand Chief Engineer of the Brotherhood of Locomotive Engineers, is on record as follows:

"I do not believe in forcing a man to join a union. If he wants to join, all right; but it is contrary to the principles of free government and the Constitution of the United States to try to make him join. We of the engineers work willingly side by side with other engineers every day who do not belong to our union though they enjoy without any objection on our part the advantages we have obtained. Some of them we would not have in the union; others we cannot get."

In 1953, Guy L. Brown, Grand Chief of the Brotherhood of Locomotive Engineers, told a reporter for a national magazine that his union did not ask Congress for the union shop and had actually opposed it as a matter of policy. He went on to say:

"We support it now only on individual roads where other unions have put it into effect. Engineers just simply resent being told they must join anything. We still think that labor in the long run has a good-enough product that you won't have to force men to join. We must go along on a 'union shop' in some instances where it is necessary because of the possible encroachment upon our membership by some other organization." (*U.S. News & World Report,* December 11, 1953, p. 71.)

*   *   *

THE NON-UNION MAN IS NOT A FREE RIDER

To justify compulsory membership the unions claim that the non-member should not be allowed to be a free rider—to accept the benefit of union bargaining without paying his share of the expenses.

At the same time they say that the present dues are light and far from burdensome on members. If so, these present members cannot be said to be suffering heavy burdens from which they need relief.

Throughout the length and breadth of the country there are thousands of voluntary associations of every description whose activities benefit members and non-members alike. But universally they are supported by voluntary dues and contributions. The idea of forced payments to private organizations is fundamentally incompatible with the voluntary character of their association.

Forced payments are equivalent to taxes. Taxation is a sovereign power and may be exercised by the government only, and not by a labor union or any other type of private association.

The free rider complaint, even if it were justified, would not entitle the unions to the form of relief they ask— which is to compel non-members to join the union. Full relief would be afforded by requiring the non-member to pay a fee for the services of the union as collective bargaining representative. To go further and to compel him to join and support all of the union's other ventures—its political activities, its insurance schemes, and other enterprises—would go far beyond what could be sustained on any version of the free rider theory. The Supreme Court of Nebraska so held in *Hanson v. Union Pacific,* 160 Neb. 669, 71 N. W. 2d 526 (1955), citing it as one of the principal grounds for holding unconstitutional the compulsory union membership feature of the Railway Labor Act.

It is said that the political activities, the insurance schemes, and the other ventures are all conducted in the interest of the union and for the welfare of the workers. But the worker under our system of government is entitled to make his own political decisions. He has the right not only to vote as he pleases, but to determine for himself whether to use his funds to support political candidates and causes. No one has the right to make the determination for him or to appropriate his political franchise or any part of it. . . .

But apart from these considerations, there is no adequate reason why the non-members should pay anything at all for the services of the union as collective bargaining representative.

The unions years ago sought and got the right to speak for and bind not only their own members but all others in the bargaining unit as well. They saw the enormous amount of power wrapped up in the bargaining monopoly it gives them. Now they would have us believe that this power is somehow an unjust burden.

This so-called burden was characterized as a tremendously valuable statutory privilege by the Supreme Court in *American Communications Assn.* v. *Douds,* 339 U.S. 382, 401-2 (1950). The unions asked for the privilege with their eyes open well knowing what it entailed. Now that they have gotten what they asked for, they have no moral or equitable claim for compensation from those who have not sought and do not want the services that are thrust upon them.

Those people who are required by law to accept a particular union's representation, whether or not they want it, are not free riders at all. They are deprived of their right to bargain for themselves. They are in truth forced followers.

The non-members actually do not get something for nothing. When they are required to surrender their right to bargain for themselves and their right to be represented by a union of their own choice, they have given a *quid pro quo.* In some cases at least they get the worst of the bargain.

*   *   *

THE PRINCIPLE OF MAJORITY RULE DOES NOT JUSTIFY COMPULSORY UNION MEMBERSHIP

It is often stoutly maintained that the principle of majority rule justifies compulsory unionism. Thus it is said that if the majority of employees unite in organizing a union, democratic principles require that their selection of that particular union should be binding on all. But there are a number of reasons why this conclusion does not follow.

In the first place, while majority rule is properly applicable for controlling the internal affairs of a private association or a business organization, as well as those of an agency of government, it may not properly be invoked to force unwilling persons into membership in a private organization. The right to use force to compel adherence and submission to rule is limited to the government. No private organization like a labor union can lay claim to this prerogative of sovereignty.

*   *   *

The legal thinkers in the labor movement have been aware of this difficulty. When they assailed the constitutionality of right to work laws in *Lincoln Union* v. *Northwestern Co.,* 335 U.S. 525 (1949), they claimed that these laws interfered with the proper prerogatives of a labor union, which they said has in a sense the powers of government. The American Federation of Labor, in its brief in that case, said:

> "The common rule of collective bargaining carries with it the legal doctrine that the union is the common authority for government of a society of workers. It has in a sense the powers and responsibilities of a government."

This argument that the union is a state within a state is apparently what the Court had in mind when characterizing some of the contentions of appellants as "startling." It rejected them in holding that right to work laws offend against no constitutional principles. The Court said there is no constitutional right to drive from employment those who are not members of a union.

The idea of the union as a state

within a state, with its emphasis on the duty of the worker to the union and its de-emphasis of the rights of the individual, lead to the conclusion that it is the duty of every worker to become a member of a union and to subject himself to its rule. This is reminiscent of the philosophy of the corporative state and is really a totalitarian philosophy utterly alien to our American heritage of freedom.

Even in affairs of government, majority rule is not absolute. The very purpose of the Bill of Rights is to lay restraints upon the majority for the protection of the fundamental rights of minorities. Under constitutional government majority rule cannot be employed as an instrument for the obliteration of minority rights.

Majority rule in governmental affairs is exercised under conditions far different from those found in labor organizations. It is exercised within a democratic framework, with general elections at frequent and regular intervals, and subject to a strong system of checks and balances. There is no correspondingly adequate system of checks and balances in labor unions, nor are democratic practices universally observed. Some unions are subject to autocratic or oligarchic control and in still others democratic processes are not fully developed. It is fairly common to throw serious obstacles into the path of opposition to the group in power, and to curtail in other ways the rights of members.

COMPULSORY UNION MEMBERSHIP MAKES NO WORTH-WHILE CONTRIBUTION TO LABOR PEACE

Proponents of compulsory unionism sometimes claim that it is desirable as a means of reducing friction among employees, of introducing discipline, of promoting morale and productivity— in short as an important measure of labor peace and efficiency. There is little basis for these claims.

No one is more interested in labor peace and productivity than employers, but they have no faith in compulsory membership as an instrument of achieving those very desirable ends. Studies of the record of businesses with, as compared with those without, compulsory union membership, have failed to show any advantages derived from compulsion. In fact, the showing has been just to the contrary.

*　　*　　*

Whether introduction of compulsory unionism would solve anything in a plant or industry where unrest might be found because of the presence of non-union men is questionable at best. If union men clash with non-union men, it is doubtful whether relations between them would be much improved by forcing those not members to join the union or be fired from their jobs. The nonunion man who is discharged for refusal to join a union will hardly be a peaceful element on the industrial scene. And he will be little different if he joins the union unwillingly and only in order to save his job. In the last analysis, it is difficult to believe that compulsory unionism does or can make any substantial contribution to labor peace.

78. *Retail Clerks International Association, Local 1625 v. Alberta Schermerhorn*

84 S.Ct. 219 (1963)

SUIT by nonunion employees to have agency shop clause declared illegal, for an injunction against enforcement of it, and for an accounting. From an adverse judgment of the Circuit Court of Florida for Dade County, the plaintiffs appealed. . . . The Florida Supreme Court, 141 So. 2d 269, reversed and remanded, and certiorari was granted. The United States Supreme Court . . . held that state courts, rather than solely the National Labor Relations Board, were tribunals with jurisdiction to enforce state's prohibition against an "agency shop" clause in a collective bargaining agreement.

*   *   *

MR. JUSTICE DOUGLAS delivered the opinion of the Court.

The sole question in the case is the one we set down for reargument in 373 U.S. 746, 747-748, 83 S.Ct. 1461, 10 L. Ed. 678: "whether the Florida courts, rather than solely the National Labor Relations Board, are tribunals with jurisdiction to enforce the State's prohibition" against an "agency shop" clause in a collective bargaining agreement.

In this case the union and the employer negotiated a collective bargaining agreement that contained an "agency shop" clause providing that the employees covered by the contract who chose not to join the union were required "to pay as a condition of employment, an initial service fee and monthly service fees" to the union. Nonunion employees brought suit in a Florida court to have the agency shop clause declared illegal. . . . The Florida Supreme Court held that this negotiated and executed union-security agreement violates the "right to work" provision of the Florida Constitution and that the state courts have jurisdiction to afford a remedy. Fla., 141 So.2d 269.

We agree with that view.

While sec. 8(a) of the Taft-Hartley Act provides that it is not an unfair labor practice for an employer and a union to require membership in a union as a condition of employment provided the specified conditions are met, sec. 14(b) (61 Stat. 151, 29 U.S.C. sec. 165(b)) provides:

> "Nothing in this Act shall be construed as authorizing the execution or application of agreements requiring membership in a labor organization in any State or Territory in which such execution or application is prohibited by State or Territorial law."

We start from the premise that, while Congress could preempt as much or as little of [t]his interstate field as it chose, it would be odd to construe sec. 14(b) as permitting a state to prohibit the agency clause but barring it from implementing its own law with sanctions of the kind involved here.

*   *   *

By the time sec. 14(b) was written into the Act, twelve States had statutes or constitutional provisions outlawing or restricting the closed shop and related devices—a state power which we sustained in Lincoln Federal Labor Union v. Northwestern Iron & Metal Co., 335 U.S. 525, 69 S.Ct. 251, 93 L.Ed. 212. . . .

*   *   *

Affirmed.

Index